T0265198

NEUROPSYCHOLOGICAL ASSESSMENT OF WORK-RELATED INJURIES

Neuropsychological Assessment of Work-Related Injuries

Edited by
**Shane S. Bush
Grant L. Iverson**

THE GUILFORD PRESS
New York   London

© 2012 The Guilford Press
A Division of Guilford Publications, Inc.
72 Spring Street, New York, NY 10012
www.guilford.com

Printed in the United States of America

This book is printed on acid-free paper.

Last digit is print number: 9   8   7   6   5   4   3   2   1

The authors have checked with sources believed to be reliable in their efforts to provide
information that is complete and generally in accord with the standards of practice that
are accepted at the time of publication. However, in view of the possibility of human error
or changes in behavioral, mental health, or medical sciences, neither the authors, nor the
editors and publisher, nor any other party who has been involved in the preparation or
publication of this work warrants that the information contained herein is in every respect
accurate or complete, and they are not responsible for any errors or omissions or the
results obtained from the use of such information. Readers are encouraged to confirm the
information contained in this book with other sources.

Library of Congress Cataloging-in-Publication Data is available from the publisher.
ISBN 978-1-4625-0227-1

*To Dana, Sarah, and Megan,
who greet me with smiles, hugs, and kisses
every time I walk in the door*
—S. S. B.

*Special thanks to Angela, Ila, and Annalise
for support, encouragement, and inspiration*
—G. L. I.

About the Editors

Shane S. Bush, PhD, ABPP, ABN, is Director of Long Island Neuropsychology; P. C.; a neuropsychologist with the VA New York Harbor Healthcare System; and Clinical Assistant Professor in the Department of Psychiatry and Behavioral Science at Stony Brook University School of Medicine. He is board certified in neuropsychology and rehabilitation psychology, a Fellow of the American Psychological Association and the National Academy of Neuropsychology, and immediate Past President of the National Academy of Neuropsychology. Dr. Bush has published numerous articles, book chapters, and books, as well as two special journal issues. He presents frequently at professional conferences.

Grant L. Iverson, PhD, RPsych, is Professor in the Faculty of Medicine, Department of Psychiatry, at the University of British Columbia. He served as Chair of the Canadian Psychological Association Section on Clinical Neuropsychology from 2003 to 2010, and is a founding member of the Traumatic Brain Injury Subcommittee of the Defense Health Board, a civilian advisory board to the U.S. Secretary of Defense. Dr. Iverson has published more than 225 empirical articles, reviews, and book chapters. He has conducted significant research into outcome from traumatic brain injury in athletes, civilians, service members, and veterans. He is also engaged in a multiyear research program designed to develop and evaluate evidence-based psychometric guidelines for identifying mild cognitive impairment in psychiatry and neurology.

Shane S. Bush, PhD, ABPP, ABN, has not received research funding from any organization or company. He has an independent practice in clinical and forensic neuropsychology.

Grant L. Iverson, PhD, RPsych, has been reimbursed by the U.S. government, professional scientific bodies, and commercial organizations for discussing or presenting research related to mild traumatic brain injury (TBI) and sport-related concussion at meetings, scientific conferences, and symposiums. These include, but are not limited to, the National Academy of Neuropsychology, American Academy of Clinical Neuropsychology, International Neuropsychological Society, U.S. Department of Defense, Australasian Faculties of Rehabilitation Medicine and Occupational and Environmental Medicine, and Swiss Accident Insurance Fund. Dr. Iverson maintains a clinical practice in forensic neuropsychology involving individuals who have sustained mild TBIs. He has received research funding from several test publishing companies, including ImPACT Applications, Inc., CNS Vital Signs, and Psychological Assessment Resources, Inc. He has received honoraria for serving on research panels that provide scientific peer review of programs (e.g., the Military Operational Medicine Research Program). Dr. Iverson is a co-investigator, collaborator, or consultant on grants funded by several organizations, including, but not limited to, the Canadian Institute of Health Research, Alcohol Beverage Medical Research Council, Rehabilitation Research and Development Service of the U.S. Department of Veterans Affairs, AstraZeneca Canada, and Lundbeck Canada.

The editors note that the views expressed in this book are those of the authors and do not reflect the official policy of the U.S. Department of Defense or the U.S. government.

Contributors

Brian L. Brooks, PhD, Neurosciences Program, Alberta Children's Hospital, University of Calgary, Calgary, Alberta, Canada

Richard A. Bryant, PhD, School of Psychology, University of New South Wales, Sydney, Australia

Shane S. Bush, PhD, VA New York Harbor Healthcare System, Brooklyn, New York, and Department of Psychiatry and Behavioral Science, Stony Brook University School of Medicine, Stony Brook, New York

Kyle E. Ferguson, PhD, Department of Psychiatry, University of British Columbia, Vancouver, British Columbia, Canada

Joseph W. Fink, PhD, Department of Psychiatry and Behavioral Neuroscience, University of Chicago Medical Center, Chicago, Illinois

Robert Fraser, PhD, Department of Rehabilitation Medicine, University of Washington Medical Center, University of Washington, Seattle, Washington

Louis M. French, PsyD, Defense and Veterans Brain Injury Center, Walter Reed National Military Medical Center, and Uniformed Services University of the Health Sciences, Washington, DC

Brad K. Grunert, PhD, Department of Plastic Surgery, Medical College of Wisconsin, Milwaukee, Wisconsin

Robert L. Heilbronner, PhD, Chicago Neuropsychology Group, Chicago, Illinois

George K. Henry, PhD, Los Angeles Neuropsychology Group, Los Angeles, California

James A. Holdnack, PhD, Pearson Assessments and Information, San Antonio, Texas

Grant L. Iverson, PhD, Department of Psychiatry, University of British Columbia, Vancouver, British Columbia, Canada; and Veterans Brain Injury Center, Washington, DC.

Curt Johnson, MS, CRC, ATP, Department of Rehabilitation Medicine, University of Washington, Seattle, Washington

Erica Johnson, PhD, CRC, Department of Rehabilitation Counseling, Western Washington University, Bellingham, Washington

Greg J. Lamberty, PhD, Noran Neurological Clinic, Minneapolis, Minnesota

Rael T. Lange, PhD, Defense and Veterans Brain Injury Center, Walter Reed National Military Medical Center, Washington, DC

Scott A. Langenecker, PhD, Department of Psychiatry, University of Michigan Medical School, Ann Arbor, Michigan

David W. Lovejoy, PsyD, Department of Neurosurgery, Hartford Hospital, Hartford, Connecticut, and Department of Traumatology and Emergency Medicine, University of Connecticut School of Medicine, Farmington, Connecticut

Mark R. Lovell, PhD, Sports Medicine Concussion Program, University of Pittsburgh Medical Center, Pittsburgh, Pennsylvania

Robert J. McCaffrey, PhD, Department of Psychology, University at Albany, State University of New York, and Albany Neuropsychological Associates, Albany, New York

Lance M. McCracken, PhD, Health Psychology Section, Psychology Department, Institute of Psychiatry, Kings College, London, United Kingdom

Andrea S. Miele, MA, Department of Psychology, University at Albany, State University of New York, Albany, New York

Howard J. Oakes, PsyD, Department of Neurosurgery, Hartford Hospital, Hartford, Connecticut

Neil H. Pliskin, PhD, Neuropsychology Division, College of Medicine, University of Illinois, Chicago, Illinois

Lauren Rog, MS, Illinois Institute of Technology, Chicago, Illinois

Gerald M. Rosen, PhD, Departments of Psychology and Psychiatry, University of Washington, Seattle, Washington

David Strand, MA, CRC, Department of Rehabilitation Medicine, University of Washington, Seattle, Washington

Miles Thompson, DClinPsy, Bath Centre for Pain Services, Royal National Hospital for Rheumatic Diseases, Bath, United Kingdom

Allan H. Young, MB ChB, PhD, Institute of Mental Health, Department of Psychiatry, University of British Columbia, Vancouver, British Columbia, Canada

Acknowledgments

We are very grateful to the chapter authors for their contributions to this book. They each brought their unique expertise to their writing, skillfully integrating their professional experience with the scientific literature. It will be immediately evident to readers that a project such as this could not have been completed without the commitment of such esteemed professionals. We also are thankful to Rochelle Serwator, Editor at The Guilford Press, for her confidence in the value of this book and her support in bringing our idea for the book to fruition. It has been a pleasure to work with Rochelle and The Guilford Press.

Contents

NEUROPSYCHOLOGICAL ASSESSMENT OF WORK-RELATED INJURIES

Introduction

Shane S. Bush
Grant L. Iverson

Cognitive impairment following workplace injuries can be time-limited or permanent. Traumatic brain injuries, electrical injuries, neurotoxic exposure, depression, anxiety disorders, and chronic pain can be associated with subjectively reported and/or objectively documented cognitive problems. The challenge for neuropsychologists who evaluate injured workers lies in accurately identifying problems with cognition, quantifying the deficits, estimating the impact on day-to-day functioning, and apportioning causation. A goal of this book is to promote and encourage evidence-based neuropsychological assessment following work-related injuries.

SCOPE OF THE PROBLEM

Work-related injuries affect the lives of millions of people every year and are a significant public health problem. In 2006 alone, more than 3.9 million U.S. private-sector workers sustained nonfatal injuries (U.S. Department of Labor Bureau of Labor Statistics, 2007). These numbers do not include the 22% of the workforce that is not employed in the private sector. The National Institute for Occupational Safety and Health (NIOSH) defines work-related traumatic injury as "any damage inflicted to the body by energy transfer during work with a short duration between exposure and health event" (NIOSH, 2009, p. 3). Such a definition includes a wide array of physical injuries and medical problems that may be associated with cognitive and/or emotional symptoms and fall under the clinical or forensic purview of neuropsychologists. The NIOSH definition does not include injuries that are purely the result of an emotional reaction to an acute psychological trauma or stressor in the workplace, nor does it include disorders that emerge over time as the result of prior exposure to disease-causing agents or situations. However, the *Occupational Injury and Illness Classification Manual*, developed by the U.S. Department of Labor's Bureau of Labor Statistics (1992), includes a broader range of injuries and illnesses of interest to neuropsychologists.

Work-related psychosocial stressors, injuries, and illnesses have been a specific focus of international attention (NIOSH, 2002; World Health Organization [WHO], 2010). Depression is a leading cause of disability and is projected by the WHO to become the second leading cause of the global burden of disease by 2020 (Murray & Lopez, 1996). As stated in the WHO report:

> There is strong evidence to indicate an association between work-related health complaints and exposure to psychosocial hazards, or to an interaction between physical and psychosocial hazards, to an array of health outcomes at the individual level and at the organisational level (Cox, Griffiths, & Rial-Gonzalez, 2000). Specifically, psychosocial risks in the workplace have been demonstrated to have a possible detrimental impact on workers' physical, mental and social health (e.g., Bonde, 2008; Bosma, Peter, Siegrist, & Marmot, 1998; Chen, Yu, & Wong, 2005; Fischer et al., 2005; Tennant, 2001; Wieclaw et al., 2008); in addition. . . . Exposure to physical and psychosocial hazards may affect psychological as well as physical health. The evidence suggests that such effects on health may be mediated by, at least, two processes: first, a direct pathway, and second, an indirect stress-mediated pathway. (Cox et al., 2000, p. 2)

PROFESSIONAL AND ETHICAL ISSUES

Persons who have sustained injuries in the workplace often experience complex and multifaceted disorders and syndromes. This complexity results from interactions between (1) the person's developmental, characterological, medical, and psychological status before the injury; (2) the biological aspects of the injury; (3) the timing and quality of healthcare following the injury; (4) psychosocial support following the injury; (5) treatment by the employer before and after the injury; (6) the degree of satisfaction with the workers' compensation system; and (7) litigation status. Neuropsychologists who evaluate and/or treat persons who have experienced work-related injuries examine this complexity when making diagnostic determinations, considering causality, determining disability status, offering treatment recommendations, and providing treatment.

The ethics codes of professional organizations (e.g., American Psychological Association [APA]; Canadian Psychological Association [CPA]) require clinicians to be familiar with the neuropsychological manifestations, probable etiologies, and expected recovery courses of the work-related injuries experienced by their patients, and to be skilled in the evaluation or treatment services they provide (APA Ethical Standard 2.01, Boundaries of Competence; CPA Principle II: Responsible Caring). Similarly, clinicians who strive to learn about and understand *the person* who has sustained a work-related neuropsychological injury face a challenging task and must draw upon multiple methods, procedures, and sources of information to assist in their endeavor (APA Ethical Standards 2.04, Bases for Scientific and Professional Judgments, and 9.01, Bases for Assessments). The evolution of the field has led in recent years to an increased appreciation of the need for a biopsychosocial conceptualization of functioning, disability, and health; a need to consider the potential complexity of suboptimal performance during neuropsychological evaluations; and the impact of psychological distress and dynamics on patient functioning (Schultz, 2009). The best neuropsychological evaluations of people with work-related injuries demonstrate, through procedures and analyses, an understanding of these advances.

Clinicians explain to their patients and examinees, or their legal representatives, the nature of the neuropsychological services, including potential risks and benefits, and the foreseeable uses to which the results will be put, including who may receive the results and copies of reports (APA Ethical Standards 3.10, Informed Consent, and 9.03, Informed Consent in Assessments: CPA Principle I: Respect for the Dignity of Persons). This information allows patients to make informed decisions regarding participation in neuropsychological services (APA General Principle E, Respect for Peoples Rights and Dignity; CPA Principle I: Respect for the Dignity of Persons).

Because neuropsychological services for work-related injuries in the United States are commonly financed by workers' compensation, which may become an adversarial process, and may evolve to litigation, practitioners determine at the outset of their involvement whether their services are best conceptualized as clinical or forensic, or clinical with the potential to become forensic at a later time. Such determinations have implications for informed consent, privacy, and confidentiality, and potentially for other aspects of the evaluation or treatment provided (Bush & NAN Policy and Planning Committee, 2005).

Chibnall and Tait (2010) found that injured workers who retained the services of attorneys because of dissatisfaction with workers' compensation medical care, compared to those who did not retain an attorney or who did so for other reasons, experienced higher levels of disability and catastrophizing and had worse psychological adjustment, both in the short term and over time. Perceived injustice can be associated with greater levels of psychological distress (Sullivan et al., 2009). Moreover, people involved in compensation claims often experience a strong sense of entitlement; perceived injustice; and stress related to the claims process, an inability to move on with life during this process, and a perceived lack of trust about having to prove impairment or disability (Murgatroyd, Cameron, & Harris, 2010). The compensation process can have an adverse effect on recovery trajectories for pain and psychological distress in some people (Sterling, Hendrikz, & Kenardy, 2010). The forensic context challenges clinicians in ways that are not experienced in many clinical settings. Schultz (2009) described the essence of such challenges: "Practitioners in forensic psychology and neuropsychology, more often than in other applied specialties in psychology, are forced to answer complex, high-stakes clinical questions that require operating on the cutting edge of science. They are even pressured to move beyond the boundaries of science where empirical and evidentiary support is absent or where lack of clarity still reigns" (p. 200).

Regardless of the context, neuropsychologists approach those receiving neuropsychological services with an attitude of "responsible caring":

> Psychologists accept as fundamental the principle of respect for the dignity of persons; that is, the belief that each person should be treated primarily as a person or an end in him/herself, not as an object or a means to an end. . . . Although psychologists have a responsibility to respect the dignity of all persons with whom they come in contact in their role as psychologists, the nature of their contract with society demands that their greatest responsibility be to those persons in the most vulnerable position. . . . This responsibility is almost always greater than their responsibility to those indirectly involved (e.g., employers, third party payers, the general public). (CPA, 2003, p. 13)

PURPOSE AND PROCESS OF THIS BOOK

The scientific research literature has much to offer practitioners who strive to understand the experience of each patient or forensic examinee. However, "the accumulation of knowledge in diagnostically defined domains of inquiry, such as depression, posttraumatic stress disorder (PTSD), traumatic brain injury (TBI), and pain disorders, proceeds more rapidly than researcher and practitioner ability to integrate the new data, develop cross-diagnostic or transdiagnostic knowledge of disability, and improve clinical practices" (Schultz, 2009, p. 20).

The goal of this book is to provide the reader with an understanding of the neuropsychological science and professional practice issues associated with work-related injuries. Part I describes common injuries that are sustained in the workplace and encountered by neuropsychologists in clinical and forensic settings. Experienced and knowledgeable researchers, clinicians, and forensic experts contributed chapters on topics such as traumatic brain injury, sports concussion, electrical injury, exposure to neurotoxic substances, and brain and psychological injuries experienced in combat.

Part II is devoted to mental health problems and chronic pain. Chapters on depression, posttraumatic stress disorder, and chronic pain are provided. The chapters in Parts I and II of this book reflect both traditional and contemporary topics of concern for clinicians, and the authors apply their knowledge of recent research in their reviews. Part III of this book is focused on professional practice issues. These chapters provide a tremendous amount of practical information relating to conducting work-related neuropsychological evaluations. By design, there is considerable overlap of topics addressed across the first three chapters, though the individual "voices" and style of the authors are nicely distinctive. Chapter 12 provides important insights into the disability determination process. Chapter 13 helps focus the clinician on the importance of writing reports that are relevant for vocational rehabilitation planning. The final chapter of the book, Chapter 14, is designed to promote and encourage evidence-based neuropsychological assessment. It provides clinicians with new psychometric information to improve their accuracy in identifying and quantifying acquired cognitive problems in daily practice. It is our hope that this information will help strengthen the scientific underpinnings of clinical judgment.

REFERENCES

American Psychological Association. (2002). *Ethical principles of psychologists and code of conduct*. Retrieved from *www.apa.org/ethics/code2002.html*.

Bonde, J. P. (2008). Psychosocial factors at work and risk of depression: A systematic review of the epidemiological evidence. *Occupational and Environmental Medicine, 65*(7), 438–445.

Bosma, H., Peter, R., Siegrist, J., & Marmot, M. (1998). Two alternative job stress models and the risk of coronary heart disease. *American Journal of Public Health, 88*(1), 68–74.

Bush, S. S., & NAN Policy and Planning Committee. (2005). Independent and court-ordered forensic neuropsychological examinations: Official statement of the National Academy of Neuropsychology. *Archives of Clinical Neuropsychology, 20*(8), 997–1007.

Canadian Psychological Association. (2003). *Canadian Code of Ethics for Psychologists, 3rd edition*. Retrieved February 5, 2011, from *www.cpa.ca/cpasite/user-files/Documents/Canadian%20Code%20of%20Ethics%20for%20Psycho.pdf*.

Chen, W. Q., Yu, I. T., & Wong, T. W. (2005). Impact of occupational stress and other psychosocial factors on musculoskeletal pain among Chinese offshore oil installation workers. *Occupational and Environmental Medicine, 62*(4), 251–256.

Chibnall, J. T., & Tait, R. C. (2010). Legal representation and dissatisfaction with workers' compensation: Implications for claimant adjustment. *Psychological Injury and Law, 3*, 230–240.

Cox, T., Griffiths, A., & Rial-Gonzalez, E. (2000). *Research on work related stress*. Luxembourg: Office for Official Publications of the European Communities.

Fischer, F. M., Oliveira, D. C., Nagai, R., Teixeira, L. R., Lombardi Júnior, M., Latorre

Mdo, R., et al. (2005). [Job control, job demands, social support at work and health among adolescent workers]. *Revista Saúde Pública, 39*(2), 245–253.

Murgatroyd, D. F., Cameron, I. D., & Harris, I. A. (2010). Understanding the effect of compensation on recovery from severe motor vehicle crash injuries: A qualitative study. *Injury Prevention: Journal of the International Society for Child and Adolescent Injury Prevention, 17*(4), 222–227.

Murray, C. J. L., & Lopez, A. (1996). *Global Health Statistics: A compendium of incidence, prevalence and mortality estimates for over 2000 conditions.* Cambridge, MA: Harvard School of Public Health.

National Institute for Occupational Safety and Health. (2002). *The changing organization of work and the safety and health of working people: Knowledge gaps and research directions.* Retrieved February 5, 2011, from *www.cdc.gov/niosh/docs/2002-116/pdfs/2002-116.pdf.*

National Institute for Occupational Safety and Health. (2009). *Traumatic injury research at NIOSH.* Retrieved June 29, 2011, from *nap.edu/catalog/12459.html.*

Schultz, I. Z. (2009). Determining disability: New advances in conceptualization and research. *Psychological Injury and Law, 2,* 199–204.

Sterling, M., Hendrikz, J., & Kenardy, J. (2010). Compensation claim lodgement and health outcome developmental trajectories following whiplash injury: A prospective study. *Pain, 150*(1), 22–28.

Sullivan, M. J., Thibault, P., Simmonds, M. J., Milioto, M., Cantin, A. P., & Velly, A. M. (2009). Pain, perceived injustice and the persistence of post-traumatic stress symptoms during the course of rehabilitation for whiplash injuries. *Pain, 145*(3), 325–331.

Tennant, C. (2001). Work-related stress and depressive disorders. *Journal of Psychosomatic Research, 51*(5), 697–704.

U.S. Department of Labor, Bureau of Labor Statistics. (1992). *Occupational Injury and Illness Classification Manual.* Retrieved February 5, 2011, from *www.bls.gov/iif/oshwc/oiicm.pdf.*

U.S. Department of Labor, Bureau of Labor Statistics. (2007). *News release: Workplace injuries and illnesses in 2006.* Washington, DC: Author.

Wieclaw, J., Agerbo, E., Mortensen, P. B., Burr, H., Tuchsen, F., & Bonde, J. P. (2008). Psychosocial working conditions and the risk of depression and anxiety disorders in the Danish workforce. *BMC Public Health, 8,* 280.

World Health Organization. (2010). *Health impact of psychological stressors at work: An overview.* Retrieved February 5, 2011, from *whqlibdoc.who.int/publications/2010/9789241500272_eng.pdf.*

PART I

Work-Related Injuries

CHAPTER 1

Traumatic Brain Injury in the Workplace

Grant L. Iverson
Rael T. Lange

Traumatic brain injuries (TBIs) occur on a broad continuum of severity, from very mild transient injuries to catastrophic injuries resulting in death or severe disability. As a general rule, as injury severity increases, the magnitude of impairment increases. Moderate and severe brain injuries can result in temporary, prolonged, or permanent neurological or neuropsychiatric problems (e.g., motor impairments, poor balance and dizziness, visual impairments, cranial nerve impairments, headaches). Mild TBIs (MTBIs) tend to result in time-limited symptoms, and permanent impairment is unlikely.

This chapter provides an overview of TBI with an emphasis on return-to-work issues. This chapter is divided into the following sections: (1) classification of injury severity, (2) epidemiology, (3) pathophysiology, (4) neurological and neuropsychiatric problems, (5) substance abuse and TBI, (6) functional and neuropsychological outcome, (7) postconcussion syndrome, (8) assessment methodology: interview versus questionnaire for residual symptoms, (9) exaggerated symptoms and poor effort on testing, (10) early intervention and following MTBI, (11) return to work, and (12) conclusions.

CLASSIFICATION OF INJURY SEVERITY

Brain injuries can result from an open- or closed-head injury. Most TBIs arise from closed-head injuries (open-head injuries involve penetration of the skull). Traumatic injuries to the brain occur as the result of acceleration–deceleration forces (linear or angular), blunt trauma, or both. These injuries fall on a broad continuum of severity, from very mild transient injuries to catastrophic injuries resulting in death or severe disability (Figure 1.1).

9

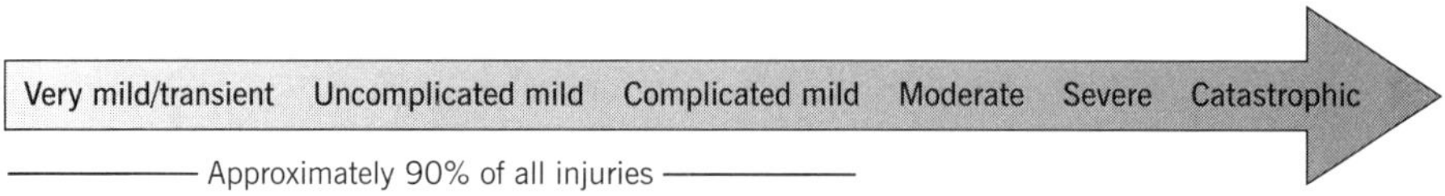

| Very mild/transient | Uncomplicated mild | Complicated mild | Moderate | Severe | Catastrophic |

——————— Approximately 90% of all injuries ———————

■ **FIGURE 1.1.** Continuum of TBI severity.

By convention, TBIs are typically classified as mild, moderate, or severe, using Glasgow Coma Scale (GCS) scores, duration of loss of consciousness (LOC), and posttraumatic amnesia (PTA). The classification system based on GCS scores is widely, but not universally, used in clinical practice and research. There is less agreement for classification categories using LOC or PTA. A commonly used system for classifying TBI severity is summarized in Table 1.1.

The pathophysiology of MTBI is heterogeneous, ranging from very mild neurometabolic changes in the brain with rapid recovery to permanent problems due to structural brain damage. Some researchers have proposed two important subtypes to further classify MTBIs based on the presence ("complicated" MTBI) or absence ("uncomplicated" MTBI) of macroscopic, structural, trauma-related abnormalities visible on computed tomography (CT) or magnetic resonance imaging (MRI) (Williams, Levin, & Eisenberg, 1990). Williams and colleagues noted that patients with complicated MTBIs are more likely to have worse cognitive functioning acutely compared to uncomplicated MTBI, and their 6-month functional recovery pattern is more similar to persons with moderate brain injuries. Worse outcome associated with complicated MTBIs has been reported by some (Iverson, 2006a; Lange, Iverson, & Franzen, 2009; Temkin, Machamer, & Dikmen, 2003; van der Naalt, Hew, van Zomeren, Sluiter, & Minderhoud, 1999a; Williams, Levin, & Eisenberg, 1990; Wilson, Hadley, Scott, & Harper, 1996), but not all (Hofman et al., 2001; Hughes et al., 2004; McCauley, Boake, Levin, Contant, & Song, 2001), researchers.

■ **TABLE 1.1. Common Classification System for TBI**

Classification	Duration of unconsciousness	Glasgow Coma Scale	Posttraumatic amnesia
Mild	< 30 minutes	13–15[a]	< 24 hours
Moderate	30 minutes–24 hours	9–12	1–7 days
Severe	> 24 hours	3–8	> 7 days

Note. This is not a universally agreed-upon classification system.
[a]Defined as the lowest GCS score obtained 30 minutes or more postinjury.

As technology evolves, it will be interesting to see if the criteria for complicated MTBI change. In the past, intracranial abnormalities were identified using CT or conventional MRI. Over time, smaller and smaller abnormalities can be detected using structural imaging. For example, the area of hemosiderin (iron-rich staining of tissue from an area with past blood) shown in Figure 1.2 using multi-echo susceptibility weighted imaging (SWI) with 5 echoes (Denk & Rauscher, 2010; Rauscher et al., 2008) on a 3-Tesla MRI scanner would be undetectable with a modern CT scan and would likely be missed using 1.5- or 3.0-Tesla MRI conventional sequences (Tong et al., 2003). As such, in previous studies this person would be classified as having an uncomplicated MTBI, but in future studies this abnormality might qualify for classification as a complicated MTBI. However, this subject was actually a control subject in one of our studies. He had no known history of an injury to his brain. Thus, not only might the criteria for a complicated MTBI evolve to include smaller and smaller abnormalities, but some of these abnormalities might not be related to the MTBI, thus resulting in misdiagnosis.

Other researchers have recommended differentiating MTBIs based on GCS scores (i.e., GCS 15 and GCS 13–14). In a large-scale study of 2,484

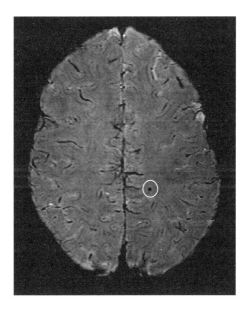

■ **FIGURE 1.2.** Hemosiderin detected with multi-echo SWI using a 3-Tesla scanner. Multi-echo SWI image (Philips Achieva 3T; 5 echoes; voxel size = 0.32 × 0.32 × 0.75 mm^3) courtesy of Alexander Rauscher, PhD, University of British Columbia MRI Research Centre, Department of Radiology, University of British Columbia, Vancouver, Canada.

consecutive patients who presented to an emergency unit in Spain following MTBI, Gomez, Lobato, Ortega, and De La Cruz (1996) found that patients with GCS scores of 13–14 "had a significantly higher incidence of initial loss of consciousness, of skull fracture, abnormal CT findings, need for hospital admission, delayed neurological deterioration, and need for operation" compared to those patients with a GCS score of 15 (p. 453).

EPIDEMIOLOGY

It is very difficult to determine the incidence and prevalence of TBI because many people who sustain an MTBI do not seek medical attention after their injury and thus are not evaluated in an emergency department or admitted to a hospital (Sosin, Sniezek, & Thurman, 1996). This substantial minority of injuries is not captured in most surveillance estimates (see Figure 1.3). Based on hospital surveillance statistics, the Centers for Disease Control and Prevention estimated that at least 1.4 million people sustain a TBI *each year* in the United States. Approximately 1.1 million (79.6%) are treated and released from emergency departments, 235,000 (16.8%) are hospitalized, and 50,000 (3.6%) die (Langlois, Rutland-Brown, & Thomas, 2006). The basic epidemiological characteristics of TBI in the United States, based on hospital surveillance statistics, are presented in Table 1.2.

Brain Injury in the Workplace

Brain injuries in the workplace can result in temporary deficits, permanent impairment, disability, or death (Heyer & Franklin, 1994; Kristman et al., 2008; Wrona, 2006). A substantial percentage of work-related fatalities

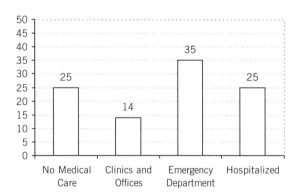

▪ **FIGURE 1.3.** Location of medical care following mild–moderate TBI (percentages). Data from Sosin et al. (1996).

▨ TABLE 1.2. Epidemiological Characteristics of TBI in the United States

- Injuries resulting in emergency department visits are more common in men than women (approximately 60% vs. 40% between the ages of 20 and 44).
- Between the ages of 45 and 54, the injury rate was approximately 48% men and 52% women.
- The rate of hospitalization following TBI in adults is approximately 70% men and 30% women, and motor vehicle accidents are the most common mechanism of injury leading to hospitalization.
- The primary mechanisms of injury are falls (28%), motor vehicle accidents (20%), being struck by or against an object (19%), assaults (11%), "other" (13%), and unknown (9%).
- The anticipated payment sources for hospitalizations were as follows: 43–53% private, 10–13% Medicaid, 4–6% workers' compensation, and 23–39% other/unknown.
- The majority of those who die are men (77–82%), and motor vehicle accidents are the most common mechanism of injury in TBI-related deaths (26–45% across working adult age groups).

Note. From Langlois, Rutland-Brown, and Thomas (2006).

have associated TBIs, and they occur most commonly in primary industry, agriculture, and construction (Tricco, Colantonio, Chipman, Liss, & McLellan, 2006). Men sustain the vast majority of workplace injuries (e.g., 94% in one study), and common mechanisms of on-the-job injury include falls (45.3%), motor vehicle accidents (20.7%), and being struck by or against an object (15.6%; Kim, Colantonio, & Chipman, 2006). Mechanisms of injury by occupational category are presented in Figure 1.4.

PATHOPHYSIOLOGY

TBI is associated with both primary and secondary pathophysiologies. Primary damage involves axonal injury, vascular injury, and hemorrhage. When the brain is subjected to considerable force, the vascular system is at risk for compromise. Thus, tiny, small, or large amounts of bleeding can occur within or around the brain. Due to the intricate and pervasive nature of the vascular system (see Figure 1.5), blood within the brain (detectable using CT or MRI) is often considered a marker for traumatic axonal injury, too. The anterior portion of the brain is most likely to be contused (i.e., frontal and temporal regions), but most parts of the brain are vulnerable to TBI.

Secondary pathophysiology can relate to the endogenous evolution of cellular damage or from secondary systemic processes, such as hypotension or hypoxia. The endogenous secondary pathophysiologies include (1) ischemia, excitotoxicity, energy failure, and cell death cascades (e.g., necrosis

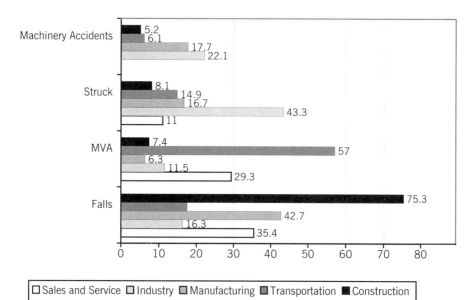

■ **FIGURE 1.4.** Mechanisms of injury by occupational category (percentages of injuries). Data from Kim et al. (2006).

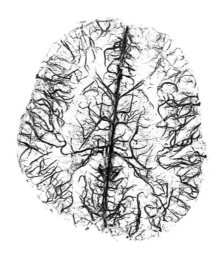

■ **FIGURE 1.5.** Venogram of the human brain. Maximum-intensity projection over 4.2 cm of a multi-echo SWI venogram (Philips Achieva 3T; 7 echoes; voxel size = $0.32 \times 0.32 \times 0.75$ mm^3) courtesy of Alexander Rauscher, PhD, University of British Columbia MRI Research Centre, Department of Radiology, University of British Columbia, Vancouver, Canada.

and apoptosis); (2) edema; (3) traumatic axonal injury; and (4) inflammation (Kochanek, Clark, & Jenkins, 2007).

Ventricular dilation, also referred to as hydrocephalus ex vacuo, can occur gradually following severe traumatic brain injury. Gradually, damaged cells essentially shrink and many are removed, with the residual space being filled by the expanding ventricles. Cortical atrophy (shrinking) and ventricular dilation have been identified in patients with traumatic brain injuries through neuroimaging conducted 6 weeks to 1 year postinjury (Anderson & Bigler, 1995; Bigler, Kurth, Blatter, & Abildskov, 1992).

Traumatic Axonal Injury

Traumatic axonal injuries are often referred to as diffuse axonal injuries, shearing injuries, or deep white matter injuries. Traumatic axonal injury is the preferred terminology in neuroscience research. Axonal injuries result from severe rotational and/or linear acceleration/deceleration forces on the brain. These injuries typically occur in specific brain regions such as the gray and white matter interfaces of the cerebral cortex, the long fibers of the internal capsule (part of the corticospinal tract) that carry motor information (see Figure 1.6), the crossing fibers that connect the two cerebral hemispheres (corpus callosum, see Figure 1.6), and the upper brainstem (Gentry, Godersky, & Thompson, 1988; Orrison et al., 1994).

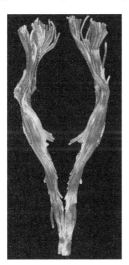 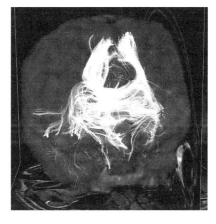

▓ **FIGURE 1.6.** Images of the corticospinal tract (left) and corpus callosum (right). Image of the corticospinal tract courtesy of Ullamari Hakulinen, MSc, Department of Radiology, Tampere University Hospital, Tampere, Finland. Image of the corpus callosum courtesy of Burkhard Mädler, PhD, University of Bonn—Medical Center, Cologne Area, Germany.

In general, unless exposed to very strong forces, axons do not "shear" at the point of injury. What was originally conceptualized as "shearing" in patients with severe to catastrophic brain injuries (Nevin, 1967; Peerless & Rewcastle, 1967; Strich, 1961) is actually a gradual process where stretched and badly damaged axons swell and eventually separate (Povlishock, Becker, Cheng, & Vaughan, 1983). The pathophysiologic sequence that leads to traumatic injury to neurons is "a process, not an event" (Gennarelli & Graham, 1998, p. 163). However, it is important to appreciate that axons can stretch and twist without being sheared or torn (Christman, Grady, Walker, Holloway, & Povlishock, 1994; Povlishock & Becker, 1985; Povlishock et al., 1983; Yaghmai & Povlishock, 1992), even after repeated stretch injuries (Slemmer, Matser, De Zeeuw, & Weber, 2002). In other words, stretch causes a temporary deformation of an axon that gradually returns to the original orientation and morphology even though internal damage might have been sustained (Smith, Wolf, Lusardi, Lee, & Meaney, 1999).

Axons contain numerous microscopic elements including microtubules and neurofilaments. Microtubules are thick cytoskeletal fibers and consist of long polar polymers constructed of protofilaments packed in a long tubular array. They are oriented longitudinally in relation to the axon and are associated with fast axonal transport (Schwartz, 1991). Neurofilaments are essentially the "bones" of the axon and are the most abundant intracellular structural element in axons (Schwartz, 1991). Following axonal stretch, ions enter the axons. This initiates metabolic dysfunction, and when acceleration–deceleration forces are sufficiently high, a progressive series of intracellular events will occur that result in damage to the cytoskeleton and microtubules (Christman et al., 1994; Erb & Povlishock, 1991; Grady et al., 1993; Pettus, Christman, Giebel, & Povlishock, 1994; Povlishock & Becker, 1985; Povlishock et al., 1983; Yaghmai & Povlishock, 1992).

Various characteristics of neurons themselves appear to make them more susceptible to injury. Where axons change direction, enter target nuclei, or decussate, they can be more easily damaged (Adams, Mitchell, Graham, & Doyle, 1977; Grady et al., 1993; Oppenheimer, 1968; Povlishock, 1993; Yaghmai & Povlishock, 1992). Large-caliber neurons are injured more often than smaller neurons that surround them (Yaghmai & Povlishock, 1992). Injured axons are observed more often where a change in tissue density occurs, such as at the gray/white matter interface near the cerebral cortex (Gentry, Godersky, Thompson, & Dunn, 1988; Grady et al., 1993; Peerless & Rewcastle, 1967; Povlishock, 1993). In summary, a TBI might result in (1) no apparent change in structure or function, (2) functional or metabolic change, (3) eventual structural change in the axon, or (4) frank separation of the axon into proximal and distal segments. These outcomes are dependent on the force applied to the brain.

Pathophysiology of MTBI

Most MTBIs are not associated with structural pathoanatomy. The neuro-biology of MTBI, especially injuries on the milder end of the MTBI severity continuum, has been extrapolated mostly from the animal literature (Giza & Hovda, 2001, 2004; Iverson, 2005; Iverson, Lange, Gaetz, & Zasler, 2007a). Giza and Hovda described the complex interwoven cellular and vascular changes that occur following concussion as a multilayered neuro-metabolic cascade. The primary mechanisms include ionic shifts, abnormal energy metabolism, diminished cerebral blood flow, and impaired neu-rotransmission. The stretching of axons due to mechanical force results in an indiscriminate release of neurotransmitters and uncontrolled ionic fluxes. Mechanoporation allows calcium (Ca^{2+}) influx and potassium (K) efflux, contributing to rapid and widespread depolarization. Cells respond by activating ion pumps in an attempt to restore the normal membrane potential. This pump activation increases glucose utilization (i.e., acceler-ated glycolysis). There also appears to be impaired oxidative metabolism. These factors contribute to a state of hypermetabolism, which occurs in tandem with decreased cerebral blood flow, further compounding the hypermetabolism.

The sustained influx of Ca^{2+} can result in mitochondrial accumula-tions of this ion and contribute to metabolic dysfunction and energy fail-ure. The energy production of the cell is compromised further by overuti-lization of anaerobic energy pathways and elevated lactate as a by-product. Moreover, intracellular magnesium levels appear to decrease significantly and remain depressed for several days following injury. This change is important because magnesium is essential for the generation of adenosine triphosphate (ATP; energy production). Magnesium is also essential for the initiation of protein synthesis and the maintenance of the cellular mem-brane potential. Fortunately, for the vast majority of affected cells, this appears to be a reversible series of neurometabolic events.

The ultimate fate of neurons following more serious forms of MTBI, moderate TBI, and severe TBI is related to the extent of traumatic axonal injury (Buki & Povlishock, 2006; Farkas & Povlishock, 2007; Raghupathi, 2004). High intracellular Ca^{2+} levels, combined with stretch injury, can initiate an irreversible process of destruction of microtubules within axons. The disruption of the microtubular and neurofilament components contrib-utes to axonal swelling and detachment (i.e., secondary axotomy). Some, but not all, cells that experience secondary axotomy will degenerate and die through necrotic or apoptotic mechanisms. In general, however, most injured cells, especially following MTBI, do not undergo secondary axo-tomy, and they appear to recover normal cellular function. Following most MTBIs, it appears as if the brain undergoes dynamic restoration, and the injured person returns, in due course, to normal functioning.

Diffusion Tensor Imaging in MTBI

As previously noted, some MTBIs are characterized by structural damage to the brain. Structural damage can be macroscopic (e.g., visible to the naked eye on CT or MRI) or microscopic (visible through diffusion tensor imaging). Researchers have reported that the anterior region of the brain, especially the prefrontal cortex and temporal poles, is particularly susceptible to contusions in brain injuries of all severities. It has been reported that 10–20% of consecutively scanned patients presenting to the hospital with an MTBI will have a macroscopic intracranial abnormality visible on day-of-injury CT (Iverson, Lovell, Smith, & Franzen, 2000; Livingston, Loder, Koziol, & Hunt, 1991; Stein & Ross, 1992; Stiell et al., 2005).

Diffusion tensor imaging (DTI) is a relatively recent MRI technique that is able to examine the integrity of white matter in the brain at a microstructural level (as opposed to a macrostructural level as examined by structural MRI scans). Thermal energy causes molecules to intermingle and migrate, a process called diffusion. MRI can be used to measure the diffusion of water molecules because this diffusion along a field gradient reduces the MR signal. DTI can be used to measure both the directionality and the magnitude of water diffusion in white matter in the human brain. Fractional anisotropy (FA) is a mathematical measurement used in physics to estimate diffusion at the level of a voxel,[1] with values ranging from zero ("isotropic" equal in all directions) to one ("anisotropic" highly directional and linear). Thus, reduced FA is believed to represent white matter that is reduced in directionality, and mean diffusivity is a measure of the total diffusion within a voxel. These complementary measures, at certain levels, might reflect disintegrative changes in white matter. As such, this technology can be used to estimate damage to white matter. White matter is extensive in the brain, as illustrated in Figure 1.7.

DTI is superior for detecting diffuse white matter changes in the brain, and this technology is becoming increasingly important in the evaluation of MTBI. Researchers have reported differences between MTBI samples and healthy control subjects on DTI within the early (i.e., 2 weeks to 3 months) (Inglese et al., 2005a; Kumar et al., 2009; Rutgers et al., 2008a) and late (i.e., 2 or more years) stages of the recovery trajectory (Inglese et al., 2005b; Kraus et al., 2007; Lipton et al., 2008, 2009). Most researchers have reported reduced FA and increased mean diffusivity (MD) in large white matter structures such as the centrum semiovale (Inglese et al., 2005b; Lipton et al., 2008), internal capsule (Inglese et al., 2005b; Lipton et al., 2008), and the corpus callosum (Lipton et al., 2008; Rutgers et al., 2008b), particularly in the splenium (Inglese et al., 2005b; Kumar et al., 2009) and genu (Kumar et al., 2009; Rutgers et al., 2008a). Researchers have reported that symptomatic patients scanned 3–6 years following MTBI had decreased FA and/or increased MD in the corpus callosum, internal capsule (Inglese

■ **FIGURE 1.7.** White matter tracts in the brain: DTI tractography. Image courtesy of Burkhard Mädler, PhD, University of Bonn-Medical Centre, Cologne Area, Germany.

et al., 2005b; Lipton et al., 2008; Niogi et al., 2008), centrum semiovale, deep cerebellar white matter (Lipton et al., 2008), anterior corona radiata, uncinate fasciculus, and cingulum bundle (Niogi et al., 2008) compared to healthy controls.

Given the possibility of widespread microstructural changes, DTI holds great promise for better understanding the potential biological underpinnings of poor outcome following moderate-severe TBI, and more serious forms of MTBI. However, there are several important factors to consider when reviewing the literature relating to DTI in MTBI. First, it is important to appreciate that microstructural abnormalities in white matter can be associated with numerous preexisting conditions. For example, researchers have found microstructural abnormalities in white matter in patients with (1) learning disorders (e.g., Carter et al., 2009; Odegard, Farris, Ring, McColl, & Black, 2009; Rimrodt, Peterson, Denckla, Kaufmann, & Cutting, 2010), (2) attention-deficit/hyperactivity disorder (ADHD) (e.g., Cao et al., 2010; Konrad et al., 2010), (3) substance abuse (e.g., Jacobus et al., 2009; Ma et al., 2009; Yeh, Simpson, Durazzo, Gazdzinski, & Meyerhoff, 2009), and (4) depression (e.g., Dalby et al., 2010). Researchers might not consider common comorbidities when defining groups (e.g., Ashtari et al., 2009; Carter et al., 2009). Second, much of the DTI literature has methodological limitations that restrict our ability to draw confident conclusions. For example, some studies (1) examine groups with sample sizes less than n = 10 (e.g., Carter et al., 2009; Widjaja et al., 2010; Xu, Rasmussen, Lagopoulos, & Haberg, 2007; Yeh et al., 2009; Zhou, Chen, Gong, Tang, & Zhou, 2010), (2) have poorly described or applied inclusion/ exclusion criteria (e.g., Carter et al., 2009; Widjaja et al., 2010; Zhou et al., 2010), or (3) have examined highly selected, nonrepresentative patient samples (e.g., Dalby et al., 2010; Liao, Zhang, Pan, Mantini, Ding, Duan, et al., 2011; Xu, Rasmussen, Lagopoulos, & Haberg, 2007). These factors are important to consider when reviewing the DTI literature.

NEUROLOGICAL AND NEUROPSYCHIATRIC PROBLEMS

Moderate and severe traumatic brain injuries can result in temporary, prolonged, or permanent neurological or neuropsychiatric problems. There are diverse motor, sensory, language, cognitive, emotional, and interpersonal problems that can be caused by such TBIs. Some of the neurological and neuropsychiatric problems that are associated with TBI are listed below (previously described by Iverson & Lange, 2011).

Motor Impairments and Movement Disorders

Motor impairments, such as weakness (paresis) or paralysis (plegia), sometimes occur following severe TBI. Some patients experience spasticity (increased muscle tone and exaggerated reflexes) or ataxia (loss of muscle coordination). Posttraumatic movement disorders manifest by either slowness or poverty of movement (hypokinesia) or by excessive involuntary movements (hyperkinesia).

Balance and Dizziness

Temporary or permanent deficits in static or dynamic balance are often associated with TBI (Campbell & Parry, 2005; Gagnon, Forget, Sullivan, & Friedman, 1998; Geurts, Ribbers, Knoop, & van Limbeek, 1996; Greenwald et al., 2001; Kaufman et al., 2006; McCrea et al., 2003; Rinne et al., 2006). Dizziness is a common complaint in patients who have sustained TBIs of all severities. Vertigo (i.e., a spinning sensation) is less common than dizziness and typically is caused by a peripheral injury to the vestibular system. Imbalance and dizziness can be related to multiple potential causes such as damage to the vestibular system, visual system, somatosensory system, proprioceptive system, brainstem, or cerebellum. However, peripheral damage to the vestibular system is a common etiology.

Visual Impairments

Visual impairments following injuries to the head, brain, or both, can include blurred vision, binocular vision problems (e.g., double vision [diplopia], changes in depth perception, or difficulty localizing objects in space), nystagmus, difficulty with visual tracking (i.e., deficit of smooth pursuit), or difficulty reading or rapidly localizing objects in space (i.e., deficit of saccadic movement). These visual impairments and ocular abnormalities may be caused by orbital fractures; cornea, lens, or retinal injuries; cranial neuropathies; brainstem damage; or damage to subcortical or cortical regions involved with the visual system (Kapoor & Ciuffreda, 2005; Padula et al., 2007). Although uncommon following TBI, it is possible to have a visual field defect.

Cranial Nerve Impairments

Cranial nerves can be damaged due to skull fractures (e.g., olfactory, optic, facial, and auditory-vestibular), shearing forces (e.g., at the level of the cribriform plate for olfaction), intracranial hemorrhages or hematomas, or uncal herniation. Damage to a cranial nerve can cause problems with olfaction, vision, hearing, balance, eye movements, facial sensation, facial movement, swallowing, tongue movements, and neck strength.

Damage to the olfactory system is often underappreciated by clinicians. It is particularly important to neuropsychologists given its anatomical proximity to the orbitomedial frontal lobes (the gyrus rectus is the cortex medial to the olfactory tracts, and the orbital gyri are lateral to these tracts). Costanzo and Zasler (1992) listed the known and presumed mechanisms underlying impairment of sense of smell in patients with injuries to the face, head, and brain as follows: (1) traumatic damage to the nasal epithelium; (2) shearing of the olfactory fila, arising from the nasal epithelium, prior to entering the olfactory bulbs, as a presumed consequence of movement of the brain relative to, and/or fracture of, the cribriform plate; and (3) contusions or edema affecting the olfactory bulb or the lateral or medial olfactory tracts. All of these mechanisms could cause impairment in the ability to detect odors. The authors also stated that it is possible that most cases of anosmia are caused by damage to central olfactory brain regions. Thus, olfactory discrimination could be impaired without any loss in the ability to detect odors.

In closed-head injuries, the sphenoid wings, which are in very close proximity to the anterior borders of both temporal lobes, likely play a major role in producing temporal lobe damage and dysfunction. The upper border of the sphenoid bone is sharply angulated, like the edge of a shelf. In the center of the skull base, the sphenoid wings or ridges terminate in two bony projections called the anterior clinoid processes, derived from the

Latin word for "bedposts." They are adjacent and immediately anterior to the uncus on both sides and point posteriorly toward the foramen magnum. Hence, with a violent forward movement of the brain relative to the skull, the anterior clinoid processes could produce contusions in the region of the uncus. If so, the primary olfactory cortex on each side would be vulnerable to head trauma because it is located near the anteromedial part of the uncus on each side. The olfactory tract is attached to the outer aspect of the hemisphere, whereas other sensory pathways enter the hemisphere through the anterior capsule. Hence, the impact of the skull's jagged interior upon the uncus could damage the primary olfactory cortex or the terminal portion of the olfactory nerve or both (Green, Rohling, Iverson, & Gervais, 2003).

Headaches

Time-limited or chronic headaches can occur following injuries to the neck, head, or both. The most common types of headaches are: (1) muculoskeletal headaches (cap-like discomfort), (2) cervicogenic headaches (unilateral suboccipital head pain with secondary oculo-frontotemporal discomfort), (3) neuritic and neuralgic head pain (sharp and shooting pain in the occipital or parietal region of the scalp), (4) posttraumatic migraine (throbbing with associated nausea and sometimes vomiting), and (5) posttraumatic tension headache (bilateral vise-like pain in the temporal regions) (Zasler, Horn, Martelli, & Nicolson, 2007). Posttraumatic headaches typically resolve within 3 months, but are regarded as chronic if they last more than 3 or 6 months.

Sexual Dysfunction

Changes in sexuality and sexual functioning following TBIs are commonly reported by patients or spouses. These changes can involve desire, drive, arousal, and sexual functioning. Human sexuality is influenced by physical, cognitive, emotional, and social factors. Thus, TBIs can lead to changes in sexuality and functioning through multiple mechanisms such as damage to specific brain regions, neurochemical changes relating to brain damage, endocrinologic abnormalities, medication side effects, secondary medical conditions, physical limitations, cognitive impairments, emotional problems, behavioral problems, and interpersonal difficulties (Sandel, Delmonico, & Kotch, 2007). In addition, sexual problems can occur following work-related injuries that do not involve trauma to the brain.

Fatigue and Sleep Disturbance

Approximately 16–32% of patients who sustain TBIs (mostly moderate-severe) report significant problems with fatigue 1 year postinjury (Bushnik,

Englander, & Wright, 2008), 21–68% at 2 years postinjury (Bushnik et al., 2008; Hillier, Sharpe, & Metzer, 1997; Olver, Ponsford, & Curran, 1996), and 37–73% at 5 years postinjury (Hillier et al., 1997; Olver et al., 1996). Fatigue can interfere with cognitive functioning and a person's day-to-day activities.

Sleep disturbances following TBI are also common (Thaxton & Patel, 2007) and are typically characterized as (1) insomnia (difficulty initiating or maintaining sleep), (2) hypersomnia (excessive sleep or excessive day-time sleepiness), or (3) disturbed sleep–wake (circadian) cycles. Fatigue and sleep disturbances can be related to traumatic brain damage, co-occurring depression, lifestyle factors, or a combination of factors.

Depression

The estimated prevalence of depression following TBI varies widely, ranging from 11 to 77% (e.g., Jorge, Robinson, Starkstein, & Arndt, 1993; Silver, Kramer, Greenwald, & Weissman, 2001; Varney, Martzke, & Roberts, 1987). Depression is most common in the first year postinjury (Dikmen, Bombardier, Machamer, Fann, & Temkin, 2004; Jorge et al., 2004), with rates generally decreasing over time (Ashman et al., 2004; Dikmen et al., 2004). It is likely that depression can (1) arise directly or indirectly from the biological consequences of the TBI, (2) be a psychological reaction to deficits and problems associated with having a brain injury, (3) be a psychological reaction to the trauma of the accident and/or nonbrain injuries, or (4) result from a combination of these factors. It can also arise de novo, incidentally, sometimes postinjury; such as in response to life stressors. It can also arise as part of a preexisting chronic relapsing and remitting condition.

Anxiety Disorders

The most commonly experienced anxiety disorders following TBI include generalized anxiety disorder (8–24%), panic disorder (2–7%), obsessive compulsive disorder (1–9%), specific phobias (e.g., driving; <25%), and posttraumatic stress disorder (0–42%). However, it is important to note that these reported prevalence rates include patients with mild TBI. The prevalence rates of these disorders in moderate to severe TBI alone is not known (Warden & Labbate, 2005). Exacerbation of preinjury anxiety problems in people who sustain an MTBI is commonly seen in clinical settings.

Posttraumatic Stress Disorder

A particularly controversial and confusing issue is whether a person who sustains a TBI can develop PTSD when that person has no memory for the traumatic event. Researchers have reported that individuals with marked amnesia around the time of the event are at relatively low risk for developing PTSD (Bombardier et al., 2006; Gil, Caspi, Ben-Ari, Koren, & Klein, 2005; Levin et al., 2001; Sbordone & Liter, 1995; Warden & Labbate, 2005). Other researchers have reported that PTSD can exist as a comorbid condition with TBI (Harvey & Bryant, 2000; Hickling, Gillen, Blanchard, Buckley, & Taylor, 1998; Mather, Tate, & Hannan, 2003; Mayou, Black, & Bryant, 2000). Despite the absence of memory for the traumatic event, it is hypothesized that some injured people can develop PTSD because (1) they experience some degree of fear conditioning even while in a state of posttraumatic amnesia or confusion, (2) they reconstruct their traumatic experiences over time, or (3) the person experiences traumatic events as they are emerging from posttraumatic amnesia.

Psychotic Disorders

Psychotic disorders following TBI are generically referred to as *posttraumatic psychosis* (American Psychiatric Association, 2000). It is difficult to definitively demonstrate that TBI directly causes any one case of posttraumatic psychosis. However, some researchers have reported that the prevalence of posttraumatic psychosis tends to be higher in individuals who have sustained a TBI than in the general population (Achte, Jarho, Kyykka, & Vesterinen, 1991; Hillbom, 1960; Thomsen, 1984). Similarly, other researchers have reported that individuals with psychotic disorders are more likely to have had a prior TBI than the general population (Abdel-Malik, Husted, Chow, & Bassett, 2003; Gureje, Bamidele, & Raji, 1994; Malaspina et al., 2001). Potential risk factors may include: (1) injuries to the left hemisphere, particularly the temporal and parietal lobes; (2) increased severity of brain injury; (3) closed-head injury, as opposed to a penetrating head injury; (4) vulnerability and/or predisposition to psychosis (e.g., having a first-degree relative with a psychotic disorder); (5) presence of premorbid neurological or neuropsychiatric conditions (e.g., prior brain injury, seizures, ADHD); and (6) posttraumatic epilepsy (Corcoran, McAllister, & Malaspina, 2005).

Personality Changes, Apathy, and Motivation

Personality changes following moderate or severe TBI can result from structural damage to specific regions of the brain, from secondary reactions to impairment or loss, or both (Lezak, Howieson, & Loring, 2004). Depression, anxiety, irritability, restlessness, low frustration tolerance, and apathy are common secondary reactions (O'Shanick & O'Shanick, 2005). Impulsivity, emotional liability, socially inappropriate behaviors, apathy, decreased spontaneity, lack of interest, and emotional blunting are associated with damage to the frontal lobes. Similarly, episodic hyperirrita-bility, aggressive outbursts, or dysphoric mood states are sometimes associ-ated with damage to the temporal lobes (Lucas, 1998).

Lack of Awareness

Up to 45% of people who sustain moderate to severe TBIs are reported to have reduced awareness of medical, physical, and/or cognitive deficits (Flashman & McAllister, 2002). Lack of awareness tends to be function specific, in which some deficits may be accurately assessed by the patient (e.g., hemiplegia), while other deficits are assessed less reliably (e.g., cogni-tive skills). In general, patients tend to underestimate the severity of their cognitive and behavioral impairments when compared to ratings of fam-ily members. In addition, although many patients generally exhibit some awareness of cognitive and speech deficits, they are less likely to report changes in personality and behavior.

SUBSTANCE ABUSE AND TBI

Substance abuse following moderate–severe TBI is common and can inter-fere with rehabilitation. The prevalence of substance abuse in patients following TBI is typically higher than in those without TBI (Silver et al., 2001). Silver and colleagues reported that the prevalence of alcohol and drug abuse disorders was 25% and 11%, respectively, in persons with a history of TBI, compared to 10% and 5% in those without a history of TBI (Silver et al., 2001). Other researchers have reported much higher preva-lence rates of preinjury alcohol abuse problems (43–58%) and illicit drug abuse problems (29.39%) in TBI rehabilitation populations (Bombardier, Temkin, Machamer, & Dikmen, 2003; Corrigan, Bogner, Lamb-Hart, & Sivik-Sears, 2003; Corrigan, Bogner, Mysiw, Clinchot, & Fugate, 2001). Risk factors for substance abuse following TBI include (1) preinjury history of substance abuse, (2) onset of depression postinjury, (3) better physical functioning, (4) male gender, (5) younger age, (6) being uninsured, and (7) not being married (Horner et al., 2005). Combinations of these factors might be related to resumption of, or development of, a substance abuse problem following a TBI.

    For the majority of people, substance abuse problems following TBI reflect the *resumption* of substance use patterns that existed prior to the injury. Patients will typically consume less alcohol during the acute stages of recovery and during the first year postinjury (Bombardier et al., 2003; Corrigan, Lamb-Hart, & Rust, 1995; Jones, 1989; Kreutzer, Witol, & Marwitz, 1996) followed by incremental increases in consumption back to preinjury levels by 3 years postinjury (Bombardier et al., 2003; Corrigan,

Smith-Knapp, & Granger, 1998; Kreutzer et al., 1996). Resumption of illicit drug use is much slower than that of alcohol, with fewer than 25% of previous users reporting any use after 2 years (Kreutzer et al., 1996).

Although the large majority of substance abuse problems following TBI may be related to the resumption of preinjury usage patterns, some individuals who did not have a history of substance abuse may develop problems following injury (Corrigan, 2007). Bombardier and colleagues reported that 14.8% of persons who reported an abstinence or only light consumption of alcohol before injury were reporting consuming moderate or heavy amounts of alcohol at one-year postinjury (Bombardier et al., 2003). Increases in alcohol use postinjury may be related to self-medication attempts to alleviate pain, depression, and/or anxiety (Corrigan, 2007), though causation has received little research to date and is poorly understood.

Substance use disorders following TBI can adversely affect neuropsychological functioning, subjective well-being, employment, and involvement with the criminal justice system (Corrigan, Smith-Knapp, & Granger, 1997; Kreutzer, Wehman, Harris, Burns, & Young, 1991; Kreutzer et al., 1996; Sherer, Bergloff, High, & Nick, 1999). The adverse effects of alcoholism on neuropsychological functioning are well documented. Numerous studies show that chronic alcoholics perform worse on a variety of cognitive measures (e.g., attention, memory, processing speed, executive functioning [e.g., Brandt, Butters, Ryan, & Bayog, 1983; Errico, Parsons, & King, 1991; Gordon, Kennedy, & McPeake, 1988; Grant, 1987; Nixon, 1999; Parsons & Nixon, 1993]) and have structural and functional changes in the brain (e.g., Muuronen, Bergman, Hindmarsh, & Telakivi, 1989; Pfefferbaum et al., 1992; Sullivan, Marsh, Mathalon, Lim, & Pfefferbaum, 1996), such as white matter atrophy (Harper, Kril, & Holloway, 1985; Pfefferbaum et al., 1992, 2000; Pfefferbaum & Sullivan, 2002; Sullivan et al., 1996). Chronic alcohol abuse affects the corpus callosum (Pfefferbaum, Rosenbloom, & Sullivan, 2002; Rosenbloom, Sullivan, & Pfefferbaum, 2003; Sullivan & Pfefferbaum, 2003), and in particular the areas of the genu and splenium (Ma et al., 2005; Pfefferbaum, Adalsteinsson, & Sullivan, 2006; Pfefferbaum & Sullivan, 2002, 2005; Pfefferbaum et al., 2000).

FUNCTIONAL AND NEUROPSYCHOLOGICAL OUTCOME

Injury severity affects all aspects of recovery and outcome from TBI. However, cognitive impairment following TBI is highly individualized and difficult to predict. As a general rule, when considering groups of patients, severe brain injuries are *likely* to result in persisting impairment, and MTBIs are *unlikely* to have persisting impairment (Dikmen, Machamer, & Temkin, 2001; Dikmen, Machamer, Winn, & Temkin, 1995; Schretlen & Shapiro, 2003).

Without question, moderate or severe TBIs frequently result in persistent neuropsychological impairment (neurocognitive and neurobehavioral), functional disability (e.g., difficulty managing day-to-day affairs), and poor return to work rates (Dikmen, Machamer, & Temkin, 1993; Dikmen et al., 1994). Common neurobehavioral changes include personality changes, problems regulating one's emotions, apathy, disinhibition, and anosognosia (loss of awareness of deficits and limitations). Neurocognitive impairments are most notable in, but certainly not restricted to, attention, concentration, working memory, speed of processing, and memory domains (Dikmen et al., 1995, 2001; Dikmen, Machamer, Powell, & Temkin, 2003; Dikmen, McLean, Temkin, & Wyler, 1986; Iverson, 2005; Lezak et al., 2004; Mearns & Lees-Haley, 1993; Spikman, Timmerman, Zomeren van, & Deelman, 1999; Whyte, Schuster, Polansky, Adams, & Coslett, 2000). As injury severity increases, there is a greater likelihood of global cognitive deficit that may include motor skills, verbal and visual-spatial ability, and reasoning skills (Dikmen et al., 1995). As a rule, the vast majority of recovery from moderate to severe TBI occurs within the first year, although some additional recovery can occur during the second year. Substantial improvements after 2 years are not realistic for most patients. However, improvement in functioning can and does occur as the result of learned accommodations and compensations in the years following injury.

Neurocognitive outcome from uncomplicated MTBI is well documented. Injured athletes and trauma patients perform more poorly on neuropsychological tests in the initial days (Bleiberg et al., 2004; Hughes et al., 2004; Lovell, Collins, Iverson, Johnston, & Bradley, 2004; Macciocchi, Barth, Alves, Rimel, & Jane, 1996; McCrea et al., 2003; McCrea, Kelly, Randolph, Cisler, & Berger, 2002) and up to the first month following the injury (Hugenholtz, Stuss, Stethem, & Richard, 1988; Levin et al., 1987; Macciocchi et al., 1996; Mathias, Beall, & Bigler, 2004; Ponsford et al., 2000). As a result of natural recovery, neurocognitive deficits typically are not seen in athletes after 1–3 weeks (Bleiberg et al., 2004; Lovell et al., 2004; Macciocchi et al., 1996; McCrea et al., 2003; McCrea, Hammeke, Olsen, Leo, & Guskiewicz, 2004; Pellman, Lovell, Viano, Casson, & Tucker, 2004) and in trauma patients after 1–3 months (Gentilini et al., 1985; Lahmeyer & Bellur, 1987; Ponsford et al., 2000) in prospective group studies.

Following MTBI, it seems logical to assume that worse short-, medium-, and long-term neuropsychological and functional outcome would result from structural damage to the brain (i.e., complicated MTBI) compared to those patients without obvious structural damage (uncomplicated MTBI). However, the research findings are mixed. Patients who sustained complicated MTBIs tend to perform more poorly on neuropsychological tests in the first 2 months following injury, but only on a small number of tests rather than globally depressed scores (Borgaro, Prigatano, Kwasnica, & Rexer, 2003; Iverson, 2006a; Iverson, Franzen, & Lovell, 1999; Kurca,

Sivak, & Kucera, 2006; Lange, Iverson, Zakrzewski, Ethel-King, & Franzen, 2005; Williams et al., 1990). These differences appear to diminish at 6 months postinjury (Hanlon, Demery, Martinovich, & Kelly, 1999; Hofman et al., 2001). When differences do occur between groups, the effect sizes of these differences are lower than expected (i.e., medium to medium-large effect sizes or lower [Borgaro et al., 2003; Hofman et al., 2001; Iverson, 2006a; Iverson et al., 1999; Lange et al., 2009; Lange et al., 2005; Williams et al., 1990]; see Borgaro and colleagues, 2003, for an exception).

It has also been reported that patients who sustained complicated MTBIs have worse 6–12 month functional outcome (i.e., Glasgow Outcome Scale) compared to patients who sustained uncomplicated MTBIs (van der Naalt et al., 1999a; Williams et al., 1990; Wilson et al., 1996) and have similar 3–5 year outcome (i.e., Functional Status Examination) to patients with a history of moderate and severe TBI (Temkin et al., 2003). There are some exceptions, however. McCauley and colleagues reported that CT abnormalities were not associated with increased risk for postconcussion syndrome at 3 months postinjury (McCauley et al., 2001). Similarly, Lee and colleagues (2008) reported that CT and conventional 3T MRI imaging findings do not predict neurocognitive functioning at 1 or 12 months postinjury, nor functional outcome at 1-year postinjury. It is becoming increasingly clear that complicated MTBIs represent a fairly broad spectrum of injury, with some people having very small abnormalities and excellent functional outcome and other people requiring inpatient rehabilitation and having poor outcome.

POSTCONCUSSION SYNDROME

Following an MTBI, it is well established in the literature that many people experience a cluster of symptoms such as headaches, subjective dizziness, fatigue, sleep disturbance, difficulty thinking (e.g., concentration or memory), and/or emotional changes (e.g., irritability). Of course, not everyone experiences all symptoms, or symptoms to the same degree, but a core set of symptoms is commonly experienced acutely.

There are two mainstream sets of research criteria for the postconcussion syndrome. Although the symptom criteria are similar, the overall criteria differ in important ways. The *Diagnostic and Statistical Manual of Mental Disorders*, fourth edition, criteria (DSM-IV; American Psychiatric Association, 1994) are much more stringent than the ICD-10 criteria (World Health Organization, 1992) in that they require objective evidence of neurocognitive deficits and significant impairment in social or occupational functioning. Not surprisingly, when the ICD-10 and DSM-IV criteria are compared in the same set of patients, relatively low rates of diagnoses are obtained using DSM-IV (i.e., 11 to 17%) compared to ICD-10 criteria

(54 to 64%; [Boake et al., 2004; McCauley et al., 2005]). It is important to note that postconcussional disorder is not an official ICD-10 or DSM-IV diagnostic category. These are research criteria, presented in an effort to provide a common language for researchers and clinicians who are interested in studying this disorder.

The etiology, pathophysiology, definition, and diagnostic criteria for the *persistent* postconcussion syndrome have not been universally agreed upon (see Bigler, 2008; Evered, Ruff, Baldo, & Isomura, 2003; Iverson, 2005; and Ryan & Warden, 2003, for reviews). The syndrome continues to be controversial and poorly understood (Cook, 1972; Lees-Haley, Fox, & Courtney, 2001; Mickeviciene et al., 2002, 2004; Rutherford, Merrett, & McDonald, 1979; Satz et al., 1999). In prospective studies, the syndrome is rare (Alves, Macciocchi, & Barth, 1993; Rutherford et al., 1979), and concerns regarding the role of financial compensation on symptom reporting have been expressed for many years (Binder & Rohling, 1996; Cook, 1972; Miller, 1961; Paniak et al., 2002; Reynolds, Paniak, Toller-Lobe, & Nagy, 2003). Most researchers suggest that the postconcussion syndrome is the result of the biological effects of the injury, psychological factors, psychosocial factors (broadly defined), chronic pain, or a combination of factors (Bijur, Haslum, & Golding, 1990; Binder, 1986; Brown, Fann, & Grant, 1994; Cicerone & Kalmar, 1995; Heilbronner, 1993; Larrabee, 1997; Lishman, 1986; Mittenberg & Strauman, 2000; Youngjohn, Burrows, & Erdal, 1995). The perception and reporting of symptoms long after an MTBI can be influenced by a diverse range of biological, psychological, and social-psychological factors. These factors are illustrated in Figure 1.8 (and some of them are defined in Table 1.3).

When considering long-term outcome, it is important to appreciate that a mild injury to the head or brain is not necessary (and often not sufficient) to produce the constellation of symptoms and problems that comprise the postconcussion syndrome. These symptoms and problems are nonspecific and are commonly found in healthy, community-dwelling adults (Garden & Sullivan, 2010; Gouvier, Uddo-Crane, & Brown, 1988; Iverson & Lange, 2003; Machulda, Bergquist, Ito, & Chew, 1998; Mittenberg, DiGiulio, Perrin, & Bass, 1992; Sawchyn, Brulot, & Strauss, 2000; Trahan, Ross, & Trahan, 2001; Wong, Regennitter, & Barrios, 1994). These symptoms can also commonly arise from other conditions, singly or in combination, such as chronic headaches, chronic bodily pain (Gasquoine, 2000; Iverson & McCracken, 1997; Radanov, Dvorak, & Valach, 1992; Smith-Seemiller, Fow, Kant, & Franzen, 2003), heterogeneous mental health problems (Fox, Lees-Haley, Ernest, & Dolezal-Wood, 1995), depression (Garden & Sullivan, 2010; Iverson, 2006b), and posttraumatic stress disorder (Foa, Cashman, Jaycox, & Perry, 1997). Larrabee (2005), noting the nonspecific nature of symptoms associated with postconcussion syndrome (PCS), stated "There is increasing evidence that questions the

■ **FIGURE 1.8.** Factors that can influence postconcussion-like symptom reporting postacutely or long after an MTBI. From Iverson, Langlois, McCrea, and Kelly (2009). Copyright 2009 by Taylor & Francis. Reprinted by permission.

validity of the PCS symptom constellation" (p. 222). He further observed that failure to appreciate the nonspecific nature of postconcussion symptoms can lead to misdiagnosis and iotrogenesis.

If the postconcussion syndrome is diagnosed, it should not be assumed, uncritically, that the problems are predominately related to traumatically induced cellular damage. Traumatically induced cellular damage, with resulting cognitive and psychological dysfunction, might be a partial causal factor in some patients. However, experienced clinicians who work with this patient population know that the only reasonable perspective is biopsychosocial. The postconcussion syndrome should be considered a diagnosis

▪ TABLE 1.3. Factors Relating to the Perception and Reporting of Symptoms

Personality characteristics and disorders

Personality characteristics influence the development and maintenance of the postconcussion syndrome (Evered et al., 2003; Greiffenstein & Baker, 2001; Hibbard et al., 2000). Personality characteristics influence how people respond to illness, injury, or disease. Kay, Newman, Cavallo, Ezrachi, and Resnick (1992) proposed three personality factors that may influence the development and maintenance of symptoms following MTBI: (1) *Differences in individual response style to trauma.* Some individuals tend to overemphasize cognitive and physical symptoms, whereas others tend to deemphasize them; (2) *Differences in the emotional significance of an event.* For some people the injury can trigger old, unresolved emotional issues; and (3) *Vulnerable personality styles.* These include overachievement, dependency, insecurity, grandiosity, and borderline personality characteristics (not disorder).

Expectation as etiology

Expectation as etiology is a term coined by Mittenberg and colleagues (1992) who proposed that for some people the presence of PCS symptoms following MTBI may be due to "the anticipation, widely held by individuals who have had no opportunity to observe or experience postconcussive symptoms, that PCS will occur following mild head injury" (p. 202). Following an injury, people's anticipation or expectation of certain symptoms might cause them to misattribute future normal, everyday symptoms to the remote injury—or fail to appreciate the relation between more proximal factors (e.g., life stress, poor sleep, and mild depression) and their symptoms (Ferguson, Mittenberg, Barone, & Schneider, 1999; Gunstad & Suhr, 2001).

Nocebo effect (see Gunstad & Suhr, 2001)

The nocebo effect is the causation of sickness by the expectations of sickness and by associated emotional states. That is, the sickness is, essentially, caused by expectation of sickness (Hahn, 1997).

Good-old-days bias

The tendency to view oneself as healthier in the past and to underestimate past problems is referred to as the "good old days" bias. In some studies, patients with back injuries, general trauma, and patients who have sustained MTBIs appear to overestimate the actual degree of change that has taken place postinjury by retrospectively recalling fewer pre-injury symptoms than the base rate of symptoms in healthy adults (Davis, 2002; Gunstad & Suhr, 2001, 2004; Hilsabeck et al., 1998; Mittenberg et al., 1992). This bias is further complicated by involvement in personal injury litigation (e.g., Lees-Haley, Williams, & English, 1996; Lees-Haley et al., 1997) and poor effort on neuropsychological testing (Iverson et al., 2010b). This response bias, combined with an expectation of certain symptoms following MTBI, can have a potent impact on symptom reporting.

Diagnosis threat

The concept of *diagnosis threat* was proposed by Suhr and Gunstad (2002), who adapted the social psychological concept of *stereotype threat* (e.g., Aronson, Lustina, & Good, 1999; Levy, 1996; Leyens, Desert, & Croizet, 2000; Spencer, Steele, & Quinn, 1999; Steele & Aronson, 1995; Walsh, Hickey, & Duffy, 1999). Stereotype threat proposes that the threat of an inferior and/or negative stereotype can adversely affect an individual's performance on a particular task (Steele & Aronson, 1995;

(cont.)

■ **TABLE 1.3.** *(cont.)*

Suhr & Gunstad, 2005). For example, men perform better than women at using a map to navigate. Applied to MTBI, diagnosis threat is the tendency for individuals to perform worse on neuropsychological testing when attention is called to their history of MTBI and the potential negative effects MTBI might have on cognition. That is, Suhr and Gunstad (2002, 2005) reported that university students who are told they are being tested to look for problems relating to a remote MTBI actually perform more poorly than those tested following neutral instructions. Quite remarkably, the psychological effect of "diagnosis threat" has a large, adverse effect on neuropsychological test performance.

Iatrogenesis

A state of ill health or adverse effect caused by medical treatment. For example, diagnosing "brain damage" as an explanation for persistent problems seen long after a mild concussion can be iatrogenic for some people. Telling her she has brain damage and that she will need to cope and compensate, when in fact the probability of permanent brain damage is very low and the probability of an anxiety disorder and sleep disturbance is high, can be iatrogenic. It can also, of course, result in failure to provide the most effective treatment.

of exclusion. The clinician should carefully study the history and progression of the symptoms and problems, and systematically attempt to rule out the most obvious differential diagnoses or competing explanations for the symptoms. Once identified, the differential diagnosis should be treated. If no obvious differential diagnosis can be identified and treated, then the clinician should attempt to conceptualize the person's symptoms and problems broadly and descriptively. Then, treatment (psychological and pharmacological) can be implemented that targets the breadth and depth of factors that might be causing and maintaining a person's symptom reporting and problems in daily life.

ASSESSMENT METHODOLOGY: INTERVIEW VERSUS QUESTIONNAIRE FOR RESIDUAL SYMPTOMS

When evaluating a person following a work-related MTBI, two specialists, in close proximity, can easily come to different conclusions. Different symptoms can be documented, and different conditions can be diagnosed. The reasons for this variability relate to expertise, "focus" (e.g., neurological versus mental health), context (e.g., brief medical appointment with general physician, psychiatric consultation, or forensic evaluation), and methodology (i.e., how information is gathered). Checklists and questionnaires are commonly used to document postconcussion symptoms. They can be a rapid and efficient method for collecting information. However, researchers have found that there is a tendency for MTBI patients to over-endorse symptoms and problems when responding to a list of symptoms compared to spontaneous recall (Gerber & Schraa, 1995; Iverson, Brooks, Ashton, & Lange, 2010a; Nolin, Villemure, & Heroux, 2006). For example, Iverson and colleagues found that injured workers spontaneously endorsed an average of 3.3 symptoms during clinical interview versus 9.1 symptoms when given a questionnaire to complete. More strikingly, it was common for them to endorse symptoms as *moderate or severe* on the questionnaire, despite *not* spontaneously reporting those symptoms during the interview.

There are several possible reasons why people report more symptoms on a questionnaire than during the interview. For example, the questionnaire might remind patients of a symptom or encourage patients to report a symptom that they did not think was of interest to the clinician. Moreover, some patients are not very good at articulating their symptoms during an interview, and anxiety or simply feeling rushed or uncomfortable might exacerbate that problem. There are also several reasons to question the accuracy of questionnaire results. For example, clinicians need to be aware of the possibility of (1) nonspecific symptom endorsement (e.g., symptoms due to other causes), (2) symptom exaggeration and overendorsement (especially in the context of a compensation-related evaluation), (3) symptom expectations influencing symptom endorsement, (4) the "good old days" bias (Davis, 2002; Gunstad & Suhr, 2001, 2004; Hilsabeck, Gouvier, & Bolter, 1998; Iverson, Lange, Brooks, & Ashton Rennison, 2010b; Mittenberg et al., 1992), and (5) the nocebo effect (sickness that is, essentially, caused by expectation of sickness). Moreover, patients periodically do not understand the meaning of a symptom, do not ask for clarification, and simply endorse it. It is also fairly common for patients to report past symptoms as if they are current symptoms (i.e., not properly considering the time frame of the questionnaire). Therefore, it is easy to misdiagnose the postconcussion syndrome when using a symptom questionnaire.

EXAGGERATED SYMPTOMS AND POOR EFFORT ON TESTING

Effort testing is standard practice in forensic neuropsychology (Bush et al., 2005; Heilbronner, Sweet, Morgan, Larrabee, & Millis, 2009). Workers' compensation claims and litigation are potential external incentives for providing poor effort or exaggerating symptoms and problems during an evaluation. Failure to carefully consider these factors may result in the clinician or researcher misattributing a poor performance on testing to an underlying deficit when, in fact, the individual has simply failed to give adequate effort.

Without question, the *context* of the evaluation is critically important. Gervais and colleagues (2001) examined 96 patients with fibromyalgia (FM) with two effort tests. Approximately half of the patients were seen in the context of a disability-related evaluation ($N = 46$). For the 50 patients who were not involved in a disability-related evaluation, 4% failed one effort test and none of them failed the other effort test. In contrast, effort test failure ranged from 24 to 30% of patients seeking disability benefits. In a follow-up study, Gervais and colleagues (2004) reported that failure rates on different effort tests in a sample of 326 patients being evaluated within a compensation context (e.g., workers' compensation or personal injury) ranged from 17 to 43%. None of these patients were being evaluated for the lingering effects of a brain injury or toxic exposure. They were all being evaluated for chronic pain, psychological problems, or both.

Iverson and colleagues (2007b) recruited 54 community-dwelling adults with FM to participate in a study (these were not clinical referrals, and no reports were generated). These subjects reported high levels of depression, chronic pain, and disability on questionnaires. In stark contrast to the Gervais studies, however, not a single research subject failed effort testing. Etherton and colleagues induced moderate pain in healthy young adults, using the cold-presser technique, and demonstrated that this acute pain did not have an adverse effect on effort test results (Etherton, Bianchini, Ciota, & Greve, 2005; Etherton, Bianchini, Greve, & Ciota, 2005). These two studies clearly illustrate that acute and chronic pain, in isolation, does not lead to effort test failure. However, effort test failure is common in patients with chronic pain who are involved in a compensation-related evaluation.

Whitney and colleagues (2009) conducted a retrospective chart review study of Operation Iraqi Freedom/Operation Enduring Freedom patients at a Polytrauma Network Site who were referred for a neuropsychological evaluation. Of the 23 military personnel and veterans evaluated, four (17%) failed effort testing. The patients who failed effort testing had experienced, at most, mild traumatic brain injuries characterized by brief or no loss of consciousness and posttraumatic amnesia lasting less than 10 minutes. In a more recent study, Armistead-Jehle (2010) reported a remarkably high 57.8% failure rate on the Medical Symptom Validity Test in 45 US veterans who screened positive on the Veterans Health Administration TBI screening measure.

As part of an early intervention program for MTBI, we conduct cognitive screening evaluations that include effort testing. These patients are referred to the early intervention program by their workers' compensation case managers because they are slow to recover. The patients were evaluated, on average, 2.1 months ($SD = 1.3$; Range = 1–6) postinjury. Nearly all endorsed symptoms severe enough to warrant an ICD-10 diagnosis of postconcussion syndrome, none were working, and all were receiving benefits. Cognitive test results, based on the Neuropsychological Assessment Battery Screening Module (NAB; Stern & White, 2003), stratified by effort test results, are presented in Figure 1.9. Based on the first 40 evaluations that we conducted, 25% failed effort testing. Their performance was compared to that of clinical groups (i.e., ADHD, TBI, multiple sclerosis, and dementia) from the NAB Psychometric and Technical Manual. As seen in Figure 1.9, effort test failure had a dramatic effect on neuropsychological test results. On average, patients who passed effort testing had broadly normal cognitive functioning, and those who failed had impaired cognitive functioning, consistent with that of the mild dementia sample.

Clinicians should not assume, however, that poor effort occurs only in a forensic context. Poor effort can occur in a research context and, as such, contaminate the findings. This was illustrated, unexpectedly and persuasively, by Stulemeijer and colleagues (2007). These researchers sent a letter and questionnaire to 618 consecutive patients who attended the emergency department as part of a longitudinal prospective cohort study on outcome after MTBI. The information was sent at 6 months postinjury. Of the 299 patients who returned the questionnaire, 113 patients were also willing to undergo a neuropsychological evaluation. The final sample consisted of 110 patients. In this sample of research participants with a history of MTBI, 27% failed effort testing. Poor effort was associated with significantly worse performance on neuropsychological testing. Poor effort was also associated with increased reporting of symptoms of psychological distress. The results of this study are very troubling; they suggest that some of the past research relating to MTBI that did not involve effort testing was likely contaminated by poor effort.

Practitioners are encouraged to conceptualize poor effort, exaggeration, and malingering not in simple dichotomous terms, but in continuous terms, through probabilistic considerations. Clinicians need to identify and explain test scores that simply do not make biological or psychometric sense. If the examinee demonstrates clear evidence of poor effort on any test within the evaluation, the entire set of test results is questionable. The results might not be "invalid," but one should have less confidence in their reliability and validity. In that situation, one cannot assume that even broadly normal test scores represent the person's *true* ability. Some broadly normal scores might also be diminished owing to variable effort. Accordingly, the more conservative conclusion would be that the obtained scores represent the examinee's minimum *overall* performance at the time of the evaluation. Practitioners should avoid trying to use clinical judgment (i.e., make "educated" guesses) to determine which test performances are valid, questionable, or biased. In general, psychologists should avoid overstating effort test results in either direction ("excellent" effort or poor effort).

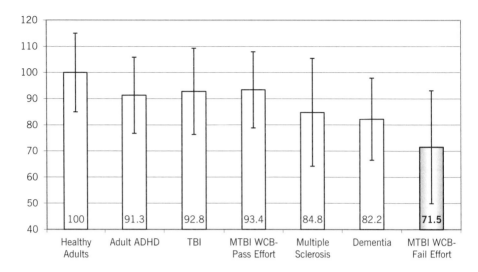

■ **FIGURE 1.9.** Effects of poor effort on cognitive test results in workers' compensation patients with ICD-10 postconcussion syndrome. Scores are for the Attention Index from the NAB Screening Module. The sample size for the MTBI WCB group was 40, 10 of whom failed the Test of Memory Malingering (TOMM; Tombaugh, 1996). Healthy adults: That represents the mean (100) and standard deviation (15) for the S-NAB Attention Index. Test scores for adults with attention-deficit/hyperactivity disorder (ADHD) (N = 30), TBI (N = 31), multiple sclerosis (N = 31), and dementia (N = 20) were derived from the NAB Psychometric and Technical Manual (White & Stern, 2003). The majority of the ADHD participants (63%) were taking stimulant medication at the time of testing. The TBI group from the NAB manual consisted of patients with varying severity of TBIs. Positive CT or MRI results were found in 39% of the sample. Nearly 75% of the patients had less than one day of posttraumatic amnesia. Time between injury and assessment varied across the group, with 15% examined within 3 months, more than one-third examined within the first year, one-third examined within the second year, and 12% examined after more than 2 years. Although 85% of the TBI sample was involved in litigation at the time of testing, all patients performed adequately on a measure of effort. Of the 31 participants with MS, 23 had relapsing/remitting form of MS, 1 had primary progressive, 6 had secondary progressive, and 1 had an unclear subtype. Participants in the dementia sample were community-dwelling older adults who had Clinical Dementia Ratings between 0.5 (questionable dementia) and 1.5 (mild-to-moderate dementia), with the majority having a 1.0 rating (mild dementia). They were tested either in their homes or in an outpatient clinic.

Rather, psychologists should use phraseology that is clear, objective, reasoned, and unambiguous.

EARLY INTERVENTION FOLLOWING MTBI

MTBI early intervention programs are designed to promote recovery and resumption of normal activities. These programs typically consist of educational brochures or sessions that provide information regarding common symptoms, likely time course of recovery, reassurance of recovery, and suggested coping strategies following MTBI (e.g., Mittenberg, Tremont, Zielinski, Fichera, & Rayls, 1996; Paniak, Toller-Lobe, Reynolds, Melnyk, & Nagy, 2000; Ponsford et al., 2002; Wade, King, Wenden, Crawford, & Caldwell, 1998). There is reasonably good evidence that early intervention programs can reduce the severity of postconcussion symptoms (Minderhoud, Boelens, Huizenga, & Saan, 1980) and increase return to work rates (Relander, Troupp, & Af Bjorkesten, 1972). Researchers have found that patients participating in early intervention programs consisting of educational materials as well as various additional treatments and/or assessments (e.g., neuropsychological testing, meeting with a therapist, reassurance, access to a multidisciplinary team) report fewer postconcussion symptoms at 3 months postinjury (Ponsford et al., 2001, 2002) and at 6 months postinjury (Minderhoud et al., 1980; Mittenberg et al., 1996; Wade et al., 1998) compared to patients who received standard hospital treatment.

RETURN TO WORK

Vocational outcome following TBI is important for patients and society as a whole. Individuals who have sustained TBIs and have more confidence in their ability to meet the demands of employment report better quality of life (Tsaousides et al., 2009). For many individuals, the inability to return to work results in a number of economic, social, family, and interpersonal problems (Dikmen et al., 1994; Kraus et al., 2005; Wrightson & Gronwall, 1981). In addition, the economic burden placed on society is of serious concern (e.g., long-term sickness benefits and unemployment benefits), particularly because many individuals who sustain a TBI tend to be young and have their whole working lives ahead of them (Ruffolo, Friedland, Dawson, Colantonio, & Lindsay, 1999).

Severity of injury is related to successful return to work. Individuals who have sustained moderate or severe TBIs have consistently lower return-to-work rates when compared to individuals who have sustained an MTBI (e.g., Asikainen, Kaste, & Sarna, 1996; Dawson, Levine, Schwartz, & Stuss, 2004; Dikmen et al., 1994; Hawley, Ward, Magnay, & Mychalkiw, 2004; Stambrook, Moore, Peters, Deviaene, & Hawryluk, 1990; Uzzell, Langfitt, & Dolinskas, 1987). For example, Dikmen and colleagues (1994) reported successful return-to-work rates after 2 years postinjury in 38% of those with severe TBIs, 66% for moderate TBIs, and 80% for MTBIs.

Return-to-work rates following MTBI vary substantially in the literature. Employment rates have ranged from: (1) 25 to 100% within the first month postinjury (e.g., Dikmen et al., 1994; Haboubi, Long, Koshy, & Ward, 2001; Stranjalis et al., 2004; Wrightson & Gronwall, 1981), (2) 38 to 83% 6 to 9 months postinjury (Dikmen et al., 1994; Drake, Gray, Yoder, Pramuka, & Llewellyn, 2000; Friedland & Dawson, 2001; Hughes et al., 2004; Kraus et al., 2005; McCullagh, Oucherlony, Protzner, Blair, & Feinstein, 2001), (3) 47 to 83% 1 to 2 years postinjury (Dawson et al., 2004; Dikmen et al., 1994; Uzzell et al., 1987; van der Naalt, van Zomeren, Sluiter, & Minderhoud, 1999b) and (4) 62 to 88% 3 or more years postinjury (Asikainen et al., 1996; Dawson et al., 2004; Edna & Cappelen, 1987; Stambrook et al., 1990; Vanderploeg, Curtiss, Duchnick, & Luis, 2003). Iverson et al. (2007a) provided a comprehensive review of this literature. The variability in return-to-work rates is due in large part to methodological differences across studies (e.g., differences in definitions of return to work, inclusion/exclusion criteria, and comparisons to preinjury employment status).

Return-to-work rates following moderate to severe TBI (see Table 1.4 on pp. 40–45) reported in the literature range from (1) 13–44% within the first 6 months, (2) 26–56% after 1 year, (3) 37–64% after 2 years, and (4) 35–77% after 4–5 years (Dawson et al., 2004; Dikmen et al., 1994; Greenspan, Wrigley, Kresnow, Branche-Dorsey, & Fine, 1996; Mazaux et al., 1997; Olver et al., 1996; Ponsford, Olver, Curran, & Ng, 1995; Ruff et al., 1993; Stambrook et al., 1990). Factors that might statistically increase the risk of *poor* return to work include: (1) being married, male, age greater than 40, or having low education; (2) previous employment in semiskilled or unskilled manual jobs; (3) starting a new job; (4) low level of social support; (5) greater cognitive, physical, and psychosocial impairment; (6) changes in personality; and (7) a history of substance abuse (see Table 1.5 on pp. 46–47). Factors that might increase the probability of a *successful* return to work include: (1) using a multidisciplinary team approach during the acute rehabilitation stage, (2) providing a socially inclusive work environment, (3) having health insurance, (4) having social interaction on the job, (5) returning to a job with greater decision-making latitude, (6) providing environmental modifications, and (7) focusing the position on the vocational strengths of the individual (West, Targett, Yasuda, & Wehman, 2007).

CONCLUSIONS

Traumatic brain injuries are common. These injuries occur on a broad continuum of severity, from very mild to catastrophic. The vast majority (at least 80%) are mild in severity. The severity of injury typically is classified based on combinations of severity criteria derived from the duration of unconsciousness, Glasgow Coma Scale score, duration of posttraumatic amnesia, and, sometimes, the results of neuroimaging.

Without question, moderate and severe TBI can result in permanent neurocognitive impairments. Many individuals with severe brain injuries have persistent functional disabilities (e.g., managing day-to-day affairs) and poor return-to-work rates. Problems associated with returning to work result in a number of economic, social, family, and interpersonal problems for the patients. In addition, there is an increased economic burden on society because many of these individuals are young and have their whole working lives ahead of them.

In general, a linear relationship exists between injury severity and risk for cognitive impairment. Impairments are most notable in attention, concentration, working memory, speed of processing, and memory. As injury severity increases, there is a greater likelihood of widespread cognitive deficits. As a rule, the vast majority of recovery from moderate to severe TBI occurs within the first year, with some additional recovery expected during the second year. Substantial improvements after 2 years are not expected for most patients. However, improvement in functioning can and does occur as the result of learned accommodations and compensations in the years following injury.

It is incorrect to assume that MTBIs *cannot* cause permanent brain damage, and it is incorrect to assume that MTBIs *typically* cause permanent brain damage. This is a highly individualized injury—most people recover relatively quickly and fully. However, some people have long-term problems. These long-term problems can be caused or maintained by multiple factors. Brain damage, although possible, is probably not the root cause of long-term problems in most patients (although it can be in some of the more seriously injured). Instead, a diverse set of preexisting and co-occurring conditions and factors likely cause and/or maintain symptoms and problems in most patients (e.g., personality characteristics; preexisting health and mental health problems; comorbid chronic pain, depression, anxiety disorders; social psychological factors; and litigation). It is important to carefully consider a multitude of factors that can cause or maintain symptom reporting long after an MTBI before concluding that a person is likely to have permanent damage to brain function.

(text resumes on page 47)

■ **TABLE 1.4. Return-to-Work Rates Following Moderate to Severe TBI**

First author (year)	Setting	N	Country	Time postinjury	% RTW	TBI definition	RTW definition	Preinjury work status
					Severe TBI			
Inzaghi (2005)	Rehabilitation center	16	Italy	9.7 years (range = 5.8–16.4)	50%	Severe TBI (GCS = 3–7 [GCS <5 in 69% of sample]; LOC = 24 hours–>1 month [LOC >1 week in 94% of sample])	Returned to some meaningful activity (usually at a lower level; no info re: FT/PT status)	14 workers, 2 students (no info re: FT/PT status)
Wood (2006)	Medicolegal practice and hospital	80	UK	17 years (range = 10–32)	53.7%	Severe TBI (PTA: M = 19.3 days, median = 14 days; SD = 23.2 days)	FT, PT, or retired	91.3% FT preinjury
Lippert-Gruner (2007)	Rehabilitation center	51	Germany	12 months	28%	Severe TBI (GCS = < 9 for at least 24 hours)	FT work	Not indicated
Lippert-Gruner (2007)	Rehabilitation center	51	Germany	24 months	40%	Severe TBI (GCS = < 9 for at least 24 hours)	FT work	Not indicated
Doctor (2005)	Level 1 trauma	87	US	1 year	37.9%	Severe TBI (GCS = 3–8)	Worked within 7 days of interview	Employed before TBI
Murphy (2006)	Vocational rehabilitation program	214[a]	UK	5.5 years (SD = 6, range = 7 months–35 years)	59%[b]	Severe TBI (PTA >24 hours)	Paid employment or enrollment in a recognized training course	70% competitive employment, 19% students, 11% unemployed

Study	Setting	N	Country	Time postinjury	%	Severity	Definition of return to work	Outcome
Murphy (2006)	Vocational rehabilitation program	214[a]	UK	5.5 years (SD = 6, range = 7 months–35 years)	72%[b]	Severe TBI (PTA >24 hours)	Paid employment, volunteer work, or enrollment in a recognized training course	70% competitive employment, 19% students, 11% unemployed
Fabiano (1995)	Trauma center	94	US	≤ 1 year	29.8%	Severe TBI (length of coma ≥ 24 hours; M = 20 days, SD = 20 days, range = 1–60 days)	FT or college	75.6% FT, 8.5% PT, 6.4% high school, 7.4% college, 2.1% unemployed/not student
Fabiano (1995)	Trauma center	94	US	≥ 1 year	45.7%	Severe TBI (coma ≥ 24 hours; M = 20 days, range = 1–60 days)	FT, PT, or college	75.6% FT, 8.5% PT, 6.4% high school, 7.4% college, 2.1% unemployed/not student
Asikainen (1996)	Hospital outpatient clinic	285	Finland	12 years (range = 5–20)	41.1%	Severe TBI (GCS = 3–8)	Returned to independent work only	No apparent exclusions
Asikainen (1996)	Hospital outpatient clinic	285	Finland	12 years (range = 5–20)	71.6%	Severe TBI (GCS = 3–8)	Returned to independent work or subsidized employment or education continuation	No apparent exclusions
Mazaux (1997)	Trauma center	17	France	5 years	47%	Severe TBI (GCS = 3–8)	Returned to previous work	Employed prior to injury
Stambrook (1990)	Tertiary trauma center	41	Canada	1–8 years	58.5%	Severe TBI (GCS = 3–8)	Returned to same status	FT work, PT work, or student

(cont.)

41

■ **TABLE 1.4.** (cont.)

First author (year)	Setting	N	Country	Time postinjury	% RTW	TBI definition	RTW definition	Preinjury work status
				Moderate TBI				
Doctor (2005)	Level 1 trauma	84	US	1 year	54.6%	Moderate TBI (GCS = 9–12)	Worked within 7 days of interview	Employed before TBI
Asikainen (1996)	Hospital outpatient clinic	82	Finland	13 years (range = 5–20)	51.21%	Moderate TBI (GCS = 9–12)	Return to independent work only	No apparent exclusions
Asikainen (1996)	Hospital outpatient clinic	82	Finland	15 years (range = 5–20)	69.2%	Moderate TBI (GCS = 9–12)	Returned to independent work or subsidized employment or education continuation	No apparent exclusions
Stambrook (1990)	Tertiary trauma center	51	Canada	1–8 years	68.6%	Moderate TBI (GCS = 9–12)	Returned to same status	FT work, PT work, or student
				Moderate and severe TBI				
Schoenberg (2008)	Rehabilitation program	19	US	59 months (SD = 56)	57.9%	Moderate–severe TBI; cognitive therapy group (telehealth)	31 or more hours of either paid or volunteer work or school class time	Not indicated
Schoenberg (2008)	Rehabilitation program	20	US	28.4 months (SD = 22.5)	65%	Moderate–severe TBI; cognitive therapy group (face-to-face)	31 or more hours of either paid or volunteer work or school class time	Not indicated

Study	Setting	N	Country	Time since injury	%	Severity	Return-to-work definition	Employment status
Hanlon (2005)	Neurological rehabilitation program	24	US	1 year	0%	Moderate–severe TBI (GCS = 3–8; 67% severe, 33% moderate)	Returned to premorbid occupation in previous capacity	Not indicated
Avesani (2005)	Rehabilitation unit	230	Italy	2–10 years	54.3%	Moderate–severe TBI (PTA > 1 day); includes 1.9% mild TBI (PTA < 1 day); GCS $M = 6.7$, $SD = 2.8$	Involved in a work activity for at least a year or more (not necessarily the same job and the same level preinjury)	Employed before TBI
Hanlon (2005)	Neurological rehabilitation program	24	US	1 year	42%	Moderate–severe TBI (GCS = 3–8; 67% severe, 33% moderate)	Returned to premorbid occupation in different or previous capacity, or return to some other occupation	Not indicated
Hanlon (2005)	Neurological rehabilitation program	24	US	1 year	0%	Moderate–severe TBI (GCS = 3–8; 67% severe, 33% moderate)	Returned to premorbid occupation in previous capacity	Not indicated
Tomberg (2005)	Level 1 trauma	61	Estonia	2.3 years (range = 9 months–3 years)	41%	Moderate–severe TBI (GCS = 3–8)	Returned to previous professional occupation or studies	Employed or studying preinjury
Tomberg (2005)	Level 1 trauma	62	Estonia	2.3 years (range = 9 months–3 years)	53%	Moderate–severe TBI (GCS = 3–8)	Returned to previous professional occupation or studies (FT or PT)	Employed or studying preinjury

(cont.)

■ TABLE 1.4. (cont.)

First author (year)	Setting	N	Country	Time postinjury	% RTW	TBI definition	RTW definition	Preinjury work status
Nybo (2005)	Insurance rehabilitation association referrals	19	Finland	34.6 years (SD = 3.1, range = 31–42)	15.8%	Moderate–severe TBI (LOC > 24 hours); childhood injuries	FT work	Not indicated
Nybo (2005)	Insurance rehabilitation association referrals	19	Finland	34.6 years (SD = 3.1, range = 31–42)	26.3%	Moderate–severe TBI (LOC > 24 hours); childhood injuries	FT or subsidized work (PT + compensation)	Not indicated
Vanderploeg (2008)	VA medical center	180	US	1 year	38.9%	Moderate–severe TBI (GCS = <13, or coma of 12 hours or more, or PTA of 24 hours or more, and/ or intracranial abnormality on neuroimaging); cognitive rehabilitation group	Returned to current status of paid employment or school enrolment, either FT or PT, not sheltered workshop	Not indicated
Vanderploeg (2008)	VA medical center	180	US	1 year	35.4%	Moderate–severe TBI (GCS = <13, or coma of 12 hours or more, or	Returned to current status of paid employment or school enrolment, either FT	Not indicated

						PTA of 24 hrs or more, and/ or intracranial abnormality on neuroimaging; functional rehabilitation group	or PT, not sheltered workshop	
Andelic (2009)	Level 1 trauma	62	Norway	9.7 years (*SD* = 0.5, range = 9–10)	58%	Moderate–severe TBI (GCS = 3–12)	FT or PT employment or student	81% FT employment or student preinjury
Olver (1996)	Inpatient rehabilitation hospital	68	Australia	2 years	50%	Moderate–severe TBI (PTA ≥ 1 day or GCS = <13)	Employed FT or PT	Employed at time of injury (FT or PT)
Olver (1996)	Inpatient rehabilitation hospital	68	Australia	5 years	40%	Moderate–severe TBI (PTA ≥ 1 day or GCS = <13)	Employed FT or PT	Employed at time of injury (FT or PT)
Ponsford (2006)	Outpatient rehabilitation program	77	Australia	2 years	46%	Moderate–severe TBI (PTA ≥ 1 day or GCS = <13)	Employed or studying	No apparent exclusions
Ponsford (2006)	Outpatient rehabilitation program	60[c]	Australia	2 years	53%	Moderate–severe TBI (PTA ≥ 1 day or GCS = <13)	Employed or studying	Employed or studying

[a]Estimate based on percentages reported in paper.

[b]Average of three percentages.

[c]A subsample of the original sample calculated based on percentages reported in paper.

■ TABLE 1.5. Factors That Might Influence Return to Work Following TBI

Possible negative influence

- Age greater than 40 years at the time of injury (Dikmen et al., 1994; Humphrey & Oddy, 1980; Ip, Dornan, & Schentag, 1995; McMordie, Barker, & Paolo, 1990; Ponsford et al., 1995; Rao et al., 1990; Sander, Kreutzer, Rosenthal, Delmonico, & Young, 1996; Stambrook et al., 1990)
- Married (vs. single) (Ip et al., 1995)
- Low education level (Brooks, McKinlay, Symington, Beattie, & Campsie, 1987; Ip et al., 1995; Keyser-Marcus et al., 2002)
- Individuals whose pre-injury employment is classified as semi- or unskilled manual labor (MacKenzie et al., 1987)
- Minority status/minorities with disabilities (Greenspan et al., 1996; Rosenthal et al., 1996; Skord & Miranti, 1994; Wright, 1988)
- A low level of social support (MacKenzie et al., 1987; Oddy, Coughlan, Tyerman, & Jenkins, 1985)
- Cognitive deficits such as new learning and memory, impaired self-awareness, preexisting and postinjury dysfunctional behaviors (Godfrey, Bishara, Partridge, & Knight, 1993; Wehman, West, Kregel, Sherron, & Kreutzer, 1995)
- Cognitive impairment (Martin-Tamer, 1988; Ryan, Sautter, Capps, Meneese, & Barth, 1992)
- Motor and cognitive impairments (Greenspan et al., 1996)
- Lower IQ (Cattelani, Tanzi, Lombardi, & Mazzucchi, 2002)
- Physical disability (McKinlay, Brooks, & Bond, 1983)
- Psychosocial impairment (Thomsen, 1984)
- History of alcohol abuse (Ip et al., 1995; Sherer et al., 1999)
- Deficits in social behavior, cognitive functioning and personality (Ben-Yishay, Silver, Piasetsky, & Rattok, 1987; Thomsen, 1984)
- Cognitive deficits and personality change (Brooks et al., 1987; Humphrey & Oddy, 1980; Wehman et al., 1993)
- High Disability Rating Scale discharge scores (Gollaher et al., 1998; Wright, 2000)
- Longer length of stay (Keyser-Marcus et al., 2002)
- Psychiatric history, violent mechanism of injury, and prior alcohol or drug use (Wagner, Hammond, Sasser, & Wiercisiewski, 2002)

Possible positive influence

- Shorter duration of coma postinjury (Dikmen et al., 1994; Rao et al., 1990)
- Higher Glasgow Coma Scale scores on admission (Cifu et al., 1997; Stambrook et al., 1990)
- Shorter duration of inpatient rehabilitation (Dikmen et al., 1994; Heaton, Thompson, Nelson, Filly, & Franklin, 1990)
- Age greater than 60 years at time of injury (Crepeau & Scherzer, 1993)
- Younger versus older aged individuals (Ip et al., 1995; Rao et al., 1990)
- Female (McMordie et al., 1990)
- Individuals whose pre-injury employment included structural occupations such as building and trades (compared to professional, managerial, clerical, or service workers) (Fraser, Dikmen, McLean, Miller, & Temkin, 1988)

(cont.)

▥ **TABLE 1.5.** *(cont.)*

- Individuals with more education and technical skills (Vogenthaler, Smith, & Goldfader, 1989)
- Individuals who are hired by their previous employer postinjury (Fabiano, Crewe, & Goran, 1995)
- Occupational category pre-injury (Orr, Walker, Marwitz, & Kreutzer, 2003)
- Level of social interaction on the job and return to jobs with greater decision-making latitude (Ruffolo et al., 1999)
- Environmental modifications and focusing on vocational strengths of the individual (Kowalske, Plenger, Lusby, & Hayden, 2000)
- Individuals with premorbid occupations that were managerial or professional (Walker, Marwitz, Kreutzer, Hart, & Novack, 2006)
- Individuals who are employed prior to injury (Keyser-Marcus et al., 2002)
- Greater self-awareness (Sherer et al., 1998)
- Socially inclusive work environments and availability of health insurance (West, 1995)

ACKNOWLEDGMENT

The views expressed in this chapter are those of the authors and do not reflect the official policy of the Department of Army, Department of Defense, or U.S. Government.

NOTE

1. A voxel is a volume region in three-dimensional space that corresponds to a picture element (i.e., "pixel") for a specific slice thickness. Pixels are used to estimate the resolution of an image.

REFERENCES

AbdelMalik, P., Husted, J., Chow, E. W., & Bassett, A. S. (2003). Childhood head injury and expression of schizophrenia in multiply affected families. *Archives of General Psychiatry, 60*(3), 231–236.

Achte, K., Jarho, L., Kyykka, T., & Vesterinen, E. (1991). Paranoid disorders following war brain damage. Preliminary report. *Psychopathology, 24*(5), 309–315.

Adams, H., Mitchell, D. E., Graham, D. I., & Doyle, D. (1977). Diffuse brain damage of immediate impact type: Its relationship to "primary brain-stem damage" in head injury. *Brain, 100*(3), 489–502.

Alves, W., Macciocchi, S. N., & Barth, J. T. (1993). Postconcussive symptoms after uncomplicated mild head injury. *Journal of Head Trauma Rehabilitation, 8*, 48–59.

American Psychiatric Association. (1994). *Diagnostic and statistical manual of mental disorders* (4th ed.). Washington, DC: Author.

American Psychiatric Association. (2000). *Diagnostic and statistical manual of mental disorders* (4th ed., text rev.). Washington, DC: Author.

Andelic, N., Hammergren, N., Bautz-Holter, E., Sveen, U., Brunborg, C., & Roe, C. (2009). Functional outcome and health-related quality of life 10 years after moderate-to-severe traumatic brain injury. *Acta Neurologica Scandinavica, 120*(1), 16–23.

Anderson, C. V., & Bigler, E. D. (1995). Ventricular dilation, cortical atrophy, and neuropsychological outcome following traumatic brain injury. *Journal of Neuropsychiatry and Clinical Neurosciences, 7*(1), 42–48.

Armistead-Jehle, P. (2010). Symptom validity test performance in U.S. veterans referred for evaluation of mild TBI. *Applied Neuropsychology, 17*(1), 52–59.

Aronson, J., Lustina, M. J., & Good, C. (1999). When white men can't do math: Necessary and sufficient factors in stereotype threat. *Journal of Experimental Social Psychology, 35*(1), 29–46.

Ashman, T. A., Spielman, L. A., Hibbard, M. R., Silver, J. M., Chandna, T., & Gordon, W. A. (2004). Psychiatric challenges in the first 6 years after traumatic brain injury: Cross-sequential analyses of Axis I disorders. *Archives of Physical Medicine and Rehabilitation, 85*(4, Suppl. 2), S36–S42.

Ashtari, M., Cervellione, K., Cottone, J., Ardekani, B. A., Sevy, S., & Kumra, S. (2009). Diffusion abnormalities in adolescents and young adults with a history of heavy cannabis use. *Journal of Psychiatric Research, 43*(3), 189–204.

Asikainen, I., Kaste, M., & Sarna, S. (1996). Patients with traumatic brain injury referred to a rehabilitation and re-employment programme: Social and professional outcome for 508 Finnish patients 5 or more years after injury. *Brain Injury, 10*(12), 883–899.

Avesani, R., Salvi, L., Rigoli, G., & Gambini, M. G. (2005). Reintegration after severe brain injury: A retrospective study. *Brain Injury, 19*(11), 933–939.

Ben-Yishay, Y., Silver, S. M., Piasetsky, E., & Rattok, J. (1987). Relationship between employability and vocational outcome after intensive holistic cognitive rehabilitation. *Journal of Head Trauma Rehabilitation, 2*(1), 35–48.

Bigler, E. D. (2008). Neuropsychology and clinical neuroscience of persistent postconcussive syndrome. *Journal of the International Neuropsychological Society, 14*(1), 1–22.

Bigler, E. D., Kurth, S. M., Blatter, D., & Abildskov, T. J. (1992). Degenerative changes in traumatic brain injury: Post-injury magnetic resonance identified ventricular expansion compared to pre-injury levels. *Brain Research Bulletin, 28*(4), 651–653.

Bijur, P. E., Haslum, M., & Golding, J. (1990). Cognitive and behavioral sequelae of mild head injury in children. *Pediatrics, 86*(3), 337–344.

Binder, L. M. (1986). Persisting symptoms after mild head injury: A review of the postconcussive syndrome. *Journal of Clinical and Experimental Neuropsychology, 8*(4), 323–346.

Binder, L. M., & Rohling, M. L. (1996). Money matters: A meta-analytic review of the effects of financial incentives on recovery after closed-head injury. *American Journal of Psychiatry, 153*(1), 7–10.

Bleiberg, J., Cernich, A. N., Cameron, K., Sun, W., Peck, K., Ecklund, P. J., et al. (2004). Duration of cognitive impairment after sports concussion. *Neurosurgery, 54*(5), 1073–1078; discussion 1078–1080.

Boake, C., McCauley, S. R., Levin, H. S., Contant, C. F., Song, J. X., Brown, S. A., et al. (2004). Limited agreement between criteria-based diagnoses of postconcussional syndrome. *Journal of Neuropsychiatry and Clinical Neurosciences, 16*(4), 493–499.

Bombardier, C. H., Fann, J. R., Temkin, N., Esselman, P. C., Pelzer, E., Keough, M., et al. (2006). Posttraumatic stress disorder symptoms during the first six months after traumatic brain injury. *Journal of Neuropsychiatry and Clinical Neurosciences, 18*(4), 501–508.

Bombardier, C. H., Temkin, N. R., Machamer, J., & Dikmen, S. S. (2003). The natural history of drinking and alcohol-related problems after traumatic brain injury. *Archives of Physical Medicine and Rehabilitation, 84*(2), 185–191.

Borgaro, S. R., Prigatano, G. P., Kwasnica, C., & Rexer, J. L. (2003). Cognitive and affective sequelae in complicated and uncomplicated mild traumatic brain injury. *Brain Injury, 17*(3), 189–198.

Brandt, J., Butters, N., Ryan, C., & Bayog, R. (1983). Cognitive loss and recovery in long-term alcohol abusers. *Archives of General Psychiatry, 40*(4), 435–442.

Brooks, N., McKinlay, W., Symington, C., Beattie, A., & Campsie, L. (1987). Return to work within the first seven years of severe head injury. *Brain Injury, 1*(1), 5–19.

Brown, S. J., Fann, J. R., & Grant, I. (1994). Postconcussional disorder: Time to acknowledge a common source of neurobehavioral morbidity. *Journal of Neuropsychiatry and Clinical Neurosciences, 6*(1), 15–22.

Buki, A., & Povlishock, J. T. (2006). All roads lead to disconnection?—Traumatic axonal injury revisited. *Acta Neurochirurgica (Wien), 148*(2), 181–193; discussion 193–184.

Bush, S. S., Ruff, R. M., Troster, A. I., Barth, J. T., Koffler, S. P., Pliskin, N. H., et al. (2005). Symptom validity assessment: Practice issues and medical necessity NAN Policy and Planning Committee. *Archives of Clinical Neuropsychology, 20*(4), 419–426.

Bushnik, T., Englander, J., & Wright, J. (2008). The experience of fatigue in the first 2 years after moderate-to-severe traumatic brain injury: A preliminary report. *Journal of Head Trauma Rehabilitation, 23*(1), 17–24.

Campbell, M., & Parry, A. (2005). Balance disorder and traumatic brain injury: Preliminary findings of a multi-factorial observational study. *Brain Injury, 19*(13), 1095–1104.

Cao, Q., Sun, L., Gong, G., Lv, Y., Cao, X., Shuai, L., et al. (2010). The macrostructural and microstructural abnormalities of corpus callosum in children with attention deficit/hyperactivity disorder: A combined morphometric and diffusion tensor MRI study. *Brain Research, 1310*, 172–180.

Carter, J. C., Lanham, D. C., Cutting, L. E., Clements-Stephens, A. M., Chen, X., Hadzipasic, M., et al. (2009). A dual DTI approach to analyzing white matter in children with dyslexia. *Psychiatry Research, 172*(3), 215–219.

Cattelani, R., Tanzi, F., Lombardi, F., & Mazzucchi, A. (2002). Competitive re-employment after severe traumatic brain injury: Clinical, cognitive and behavioural predictive variables. *Brain Injury, 16*(1), 51–64.

Christman, C. W., Grady, M. S., Walker, S. A., Holloway, K. L., & Povlishock, J. T. (1994). Ultrastructural studies of diffuse axonal injury in humans. *Journal of Neurotrauma, 11*(2), 173–186.

Cicerone, K. D., & Kalmar, K. (1995). Persistent postconcussion syndrome: The structure of subjective complaints after mild traumatic brain injury. *Journal of Head Trauma Rehabilitation, 10*, 1–7.

Cifu, D. X., Keyser-Marcus, L., Lopez, E., Wehman, P., Kreutzer, J. S., Englander, J., et al. (1997). Acute predictors of successful return to work 1 year after traumatic brain injury: A multicenter analysis. *Archives of Physical Medicine and Rehabilitation, 78*(2), 125–131.

Cook, J. B. (1972). The post-concussional syndrome and factors influencing recovery after minor head injury admitted to hospital. *Scandinavian Journal of Rehabilitation and Medicine, 4*(1), 27–30.

Corcoran, C., McAllister, T. W., & Malaspina, D. (2005). Psychotic disorders. In J. M. Silver, T. W. McAllister, & S. C. Yudofsky (Eds.), *Textbook of traumatic brain injury* (pp. 213–229). Arlington, VA: American Psychiatric Publishing.

Corrigan, J. D. (2007). The treatment of substance abuse in persons with TBI. In N. D. Zasler, D. I. Katz, & R. D. Zafonte (Eds.), *Brain injury medicine* (pp. 1105–1115). New York: Demos.

Corrigan, J. D., Bogner, J., Lamb-Hart, G., & Sivik-Sears, N. (2003). *Technical report on problematic substance use variables.* The Center for Outcome Measurement in Brain Injury. Retrieved March 18, 2008, from *www.tbims.org/combi/subst.*

Corrigan, J. D., Bogner, J. A., Mysiw, W. J., Clinchot, D., & Fugate, L. (2001). Life satisfaction after traumatic brain injury. *Journal of Head Trauma Rehabilitation, 16*(6), 543–555.

Corrigan, J. D., Lamb-Hart, G. L., & Rust, E. (1995). A programme of intervention for substance abuse following traumatic brain injury. *Brain Injury, 9*(3), 221–236.

Corrigan, J. D., Smith-Knapp, K., & Granger, C. V. (1997). Validity of the functional independence measure for persons with traumatic brain injury. *Archives of Physical Medicine and Rehabilitation, 78*(8), 828–834.

Corrigan, J. D., Smith-Knapp, K., & Granger, C. V. (1998). Outcomes in the first 5 years after traumatic brain injury. *Archives of Physical Medicine and Rehabilitation, 79*(3), 298–305.

Costanzo, R. M., & Zasler, N. D. (1992). Epidemiology and pathophysiology of olfactory and gustatory dysfunction in head trauma. *Journal of Head Trauma Rehabilitation, 7*(1), 15–24.

Crepeau, F., & Scherzer, P. (1993). Predictors and indicators of work status after traumatic brain injury: A meta-analysis. *Neuropsychological Rehabilitation, 3*, 5–35.

Dalby, R. B., Frandsen, J., Chakravarty, M. M., Ahdidan, J., Sorensen, L., Rosenberg, R., et al. (2010). Depression severity is correlated to the integrity of white matter fiber tracts in late-onset major depression. *Psychiatry Research, 184*(1), 38–48.

Davis, C. H. (2002). Self-perception in mild traumatic brain injury. *American Journal of Physical Medicine and Rehabilitation, 81*(8), 609–621.

Dawson, D. R., Levine, B., Schwartz, M. L., & Stuss, D. T. (2004). Acute predictors of real-world outcomes following traumatic brain injury: A prospective study. *Brain Injury, 18*(3), 221–238.

Denk, C., & Rauscher, A. (2010). Susceptibility weighted imaging with multiple echoes. *Journal of Magnetic Resonance Imaging (JMRI), 31*(1), 185–191.

Dikmen, S., Bombardier, C. H., Machamer, J. E., Fann, J. R., & Temkin, N. R. (2004). Natural history of depression in traumatic brain injury. *Archives of Physical Medicine and Rehabilitation, 85*(9), 1457–1464.

Dikmen, S., Machamer, J., & Temkin, N. (1993). Psychosocial outcome in patients with moderate to severe head injury: 2-year follow-up. *Brain Injury, 7*(2), 113–124.

Dikmen, S., Machamer, J., & Temkin, N. (2001). Mild head injury: Facts and artifacts. *Journal of Clinical and Experimental Neuropsychology, 23*(6), 729–738.

Dikmen, S., Machamer, J. E., Powell, J. M., & Temkin, N. R. (2003). Outcome 3 to 5 years after moderate to severe traumatic brain injury. *Archives of Physical Medicine and Rehabilitation, 84*(10), 1449–1457.

Dikmen, S., Machamer, J. E., Winn, R., & Temkin, N. R. (1995). Neuropsychological outcome 1-year post head injury. *Neuropsychology, 9,* 80–90.

Dikmen, S., McLean, A., Jr., Temkin, N. R., & Wyler, A. R. (1986). Neuropsychologic outcome at one-month postinjury. *Archives of Physical Medicine and Rehabilitation, 67*(8), 507–513.

Dikmen, S., Temkin, N. R., Machamer, J. E., Holubkov, A. L., Fraser, R. T., & Winn, H. R. (1994). Employment following traumatic head injuries. *Archives of Neurology, 51*(2), 177–186.

Doctor, J. N., Castro, J., Temkin, N. R., Fraser, R. T., Machamer, J. E., & Dikmen, S. S. (2005). Workers' risk of unemployment after traumatic brain injury: A normed comparison. *Journal of the International Neuropsychological Society, 11*(6), 747–752.

Drake, A. I., Gray, N., Yoder, S., Pramuka, M., & Llewellyn, M. (2000). Factors predicting return to work following mild traumatic brain injury: A discriminant analysis. *Journal of Head Trauma Rehabilitation, 15*(5), 1103–1112.

Edna, T. H., & Cappelen, J. (1987). Return to work and social adjustment after traumatic head injury. *Acta Neurochirurgica (Wien), 85*(1–2), 40–43.

Erb, D. E., & Povlishock, J. T. (1991). Neuroplasticity following traumatic brain injury: A study of GABAergic terminal loss and recovery in the cat dorsal lateral vestibular nucleus. *Experimental Brain Research, 83*(2), 253–267.

Errico, A. L., Parsons, O. A., & King, A. C. (1991). Assessment of verbosequential and visuospatial cognitive abilities in chronic alcoholics. *Psychological Assessment, 3,* 305–308.

Etherton, J. L., Bianchini, K. J., Ciota, M. A., & Greve, K. W. (2005). Reliable digit span is unaffected by laboratory-induced pain: Implications for clinical use. *Assessment, 12*(1), 101–106.

Etherton, J. L., Bianchini, K. J., Greve, K. W., & Ciota, M. A. (2005). Test of Memory Malingering Performance is unaffected by laboratory-induced pain: Implications for clinical use. *Archives of Clinical Neuropsychology, 20*(3), 375–384.

Evered, L., Ruff, R., Baldo, J., & Isomura, A. (2003). Emotional risk factors and postconcussional disorder. *Assessment, 10*(4), 420–427.

Fabiano, R. J., & Crewe, N. (1995). Variables associated with employment following severe traumatic brain injury. *Rehabilitation Psychology, 40*(3), 223–231.

Fabiano, R. J., Crewe, N., & Goran, D. A. (1995). Differences between elapsed time to employment and employer selection in vocational outcome following severe traumatic brain injury. *Journal of Applied Rehabilitation Councelling, 26*(4), 17–20.

Farkas, O., & Povlishock, J. T. (2007). Cellular and subcellular change evoked by diffuse traumatic brain injury: A complex web of change extending far beyond focal damage. *Progress in Brain Research, 161,* 43–59.

Ferguson, R. J., Mittenberg, W., Barone, D. F., & Schneider, B. (1999). Postconcussion syndrome following sports-related head injury: Expectation as etiology. *Neuropsychology, 13*(4), 582–589.

Flashman, L. A., & McAllister, T. W. (2002). Lack of awareness and its impact in traumatic brain injury. *NeuroRehabilitation, 17*(4), 285–296.

Foa, E. B., Cashman, L., Jaycox, L., & Perry, K. (1997). The validation of a self-report measure of posttraumatic stress disorder: The Posttraumatic Diagnostic Scale. *Psychological Assessment, 9*(4), 445–451.

Fox, D. D., Lees-Haley, P. R., Ernest, K., & Dolezal-Wood, S. (1995). Post-concussive symptoms: Base rates and etiology in psychiatric patients. *The Clinical Neuropsychologist, 9,* 89–92.

Fraser, R. T., Dikmen, S. S., McLean, A., Miller, B., & Temkin, N. R. (1988). Employ-ability of head injury survivors: First year post-injury. *Rehabilitation Counselling Bulletin, 31,* 276–288.

Friedland, J. F., & Dawson, D. R. (2001). Function after motor vehicle accidents: A pro-spective study of mild head injury and posttraumatic stress. *Journal of Nervous and Mental Disease, 189*(7), 426–434.

Gagnon, I., Forget, R., Sullivan, S. J., & Friedman, D. (1998). Motor performance following a mild traumatic brain injury in children: An exploratory study. *Brain Injury, 12*(10), 843–853.

Garden, N., & Sullivan, K. A. (2010). An examination of the base rates of post-concussion symptoms: The influence of demographics and depression. *Applied Neuropsychology, 17*(1), 1–7.

Gasquoine, P. G. (2000). Postconcussional symptoms in chronic back pain. *Applied Neuropsychology, 7*(2), 83–89.

Gennarelli, T. A., & Graham, D. I. (1998). Neuropathology of the head injuries. *Semi-nars in Clinical Neuropsychiatry, 3*(3), 160–175.

Gentilini, M., Nichelli, P., Schoenhuber, R., Bortolotti, P., Tonelli, L., Falasca, A., et al. (1985). Neuropsychological evaluation of mild head injury. *Journal of Neurology, Neurosurgery and Psychiatry, 48*(2), 137–140.

Gentry, L. R., Godersky, J. C., & Thompson, B. (1988). MR imaging of head trauma: Review of the distribution and radiopathologic features of traumatic lesions. *American Journal of Roentgenology, 150*(3), 663–672.

Gentry, L. R., Godersky, J. C., Thompson, B., & Dunn, V. D. (1988). Prospective com-parative study of intermediate-field MR and CT in the evaluation of closed head trauma. *American Journal of Roentgenology, 150*(3), 673–682.

Gerber, D. J., & Schraa, J. C. (1995). Mild traumatic brain injury: Searching for the syndrome. *Journal of Head Trauma Rehabilitation, 10*(4), 28–40.

Gervais, R. O., Rohling, M. L., Green, P., & Ford, W. (2004). A comparison of WMT, CARB, and TOMM failure rates in non-head injury disability claimants. *Archives of Clinical Neuropsychology, 19*(4), 475–487.

Gervais, R. O., Russell, A. S., Green, P., Allen, L. M., 3rd, Ferrari, R., & Pieschl, S. D. (2001). Effort testing in patients with fibromyalgia and disability incentives. *Journal of Rheumatology, 28*(8), 1892–1899.

Geurts, A. C., Ribbers, G. M., Knoop, J. A., & van Limbeek, J. (1996). Identification of static and dynamic postural instability following traumatic brain injury. *Archives of Physical Medicine and Rehabilitation, 77*(7), 639–644.

Gil, S., Caspi, Y., Ben-Ari, I. Z., Koren, D., & Klein, E. (2005). Does memory of a traumatic event increase the risk for posttraumatic stress disorder in patients with traumatic brain injury? A prospective study. *American Journal of Psychiatry, 162*(5), 963–969.

Giza, C. C., & Hovda, D. A. (2001). The neurometabolic cascade of concussion. *Jour-nal of Athletic Training, 36*(3), 228–235.

Giza, C. C., & Hovda, D. A. (2004). The pathophysiology of traumatic brain injury. In M. R. Lovell, R. J. Echemendia, J. T. Barth, & M. W. Collins (Eds.), *Traumatic brain injury in sports* (pp. 45–70). Lisse, Netherlands: Swets & Zeitlinger.

Godfrey, H. P., Bishara, S. N., Partridge, F. M., & Knight, R. G. (1993). Neuropsy-chological impairment and return to work following severe closed head injury: Implications for clinical management. *New Zealand Medical Journal, 106*(960), 301–303.

Gollaher, K., High, W., Sherer, M., Bergloff, P., Boake, C., Young, M. E., et al. (1998).

Prediction of employment outcome one to three years following traumatic brain injury (TBI). *Brain Injury, 12*(4), 255–263.

Gomez, P. A., Lobato, R. D., Ortega, J. M., & De La Cruz, J. (1996). Mild head injury: Differences in prognosis among patients with a Glasgow Coma Scale score of 13 to 15 and analysis of factors associated with abnormal CT findings. *British Journal of Neurosurgery, 10*(5), 453–460.

Gordon, S. M., Kennedy, B. P., & McPeake, J. D. (1988). Neuropsychologically impaired alcoholics: Assessment, treatment considerations, and rehabilitation. *Journal of Substance Abuse Treatment, 5*(2), 99–104.

Gouvier, W. D., Uddo-Crane, M., & Brown, L. M. (1988). Base rates of postconcussional symptoms. *Archives of Clinical Neuropsychology, 3*, 273–278.

Grady, M. S., McLaughlin, M. R., Christman, C. W., Valadka, A. B., Fligner, C. L., & Povlishock, J. T. (1993). The use of antibodies targeted against the neurofilament subunits for the detection of diffuse axonal injury in humans. *Journal of Neuropathology and Experimental Neurology, 52*(2), 143–152.

Grant, I. (1987). Alcohol and the brain: Neuropsychological correlates. *Journal of Consulting and Clinical Psychology, 55*(3), 310–324.

Green, P., Rohling, M. L., Iverson, G. L., & Gervais, R. O. (2003). Relationships between olfactory discrimination and head injury severity. *Brain Injury, 17*(6), 479–496.

Greenspan, A. I., Wrigley, J. M., Kresnow, M., Branche-Dorsey, C. M., & Fine, P. R. (1996). Factors influencing failure to return to work due to traumatic brain injury. *Brain Injury, 10*(3), 207–218.

Greenwald, B. D., Cifu, D. X., Marwitz, J. H., Enders, L. J., Brown, A. W., Englander, J. S., et al. (2001). Factors associated with balance deficits on admission to rehabilitation after traumatic brain injury: A multicenter analysis. *Journal of Head Trauma Rehabilitation, 16*(3), 238–252.

Greiffenstein, F. M., & Baker, J. W. (2001). Comparison of premorbid and postinjury mmpi-2 profiles in late postconcussion claimants. *The Clinical Neuropsychologist, 15*(2), 162–170.

Gunstad, J., & Suhr, J. A. (2001). "Expectation as etiology" versus "the good old days": Postconcussion syndrome symptom reporting in athletes, headache sufferers, and depressed individuals. *Journal of the International Neuropsychological Society, 7*(3), 323–333.

Gunstad, J., & Suhr, J. A. (2004). Cognitive factors in Postconcussion Syndrome symptom report. *Archives of Clinical Neuropsychology, 19*(3), 391–405.

Gureje, O., Bamidele, R., & Raji, O. (1994). Early brain trauma and schizophrenia in Nigerian patients. *American Journal of Psychiatry, 151*(3), 368–371.

Haboubi, N. H., Long, J., Koshy, M., & Ward, A. B. (2001). Short-term sequelae of minor head injury (6 years experience of minor head injury clinic). *Disability and Rehabilitation, 23*(14), 635–638.

Hahn, R. A. (1997). The nocebo phenomenon: Concept, evidence, and implications for public health. *Preventive Medicine, 26*(5, Pt. 1), 607–611.

Hanlon, R. E., Demery, J. A., Kuczen, C., & Kelly, J. P. (2005). Effect of traumatic subarachnoid haemorrhage on neuropsychological profiles and vocational outcome following moderate or severe traumatic brain injury. *Brain Injury, 19*(4), 257–262.

Hanlon, R. E., Demery, J. A., Martinovich, Z., & Kelly, J. P. (1999). Effects of acute injury characteristics on neurophysical status and vocational outcome following mild traumatic brain injury. *Brain Injury, 13*(11), 873–887.

Harper, C. G., Kril, J. J., & Holloway, R. L. (1985). Brain shrinkage in chronic alcoholics: A pathological study. *British Medical Journal (Clinical Research Edition), 290*(6467), 501–504.

Harvey, A. G., & Bryant, R. A. (2000). Two-year prospective evaluation of the relationship between acute stress disorder and posttraumatic stress disorder following mild traumatic brain injury. *American Journal of Psychiatry, 157*(4), 626–628.

Hawley, C. A., Ward, A. B., Magnay, A. R., & Mychalkiw, W. (2004). Return to school after brain injury. *Archives of Disease in Childhood, 89*(2), 136–142.

Heaton, R. K., Thompson, L. L., Nelson, L. M., Filly, C. M., & Franklin, G. M. (1990). Brief and intermediate length screening of neuropsychological impairment in multiple sclerosis. In S. M. Rao (Ed.), *Multiple sclerosis: A psychological perspective* (pp. 149–160). New York: Oxford University Press.

Heilbronner, R. L. (1993). Factors associated with postconcussion syndrome: Neurological, psychological, or legal? *Trial Diplomacy Journal, 16*, 161–167.

Heilbronner, R. L., Sweet, J. J., Morgan, J. E., Larrabee, G. J., & Millis, S. R. (2009). American Academy of Clinical Neuropsychology Consensus Conference Statement on the neuropsychological assessment of effort, response bias, and malingering. *The Clinical Neuropsychologist, 23*(7), 1093–1129.

Heyer, N. J., & Franklin, G. M. (1994). Work-related traumatic brain injury in Washington State, 1988 through 1990. *American Journal of Public Health, 84*(7), 1106–1109.

Hibbard, M. R., Bogdany, J., Uysal, S., Kepler, K., Silver, J. M., Gordon, W. A., et al. (2000). Axis II psychopathology in individuals with traumatic brain injury. *Brain Injury, 14*(1), 45–61.

Hickling, E. J., Gillen, R., Blanchard, E. B., Buckley, T., & Taylor, A. (1998). Traumatic brain injury and posttraumatic stress disorder: A preliminary investigation of neuropsychological test results in PTSD secondary to motor vehicle accidents. *Brain Injury, 12*(4), 265–274.

Hillbom, E. (1960). After-effects of brain-injuries. Research on the symptoms causing invalidism of persons in Finland having sustained brain-injuries during the wars of 1939–1940 and 1941–1944. *Acta Psychiatrica Scandinavica. Supplementum, 35*(142), 1–195.

Hillier, S. L., Sharpe, M. H., & Metzer, J. (1997). Outcomes 5 years post-traumatic brain injury (with further reference to neurophysical impairment and disability). *Brain Injury, 11*(9), 661–675.

Hilsabeck, R. C., Gouvier, W. D., & Bolter, J. F. (1998). Reconstructive memory bias in recall of neuropsychological symptomatology. *Journal of Clinical and Experimental Neuropsychology, 20*(3), 328–338.

Hofman, P. A., Stapert, S. Z., van Kroonenburgh, M. J., Jolles, J., de Kruijk, J., & Wilmink, J. T. (2001). MR imaging, single-photon emission CT, and neurocognitive performance after mild traumatic brain injury. *American Journal of Neuroradiology, 22*(3), 441–449.

Horner, M. D., Ferguson, P. L., Selassie, A. W., Labbate, L. A., Kniele, K., & Corrigan, J. D. (2005). Patterns of alcohol use 1 year after traumatic brain injury: A population-based, epidemiological study. *Journal of the International Neuropsychological Society, 11*(3), 322–330.

Hugenholtz, H., Stuss, D. T., Stethem, L. L., & Richard, M. T. (1988). How long does it take to recover from a mild concussion? *Neurosurgery, 22*(5), 853–858.

Hughes, D. G., Jackson, A., Mason, D. L., Berry, E., Hollis, S., & Yates, D. W. (2004).

Abnormalities on magnetic resonance imaging seen acutely following mild traumatic brain injury: Correlation with neuropsychological tests and delayed recovery. *Neuroradiology, 46*(7), 550–558.

Humphrey, M., & Oddy, M. (1980). Return to work after head injury: A review of postwar studies. *Injury, 12*(2), 107–114.

Inglese, M., Bomsztyk, E., Gonen, O., Mannon, L. J., Grossman, R. I., & Rusinek, H. (2005a). Dilated perivascular spaces: Hallmarks of mild traumatic brain injury. *American Journal of Neuroradiology, 26*(4), 719–724.

Inglese, M., Makani, S., Johnson, G., Cohen, B. A., Silver, J. A., Gonen, O., et al. (2005b). Diffuse axonal injury in mild traumatic brain injury: A diffusion tensor imaging study. *Journal of Neurosurgery, 103*(2), 298–303.

Inzaghi, M. G., De Tanti, A., & Sozzi, M. (2005). The effects of traumatic brain injury on patients and their families. A follow-up study. *Europa Medicophysica, 41*(4), 265–273.

Ip, R. Y., Dornan, J., & Schentag, C. (1995). Traumatic brain injury: Factors predicting return to work or school. *Brain Injury, 9*(5), 517–532.

Iverson, G., & Lange, R. T. (2011). Moderate–severe traumatic brain injury. In M. R. Schoenberg & J. G. Scott (Eds.), *The black book of neuropsychology: A syndrome-based approach* (pp. 663–696). New York: Springer.

Iverson, G. L. (2005). Outcome from mild traumatic brain injury. *Current Opinion in Psychiatry, 18*, 301–317.

Iverson, G. L. (2006a). Complicated vs. uncomplicated mild traumatic brain injury: Acute neuropsychological outcome. *Brain Injury, 20*(13–14), 1335–1344.

Iverson, G. L. (2006b). Misdiagnosis of persistent postconcussion syndrome in patients with depression. *Archives of Clinical Neuropsychology, 21*(4), 303–310.

Iverson, G. L., Brooks, B. L., Ashton, V. L., & Lange, R. T. (2010a). Interview vs. questionnaire symptom reporting in people with post-concussion syndrome. *Journal of Head Trauma Rehabilitation, 25*(1), 25–30.

Iverson, G. L., Franzen, M. D., & Lovell, M. R. (1999). Normative comparisons for the controlled oral word association test following acute traumatic brain injury. *The Clinical Neuropsychologist, 13*(4), 437–441.

Iverson, G. L., & Lange, R. T. (2003). Examination of "postconcussion-like" symptoms in a healthy sample. *Applied Neuropsychology, 10*(3), 137–144.

Iverson, G. L., Lange, R. T., Brooks, B. L., & Ashton Rennison, L. V. (2010b). "Good Old Days" bias following mild traumatic brain injury. *The Clinical Neuropsychologist, 24*(1), 17–37.

Iverson, G. L., Lange, R. T., Gaetz, M., & Zasler, N. D. (2007a). Mild TBI. In N. D. Zasler, H. T. Katz, & R. D. Zafonte (Eds.), *Brain injury medicine: Principles and practice* (pp. 333–371). New York: Demos.

Iverson, G. L., Langlois, J. A., McCrea, M. A., & Kelly, J. P. (2009). Challenges associated with post-deployment screening for mild traumatic brain injury in military personnel. *The Clinical Neuropsychologist, 23*(8), 1299–1314.

Iverson, G. L., LePage, J., Koehler, B. E., Shojania, K., & Badii, M. (2007b). TOMM scores are not affected by chronic pain or depression in patients with fibromyalgia. *The Clinical Neuropsychologist, 21*(3), 532–546.

Iverson, G. L., Lovell, M. R., Smith, S., & Franzen, M. D. (2000). Prevalence of abnormal CT-scans following mild head injury. *Brain Injury, 14*(12), 1057–1061.

Iverson, G. L., & McCracken, L. M. (1997). "Postconcussive" symptoms in persons with chronic pain. *Brain Injury, 11*(11), 783–790.

Jacobus, J., McQueeny, T., Bava, S., Schweinsburg, B. C., Frank, L. R., Yang, T. T., et al. (2009). White matter integrity in adolescents with histories of marijuana use and binge drinking. *Neurotoxicology and Teratology, 31*(6), 349–355.

Jones, G. A. (1989). Alcohol abuse and traumatic brain injury. *Alcohol Health and Research World, 13*(2), 104–109.

Jorge, R. E., Robinson, R. G., Moser, D., Tateno, A., Crespo-Facorro, B., & Arndt, S. (2004). Major depression following traumatic brain injury. *Archives of General Psychiatry, 61*(1), 42–50.

Jorge, R. E., Robinson, R. G., Starkstein, S. E., & Arndt, S. V. (1993). Depression and anxiety following traumatic brain injury. *Journal of Neuropsychiatry and Clinical Neurosciences, 5*(4), 369–374.

Kapoor, N., & Ciuffreda, K. J. (2005). Vision problems. In J. M. Silver, T. W. McAllister, & S. C. Yudofsky (Eds.), *Textbook of traumatic brain injury* (pp. 405–415). Arlington, VA: American Psychiatric Publishing.

Kaufman, K. R., Brey, R. H., Chou, L. S., Rabatin, A., Brown, A. W., & Basford, J. R. (2006). Comparison of subjective and objective measurements of balance disorders following traumatic brain injury. *Medical Engineering and Physics, 28*(3), 234–239.

Kay, T., Newman, B., Cavallo, M., Ezrachi, O., & Resnick, M. (1992). Toward a neuropsychological model of functional disability after mild traumatic brain injury. *Neuropsychology, 6*(4), 371–384.

Keyser-Marcus, L. A., Bricout, J. C., Wehman, P., Campbell, L. R., Cifu, D. X., Englander, J., et al. (2002). Acute predictors of return to employment after traumatic brain injury: A longitudinal follow-up. *Archives of Physical Medicine and Rehabilitation, 83*(5), 635–641.

Kim, H., Colantonio, A., & Chipman, M. (2006). Traumatic brain injury occurring at work. *NeuroRehabilitation, 21*(4), 269–278.

Kochanek, P. M., Clark, R. S. B., & Jenkins, L. W. (2007). TBI: Pathobiology. In N. D. Zasler, D. I. Katz, & R. D. Zafonte (Eds.), *Brain injury medicine: Principles and practice* (pp. 81–96). New York: Demos.

Konrad, A., Dielentheis, T. F., El Masri, D., Bayerl, M., Fehr, C., Gesierich, T., et al. (2010). Disturbed structural connectivity is related to inattention and impulsivity in adult attention deficit hyperactivity disorder. *European Journal of Neuroscience, 31*(5), 912–919.

Kowalske, K., Plenger, P. M., Lusby, B., & Hayden, M. E. (2000). Vocational reentry following TBI: An enablement model. *Journal of Head Trauma Rehabilitation, 15*(4), 989–999.

Kraus, J., Schaffer, K., Ayers, K., Stenehjem, J., Shen, H., & Afifi, A. A. (2005). Physical complaints, medical service use, and social and employment changes following mild traumatic brain injury: A 6-month longitudinal study. *Journal of Head Trauma Rehabilitation, 20*(3), 239–256.

Kraus, M. F., Susmaras, T., Caughlin, B. P., Walker, C. J., Sweeney, J. A., & Little, D. M. (2007). White matter integrity and cognition in chronic traumatic brain injury: A diffusion tensor imaging study. *Brain, 130*(Pt. 10), 2508–2519.

Kreutzer, J. S., Wehman, P. H., Harris, J. A., Burns, C. T., & Young, H. F. (1991). Substance abuse and crime patterns among persons with traumatic brain injury referred for supported employment. *Brain Injury, 5*(2), 177–187.

Kreutzer, J. S., Witol, A. D., & Marwitz, J. H. (1996). Alcohol and drug use among young persons with traumatic brain injury. *Journal of Learning Disabilities, 29*(6), 643–651.

Kristman, V. L., Cote, P., Van Eerd, D., Vidmar, M., Rezai, M., Hogg-Johnson, S., et al. (2008). Prevalence of lost-time claims for mild traumatic brain injury in the working population: Improving estimates using workers compensation databases. *Brain Injury, 22*(1), 51–59.

Kumar, R., Gupta, R. K., Husain, M., Chaudhry, C., Srivastava, A., Saksena, S., et al. (2009). Comparative evaluation of corpus callosum DTI metrics in acute mild and moderate traumatic brain injury: Its correlation with neuropsychometric tests. *Brain Injury, 23*(7), 675–685.

Kurca, E., Sivak, S., & Kucera, P. (2006). Impaired cognitive functions in mild traumatic brain injury patients with normal and pathologic magnetic resonance imaging. *Neuroradiology, 48*(9), 661–669.

Lahmeyer, H. W., & Bellur, S. N. (1987). Cardiac regulation and depression. *Journal of Psychiatry Research, 21*(1), 1–6.

Lange, R. T., Iverson, G. L., & Franzen, M. D. (2009). Neuropsychological functioning following complicated vs. uncomplicated mild traumatic brain injury. *Brain Injury, 23*(2), 83–91.

Lange, R. T., Iverson, G. L., Zakrzewski, M. J., Ethel-King, P. E., & Franzen, M. D. (2005). Interpreting the trail making test following traumatic brain injury: Comparison of traditional time scores and derived indices. *Journal of Clinical and Experimental Neuropsychology, 27*(7), 897–906.

Langlois, J. A., Rutland-Brown, W., & Thomas, K. E. (2006). *Traumatic brain injury in the United States: Emergency department visits, hospitalizaitons, and deaths.* Atlanta, GA: Centers for Disease Control and Prevention, National Center for Injury Prevention and Control.

Larrabee, G. J. (1997). Neuropsychological outcome, post concussion symptoms, and forensic considerations in mild closed head trauma. *Seminars in Clinical Neuropsychiatry, 2*(3), 196–206.

Larrabee, G. J. (2005). Mild traumatic brain injury. In G. J. Larrabee (Ed.), *Forensic neurospychology: A scientific approach* (pp. 209–236). New York: Oxford University Press.

Lee, H., Wintermark, M., Gean, A. D., Ghajar, J., Manley, G. T., & Mukherjee, P. (2008). Focal lesions in acute mild traumatic brain injury and neurocognitive outcome: CT versus 3T MRI. *Journal of Neurotrauma, 25*(9), 1049–1056.

Lees-Haley, P. R., Fox, D. D., & Courtney, J. C. (2001). A comparison of complaints by mild brain injury claimants and other claimants describing subjective experiences immediately following their injury. *Archives of Clinical Neuropsychology, 16*(7), 689–695.

Lees-Haley, P. R., Williams, C. W., & English, L. T. (1996). Response bias in self-reported history of plaintiffs compared with nonlitigating patients. *Psychological Reports, 79*(3, Pt. 1), 811–818.

Lees-Haley, P. R., Williams, C. W., Zasler, N. D., Marguilies, S., English, L. T., & Stevens, K. B. (1997). Response bias in plaintiffs' histories. *Brain Injury, 11*(11), 791–799.

Levin, H. S., Brown, S. A., Song, J. X., McCauley, S. R., Boake, C., Contant, C. F., et al. (2001). Depression and posttraumatic stress disorder at three months after mild to moderate traumatic brain injury. *Journal of Clinical and Experimental Neuropsychology, 23*(6), 754–769.

Levin, H. S., Mattis, S., Ruff, R. M., Eisenberg, H. M., Marshall, L. F., Tabaddor, K., et al. (1987). Neurobehavioral outcome following minor head injury: A three-center study. *Journal of Neurosurgery, 66*(2), 234–243.

Levy, B. (1996). Improving memory in old age through implicit self-stereotyping. *Journal of Personality and Social Psychology, 71*(6), 1092–1107.

Leyens, J. P., Desert, M., & Croizet, J. C. (2000). Stereotype treat: Are lower status and history of stigmatization preconditions of stereotype threat? *Personality and Social Psychology Bulletin, 26*(10), 1189–1199.

Lezak, M. D., Howieson, D. B., & Loring, D. W. (2004). *Neuropsychological assessment* (4th ed.). New York: Oxford University Press.

Liao, W., Zhang, Z., Pan, Z., Mantini, D., Ding, J., Duan, X., et al. (2011). Default mode network abnormalities in mesial temporal lobe epilepsy: A study combining fMRI and DTI. *Human Brain Mapping, 32*(6), 883–895.

Lippert-Gruner, M., Lefering, R., & Svestkova, O. (2007). Functional outcome at 1 vs. 2 years after severe traumatic brain injury. *Brain Injury, 21*(10), 1001–1005.

Lipton, M. L., Gellella, E., Lo, C., Gold, T., Ardekani, B. A., Shifteh, K., et al. (2008). Multifocal white matter ultrastructural abnormalities in mild traumatic brain injury with cognitive disability: A voxel-wise analysis of diffusion tensor imaging. *Journal of Neurotrauma, 25*(11), 1335–1342.

Lipton, M. L., Gulko, E., Zimmerman, M. E., Friedman, B. W., Kim, M., Gellella, E., et al. (2009). Diffusion-tensor imaging implicates prefrontal axonal injury in executive function impairment following very mild traumatic brain injury. *Radiology, 252*(3), 816–824.

Lishman, W. A. (1986). Physiogenisis and psychogenisis in the "post-concussional syndrome." *British Journal of Psychiatry, 153*, 460–469.

Livingston, D. H., Loder, P. A., Koziol, J., & Hunt, C. D. (1991). The use of CT scanning to triage patients requiring admission following minimal head injury. *Journal of Trauma, 31*(4), 483–487; discussion 487–489.

Lovell, M. R., Collins, M. W., Iverson, G. L., Johnston, K. M., & Bradley, J. P. (2004). Grade 1 or "ding" concussions in high school athletes. *American Journal of Sports Medicine, 32*(1), 47–54.

Lucas, J. A. (1998). Traumatic brain injury and post concussive syndrome. In P. J. Snyder & P. D. Nussbaum (Eds.), *Clinical Neuropsychology* (pp. 243–265). Washington, DC: American Psychological Association.

Ma, L., Hasan, K. M., Steinberg, J. L., Narayana, P. A., Lane, S. D., Zuniga, E. A., et al. (2009). Diffusion tensor imaging in cocaine dependence: Regional effects of cocaine on corpus callosum and effect of cocaine administration route. *Drug Alcohol Depend, 104*(3), 262–267.

Ma, X., Coles, C. D., Lynch, M. E., Laconte, S. M., Zurkiya, O., Wang, D., et al. (2005). Evaluation of corpus callosum anisotropy in young adults with fetal alcohol syndrome according to diffusion tensor imaging. *Alcoholism: Clinical and Experimental Research, 29*(7), 1214–1222.

Macciocchi, S. N., Barth, J. T., Alves, W., Rimel, R. W., & Jane, J. A. (1996). Neuropsychological functioning and recovery after mild head injury in collegiate athletes. *Neurosurgery, 39*(3), 510–514.

Machulda, M. M., Bergquist, T. F., Ito, V., & Chew, S. (1998). Relationship between stress, coping, and post concussion symptoms in a healthy adult population. *Archives of Clinical Neuropsychology, 13*, 415–424.

MacKenzie, E. J., Shapiro, S., Smith, R. T., Siegel, J. H., Moody, M., & Pitt, A. (1987). Factors influencing return to work following hospitalization for traumatic injury. *American Journal of Public Health, 77*(3), 329–334.

Malaspina, D., Goetz, R. R., Friedman, J. H., Kaufmann, C. A., Faraone, S. V., Tsuang, M., et al. (2001). Traumatic brain injury and schizophrenia in members of schizophrenia and bipolar disorder pedigrees. *American Journal of Psychiatry, 158*(3), 440–446.

Martin-Tamer, P. (1988). Differential vocational outcome following traumatic head injury. *Dissertation Abstract International, 49*(5), 508B.

Mather, F. J., Tate, R. L., & Hannan, T. J. (2003). Post-traumatic stress disorder in children following road traffic accidents: A comparison of those with and without mild traumatic brain injury. *Brain Injury, 17*(12), 1077–1087.

Mathias, J. L., Beall, J. A., & Bigler, E. D. (2004). Neuropsychological and information processing deficits following mild traumatic brain injury. *Journal of the International Neuropsychological Society, 10*(2), 286–297.

Mayou, R. A., Black, J., & Bryant, B. (2000). Unconsciousness, amnesia and psychiatric symptoms following road traffic accident injury. *British Journal of Psychiatry, 177*, 540–545.

Mazaux, J. M., Masson, F., Levin, H. S., Alaoui, P., Maurette, P., & Barat, M. (1997). Long-term neuropsychological outcome and loss of social autonomy after traumatic brain injury. *Archives of Physical Medicine and Rehabilitation, 78*(12), 1316–1320.

McCauley, S. R., Boake, C., Levin, H. S., Contant, C. F., & Song, J. X. (2001). Postconcussional disorder following mild to moderate traumatic brain injury: Anxiety, depression, and social support as risk factors and comorbidities. *Journal of Clinical and Experimental Neuropsychology, 23*(6), 792–808.

McCauley, S. R., Boake, C., Pedroza, C., Brown, S. A., Levin, H. S., Goodman, H. S., et al. (2005). Postconcussional disorder: Are the DSM-IV criteria an improvement over the ICD-10? *Journal of Nervous and Mental Disease, 193*(8), 540–550.

McCrea, M., Guskiewicz, K. M., Marshall, S. W., Barr, W., Randolph, C., Cantu, R. C., et al. (2003). Acute effects and recovery time following concussion in collegiate football players: The NCAA Concussion Study. *Journal of the American Medical Association, 290*(19), 2556–2563.

McCrea, M., Hammeke, T., Olsen, G., Leo, P., & Guskiewicz, K. (2004). Unreported concussion in high school football players: Implications for prevention. *Clinical Journal of Sport Medicine, 14*(1), 13–17.

McCrea, M., Kelly, J. P., Randolph, C., Cisler, R., & Berger, L. (2002). Immediate neurocognitive effects of concussion. *Neurosurgery, 50*(5), 1032–1040.

McCullagh, S., Oucherlony, D., Protzner, A., Blair, N., & Feinstein, A. (2001). Prediction of neuropsychiatric outcome following mild trauma brain injury: An examination of the Glasgow Coma Scale. *Brain Injury, 15*(6), 489–497.

McKinlay, W. W., Brooks, D. N., & Bond, M. R. (1983). Post-concussional symptoms, financial compensation and outcome of severe blunt head injury. *Journal of Neurology, Neurosurgery and Psychiatry, 46*(12), 1084–1091.

McMordie, W. R., Barker, S. L., & Paolo, T. M. (1990). Return to work (RTW) after head injury. *Brain Injury, 4*(1), 57–69.

Mearns, J., & Lees-Haley, P. R. (1993). Discriminating neuropsychological sequelae of head injury from alcohol-abuse-induced deficits: A review and analysis. *Journal of Clinical Psychology, 49*(5), 714–720.

Mickeviciene, D., Schrader, H., Nestvold, K., Surkiene, D., Kunickas, R., Stovner, L. J., et al. (2002). A controlled historical cohort study on the post-concussion syndrome. *European Journal of Neurology, 9*(6), 581–587.

Mickeviciene, D., Schrader, H., Obelieniene, D., Surkiene, D., Kunickas, R., Stovner, L. J., et al. (2004). A controlled prospective inception cohort study on the post-concussion syndrome outside the medicolegal context. *European Journal of Neurology, 11*(6), 411–419.

Miller, H. (1961). Accident neurosis. *British Medical Journal, 1*, 919–925, 992–998.

Minderhoud, J. M., Boelens, M. E., Huizenga, J., & Saan, R. J. (1980). Treatment of minor head injuries. *Clinical Neurology and Neurosurgery, 82*(2), 127–140.

Mittenberg, W., DiGiulio, D. V., Perrin, S., & Bass, A. E. (1992). Symptoms following mild head injury: Expectation as aetiology. *Journal of Neurology, Neurosurgery and Psychiatry, 55*, 200–204.

Mittenberg, W., & Strauman, S. (2000). Diagnosis of mild head injury and the postconcussion syndrome. *Journal of Head Trauma Rehabilitation, 15*(2), 783–791.

Mittenberg, W., Tremont, G., Zielinski, R. E., Fichera, S., & Rayls, K. R. (1996). Cognitive-behavioral prevention of postconcussion syndrome. *Archives of Clinical Neuropsychology, 11*(2), 139–145.

Murphy, L., Chamberlain, E., Weir, J., Berry, A., Nathaniel-James, D., & Agnew, R. (2006). Effectiveness of vocational rehabilitation following acquired brain injury: Preliminary evaluation of a UK specialist rehabilitation programme. *Brain Injury, 20*(11), 1119–1129.

Muuronen, A., Bergman, H., Hindmarsh, T., & Telakivi, T. (1989). Influence of improved drinking habits in brain atrophy and cognitive performance in alcoholic patients: A 5-year follow-up study. *Alcoholism: Clinical and Experimental Research, 13*, 137–141.

Nevin, N. C. (1967). Neuropathological changes in the white matter following head injury. *Journal of Neuropathology and Experimental Neurology, 26*(1), 77–84.

Niogi, S. N., Mukherjee, P., Ghajar, J., Johnson, C., Kolster, R. A., Sarkar, R., et al. (2008). Extent of microstructural white matter injury in postconcussive syndrome correlates with impaired cognitive reaction time: A 3T diffusion tensor imaging study of mild traumatic brain injury. *American Journal of Neuroradiology, 29*(5), 967–973.

Nixon, S. J. (1999). Neurocognitive performance in alcoholics: Is polysubstance abuse important? *Psychological Science, 10*, 181–185.

Nolin, P., Villemure, R., & Heroux, L. (2006). Determining long-term symptoms following mild traumatic brain injury: Method of interview affects self-report. *Brain Injury, 20*(11), 1147–1154.

Nybo, T., Sainio, M., & Muller, K. (2005). Middle age cognition and vocational outcome of childhood brain injury. *Acta Neurologica Scandinavica, 112*(5), 338–342.

O'Shanick, G. J., & O'Shanick, A. M. (2005). Personality disorders. In J. M. Silver, T. W. McAllister, & S. C. Yudofsky (Eds.), *Textbook of traumatic brain injury* (pp. 245–258). Arlington, VA: American Psychiatric Publishing.

Oddy, M., Coughlan, T., Tyerman, A., & Jenkins, D. (1985). Social adjustment after closed head injury: A further follow-up seven years after injury. *Journal of Neurology, Neurosurgery and Psychiatry, 48*(6), 564–568.

Odegard, T. N., Farris, E. A., Ring, J., McColl, R., & Black, J. (2009). Brain connectivity in non-reading impaired children and children diagnosed with developmental dyslexia. *Neuropsychologia, 47*(8–9), 1972–1977.

Olver, J. H., Ponsford, J. L., & Curran, C. A. (1996). Outcome following traumatic brain injury: A comparison between 2 and 5 years after injury. *Brain Injury, 10*(11), 841–848.

Oppenheimer, D. R. (1968). Microscopic lesions in the brain following head injury. *Journal of Neurology, Neurosurgery and Psychiatry, 31*(4), 299–306.

Orr, M. R., Walker, W. C., Marwitz, J. H., & Kreutzer, J. (2003). Occupational categories and return to work after traumatic brain injury. *Archives of Physical Medicine and Rehabilitation, 84*(9), A5.

Orrison, W. W., Gentry, L. R., Stimac, G. K., Tarrel, R. M., Espinosa, M. C., & Cobb, L. C. (1994). Blinded comparison of cranial CT and MR in closed head injury evaluation. *American Journal of Neuroradiology, 15*(2), 351–356.

Padula, W., Wu, L., Vicci, V., Thomas, J., Nelson, C., Gottlieb, D., et al. (2007). Evaluating and treating visual dysfunction. In N. D. Zasler, D. I. Katz, & R. D. Zafonte (Eds.), *Brain injury medicine* (pp. 511–528). New York: Demos.

Paniak, C., Reynolds, S., Toller-Lobe, G., Melnyk, A., Nagy, J., & Schmidt, D. (2002). A longitudinal study of the relationship between financial compensation and symptoms after treated mild traumatic brain injury. *Journal of Clinical and Experimental Neuropsychology, 24*(2), 187–193.

Paniak, C., Toller-Lobe, G., Reynolds, S., Melnyk, A., & Nagy, J. (2000). A randomized trial of two treatments for mild traumatic brain injury: 1 year follow-up. *Brain Injury, 14*(3), 219–226.

Parsons, O. A., & Nixon, S. J. (1993). Neurobehavioural sequelae of alcoholism. *Behavioral Neurology, 11*, 205–218.

Peerless, S. J., & Rewcastle, N. B. (1967). Shear injuries of the brain. *Canadian Medical Association Journal, 96*(10), 577–582.

Pellman, E. J., Lovell, M. R., Viano, D. C., Casson, I. R., & Tucker, A. M. (2004). Concussion in professional football: Neuropsychological testing—part 6. *Neurosurgery, 55*(6), 1290–1305.

Pettus, E. H., Christman, C. W., Giebel, M. L., & Povlishock, J. T. (1994). Traumatically induced altered membrane permeability: Its relationship to traumatically induced reactive axonal change. *Journal of Neurotrauma, 11*(5), 507–522.

Pfefferbaum, A., Adalsteinsson, E., & Sullivan, E. V. (2006). Dysmorphology and microstructural degradation of the corpus callosum: Interaction of age and alcoholism. *Neurobiology of Aging, 27*(7), 994–1009.

Pfefferbaum, A., Lim, K. O., Zipursky, R. B., Mathalon, D. H., Rosenbloom, M. J., Lane, B., et al. (1992). Brain gray and white matter volume loss accelerates with aging in chronic alcoholics: A quantitative MRI study. *Alcoholism: Clinical and Experimental Research, 16*(6), 1078–1089.

Pfefferbaum, A., Rosenbloom, M., & Sullivan, E. V. (2002). Alcoholism and AIDS: Magnetic resonance imaging approaches for detecting interactive neuropathology. *Alcoholism: Clinical and Experimental Research, 26*(7), 1031–1046.

Pfefferbaum, A., & Sullivan, E. V (2002). Microstructural but not macrostructural disruption of white matter in women with chronic alcoholism. *Neuroimage, 15*(3), 708–718.

Pfefferbaum, A., & Sullivan, E. V. (2005). Disruption of brain white matter microstructure by excessive intracellular and extracellular fluid in alcoholism: Evidence from diffusion tensor imaging. *Neuropsychopharmacology, 30*(2), 423–432.

Pfefferbaum, A., Sullivan, E. V., Hedehus, M., Adalsteinsson, E., Lim, K. O., & Moseley, M. (2000). In vivo detection and functional correlates of white matter microstructural disruption in chronic alcoholism. *Alcoholism: Clinical and Experimental Research, 24*(8), 1214–1221.

Ponsford, J., Harrington, H., Olver, J., & Roper, M. (2006). Evaluation of a community-based model of rehabilitation following traumatic brain injury. *Neuropsychological Rehabilitation, 16*(3), 315–328.

Ponsford, J., Willmott, C., Rothwell, A., Cameron, P., Ayton, G., Nelms, R., et al. (2001). Impact of early intervention on outcome after mild traumatic brain injury in children. *Pediatrics, 108*(6), 1297–1303.

Ponsford, J., Willmott, C., Rothwell, A., Cameron, P., Kelly, A. M., Nelms, R., et al. (2000). Factors influencing outcome following mild traumatic brain injury in adults. *Journal of the International Neuropsychological Society, 6*(5), 568–579.

Ponsford, J., Willmott, C., Rothwell, A., Cameron, P., Kelly, A. M., Nelms, R., et al.

(2002). Impact of early intervention on outcome following mild head injury in adults. *Journal of Neurology, Neurosurgery and Psychiatry, 73*(3), 330–332.

Ponsford, J. L., Olver, J. H., Curran, C., & Ng, K. (1995). Prediction of employment status 2 years after traumatic brain injury. *Brain Injury, 9*(1), 11–20.

Povlishock, J. T. (1993). Pathobiology of traumatically induced axonal injury in animals and man. *Annals of Emergency Medicine, 22*(6), 980–986.

Povlishock, J. T., & Becker, D. P. (1985). Fate of reactive axonal swellings induced by head injury. *Laboratory Investigation, 52*(5), 540–552.

Povlishock, J. T., Becker, D. P., Cheng, C. L., & Vaughan, G. W. (1983). Axonal change in minor head injury. *Journal of Neuropathology and Experimental Neurology, 42*(3), 225–242.

Radanov, B. P., Dvorak, J., & Valach, L. (1992). Cognitive deficits in patients after soft tissue injury of the cervical spine. *Spine, 17*(2), 127–131.

Raghupathi, R. (2004). Cell death mechanisms following traumatic brain injury. *Brain Pathology, 14*(2), 215–222.

Rao, N., Rosenthal, M., Cronin-Stubbs, D., Lambert, R., Barnes, P., & Swanson, B. (1990). Return to work after rehabilitation following traumatic brain injury. *Brain Injury, 4*(1), 49–56.

Rauscher, A., Barth, M., Herrmann, K. H., Witoszynskyj, S., Deistung, A., & Reichenbach, J. R. (2008). Improved elimination of phase effects from background field inhomogeneities for susceptibility weighted imaging at high magnetic field strengths. *Magnetic Resonance Imaging, 26*(8), 1145–1151.

Relander, M., Troupp, H., & Af Bjorkesten, G. (1972). Controlled trial of treatment for cerebral concussion. *British Medical Journal, 4*(843), 777–779.

Reynolds, S., Paniak, C., Toller-Lobe, G., & Nagy, J. (2003). A longitudinal study of compensation-seeking and return to work in a treated mild traumatic brain injury sample. *Journal of Head Trauma Rehabilitation, 18*(2), 139–147.

Rimrodt, S. L., Peterson, D. J., Denckla, M. B., Kaufmann, W. E., & Cutting, L. E. (2010). White matter microstructural differences linked to left perisylvian language network in children with dyslexia. *Cortex, 46*(6), 739–749.

Rinne, M. B., Pasanen, M. E., Vartiainen, M. V., Lehto, T. M., Sarajuuri, J. M., & Alaranta, H. T. (2006). Motor performance in physically well-recovered men with traumatic brain injury. *Journal of Rehabilitation Medicine, 38*(4), 224–229.

Rosenbloom, M., Sullivan, E. V., & Pfefferbaum, A. (2003). Using magnetic resonance imaging and diffusion tensor imaging to assess brain damage in alcoholics. *Alcohol Research and Health, 27*(2), 146–152.

Rosenthal, M., Dijkers, M., Harrison-Felix, C., Nabors, N., Witol, A. D., Young, M. E., et al. (1996). Impact of minority status on functional outcome and community integration following traumatic brain injury. *Journal of Head Trauma Rehabilitation, 11*(5), 40–57.

Ruff, R. M., Marshall, L. F., Crouch, J., Klauber, M. R., Levin, H. S., Barth, J., et al. (1993). Predictors of outcome following severe head trauma: Follow-up data from the Traumatic Coma Data Bank. *Brain Injury, 7*(2), 101–111.

Ruffolo, C. F., Friedland, J. F., Dawson, D. R., Colantonio, A., & Lindsay, P. H. (1999). Mild traumatic brain injury from motor vehicle accidents: Factors associated with return to work. *Archives of Physical Medicine and Rehabilitation, 80*(4), 392–398.

Rutgers, D. R., Fillard, P., Paradot, G., Tadie, M., Lasjaunias, P., & Ducreux, D. (2008a). Diffusion tensor imaging characteristics of the corpus callosum in mild, moderate, and severe traumatic brain injury. *American Journal of Neuroradiology, 29*(9), 1730–1735.

Rutgers, D. R., Toulgoat, F., Cazejust, J., Fillard, P., Lasjaunias, P., & Ducreux, D. (2008b). White matter abnormalities in mild traumatic brain injury: A diffusion tensor imaging study. *American Journal of Neuroradiology, 29*(3), 514–519.

Rutherford, W. H., Merrett, J. D., & McDonald, J. R. (1979). Symptoms at one year following concussion from minor head injuries. *Injury, 10*(3), 225–230.

Ryan, L. M., & Warden, D. L. (2003). Post concussion syndrome. *International Review of Psychiatry, 15*(4), 310–316.

Ryan, T. V., Sautter, S. W., Capps, C. F., Meneese, W., & Barth, J. T. (1992). Utilizing neuropsychological measures to predict vocational outcome in a head trauma population. *Brain Injury, 6*(2), 175–182.

Sandel, M. E., Delmonico, R., & Kotch, M. J. (2007). Sexuality, reproduction, and neuroendocrine disorders following TBI. In N. D. Zasler, D. I. Katz, & R. D. Zafonte (Eds.), *Brain injury medicine* (pp. 673–695). New York: Demos.

Sander, A. M., Kreutzer, J., Rosenthal, M., Delmonico, R., & Young, M. E. (1996). A multicenter longitudinal investigation of return to work and community integration following traumatic brain injury. *Journal of Head Trauma Rehabilitation, 11*(5), 70–84.

Satz, P. S., Alfano, M. S., Light, R. F., Morgenstern, H. F., Zaucha, K. F., Asarnow, R. F., et al. (1999). Persistent post-concussive syndrome: A proposed methodology and literature review to determine the effects, if any, of mild head and other bodily injury. *Journal of Clinical and Experimental Neuropsychology, 21*(5), 620–628.

Sawchyn, J. M., Brulot, M. M., & Strauss, E. (2000). Note on the use of the Postconcussion Syndrome Checklist. *Archives of Clinical Neuropsychology, 15*, 1–8.

Sbordone, R. J., & Liter, J. C. (1995). Mild traumatic brain injury does not produce post-traumatic stress disorder. *Brain Injury, 9*, 405–412.

Schoenberg, M. R., Ruwe, W. D., Dawson, K., McDonald, N. B., Houston, B., & Forducey, P. G. (2008). Comparison of functional outcomes and treatment cost between a computer-based cognitive rehabilitation teletherapy program and face-to-face rehabilitation program. *Professional Psychology: Research and Practice, 39*(2), 169–175.

Schretlen, D. J., & Shapiro, A. M. (2003). A quantitative review of the effects of traumatic brain injury on cognitive functioning. *International Review of Psychiatry, 15*(4), 341–349.

Schwartz, J. H. (1991). Synthesis and trafficking of neural proteins. In E. R. Kandel, J. H. Schwartz, & T. M. Jessell (Eds.), *Principles of neural science* (3rd ed., pp. 49–65). New York: Elsevier.

Sherer, M., Bergloff, P., High, W., Jr., & Nick, T. G. (1999). Contribution of functional ratings to prediction of long-term employment outcome after traumatic brain injury. *Brain Injury, 13*(12), 973–981.

Sherer, M., Bergloff, P., Levin, E., High, W. M., Jr., Oden, K. E., & Nick, T. G. (1998). Impaired awareness and employment outcome after traumatic brain injury. *Journal of Head Trauma Rehabilitation, 13*(5), 52–61.

Silver, J. M., Kramer, R., Greenwald, S., & Weissman, M. (2001). The association between head injuries and psychiatric disorders: Findings from the New Haven NIMH Epidemiologic Catchment Area Study. *Brain Injury, 15*(11), 935–945.

Skord, K. G., & Miranti, S. V. (1994). Towards a more integrated approach to job placement and retention for persons with traumatic brain injury and premorbid disadvantages. *Brain Injury, 8*(4), 383–392.

Slemmer, J. E., Matser, E. J., De Zeeuw, C. I., & Weber, J. T. (2002). Repeated mild injury causes cumulative damage to hippocampal cells. *Brain, 125*(Pt. 12), 2699–2709.

Smith, D. H., Wolf, J. A., Lusardi, T. A., Lee, V. M., & Meaney, D. F. (1999). High tolerance and delayed elastic response of cultured axons to dynamic stretch injury. *Journal of Neuroscience, 19*(11), 4263–4269.

Smith-Seemiller, L., Fow, N. R., Kant, R., & Franzen, M. D. (2003). Presence of post-concussion syndrome symptoms in patients with chronic pain vs. mild traumatic brain injury. *Brain Injury, 17*(3), 199–206.

Sosin, D. M., Sniezek, J. E., & Thurman, D. J. (1996). Incidence of mild and moderate brain injury in the United States, 1991. *Brain Injury, 10*(1), 47–54.

Spencer, S. J., Steele, C. M., & Quinn, D. M. (1999). Stereotype threat and women's math performance. *Journal of Experimental Social Psychology, 35*(1), 4–28.

Spikman, J. M., Timmerman, M. E., Zomeren van, A. H., & Deelman, B. G. (1999). Recovery versus retest effects in attention after closed head injury. *Journal of Clinical and Experimental Neuropsychology, 21*(5), 585–605.

Stambrook, M., Moore, A. D., Peters, L. C., Deviaene, C., & Hawryluk, G. A. (1990). Effects of mild, moderate and severe closed head injury on long-term vocational status. *Brain Injury, 4*(2), 183–190.

Steele, C. M., & Aronson, J. (1995). Stereotype threat and the intellectual test performance of African Americans. *Journal of Personality and Social Psychology, 69*(5), 797–811.

Stein, S. C., & Ross, S. E. (1992). Mild head injury: A plea for routine early CT scanning. *Journal of Trauma, 33*(1), 11–13.

Stern, R. A., & White, T. (2003). *Neuropsychological Assessment Battery.* Lutz, FL: Psychological Assessment Resources.

Stiell, I. G., Clement, C. M., Rowe, B. H., Schull, M. J., Brison, R., Cass, D., et al. (2005). Comparison of the Canadian CT Head Rule and the New Orleans Criteria in patients with minor head injury. *Journal of the American Medical Association, 294*(12), 1511–1518.

Stranjalis, G., Korfias, S., Papapetrou, C., Kouyialis, A., Boviatsis, E., Psachoulia, C., et al. (2004). Elevated serum S-100B protein as a predictor of failure to short-term return to work or activities after mild head injury. *Journal of Neurotrauma, 21*(8), 1070–1075.

Strich, S. J. (1961). Shearing of nerve fibers as a cause of brain damage due to head injury. *Lancet, 2*, 443–438.

Stulemeijer, M., Andriessen, T. M., Brauer, J. M., Vos, P. E., & Van Der Werf, S. (2007). Cognitive performance after mild traumatic brain injury: The impact of poor effort on test results and its relation to distress, personality and litigation. *Brain Injury, 21*(3), 309–318.

Suhr, J. A., & Gunstad, J. (2002). "Diagnosis Threat": The effect of negative expectations on cognitive performance in head injury. *Journal of Clinical and Experimental Neuropsychology, 24*(4), 448–457.

Suhr, J. A., & Gunstad, J. (2005). Further exploration of the effect of "diagnosis threat" on cognitive performance in individuals with mild head injury. *Journal of the International Neuropsychological Society, 11*(1), 23–29.

Sullivan, E. V., Marsh, L., Mathalon, D. H., Lim, K. O., & Pfefferbaum, A. (1996). Relationship between alcohol withdrawal seizures and temporal lobe white matter volume deficits. *Alcoholism: Clinical and Experimental Research, 20*(2), 348–354.

Sullivan, E. V., & Pfefferbaum, A. (2003). Diffusion tensor imaging in normal aging and neuropsychiatric disorders. *European Journal of Radiology, 45*(3), 244–255.

Temkin, N. R., Machamer, J. E., & Dikmen, S. S. (2003). Correlates of functional status 3–5 years after traumatic brain injury with CT abnormalities. *Journal of Neurotrauma, 20*(3), 229–241.

Thaxton, L. L., & Patel, A. R. (2007). Sleep disturbance: Epidemiology, assessment, and treatment. In N. D. Zasler, D. I. Katz, & R. D. Zafonte (Eds.), *Brain injury medicine* (pp. 557–575). New York: Demos.

Thomsen, I. V. (1984). Late outcome of very severe blunt head trauma: A 10–15 year second follow-up. *Journal of Neurology, Neurosurgery and Psychiatry, 47*(3), 260–268.

Tombaugh, T. N. (1996). *Test of memory malingering.* North Tonawanda, NY: Multi-Health Systems.

Tomberg, T., Toomela, A., Pulver, A., & Tikk, A. (2005). Coping strategies, social support, life orientation and health-related quality of life following traumatic brain injury. *Brain Injury, 19*(14), 1181–1190.

Tong, K. A., Ashwal, S., Holshouser, B. A., Shutter, L. A., Herigault, G., Haacke, E. M., et al. (2003). Hemorrhagic shearing lesions in children and adolescents with posttraumatic diffuse axonal injury: Improved detection and initial results. *Radiology, 227*(2), 332–339.

Trahan, D. E., Ross, C. E., & Trahan, S. L. (2001). Relationships among postconcussional-type symptoms, depression, and anxiety in neurologically normal young adults and victims of brain injury. *Archives of Clinical Neuropsychology, 16*, 435–445.

Tricco, A. C., Colantonio, A., Chipman, M., Liss, G., & McLellan, B. (2006). Work-related deaths and traumatic brain injury. *Brain Injury, 20*(7), 719–724.

Tsaousides, T., Warshowsky, A., Ashman, T. A., Cantor, J. B., Spielman, L., & Gordon, W. A. (2009). The relationship between employment-related self-efficacy and quality of life following traumatic brain injury. *Rehabilitation Psychology, 54*(3), 299–305.

Uzzell, B. P., Langfitt, T. W., & Dolinskas, C. A. (1987). Influence of injury severity on quality of survival after head injury. *Surgical Neurology, 27*(5), 419–429.

van der Naalt, J., Hew, J. M., van Zomeren, A. H., Sluiter, W. J., & Minderhoud, J. M. (1999a). Computed tomography and magnetic resonance imaging in mild to moderate head injury: Early and late imaging related to outcome. *Annals of Neurology, 46*(1), 70–78.

van der Naalt, J., van Zomeren, A. H., Sluiter, W. J., & Minderhoud, J. M. (1999b). One year outcome in mild to moderate head injury: The predictive value of acute injury characteristics related to complaints and return to work. *Journal of Neurology, Neurosurgery and Psychiatry, 66*(2), 207–213.

Vanderploeg, R. D., Curtiss, G., Duchnick, J. J., & Luis, C. A. (2003). Demographic, medical, and psychiatric factors in work and marital status after mild head injury. *Journal of Head Trauma Rehabilitation, 18*(2), 148–163.

Vanderploeg, R. D., Schwab, K., Walker, W. C., Fraser, J. A., Sigford, B. J., Date, E. S., et al. (2008). Rehabilitation of traumatic brain injury in active duty military personnel and veterans: Defense and Veterans Brain Injury Center randomized controlled trial of two rehabilitation approaches. *Archives of Physical Medicine and Rehabilitation, 89*(12), 2227–2238.

Varney, N., Martzke, J., & Roberts, R. (1987). Major depression in patients with closed head injury. *Neuropsychology, 1*, 7–8.

Vogenthaler, D. R., Smith, K. R., Jr., & Goldfader, P. (1989). Head injury, a multivariate study: Predicting long-term productivity and independent living outcome. *Brain Injury, 3*(4), 369–385.

Wade, D. T., King, N. S., Wenden, F. J., Crawford, S., & Caldwell, F. E. (1998). Routine follow up after head injury: A second randomised controlled trial. *Journal of Neurology, Neurosurgery and Psychiatry, 65*(2), 177–183.

Wagner, A. K., Hammond, F. M., Sasser, H. C., & Wiercisiewski, D. (2002). Return to productive activity after traumatic brain injury: Relationship with measures of disability, handicap, and community integration. *Archives of Physical Medicine and Rehabilitation, 83*(1), 107–114.

Walker, W. C., Marwitz, J. H., Kreutzer, J. S., Hart, T., & Novack, T. A. (2006). Occupational categories and return to work after traumatic brain injury: A multicenter study. *Archives of Physical Medicine and Rehabilitation, 87*(12), 1576–1582.

Walsh, M., Hickey, C., & Duffy, J. (1999). Influence of item content and stereotype situation on gender differences in mathematical problem solving. *Sex Roles, 41*(3–4), 219–240.

Warden, D. L., & Labbate, L. A. (2005). Posttraumatic stress disorder and other anxiety disorders. In J. M. Silver, T. W. McAllister, & S. C. Yudofsky (Eds.), *Textbook of traumatic brain injury* (pp. 231–243). Arlington, VA: American Psychiatric Publishing.

Wehman, P., Sherron, P., Kregel, J., Kreutzer, J., Tran, S., & Cifu, D. (1993). Return to work for persons following severe traumatic brain injury. Supported employment outcomes after five years. *American Journal of Physical Medicine and Rehabilitation, 72*(6), 355–363.

Wehman, P., West, M., Kregel, J., Sherron, P., & Kreutzer, J. (1995). Return to work for persons with severe traumatic brain injury: A data-based approach to program development. *Journal of Head Trauma Rehabilitation, 10*(1), 27–39.

West, M., Targett, P., Yasuda, S., & Wehman, P. (2007). Return to work following TBI. In N. D. Zasler, D. I. Katz, & R. D. Zafonte (Eds.), *Brain injury medicine* (pp. 1131–1147). New York: Demos.

West, M. D. (1995). Aspects of the workplace and return to work for persons with brain injury in supported employment. *Brain Injury, 9*(3), 301–313.

White, T., & Stern, R. A. (2003). *Neuropsychological assessment battery: Psychometric and technical manual.* Lutz, FL: Psychological Assessment Resources.

Whitney, K. A., Shepard, P. H., Williams, A. L., Davis, J. J., & Adams, K. M. (2009). The Medical Symptom Validity Test in the evaluation of Operation Iraqi Freedom/Operation Enduring Freedom soldiers: A preliminary study. *Archives of Clinical Neuropsychology, 24*(2), 145–152.

Whyte, J., Schuster, K., Polansky, M., Adams, J., & Coslett, H. B. (2000). Frequency and duration of inattentive behavior after traumatic brain injury: Effects of distraction, task, and practice. *Journal of the International Neuropsychological Society, 6*(1), 1–11.

Widjaja, E., Simao, G., Mahmoodabadi, S. Z., Ochi, A., Snead, O. C., Rutka, J., et al. (2010). Diffusion tensor imaging identifies changes in normal-appearing white matter within the epileptogenic zone in tuberous sclerosis complex. *Epilepsy Research, 89*(2–3), 246–253.

Williams, D. H., Levin, H. S., & Eisenberg, H. M. (1990). Mild head injury classification. *Neurosurgery, 27*(3), 422–428.

Wilson, J. T. L., Hadley, D. M., Scott, L. C., & Harper, A. (1996). Neuropsychological significance of contusional lesions identified by MRI. In B. P. Uzzell & H. H. Stonnington (Eds.), *Recovery after traumatic brain injury* (pp. 29–50). Mahwah, NJ: Erlbaum.

Wong, J. L., Regennitter, R. P., & Barrios, F. (1994). Base rate and simulated symptoms of mild head injury among normals. *Archives of Clinical Neuropsychology, 9*, 411–425.

Wood, R. L., & Rutterford, N. A. (2006). Psychosocial adjustment 17 years after severe brain injury. *Journal of Neurology, Neurosurgery and Psychiatry, 77*(1), 71–73.

World Health Organization. (1992). *International statistical classification of diseases and related health problems* (10th ed.). Geneva, Switzerland: World Health Organization.

Wright, J. (2000). *The Disability Rating Scale*. Retrieved July 9, 2009, from *www.tbims.org/combi/drs*.

Wright, T. J. (1988). Enhancing the professional preparation of rehabilitation counselors for improved services to ethnic minorities with disabilities. *Journal of Applied Rehabilitation Councelling, 19*(4), 4–9.

Wrightson, P., & Gronwall, D. (1981). Time off work and symptoms after minor head injury. *Injury, 12*(6), 445–454.

Wrona, R. M. (2006). The use of state workers' compensation administrative data to identify injury scenarios and quantify costs of work-related traumatic brain injuries. *Journal of Safety Research, 37*(1), 75–81.

Xu, J., Rasmussen, I. A., Lagopoulos, J., & Haberg, A. (2007). Diffuse axonal injury in severe traumatic brain injury visualized using high-resolution diffusion tensor imaging. *Journal of Neurotrauma, 24*(5), 753–765.

Yaghmai, A., & Povlishock, J. (1992). Traumatically induced reactive change as visualized through the use of monoclonal antibodies targeted to neurofilament subunits. *Journal of Neuropathology and Experimental Neurology, 51*(2), 158–176.

Yeh, P. H., Simpson, K., Durazzo, T. C., Gazdzinski, S., & Meyerhoff, D. J. (2009). Tract-Based Spatial Statistics (TBSS) of diffusion tensor imaging data in alcohol dependence: Abnormalities of the motivational neurocircuitry. *Psychiatry Research, 173*(1), 22–30.

Youngjohn, J. R., Burrows, L., & Erdal, K. (1995). Brain damage or compensation neurosis? The controversial post-concussion syndrome. *The Clinical Neuropsychologist, 9*, 112–123.

Zasler, N. D., Horn, L. J., Martelli, M. F., & Nicolson, K. (2007). Post-traumatic pain disorders: Medical assessment and management. In N. D. Zasler, D. I. Katz, & R. D. Zafonte (Eds.), *Brain injury medicine* (pp. 697–721). New York: Demos.

Zhou, B., Chen, Q., Gong, Q., Tang, H., & Zhou, D. (2010). The thalamic ultrastructural abnormalities in paroxysmal kinesigenic choreoathetosis: A diffusion tensor imaging study. *Journal of Neurology, 257*(3), 405–409.

CHAPTER 2

Assessment of Mild Traumatic Brain Injury in the Professional Athlete

Mark R. Lovell

Neuropsychology has been involved in professional sports since the mid-1990s. Neuropsychological assessment programs have evolved from earlier work in the 1980s with college athletes to presently encompass almost all professional sports in the United States. This chapter describes the evolution of neuropsychological assessment in professional athletics and reviews current management strategies.

The first large-scale research study of concussion that utilized athletes as subjects was conducted by the University of Virginia, and also involved the Ivy League schools and the University of Pittsburgh. The study examined concussion in college football players and utilized baseline testing and serial postconcussive testing to track recovery (Macciocchi, Barth, Alves, Rimel, & Jane, 1996). The research design of this study provided the framework for the subsequent development of clinical assessment models in professional sports. Prior to the initial publication of the University of Virginia study, return-to-play guidelines relied mostly on subjective athlete report of symptoms. In addition, early-return-to-play guidelines placed an overemphasis on loss of consciousness as an indicator of concussion severity. This methodology would later be reevaluated based on published studies that illustrated the importance of other markers of severity such as duration of amnesia (Collins et al., 2003b). With the inclusion of neuropsychological assessment, the concussion assessment process became more thorough and objective.

THE NATIONAL FOOTBALL LEAGUE PROGRAM: 1995–PRESENT

An objective management approach that emphasized neuropsychological assessment was introduced by this author and his colleagues with the Pittsburgh Steelers in 1993 (Lovell, 1999). Initially, this model utilized available standardized "paper-and-pencil" neuropsychological tests. The Steelers neuropsychological testing program emphasized a preseason baseline assessment paradigm with postinjury follow-up testing within 24 to 48 hours of injury. Following injury, the athlete was then reevaluated until his scores approximated his preinjury baseline test results.

In 1994, the National Football League (NFL) formed the Subcommittee on Mild Traumatic Brain Injury (MTBI), which includes NFL team physicians; athletic trainers; equipment managers; and neurosurgical, biomechanical, and neuropsychological consultants. Since its inception, the subcommittee has overseen multiple studies and projects on various topics. Numerous studies supported by the NFL Charities have examined concussion in professional football. A summary of some of that research follows next. (For a complete review, see Pellman & Viano, 2006.)

In an attempt to understand the biomechanics of injury, videotapes of NFL concussions from 1996 to 2001 were examined to study impact types and the physics of injury (Viano & Pellman, 2005). Specifically, translational and rotational accelerations were measured, and results indicated that impacts to the facemask (or side) and back of the helmet (from falls) were the primary cause of concussion. Sixty-one percent of the concussions were due to helmet-to-helmet impact, and most were due to translational forces, striking the facemask at an oblique to lateral (0- to 45-degree) angle. Helmets (shell/padding) appear to lower the risk for more serious injuries to the skull and brain likely because helmets distribute the impact. A second study using the 1996 to 2001 concussion data (Pellman, Viano, Tucker, & Casson, 2003) also linked facemask impacts at an oblique angle to concussion; this finding suggests that translational head acceleration needs to be addressed in future research.

Further examining the 1996 to 2001 NFL concussion data, researchers found quarterbacks to be at highest risk for concussions, then wide receivers, tight ends, and defensive secondary players (Pellman et al., 2004b). The most common symptoms were headaches (55%) and dizziness (41.8%). Loss of consciousness occurred in only 9.3% of reported cases. Over 90% of players returned to practice in fewer than 7 days, suggesting that most NFL concussions are mild (Pellman et al., 2004b). At that time the return-to-play protocol was team specific, not standardized—the MTBI subcommittee did not interfere with the clinical decision making process. This was a methodological limitation in that study. Thus, to better understand length of recovery time, future research should focus on a standard management process for returning to play following concussion.

As a result of increasing concerns regarding the effects of multiple concussions and a potential link to long-term neurocognitive problems, a series of additional analyses were conducted from 1996 to 2001. A total of 887 concussions were reported by 650 NFL players (Pellman et al., 2004c). A second concussion occurred in 160 players (24.6%), and 51 (31.9%) reported three or more concussions. Only six repeat concussions occurred within 2 weeks of an initial concussion. Those at highest risk for repeat concussions included special team ball returners and quarterbacks because they most often experience higher impact accelerations in either the open field or blind side situations. Overall, there were no significant differences between single and repeat concussions related to severity of symptoms, management of the injury, and time taken to return to play. Also, there were no cases of severe disability or death during this time period. Unfortunately, concussions that occurred prior to 1996 (sport-related or otherwise) were not recorded and may or may not have influenced the incidence or phenomenology of concussions occurring during the study.

In a study examining impact velocities (Viano, Hamberger, Bolouri, & Saljo, 2009), researchers used an animal model to characterize concussive forces that might be affecting NFL athletes. The researchers reported head impacts in the NFL that were below the threshold where diffuse axonal injury (DAI) usually occurs. However, repeat impacts at the highest velocity resulted in DAI in the cerebral cortex and hippocampus. Thus, it was assumed that the vast majority of NFL head collisions were not at a level to cause frank changes in cellular morphology. The obvious limitation of this study is its comparison of head trauma in a rat to that in a helmeted human brain.

Several studies have been published on neuropsychological deficits in NFL players. Pellman, Lovell, Viano, Casson, and Tucker (2004a) found limited evidence of neuropsychological deficits in a sample of concussed NFL athletes. Specifically, a relationship was found between memory difficulties diagnosed on the field of play and postinjury performance on standardized memory assessment tools within the first few days of injury. This study, however, was based on a relatively small number of subjects. The NFL MTBI subcommittee later published a study that compared NFL athletes with a sample of concussed high school athletes, with both groups being evaluated within several days of injury utilizing computer-based assessment (Pellman, Lovell, Viano, & Casson, 2006). The NFL group had faster recovery, as indexed by their performance on the ImPACT computer-based test battery. Currently, a study is taking place that involves the evaluation of retired NFL players utilizing both paper/pencil and computer-based assessment. Players in this study are also undergoing sophisticated brain imaging as well as a formal neurological exam. The data for the first 45 subjects is now being analyzed.

The NFL Neuropsychological Assessment Model

The original NFL test battery involved traditional paper/pencil assessment tools. It was designed to be brief, but also to examine multiple cognitive domains (Lovell & Collins, 1998). The battery, presented in Table 2.1, includes orientation questions, the Hopkins Verbal Learning Test (HVLT; Brandt, 1991), the Brief Visuospatial Memory Test—Revised (BVMT-R; Benedict, 1997), the Trail Making Test, the Controlled Oral Word Association Test (Benton & Hamsher, 1978), the Post-Concussion Symptom Scale (Lovell, 1999, p. 206; Lovell et al., 2006), and the Digit Span, Digit Symbol, and Symbol Search subtests from the Wechsler Adult Intelligence Scale (WAIS III; Wechsler, 1997). More extensive neuropsychological test batteries are used, but usually for athletes with a complex history of concussions, longstanding neurocognitive deficits, or to reduce practice effects following numerous computer administrations. Extensive normative data gathered on a large NFL sample is currently in the process of being published (Lovell & Solomon, 2011).

In 2007, the NFL mandated baseline neurocognitive computer-based testing without specification of a particular testing measure. Currently, all NFL teams have adopted the ImPACT test battery for completing baseline evaluations, and ImPACT (Maroon et al., 2000) has been instituted at the NFL Scouting Combine in Indianapolis. However, many NFL consulting neuropsychologists continue to utilize a flexible test battery approach in the event of injury as well as repeat computer-based assessment.

▨ **TABLE 2.1. NFL and NHL Neuropsychological Test Batteries**

NFL test battery	NHL test battery
Hopkins Verbal Learning Test	Hopkins Verbal Learning Test
Brief Visuospatial Memory Test—Revised	Brief Visuospatial Memory Test—Revised
Trail Making Test (parts A and B)	Color Trail Making
Controlled Oral Word Association Test	Controlled Oral Word Association Test[a]
WAIS-III Symbol Search	Penn State Cancellation Test
WAIS-III Digit Symbol	Symbol Digit Modalities
WAIS-III Digit Span	

[a]Suggested for English-speaking athletes only.

THE NATIONAL HOCKEY LEAGUE PROGRAM: 1997–PRESENT

The National Hockey League (NHL) initiated a concussion management program in 1997 and included representatives of the Team Physicians Society, the NHL players association, athletic trainers, and a network of consulting neuropsychologists. This program continues to evolve and expand.

The NHL program grew out of a desire among both the athletes and the league to protect hockey athletes from potentially career-ending injuries (Lovell & Burke, 2000). This program has been structured to identify athletes immediately after injury and to avoid exposing them to further injury during the recovery period by premature return to play. The NHL program was also initially developed to answer a number of important research questions regarding recovery from injury.

Neuropsychologists play an important role in the assessment and management of concussions in hockey. A paper published under the auspices of the International Ice Hockey Federation, FIFA, and the International Olympic Committee highlighted neuropsychological assessment as a "cornerstone" of the concussion evaluation process (Aubry et al., 2002). The role of neuropsychologists in sports continued to be emphasized over the course of two subsequent meetings of these committees (see McCrory et al., 2005, 2009). The emphasis on cognitive testing has contributed to a demand for an increasing number of neuropsychologists within both amateur and professional sports. Within the context of the NHL, neuropsychologists have come to play an important role in both the baseline assessment and postinjury evaluation of injured athletes, and have become increasingly involved in making return-to-play decisions.

Unique Biomechanics of Ice Hockey Injuries

Today's professional hockey players are typically bigger, faster, and better conditioned than players in past generations, resulting in a fast-paced and sophisticated game that affords multiple opportunities for injury. NHL rosters typically are made up of athletes who weigh over 200 pounds. Furthermore, a modern NHL player may reach speeds of almost 30 miles per hour during a game situation. In addition, the continuous substitution of rested players into the game maintains a high level of physicality and intensity throughout the game.

Most of the concussions sustained by professional hockey athletes are the result of high-speed collisions. This type of collision might result in both deceleration and rotational forces during which axons are stretched and injured (Povlishock & Coburn, 1989); also, it likely results in significant metabolic dysfunction within the brain (Hovda et al., 1998; Lovell et al., 2007). Concussive injuries in ice hockey are not necessarily prevented through the use of protective headgear, which is designed primarily to prevent skull fractures and more severe brain injury. In addition, direct contact of the head with the glass, boards, stick, elbow, or ice may result in direct trauma to the skull as well as contusion of the brain in more severe cases. Finally, periodic fights on the ice may also result in a concussion, although no published data directly links periodic fights on the ice to long-term problems in professional hockey players.

Neuropsychological Assessment Component of the NHL Program

For the first 10 years of the program, the formal neuropsychological evaluation of the athlete was structured to take place within 24 to 48 hours of the suspected concussion, whenever possible. Follow-up neuropsychological evaluation was recommended within 5 to 7 days after injury if any abnormalities were present at the time of initial evaluation. This time interval was thought to represent a useful and practical time span, and it appeared to be consistent with animal brain metabolism studies at the time that had demonstrated metabolic changes that persist for days following injury (Hovda et al., 1998).

In designing a league-wide neuropsychological evaluation program, a number of factors were considered. First, time is always a factor for professional athletes and is a particularly significant issue in ice hockey. Unlike professional football athletes, professional hockey players often play more than one game per week and are therefore at greater risk for overlapping injuries. In addition, multiple languages are spoken within the NHL, and some athletes have limited English proficiency. Therefore, a number of neuropsychological tests were selected based on the requirement of minimal translation into English. In addition, English-based tests such as word lists and verbal fluency tasks were omitted with non-native English speakers.

In 2007, the National Hockey League instituted computer-based neuropsychological assessment that was implemented to streamline the process of obtaining baseline assessment information. One advantage of this approach was the formal translation of the battery into multiple languages. At the current time, computer-based assessment is accessible in all languages spoken by NHL athletes, including English, French, Russian, Czech, German, Finnish, Swedish, and Norwegian.

In addition to language-related issues, the logistics of a typical professional hockey travel schedule (which often includes 2-week road trips) required the development of a "network approach" through which injured players could be evaluated at any point in time during a road trip. If a player is injured away from his home city, the athletic trainer under the supervision of the opponent's team physician completes the initial rink-side evaluation. If neuropsychological testing is indicated, the neuropsychological consultant for the opponent's team completes the evaluation and sends the results to the neuropsychologist from the player's team. The neuropsychologist then provides consultation to the athlete's team physician who makes the return-to-play decision. This network approach has been highly successful and has been maintained and expanded since the program began in 1997.

The NHL test battery was developed by the Neuropsychological Advisory Board, which serves as supervisors of the neuropsychological testing component of the program. This group was initially directed by this author (1997–2007). The program is currently directed by Dr. Ruben Echemendia (2007–present). The NHL test battery can be administered in approximately 30 minutes. The ImPACT test battery takes an additional 25 minutes to complete. The specific tests that make up the battery are listed in Table 2.1 and are similar to tests utilized in the NFL program. The test battery was constructed to evaluate the athlete's functioning in the areas of attention, information-processing speed, fluency, and memory. In addition, tests were selected that have equivalent forms or that have been researched with regards to the expected "practice effects."

In addition to the neuropsychological test results, the neuropsychologists are also trained to evaluate noncognitive symptoms of concussion. To this end, the NHL program utilizes a *Symptom Self-Rating* Inventory, which is administered at the time of the initial evaluation and at every subsequent follow-up evaluation. This inventory is based on the original work of Lovell with professional football athletes (Lovell, 1999).

Current Status of the NHL Program

The current NHL protocol dictates that the athlete be symptom free prior to completing neuropsychological testing. This procedure is different than the original design (1997–2006) that dictated evaluation within 24–48 hours of the injury. Following injury, physical and cognitive exertion is limited, and the athlete is evaluated by the team or network neuropsychologist (if the team is traveling), only after the athlete becomes asymptomatic. All assessment takes place under the supervision of a properly licensed and trained neuropsychologist, and test results are then communicated to the team physician and athletic training staff.

Consistent with recent international guidelines, when an athlete is asymptomatic at rest, a graded return to exertion is necessary to monitor any return of symptoms and hopefully to avoid severe exacerbation of symptoms. Exertional testing begins with light/mild (e.g., walking on treadmill or light jogging) to moderate (running on treadmill or riding stationary bicycle) to heavy (or game pace noncontact exertion) to practice and scrimmage activities. If the athlete is asymptomatic, but neurocognitive testing has not returned to baseline levels, then the athlete is not returned to play. If the athlete displays deficits on testing, an additional examination is recommended to occur within 5 to 7 days of the initial evaluation. Should the athlete continue to exhibit symptoms and/or test deficits, additional follow up testing is recommended. The nature and extent of such testing varies based on the severity of the individual athlete's injury and problems because concussion management is a dynamic process.

Prior to returning an athlete to play, multiple individual preinjury factors should also be considered along with current symptom status and neurocognitive test results. Thus, one should document each athlete's medical history (e.g., prior concussions, preinjury headaches). Research suggests that multiple concussions might result in a permanent decline in neurocognitive abilities in some athletes (Collins et al., 1999; Gronwall & Wrightson, 1975). Other studies have linked a potential relationship between headache/migraine history and increased severity and/or prolonged recovery of concussion symptoms (Collins et al., 2003a).

Current Research Questions in Professional Hockey

In addition to providing important clinical data to the team physician, the NHL program has been structured to help answer a number of research questions regarding sports-related concussion. This project should eventually allow the NHL to track the rate of concussion from season to season, team to team, and conference to conference and will promote evidence-based decision-making. In addition, one of the primary goals of this project is to help answer basic return-to-play questions such as:

1. How long should an athlete wait to return to maximize safety or prevent further injury?
2. How many concussions during any given season can a player experience before terminating play for that season?
3. What specific criteria should be used in making return-to-play decisions?

For instance, is loss of consciousness an important factor in determining recovery, or are other factors such as duration of amnesia or concussion symptoms relatively more important? Although not a stated goal of the NHL program, this project might eventually improve evidence-based concussion strategies that are based on a number of factors, including the results of neuropsychological testing.

The NHL concussion project will promote a better understanding of the role of neuropsychological testing in the assessment of athletes. The project will address questions such as:

1. Which neuropsychological tests are sufficiently reliable and valid to allow their continued and more widespread use throughout organized athletics?
2. Which neuropsychological cutoff scores should be used for making return-to-play decisions, and what confidence intervals will be utilized?
3. To what extent do players' self-report symptoms correlate with objective neuropsychological test results?

The correlation between neuropsychological test results and subjective symptoms is an imperfect one. The discrepancy may be a function of a variety of factors, which include both neurological and non-neurological processes (e.g., brain vs. vestibular system), limitations of current testing, or other processes. Hopefully, the NHL project will help to answer some of these questions in the future.

USE OF NEUROPSYCHOLOGICAL ASSESSMENT IN OTHER PROFESSIONAL SPORTS ORGANIZATIONS

The NFL and NHL programs were the first league-wide initiatives in professional sports. A number of other professional organizations now have programs designed to monitor cognitive functioning and symptoms following a suspected injury. For instance, Major League Baseball, Major League Soccer, and the US Ski/Snowboard teams have sport-specific neuropsychological testing protocols that emphasize preseason baseline and postinjury assessment. In addition, in 2002, the Indianapolis Racing League began conducting baseline studies to help make decisions regarding a professional driver's return to the race track after a suspected concussion. More recently, Formula 1 Racing has begun to utilize the ImPACT program. Finally, a number of National Basketball Association teams have begun to conduct neuropsychological assessments, pre- and postconcussion.

CURRENT CONTROVERSIES AND REMAINING RESEARCH QUESTIONS

Given the rapid development of the field of sports neuropsychology and the relatively recent focus on short- and long-term outcome in professional athletes, many important research questions remain unanswered. At the current time, clinical return-to-play decisions are being made based on incomplete evidence regarding possible long-term implications of playing professional sports. Most prominently, a debate currently rages regarding the prevalence of dementia and its relationship to sport-related trauma.

This debate has been fueled primarily by the release of case studies on a relatively small series of autopsies conducted on professional football athletes (McKee et al., 2009). Although of great interest and importance, public media attention to these cases has led some to assume a clear relationship between trauma and dementia without fully considering other moderating factors that might play a role in the development of dementia (e.g., genetic factors, drug or alcohol abuse, the effects of other as yet unknown factors). In addition, self-report survey studies have been published that have suggested that athletes who have experienced multiple concussions have a higher incidence of both premature dementia (Guskiewicz et al., 2005) and depression (Guskiewicz et al., 2007). However, given the inherent limitations of self-report based on retrospective recall of concussion history decades after injury, these studies have yet to be verified via careful "face-to-face" evaluation of the retired athlete. It is hoped that future research will help clarify these matters.

SUMMARY

This chapter has provided a summary of current neuropsychological assessment programs in professional sports and has focused on important issues regarding the evaluation and management of the concussed athlete. The utilization of neuropsychological assessment in professional sports has been a relatively recent development, and it is expected that the role of the neuropsychologist in this arena will continue to expand rapidly in the near future.

Neuropsychologists play a unique role in making complicated and important return-to-play decisions and retirement decisions. Given our training in disentangling complicated clinical research issues, our field is well placed in the professional sports arena. It is hoped that neuropsychologists increasingly view their involvement in sports as an area of interest.

ACKNOWLEDGMENT

The author is the developer of, and has a commercial interest in, a computerized neurocognitive screening battery called ImPACT. This battery is widely used in professional and amateur sports.

REFERENCES

Aubry, M., Cantu, R., Dvorak, J., Graf-Baumann, T., Johnston, K., Kelly, J., et al. (2002). Summary of the first international conference on concussion in sport, Vienna Austria. *The Physician and Sportsmedicine, 30*(3), 1–11.

Benedict, R. H. B. (1997). *Brief Visuospatial Memory Test—Revised professional manual*. Odessa, FL: Psychological Assessment Resources.

Benton, A., & Hamsher, K. (1978). *Multilingual aphasia examination*. Iowa City: University of Iowa Press.

Brandt, J. (1991). The Hopkins Verbal Learning Test: Development of a new memory test with six equivalent forms. *The Clinical Neuropsychologist, 5*, 125–142.

Collins, M. W., Field, M., Lovell, M. R., Iverson, G., Johnston, K. M., Maroon, J., et al. (2003a). Relationship between postconcussion headache and neuropsychological test performance in high school athletes. *American Journal of Sports Medicine, 31*(2), 168–173.

Collins, M. W., Grindel, S. H., Lovell, M. R., Dede, D. E., Moser, D. J., Phalin, B. R., et al. (1999). Relationship between concussion and neuropsychological performance in college football players. *Journal of the American Medical Association, 282*(10), 964–970.

Collins, M. W., Iverson, G. L., Lovell, M. R., McKeag, D. B., Norwig, J., & Maroon, J. (2003b). On-field predictors of neuropsychological and symptom deficit following sports-related concussion. *Clinical Journal of Sport Medicine, 13*(4), 222–229.

Gronwall, D., & Wrightson, P. (1975). Cumulative effect of concussion. *Lancet, 2*(7943), 995–997.

Guskiewicz, K. M., Marshall, S. W., Bailes, J., McCrea, M., Cantu, R. C., Randolph, C., et al. (2005). Association between recurrent concussion and late-life cognitive impairment in retired professional football players. *Neurosurgery, 57*(4), 719–726; discussion 719–726.

Guskiewicz, K. M., Marshall, S. W., Bailes, J., McCrea, M., Harding, H. P., Jr., Matthews, A., et al. (2007). Recurrent concussion and risk of depression in retired professional football players. *Medicine and Science in Sports and Exercise, 39*(6), 903–909.

Hovda, D. A., Prins, M., Becker, D. P., Lee, S., Bergneider, M., & Martin, N. (1998). Neurobiology of concussion. In J. Bailes, M. R. Lovell, & J. C. Maroon (Eds.), *Sports-related concussion*. St. Louis, MO: Quality Medical Publishers.

Lovell, M. R. (1999). Evaluation of the professional athlete. In J. E. Bailes, M. R. Lovell, & J. C. Maroon (Eds.), *Sports-related concussion*. St. Louis, MO: Quality Medical Publishing.

Lovell, M. R., & Burke, C. J. (2000). Concussion in the professional athlete: The NHL program. In R. E. Cantu (Ed.), *Neurologic athletic head and spine injuries*. Philadelphia: W. B. Saunders.

Lovell, M. R., & Collins, M. W. (1998). Neuropsychological assessment of the college football player. *Journal of Head Trauma Rehabilitation, 13*(2), 9–26.

Lovell, M. R., Iverson, G. L., Collins, M. W., Podell, K., Johnston, K. M., Pardini, D., et al. (2006). Measurement of symptoms following sports-related concussion: Reliability and normative data for the post-concussion scale. *Applied Neuropsychology, 13*(3), 166–174.

Lovell, M. R., Pardini, J. E., Welling, J., Collins, M. W., Bakal, J., Lazar, N., et al. (2007). Functional brain abnormalities are related to clinical recovery and time to return-to-play in athletes. *Neurosurgery, 61*(2), 352–359; discussion 359–360.

Lovell, M. R., & Solomon, G. (2011). Psychometric data for the NFL neuropsychological test battery. *Applied Neuropsychology, 18*(3), 197–209.

Macciocchi, S. N., Barth, J. T., Alves, W., Rimel, R. W., & Jane, J. A. (1996). Neuropsychological functioning and recovery after mild head injury in collegiate athletes. *Neurosurgery, 39*(3), 510–514.

Maroon, J. C., Lovell, M. R., Norwig, J., Podell, K., Powell, J. W., & Hartl, R. (2000). Cerebral concussion in athletes: Evaluation and neuropsychological testing. *Neurosurgery*, 47(3), 659–669; discussion 669–672.

McCrory, P., Johnston, K., Aubry, M., Cantu, R., Dvorak, J., Graf-Baumann, T., et al. (2005). Summary of the second international conference on concussion in sport, Prague, Czech Republic. *Clinical Journal of Sport Medicine*, 15(2), 48–55.

McCrory, P., Meeuwisse, W., Johnston, K., Dvorak, J., Aubry, M., Molloy, M., et al. (2009). Consensus statement on concussion in sport—the Third International Conference on Concussion in Sport held in Zurich, November 2008. *Phys Sportsmed*, 37(2), 141–159.

McKee, A. C., Cantu, R. C., Nowinski, C. J., Hedley-Whyte, E. T., Gavett, B. E., Budson, A. E., et al. (2009). Chronic traumatic encephalopathy in athletes: Progressive tauopathy after repetitive head injury. *Journal of Neuropathology and Experimental Neurology*, 68(7), 709–735.

Pellman, E. J., Lovell, M. R., Viano, D. C., & Casson, I. R. (2006). Concussion in professional football: Recovery of NFL and high school athletes assessed by computerized neuropsychological testing-part 12. *Neurosurgery*, 58(2), 263–274; discussion 263–274.

Pellman, E. J., Lovell, M. R., Viano, D. C., Casson, I. R., & Tucker, A. M. (2004a). Concussion in professional football: Neuropsychological testing—Part 6. *Neurosurgery*, 55(6), 1290–1303; discussion 1303–1295.

Pellman, E. J., Powell, J. W., Viano, D. C., Casson, I. R., Tucker, A. M., Feuer, H., et al. (2004b). Concussion in professional football: Epidemiological features of game injuries and review of the literature—Part 3. *Neurosurgery*, 54(1), 81–94; discussion 94–86.

Pellman, E. J., Powell, J. W., Viano, D. C., Casson, I. R., Tucker, A. M., Feuer, H., et al. (2004c). Concussion in professional football: Epidemiological features of game injuries and review of the literature—Part 3. *Neurosurgery*, 54(1), 81–94; discussion 94–96.

Pellman, E. J., & Viano, D. C. (2006). Concussion in professional football: Summary of the research conducted by the National Football League's Committee on Mild Traumatic Brain Injury. *Neurosurgical Focus*, 21(4), E12.

Pellman, E. J., Viano, D. C., Tucker, A. M., & Casson, I. R. (2003). Concussion in professional football: Location and direction of helmet impacts—Part 2. *Neurosurgery*, 53(6), 1328–1340; discussion 1340–1321.

Povlishock, J. T., & Coburn, T. H. (1989). Morphopathological change associated with mild head injury. In H. S. Levin, H. M. Eisenberg, & A. L. Benton (Eds.), *Mild head injury*. New York: Oxford University Press.

Viano, D. C., Hamberger, A., Bolouri, H., & Saljo, A. (2009). Concussion in professional football: Animal model of brain injury—Part 15. *Neurosurgery*, 64(6), 1162–1173; discussion 1173.

Viano, D. C., & Pellman, E. J. (2005). Concussion in professional football: Biomechanics of the striking player—Part 8. *Neurosurgery*, 56(2), 266–280; discussion 266–280.

Wechsler, D. (1997). *Wechsler Adult Intelligence Scale—Third edition*. San Antonio, TX: Psychological Corporation.

CHAPTER 3

Electrical Injury in the Workplace

Joseph W. Fink
Lauren Rog
Shane S. Bush
Neil H. Pliskin

Electricity permeates modern society, and the modern workplace largely runs on electricity. Although electrical power is virtually omnipresent in the workplace, it is normally a silent and invisible force that functions safely and dependably in the background to power day-to-day business (Capelli-Schellpfeffer, 2005). However, since the first work-related electrical accident fatality due to commercially generated electricity in the late 19th century (Duff & McCaffrey, 2001), electricity has been recognized as a potential workplace hazard that can cause death, injury, and disability. Indeed, most electrical injuries (EIs) requiring medical attention occur in the workplace (Brett et al., 2004; Gourbiere, Corbut, & Bazin, 1994; Tredget, Shankowsky, & Tilley, 1999). Moreover, electricity produces work-related injuries that, despite their lower base rates of occurrence relative to some other types of injuries, result in disproportionately high economic costs (Fordyce, Kelsh, Lu, Sahl, & Yager, 2007) and fatalities (Cawley & Homce, 2003).

EIs are sometimes poorly understood by neuropsychologists, as well as by physicians, other clinicians, workers' compensation representatives, and attorneys. Despite the ubiquity of electricity in the workplace, relative to other types of work accidents electrical injuries are comparatively rare, accounting for only 0.22% of nonfatal claims in a survey of workers' compensation claims during the year 2002 (Lombardi, Matz, Brennan, Smith, & Courtney, 2009). Because of the relatively low base rate of electrical injury, some neuropsychologists may have little or no knowledge of EI dynamics and issues when they first encounter a patient with such an injury. Neuropsychologists, like many other clinicians and care managers, may be uninformed about the nature of electrical injury and, in particular, the range of neurobehavioral presentations that can be expected. Some of the peri-injury parameters (e.g., presence and duration of loss of consciousness, Glasgow Coma Scale, posttraumatic amnesia) that serve as clinically useful conventions to guide clinicians' understanding of other traumatic injuries to the central nervous system tend not to apply as clearly to electrical injury. Indeed, in electrical injury some of the event parameters that are often known following accidents, such as whether loss of consciousness occurred or the presumed level of exposure voltage, do not serve as reliable predictors of clinical sequelae (Pliskin et al., 1998, 2006; Primeau, Engelstatter, & Bares, 1995). Following electrical shocks, the spectrum of possible overt manifestations is wide, ranging from death or gross disfigurement to absence of any obvious external signs of injury.

EI survivors may ultimately see numerous clinicians from various disciplines and specialties. Because of the low incidence of this type of injury and the fact that the visible sequelae may appear to be minimal, it is often difficult for patients to obtain a comprehensive assessment that integrates an understanding of the "invisible" neurocognitive, emotional, and behavioral sequelae that can ensue (Tkachenko, Kelley, Pliskin, & Fink, 1999). Moreover, a high proportion of work-related electrical injuries occur in a compensable context (Bianchini, Love, Greve, & Adams, 2005; Heilbronner & Pliskin, 1993), in which the possibility of malingering may become salient. Thus, assessment of the electrically injured patient typically requires a sophisticated and comprehensive neuropsychological evaluation that combines knowledge of electrical injury dynamics with patient history data, neurocognitive profile analysis, and careful consideration of personality/emotional functioning and effort/motivation issues. Particularly when there are few overt manifestations (e.g., burns, disfigurement), the role of neuropsychological assessment is often central to guiding clinical management and medical–legal decisions.

In this chapter, we review the epidemiology of work-related electrical injuries and consider some of the known and poorly understood aspects of the pathophysiology of these injuries. We review the patterns of symptom presentation, typical course, comorbid conditions, and complicating factors. Finally, we consider key issues guiding neuropsychological assessment and treatment planning for electrical injury patients.

EPIDEMIOLOGY

Although EIs may be relatively uncommon, their impact on individuals and the workplace is often great. As will be reviewed, the modal electrical accident victim is a young man shocked while working in the electrical or construction trades, and these accident events bring disproportionately high economic costs and risks for death and disability as compared to many other work-related injuries.

In a National Institute for Occupational Safety and Health (NIOSH) review of U.S. Bureau of Labor Statistics for occupational electrical injuries from 1992 to 1998 (Cawley & Homce, 2003), the total of 2,267 fatal incidents involving electricity ranked sixth among all causes of work-related deaths in the United States, accounting for 5.2% of all deaths. This figure is similar to a 15-year NIOSH study from 2000 that showed electricity accounted for 7.1% of work-related deaths in men and 0.7% in women during the years 1980–1995 (Capelli-Schellpfeffer, 2005). Electrical incidents were shown to be relatively rare but disproportionately fatal when they occurred. For example, in 1997 only 1 in 494 days away from work due to injury/illness were attributed to electrical exposure, yet approximately 1 in 20 occupational deaths were caused by electricity (Cawley & Homce, 2003). In this same study, the leading accident scenario, accounting for 41% of electrical fatalities, was contact with overhead power lines. This study also showed that construction workers (representing approximately 7% of the U.S. workforce) sustained 44% of the electrical fatalities. Another analysis of electrical fatalities among U.S. construction workers from 1980 to 1991 found 2,000 electrical fatalities, which represented the highest mean mortality rate and the second highest age-adjusted rate of all industries (Ore & Casini, 1996). The construction industry accounted for approximately 40% of the total fatal electrical accidents in all industries combined, such that construction workers were found to be four times more likely to be electrocuted (i.e., killed by electricity) at work than workers in all other industries combined.

Considering nonfatal electrical accidents, the U.S. Bureau of Labor Statistics study indicated that 32,309 nonfatal electrical injuries in private industry were reported during 1992–1998, representing an average of 4,687 reported injuries per year. Such figures underestimate the actual incidence of work-related electrical trauma to some extent, because groups such as the self-employed and small businesses are not included in these totals (Capelli-Schellpfeffer, Miller, & Humilier, 1999). The two leading industry sectors for nonlethal electrical injury were construction and manufacturing. In an analysis of 586,567 workers' compensation claims from Liberty Mutual insurance in 2002, fatal electrical accidents accounted for 1.2% and nonfatal electrical-related injuries accounted for 0.22% of the claims. Similar to other surveys, the victims were disproportionately male (72.3%), with an average age of 36 years.

Further descriptive data are available from surveys of burn unit admissions. A 1999 survey from a Canadian burn unit showed that across ten years electrical injuries comprised 5.3% of all admissions, and 95.9% of the electrically injured were males with a mean age of 33.9 years (Tredget et al., 1999). Whereas 74.3% of the electrically injured cases were work-related, only 27.3% of all thermal burn admissions were work-related. In a more recent analysis of burn center admissions over a 20-year period (Brett et al., 2004), work-related activity was likewise responsible for the major-ity of electrical injury admissions, with linemen and electricians being the most common occupations.

Gourbiere et al. (1994) studied electrical accidents from a French elec-trical power company between 1970 and 1989 and found an average of 104 victims per year, 99.9% of whom were male and the mean age was 35. Of these accidents, 18% were considered high-voltage ($\geq$ 1,000 volts), 57% were deemed "low-voltage" ($\leq$1,000 volts), and for 25% the volt-age was unknown. A total of 2.7% of the total cases were fatal, and of the remaining (nonfatal) cases approximately 73% were deemed to have a complete recovery. Approximately 25% of the cases showed long-term effects, including sequelae directly related to burns in 63% of the cases and neuropsychiatric sequelae in 18% of the cases.

In a more recent analysis of thermal and burn injuries among electri-cal utility workers from 1995 to 2004 documented in the Electric Power Research Institute (EPRI) Occupational Health and Safety Database (OHSD), electrical injuries accounted for 45.8% of the 872 burn-related injuries reported during this period (Fordyce et al., 2007). Males accounted for approximately 97% of the electrical injuries for the cases in which gen-der was reported, though they comprised only 72% of the OHSD dataset. Burn and electric shock injuries constituted approximately 13% of all of the medical claim costs, with an average of $14,121 per electrical injury. Finally, in a retrospective review of 291 fatalities caused by electricity in Bulgaria, Dokov (2009) found that most deaths by electrocution in that country were due to contact with high-voltage power transmission wires (41.24%) and from lightning (32.3%). Contact with construction/repair electrical devices (7.56%) and electrical railway infrastructure (6.9%) accounted for most of the remaining fatalities.

PATHOPHYSIOLOGY

EI patterns are considered to be complex and variable, depending on a multitude of factors, including current density, pathway through the body, and variations in body size, body position, and use of protective gear (Lee, 1997; Lee, Zhang, & Hannig, 2000). Electricity is the flow of electrons through a conductor (Koumbourlis, 2002). Electricity generated for use in industrial and residential settings is either in the form of direct current (DC) or, more commonly, alternating current (AC). DC refers to a continu-ous flow of electrons in one direction, while AC refers to a pattern of con-tinuous reversal of electrons (Koumbourlis, 2002; Lee, 1997).

AC is considered to be three to four times more dangerous than DC of similar voltage for two primary reasons. First, AC can cause tetanic muscle spasms leading to repetitive contractions of the affected muscles, particularly at low voltages (Ressijac, 1986). If the victim's hand comes into contact with AC, the muscles in the hand may contract, leading to what is referred to as the "no let-go" phenomenon, in which the victim is unable to release contact with the electrical source. This situation is particularly dangerous because it increases the duration of electrical contact. Second, AC appears to have a greater effect on cardiac and respiratory systems than DC, and thus accidents involving AC are more likely to lead to severe injury or death (Silversides, 1964; Wilbourn, 1995).

Physics of EI

The physics of EI involves several factors, including voltage, amperage, tissue resistance, current pathway, distance from the source, surface area of the body exposed, and duration of electrical contact (Capelli-Schellpfeffer et al., 1999; Selvaggi, Monstrey, Van Landuyt, Hamdi, & Blondeel, 2005). Voltage is described as a unit of force that causes current to flow along a conductor. In grouping clinical cases, high voltage is typically considered to refer to any value at or above 1,000 volts, whereas low voltage refers to values below that point (e.g., Capelli-Schellpfeffer, Toner, Lee, & Astumian, 1995; Gourbiere et al., 1994). The injury effects of different voltages have been reported to vary widely. Although voltage is one factor affecting the amount of damage caused by electrical contact, it is by no means the only determinant. For example, amperage, which refers to the number of electrons per second passing over a given point, is thought to be related to deep tissue damage and mortality associated with EI (Hunt, Mason, Masterson, & Pruitt, 1976).

Tissue resistance is another important factor that affects the extent of electrical injury. Resistance is a unit of force that opposes the flow of electric current. Electric current travels along the path of least resistance; when resistance is met, heat is generated, leading to tissue damage when living organisms are subjected to electrical current. Resistance levels of different tissues vary (from most to least resistance: bone, fat, tendon, skin, muscle, blood, nerves; Christensen, Sherman, Balis, & Wuamett, 1980; Cooper, 1995). The first tissue to come into contact with electric current is typically skin, which has varying levels of resistance that depend on a number of factors. For example, while a clean and dry adult human hand has a resistance of approximately 5,000 ohms, a dirty or wet hand is less resistant (1,000 ohms), and a heavily calloused hand may have much more resistance (up to 1 million ohms). When current overcomes resistance of the skin, it preferentially follows those tissues with the least resistance, typically nerves and blood vessels (Christensen et al., 1980; Cooper, 1995). Due to the low resistance of nervous system tissue, EI often causes damage to the central nervous system (CNS) and is known to affect the brain and the spinal cord. Neurologic symptoms can therefore be observed in victims of EI regardless of whether the head was a point of direct contact with the electrical current (Pliskin et al., 1994). Vasculature also is preferentially affected due to its high water content, and smaller vessels are particularly affected by coagulation necrosis (Koumbourlis, 2002).

Mechanisms of Injury

Electricity can be transmitted via direct or indirect contact with the electrical source. Direct contact occurs when a person physically touches a power source, whereas indirect contact can occur in several ways, including arcing, capacitative coupling, magnetic fields, or thermoacoustic effects. Victims of EI commonly suffer more than one type of injury (Capelli-Schellpfeffer et al., 1995; Lee & Dougherty, 2003).

Direct electric current traveling through the body can lead to damage on a cellular level due to the disruption of the electrically polarized components of cells (Lee, 1997; Lee & Kolodney, 1987). Electroporation refers to one type of cellular damage in which cell membranes become permeable due to the formation of pores in the lipid and protein bilayer. Electroporation of cells can be transient if pores seal spontaneously, or stable if they do not. Loss of cell function is the typical result of electroporation, and nonporated or less severely porated cells must work harder to maintain homeostasis, ultimately leading to cell death in some instances by means of energy starvation (Capelli-Schellpfeffer et al., 1995; Lee et al., 1995, 2000).

The second type of electrical injury, thermal injury, can result from joule heating of tissues as a consequence of electric current resistance. Such injuries can cause deep burns within the victim's body, resulting in tissue coagulation and necrosis that can progress for several weeks after injury (Lee, 1997; Lee & Dougherty, 2003; Tredget et al., 1999). A victim also may sustain thermal injuries from an electric arc injury, which occurs when a powerful electrical source jumps the air gap between the source and the individual. Arcing often occurs when very high voltages are involved; if the victim is grounded, electrical contact is more likely to be mediated by an arc before direct mechanical contact is made (Capelli-Schellpfeffer et al., 1995; Lee, 1997). Because high temperatures (up to 5,000°C) are often reached, electric arcs can lead to burns on the skin or an igniting of the victim's clothing (Koumbourlis, 2002; Lee, 1997). In addition, thermoacoustic injury is a common consequence of an electric arc event. Thermoacoustic injury (also referred to as "blast" injury) is a form of barotrauma that occurs when electrical energy is transformed into explosive heat (thermal) and pressure (acoustic) waves to which the victim is exposed (Lee, 1997). Thus, it is extremely relevant to determine if an explosion occurred as part of an electrical accident scenario, especially when accidents take place in closed spaces. Indeed, the cognitive effects of blast injuries have begun to attract greater attention given their ever-increasing number in modern warfare (Belanger, Kretzmer, Yoash-Gantz, Pickett, & Tupler, 2009).

Common consequences of electric arc injury are "flash" injuries and barotraumas. The term *flash* injury is used to describe instances in which there are burns to the skin in the absence of any focal contact wounds (Lee, 1997). Barotrauma from acoustic or blast injuries is not always readily apparent immediately following the accident, and victims may present with impairments (e.g., neurological) in the absence of external signs of electrical contact (Chico, Capelli-Schellpfeffer, Kelley, & Lee, 1999). Victims may experience blunt trauma due to being thrown down from the force of acoustic pressure waves, or as a result of falls (e.g., from a ladder or pole), resulting in head injuries, fractures, or dislocations (Heilbronner & Pliskin, 1999). Using a two-dimensional simulation of an electric arc event, Capelli-Schellpfeffer et al. (1999) demonstrated that the thermoacoustic effects of such an event are sufficient to cause a worker to be thrown to the ground, increasing the possibility that the victim may suffer head trauma due to mechanical forces.

Cardiac arrest or arrhythmias (e.g., atrial fibrillation) may result from disturbance of the heart's electrical conduction. The extent of myocardial injury depends in part on the voltage and type of current, with higher voltages and AC leading to more severe injury (Capelli-Schellpfeffer et al., 1995; Jost, Schonrock, & Cherington, 2005; Lee, 1997). Respiratory muscle spasms also may occur when electrical current flows through the chest, as is the case when electricity enters through one hand and exits through the other (Lee, 1997). Herlevsen and Andersen (1987) reported a case in which an EI patient with premorbid vasovagal symptom history fainted soon after experiencing a 220-volt AC injury, with very brief loss of consciousness (10–15 seconds). One hour postinjury, the patient suffered sinus bradycardia leading to sinus arrest in response to a situation he found anxiety-provoking (having his blood drawn). The authors speculated that patients with vasovagal symptom histories may be at increased risk for cardiac arrest following an electrical injury. Because of these various causes of neurologic impairment, Bush (2008) proposed the following descriptive terms in an attempt to help clarify the nature of the electricity-related brain injury (EBI) for a given patient: EBI–head contact, EBI–peripheral contact, EBI–TBI, EBI–anoxia, EBI–combined, or EBI–undetermined origin. Research is needed to establish the clinical value of such classifications.

Central Nervous System Damage

Damage to the central nervous system (CNS) may occur by a number of means, including the direct thermal and mechanical effects of the electric current passing through the body. Histopathological changes to the CNS may include coagulation necrosis (i.e., death of tissue as a result of clotted blood vessels), demyelination (destruction of the protein sheaths that cover many nerves), reactive gliosis (injury-responsive increase in non-neural support cells), perivascular hemorrhage (areas of bleeding), and vacuolization (small holes in brain tissue; Daniel, Haban, Hutcherson, Bolter, & Long, 1985; DiVincenti, Moncrief, & Pruitt, 1969; Pliskin et al., 1994; Pruitt &

Mason, 1979; Wilkinson & Wood, 1978). Indirectly, victims may experience anoxic injury as a result of cardiac or respiratory damage, or may suffer traumatic brain injury as a result of either blunt head trauma or "blast" injury (Gualtieri & Johnson, 1999).

Pathways

In the case of DC current, electric current enters a victim at contact points on the body at an "entrance" point, and after traveling along a pathway through the body, leaves through an "exit" point. In the case of AC current, which repeatedly changes its directional flow, there are technically no "entrance" and "exit" points but simply "contact points." Contact wounds are one indication that the body has conducted a significant amount of electrical energy to cause injury. The presence of contact wounds does not necessarily indicate that CNS damage occurred, just as contact wounds may be absent in someone who suffered EI (Bianchini et al., 2005).

The initial electrical contact point may come into direct or indirect contact with the electrical source; the most common body sites are the hands, followed by the head and chest (Cooper, 1995; Janus & Barrash, 1996; Wilkinson & Wood, 1978). In the case of a head contact point, there may be considerable damage to the CNS because the current often is dense enough to pass through the skull. The current is likely to generate substantial heat as it travels through the meninges, cortex, and cerebrospinal fluid (Christensen et al., 1980). Other contact point(s) are created when electrical current leaves the body in search of a grounding source (i.e., earth). The specific location of a grounding contact point depends on the path of electrical current, though common points are feet, hands, legs, and trunk of the body (Janus & Barrash, 1996; Wilkinson & Wood, 1978).

In general, common pathways for electricity through the body are hand-to-hand, hand-to-foot, or head-to-foot. When a person comes into contact with AC, the electrical current continuously flows into and out of the body through the same points (Lee, 1997). Hooshmand, Radfar, and Beckner (1989) reported 2 cases in which current passed through a hand-to-hand pathway, and 14 cases of patients experiencing hand-to-foot pathways. Importantly, the pathway of electrical current through the body affects the number and types of organs affected, and therefore the severity and types of injury sustained in the accident (Koumbourlis, 2002).

Neurodiagnostic Testing

Electroencephalogram (EEG) abnormalities have been reported in EI patients in both the presence and absence of measurable symptoms (Gourbiere et al., 1994; Hooshmand et al., 1989; Janus & Barrash, 1996). Specific findings include mild generalized slowing, polyspike and wave ictal bursts, and seizure activity. Brainstem auditory evoked response (BAER) abnormalities have been reported in some cases and suggest lower brain-stem dysfunction (Hooshmand et al., 1989). Somatosensory evoked potential (SEP) abnormalities include peripheral nerve involvement in the burned extremity and cervical spinal cord dysfunction. CT of the head has been reported to be generally within normal limits in EI patients, though there have been reports of mild generalized cerebral atrophy (Hooshmand et al., 1989; Janus & Barrash, 1996). MRI of the brain has typically been negative in the majority of EI patients, though small, unspecified T2 hyperintensities have been noted in multiple patients (Ramati et al., 2009a). EI patients have been found to be less likely than TBI patients to show structural abnormalities on MRI and CT (Barrash, Kealey, & Janus, 1996).

In a functional MRI study using oculomotor tasks to assess working memory and learning performance, EI patients demonstrated increased activation in neocortical sensorimotor systems during a visual sensorimotor task, as well as increased activation in prefrontal systems during a spatial working memory task, compared to controls (Ramati et al., 2009a). This pattern of increased activation suggests inefficiency and subsequent compensatory increases in neurophysiological activity in these brain regions. EI patients also demonstrated less activation in frontostriatal systems during a procedural learning task, possibly reflecting inefficiencies in automatic processes associated with procedural learning. Despite these findings, EI patients and controls in this study did not differ in their performances on standard neuropsychological measures of working memory.

Single photon emission computed tomography (SPECT) performed on seven high-voltage electrical injury patients was abnormal in two cases, with hypoperfusion in the right mesial-temporal region in one patient and hyperperfusion in the left caudate nucleus with global cortical uptake in the other patient (Deveci, Bozkurt, Arslan, & Sengezer, 2002). Both patients with abnormal imaging had related neurological complications.

In an analysis of 12 EEG and imaging studies on EI and lightning injury patients (Duff & McCaffrey, 2001), 80% of EEG and evoked potential (EP) findings were abnormal, including mild slowing, suspicious theta activity, and atonic/myoclonic attacks. Thirty-two percent of CT/MRI results were abnormal, with findings including cerebral edema, mild atrophy, and basal ganglia hematoma.

SYMPTOM PRESENTATION

Because there are multiple means of injury in electrical accidents, symptom presentations can be highly variable. Physical, cognitive, and emotional/behavioral symptoms are all common in victims of EI and may result from either direct or indirect electric current damage (Cooper, 1995; Heilbronner & Pliskin, 1999; Primeau, 2005) and/or psychiatric factors. The severity of injury from an electrical accident can range widely from minimal (e.g., minor burns, transient confusion) to very severe (e.g., paraplegia, permanent memory loss, death).

The nervous system can be particularly vulnerable to electrical injury due to its low-resistance properties, and neurological symptoms are the major cause of morbidity and mortality in high-voltage electrical injury (Barrash et al., 1996; Deveci et al., 2002). Central nervous system sequelae can occur whether or not the head is in the pathway of electrical current (Lee, 1997; Pliskin et al., 1999, 2006; Ramati et al., 2009a), though there currently is no definitive neuropathological model to explain how electrical exposure to the peripheral nervous system leads to CNS deficits. One hypothesis is that electricity is transmitted via the spinal cord to the brain, perhaps preferentially along white matter tracks, and may be responsible for complex spinal and supraspinal interactions that lead to cognitive dysfunction (Ramati et al., 2009a). Indeed, there is a growing body of research demonstrating that functional changes in key cortical and subcortical areas occur following different kinds of lesions to the peripheral nervous system (PNS; Kaas et al., 2008; Schlaier et al., 2007).

Somatic Symptoms

Physical injury caused by electrical accidents can take many forms, and multiple organ systems may be affected, including nervous, cardiovascular, respiratory, ocular, and renal systems (Fish, 1993; Koumbourlis, 2002; Lee, 1997; Yarnell & Lammertse, 1995). Dermal and subcutaneous burns are among the most common acute symptoms in EI and often lead to pain, scarring, fibrosis, and joint stiffness (Gourbiere et al., 1994). Limb amputation may be necessary as a result of thermal and nonthermal tissue damage, with amputation rates in EI survivors reported from 14% (Gourbiere et al., 1994) to 60% (Butler & Gant, 1977) in some clinical samples. In the case of electric arc events, possible injuries resulting from barotrauma include perforated eardrums, blast lung, abdominal blast injury, acceleration–deceleration head injury, and blunt head trauma from falling or being hit by explosion shrapnel. Ocular injuries (e.g., cataracts, keratitis) and other auditory sequelae (e.g., hearing loss, tinnitus, vertigo) also are common (Capelli-Schellpfeffer et al., 1999; Gourbiere et al., 1994; Lee & Dougherty, 2003). Cardiac complications (e.g., arrhythmias; cardiac arrest) may occur, particularly when AC or high voltages are involved (Barrash et al., 1996; Janus & Barrash, 1996).

In terms of neurological symptoms, loss of consciousness can occur following the injury (Barrash et al., 1996; Hooshmand et al., 1989; Ramati et al., 2009a). Damage to peripheral and sensory nerves can lead to a range of sensory and motor symptoms, including paresthesia and dysesthesia (Koumbourlis, 2002; Lee, 1997). Victims of EI have been reported to experience isolated seizures shortly following the accident, as well as recurring seizures that may last for years after injury (Daniel et al., 1985;

Hooshmand et al., 1989). In a study of 13 patients who sustained electrical injury, emergency department neurology records indicated normal neurological function in nine patients and abnormal functioning in four patients (e.g., cranial nerve dysfunction, facial nerve palsy, and diffuse weakness; Janus & Barrash, 1996).

In the postacute and long-term phases (reported as 1 month to 5 or more years postinjury), common physical complaints include pain, headache, motor weakness, coordination problems, blurred vision, dizziness, insomnia, contracture, and paresthesia (Daniel et al., 1985; Hooshmand et al., 1989; Ramati et al., 2009a, 2009b; Theman, Singerman, Gomez, & Fish, 2008). In a study involving 65 acute and postacute EI patients evaluated by the University of Chicago Electrical Trauma Research Program, Pliskin et al. (1998) found that EI patients endorsed significantly more symptoms on the Neuropsychological Symptom Checklist than electrician control subjects. The most common somatic complaints were paresthesia, headaches, muscle spasms and weakness, pain, loss of feeling, burning skin, and numbness.

Cognitive Symptoms

The most frequent cognitive complaint reported in EI patients is memory dysfunction, with impairment also commonly reported in attention and concentration, learning, planning, and organizing. Patients often complain of difficulty recalling recent events, forgetting names, word-finding difficulties, getting lost in familiar places, distractibility, and slowed thinking. They report that more effort than usual is required to sustain attention and concentrate, and that these functions are less automatic (Daniel et al., 1985; Heilbronner & Pliskin, 1999; Pliskin et al., 2006).

Most studies examining the neuropsychological profiles of EI patients have not found a singularly unique symptom pattern, though impaired cognitive functioning is often documented (Daniel et al., 1985; Janus & Barrash, 1996; Martin, Salvatore, & Johnstone, 2003; Pliskin et al., 1999, 2006). One sample of 14 high-voltage electrical injury patients found impairments in memory and attention to be most frequent, and verbal memory was found to be particularly affected (Janus & Barrash, 1996). All patients with neuropsychological deficits displayed problems with memory and attention. Less frequently, patients displayed impairments in processing speed, expressive language, reasoning, executive function, auditory processing, and visuoperception/construction. Similar findings are reported in case study reports (Crews, Barth, Brelsford, Francis, & McArdle, 1997; Hopewell, 1983; Martin et al., 2003).

Pliskin et al. (1999) compared the profiles of 45 EI patients with 29 electrician controls and found that EI patients had significantly lower full-scale IQ (FSIQ) scores than controls. This finding was replicated in a study by Pliskin et al. (2006) comparing the neuropsychological profiles of 29 EI patients who passed cognitive effort testing to a sample of demographically matched electrician controls. Although the control group's current FSIQ scores were significantly higher than EI patients' scores, the groups did not differ in their estimated premorbid IQ scores, suggesting a decline in intellectual functioning in the patient group. Indeed, EI patients showed a greater difference between their estimated premorbid and current IQ than controls. The EI group also performed significantly worse than controls on measures of sustained and divided attention, as well as mental processing and psychomotor speed. Pliskin et al. (1999) previously reported similar results, in addition to poorer memory performance in EI patients, particularly visual learning and memory. Similarly, verbal memory deficits also have been reported in acute and postacute EI patients, with acquisition and retrieval processes more affected than retention (Primeau et al., 1995).

In an overview analysis of eight studies involving 65 EI and lightning injury patients, impaired cognitive performance was evident across all domains assessed: (1) overall neuropsychological functioning, (2) intelligence, (3) attention/concentration, (4) speech/language, (5) sensory/motor, (6) visual motor, (7) memory, and (8) executive functioning (Duff & McCaffrey, 2001). Memory impairment was most common (37% of impaired results), followed by deficits in attention (15%), sensory/motor functions (13%), visual motor abilities (13%), speech/language skills (10%), executive functioning (5%), and intelligence/achievement (5%).

A number of non-neurological factors may complicate a patient's cognitive presentation, including motivation, effort, stress, pain, pain medications, emotional state, and personality traits. In a sample of 14 EI patients seeking financial compensation for their injuries, 5 did not meet the criteria for malingering neurocognitive dysfunction (MND), while 8 met the criteria for probable MND and 1 for definite MND (Bianchini et al., 2005). The authors concluded that malingering in EI patients is similar to what is reported in litigating TBI patients. In both groups, patients with more ambiguous neurological sequelae are more likely to meet criteria for MND, though patients with demonstrable neurological injuries were also found to meet criteria. However, other studies demonstrated that litigating and nonlitigating EI patients have not been found to differ in cognitive domain performance, depressive symptoms, or self-report somatic, cognitive, and emotional symptoms (Pliskin et al., 1999, 2006; Ramati et al., 2009b).

Emotional Symptoms

Emotional disturbance is one of the symptoms most frequently reported by EI patients and has been found to be more common in victims of EI than in electrician controls (Pliskin et al., 1998, 2006). The rates of significant psychiatric symptomatology in EI are reported to range from 57% (Kelley, Pliskin, Meyer, & Lee, 1994) to 87.5% (Hooshmand et al., 1989). Depression, anxiety, posttraumatic stress disorder (PTSD), adjustment disorders, irritability, attitude change, and decreased frustration tolerance are commonly reported (Barrash et al., 1996; Daniel et al., 1985; Gourbiere et al., 1994; Hooshmand et al., 1989; Kelley, Tkachenko, Pliskin, Fink, & Lee, 1999; Mancusi-Ungaro, Tarbox, & Wainwright, 1986; Pliskin et al., 1998, 1999; Primeau et al., 1995; Ramati et al., 2009b; Theman et al., 2008). Barrash et al. (1996) found assaultive behavior to be relatively common among patients with affective disturbance. Similarly, a meta-analysis of 28 studies involving 2,738 patients found the most prevalent psychiatric complaints to be (in descending order of frequency) depression, phobias/fears, irritability, sleep disturbances, and occupational difficulties (Duff & McCaffrey, 2001).

The development of PTSD and phobias in EI patients have been described as akin to a single-trial aversive conditioning paradigm that is difficult to extinguish and may lead to chronic and progressive distress (Mancusi-Ungaro et al., 1986). Rates of PTSD in EI samples have been reported to be 44–50% (Kelley et al., 1999; Primeau, 2005). Emotional distress has often been reported to persist over time, and difficulty with psychological adjustment has been reported in patients on longitudinal follow-up at an average of 4 years postinjury (Fink et al., 1999).

The most commonly elevated subscales for EI patients on the Minnesota Multiphasic Personality Inventory (MMPI) are 1 (Hs), 2 (D), 3 (Hy), 7 (Pt), and 8 (Sc), suggesting the presence of somatic symptoms, depression, anxiety, and abnormal cognitive experiences (Crews et al., 1997; Daniel et al., 1985; Mancusi-Ungaro et al., 1986; Wicklund et al., 2008). MMPI profiles of EI patients have been found to be similar to the profiles of TBI patients. EI patients, however, had significantly higher scores (medium effect sizes) than chronic pain patients on scales 1 and 3 (Wicklund et al., 2008).

Clinical Presentation of CNS Dysfunction in EI

There is not a particular clinical presentation that is considered pathognomonic of nervous system damage due to EI. As is the case in EI generally, EI to the CNS can occur directly (e.g., passage of current through the body) or indirectly (e.g., blunt head or cardiac trauma; Koumbourlis, 2002). EI symptom patterns have been compared to patterns seen in diffuse cerebral injury, damage to the limbic system or the hypothalamic–pituitary axis, and in electroconvulsive therapy (ECT; Pliskin et al., 1998, 1999). It has been hypothesized that EI leads to electrochemical alterations in brain systems, and ECT has been used as a model to explain possible changes to the central nervous system in EI (Pliskin et al., 2006). ECT exposes the central nervous system to a relatively small electrical field, and recipients of ECT often experience disturbance of cognition, including confusion, disorientation, and anterograde memory disturbance (Pliskin et al., 2006; Rosen, Reznik, Sluvis, Kaplan, & Mester, 2003). Negative MRI findings in examining the effects of ECT on the brain have led investigators to suspect that the neuropsychiatric and neurocognitive changes that occur following ECT are due to electrochemical changes that occur on a neuronal level (Coffey et al., 1991; Rami-Gonzalez et al., 2003).

Based on the findings in the EI and ECT literature, it has been suggested that EI pathophysiology is similar to that of ECT, although it is more severe when associated with greater electrical field strength exposure (Pliskin et al., 2006; Primeau et al., 1995). The diffuse patterns of cognitive dysfunction often seen in EI have been compared to presentations of patients with traumatic brain injuries due to mechanical forces, though unlike TBI patients, EI patients' symptoms have been reported to sometimes worsen over time (Bianchini et al., 2005; Chico et al., 1999).

Relationship between Cognitive and Emotional Symptoms

The co-occurrence of cognitive dysfunction and emotional distress has been reported in samples of EI patients (e.g., Barrash et al., 1996; Daniel et al., 1985). Barrash et al. (1996) suggested several possible explanations for this relationship: (1) neuropathological cognitive dysfunction may lead to emotional distress; (2) both may be the result of neurological dysfunction; (3) posttraumatic affective disorder may lead to compromised cognitive functioning; or (4) both may be the results of physical pain/injury. Janus and Barrash (1996) found cognitive and affective disturbances to occur together in their sample, but concluded that they were not proportional, as emotional symptoms were typically more severe than cognitive symptoms. The authors theorized that the sample's clinical pictures reflected both neuropathological effects and psychological reactions. In support of this theory, Pliskin et al. (2006) found that impairment in attention and processing speed was independent of self-report depression symptoms.

Distress is likely to be a manifestation of the traumatic experience of EI that may or may not contribute significantly to cognitive dysfunction. At the same time, it is possible that new-onset emotional disturbance (e.g., depression) may also reflect CNS damage. Ammar et al. (2006) found that EI patients with PTSD had poorer memory performances than EI patients without PTSD, suggesting a possible psychological contribution to the cognitive profile in EI. Ramati et al. (2009b) similarly reported that EI patients with two psychiatric diagnoses (most often depression and PTSD) performed significantly worse on cognitive testing than patients with one or no diagnosis, and also reported an increased rate of symptom concerns.

COURSE

EI patients sometimes report worsening physical, cognitive, and emotional symptoms over time. Cherington (1995) described three symptom courses in EI: (1) *immediate and transient*: symptoms begin at the time of the injury and remit shortly thereafter (e.g., days); (2) *immediate and prolonged/ permanent*: symptoms that begin at the time of injury and persist long-term (e.g., months, years, indefinitely); and (3) *delayed and progressive*: symptoms that appear sometime after the injury and worsen over time. Symptoms have been reported to develop weeks, months, or (less typically) years after injury (Farrell & Starr, 1968). Possible causes for delayed and progressive neurological symptoms include demyelinating disorders or thrombosis (Christensen et al., 1980), emotional adjustment problems, and litigation (Binder & Rohling, 1996; Suhr, Tranel, Wefel, & Barrash, 1997). Late development of tissue fibrosis around the injured area may explain increased physical complaints (e.g., pain) over time (Selvaggi et al., 2005). Spinal cord injury has been documented to lead to quadriplegia 6 weeks postinjury, and some delayed neurologic injuries that are reported may be attributed to spinal cord injury (Janus & Barrash, 1996; Wilbourn, 1995).

Barrash et al. (1996) reported increased distress in their high-voltage EI sample that began a few months postinjury. The authors stated that the patients' clinical pictures most closely reflected interactions between physical and psychosocial consequences of the injury and their emotional reactions to the injury and its consequences. They suggested that an increase in mood disturbance may have been seen over time as patients became more concerned that their conditions had not yet resolved. Patients in the postacute phase of recovery (i.e., more than 3 months postinjury) are more likely to report physical complaints (headaches, muscle spasms, balance problems, pain); cognitive difficulties (poor memory, distractibility, word-finding problems, slowed thinking); and emotional symptoms (anxiety, depression, change in attitude) than acute patients (i.e., within 3 months of injury; Pliskin et al., 1998).

One possibility for a more severe clinical picture over time is CNS dysfunction caused by the progressive effects of EI. However, deterioration in functioning over time due to progressive effects of the original injury on the CNS is speculative, and clinicians should be careful to not evoke this explanation in the absence of (1) clear evidence of CNS injury acutely and (2) corroborating medical or neuroimaging evidence to support the theory.

It may also be the case that the patient does not become aware of neuropsychological problems until he or she later attempts to return to pre-injury roles and responsibilities in the home and workplace. This symptom pattern also may be primarily psychological in nature and associated with trauma experiences (Pliskin et al., 1999). In addition, litigation has been associated with neuropsychological symptom presentation in persons who sustained traumatic neurological injuries (Binder & Rohling, 1996; Suhr et al., 1997); its potential impact should be considered in cases of work-related electrical brain injury.

Neuropsychological testing has offered some corroboration of patient reports of a progressive decline in cognitive and emotional functioning, including case study reports (e.g., Crews et al., 1997; Daniel et al., 1985; Martin et al., 2003) and between-group comparisons (e.g., Pliskin et al., 1999). Patients later in their postinjury course (i.e., 9 months to 4 years postinjury) have been found to perform worse than patients earlier in their course (i.e., 1 to 57 days postinjury) on a measure of verbal learning and memory. This finding remained when controlling for symptoms of depression.

Postacute patients (more than 3 months postinjury) also have shown greater elevations on MMPI scales 1 (*Hs*), 2 (*D*), and 3 than acute patients (*Hy*; Wicklund et al., 2008). Ramati et al. (2009b) found that time since injury was a predictor of psychiatric diagnosis, with long-term patients (more than 2 years postinjury) more likely than acute patients (within 3 months of injury) and postacute patients (3 months to 2 years postinjury) to have one or more psychiatric diagnoses. In the acute phase of recovery the most prevalent diagnosis was adjustment disorder, and in the postacute phase depression was most common. Long-term patients most commonly had a comorbid diagnosis of PTSD and depression. Noble, Gomez, and Fish (2006) did not find differences in reported quality of life, coping strategies, or pain symptoms when comparing patients within 5 years of injury and those more than 5 years postinjury, with results indicating a stable course with little symptom improvement in these areas. Some authors have suggested that the argument for a progressive symptom course in EI is weakened by the methodological limitations of some studies, particularly lack of symptom validity testing or malingering assessment (Bianchini et al., 2005; Bush, 2008).

Effects of El Parameters on Symptoms

Sufficient data are lacking to support a relationship between cognitive and emotional symptoms and injury parameters such as voltage, current, loss of consciousness, cardiac arrest, surgery, and hospitalization (Martin et al., 2003; Pliskin et al., 1998). One study examining the neuropsychological profiles of high-voltage EI patients found no difference between patients who experienced cardiac arrest as a result of their injury and those who did not (Barrash et al., 1996). The authors reported that although cardiac arrest patients had more impaired delayed recall scores, the difference was not significant ($p = .10$; Cohen's $d = 0.85$, large effect[1]). Although there are relatively few well-controlled prospective studies relating to cognitive impairment and cardiac arrest (Moulaert, Verbunt, van Heugten, & Wade,

2009), it clearly should be considered a major risk factor (Lim, Alexander, LaFleche, Schnyer, & Verfaellie, 2004).

Regardless of litigation status, lower voltage injury was found to be predictive of greater complaints of physical, cognitive, and emotional symptoms in a sample of 30 EI patients assessed an average of nearly 4 years postinjury (Fink et al., 1999). On the other hand, Noble et al. (2006) found higher levels of anxiety reported by patients who experienced high-voltage injuries than those who experienced low-voltage injuries, and others did not find voltage to be related to cognitive or psychiatric symptoms (Daniel et al., 1985; Pliskin et al., 1999; Ramati et al., 2009b). In terms of injury type, patients with low-voltage electrical contact injuries reported more psychological and neurological symptoms than patients with low-voltage electrical flash injuries; depression, insomnia, memory loss, headache, fatigue, and chronic pain were more frequently reported in contact injuries (Theman et al., 2008).

Effects of Demographic and Other Factors on Symptoms

The majority of samples in EI research are comprised predominantly of males, a reflection of employee demographics in professions where workers are susceptible to electrical injury. The existing research involving female EI patients (Miller, 1993; Morse & Morse, 2005) suggests that overall symptom profiles are relatively similar between males and females, though in one sample of 34 females and 59 males who experienced low-voltage injury (Morse & Morse, 2005), males more commonly reported unexplained moodiness, short-term memory loss, and dizziness, while females more often reported chronic pain syndrome. Previous psychiatric history does not appear to be related to cognitive or psychiatric symptom profiles in EI patients, including depression and PTSD (Kelley et al., 1999; Pliskin et al., 1999; Ramati et al., 2009b). Age also has been found to be unrelated to symptom presentation (Daniel et al., 1985). Patients' current pain levels, use of pain medications, and use of psychotropic medications were all unrelated to symptoms in one recent study (Ramati et al., 2009b).

NEUROPSYCHOLOGICAL ASSESSMENT

An adequate understanding of a given electrically injured patient's neurocognitive and psychological functioning typically requires a comprehensive evaluation (Heilbronner, 1994). Although briefer evaluations or screening evaluations may be sufficient in acute inpatient settings or in other contexts with severely impaired patients, the breadth and depth of assessment afforded by comprehensive evaluations is usually needed to address most outpatient referral questions. Neuropsychologists have an ethical responsibility to select the assessment measures that they determine to be appropriate for a given patient and situation (Ethical Standard 9.01, Bases for Assessment; American Psychological Association, 2002).

The selection of assessment measures and procedures takes into consideration at least two primary questions. First, consider the purpose of the evaluation. Specifically, what does the referral source want or need to know? A specific focus identified by the referral source may influence the emphasis placed by the clinician on certain neurocognitive domains, emotional states, personality traits, or other factors that may affect the patient's presentation, such as effort and honesty. The clinician's assessment measures and procedures may be influenced by the nature of the referral questions or other requests from the referral source. However, there is no need for clinicians to allow themselves to be pressured by referral sources into using certain psychological or neuropsychological tests when clinical justification is lacking or professional judgment suggests otherwise.

Second, consider the nature of the neuropsychological impairment expected from the suspected or known cerebral insult(s). Specifically, what neuropsychological profile and extent of impairment are expected from the type of injury sustained by the patient? Such questions can be valuable for ensuring that important domains are not overlooked. However, caution is warranted to reduce the possibility that "unexpected" deficits are missed. Also, as previously described in this chapter, persons who have sustained EIs often have multiple injuries (e.g., traumatic brain injury, cardiac arrest) that could cause cerebral impairment that alone or in combination affect neuropsychological functioning in ways that would differ from EI alone. With those cautions noted, research (Pliskin et al., 2006) indicates that a comprehensive neuropsychological evaluation that does not include thorough evaluation of attention, mental processing speed, and motor skills would be considered incomplete. For assessment of a domain to be considered thorough, multiple well-validated assessment measures are typically needed.

Neurocognitive testing is only one component of a comprehensive evaluation of patients who have experienced EIs. Symptom validity assessment, including consideration of multiple empirically derived measures and embedded indicators, is also an important part of the evaluation of these patients. Secondary gain contexts further increase the importance of a comprehensive approach to the assessment of symptom validity (Bush et al., 2005; Slick, Sherman, & Iverson, 1999). (Additional information about neuropsychological evaluation methods and procedures in forensic contexts can be found in other chapters in this volume.)

Evaluations of patients who have sustained EIs also include measures of mood and personality. Measures of posttraumatic stress, specific phobias, depression, and somatic preoccupation are particularly valuable (Daniel et al., 1985; Grossman, Tempereau, Brones, Kulber, & Pembrook,

1993; Kelley et al., 1994, 1999; Mancusi-Ungaro et al., 1986). Measures of mood and personality preferably include well-validated symptom validity scales. In addition, quantification of pain frequency, intensity, and duration, including pain severity at the time of neurocognitive testing, is often an important component of the neuropsychological evaluation (Kim & Bryant, 2001; McCracken & Iverson, 2001).

In EI evaluation contexts, nontest-based methods and procedures often provide valuable information for understanding the patient's injury, recovery course, symptoms, and abilities. Review of records, particularly those from emergency medical personnel at the scene of the injury and those from emergency departments, can be particularly valuable for understanding the characteristics of the injury or injuries, related complications, and medical interventions. Interviews of collateral sources can also provide useful information, particularly related to pre- and postinjury daily functioning. Observations of patients within and outside of the office setting are another important source of information about neuropsychological and physical functioning. Consideration of collateral neurodiagnostic studies (e.g., EEG, MRI) is likewise important, though such studies are often negative even when genuine neurocognitive dysfunction is verified on neuropsychological testing.

When damage to the CNS is medically documented, the clinician can have increased confidence that neurocognitive dysfunction is, in whole or part, causally related to this damage. However, in the absence of evidence of neurological injury, and the presence of comorbidities (e.g., depression, traumatic stress, insomnia, and/or chronic pain), the causal contribution of possible neurological injury becomes less clear. The cause of subjectively experienced cognitive impairment is very likely to be multifactorial as the burden of comorbidities increases.

TREATMENT

Persons who sustain EIs may experience a variety of wounds and other injuries as the direct or indirect effects of the electrical contact. The nature and extent of treatment will necessarily depend on the nature of the injuries. Initial acute treatment following EI focuses on emergent clinical issues, such as restoring and maintaining cardiopulmonary stability. Treatment then involves aggressive management of wounds and other injuries, including brain injuries that require surgical intervention, and control of pain. Establishing adequate nutritional intake is also a vital early step in the treatment process. Clinicians typically begin to turn attention toward cognitive, emotional, and behavioral symptoms only after the acute effects of the injury have been addressed.

Yarnell (2005) described three categories of brain injuries associated with electrical or lightning injuries, with different expectations for recovery and different treatment needs: (1) global dysfunction following cardiac arrest, (2) focal brain injuries from direct lightning strike to the head or from falls, and (3) behavioral-cognitive sequelae without gross physical signs. According to Yarnell (2005), the approach to rehabilitation following lightning and electrical brain injuries is similar to that taken with more common traumatic brain injuries and stroke. With the goal of maximizing functioning, rehabilitation efforts should begin as soon as possible and, to the extent needed, involve multiple healthcare disciplines. Because of the relatively limited amount of research on electrical brain injuries compared to mechanical traumatic brain injuries, careful consideration is needed when determining a given patient's expected recovery and treatment needs. Treatment is typically focused on alleviating symptoms and compensating for persisting deficits. Patients may be well served when clinicians are "selective and inventive" when adopting and applying therapeutic interventions (Primeau, 2005).

Neuropsychological treatment on an outpatient basis frequently addresses physical (e.g., pain), cognitive, emotional, and behavioral problems. An individualized, biopsychosocial conceptualization and treatment approach addresses the comprehensive needs of patients who have sustained electrical brain injuries. Such an approach benefits from structure. A stepwise, hierarchically arranged approach to the treatment of neuropsychological problems following polytrauma that includes TBI and PTSD has been proposed (Brenner, Vanderploeg, & Terrio, 2009; Terrio et al., 2009). The steps consist of the following: (1) education: pattern of recovery, (2) behavioral health issues, (3) somatic complaints/self-care routines, (4) irritability/impulsivity, and (5) cognitive issues.

The foundation of recovery lies in the expectations for recovery that are established and reinforced by clinicians. Psychoeducation about typical recovery patterns allows patients to blend hope with a realistic assessment of the challenges that may be encountered on the road to maximum recovery. A problem with education about recovery lies in the variable recovery trajectories reported in the EI literature (Heilbronner & Pliskin, 1999). For example, although much of the research suggests improvement over time, one case study reported a late-onset and progressively deteriorating cognitive profile (Martin et al., 2003); however, methodical problems limit the confidence that can be placed in the conclusions of that case study. Yarnell (2005) noted that the complexities and challenges associated with atypical complaints require clinicians to try to distinguish between unusual injury effects, unconscious somatoform processes, and intentional exaggeration or fabrication of symptoms. At times, a combination of these issues may be present. In the context of veterans with comorbid TBI and PTSD, Brenner et al. (2009) advise treating symptoms regardless of etiology.

With the foundation of education established, treatment of the higher steps in the model can be addressed. Extrapolated from research with general TBI populations, combined psychotherapeutic and cognitive rehabilitative approaches allow clinicians to address each patient's unique neuropsychological symptom profile. A variety of psychotherapeutic approaches, including cognitive-behavior therapy (Kelley et al., 1999; Lamberty, 2007; Mittenberg, Tremont, Zielinski, Fichera, & Rayls, 1996), appear to hold value depending on the specific goals of the intervention.

Similarly, numerous approaches to cognitive rehabilitation have the potential to benefit patients who have sustained EIs (e.g., Cicerone et al., 2000; National Institutes of Health, 1998; Sohlberg & Mateer, 2001). A focus on compensatory strategies may be particularly valuable (Carney et al., 1999). Family education and support, encouragement of a return to social activities, and spiritual or religious supports can also be important components of the biopsychosocial treatment approach. In addition, pharmacologic interventions can be a valuable part of the treatment plan for persons who experience neuropsychological problems following electrical trauma (Kelley et al., 1999). A multidisciplinary approach to neurorehabilitation following electrical trauma is often preferred (Heilbronner, 1994). More research is needed on the neuropsychological treatment of persons who have sustained electrical brain injuries.

CONCLUSIONS

As modern society in general, and the workplace in particular, has an ever-increasing reliance on electricity to power daily productivity, electrical injuries will be inevitable. These injuries can be enigmatic in the diverse and at times unpredictable ways that they affect the human body and mind. The worker injured by electricity deserves comprehensive care to help restore any lost function and to increase the chances for full resumption of work productivity and quality of life. Neuropsychologists play a prominent role in the understanding and care of workers who sustain electrical injuries.

NOTE

1. The effect size was not reported in the original article. The nonsignificance of the null hypothesis test was likely due to very small sample sizes.

REFERENCES

American Psychological Association. (2002). Ethical principles of psychologists and code of conduct. *American Psychologist, 57*(12), 1060–1073.
Ammar, A. N., Fink, J. W., Malina, A. C., Ramati, A., Kelley, K. M., Crawford, I., et al. (2006). Memory functioning in electrically injured patients with and without PTSD. *Acta Neuropsychologica, 4,* 119–124.
Barrash, J., Kealey, G. P., & Janus, T. J. (1996). Neurobehavioral sequelae of high

voltage electrical injuries: Comparison with traumatic brain injury. *Applied Neuropsychology, 3*(2), 75–81.

Belanger, H. G., Kretzmer, T., Yoash-Gantz, R., Pickett, T., & Tupler, L. A. (2009). Cognitive sequelae of blast-related versus other mechanisms of brain trauma. *Journal of the International Neuropsychological Society, 15*(1), 1–8.

Bianchini, K. J., Love, J. M., Greve, K. W., & Adams, D. (2005). Detection and diagnosis of malingering in electrical injury. *Archives of Clinical Neuropsychology, 20*(3), 365–373.

Binder, L. M., & Rohling, M. L. (1996). Money matters: A meta-analytic review of the effects of financial incentives on recovery after closed-head injury. *American Journal of Psychiatry, 153*(1), 7–10.

Brenner, L. A., Vanderploeg, R. D., & Terrio, H. (2009). Assessment and diagnosis of mild traumatic brain injury, posttraumatic stress disorder, and other polytrauma conditions: Burden of adversity hypothesis. *Rehabilitation Psychology, 54*(3), 239–246.

Brett, A., Purdue, G. F., Kowalske, K., Helm, P., Burris, A., & Hunt, J. L. (2004). Electrical injuries: A 20-year review. *Journal of Burn Care and Rehabilitation, 25*(6), 479–484.

Bush, S. S. (2008). Electrical brain injury: A case of examiner shock. In R. L. Heilbronner (Ed.), *Neuropsychology in the courtroom: Expert analysis of reports and testimony* (pp. 79–94). New York: Guilford Press.

Bush, S. S., Ruff, R. M., Troster, A. I., Barth, J. T., Koffler, S. P., Pliskin, N. H., et al. (2005). Symptom validity assessment: Practice issues and medical necessity NAN policy and planning committee. *Archives of Clinical Neuropsychology, 20*(4), 419–426.

Butler, E. D., & Gant, T. D. (1977). Electrical injuries, with special reference to the upper extremities: A review of 182 cases. *American Journal of Surgery, 134*(1), 95–101.

Capelli-Schellpfeffer, M. (2005). Fair warning. *IEEE Industry Applications Magazine, January/February*, 36–51.

Capelli-Schellpfeffer, M., Miller, G. H., & Humilier, M. (1999). Thermoacoustic energy effects in electrical arcs. *Annals of the New York Academy of Sciences, 888*, 19–32.

Capelli-Schellpfeffer, M., Toner, M., Lee, R. C., & Astumian, R. D. (1995). Advances in the evaluation and treatment of electrical and thermal injury emergencies. *IEEE Transactions on Industry Applications, 31*, 1147–1152.

Carney, N., Chesnut, R. M., Maynard, H., Mann, N. C., Patterson, P., & Helfand, M. (1999). Effect of cognitive rehabilitation on outcomes for persons with traumatic brain injury: A systematic review. *Journal of Head Trauma Rehabilitation, 14*(3), 277–307.

Cawley, J. C., & Homce, G. T. (2003). Occupational electrical injuries in the United States, 1992–1998, and recommendations for safety research. *Journal of Safety Research, 34*(3), 241–248.

Cherington, M. (1995). Central nervous system complications of lightning and electrical injuries. *Seminars in Neurology, 15*(3), 233–240.

Chico, M. S., Capelli-Schellpfeffer, M., Kelley, K. M., & Lee, R. C. (1999). Management and coordination of postacute medical care for electrical trauma survivors. *Annals of the New York Academy of Sciences, 888*, 334–342.

Christensen, J. A., Sherman, R. T., Balis, G. A., & Wuamett, J. D. (1980). Delayed neurologic injury secondary to high-voltage current, with recovery. *Journal of Trauma, 20*(2), 166–168.

Cicerone, K. D., Dahlberg, C., Kalmar, K., Langenbahn, D. M., Malec, J. F., Bergquist, T. F., et al. (2000). Evidence-based cognitive rehabilitation: Recommendations for clinical practice. *Archives of Physical Medicine and Rehabilitation, 81*(12), 1596–1615.

Coffey, C. E., Weiner, R. D., Djang, W. T., Figiel, G. S., Soady, S. A., Patterson, L. J., et al. (1991). Brain anatomic effects of electroconvulsive therapy: A prospective magnetic resonance imaging study. *Archives of General Psychiatry, 48*(11), 1013–1021.

Cooper, M. A. (1995). Emergent care of lightning and electrical injuries. *Seminars in Neurology, 15*(3), 268–278.

Crews, W. D., Jr., Barth, J. T., Brelsford, T. N., Francis, J. P., & McArdle, P. A. (1997). Neuropsychological dysfunction in severe accidental electrical shock: Two case reports. *Applied Neuropsychology, 4*(4), 208–219.

Daniel, M., Haban, G. F., Hutcherson, W. L., Bolter, J., & Long, C. (1985). Neuropsychological and emotional consequences of accidental high-voltage electrical shock. *International Journal of Clinical Neuropsychology, 7*, 102–106.

Deveci, M., Bozkurt, M., Arslan, N., & Sengezer, M. (2002). Nuclear imaging of the brain in electrical burn patients. *Burns, 28*(6), 591–594.

DiVincenti, F. C., Moncrief, J. A., & Pruitt, B. A., Jr. (1969). Electrical injuries: A review of 65 cases. *Journal of Trauma, 9*(6), 497–507.

Dokov, W. (2009). Assessment of risk factors for death in electrical injury. *Burns, 35*(1), 114–117.

Duff, K., & McCaffrey, R. J. (2001). Electrical injury and lightning injury: A review of their mechanisms and neuropsychological, psychiatric, and neurological sequelae. *Neuropsychology Reviews, 11*(2), 101–116.

Farrell, D. F., & Starr, A. (1968). Delayed neurological sequelae of electrical injuries. *Neurology, 18*(6), 601–606.

Fink, J. W., Pliskin, N., Moran, S., Capelli-Schellpfeffer, M., Lee, R., & Kelley, K. (1999). Longitudinal follow-up of electrically injured patients: Neuropsychological and injury parameters in a select group of patients. *Journal of the International Neuropsychological Society, 5*, 131.

Fish, R. (1993). Electric shock, Part I: Physics and pathophysiology. *Journal of Emergency Medicine, 11*(3), 309–312.

Fordyce, T. A., Kelsh, M., Lu, E. T., Sahl, J. D., & Yager, J. W. (2007). Thermal burn and electrical injuries among electric utility workers, 1995–2004. *Burns, 33*(2), 209–220.

Gourbiere, E., Corbut, J. P., & Bazin, Y. (1994). Functional consequence of electrical injury. *Annals of the New York Academy of Sciences, 720*, 259–271.

Grossman, A. R., Tempereau, C. E., Brones, M. F., Kulber, H. S., & Pembrook, L. J. (1993). Auditory and neuropsychiatric behavior patterns after electrical injury. *Journal of Burn Care and Rehabilitation, 14*(2, Pt. 1), 169–175.

Gualtieri, C. T., & Johnson, L. G. (1999). Traumatic brain injury: Special issues in psychiatric assessment. *NeuroRehabilitation, 13*, 103–115.

Heilbronner, R. L. (1994). Rehabilitation of the neuropsychological sequelae associated with electrical trauma. *Annals of the New York Academy of Sciences, 720*, 224–229.

Heilbronner, R. L., & Pliskin, N. H. (1993). Brain injury from electrical trauma. *NeuroLaw Newsletter, 3*, 1.

Heilbronner, R. L., & Pliskin, N. H. (1999). Psychological issues in the neurorehabilitation of electrical injuries. *NeuroRehabilitation, 13*, 127–132.

Herlevsen, P., & Andersen, P. T. (1987). Constitutional predisposition to vasovagal syncope: An additional risk factor in patients exposed to electrical injuries? *British Heart Journal, 57*(3), 284–285.

Hooshmand, H., Radfar, F., & Beckner, E. (1989). The neurophysiological aspects of electrical injuries. *Clinical Electroencephalography, 20*(2), 111–120.

Hopewell, C. A. (1983). Serial neuropsychological assessment in a case of reversible electrocution encephalopathy. *Clinical Neuropsychology, 5*, 61–65.

Hunt, J. L., Mason, A. D., Jr., Masterson, T. S., & Pruitt, B. A., Jr. (1976). The pathophysiology of acute electric injuries. *Journal of Trauma, 16*(5), 335–340.

Janus, T. J., & Barrash, J. (1996). Neurologic and neurobehavioral effects of electric and lightning injuries. *Journal of Burn Care and Rehabilitation, 17*(5), 409–415.

Jost, W. H., Schonrock, L. M., & Cherington, M. (2005). Autonomic nervous system dysfunction in lightning and electrical injuries. *NeuroRehabilitation, 20*(1), 19–23.

Kaas, J. H., Qi, H. X., Burish, M. J., Gharbawie, O. A., Onifer, S. M., & Massey, J. M. (2008). Cortical and subcortical plasticity in the brains of humans, primates, and rats after damage to sensory afferents in the dorsal columns of the spinal cord. *Experimental Neurology, 209*(2), 407–416.

Kelley, K. M., Pliskin, N., Meyer, G., & Lee, R. C. (1994). Neuropsychiatric aspects of electrical injury. The nature of psychiatric disturbance. *Annals of the New York Academy of Sciences, 720*, 213–218.

Kelley, K. M., Tkachenko, T. A., Pliskin, N. H., Fink, J. W., & Lee, R. C. (1999). Life after electrical injury. Risk factors for psychiatric sequelae. *Annals of the New York Academy of Sciences, 888*, 356–363.

Kim, C. T., & Bryant, P. (2001). Complex regional pain syndrome (type I) after electrical injury: A case report of treatment with continuous epidural block. *Archives of Physical Medicine and Rehabilitation, 82*(7), 993–995.

Koumbourlis, A. C. (2002). Electrical injuries. *Critical Care Medicine, 30*(11, Suppl.), S424–S430.

Lamberty, G. J. (2007). *Understanding somatization in the practice of clinical neuropsychology.* New York: Oxford University Press.

Lee, R. C. (1997). Injury by electrical forces: Pathophysiology, manifestations, and therapy. *Current Problems in Surgery, 34*(9), 677–764.

Lee, R. C., Aarsvold, J. N., Chen, W., Astumian, R. D., Capelli-Schellpfeffer, M., Kelley, K. M., et al. (1995). Biophysical mechanisms of cell membrane damage in electrical shock. *Seminars in Neurology, 15*(4), 367–374.

Lee, R. C., & Dougherty, W. (2003). Electrical injury: Mechanisms, manifestations, and therapy. *IEEE Transactions on Dielectrics and Electrical Insulation, 10*, 810–819.

Lee, R. C., & Kolodney, M. S. (1987). Electrical injury mechanisms: Electrical breakdown of cell membranes. *Plastic Reconstruction Surgery, 80*(5), 672–679.

Lee, R. C., Zhang, D., & Hannig, J. (2000). Biophysical injury mechanisms in electrical shock trauma. *Annual Review of Biomedical Engineering, 2*, 477–509.

Lim, C., Alexander, M. P., LaFleche, G., Schnyer, D. M., & Verfaellie, M. (2004). The neurological and cognitive sequelae of cardiac arrest. *Neurology, 63*(10), 1774–1778.

Lombardi, D. A., Matz, S., Brennan, M. J., Smith, G. S., & Courtney, T. K. (2009). Etiology of work-related electrical injuries: A narrative analysis of workers' compensation claims. *Journal of Occupational and Environmental Hygiene, 6*(10), 612–623.

Mancusi-Ungaro, H. R., Jr., Tarbox, A. R., & Wainwright, D. J. (1986). Posttraumatic stress disorder in electric burn patients. *Journal of Burn Care and Rehabilitation, 7*(6), 521–525.

Martin, T. A., Salvatore, N. F., & Johnstone, B. (2003). Cognitive decline over time following electrical injury. *Brain Injury, 17*(9), 817–823.

McCracken, L. M., & Iverson, G. L. (2001). Predicting complaints of impaired cognitive functioning in patients with chronic pain. *Journal of Pain and Symptom Management, 21*(5), 392–396.

Miller, L. (1993). Toxic torts: Clinical, neuropsychological, and forensic aspects of chemical and electrical injuries. *Journal of Cognitive Rehabilitation, 49*, 6–18.

Mittenberg, W., Tremont, G., Zielinski, R. E., Fichera, S., & Rayls, K. R. (1996). Cognitive-behavioral prevention of postconcussion syndrome. *Archives of Clinical Neuropsychology, 11*(2), 139–145.

Morse, J. S., & Morse, M. S. (2005). Diffuse electrical injury: Comparison of physical and neuropsychological symptom presentation in males and females. *Journal of Psychosomatic Research, 58*(1), 51–54.

Moulaert, V. R., Verbunt, J. A., van Heugten, C. M., & Wade, D. T. (2009). Cognitive impairments in survivors of out-of-hospital cardiac arrest: A systematic review. *Resuscitation, 80*(3), 297–305.

National Institutes of Health. (1998). Rehabilitation of persons with traumatic brain injury. *NIH Consensus Statement, 16*(1), 1–41.

Noble, J., Gomez, M., & Fish, J. S. (2006). Quality of life and return to work following electrical burns. *Burns, 32*(2), 159–164.

Ore, T., & Casini, V. (1996). Electrical fatalities among U.S. construction workers. *Journal of Occupational and Environmental Medicine, 38*, 587–592.

Pliskin, N. H., Ammar, A. N., Fink, J. W., Hill, S. K., Malina, A. C., Ramati, A., et al. (2006). Neuropsychological changes following electrical injury. *Journal of the International Neuropsychological Society, 12*(1), 17–23.

Pliskin, N. H., Capelli-Schellpfeffer, M., Law, R. T., Malina, A. C., Kelley, K. M., & Lee, R. C. (1998). Neuropsychological symptom presentation after electrical injury. *Journal of Trauma, 44*(4), 709–715.

Pliskin, N. H., Fink, J., Malina, A., Moran, S., Kelley, K. M., Capelli-Schellpfeffer, M., et al. (1999). The neuropsychological effects of electrical injury: New insights. *Annals of the New York Academy of Sciences, 888*, 140–149.

Pliskin, N. H., Meyer, G. J., Dolske, M. C., Heilbronner, R. L., Kelley, K. M., & Lee, R. C. (1994). Neuropsychiatric aspects of electrical injury: A review of neuropsychological research. *Annals of the New York Academy of Sciences, 720*, 219–223.

Primeau, M. (2005). Neurorehabilitation of behavioral disorders following lightning and electrical trauma. *NeuroRehabilitation, 20*(1), 25–33.

Primeau, M., Engelstatter, G. H., & Bares, K. K. (1995). Behavioral consequences of lightning and electrical injury. *Seminars in Neurology, 15*(3), 279–285.

Pruitt, B. A., Jr., & Mason, A. D., Jr. (1979). High-tension electrical injury. *Lancet, 1*(8110), 271.

Ramati, A., Pliskin, N. H., Keedy, S., Erwin, R. J., Fink, J. W., Bodnar, E. N., et al. (2009a). Alteration in functional brain systems after electrical injury. *Journal of Neurotrauma, 26*(10), 1815–1822.

Ramati, A., Rubin, L. H., Wicklund, A., Pliskin, N. H., Ammar, A. N., Fink, J. W., et al. (2009b). Psychiatric morbidity following electrical injury and its effects on cognitive functioning. *General Hospital Psychiatry, 31*(4), 360–366.

Rami-Gonzalez, L., Salamero, M., Boget, T., Catalan, R., Ferrer, J., & Bernardo, M.

(2003). Pattern of cognitive dysfunction in depressive patients during maintenance electroconvulsive therapy. *Psychological Medicine, 33*(2), 345–350.

Ressijac, R. H. (1986). High voltage electrical injuries. *Issues in Comprehensive Pediatric Nursing, 9*(6), 383–389.

Rosen, Y., Reznik, I., Sluvis, A., Kaplan, D., & Mester, R. (2003). The significance of the nitric oxide in electro-convulsive therapy: A proposed neurophysiological mechanism. *Medical Hypotheses, 60*(3), 424–429.

Schlaier, J. R., Eichhammer, P., Langguth, B., Doenitz, C., Binder, H., Hajak, G., et al. (2007). Effects of spinal cord stimulation on cortical excitability in patients with chronic neuropathic pain: A pilot study. *European Journal of Pain, 11*(8), 863–868.

Selvaggi, G., Monstrey, S., Van Landuyt, K., Hamdi, M., & Blondeel, P. (2005). Rehabilitation of burn injured patients following lightning and electrical trauma. *NeuroRehabilitation, 20,* 35–42.

Silversides, J. (1964). The neurological sequelae of electrical injury. *Canadian Medical Association Journal, 91,* 195–204.

Slick, D., Sherman, E. M., & Iverson, G. L. (1999). Diagnostic criteria for malingered neurocognitive dysfunction: Proposed standards for clinical practice and research. *The Clinical Neuropsychologist, 13*(4), 545–561.

Sohlberg, M. M., & Mateer, C. A. (2001). *Cognitive rehabilitation: An integrative neuropsychological approach.* New York: Guilford Press.

Suhr, J., Tranel, D., Wefel, J., & Barrash, J. (1997). Memory performance after head injury: Contributions of malingering, litigation status, psychological factors, and medication use. *Journal of Clinical and Experimental Neuropsychology, 19*(4), 500–514.

Terrio, H., Brenner, L. A., Ivins, B., Cho, J. M., Helmick, K., Schwab, K., et al. (2009). Traumatic brain injury screening: Preliminary findings in a U.S. Army Brigade combat team. *Journal of Head Trauma Rehabilitation, 24*(1), 14–23.

Theman, K., Singerman, J., Gomez, M., & Fish, J. S. (2008). Return to work after low voltage electrical injury. *Journal of Burn Care Research, 29*(6), 959–964.

Tkachenko, T. A., Kelley, K. M., Pliskin, N. H., & Fink, J. W. (1999). Electrical injury through the eyes of professional electricians. *Annals of the New York Academy of Sciences, 888,* 42–59.

Tredget, E. E., Shankowsky, H. A., & Tilley, W. A. (1999). Electrical injuries in Canadian burn care: Identification of unsolved problems. *Annals of the New York Academy of Sciences, 888,* 75–87.

Wicklund, A. H., Ammar, A., Weitlauf, J. C., Heilbronner, R. L., Fink, J., Lee, R. C., et al. (2008). MMPI-2 patterns in electrical injury: A controlled investigation. *The Clinical Neuropsychologist, 22*(1), 98–111.

Wilbourn, A. J. (1995). Peripheral nerve disorders in electrical and lightning injuries. *Seminars in Neurology, 15*(3), 241–255.

Wilkinson, C., & Wood, M. (1978). High-voltage electrical injury. *American Journal of Surgery, 136,* 693–696.

Yarnell, P. R. (2005). Neurorehabilitation of cerebral disorders following lightning and electrical trauma. *NeuroRehabilitation, 20*(1), 15–18.

Yarnell, P. R., & Lammertse, D. P. (1995). Neurorehabilitation of lightning and electrical injuries. *Seminars in Neurology, 15*(4), 391–396.

CHAPTER 4

Neurotoxic Exposure Injuries in the Workplace

Robert J. McCaffrey
Andrea S. Miele

Occupational exposure to gases (e.g., carbon monoxide), solvents (e.g., n-hexane, toluene, and xylene), metals (e.g., lead, mercury, arsenic, and cadmium), and insecticides can be neurotoxic. The Environmental Protection Agency (EPA) defines neurotoxicity as "an adverse change in the structure or function of the central and/or peripheral nervous system following exposure to a chemical, physical, or biological agent" (EPA, 1998). Neurotoxic substances can enter the body via inhalation, contact with the skin, ingestion, or injection.

Exposure to toxins in occupational settings is of concern to healthcare professionals. In fact, "accidental exposure to chemicals represents the most common cause of acute medical illness in developed countries, while they are the second most common cause of death, after infectious diseases, in many developing countries" (Abou-Donia, 2000, p. ii). Toxins are generally defined as poisonous substances that are capable of causing disease, and exist as solids, liquids, and gases. In work settings, calculable risk of exposure varies widely based on occupation type. Numerous government agencies play a role in the classification and regulation of toxic chemicals. For example, the EPA, the Occupational Safety and Health Administration (OSHA; part of the Department of Labor), the National Institute of Occupational Safety and Health (NIOSH; part of the Centers for Disease Control and Prevention [CDC]), and the Agency for Toxic Substances and Disease Registry (ATSDR; part of the Department of Health and Human Services) all provide publicly available information that integrates the latest research into federally mandated safety regulations and protocols. The

United States government has funded a number of large-scale research initiatives in order to better document the scope of occupational exposure risk and health effects associated with exposure (see Appendix 4.1). Although the most recent data published is still preliminary, the rates of fatal and nonfatal occupational injuries and illnesses resulting from toxins have declined since 2000 and 2003, respectively (Bureau of Labor Statistics, 2009a, 2009b).

Although careful questioning can help achieve a somewhat more accurate reporting and documentation of the exposure event, it can be difficult for healthcare professionals to document exposure to neurotoxic substances and to assess the consequences of that exposure. First, determining the true location of an exposure is often difficult, especially in the absence of an acute event. Are a person's current symptoms the result of occupational exposure, or does the source of exposure actually exist in another setting or even at multiple sites? For example, faulty home heating systems and some hobbies that require the use of certain chemicals are also sources of exposure. Second, the symptom presentation following an exposure is often nonspecific and may also be explained by other, nonexposure-related causes. Are a person's headaches the result of stress or of acute carbon monoxide exposure? The nonspecific nature of symptoms likely results in prevalence rates that underestimate true rates of exposure, possibly because workers do not seek medical help for symptoms or because an exposure diagnosis is missed. Lastly, most of the data regarding work-exposure standards is derived from animal models, and generalizability of animal-based models to the individual worker seen for an exposure-related event is of uncertain value. These issues, among others discussed in this chapter, greatly increase the difficulty of determining the actual health hazard potential for toxins that are used in occupational settings. As a result, the number of adverse health effects is largely still unpredictable. In this chapter, we will discuss a range of issues relating to neurotoxin exposure in the workplace including documentation of exposure limits, routes and levels of exposure, epidemiology, pathophysiology, and assessment issues.

DOCUMENTATION OF EXPOSURE LIMITS

Since its inception in 1970, the Occupational Health Safety Act has sought to ensure "safe and healthful working conditions" (Occupational Safety and Health Act of 1970). These federal safety regulations are based on three types of exposure limits: permissible exposure limits (PELs; OSHA, 2006), threshold limit values (TLVs; American Conference of Industrial Government Hygienists, 2009), and recommended exposure limits (RELs; NIOSH, 1992) (see Table 4.1).

▓ **TABLE 4.1. Types of Exposure Limits**

	Permissible exposure limits	Threshold limit values	Recommended exposure limits	Occupational exposure limits
Enforced by	OSHA	—	—	OSHA
Informed by	ACGIH and NIOSH	ACGIH	NIOSH	ACGIH, NIOSH, AIHA
How many exist today?	500	642	600 (approx.)	Not reported

Note. OSHA, Occupational Health and Safety Administration; ACGIH, American Conference of Governmental and Industrial Hygienists; NIOSH, National Institute of Occupational Safety and Health; AIHA, American Industrial Hygiene Association.

Permissible Exposure Limits

PELs are legal regulatory limits in the United States depicting the amount or concentration of a substance in the air. PELs may also contain a skin designation. They usually are based on an 8-hour time-weighted average exposure. Recommendations from the American Conference of Governmental Industrial Hygienists and/or NIOSH inform the establishment and revisions of PELs (Feldman, 1999), which are then legally enforced by OSHA. In instances when workplace chemicals are not covered by PELs, OSHA may refer to occupational exposure limits (OSHA, 2003) to evaluate the safety of the chemical agent. These additional values are established by recommendations from NIOSH, the American Conference of Governmental Industrial Hygienists, and the American Industrial Hygiene Association.

Threshold Limit Values

A committee of the American Conference of Governmental Industrial Hygienists published the first *Documentation of the Threshold Limit Values* in 1962. Today the list includes 642 chemical and physical agents (American Conference of Industrial Government Hygienists, 2009). There are three types of TLVs: (1) short-term exposure limits, (2) time-weighted averages, and (3) ceilings. A short-term exposure limit is defined as a period of time lasting no longer than 15 minutes. Generally, a short-term exposure limit reflects a concentration to which workers may be exposed for a short period of time without suffering any adverse effects. Currently, repeated exposures to short-term exposure limits should not exceed four 15-minute intervals within a single 8-hour workday, and there should be at least one hour between each of the four short-term exposures. Time-weighted averages provide information regarding the concentration of a chemical to which workers may be exposed repeatedly during an 8-hour workday and

40-hour workweek without suffering any adverse effects. The threshold limit value-ceiling defines the upper limit of a concentration of a specific chemical to which no worker should *ever* be exposed.

Recommended Exposure Limits

RELs are "occupational exposure limits recommended by NIOSH as being protective of worker health and safety over a working lifetime" (NIOSH, 1992). According to the CDC and NIOSH, a "working lifetime" is approximately 40 to 45 years. Presented in tabular form, readers are provided with the hazardous chemical name, Chemical Abstracts Service (CAS) and Registry of Toxic Effects of Chemical Substances (RTECS) numbers, NIOSH recommended exposure limit, and observed health effects. These RELs are usually presented as time-weighted averages for exposures lasting up to 10 hours during a 40-hour workweek. Short-term exposure limits that should never be exceeded except for a specified short period of time are also indicated, as well as some short-term exposure limits that should never be exceeded, even instantaneously (NIOSH, 1992). In addition, the document itself, which is available to the public (*www.cdc.gov/niosh/92-100.html*), contains a list of all relevant documents compiled by NIOSH in order to arrive at the RELs for each chemical.

ROUTES AND LEVELS OF EXPOSURE

Toxins can enter the body in several ways. Routes of exposure include inhalation, contact with the skin, ingestion, or injection. Generally, "in the occupational setting, inhalation is the most important route of entry" (Hathaway & Proctor, 2004, p. 4), as the toxin enters the bloodstream via the lungs. This type of absorption can bring a more potent amount of the toxin into the body than the gastrointestinal tract and at a much faster rate than cutaneous absorption. Occupational exposure is often classified by duration (Hathaway & Proctor, 2004). Generally, *acute* refers to a period of exposure lasting no longer than 24 hours. *Subacute* exposure is repeated exposure for no more than 1 month. *Subchronic* exposure is repeated exposure for 1–3 months, while *chronic* exposure is repeated exposure for longer than 3 months.

   Depending on the route of entry into the body, OSHA defines chemicals as "highly toxic" in three ways based on animal studies. Following *oral ingestion*, a highly toxic chemical is one in which the median lethal dose is 50 milligrams or less per kilogram of body weight when administered to albino rats weighing between 200 and 300 grams. Similarly, a chemical is considered highly toxic if the median lethal dose *inhaled* is 200 parts per million per liter or less of mist, fume, or dust. A chemical is considered highly toxic if administered by *continuous contact* with the bare skin of albino rabbits weighing between 2 and 3 kilograms each for 24 hours or less, and the median lethal dose is 200 milligrams or less per kilogram of body weight (see Federal Regulations for Occupational Safety and Health Standards of Toxic and Hazardous Substances, 1996).

EPIDEMIOLOGY OF OCCUPATIONAL EXPOSURE TO NEUROTOXINS

The EPA defines neurotoxicity as "an adverse change in the structure or function of the central and/or peripheral nervous system following exposure to a chemical, physical, or biological agent" (EPA, 1998). Anger and Johnson (1985, p. 55) estimated that evidence of neurotoxicity exists for at least 850 chemicals that may be encountered in the workplace, of which 65 are "well established toxic chemicals." In addition, NIOSH's National Occupational Hazard Survey (see Appendix 4.1) identified 197 chemicals to which over 1 million persons were believed exposed in U.S. workplaces. Anger (1984) reported that nearly 30% of the chemicals listed by the American Conference of Governmental Industrial Hygienists affect the nervous system. Neurotoxic disorders have repeatedly been listed "among the ten leading work-related diseases and injuries" (NIOSH, 1987). There are generally four classes of neurotoxic chemicals: gases, solvents, metals, and insecticides. Annual safe disposal/storage for these chemicals is monitored by the EPA's Toxics Release Inventory Program (EPA, 2007; see Appendix 4.1).

Gases

Gaseous neurotoxins are often recognized by their odor. Carbon monoxide is a colorless and odorless gas produced anywhere carbon-containing fuels are not burned completely. Information from the Injuries/Illness and Fatal Injuries Database indicates that from 2005 to 2007 at least 1,650 employees missed at least one day of work due to carbon monoxide exposure (Bureau of Labor Statistics, 2007). Hydrogen sulfide, another colorless gas, is known for its rotten egg-like smell. This gas occurs naturally in the environment, and it is produced from petroleum refineries, as well as in the food processing, tanning, and paper mill industries. At least 50 workers missed at least one day of work due to hydrogen sulfide exposure between 2005 and 2007 (Bureau of Labor Statistics, 2007).

Ethylene oxide, another naturally occurring and synthetic gas, is flammable, colorless, and has a sweet odor, and is used in producing ethylene glycol (antifreeze) and lubricants and in sterilizing equipment. Using their Toxics Release Inventory database (EPA, 2007; see Appendix 4.1), the

▨ TABLE 4.2. Potential Exposure to Four Neurotoxins from the National Occupational Exposure Survey (1981–1983)

Gases	NOES data estimating number of *potentially* exposed workers
Carbon monoxide	68,500
Hydrogen sulfide	94,900
Ethylene oxide	270,700
Carbon disulfide	45,700

Note. Exposure by two-digit Standard Industrial Classification (SIC) number rounded to nearest hundred.

EPA reported that nearly 311,000 pounds of this chemical were disposed of in 2007. Volatile liquids such as carbon disulfide, which is used in the manufacturing of viscose rayon, adhesives, resins, and cellophane, have an unpleasant odor "similar to decaying cabbage" (Abou-Donia, 2000). Interestingly, carbon disulfide has an "ethereal" (O'Donoghue, 1985) odor in its pure form. Although this neurotoxin is a liquid, exposure can occur from inhalation. Nearly 9 million pounds of this chemical were disposed of in 2007 (EPA, 2007). See Table 4.2 for the latest estimated number of people exposed to the above neurotoxins from 1981 to 1983.

Solvents

Solvents are organized according to chemical composition. Some of the most neurotoxic include the liquid aliphatic hydrocarbons such as n-hexane, ketones like methyl n-butyl ketone, halogenated hydrocarbons such as carbon tetrachloride, unsaturated chlorinated hydrocarbons like trichloroethylene, and aromatic hydrocarbons such as toluene, styrene, and xylene. These chemicals have many commercial uses and in addition to their use as cleaning agents, can be found in glues, paints, varnishes and lacquers. These sources of exposure are particularly complex in that "exposures are commonly to multicomponent solvent systems which may result in toxic interactions" (O'Donoghue, 1985, p. 62). According to Toxics Release Inventory Explorer data (EPA, 2007), toluene and styrene required the most disposal in 2007 (nearly 42 million pounds each), followed closely by n-hexane and xylene (over 35 million pounds and nearly 26 million pounds, respectively). At least 20 workers missed one day of work due to toluene exposure, and 70 workers due to xylene exposure between 2005 and 2007 (Bureau of Labor Statistics, 2007). During some of the same time period, it was necessary to dispose of 4.5 million pounds of trichloroethylene (EPA, 2007). Compared to the gases, it would seem that higher quantities of organic solvents are more readily used in industry; however,

▦ **TABLE 4.3. Potential Exposure to Solvents from the National Occupational Exposure Survey (1981–1983)**

Solvents	NOES data estimating number of *potentially* exposed workers
n-hexane	643,200
Methyl n-butyl ketone	Not reported
Carbon tetrachloride	104,200
Trichloroethylene	401,400
Toluene	2,015,900
Styrene	333,200
Xylene	2,145,000

Note. Exposure by two-digit Standard Industrial Classification (SIC) number rounded to nearest hundred.

these numbers may reflect the disposal requirements of liquids. See Table 4.3 for the estimated number of people exposed to the above neurotoxins from 1981 to 1983.

Metals

The CDC defines metals as "agents that consist of metallic poisons" (CDC, Metals). Heavy metals such as lead, mercury, arsenic, and cadmium are all listed under OSHA's toxic metals (OSHA, 2009) and are considered potent neurotoxins. These metals are frequently found in welding, smelting, or other industrial workplaces. Of these metals, exposure to lead has received considerable attention recently, especially because 95% of reported elevated blood lead levels are work-related (Alarcon, Roscoe, Calvert, & Graydon, 2009). Information regarding exposure rates has been federally monitored since 1987 through the Adult Blood Lead Epidemiology and Surveillance Program (ABLES), which oversees state-based mandated reporting of blood lead levels (Roscoe et al., 2002). ABLES defines elevated blood lead levels as concentrations ≥ 25 mg/dL. In 2007, national rates of elevated blood lead levels were 7.8% per 100,000 employed adults (ages ≥ 16); rates of blood lead levels ≥ 40 mg/dL ranged from 0.1 to 9.1 per 100,000 state resident adults, with the highest levels reported in the state of Alabama (Alarcon et al., 2009). ABLES data is also publicly available in an interactive database (see Appendix 4.1).

The Toxics Release Inventory program controls the extent of regulated toxicants for which safe disposal/storage is mandated. In 2007, nearly 21 million pounds of lead required disposal. In contrast, disposal of only 102,500 pounds of mercury were reported in the same year (EPA, 2007). Other metals such as aluminum, manganese, and thallium, found

▦ **TABLE 4.4. Potential Exposure to Solvents from the National Occupational Exposure Survey (1981–1983)**

Metals	NOES data estimating number of *potentially* exposed workers
Arsenic	27,300
Cadmium	167,400
Lead	381,900
Mercury	71,900
Aluminum	See source for details
Manganese	467,270
Thallium	1,700

Note. Exposure by two-digit Standard Industrial Classification (SIC) number rounded to nearest hundred.

throughout the manufacturing and automotive industries, are also neurotoxic. Much more aluminum and manganese was disposed of than thallium in 2007 (EPA, 2007). Four people died from metallic particulates, trace elements, dusts, powders, and fumes, while 23 died from nonstructural metal materials during 2005–2007 (Bureau of Labor Statistics, 2007). See Table 4.4 for the most recent estimates of the number of people exposed to the above neurotoxins from 1981 to 1983.

Insecticides

The most dangerous insecticides are those that contain neurotoxic organophosphates or carbamates. These are synthetic and can be used in any type of agricultural work. Organophosphates have been used as potential nerve agents in warfare (Abou-Donia, 2000).

EPIDEMIOLOGY OF OCCUPATIONAL ILLNESS AND INJURY FROM EXPOSURE

In order to better understand the scope of occupational hazards encountered by the U.S. workforce, statistics were compiled from the most recent *Worker Health Chartbook* (NIOSH, 2004). From its sample of approximately 135 million workers, NIOSH estimates that around 13 million currently work in the "high-risk" industries of agriculture, mining, and construction. Approximately 18 million workers were employed in manufacturing of both durable and nondurable goods. In private industry, a greater number of occupational injuries were reported than illnesses. Of selected occupational injuries, workers had the same rate of disorder due to a physical agent as respiratory condition due to a toxic agent (approximately 2 per 10,000). Less than 1 per 10,000 workers reported poisoning. Exposure to harmful substances accounted for 4.4% of injuries and illnesses that resulted in missed days of work, while contact with objects and equipment accounted for 26%. Approximately 35% of all fatal injuries reported in 2002 occurred in the operator, fabricator, and labor industries, and just over 20% of all fatal injuries were found in the precision production, craft, and repair industries. Of all fatal injuries, 9.7% reportedly resulted from "exposure to harmful environments."

In an effort to prevent workplace poisoning and pesticide-related illnesses, exposures to these kinds of chemicals and potential neurotoxins are complied in an *Annual Survey of Employers: Reports of Occupational Poisonings* (which is also included in the chartbook: NIOSH, 2004). This survey includes exposures to the broad categories of metals, gases, organic solvents, insecticide sprays, and other chemicals. Welding exposures, polymers, hydrocarbons, and solvents each contributed a similar percentage to cases of work-related asthma (4.3%, 5.3%, 6.1%, and 8.2%, respectively), while exposure to "miscellaneous chemicals" accounted for nearly 20% of all work-related asthma cases. The number of these types of occupational exposures has decreased significantly, from 7,600 cases in 1993, to 4,400 cases in 1999, and 2,800 cases in 2001. Texas, California, South Carolina, Missouri, Illinois, Indiana, and Michigan reported the most cases (>199 per state).

The EPA also partially funds the Sentinel Event Notification System for Occupational Risk (SENSOR), a program that focuses its surveillance efforts on pesticide exposure (NIOSH, 2004). Although not all 50 states participated in the data collection, 1,009 cases of acute pesticide-related occupational injury were reported from 1998 to 1999. Of the 4.9 million injuries reported in 2001, over 500,000 injuries or illnesses were classified as "musculoskeletal disorders" resulting in missed days of work. Specific nervous system injury was not reported. Over 25,000 total cases of burns were reported in 2001, including those caused by chemicals and radiation.

In an effort to better document exposures resulting in central nervous system damage, the following statistics were compiled from the Occupational Injuries/Illnesses and Fatal Injuries Profiles database (Bureau of Labor Statistics, 2007). Approximately 16,500 nonfatal occupational injuries and illnesses of the "nervous system and sense organs" were documented in the private industry. Of these, nearly 3,000 were caused by "exposure to a harmful substance or environment." Approximately half of all nonspecific "symptoms, signs and ill-defined conditions," and roughly 30% of reported "mental disorders or syndromes," including unspecified, were caused by "exposure to a harmful substance or environment."

A total of 6,420 nonfatal occupational injuries involving days away from work were attributed to the "brain," with almost 15% of these caused by "parts and materials." Surprisingly, none of these brain injuries were reported as resulting from "chemicals and chemical products" or from "exposure to harmful substance or environment." Given that brain injury is known to occur following exposure to some substances, the absence of neurological injury in this dataset may result from coding of the incidents. Here, brain injury likely results from blunt force trauma (i.e., "traumatic brain injury"), rather than from other disease processes or other sources including toxins. In addition, the information presented here was only gathered for a single year, and the exposed worker must have missed at least one day of work.

PATHOPHYSIOLOGY AND CLINICAL PRESENTATION

Physiological changes vary widely depending on numerous factors, including class of neurotoxin and duration and amount of exposure. In addition, exposure can affect numerous levels of nervous system organization. Government agencies typically document behavioral effects, as well as anatomical, physiological, and neurochemical changes, although "at present, relatively few neurotoxic syndromes have been thoroughly characterized in terms of the initial neurochemical change, structural alterations, physiological consequence and behavioral effects" (EPA, 1998). Markers in several body systems are used as endpoints that indicate possible neurotoxic exposure. Behavioral changes, including cognitive impairment, are often the most obvious.

The presence of these changes may indicate underlying pathology. For example, structural changes may be evident in the morphology of the brain or its constituents and may present as encephaolopathy, neuropathy, or myelinopathy. Changes in neurotransmitter system functioning, including the synthesis, release, uptake, and degradation, as well as second messenger system activation, may also indicate neurotoxic exposure (EPA, 1998). Neurophysiological indicators may be found in abnormal electroencephalogram patterns or changes in nerve conduction capability.

Symptom presentation also depends on details of the exposure; the effects of chronic exposures are usually different from those that appear following an acute exposure. Chronic exposure to some neurotoxins induces relatively specific effects on the nervous system and is frequently detected in the form of neurological signs, neuropathies, the emergence of a neurological disorder, or the presence of cognitive decline. For example, chronic exposure to certain metal dusts or fumes, solvent vapors, or insecticides can produce peripheral neuropathy (Feldman, 1999). Generally, weakness, numbness, or tingling in the extremities following exposure is an early indicator of damage to the peripheral nerves. In addition, chronic exposure to some solvents can result in parkinsonism; declines in attention, memory, and visuospatial skills; and alterations in color vision and smell. Parkinsonian symptoms have also been noted following chronic exposure to some metals such as manganese (Olanow, 2004).

Although the symptoms of acute exposure are usually different from those following chronic exposure, they are frequently nonspecific and similar, despite the class of chemical. For example, headache and dizziness are very commonly reported, as are gastrointestinal symptoms such as nausea. Seizures, disorientation, and changes in affect may also occur, and are usually dose and duration related.

Numerous factors influence and complicate a patient's presentation following neurotoxic exposure (EPA, 1998). First, and perhaps most obvious, is the health and age of the individual at the time of exposure. Younger and older generations may be more susceptible to neurotoxic injury, due to developmental factors in the younger and age-related changes in the older. Second, theories relating to the reserve capacity of the nervous system also complicate efforts to predict clinical course following neurotoxic exposure. Some theories suggest that the nervous system's adaptation to a toxin may reduce the likelihood of future nervous system injury (Tilson & Mitchell, 1982), but others suggest that repeated exposure actually results in a weakening of the nervous system's capacity to prevent future injury (Grandjean, 1991). Third, certain low-level doses of chemicals promote compensation and tolerance by the nervous system, which may offer protection from central nervous system (CNS) injury. Finally, the manner by which neurotoxins affect the nervous system is complex. Primary neurotoxic agents may exert both direct and indirect influences on the nervous system. These indirect effects involve changes carried out elsewhere in the body. Secondary neurotoxins must be metabolized before they can act directly or indirectly on the nervous system.

AN EXAMPLE OF THE PATHOPHYSIOLOGY OF EXPOSURE: CARBON MONOXIDE POISONING

In the following section, we present a detailed account of nervous system changes that can occur following exposure to carbon monoxide (CO). CO is "a colorless, tasteless, odorless, and non-irritating gas formed when carbon in fuel is not burned completely" (Raub & Benignus, 2002). This means that CO is present anywhere combustion occurs, both inside and outside. Common examples include car exhaust and emissions from heaters that are not well maintained. We emphasize CNS effects at the structural and molecular level because these are most relevant to neuropsychological injuries in the workplace. We provide a very detailed discussion because this is a relatively common form of neurotoxic exposure both in daily life and occupationally, and we wanted to illustrate the complexity of the pathophysiology.

Once considered "the unnoticed poison of the 21st century" (Crepat & Fritsch, 1998), CO has attracted greater research and public attention over the past decade. In the 1990s, an estimated 5,000 to 6,000 people died as a result of CO exposure from all sources in the United States every year (Kao & Nanagas, 2004), and between 10,000 and 40,000 people were estimated to either seek medical attention or miss work due to CO exposure from all sources (Omaye, 2002). Occupational Injuries/Illnesses and Fatal Injuries Profiles (Bureau of Labor Statistics, 2007) report that only 27 deaths occurred due to occupational CO exposure in 2007. No fatalities resulted from secondary-source CO exposure; however, 540 (out of a total of 1,158,870) workers sustained nonfatal occupational injury or illness from CO exposure. Generally, "any exposure to ambient air with CO levels greater than 100ppm is dangerous to human health" (Prockop & Chichkova, 2007, p. 126).

CO is a particularly dangerous neurotoxin because exposure can result in fairly common neurobehavioral sequelae such as headache, dizziness, or tingling. The severity of these sequelae varies and is both concentration- and dose-dependent. However, like those symptoms, many of the more serious symptoms are nonspecific, including vomiting, confusion, tachycardia, chest pain, and seizures. The severity of neurological and cognitive insults following acute exposure to CO is also difficult to predict because neurological or neuropsychiatric changes may emerge following a period of seeming recovery.

The literature refers to these cases of sudden onset of new neurological/neuropsychological symptoms as *DNS* under such headings as "delayed neuropsychiatric syndrome" (Lo et al., 2007; Prockop & Chichkova, 2007), "delayed neuropsychiatric sequelae" (Gorman, Drewry, Huang, & Sames, 2003), "delayed neuropsychologic sequelae" (Stoller, 2007), "late neurological sequelae" (Raub, Mathieu-Nolf, Hampson, & Thom, 2000), "delayed neurological sequelae" (Buckley, Isbister, Stokes, & Juurlink, 2005), or "delayed neurological syndrome" (Omaye, 2002). We use the term *DNS* to indicate the delayed onset of any neurobehavioral sequelae. The overall range of DNS based on the above reports is from 2 days to 240 days following an acute exposure. With estimates ranging from 1 to 47%, there is limited consistency in the literature regarding the base rate of these cases. This is likely partly due to the absence of a clear definition of DNS (Kao & Nanagas, 2004), or even an agreement on its name. Nevertheless, the occurrence of DNS provides evidence of the underlying complexity with which CO acts on the CNS. The clinical neuropsychological practitioner should also be cognizant of variables independent of exposure, such as litigation status, disability/compensation-seeking issues, and premorbid medical and/or emotional factors.

A review of the literature reveals that the pathophysiology of CO poisoning is indeed "more complex than initially presumed" (Kao & Nanagas,

2004). CO affects the body through numerous pathways that lead to neurological and neuropsychological injury. We first focus on the physiology of hemoglobin binding because the mechanism is well known. We then discuss two different binding patterns and CO's role in nitric oxide activity because of their hypothesized role in DNS. We refer the reader to four detailed reviews of the metabolic (Omaye, 2002), nervous system (Raub & Benignus, 2002), and other effects of CO (Kao & Nanagas, 2004; Prockop & Chichkova, 2007) because an in-depth discussion of each of these points is beyond the scope of this chapter.

Hemoglobin Binding

Once in the lungs, CO actively competes with or displaces oxygen on the hemoglobin molecule, which can result in tissue hypoxia. The affinity of hemoglobin for CO is approximately 200 to 250 times stronger than its affinity for oxygen. Once CO is bound to hemoglobin, it forms carboxyhemoglobin. This process is reversible but proceeds very slowly. The "cherry-like" skin or mucus membrane discoloration sometimes accompanying CO exposure results from the formation of large amounts of carboxyhemoglobin, which has a red color. This color change cannot be used as a biomarker of exposure levels, however, because levels of carboxyhemoglobin this high are usually only observed postmortem (Kao & Nanagas, 2004; Stoller, 2007). The presence of carboxyhemoglobin can cause tissue hypoxia in two ways. First, the brain stimulates hyperventilation due to depleted oxygen levels, which if located in an area of exposure, results in inhalation of more CO and increased formation of carboxyhemoglobin. Second, the presence of CO on any one of the oxygen sites increases the hemoglobin complex's affinity for oxygen at the remaining oxygen sites in the complex. This increased affinity for oxygen, referred to as the Haldane Effect (Omaye, 2002), causes the dissociation curve of hemoglobin to shift to the left, meaning that less oxygen is released to the tissues, or hypoxia.

Cellular Changes

CO can also induce cellular toxicity by interfering with mitochondrial cellular energy production. Omaye (2002) described the binding of CO to molecules called cytochromes because of their heme groups. One cytochrome that is a particular target for CO is cytochrome c oxidase (Complex IV), an electron transport chain enzyme. This enzyme is involved in the process of oxidative phosphorylation, which results in the synthesis of the main source of energy for cells, adenosine triphosphate (ATP). Oxidative phosphorylation is part of the aerobic process of cellular respiration, the most efficient mode of ATP production. The inhibition of the activity of cytochrome c oxidase due to the binding of CO causes disruption of the transport chain's ability to pump protons and thus inhibits production of ATP. Without the presence of oxygen, cells may instead undergo lactic acid fermentation for energy. This anaerobic process results in much less ATP and creates lactic acid as a waste product. CO poisoning leads to sustained use of this anaerobic process, which can cause lactic acidosis and cell death. This action is also hypothesized to play a role in DNS because carboxyhemoglobin levels appear to return to normal at a faster rate than does cytochrome c oxidase activity (Omaye, 2002). Thus, by limiting available oxygen and binding to cytochrome c oxidase, CO disrupts the normal mitochondrial ATP production and results in cellular toxicity.

Like hemoglobin, other globular proteins such as cardiac and muscle myoglobin also have an affinity for CO that is greater than their affinity for oxygen. This CO binding reduces the oxygen supply to the heart muscle and can lead to cardiac dysfunction, arrhythmias, angina, and impaired perfusion. Prockop and Chichkova (2007) state that the binding of CO to the intracellular myoglobin in the myocardium of the heart interferes with the delivery of oxygen to the mitochondria for oxidative phosphorylation and results in clinical CO symptoms. Thus, CO disrupts ATP production through at least two mechanisms. The return of CO poisoning symptoms may occur as myoglobin continues to release CO after the conclusion of the exposure, which leads to an increase in carboxyhemoglobin levels and subsequent binding of CO to hemoglobin (Omaye, 2002). This mechanism of action may also explain the emergence of DNS.

Nitric oxide, other oxygen free radicals, and reduced oxygen species may also play a role in CO poisoning and reperfusion injury. Kao and Nanagas (2004) hypothesized that nitric oxide may be involved in the onset of syncope because animals exposed to CO show loss of consciousness and increased nitric oxide levels. These authors also emphasized the role of nitric oxide in a "cascade of events culminating in oxidative damage to the brain" that may be responsible for DNS (Kao & Nanagas, 2004). Ultimately, nitric oxide may induce changes in the microvasculature of the brain, resulting in free-radical formation, oxidative stress and damage, and lipid peroxidation and demyelination. DNS resulting from brain lipid peroxidation may also result directly from activation of polymorphonuclear leukocytes, which normally bind to endothelial cells (Gorman et al., 2003). Alternatively, oxygen free radicals may result from hyperoxygenation, which can damage proteins and other molecules and cause reperfusion injury (Prockop & Chichkova, 2007).

In summary, CO produces cellular toxicity at numerous levels of organization that result in the clinical symptoms of CO poisoning. Not only does CO act via the bloodstream by decreasing oxygen delivery to the tissues and brain, but this action also limits energy production and utilization at the cellular level. Evidence suggests that early manifestations of DNS may occur as the body returns to homeostasis, re-oxygenating and expelling excess CO. Physiological and pathological causes for the development of delayed neurological, neuropsychological, or neuropsychiatric symptoms weeks following exposure require further investigation, especially as some investigators remain unconvinced that DNS results from brain injury. Other theories speculate that CO-exposed individuals are instead "exhibiting a reaction to an acute threat to health and hospitalization, with consequent illness beliefs" (Gorman et al., 2003, p. 34).

CNS Damage

Neurological damage can also occur following CO exposure. Most common are lesions in the cortex (Prockop & Chichkova, 2007), hippocampus (Kao & Nanagas, 2004), substantia nigra (Omaye, 2002), and bilateral globus pallidus (Kao & Nanagas, 2004). In addition, white matter lesions (Prockop & Chichkova, 2007) sometimes occur in the periventricular areas (Kao & Nanagas, 2004), basal ganglia (Prockop & Chichkova, 2007), centrum semiovale, and thalamus (Kao & Nanagas, 2004). The presence of systemic hypotension in CO poisoning is correlated with the severity of CNS structural damage, and abnormal neuroimaging findings are associated with poor prognoses (Kao & Nanagas, 2004). Lesion distribution likely reflects the "severity, suddenness and duration of oxygen deprivation" (Prockop & Chichkova, 2007, p. 124). Several sources also hypothesize that lesions are more likely to occur in poorly vascularized (watershed) areas (e.g., globus pallidus). Myelin damage is frequently noted, and varies in severity and localization depending on the duration and potency of exposure. Generally, CO intoxication usually spares the hypothalamus, the walls of the third ventricle, and the brainstem (Prockop & Chichkova, 2007).

Neuroimaging findings are likely to change following the acute period of CO exposure and are not always accurately represented by clinical symptoms (Hantson & Duprez, 2006). Moreover, the absence of acute neurological and/or neuropsychological symptoms does not preclude the subsequent development of DNS. Prockop and Chichkova (2007) recommended the use of diffusion-weighted imaging techniques rather than brain CT for detecting the early effects of CO poisoning, and, if available, the use of magnetic resonance spectroscopy, or proton magnetic resonance spectroscopy, to provide information about brain tissues and biochemistry.

ASSESSMENT CONSIDERATIONS

Exposure to toxins can result in damage to the structure and function of the brain. As such, some exposed workers will have varying degrees of cognitive diminishment or impairment that can be documented through neuropsychological assessment. Moreover, exposure to toxic substances can lead to psychological distress, worry, and somatic preoccupation in some people. In general, there is not a "typical" or "classic" pattern of neuropsychological test findings for each neurotoxic exposure. This variability may be due to the degree of exposure, the duration of exposure, as well as other factors, some of which are known while others may be unknown.

Neuropsychological assessment of workers exposed to toxic substances typically covers all major domains of cognitive functioning. It also involves psychological assessment and careful effort and symptom validity testing. Clinical neuropsychologists working within the field of toxic exposures need to be cognizant of bias and its many forms. Although attorneys engage in confirmatory bias (i.e., focusing on data that support one position vs. another) as part of the adversarial system, the clinical neuropsychologist should consider all of the data. Moreover, the interpretation of neuropsychological test findings should not be based only on a post hoc level of performance analysis of the results. Specifically, not every score that falls within a borderline or deficient range of performance relative to normative groups should be considered to reflect an underlying neurotoxic exposure-related cognitive deficit. In the past several years, it has become increasingly clear that among non-neurologically impaired groups (i.e., healthy controls among the general population), the presence of a few borderline/abnormal test findings is the norm, not the exception (e.g., Axelrod & Wall, 2007; Binder, Iverson, & Brooks, 2009; Schretlen, Testa, Winicki, Pearlson, & Gordon, 2008).

Similar incidental findings on brain MRI studies have been reported in the general population among healthy older adults (Vernooij et al., 2007). This study found that the presence of subclinical vascular pathologic changes were common in the general population. The presence of infarcts, cerebral aneurysms, and benign primary tumors, were also noted to occur in the general population. White matter hyperintensities on MRI have been documented in healthy children and adults; they also are associated with a variety of medical, psychiatric, and neurological conditions (Hopkins et al., 2006; Wen, Sachdev, Li, Chen, & Anstey, 2009).

Establishing a clear and concise link between neurotoxic exposures in the workplace and subsequent alterations in cognitive functioning can pose a significant challenge to the clinician. All clinical neuropsychologists are familiar with and routinely engage in the process of "differential diagnosis." Stedman's Medical Dictionary (Hensyl, 1990) defines the term *differential diagnosis* as "the determination of which of two or more diseases with similar symptoms is the one from which the patient is suffering" (p. 428). As such, differential diagnosis is concerned with the identification of the internal disease, or the internal process, that is the cause of the patient's symptoms and/or clinical findings.

Differential diagnosis is not directly concerned with matters of causation, and therefore, should not be used by clinical neuropsychologists solely to arrive at the ultimate issue of causation in cases of neurotoxic exposure in the workplace. Causation assessment goes beyond differential diagnosis and is a search for the ultimate cause of either a disorder or disease process that may or may not have been identified by the differential diagnostic process (Gots, 2005). This search may be complicated by factors unrelated to the exposure history per se (McCaffrey, Lynch, & Gregan, 2010).

CONCLUSIONS

Toxins can enter the body via inhalation, contact with the skin, ingestion, or injection. In occupational settings, inhalation is the most common and important route of entry. There are generally four classes of neurotoxic chemicals: gases (e.g., carbon monoxide), solvents (e.g., n-hexane, toluene, and xylene), metals (e.g., lead, mercury, arsenic, and cadmium), and insecticides. The EPA defines neurotoxicity as "an adverse change in the structure or function of the central and/or peripheral nervous system following exposure to a chemical, physical, or biological agent" (EPA, 1998). Anger and Johnson (1985) estimated that evidence of neurotoxicity exists for at least 850 chemicals that may be encountered in the workplace. Physiological changes vary widely depending on numerous factors, including class of neurotoxin and duration and amount of exposure. Exposure can affect numerous levels of nervous system organization. Behavioral changes, including cognitive impairment and/or change, are often the most obvious. Neuropsychological assessment can be helpful for documenting the nature and extent of cognitive deficits, if present, that are caused by neurotoxin exposure. Moreover, neuropsychologists are well positioned to evaluate for psychological problems that can co-occur with, mimic, or obscure cognitive deficits associated with toxin exposure.

REFERENCES

Abou-Donia, M. B. (Ed.). (2000). *Neurotoxicology*. Boca Raton, FL: CRC Press.
Agency for Toxic Substances and Disease Registry. Division of Toxicology. (1993). *Criteria for selecting toxicological profiles for development*. Guidance Document.
Alarcon, W. A., Roscoe, R. J., Calvert, G. M., & Graydon, J. R. (2009). Adult blood lead epidemiology and surveillance—United States, 2005–2007. *Morbidity and Mortality Weekly Report, 58*(14), 365–369.
Alterman, A. I., Goldstein, G., Shelly, C., Bober, B., & Tarter, R. E. (1985). The impact of mild head injury on neuropsychological capacity in chronic alcoholics. *International Journal of Neuroscience, 28*(3–4), 155–162.
American Conference of Industrial Government Hygienists. (2009). History of threshold limit values. Retrieved from *www.acgih.org/about/history.htm*.
Anger, W. K. (1984). Neurobehavioral testing of chemicals: impact on recommended standards. *Neurobehavioral Toxicology and Teratology, 6*(2), 147–153.

Anger, W. K., & Johnson, B. L. (1985). Chemicals affecting behavior. In J. L. O'Donoghue (Ed.), *Neurotoxicity of industrial and commercial chemicals* (pp. 51–148). Boca Raton, FL: CRC Press.

Axelrod, B. N., & Wall, J. R. (2007). Expectancy of impaired neuropsychological test scores in a non-clinical sample. *International Journal of Neuroscience, 117*(11), 1591–1602.

Binder, L. M., Iverson, G. L., & Brooks, B. L. (2009). To err is human: "Abnormal" neuropsychological scores and variability are common in healthy adults. *Archives of Clinical Neuropsychology, 24,* 31–46.

Buckley, N. A., Isbister, G. K., Stokes, B., & Juurlink, D. N. (2005). Hyperbaric oxygen for carbon monoxide poisoning: A systematic review and critical analysis of the evidence. *Toxicological Reviews, 24*(2), 75–92.

Bureau of Labor Statistics. (2007). *Occupational injuries and illnesses and fatal injuries (IIF) profiles database.* Retrieved from *data.bls.gov/GQT/servlet/Initial-Page.*

Bureau of Labor Statistics. (2009a). *National census of fatal occupational injuries in 2008 (USDL Publication No. 09-0979).* Retrieved November 2009, from *www.bls.gov/news.release/pdf/cfoi.pdf.*

Bureau of Labor Statistics. (2009b). *News release: Workplace injuries and illnesses (USDL Publication No. 09-1302).* Retrieved November 2009, from *www.bls.gov/news.release/pdf/osh.pdf.*

Centers for Disease Control and Prevention. *Metals: Emergency, preparedness and response.* Retrieved November 19, 2009, from *emergency.cdc.gov/agent/metals.*

Crepat, G., & Fritsch, R. (1998). *Carbon monoxide: The unnoticed poison of the 21st century.* Paper presented at the Satellite Meeting of IUTOX VIIIth International Congress of Toxicology.

Department of Health and Human Services [DHHS]. (2009). *Agency for toxic substances and disease registry (ATSDR), ToxFAQs.* Retrieved November 2009, from *www.atsdr.cdc.gov/toxfaq.html.*

Environmental Protection Agency. (1998, May 14). *Guidelines for neurotoxicity risk assessment: Federal Register, 63*(93).

Environmental Protection Agency. (2007). *Toxics release inventory program (TRI) explorer database [data file].* Retrieved from *www.epa.gov/triexplorer.*

Federal Regulations for Occupational Safety and Health Standards of Toxic and Hazardous Substances. *Health Hazard Definitions (Mandatory) (1996), 29 C.F.R., Standard Number 1910.1200 App A.* Retrieved November 19, 2009, from *www.osha.gov/pls/oshaweb/owadisp.show_document?p_table=STANDARDS&p_id=10099.*

Feldman, R. G. (1999). *Occupational and environmental neurotoxicology.* Philadelphia: Lippincott-Raven.

Gorman, D., Drewry, A., Huang, Y. L., & Sames, C. (2003). The clinical toxicology of carbon monoxide. *Toxicology, 187*(1), 25–38.

Gots, R. E. (2005, July). The distinct roles of differential diagnosis and causation assessment. *For the Defence,* 24–30.

Grandjean, P. (1991). Effects on reserve capacity: Significance for exposure limits. *Science of the Total Environment, 101*(1–2), 25–32.

Hantson, P., & Duprez, T. (2006). The value of morphological neuroimaging after acute exposure to toxic substances. *Toxicological Reviews, 25*(2), 87–98.

Hathaway, G. J., & Proctor, N. H. (2004). *Chemical hazards of the workplace* (5th ed.). Hoboken, NJ: Wiley.

Hensyl, W. R. (Ed.). (1990). *Stedman's Medical Dictionary* (25th ed.). Baltimore: Williams & Wilkins.

Hopkins, R. O., Beck, C. J., Burnett, D. L., Weaver, L. K., Victoroff, J., & Bigler, E. D. (2006). Prevalence of white matter hyperintensities in a young healthy population. *Journal of Neuroimaging, 16*(3), 243–251.

Kao, L. W., & Nanagas, K. A. (2004). Carbon monoxide poisoning. *Emergency Medicine Clinics of North America, 22*(4), 985–1018.

Lo, C. P., Chen, S. Y., Lee, K. W., Chen, W. L., Chen, C. Y., Hsueh, C. J., et al. (2007). Brain injury after acute carbon monoxide poisoning: Early and late complications. *American Journal of Roentgenology, 189*(4), W205–W211.

McCaffrey, R. J., Lynch, J. K., & Gregan, W. J. (2010, January). Lead paint injuries-Causation and discovery. *For the Defense,* 36–42, 86.

National Institute of Occupational Safety and Health. (1981–1983). *National occupational exposure [Data file].* Retrieved October 2009, from *www.cdc.gov/noes/default.html.*

National Institute of Occupational Safety and Health. (1987). *Current Intelligence Bulletin 48, Organic Solvent Neurotoxicity (DHHS Publication No. 87-104).* Retrieved August 11, 2009, from *www.cdc.gov/niosh/87104_48.html.*

National Institute of Occupational Safety and Health. (1992). *Recommended exposure limits (DHHS Publication No. 92-100).* Retrieved October 2009, from *www.cdc.gov/niosh/92-100.html.*

National Institute of Occupational Safety and Health. (1997). *Registry of toxic effects of chemical substances (NIOSH Publication No. 97-119).* Retrieved October 4, 2009, from *www.cdc.gov/niosh/97-119.html.*

National Institute of Occupational Safety and Health. (2004). *Worker health chartbook (NIOSH Publication No. 2004-146),* from *www.cdc.gov/niosh/docs/2004-146.*

O'Donoghue, J. L. (1985). *Neurotoxicity of industrial and commercial chemicals* (Vol. 1 and 2). Boca Raton, FL: CRC Press.

Occupational Health and Safety Administration. (2003). *Use of occupational exposure limits (OELs) for substances not covered by an OSHA Permissible Exposure Limit (PEL).* Retrieved October 2009, from *www.osha.gov/pls/oshaweb/owadisp.show_document?p_table=INTERPRETATIONS&p_id=24749.*

Occupational Health and Safety Administration. (2006). *Permissible exposure limits: Establishing PELs.* Retrieved October 2009, from *www.osha.gov/SLTC/pel/recognition.html.*

Occupational Health and Safety Administration. (2009). *Safety and health topics: Toxic metals.* Retrieved July 10, 2009, from *www.osha.gov/SLTC/metalsheavy/index.html.*

Occupational Safety and Health Act of 1970 (1970–2003).

Olanow, C. W. (2004). Manganese-induced parkinsonism and Parkinson's disease. *Annals of the New York Academy of Sciences, 1012,* 209–223.

Omaye, S. T. (2002). Metabolic modulation of carbon monoxide toxicity. *Toxicology, 180*(2), 139–150.

Prockop, L. D., & Chichkova, R. I. (2007). Carbon monoxide intoxication: An updated review. *Journal of Neurological Science, 262*(1–2), 122–130.

Raub, J. A., & Benignus, V. A. (2002). Carbon monoxide and the nervous system. *Neuroscience and Behavioral Reviews, 26*(8), 925–940.

Raub, J. A., Mathieu-Nolf, M., Hampson, N. B., & Thom, S. R. (2000). Carbon monoxide poisoning—a public health perspective. *Toxicology, 145*(1), 1–14.

Roscoe, R. J., Ball, W., Curran, J. J., DeLaurier, C., Falken, M. C., Fitchett, R., et al. (2002). Adult blood lead epidemiology and surveillance—United States, 1998–2001. *Morbidity and Mortality Weekly Report, 51*(SS-11), 1–10.

Schretlen, D. J., Testa, S. M., Winicki, J. M., Pearlson, G. D., & Gordon, B. (2008). Frequency and bases of abnormal performance by healthy adults on neuropsychological testing. *Journal of the International Neuropsychological Society, 14*(3), 436–445.

Stoller, K. P. (2007). Hyperbaric oxygen and carbon monoxide poisoning: A critical review. *Neurology Research, 29*(2), 146–155.

Tilson, H. G., & Mitchell, C. L. (1982). *Neurotoxicants and adaptive responses of the nervous system.* Symposium presented by the American Society for Pharmacology and Experimental Therapeutics at the 66th Annual Meeting of the Federation of American Societies for Experimental Biology, New Orleans, LA.

United States National Library of Medicine. (2009). *TOXNET hazardous substances data bank* [datafile]. Retrieved from *http://toxnet.nlm.nih.gov/cgi-bin/sis/htmlgen?HSDB*.

Vernooij, M. W., Ikram, M. A., Tanghe, H. L., Vincent, A. J., Hofman, A., Krestin, G. P., et al. (2007). Incidental findings on brain MRI in the general population. *New England Journal of Medicine, 357*(18), 1821–1828.

Wen, W., Sachdev, P. S., Li, J. J., Chen, X., & Anstey, K. J. (2009). White matter hyperintensities in the forties: Their prevalence and topography in an epidemiological sample aged 44–48. *Human Brain Mapping, 30*(4), 1155–1167.

APPENDIX 4.1. FEDERAL SURVEYS AND PUBLIC DATABASES

Toxic Chemicals and Their Health Effects

- *Toxic Substances List.* Published by NIOSH in 1971. Contained approximately 4,000 chemicals. Now revised (see next entry).

- *Registry of Toxic Effects of Chemical Substances* (NIOSH, 1997). This list contains toxicity information derived from reports of the toxic effects of nearly 140,000 chemical substances.

- *TOXNET Hazardous Substances Data Bank* (United States National Library of Medicine, 2009). This search engine features comprehensive peer-reviewed toxicology data for approximately 5,000 entries (Available *toxnet.nlm.nih.gov/cgi-bin/sis/htmlgen?HSDB*).

- *Toxicological Profiles* (ToxFAQs). Published by the Agency for Toxic Substances and Disease Registry (ATSDR) in order to provide detailed information about hazardous substances (Department of Health and Human Services [DHHS], 2009). Available at *www.atsdr.cdc.gov/toxfaq.html* or through the *Toxic Substances Portal* at *www.atsdr.cdc.gov/toxicsubstances.html*. See ATSDR (1993) for criteria used to select toxicological profiles.

National Surveys

- *National Occupational Hazard Survey (NOHS).* Carried out by NIOSH from 1972 to 1974 in order to obtain information regarding safety conditions in U.S. workplaces.

Nearly 900,000 workers from 4,600 plants containing approximately 450 different occupational categories, and over 8,000 chemicals and an estimated 80,000 unique trade name products were surveyed.

- *National Occupational Exposure Survey* (NOES, 1980–1983). Expanded upon the information retrieved from NOHS by investigating the association between potential chemical, physical, and biological exposure agents within specific occupations and industry types. Contains approximately 13,000 chemicals and over 100,000 unique trade name products collected from over 1.8 million workers in 4,500 plants. Over 500 industry types and nearly 400 occupational categories were surveyed. Data used in compiling the *Registry of Toxic Effects of Chemical Substances* and the *Hazardous Substances Data Bank*. This information also available in an interactive database located at *www. cdc.gov/noes/default.html*.
- *Worker Health Chartbook* (NIOSH, 2004). Published to act as a descriptive epidemiologic reference on occupational morbidity and mortality in the United States. Data collected by the Bureau of Labor Statistics. Available for download at *www.cdc.gov/niosh/ docs/2004-146*.
- *Adult Blood Lead Epidemiology & Surveillance (ABLES) Program (CDC/NIOSH 2002– 2005) and CDC/NIOSH 1994–2001)*. Blood lead-level data including prevalence, incidence for ≥25 mg/dL, ≥40 mg/dL and <25 mg/dL. Available for download at *www.cdc. gov/niosh/topics/ABLES/data.html*

Interactive Databases

- *Toxics Release Inventory (TRI) Program Explorer Database*. Started in 1988, contains information regarding disposal, recycling, and other releases from facilities throughout the United States in an effort to better document risk of hazard and exposure (EPA, 2007). Available at *www.epa.gov/triexplorer*. Includes 650 different chemicals and receives information from an estimated 23,000 plants. Lists of the chemicals included in the TRI Program are publicly available for reporting years 1997 until 2006 at *www. epa.gov/TRI/trichemicals/index.htm*.
- *Occupational Injuries, Illnesses and Fatalities (IIF Program)*. Provided by the Bureau of Labor Statistics. Contains information on workplace illness, injury and fatalities (located at *data.bls.gov/GQT/servlet/InitialPage*).
- *Adult Blood Lead Epidemiology & Surveillance (ABLES) Interactive Database*. Provided from the CDC through NIOSH, allows for customized searches of data beginning in 2002 by year, state, age group, exposure, blood lead level, industry sector, and gender. Located at *wwwn.cdc.gov/niosh-survapps/ables/default.aspx*.

CHAPTER 5

Neuropsychological Consequences of Injury in Military Personnel

Louis M. French
Grant L. Iverson
Rael T. Lange
Richard A. Bryant

Injuries due to wartime hazards are common. Wartime hazards generally fall into two categories: (1) hazards found in the combat operational environment and (2) hazards related to the combat itself or the actions of the enemy. Hazards related to the combat operational environment include exposure to extreme temperatures or high altitudes (e.g., altitude sickness) and exposure to toxic substances (e.g., depleted uranium). Hazards related to combat might result in injuries that are either directly or indirectly related to hostile action. Direct injuries include gunshot wounds and blast injuries. Indirect injuries include significant mental health problems that result from real or perceived threat against the individual or from witnessing highly stressful events involving other parties (i.e., posttraumatic stress disorder). Some hazards, however, fall into both categories. Infectious diseases or pathogens, for example, are indigenous to an operational environment and can also be used as an offensive weapon in biological warfare.

This chapter provides an overview of the consequences of some hazards that are either known to cause, or suspected to cause, neuropsychological injury. This chapter is not intended to be exhaustive. The nature of war is constantly changing, and we cannot address all possible weapons, injuries, or wartime threats against our service members. Rather, because the vast majority of combat operations over the last few years have taken place in Iraq and Afghanistan, we will focus on injuries common to these military locations. Injuries sustained during combat deployments that are not unique to combat experiences, such as a fall from a ladder during a construction project, are not a focus of this chapter. This chapter is divided into the following sections: (1) overview of injuries in the military, (2) stress and posttraumatic stress disorder (PTSD), (3) traumatic brain injury (TBI), (4) TBI and PTSD comorbidity, (5) amputation and blood loss, (6) sensory impairment, (7) infectious diseases or other pathogens, (8) depleted uranium, (9) environmental extremes, and (10) conclusions.

OVERVIEW OF INJURIES IN THE MILITARY

In 2008, more than three times as many service members (599,229) received medical care for a service-related injury than disease or other condition. Injuries and mental health disorders combined accounted for 54% of all hospital bed days and 43% of all medical encounters (Armed Forces Health Surveillance Center, 2009a). The conditions vary widely in terms of their overall morbidity. Back injuries, pregnancy-related conditions, and mental health disorders (including substance abuse) account for a large proportion of the morbidity burden.

The vast majority (79%) of all injuries sustained in the Iraq/Afghanistan conflict were due to explosive devices. Historically, gunshot wounds have been decreasing over the last 150 years of U.S. wars. The Iraq/Afghanistan conflict represents the lowest proportion of wounds resulting from bullet or ballistic trauma to date (Owens et al., 2008). Blast, as a mechanism of injury, has garnered significant attention because of the high frequency of polytrauma experienced by injured individuals. In an examination of the patients in the VA polytrauma system (Sayer et al., 2008) (in which 56% of those injured had blast-related injuries), for example, the pattern of injuries was different among those with blast injuries compared to wartime injuries due to other etiologies. Specifically, auditory impairments, soft tissue, eye, oral and maxillofacial, otologic, penetrating brain injuries, and symptoms of PTSD were more common in blast-injured patients.

STRESS AND PTSD

Formerly known as "shell shock" or "battle fatigue," chronic stress symptoms have often been reported by soldiers returning from combat since at least World War I (for a review see Shephard, 2001). Several large-scale surveys conducted among veterans over the last 20 years have confirmed the relation between combat experiences and posttraumatic symptoms (Hoge et al., 2004; Hoge, Terhakopian, Castro, Messer, & Engel, 2007; Kang,

Natelson, Mahan, Lee, & Murphy, 2003; Rona et al., 2009; Toomey et al., 2007). For example, in a survey of four U.S. combat infantry units, the prevalence of mental health disorders after deployment to Iraq was 27.9% (Hoge et al., 2004). In this study, 11.5 to 19.9% screened positive for PTSD using a more liberal definition, and 6.2 to 12.9% screened positive using a strict definition.[1] Respondents reported a high frequency of contact with the enemy and high rates of potentially traumatic combat experiences [e.g., seeing dead bodies or human remains (95%), knowing someone who was seriously injured or killed (43%), or being responsible for the death of an enemy combatant (48%)]. Moreover, there was a strong linear relation between the number of combat experiences and the rate of PTSD. For example, 9.3% of military personnel who were involved in one or two firefights developed PTSD, compared to 19.3% of those involved in five or more firefights (Hoge et al., 2004).

In a postdeployment telephone-based clinical interview study, Iversen and colleagues reported that 27.2% of U.K. military service members screened positive for a mental health problem and 4.8% screened positive for PTSD (Iversen et al., 2009). In a large-scale survey of 9,990 U.K. armed forces deployed to Iraq and Afghanistan between 2003 and 2009 (Fear et al., 2010), the prevalence of mental health disorders (19.7%) was lower than that reported in previous studies with the U.K. and U.S. armed forces (c.f. Hoge et al., 2004; Iversen et al., 2009). Only 4.0% of the sample reported symptoms of probable PTSD. Probable PTSD was more likely to occur in (1) personnel who were engaged in combat roles compared to supportive roles, and (2) reservists compared to regular personnel. In this study, there was no association with multiple deployments and PTSD or mental health disorders. However, deployment was associated with alcohol use (Fear et al., 2010).

In large military treatment facilities, psychiatric assessment and monitoring is part of the standard of care, regardless of the type of injury. This protocol is based on the model that any deployment with subsequent injury is likely to cause a significant stress reaction, even if it never develops into persistent emotional distress or evolves into a full-blown psychiatric disorder (Wain, Bradley, Nam, Waldrep, & Cozza, 2005).

There is also increased risk of developing PTSD after hospitalization. Zatzick and colleagues (2007), for example, found that 22% of the injured trauma survivors across the United States had symptoms consistent with the diagnosis of PTSD 12 months after hospitalization. Moreover, high levels of postinjury emotional distress, as well as physical pain, were associated with an increased risk of PTSD symptoms. Apart from PTSD, traumatic injury is also associated with increased rates of depression, generalized anxiety disorder, social phobia, agoraphobia, and panic disorder (Bryant et al., 2010). Other risk factors that have been identified as contributing to the development of depression or generalized distress include:

(1) being female; (2) having a prior Operation Endwing Freedom (OEF) or Operation Iraqi Freedom (OIF) deployment; (3) attitudinal factors such as a belief that one was not well prepared for the combat role; (4) perceiving less support from leadership; (5) and perceiving infrequent or negative contact with home during the deployment (Ferrier-Auerbach, Erbes, Polusny, Rath, & Sponheim, 2009).

Researchers have also reported a relation between the development of PTSD and having been wounded in combat. In a sample of 449 newly registered veterans in the VA healthcare system, 37% had PTSD, 37% had substance abuse, and 43% had depression. Symptoms were significantly greater in those veterans exposed to combat trauma than those who were not. In those without combat trauma exposure, 61% of individuals had no significant mental health symptoms compared to 16% of the trauma sample. The rate of depression was 60% in the trauma sample compared to 21% in the nontrauma sample, whereas the rate of substance abuse was 45% in the trauma sample and 27% in the nontrauma sample. In the trauma sample, 8.3% had PTSD only, 25% had concurrent PTSD and depression, and 5.7% had concurrent PTSD and substance abuse. None of the nontrauma sample had PTSD only, or concurrent PTSD and depression or substance abuse (Baker et al., 2009). The relation between PTSD and physical injury has been previously reported by Koren, Norman, Cohen, Berman, and Klein (2005) in injured Israeli war veterans. Koren and colleagues found that the odds of developing PTSD following physical injury during combat was approximately eight times greater than following injury-free emotional trauma.

In a recently published survey of deployed National Guard soldiers, the rates of depression and probable PTSD were 9% and 7%, respectively (Ferrier-Auerbach et al., 2009). These rates, of course, are somewhat lower than expected in light of other prevalence studies (e.g., Baker et al., 2009). However, it is important to recognize that the participants in the study by Ferrier-Auerbach and colleagues were assessed in a war theater (one month prior to returning home) rather than after they had returned to the United States, which is the method of data collection in other studies (Baker et al., 2009). It is likely that the differences in rates of depression and PTSD between these studies may reflect the onset or worsening of depressive and PTSD symptoms once the person is removed from the combat zone. A study by Grieger et al. (2006), who examined the rates of PTSD and depression among soldiers who were seriously injured and required medical evacuation and hospitalization at a tertiary military medical care center, lends some support to this notion. Approximately 4% had PTSD and/or depression at 1 month postinjury. At 4 months postinjury, these rates increased to 12.2% for PTSD and 8.9% for depression, reaching stability at approximately 7 months (12% and 9.3%, respectively). Interestingly, the majority of soldiers with PTSD or depression at 7 months did not have those conditions at the 1-month point.

Given the concerns about PTSD in a military population, educational initiatives such as "Battlemind" (*www.behavioralhealth.army.mil/battlemind/index.html*) have been recently implemented. Battlemind is a pre- and postdeployment psychoeducational program designed to facilitate the transition from combat zone deployment to civilian life. At a 4-month follow-up, involving 1,060 participants, individuals with high levels of combat exposure who received Battlemind debriefing reported fewer posttraumatic stress symptoms, depressive symptoms, and sleep problems than those in a stress-education-only group. Accordingly, this study illustrates that brief pre-and postdeployment interventions can reduce the stressful effects of combat exposure (Adler, Bliese, McGurk, Hoge, & Castro, 2009).

Neuropsychological Consequences of PTSD

Despite more than two decades of research, the scientific community has not reached a consensus on whether PTSD causes measurable cognitive deficits. Some researchers have reported that patients with PTSD perform more poorly on neuropsychological tests than healthy adults (Buckley, Blanchard, & Neill, 2000; Jelinek et al., 2006; Jenkins, Langlais, Delis, & Cohen, 2000). A study of Dutch veterans, for example, revealed that individuals with PTSD performed more poorly on neuropsychological tests compared to those without PTSD (Geuze, Vermetten, de Kloet, Hijman, & Westenberg, 2009). Moreover, among deficits reported in the literature, verbal learning and memory appear to be most commonly affected (Bremner et al., 1993, 1995; Geuze et al., 2009; Sutker, Allain, Johnson, & Butters, 1992; Vasterling, Brailey, Constans, & Sutker, 1998; Yehuda et al., 1995). In contrast, some studies have not found measurable cognitive decrements in persons with PTSD (Crowell, Kieffer, Siders, & Vanderploeg, 2002; Stein, Hanna, Vaerum, & Koverola, 1999; Twamley, Hami, & Stein, 2004).

Methodological limitations may be responsible for these mixed findings (Danckwerts & Leathem, 2003; Horner & Hamner, 2002). Depression and substance abuse are common comorbid conditions that are also associated with reduced performance on neuropsychological testing. As such, including patients in clinical samples with these conditions will tend to obscure the true causal relationship between PTSD and neurocognitive diminishment, if one indeed exists.

In a meta-analysis of the magnetic resonance imaging literature, Kitayama and colleagues concluded that there is an association between PTSD and smaller hippocampal volume (Kitayama, Vaccarino, Kutner, Weiss, & Bremner, 2005). Furthermore, in a meta-analysis of the memory literature, Brewin and colleagues reported that, overall, samples of patients with PTSD show a small decrement in memory functioning, broadly defined (i.e., an effect size of 0.2). In particular, those individuals with PTSD had a slightly greater decrement in verbal memory, although the magnitude of this decrement was modest (i.e., an effect size of 0.3) (Brewin, Kleiner,

Vasterling, & Field, 2007). In both meta-analyses, however, the cause(s) of these decrements remains unclear. In particular, the methodology did not permit determination of whether the findings predated the development of PTSD or were a consequence of PTSD (and comorbid conditions).

Increasingly, researchers are noting that people with PTSD might have lower neuropsychological test scores as a *preexisting* characteristic (Gilbertson et al., 2006; Parslow & Jorm, 2007). Additional indirect evidence for preexisting problems with verbal learning and memory can be deduced psychometrically. There is considerable evidence of differences in intelligence (IQ) in people who develop PTSD versus those who do not (Brandes et al., 2002; Macklin et al., 1998; Vasterling et al., 2002). That is, those with PTSD are more likely to have average or below-average IQs, whereas individuals exposed to traumatic events who do not develop PTSD are more likely to have high average or superior IQs. There is also evidence that reduced hippocampal volume may be a preexisting factor that increases the risk for developing PTSD, with sufficient trauma exposure. A study of hippocampal volumes in monozygotic twins, discordant for PTSD and trauma exposure, provides initial supporting evidence (Gilbertson et al., 2002). In particular, this study revealed comparable reductions in hippocampal volume in both the twin with PTSD and in the nontrauma exposed twin relative to healthy non-PTSD twin pairs—suggesting that there may be a genetic contribution to variation in hippocampal volume. From this evidence, it was proposed that smaller hippocampal volume is a preexisting risk factor for severe chronic PTSD rather than a consequence of trauma exposure per se. Consistent with this theory, in a case-controlled study of identical twins (one of which was exposed to combat in the Vietnam War), Gurvits and colleagues (2006) found that the rate of neurological soft signs was greater in both the combat-exposed twins with PTSD and their noncombat-exposed siblings, compared to the combat-exposed twin without PTSD and their noncombat-exposed siblings. These data suggest that neurological soft signs may be a preexisting genetic vulnerability factor for combat-related PTSD.

TRAUMATIC BRAIN INJURY

TBIs in military personnel predominately occur as a result of closed-head injuries. Penetrating or open-head injuries are far less common. TBIs occur on a broad spectrum of severity ranging from very mild to catastrophic injuries. TBIs are traditionally categorized into mild, moderate, or severe classifications using injury severity indicators such as the Glasgow Coma Scale (GCS; Mild = 13–15; Moderate = 9–12; Severe = 3–8), duration of loss of consciousness, and posttraumatic amnesia. However, GCS scores are often not available shortly after combat-related injuries. The classification system officially adopted by the United States Department of Defense

▪ TABLE 5.1. U.S. DoD TBI Classification System

Classification	Duration of unconsciousness	Alteration of consciousness (AOC)	Posttraumatic amnesia
Mild	< 30 minutes	A moment up to 24 hours	< 24 hours
Moderate	30 minutes– 24 hours	If AOC > 24 hours, then severity based on other criteria	1–7 days
Severe	> 24 hours		> 7 days

is summarized in Table 5.1. Note that this classification system does not use GCS scores, but is otherwise very similar to other definitions of TBI severity.

Epidemiology

Recently, the Department of Defense (DoD) released ICD-9 derived diagnoses for TBI in the DoD Health Care System. There were 27,862 brain injuries coded in 2009, 21,859 of which were classified as mild. These data reflect the most accurate official accounting of brain injuries sustained in the military, but likely underestimate the true prevalence of brain injuries in this population. These data are limited to those personnel who presented to the military healthcare system. There are likely to be many other personnel who have sustained TBIs—which, presumably, are largely on the milder end of the spectrum—who never sought medical treatment or came to the attention of healthcare providers. Military efforts aimed at screening deployed (nonmedically evacuated) service members for mild TBI during deployment suggest that as many as 10 to 20% may have suffered a concussion during deployment (TBI Task Force Report, 2008). Terrio et al. (2009) reported a 22.9% rate of mild TBI in a Brigade Combat Team who were screened after they returned to the United States. In that sample, personnel with a history of mild TBI were more likely to report postinjury and postdeployment somatic and/or neuropsychiatric symptoms compared to those without a history of brain injury.

The Defense and Veterans Brain Injury Center (DVBIC) has released official surveillance numbers for medically diagnosed TBI in the military. The surveillance numbers represent individual service members who sustained a TBI of any severity, anywhere in the world, between 2000 and 2009 (see Table 5.2). Each injured service member was counted only once in order to represent the total number of injured service members, not the total number of injuries (i.e., some service members had been injured more than once). The number of TBIs increased significantly between 2006 and 2008. The DoD did not provide an explanation for this increase, and multiple factors could have contributed, including possible changes to the methodology by which service members were screened and then clinically

■ TABLE 5.2. Traumatic Brain Injuries in the Military: 2000–2009

	2000	2001	2002	2003	2004	2005	2006	2007	2008	2009
Total	10,963	11,830	12,469	12,886	13,271	12,025	16,873	23,002	28,557	27,862
Mild	6,340	7,779	8,998	9,795	10,542	9,778	13,989	18,775	22,038	21,859
Moderate	4,141	3,536	3,058	2,618	2,240	1,803	2,328	3,456	2,999	3,059
Severe	174	186	149	167	145	151	186	194	226	258
Penetrating	271	290	223	270	310	234	299	349	420	404
Not Classifiable	37	39	41	36	34	59	71	228	2,874	2,282

Note. Defense and Veterans Brain Injury Center (retrieved May 16, 2010, from *www.dvbic.org/TBI-Numbers.aspx*). Numbers were extracted from tables.

diagnosed. An examination of trends from 2000 to 2009 showed that 1.3 to 2.5% of all injuries were penetrating and 0.8 to 1.6% of all injuries were severe. Over the years, there generally has been a gradual linear increase in the percentage of all injuries classified as mild.

Data from 1992 suggest that the age-adjusted head injury rates for ages 15–44 years were higher in active-duty individuals compared to other civilian beneficiaries (1.6 times greater for men and 2.5 times greater for women) (Ommaya, Ommaya, Dannenberg, & Salazar, 1996a). Motor vehicle crashes, falls, and fighting accounted for 80% of the total military facility cost for head injuries. More recent data, however, suggest that the incidence of hospitalization associated with TBI in the active-duty U.S. Army decreased substantially in the 1990s (Ivins, Schwab, Baker, & Warden, 2006). Although some maintain that this trend was due to increased emphasis on injury prevention and changes in U.S. Army population demographics, there were extended periods of peace during the 1990s. In an examination of hospitalization rates associated with TBI in the active-duty Army for a wartime period (2000 to 2006), incidence of TBI-related hospitalization increased 105% from 2000 to 2006. This included a 60-fold increase in the hospitalization rate of TBI due to weapons. Overall, the Army's hospitalization rates for moderate and severe TBI within this period were lower than civilian rates. In contrast, the Army's hospitalization rates for mild TBI were higher than civilian rates. This suggests that, although wartime operations appear to have had a substantial impact on TBI-related hospitalization rates, the differences between Army and civilian rates are not as excessive as might be expected.

Outcome from TBI

Another chapter in this book describes in some detail the neurocognitive, neurobehavioral, and functional outcome from mild, moderate, and severe

TBI in civilian populations (see Iverson & Lange, Chapter 1, this volume). Information from that chapter is directly applicable to military personnel who have sustained a TBI. In this section we will briefly discuss some issues that pertain to the military per se, rather than repeating information from that chapter.

The majority of individuals who sustain a mild TBI on the battlefield will have time-limited symptoms. In the short-term recovery phase, it is common for individuals to experience slowed reaction time, headache, dizziness, inattention, or other postconcussion symptoms (Fear et al., 2009). These symptoms may have implications for combat readiness, troop welfare, or safety, which have motivated the military to make significant efforts to screen for mild TBI on the battlefield. This screening process has resulted in widespread use of the Military Acute Concussion Evaluation (MACE) (French, McCrea, & Baggett, 2008) and the development of standardized DoD clinical practice guidelines, which involve the management of mild TBI. However, similar to a civilian population, it is important to appreciate that postconcussion symptoms are not specific to mild TBI and are often reported in the absence of a brain injury. For example, Fear and colleagues reported that the incidence of postconcussion-like symptoms was highest in military personnel who were exposed to depleted uranium and/or who had aided the wounded, rather than those who had been injured by blasts directly (Fear et al., 2009). Comparable rates of acute postconcussion symptoms have been reported in general trauma patients with and without TBI (Meares et al., 2008).

Polytrauma patients, even without brain injury, have high rates of neurobehavioral symptoms, including memory difficulties, irritability, mood swings, suspiciousness, amotivation, and guilt (Frenisy et al., 2006). Minimal extracranial injuries and lower reported pain predict better outcomes for return to work after MTBI (Stulemeijer et al., 2006). In a group of individuals who sustained MTBI, coupled with extracranial injuries, at 6 months postinjury, 44% of the patients with the additional injuries were still in treatment, compared to 14% of the patients with isolated MTBI. They also had lower return-to-work rates, and they reported more limitations in physical functioning. Those individuals who required ongoing treatment also reported significantly more severe postconcussive symptoms.

Although there is limited information about longer-term outcomes of neurobehavioral symptoms, employment, or interpersonal functioning among those who have sustained a TBI in the Iraq/Afghanistan conflicts, similar longitudinal data are available from peacetime and previous conflicts. In a peacetime sample, when compared to the total discharge population, the relative risk for behavioral discharge from the military was 1.8 times greater for those individuals with mild TBI. In contrast, individuals with moderate or severe TBI had similar rates of behavioral discharge as the total discharge population. Discharge for alcoholism or drug abuse in individuals with mild TBI was 2.6 times the rates of the total discharge population. Individuals with moderate TBI had 5.4 times greater substance abuse prevalence rates than the total discharge population. There was no significant difference with respect to discharge rates for alcoholism or drug abuse between individuals with severe TBI and the total discharge population. Discharge for criminal conviction was 2.7 times greater in those individuals with MTBI when compared to the total discharge population. There was no significant difference for criminal conviction discharges between individuals with moderate or severe TBI and the total discharge population (Ommaya et al., 1996b).

There have been multiple TBI outcome studies, particularly penetrating brain injury, from the Vietnam era (Grafman et al., 1988; Koenigs et al., 2008; Raymont et al., 2008; Salazar, Schwab, & Grafman, 1995; Schwab, Grafman, Salazar, & Kraft, 1993). For example, Schwab and colleagues reported several neurological, neuropsychological, and social interaction factors that related to return-to-work status following penetrating brain injury. These factors included epilepsy, paresis, visual field loss, verbal memory and reasoning deficits, visual recognition loss, self-reported violent behavior, and social isolation.

In a recent major study of civilians, Bryant and colleagues found that, after serious traumatic bodily injury, having an MTBI[2] did not increase the likelihood of suffering functional impairment in physical, psychological, social, or environmental domains (Bryant et al., 2010). In contrast, those who sustained an MTBI and had a psychiatric disorder at 12 months were between 2 and 4 times more likely to suffer functional impairment.

In a series of studies examining long-term intellectual functioning following penetrating brain injury, researchers reported that pre-injury intellectual ability is the most consistent predictor of post-injury intellectual ability at 15 years (Grafman et al., 1988) and 30 years post injury (Raymont et al., 2008). However, when pre-injury IQ was taken into account, total brain volume loss and lesion location was also found to be an important predictor 15 years post injury (Grafman et al., 1988). In addition, Raymont and colleagues reported that cognitive functioning 30 years post injury was also associated with global atrophy, tissue loss in specific regions (e.g., corpus callosum thickness, third ventricle width), and certain genetic markers (e.g., GRIN2A).

TBI/PTSD COMORBIDITY

PTSD as a comorbid condition in individuals who have sustained traumatic brain injuries with associated loss of consciousness (LOC) and posttraumatic amnesia remains controversial in the literature. Proponents on one side of the debate argue that individuals who cannot recall the traumatic event because of LOC or amnesia should also not be able to later recall the event via flashbacks or intrusive recollections. Individuals with marked amnesia around the time of the event are thus at relatively low risk for developing PTSD (Bombardier et al., 2006; Levin et al., 2001; Sbordone & Liter, 1995). A small number of studies support this notion. Low rates of PTSD have been found in individuals who have sustained TBI and who had associated LOC in both military (Warden & Labbate, 2005) and civilian populations (Gil, Caspi, Ben-Ari, Koren, & Klein, 2005; Glaesser, Neuner, Lutgehetmann, Schmidt, & Elbert, 2004). In one study, for example, Glaesser and colleagues (2004) found that the rate of PTSD was significantly lower for patients who had a LOC of more than 12 hours, compared to those who had a LOC of less than 12 hours. Another study found that longer duration of posttraumatic amnesia was associated with less severe intrusive memories immediately following exposure to trauma (Bryant et al., 2009).

Proponents on the other side of the debate maintain that the anxiety response is activated in some individuals, despite the occurrence of memory impairment. Therefore, PTSD can exist as a comorbid condition with TBI (Harvey & Bryant, 2000; Hickling, Gillen, Blanchard, Buckley, & Taylor, 1998; Mather, Tate, & Hannan, 2003; Mayou, Black, & Bryant, 2000). It is proposed that PTSD can develop following TBI via several possible mechanisms.

- *Fear conditioning.* Rauch, Shin, and Phelps (2006) proposed that extreme fear at the time of trauma is classically conditioned with stimuli associated with concomitant events and experiences, and that these associations between trauma reminders and anxiety responses can develop into PTSD. Fear conditioning may occur with varying levels of awareness of the contingency between the trauma and the consequences, which may allow for some fear conditioning following TBI. There is evidence, for example, that people can develop PTSD following severe TBI, even though these patients do not recall the trauma and do not suffer intrusive memories of the event (Bryant, Marosszeky, Crooks, & Gurka, 2000).
- *Reconstruction of traumatic experiences.* Following TBI, people can reconstruct their traumatic experiences in ways that permit them to compensate for the impoverished memory of their trauma, which can develop into PTSD. Some researchers have found that in a sample of patients who sustained a mild TBI and reported amnesia for some aspect of their accident, 40% were able to achieve full recall of the experience 2 years later (Harvey & Bryant, 2001). In a case study, Bryant (1996) described a man who developed PTSD 12 months following severe TBI (despite being densely amnesic), as a result of developing distressing and intrusive images of his

accident related to his seeing a newspaper photograph of his wrecked car. Reconstructed memories that develop in patients who have sustained TBIs can be subjectively compelling and share many of the memory attributes experienced by people who have continuous recall of their trauma (Bryant & Harvey, 1998).

• *Resolution of PTA during trauma.* Following TBI, despite experiencing amnesia for the events directly surrounding their injury, many people can experience traumatic events following the resolution of their PTA. It is common for patients, particularly those who have sustained a very mild TBI, to have full recall of being transported to a hospital or being treated by medical personnel. These experiences can be sufficiently associated with distressing emotions and contribute to PTSD symptoms.

• *Biological dysfunction.* Prevailing biological models of PTSD propose that PTSD involves exaggerated amygdala response associated with diminished regulation by the medial prefrontal cortex (Rauch et al., 2006). The amygdala is central to the development and expression of conditioned fear reactions. Human and animal studies have shown that learning to inhibit these fear reactions involves inhibition by the medial prefrontal cortex. Consistent with this model, patients with PTSD have diminished medial prefrontal cortex activation during processing of fear stimuli (Lanius, Bluhm, Lanius, & Pain, 2006). Because TBI often involves damage to the prefrontal cortex, it is possible that an individual's capacity to regulate the fear reaction may be impaired after MTBI because the neural networks involved in the regulation of anxiety may be damaged (Bryant, 2008). This theory raises the possibility that some people who suffer an MTBI may actually be more susceptible to PTSD than other trauma survivors because the neural structures involved in emotion regulation and inhibition of fear are compromised.

Without question, assessing cognition in people with a history of mild TBI, PTSD, or both, is extraordinarily complex in regards to (1) subjective symptoms, (2) objective test results, and (3) determining the cause of any particular finding. Complicating the picture, people with a history of mild TBI, PTSD, or both, can also have comorbid depression, substance abuse, or chronic pain. Table 5.3 presents a summary of studies reporting comorbid PTSD and TBI rates in Operation Iraqi Freedom (OIF) and Operation Enduring Freedom (OEF) veterans. Moreover, individuals with PTSD can have preexisting lower scores on intellectual and neuropsychological tests. PTSD itself should not lower intelligence scores. Therefore, it is essential to interpret neuropsychological test scores in people with PTSD carefully, not by simply comparing them to normative data adjusted for age, but by considering their educational attainment and level of intelligence. These factors can have a substantial impact on the interpretation of neuropsychological test results.

▪ **TABLE 5.3. Summary of Studies Reporting Screening Estimates on Comorbid PTSD and TBI Rates in OIF and OEF Veterans**

Author(s) year	N	Population	PTSD rate	TBI rate	Both rate	Neither rate
Lew et al. (2007)	62	VA PRC outpatients with TBI; 89% OIF/OEF	71%	n/a	NR	n/a
Gaylord et al. (2008)	76	Medically evacuated OIF/OEF for burns	32%	41%	18%	46%
Vasterling et al. (2006)	1,457	Surveyed OIF deployed	11.6%	7.6%[a]	NR	NR
Schneiderman et al. (2008)	2,235	Surveyed OIF/OEF in DC area; not medically evacuated	11%	12%	NR	NR
Hoge et al. (2008)	2,525	Surveyed OIF; not medically evacuated	13.9%	15.2%	NR	NR
Tanielian & Jaycox (2008)	1,965	Surveyed OIF deployed	13.8%	19.5%	1.1 %	69.3%
Nelson et al. (2009)	53	OIF/OEF veterans with mild–moderate TBI	35%	n/a	n/a	n/a
Hill et al. (2009)	95	OIF/OEF veterans screened positive for a possible TBI: VA TBI Screening Program[b]	34.7%	85.3%	29.5%	9.4%
Pietrzak et al. (2009)	277	National Guard/Reserve OIF/OEF veterans: Veterans Needs Assessment Survey	32.1%	18.8%	12.3%	61.4%[c]
Tan et al. (2009)	28	OEF/OIF veterans from Level II Polytrauma Network Site	57.1%	64.3%	39.3%	17.8%
Lew et al. (2009b)	340	OEF/OIF veterans from a VA Polytrauma Network Site	68.3%	66.8%[d]	48.9%	10.3%
Wilk et al. (2010)	3,952	Surveyed OIF/OEF National Guard and Active Duty infantry brigades, 3–6 months after returning from deployment	NR	14.9%[e]	5.0%	NR
MacGregor et al. (2010)	781	Injured OIF combatants medically evacuated	16.5%	15.8%	13.7%	NR

Note. NR, not reported
[a]As defined by LOC >15 minutes.
[b]Using a modified version of the Brief TBI Screen.
[c]Percentages calculated based on other data presented in the study.
[d]Defined by TBI and the presence of three or more postconcussion symptoms last for more than 3 months postinjury.
[e]Defined by the self-reported involvement of sustaining an injury (e.g., blast, fall, MVA, fragment), in addition to one of three self-reported symptoms: (1) dazed, confused, or "seeing stars"; (2) not remembering the injury; and (3) losing consciousness (knocked out).

AMPUTATION AND BLOOD LOSS

The use of explosive devices is a common combat tactic. Injuries caused by close exposure to an explosive device are often severe and may result in limb amputation. In a review of military healthcare records, Stansbury, Lallis, Branstetter, Bagg, and Holcomb (2008) reported that 8,058 U.S. military casualties required medical evacuation between October 2001 and June 2006. The majority of these casualties (i.e., 5,684; 70.5%) sustained major limb injuries, 423 of whom underwent major limb amputation, or amputation at or proximal to the wrist or ankle joint (i.e., 5.2% of all serious injuries; 7.4% of major limb injuries). The overwhelming majority (87%) of injuries resulting in limb amputations were caused by an explosive device. When compared to the prevalence of major limb amputations in past military conflicts (e.g., Vietnam, 7.4%), the prevalence of major limb amputations for the current conflicts in Afghanistan and Iraq is comparable (Stansbury et al., 2008).

Besides amputation, high numbers of individuals (over 90% in one sample) have sustained penetrating injuries with at least some degree of hemorrhage during the conflicts in Iraq and Afghanistan. Over 40% of patients who were medically evacuated were treated for hypotension, and more than 80% of patients treated by one U.S. Marine forward resuscitation surgical unit experienced hemorrhagic shock (Chambers et al., 2005). In cases of traumatic amputation, there is the possibility of hemorrhagic or hypoxemic posttraumatic insults to the central nervous system. Multiple studies (e.g., DeWitt & Prough, 2009) have reported that inadequate cerebral blood flow can contribute to increased morbidity after TBI. Hypotension is a significant risk factor for death following trauma, even in the absence of TBI (Shafi & Gentilello, 2005). Following TBI, the brain appears to be especially vulnerable to posttraumatic hypoxemia (DeWitt & Prough, 2009). Interventions intended for blood volume replacement following hemorrhagic hypotension, such as hypertonic saline, however, may not improve cerebral oxygen delivery after head injury (DeWitt, Prough, Deal, Vines, & Hoen, 1996). Consistent with the model of blast injury posited by Cernak and colleagues, damage to the lungs may further complicate the recovery process through reduced arterial blood pressure and reduced oxygenation (Cernak, Savic, Ignjatovic, & Jevtic, 1999). It has also been hypothesized that the primary blast wave effects, including changes in pressure, can lead to cavitation in blood vessels, which can result in air emboli causing cerebral infarction (Mayorga, 1997).

The long-term cognitive or psychological consequences of severe hemorrhage (without co-occurring TBI) are largely unknown. The clinical experience of one author (LMF) is that severe blood loss can complicate the clinical presentation of those suffering from mild TBI, such that cognitive or other symptoms may persist well beyond the period one would typically expect for an uncomplicated TBI of similar severity.

SENSORY IMPAIRMENT

Although sensory impairment does not result in neuropsychological dysfunction per se, it is a relatively common condition that may have a significant impact on an individual's overall functioning. Individuals with sensory impairments, for example, may face more challenges over the course of rehabilitation than those with intact sensory functioning. In a group of polytrauma patients who sustained blast injuries, the rate of visual impairment was more than double (52%) that of other causes of polytrauma (20%), such as motor vehicle accidents, gunshot and/or shrapnel wounds, assault, falls, or anoxia (Goodrich, Kirby, Cockerham, Ingalla, & Lew, 2007). In a group of patients at Walter Reed National Military Medical Center, explosive fragmentary munitions accounted for 79% of TBI-associated combat ocular trauma (Weichel, Colyer, Bautista, Bower, & French, 2009). Moreover, severe TBI was more frequently associated with combat ocular trauma than milder TBI. Overall, TBI occurred in two-thirds of all cases involving combat-related ocular trauma, and ocular trauma was a common finding in all TBI cases.

Lew and colleagues examined Iraq and Afghanistan veterans treated in a VA polytrauma center following a blast injury and found that 62% of patients complained of hearing loss and 38% reported tinnitus, with sensorineural loss being the most prevalent type of hearing loss (Lew, Jerger, Guillory, & Henry, 2007). This finding compares to rates of 44% with hearing loss and 18% with tinnitus in those injured through a mechanism other than blast (Lew et al., 2007). For those with dual sensory impairment (impairments in both hearing and vision), the difficulties are likely magnified. In a follow-up study, Lew and colleagues reported that hearing impairment was identified in 19% of the sample, visual impairment in 34% of the sample, and dual sensory impairment in 32% of the sample (Lew et al., 2009a). Surprisingly, only 15% of the patients in the sample had no sensory impairments in either modality. For those with dual sensory impairment, advancement in rehabilitation was limited, as reflected by an overall reduction in both total and motor Functional Impairment Measure scores at discharge. This finding is consistent with previous work with other populations, which suggests that dual sensory impairment is associated with more depressive symptoms (Capella-McDonnall, 2005) and a lower overall health-related quality of life (Chia et al., 2006).

INFECTIOUS DISEASES OR OTHER PATHOGENS

Infectious diseases have always had a significant impact on military campaigns. These diseases are related to parasites and infectious agents in the area in which combat operations occur. They are in addition to those infections arising from war wounds or those infections related to crowded conditions, breakdown of sanitation facilities, and other similar infrastructure issues that occur in wartime. Although some of these conditions may lead to severe gastroenteritis or persistent diarrhea, these conditions are not typically associated with central nervous system (CNS) effects (Aronson, Sanders, & Moran, 2006). However, infections associated with war wounds may have implications for recovery from other conditions. For example, infections can complicate recovery from TBI. Dau and colleagues (Dau, Oda, & Holodniy, 2009) reported on two cases of blast-related TBI in which the outcomes were negatively affected by bacterial and fungal infections endemic to the combat area.

Current U.S. combat operations have seen hundreds of cases of *cutaneous leishmaniasis* and at least five cases of *visceral leishmaniasis* among U.S. military personnel serving in Southwest Asia. Leishmaniasis is a sandfly-borne parasitic disease caused by protozoa that live inside mammals. The sand flies become infected after feeding on an infected animal, including humans, and can then transmit the parasite to other animals. The *cutaneous* version of leishmaniasis involves skin ulceration. The *visceral* version of leishmaniasis has more systemic consequences and can result in death in adults with compromised immune functioning (Weina, Neafie, Wortmann, Polhemus, & Aronson, 2004). Neurologic involvement in visceral leishmaniasis has been suspected, though its nature has remained elusive (Chunge, Gachihi, & Muigai, 1985; Mustafa, 1965). For example, in one case (Karak, Garg, Misra, & Sharma, 1998), a patient's onset of new neurological problems (e.g., dysarthria, ataxia, neural deafness, nystagmus, and facial palsy) were related to herpes zoster that occurred because of immunological changes in the patient, not due to the leishmaniasis per se.

Infection with *Plasmodium falciparum*, a protozoan parasite that is one of the species that causes malaria in humans, is known to cause several neurological complications (Markley & Edmond, 2009). The worst of these complications is cerebral malaria, which is much more common in children but is also found in adults (Garg, Karak, & Misra, 1999). Malaria has been reported among U.S. Army soldiers in Afghanistan, though not in Iraq (Aronson et al., 2006; Zapor & Moran, 2005).

In a study of Vietnam veterans who had been hospitalized for malarial infection while in Vietnam,[3] the infected veterans performed significantly worse than controls on memory tasks (verbal memory measures from the Wechsler Memory Scale and visual memory from the Benton Visual Retention Test) and exhibited impaired dichotic listening, consistent with the presumed disruption of subcortical white matter tracts (Richardson, Varney, Roberts, Springer, & Wood, 1997). In the same group, individuals with a history of infection manifested significant problems with depression, personality change, emotional lability, and feelings of overall distress. Half of the infected veterans (51%) had at least six clinically elevated scales on the Minnesota Multiphasic Personality Inventory (MMPI) (compared to 16% of controls), 58% met the criteria for a major depressive episode at the time of the evaluation (compared to 30% controls), and 68% endorsed more than half of the symptoms on the complex partial seizure interview (compared to 11% of the control group) (Varney, Roberts, Springer, Connell, & Wood, 1997).

It has been suggested that cognitive impairment may also occur after less severe malarial disease. Moreover, many of the drugs used in treating malaria prophylaxis have significant adverse effects, including neuropsychiatric effects (Croft, Whitehouse, Cook, & Beer, 2002). Mefloquine has been reported to have about a 29% rate of occurrence of neuropsychiatric side effects (e.g., strange dreams, insomnia, dizziness, anxiety, depression, and visual difficulties); atovaquone-proguanil has a 10 to 14% rate; and chloroquine has been associated with severe neuropsychiatric reactions, including convulsions, mania, and psychosis (Croft et al., 2002). One report of mefloquine administration to a small sample of healthy volunteers resulted in lightheadedness in all subjects, two with dizziness and impaired concentration,[4] and two with more severe incapacitation (Patchen, Campbell, & Williams, 1989).

Although chemical nerve agents are, fortunately, only rarely used in modern warfare (e.g., organophosphates), the potential impact of the pharmacologic countermeasures that are used by our service members is worth mentioning. U.S. service members are issued several automatic injector devices that deliver drugs intramuscularly for emergency treatment in the event of a nerve agent attack. In addition, service members may be given a pretreatment drug, frequently pyridostigmine bromide, as a prophylactic, under conditions where the threat of nerve agent attack may be high (McDonough, 2002). Although there have been anecdotal reports of impairment in cognitive or other functioning, it is generally believed that the effects of pyridostigmine bromide on performance appear to be negligible under most circumstances (McDonough, 2002). However, in some recent animal studies, pyridostigmine bromide has been shown to have potentially deleterious effects on performance under conditions of stress (Amourette et al., 2009; Myers et al., 2010). Other prophylactic agents, including atropine, have been shown to have marked effects on cognitive functioning, particularly short-term memory (McDonough, 2002). In a group of military helicopter pilots, a 4-mg dose of atropine affected vision, psychomotor performance, and cognitive skills, such that flight performance was considered seriously impaired. It has been suggested that lower doses in combination with sleep deprivation, fatigue, or other factors may be sufficient to cause marked neurobehavioral effects (Caldwell, Stephens, Carter, & Jones, 1992). Of note, many of the countermeasures, though effective when used in the presence of nerve agents, may have unacceptable

deleterious effects if administered in the absence of cholinesterase inhibitors (Cerasoli & Lenz, 2002).

DEPLETED URANIUM

Depleted uranium (DU) was first used in battle in the 1991 Gulf War conflict. Over 300 tons of DU were fired by U.S. and U.K. forces. Military
exposure to DU usually results from handling the munitions or battlefield
exposure. Skin contact with intact munitions or armor does not impose a
toxicological hazard, and the external radiation hazard is minimal. It has
been estimated, for example, that radiation exposure inside a DU-armored
closed-down tank carrying a full load of DU munitions for one year would
result in less than 25% of the U.S. annual occupational exposure limit
for ionizing radiations. It is estimated that it would require 250 hours of
direct skin contact to exceed U.S. occupational dose limits for skin contact.
Rather, the risk of DU poisoning results from inhalation, ingestion, and the
contamination of wounds with DU dust, or shrapnel caused by hard-target
strikes (Bolton & Foster, 2002). Although Iraqi forces did not have DU
munitions, some U.S. casualties resulted from friendly-fire incidents.

In an initial study of 29 DU exposed veterans and 38 nonexposed Gulf
War veterans at the Baltimore Veterans Affairs Medical Center more than
7 years after first exposure, DU-exposed Gulf War veterans with retained
metal fragments continued to excrete elevated concentrations of uranium
in their urine. A significant relation between increased urinary uranium
concentrations and poor performance on neuropsychological tests has been
found, though the findings are mixed. For example, urinary uranium concentrations were not found to be significant predictors of neuropsychological test performance when using traditional (i.e., pencil and paper) neuropsychological test measures, but was a good predictor when using automated
(i.e., computerized) neurocognitive measures (McDiarmid et al., 2000). In a
series of follow-up evaluations, however, the relation between urinary uranium concentration and performance on automated neuropsychological test
measures weakened. The relation was not statistically significant ($p = .098$)
between high and low urinary–uranium groups in the 1999 surveillance
after adjustment for intelligence (WRAT-3) and depression (Beck Depression Inventory) (McDiarmid et al., 2001). Later surveillance (2001, 2003,
and 2005) found no statistically significant differences between exposure
groups across neurocognitive indexes (McDiarmid et al., 2007).

The Institute of Medicine (2008) concluded that studies of military and
veteran populations have not been able to determine conclusively whether
exposure to DU is associated with worse health outcomes. The committee remarked that although many of the studies were well designed, they
lacked either an adequate sample size or accurate exposure information

to properly assess whether DU exposure is associated with adverse health outcomes. Overall, they concluded that there is inadequate and insufficient evidence to determine whether an association exists between exposure to uranium and nonmalignant diseases of the CNS. The Institute of Medicine, however, remarked that the results of studies in animal models indicate that depleted uranium is a toxicant capable of crossing the blood-brain barrier, with behavioral changes reported in some studies. The committee suggested that subtle neurological dysfunction, associated with high concentration of uranium, might be possible and that further study of the association between exposure to DU and neurological effects was warranted.

In a large-scale study of 5,869 U.K. military personnel (Fear et al., 2009) deployed to Iraq, 21% reported that they had been exposed to depleted uranium. This contrasts with a 52% self-report rate of exposure to blast and a 24% self-report rate of aiding the wounded. Fear and colleagues examined postconcussion-like symptoms across the three conditions. They generated two markers of for these symptoms: presence and severity. Military personnel were classified according to: (1) blast exposure; (2) exposure to uranium or wounded personnel; (3) both blast exposure and exposure to uranium or wounded personnel; or (4) no exposure to any of these. The presence of postconcussion-like symptoms, by group, is presented in Figure 5.1. Approximately 27% of those individuals who were blast-exposed reported three or more symptoms. However, approximately 21% of those individuals with *no* blast exposure, uranium exposure, or exposure to wounded personnel reported three or more symptoms, while 32% of those individuals who were exposed to uranium or wounded personnel reported three or more symptoms. As seen in Figure 5.2, the percentages of military personnel reporting three or more symptoms diminished considerably when only symptoms that were rated as moderate to severe were considered. Exposure to depleted uranium and/or aiding the wounded was more strongly associated with postconcussion-like symptoms than was blast exposure alone. Self-reported symptoms were more likely related to distressing experiences than to a mechanism that could cause mild TBI per se.

ENVIRONMENTAL EXTREMES

For the military service member, exposure to extremely cold temperatures can have a significant impact on comfort, combat readiness, and overall well-being. During 2008–2009, the overall rate of cold-related injuries in the military was 30.3 per 100,000 persons (Armed Forces Health Surveillance Center, 2009b). Frostbite was the most common cold-related injury. Besides local injury related to low-temperature exposure, systemic injuries can also occur. Reductions in core body temperature can alter cognitive performance and result in memory impairment, slowed response times,

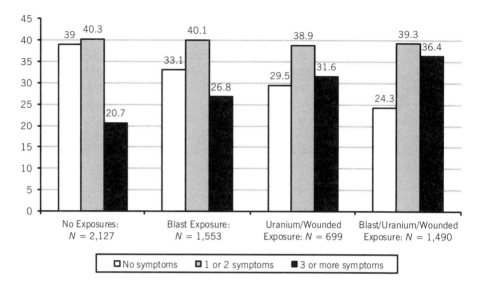

■ **FIGURE 5.1.** Percentages of U.K. military personnel reporting the presence of postconcussion-like symptoms. Data were extracted from Fear et al. (2008). "Wounded exposure" refers to aiding the wounded.

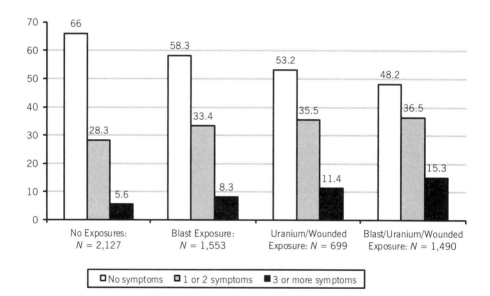

■ **FIGURE 5.2.** Percentages of U.K. military personnel reporting moderate–severe postconcussion-like symptoms. Data were extracted from Fear et al. (2008). "Wounded exposure" refers to aiding the wounded. The symptoms had to be endorsed as moderate or severe to be included in this figure.

impaired learning, decreased cognitive efficiency, and difficulties with reasoning abilities (Finnoff, 2008). Although these cognitive problems were originally postulated to be related to simple discomfort and distraction, research indicates that the cognitive dysfunction is caused by the direct temperature effects on the brain, through decreased release of central nervous system neurotransmitters in response to cold-induced catecholamine release (Shurtleff, Thomas, Schrot, Kowalski, & Harford, 1994).

Perhaps of greater concern is exposure to excessive heat. Excessive heat can result in heat exhaustion or heat stroke, exertional rhabdomyolysis, and acute hyponatremia (due to excessive water consumption in hot weather). In 2008, there were 299 cases of heat stroke and 1,467 cases of heat exhaustion among active duty service members (Armed Forces Health Surveillance Center, 2009e). The overall rate of heat stroke was 0.21 per 1,000 person-years, and the heat exhaustion rate was 1.04 per 1,000 person-years. In 2008, the rates of heat stroke and heat exhaustion were higher in combat-related personnel compared to other occupational groups, and nearly one-third higher among men than women. Even for otherwise healthy, physically active young adults, rhabdomyolysis is a significant threat during physical exertion under conditions of heat stress. Militarily relevant risk factors for exertional rhabdomyolysis, particularly among recruits, include rapid increase in physical activity, high heat and humidity, inadequate hydration, concurrent heat injury, and ongoing/recent acute infectious illness (Armed Forces Health Surveillance Center, 2009d).

Under environmental conditions of elevated temperature and heavy physical activity, some service members may dramatically increase fluid intake, which may result in acute hyponatremia. Acute hyponatremia is an osmotic imbalance between fluid outside and inside of cells. This imbalance results in an osmotic gradient in which water flows from outside to inside the cells of various organs, including the lungs and brain. The resulting cerebral edema increases intracranial pressure, which can decrease cerebral blood flow and disrupt brain function, thus potentially resulting in seizure or coma. This situation represents a neurological emergency in which the brainstem can herniate through the base of the skull, which can compromise cardiac and respiratory function and result in death (Armed Forces Health Surveillance Center, 2009c, 2009e).

Case reports of neurological and neuropsychological deficits following heat stroke in military populations have been documented (Rav-Acha, Shuvy, Hagag, Gomori, & Biran, 2007; Romero, Clement, & Belden, 2000). The neurological impairment in heat stroke is generally attributed to hyperthermia-induced neuronal damage (Rav-Acha et al., 2007). It is believed that hyperthermia can reduce cerebral blood flow during exercise, while it causes a simultaneous increase in brain metabolism. In addition, hyperthermia can cause severe hypoglycemia. This series of events can lead to brain glycogen depletion (Finnoff, 2008). Irritability, concentration problems, and delusions can occur in the postacute period following heat stroke. Historically, gait problems and cerebellar disturbances were also commonly observed (Mehta & Baker, 1970). However, a recent report described minimal cerebellar changes at follow-up (Rav-Acha et al., 2007). Neuropsychological evaluation showed reduced WAIS Digit Span backwards, impaired go/no-go, slowed performance on the Trail Making Test (Part A) and Grooved Pegboard Test, and increased perseverative errors on the Wisconsin Card Sorting Test. The deficits were described as motor and mental slowing, and frontal subcortical problems including disinhibition and perseveration. In another series of case reports, similar neuropsychological deficits were found (Romero et al., 2000).

The cognitive and psychological effects of high-altitude exposure have been known for decades (Bonnon, Noel-Jorand, & Therme, 1995; Lieberman, Protopapas, Reed, Youngs, & Kanki, 1994; Shukitt-Hale, Banderet, & Lieberman, 1991). Because of recent military operations in the mountainous areas of Afghanistan, the effects of high-altitude exposure have become a growing concern. Acute Mountain Sickness (AMS) is a syndrome associated with an inadequate adaptation to a hypoxic environment. It is manifested by a number of nonspecific symptoms, most typically headache, dizziness, fatigue, sleep disturbance, and gastrointestinal symptoms (Virues-Ortega, Buela-Casal, Garrido, & Alcazar, 2004). AMS may, however, be different from concurrent neuropsychological or behavioral alterations associated with high altitude. AMS is related to sudden ascension in the absence of adequate bodily adjustment. Neurobehavioral changes are thought to be related to the consequences of reduced oxygen regardless of the level of acclimatization. That is, neuropsychological changes may be present regardless of whether an individual displays symptoms of AMS (Virues-Ortega et al., 2004).

In addition to the altitude-related hypoxemia, there are significant alterations in cerebral blood flow. These alterations may result in increased cerebral intravascular pressure and cerebral edema (Finnoff, 2008). It has been hypothesized that there is a disruption of subcortical basal ganglia pathways leading to the prefrontal cortex, related to mild anoxia/hypoxia in these subcortical circuits (Lieberman et al., 1994). Virues-Ortega and colleagues, in a comprehensive review of the neuropsychological effects of high altitude (Virues-Ortega et al., 2004), concluded that "there is an unquestionable impairment of motor, perceptive, memory, and executive functions as an acute effect and at least with middle-term duration" (p. 217). These findings, however, have not been entirely consistent across studies. One study (Pavlicek et al., 2005), for example, involved three groups of individuals who underwent simulated high-altitude conditions at different altitudes for a 30-minute period. No differences were noted in word fluency, word association, or collateralized lexical decision performance between groups. This finding occurred despite significant oxygen desaturation and a drop in blood pressure indicating nascent hypoxia. The authors concluded that cognitive flexibility is largely insensitive to hypoxia, at least for the relatively short period to which these individuals were exposed.

In addition to cognitive degradation, psychiatric changes have been reported. New-onset anxiety-related disorders have been reported in climbers in Nepal, including individuals with no prior psychiatric history (Fagenholz, Murray, Gutman, Findley, & Harris, 2007). Perceptual changes including visual and auditory hallucinations have been reported, although social deprivation and acute stress seem to also play a role in psychiatric changes (Brugger, Regard, Landis, & Oelz, 1999).

SUMMARY AND CONCLUSIONS

The military workplace, especially the battlefield, has the potential to cause significant physical, psychological, and cognitive problems for service members. Such problems can result from a direct attack from the enemy or from exposure to the combat environment itself. Combat-related injuries include gunshot wounds and, more frequently, blast injuries. Blasts can result in orthopedic, soft tissue, facial, ocular, auditory-vestibular, closed-head, and open-head injuries. Polytrauma patients, even without brain injury, present with high rates of psychological and neurobehavioral symptoms, including memory problems, significant mood symptoms, amotivation, and guilt (Frenisy et al., 2006).

Hazards related to the combat operational environment include exposure to extreme temperatures (hot and cold), high altitudes, and exposure to toxic substances. Rhabdomyolysis and acute hyponatremia are significant threats during physical exertion under conditions of heat stress, both of which affect major organ systems, including the brain (Armed Forces Health Surveillance Center, 2009b; Romero et al., 2000). High-altitude exposure has become a growing concern during recent military operations, particularly in the mountainous regions of Afghanistan. Acute Mountain Sickness with its associated headache, dizziness, fatigue, sleep disturbance, and gastrointestinal symptoms, and altitude-related hypoxemia with its associated increased cerebral intravascular pressure and cerebral edema, are conditions related to inadequate adaptation to hypoxic environments (Virues-Ortega et al., 2004).

Other hazards related to the combat operational environment include exposure to neurotoxins, infectious diseases, and other pathogens. Neurotoxins include DU and the pharmacologic countermeasures used in response to chemical nerve agents, including those employed prophylactically. Although the risk of DU poisoning from handling DU munitions is minimal, the risk of poisoning increases substantially when individuals come in contact with DU dust or shrapnel produced by hard-target strikes

(Bolton & Foster, 2002). Regardless of actual harm, exposure to DU and/ or aiding the wounded has been associated with postdeployment reporting of physical, emotional, and cognitive symptoms (Fear et al., 2009).

Traumatic brain injuries in military personnel predominately occur as a result of closed-head trauma. Penetrating or open-head injuries are far less common. According to the DoD, there were 27,862 medically verified brain injuries coded in the DoD Health Care System in 2009, 21,859 of which were classified as mild. Minimal extracranial injuries and lower reported pain predict better outcomes for return to work after MTBI (Stulemeijer et al., 2006).

Military personnel often experience significant mental health problems, such as PTSD (Ramchand et al., 2010) and depression. There is a positive linear relation between the number of combat experiences and the rate of PTSD. Although PTSD is associated with smaller hippocampal volume (Kitayama et al., 2005) and small decrements in memory functioning (i.e., an effect size of 0.2) (Brewin et al., 2007), research methodologies do not permit us to determine definitively whether these differences existed premorbidly or developed after PTSD (and comorbid conditions). Increasingly, researchers are noting that people with PTSD might have lower neuropsychological test scores as a *preexisting* characteristic (Gilbertson et al., 2006; Parslow & Jorm, 2007). For example, there is considerable evidence of differences in intelligence in people who develop PTSD versus those who do not (Brandes et al., 2002; Macklin et al., 1998; Vasterling et al., 2002). There is also evidence that reduced hippocampal volume may be a preexisting factor that increases the risk for developing PTSD, with sufficient trauma exposure (e.g., (Gilbertson et al., 2002). PTSD has been associated with TBI, though evidence of the existence of PTSD remains inconclusive in the presence of brain injuries that include a loss of consciousness and posttraumatic amnesia. Evaluating cognition in people with a history of mild TBI, PTSD, or both, is complex in regards to (1) subjective symptoms, (2) objective test results, and (3) determining the cause of a given finding. Complicating the picture, individuals with a history of mild TBI, PTSD, or both, can also have comorbid depression, substance abuse, or chronic pain. In spite of considerable advances in our understanding of the cognitive and neurobehavioral consequences of injury in military and civilian contexts, many questions remain unanswered. Although there is mounting evidence of associations between functional impairment and environmental, physical, and psychological factors, there is a paucity of research that examines the specific mechanisms underlying these associations. In the case of MTBI, for example, postdeployment functional difficulties that are sometimes experienced may be related to psychological responses, neurological damage, or an interaction between the two. The challenge is to understand the relative contribution of each factor. In the military, understanding the mechanisms involved across the range of identified injuries will facilitate more accurate diagnostic and screening instruments and potentially shed light on better treatments that target these confounding mechanisms. Maximal outcomes can best be achieved by understanding those factors that maintain the effects of injury and stifle our efforts at rehabilitation.

ACKNOWLEDGMENT

The views expressed in this chapter are those of the authors and do not reflect the official policy of the Department of Army, Department of Defense, or U.S. government.

NOTES

1. It is important to note that 9.4% screened positive using the liberal definition and 5.0% screened positive using the strict definition *prior to deployment*. Whether these are false positive cases, or service members with significant pre-existing problems, is unclear.
2. After controlling for type of traumatic injury, Injury Severity Score, age, pain at 12 months, and prior psychiatric disorder.
3. Who had indications of cerebral involvement and who had been treated with antimalarial medications.
4. These effects lasted for 2 weeks with one patient.

REFERENCES

Adler, A. B., Bliese, P. D., McGurk, D., Hoge, C. W., & Castro, C. A. (2009). Battlemind debriefing and battlemind training as early interventions with soldiers returning from Iraq: Randomization by platoon. *Journal of Consulting and Clinical Psychology, 77*(5), 928–940.

Amourette, C., Lamproglou, I., Barbier, L., Fauquette, W., Zoppe, A., Viret, R., et al. (2009). Gulf War illness: Effects of repeated stress and pyridostigmine treatment on blood-brain barrier permeability and cholinesterase activity in rat brain. *Behavioral Brain Research, 203*(2), 207–214.

Armed Forces Health Surveillance Center. (2009a). Absolute and relative morbidity burdens attributable to various illnesses and injuries, U.S. armed forces 2008. *Medical Surveillance Monthly Report, 16*(4), 16–21.

Armed Forces Health Surveillance Center. (2009b). Cold weather-related injuries, U.S. armed forces July 2004–June 2009. *Medical Surveillance Monthly Report, 16*(9), 2–5.

Armed Forces Health Surveillance Center. (2009c). Update: Exercise-associated hyponatremia due to excessive water consumption, active component, U.S. armed forces, 1999–2008. *Medical Surveillance Monthly Report, 16*(3), 14–17.

Armed Forces Health Surveillance Center. (2009d). Update: Exertional rhabdomyolysis among active component members, U.S. armed forces, 2004–2008. *Medical Surveillance Monthly Report, 16*(3), 10–13.

Armed Forces Health Surveillance Center. (2009e). Update: Heat injuries among active component members, U.S. armed forces, 2008. *Medical Surveillance Monthly Report, 16*(3), 8–9.

Aronson, N. E., Sanders, J. W., & Moran, K. A. (2006). Emerging infections—In harms way: Infections in deployed American military forces. *Clinical Infectious Diseases, 43*(8), 1045–1051.

Baker, D. G., Heppner, P., Afari, N., Nunnink, S., Kilmer, M., Simmons, A., et al. (2009). Trauma exposure, branch of service, and physical injury in relation to mental health among U.S. veterans returning From Iraq and Afghanistan. *Military Medicine, 174*(8), 773–778.

Bolton, J. P., & Foster, C. R. (2002). Battlefield use of depleted uranium and the health of veterans. *Journal of the Royal Army Medical Corps, 148*(3), 221–229.

Bombardier, C. H., Fann, J. R., Temkin, N., Esselman, P. C., Pelzer, E., Keough, M., et al. (2006). Posttraumatic stress disorder symptoms during the first six months after traumatic brain injury. *Journal of Neuropsychiatry and Clinical Neurosciences, 18*(4), 501–508.

Bonnon, M., Noel-Jorand, M. C., & Therme, P. (1995). Psychological changes during altitude hypoxia. *Aviation, Space, and Environmental Medicine, 66*(4), 330–335.

Brandes, D., Ben-Schachar, G., Gilboa, A., Bonne, O., Freedman, S., & Shalev, A. Y. (2002). PTSD symptoms and cognitive performance in recent trauma survivors. *Psychiatry Research, 110*(3), 231–238.

Bremner, J. D., Randall, P., Scott, T. M., Capelli, S., Delaney, R., McCarthy, G., et al. (1995). Deficits in short-term memory in adult survivors of childhood abuse. *Psychiatry Research, 59*(1–2), 97–107.

Bremner, J. D., Scott, T. M., Delaney, R. C., Southwick, S. M., Mason, J. W., Johnson, D. R., et al. (1993). Deficits in short-term memory in posttraumatic stress disorder. *American Journal of Psychiatry, 150*(7), 1015–1019.

Brewin, C. R., Kleiner, J. S., Vasterling, J. J., & Field, A. P. (2007). Memory for emotionally neutral information in posttraumatic stress disorder: A meta-analytic investigation. *Journal of Abnormal Psychology, 116*(3), 448–463.

Brugger, P., Regard, M., Landis, T., & Oelz, O. (1999). Hallucinatory experiences in extreme-altitude climbers. *Neuropsychiatry, Neuropsychology, and Behavioral Neurology, 12*(1), 67–71.

Bryant, R. A. (1996). Posttraumatic stress disorder, flashbacks, and pseudomemories in closed head injury. *Journal of Traumatic Stress, 9*(3), 621–629.

Bryant, R. A. (2008). Disentangling mild traumatic brain injury and stress reactions. *New England Journal of Medicine, 358*(5), 525–527.

Bryant, R. A., Creamer, M., O'Donnell, M., Silove, D., Clark, C. R., & McFarlane, A. C. (2009). Post-traumatic amnesia and the nature of post-traumatic stress disorder after mild traumatic brain injury. *Journal of the International Neuropsychological Society, 15*(6), 862–867.

Bryant, R. A., & Harvey, A. G. (1998). Traumatic memories and pseudomemories in posttraumatic stress disorder. *Applied Cognitive Psychology, 12*(1), 81–88.

Bryant, R. A., Marosszeky, J. E., Crooks, J., & Gurka, J. A. (2000). Posttraumatic stress disorder after severe traumatic brain injury. *American Journal of Psychiatry, 157*(4), 629–631.

Bryant, R. A., O'Donnell, M. L., Creamer, M., McFarlane, A. C., Clark, C. R., & Silove, D. (2010). The psychiatric sequelae of traumatic injury. *American Journal of Psychiatry, 167*(3), 312–320.

Buckley, T. C., Blanchard, E. B., & Neill, W. T. (2000). Information processing and

PTSD: A review of the empirical literature. *Clinical Psychology Review, 20*(8), 1041–1065.

Caldwell, J. A., Jr., Stephens, R. L., Carter, D. J., & Jones, H. D. (1992). Effects of 2 mg and 4 mg atropine sulfate on the performance of U.S. Army helicopter pilots. *Aviation, Space, and Environmental Medicine, 63*(10), 857–864.

Capella-McDonnall, M. E. (2005). The effects of single and dual sensory loss on symptoms of depression in the elderly. *International Journal of Geriatric Psychiatry, 20*(9), 855–861.

Cerasoli, D. M., & Lenz, D. E. (2002). Nerve agent bioscavengers: Protection with reduced behavioral effects. *Military Psychology, 14*(2), 121–143.

Cernak, I., Savic, J., Ignjatovic, D., & Jevtic, M. (1999). Blast injury from explosive munitions. *Journal of Trauma, 47*(1), 96–103; discussion 103–104.

Chambers, L. W., Rhee, P., Baker, B. C., Perciballi, J., Cubano, M., Compeggie, M., et al. (2005). Initial experience of U.S. Marine Corps forward resuscitative surgical system during Operation Iraqi Freedom. *Archives of Surgery, 140*(1), 26–32.

Chia, E. M., Mitchell, P., Rochtchina, E., Foran, S., Golding, M., & Wang, J. J. (2006). Association between vision and hearing impairments and their combined effects on quality of life. *Archives of Ophthalmology, 124*(10), 1465–1470.

Chunge, C. N., Gachihi, G., & Muigai, R. (1985). Is neurological involvement possible in visceral leishmaniasis in Kenya. *Transactions of the Royal Society of Tropical Medicine and Hygiene, 79*(6), 872.

Croft, A. M., Whitehouse, D. P., Cook, G. C., & Beer, M. D. (2002). Safety evaluation of the drugs available to prevent malaria. *Expert Opinion on Drug Safety, 1*(1), 19–27.

Crowell, T. A., Kieffer, K. M., Siders, C. A., & Vanderploeg, R. D. (2002). Neuropsychological findings in combat-related posttraumatic stress disorder. *The Clinical Neuropsychologist, 16*(3), 310–321.

Danckwerts, A., & Leathem, J. (2003). Questioning the link between PTSD and cognitive dysfunction. *Neuropsychology Reviews, 13*(4), 221–235.

Dau, B., Oda, G., & Holodniy, M. (2009). Infectious complications in OIF/OEF veterans with traumatic brain injury. *Journal of Rehabilitation Research and Development, 46*(6), 673–684.

DeWitt, D. S., & Prough, D. S. (2009). Blast-induced brain injury and posttraumatic hypotension and hypoxemia. *Journal of Neurotrauma, 26*(6), 877–887.

DeWitt, D. S., Prough, D. S., Deal, D. D., Vines, S. M., & Hoen, H. (1996). Hypertonic saline does not improve cerebral oxygen delivery after head injury and mild hemorrhage in cats. *Critical Care Medicine, 24*(1), 109–117.

Fagenholz, P. J., Murray, A. F., Gutman, J. A., Findley, J. K., & Harris, N. S. (2007). New-onset anxiety disorders at high altitude. *Wilderness and Environmental Medicine, 18*(4), 312–316.

Fear, N. T., Jones, E., Groom, M., Greenberg, N., Hull, L., Hodgetts, T. J., et al. (2008). Symptoms of post-concussional syndrome are non-specifically related to mild traumatic brain injury in U.K. armed forces personnel on return from deployment in Iraq: An analysis of self-reported data. *Psychological Medicine*, 1–9.

Fear, N. T., Jones, E., Groom, M., Greenberg, N., Hull, L., Hodgetts, T. J., et al. (2009). Symptoms of post-concussional syndrome are non-specifically related to mild traumatic brain injury in U.K. armed forces personnel on return from deployment in Iraq: An analysis of self-reported data. *Psychological Medicine, 39*(8), 1379–1387.

Fear, N. T., Jones, M., Murphy, D., Hull, L., Iversen, A. C., Coker, B., et al. (2010).

What are the consequences of deployment to Iraq and Afghanistan on the mental health of the U.K. armed forces? A cohort study. *Lancet, 375*(9728), 1783–1797.

Ferrier-Auerbach, A. G., Erbes, C. R., Polusny, M. A., Rath, C. O. L. M., & Sponheim, S. R. (2009). Predictors of emotional distress reported by soldiers in the combat zone. *Journal of Psychiatric Research, 44*(7), 470–476.

Finnoff, J. T. (2008). Environmental effects on brain function. *Current Sports Medicine Reports, 7*(1), 28–32 10.1097/1001.CSMR.0000308669.0000399816.00003086 71.

French, L. M., McCrea, M., & Baggett, M. R. (2008). The Military Acute Concussion Evaluation (MACE). *Journal of Special Operations Medicine, 8*(1), 68–77.

Frenisy, M. C., Benony, H., Chahraoui, K., Minot, D., d'Athis, P., Pinoit, J. M., et al. (2006). Brain injured patients versus multiple trauma patients: Some neurobehavioral and psychopathological aspects. *Journal of Trauma, 60*(5), 1018–1026.

Garg, R. K., Karak, B., & Misra, S. (1999). Neurological manifestations of malaria: An update. *Neurology India, 47*(2), 85–91.

Gaylord, K. M., Cooper, D. B., Mercado, J. M., Kennedy, J. E., Yoder, L. H., & Holcomb, J. B. (2008). Incidence of posttraumatic stress disorder and mild traumatic brain injury in burned service members: Preliminary report. *Journal of Trauma, 64*(2 Suppl.), S200–205; discussion S205–S206.

Geuze, E., Vermetten, E., de Kloet, C. S., Hijman, R., & Westenberg, H. G. (2009). Neuropsychological performance is related to current social and occupational functioning in veterans with posttraumatic stress disorder. *Depression and Anxiety, 26*(1), 7–15.

Gil, S., Caspi, Y., Ben-Ari, I. Z., Koren, D., & Klein, E. (2005). Does memory of a traumatic event increase the risk for posttraumatic stress disorder in patients with traumatic brain injury? A prospective study. *American Journal of Psychiatry, 162*(5), 963–969.

Gilbertson, M. W., Paulus, L. A., Williston, S. K., Gurvits, T. V., Lasko, N. B., Pitman, R. K., et al. (2006). Neurocognitive function in monozygotic twins discordant for combat exposure: Relationship to posttraumatic stress disorder. *Journal of Abnormal Psychology, 115*(3), 484–495.

Gilbertson, M. W., Shenton, M. E., Ciszewski, A., Kasai, K., Lasko, N. B., Orr, S. P., et al. (2002). Smaller hippocampal volume predicts pathologic vulnerability to psychological trauma. *Nature Neuroscience, 5*(11), 1242–1247.

Glaesser, J., Neuner, F., Lutgehetmann, R., Schmidt, R., & Elbert, T. (2004). Posttraumatic stress disorder in patients with traumatic brain injury. *BMC Psychiatry, 4*, 5.

Goodrich, G. L., Kirby, J., Cockerham, G., Ingalla, S. P., & Lew, H. L. (2007). Visual function in patients of a polytrauma rehabilitation center: A descriptive study. *Journal of Rehabilitation Research and Development, 44*(7), 929–936.

Grafman, J., Jonas, B. S., Martin, A., Salazar, A. M., Weingartner, H., Ludlow, C., et al. (1988). Intellectual function following penetrating head injury in Vietnam veterans. *Brain, 111*(Pt. 1), 169–184.

Grieger, T. A., Cozza, S. J., Ursano, R. J., Hoge, C., Martinez, P. E., Engel, C. C., et al. (2006). Posttraumatic stress disorder and depression in battle-injured soldiers. *American Journal of Psychiatry, 163*(10), 1777–1783; quiz 1860.

Gurvits, T. V., Metzger, L. J., Lasko, N. B., Cannistraro, P. A., Tarhan, A. S., Gilbertson, M. W., et al. (2006). Subtle neurologic compromise as a vulnerability factor for combat-related posttraumatic stress disorder: Results of a twin study. *Archives of General Psychiatry, 63*(5), 571–576.

Harvey, A. G., & Bryant, R. A. (2000). Two-year prospective evaluation of the relationship between acute stress disorder and posttraumatic stress disorder following mild traumatic brain injury. *American Journal of Psychiatry, 157*(4), 626–628.

Harvey, A. G., & Bryant, R. A. (2001). Reconstructing trauma memories: A prospective study of "amnesic" trauma survivors. *Journal of Traumatic Stress, 14*(2), 277–282.

Hickling, E. J., Gillen, R., Blanchard, E. B., Buckley, T., & Taylor, A. (1998). Traumatic brain injury and posttraumatic stress disorder: A preliminary investigation of neuropsychological test results in PTSD secondary to motor vehicle accidents. *Brain Injury, 12*(4), 265–274.

Hill, J. J., III, Mobo, B. H., Jr., & Cullen, M. R. (2009). Separating deployment-related traumatic brain injury and posttraumatic stress disorder in veterans: Preliminary findings from the Veterans Affairs traumatic brain injury screening program. *American Journal of Physical Medicine and Rehabilitation, 88*(8), 605–614.

Hoge, C. W., Castro, C. A., Messer, S. C., McGurk, D., Cotting, D. I., & Koffman, R. L. (2004). Combat duty in Iraq and Afghanistan, mental health problems, and barriers to care. *New England Journal of Medicine, 351*(1), 13–22.

Hoge, C. W., McGurk, D., Thomas, J. L., Cox, A. L., Engel, C. C., & Castro, C. A. (2008). Mild traumatic brain injury in U.S. soldiers returning from Iraq. *New England Journal of Medicine, 358*(5), 453–463.

Hoge, C. W., Terhakopian, A., Castro, C. A., Messer, S. C., & Engel, C. C. (2007). Association of posttraumatic stress disorder with somatic symptoms, health care visits, and absenteeism among Iraq war veterans. *American Journal of Psychiatry, 164*(1), 150–153.

Horner, M. D., & Hamner, M. B. (2002). Neurocognitive functioning in posttraumatic stress disorder. *Neuropsychology Reviews, 12*(1), 15–30.

Institute of Medicine. (2008). *Gulf War and health: Updated literature review of depleted uranium.* Retrieved May 5, 2010, from *www.iom.edu/Reports/2008. Gulf-War-Health-Updated-Literature-Review-Depleted-Uranium.aspx.*

Iversen, A. C., van Staden, L., Hughes, J. H., Browne, T., Hull, L., Hall, J., et al. (2009). The prevalence of common mental disorders and PTSD in the U.K. military: Using data from a clinical interview-based study. *BMC Psychiatry, 9*, 68.

Ivins, B. J., Schwab, K. A., Baker, G., & Warden, D. L. (2006). Hospital admissions associated with traumatic brain injury in the U.S. Army during peacetime: 1990s trends. *Neuroepidemiology, 27*(3), 154–163.

Jelinek, L., Jacobsen, D., Kellner, M., Larbig, F., Biesold, K. H., Barre, K., et al. (2006). Verbal and nonverbal memory functioning in posttraumatic stress disorder (PTSD). *Journal of Clinical and Experimental Neuropsychology, 28*(6), 940–948.

Jenkins, M. A., Langlais, P. J., Delis, D. A., & Cohen, R. A. (2000). Attentional dysfunction associated with posttraumatic stress disorder among rape survivors. *The Clinical Neuropsychologist, 14*(1), 7–12.

Kang, H. K., Natelson, B. H., Mahan, C. M., Lee, K. Y., & Murphy, F. M. (2003). Posttraumatic stress disorder and chronic fatigue syndrome-like illness among Gulf War veterans: A population-based survey of 30,000 veterans. *American Journal of Epidemiology, 157*(2), 141–148.

Karak, B., Garg, R. K., Misra, S., & Sharma, A. M. (1998). Neurological manifestations in a patient with visceral leishmaniasis. *Postgraduate Medical Journal, 74*(873), 423–425.

Kitayama, N., Vaccarino, V., Kutner, M., Weiss, P., & Bremner, J. D. (2005). Magnetic resonance imaging (MRI) measurement of hippocampal volume in posttraumatic stress disorder: A meta-analysis. *Journal of Affective Disorders, 88*(1), 79–86.

Koenigs, M., Huey, E. D., Raymont, V., Cheon, B., Solomon, J., Wassermann, E. M., et al. (2008). Focal brain damage protects against post-traumatic stress disorder in combat veterans. *Nature Neuroscience, 11*(2), 232–237.

Koren, D., Norman, D., Cohen, A., Berman, J., & Klein, E. M. (2005). Increased PTSD risk with combat-related injury: A matched comparison study of injured and uninjured soldiers experiencing the same combat events. *American Journal of Psychiatry, 162*(2), 276–282.

Lanius, R. A., Bluhm, R., Lanius, U., & Pain, C. (2006). A review of neuroimaging studies in PTSD: Heterogeneity of response to symptom provocation. *Journal of Psychiatric Research, 40*(8), 709–729.

Levin, H. S., Brown, S. A., Song, J. X., McCauley, S. R., Boake, C., Contant, C. F., et al. (2001). Depression and posttraumatic stress disorder at three months after mild to moderate traumatic brain injury. *Journal of Clinical and Experimental Neuropsychology, 23*(6), 754–769.

Lew, H. L., Garvert, D. W., Pogoda, T. K., Hsu, P.-T., Devine, J. M., White, D. K., et al. (2009a). Auditory and visual impairments in patients with blast-related traumatic brain injury: Effect of dual sensory impairment on Functional Independence Measure. *Journal of Rehabilitation Research and Development, 46*(6), 819–826.

Lew, H. L., Jerger, J. F., Guillory, S. B., & Henry, J. A. (2007). Auditory dysfunction in traumatic brain injury. *Journal of Rehabilitation Research and Development, 44*(7), 921–928.

Lew, H. L., Otis, J. D., Tun, C., Kerns, R. D., Clark, M. E., & Cifu, D. X. (2009b). Prevalence of chronic pain, posttraumatic stress disorder, and persistent post-concussive symptoms in OIF/OEF veterans: Polytrauma clinical triad. *Journal of Rehabilitation Research and Development, 46*(6), 697–702.

Lieberman, P., Protopapas, A., Reed, E., Youngs, J. W., & Kanki, B. G. (1994). Cognitive defects at altitude. *Nature, 372*(6504), 325.

MacGregor, A. J., Shaffer, R. A., Dougherty, A. L., Galarneau, M. R., Raman, R., Baker, D. G., et al. (2010). Prevalence and psychological correlates of traumatic brain injury in Operation Iraqi Freedom. *Journal of Head Trauma Rehabilitation, 25*(1), 1–8.

Macklin, M. L., Metzger, L. J., Litz, B. T., McNally, R. J., Lasko, N. B., Orr, S. P., et al. (1998). Lower precombat intelligence is a risk factor for posttraumatic stress disorder. *Journal of Consulting and Clinical Psychology, 66*(2), 323–326.

Markley, J. D., & Edmond, M. B. (2009). Post-malaria neurological syndrome: A case report and review of the literature. *Journal of Travel Medicine, 16*(6), 424–430.

Mather, F. J., Tate, R. L., & Hannan, T. J. (2003). Post-traumatic stress disorder in children following road traffic accidents: A comparison of those with and without mild traumatic brain injury. *Brain Injury, 17*(12), 1077–1087.

Mayorga, M. A. (1997). The pathology of primary blast overpressure injury. *Toxicology, 121*(1), 17–28.

Mayou, R. A., Black, J., & Bryant, B. (2000). Unconsciousness, amnesia and psychiatric symptoms following road traffic accident injury. *British Journal of Psychiatry, 177*, 540–545.

McDiarmid, M. A., Engelhardt, S. M., Oliver, M., Gucer, P., Wilson, P. D., Kane, R., et al. (2007). Health surveillance of Gulf War I veterans exposed to depleted uranium: Updating the cohort. *Health Physics, 93*(1), 60–73.

McDiarmid, M. A., Keogh, J. P., Hooper, F. J., McPhaul, K., Squibb, K., Kane, R., et al. (2000). Health effects of depleted uranium on exposed Gulf War veterans. *Environmental Research, 82*(2), 168–180.

McDiarmid, M. A., Squibb, K., Engelhardt, S., Oliver, M., Gucer, P., Wilson, P. D., et al. (2001). Surveillance of depleted uranium exposed Gulf War veterans: Health effects observed in an enlarged "friendly fire" cohort. *Journal of Occupational and Environmental Medicine, 43*(12), 991–1000.

McDonough, J. H. (2002). Performance impacts of nerve agents and their pharmacological countermeasures. *Military Psychology, 14*(2), 93–119.

Meares, S., Shores, E. A., Taylor, A. J., Batchelor, J., Bryant, R. A., Baguley, I. J., et al. (2008). Mild traumatic brain injury does not predict acute postconcussion syndrome. *Journal of Neurology, Neurosurgery and Psychiatry, 79*(3), 300–306.

Mehta, A. C., & Baker, R. N. (1970). Persistent neurological deficits in heat stroke. *Neurology, 20*(4), 336–340.

Mustafa, D. (1965). Neurological disturbances in visceral leishmaniasis. *Journal of Tropical Medicine and Hygiene, 68*(10), 248–250.

Myers, T. M., Sun, W., Saxena, A., Doctor, B. P., Bonvillain, A. J., & Clark, M. G. (2010). Systemic administration of the potential countermeasure huperzine reversibly inhibits central and peripheral acetylcholinesterase activity without adverse cognitive-behavioral effects. *Pharmacology, Biochemistry, and Behavior, 94*(3), 477–481.

Nelson, L. A., Yoash-Gantz, R. E., Pickett, T. C., & Campbell, T. A. (2009). Relationship between processing speed and executive functioning performance among OEF/OIF veterans: Implications for postdeployment rehabilitation. *Journal of Head Trauma Rehabilitation, 24*(1), 32–40.

Ommaya, A. K., Ommaya, A. K., Dannenberg, A. L., & Salazar, A. M. (1996a). Causation, incidence, and costs of traumatic brain injury in the U.S. military medical system. *Journal of Trauma, 40*(2), 211–217.

Ommaya, A. K., Salazar, A. M., Dannenberg, A. L., Ommaya, A. K., Chervinsky, A. B., & Schwab, K. (1996b). Outcome after traumatic brain injury in the U.S. military medical system. *Journal of Trauma, 41*(6), 972–975.

Owens, B. D., Kragh, J. F., Jr., Wenke, J. C., Macaitis, J., Wade, C. E., & Holcomb, J. B. (2008). Combat wounds in Operation Iraqi Freedom and Operation Enduring Freedom. *Journal of Trauma, 64*(2), 295–299.

Parslow, R. A., & Jorm, A. F. (2007). Pretrauma and posttrauma neurocognitive functioning and PTSD symptoms in a community sample of young adults. *American Journal of Psychiatry, 164*(3), 509–515.

Patchen, L. C., Campbell, C. C., & Williams, S. B. (1989). Neurologic reactions after a therapeutic dose of mefloquine. *New England Journal of Medicine, 321*(20), 1415–1416.

Pavlicek, V., Schirlo, C., Nebel, A., Regard, M., Koller, E. A., & Brugger, P. (2005). Cognitive and emotional processing at high altitude. *Aviation, Space, and Environmental Medicine, 76*(1), 28–33.

Pietrzak, R. H., Johnson, D. C., Goldstein, M. B., Malley, J. C., & Southwick, S. M. (2009). Posttraumatic stress disorder mediates the relationship between mild traumatic brain injury and health and psychosocial functioning in veterans of Operations Enduring Freedom and Iraqi Freedom. *Journal of Nervous and Mental Disease, 197*(10), 748–753.

Ramchand, R., Schell, T. L., Karney, B. R., Osilla, K. C., Burns, R. M., & Caldarone, L. B. (2010). Disparate prevalence estimates of PTSD among service members who served in Iraq and Afghanistan: Possible explanations. *Journal of Traumatic Stress, 23*(1), 59–68.

Rauch, S. L., Shin, L. M., & Phelps, E. A. (2006). Neurocircuitry models of posttraumatic stress disorder and extinction: Human neuroimaging research—past, present, and future. *Biological Psychiatry, 60*(4), 376–382.

Rav-Acha, M., Shuvy, M., Hagag, S., Gomori, M., & Biran, I. (2007). Unique persistent neurological sequelae of heat stroke. *Military Medicine, 172*(6), 603–606.

Raymont, V., Greathouse, A., Reding, K., Lipsky, R., Salazar, A., & Grafman, J. (2008). Demographic, structural and genetic predictors of late cognitive decline after penetrating head injury. *Brain, 131*(Pt. 2), 543–558.

Richardson, E. D., Varney, N. R., Roberts, R. J., Springer, J. A., & Wood, P. S. (1997). Long-term cognitive sequelae of cerebral malaria in Vietnam veterans. *Applied Neuropsychology, 4*(4), 238–243.

Romero, J. J., Clement, P. F., & Belden, C. (2000). Neuropsychological sequelae of heat stroke: Report of three cases and discussion. *Military Medicine, 165*(6), 500–503.

Rona, R. J., Hooper, R., Jones, M., Iversen, A. C., Hull, L., Murphy, D., et al. (2009). The contribution of prior psychological symptoms and combat exposure to post Iraq deployment mental health in the UK military. *Journal of Traumatic Stress, 22*(1), 11–19.

Salazar, A. M., Schwab, K., & Grafman, J. H. (1995). Penetrating injuries in the Vietnam War. Traumatic unconsciousness, epilepsy, and psychosocial outcome. *Neurosurgery Clinics of North America, 6*(4), 715–726.

Sayer, N. A., Chiros, C. E., Sigford, B., Scott, S., Clothier, B., Pickett, T., et al. (2008). Characteristics and rehabilitation outcomes among patients with blast and other injuries sustained during the Global War on Terror. *Archives of Physical Medicine and Rehabilitation, 89*(1), 163–170.

Sbordone, R. J., & Liter, J. C. (1995). Mild traumatic brain injury does not produce post-traumatic stress disorder. *Brain Injury, 9*, 405–412.

Schneiderman, A. I., Braver, E. R., & Kang, H. K. (2008). Understanding sequelae of injury mechanisms and mild traumatic brain injury incurred during the conflicts in Iraq and Afghanistan: Persistent postconcussive symptoms and posttraumatic stress disorder. *American Journal of Epidemiology, 167*(12), 1446–1452.

Schwab, K., Grafman, J., Salazar, A. M., & Kraft, J. (1993). Residual impairments and work status 15 years after penetrating head injury: Report from the Vietnam Head Injury Study. *Neurology, 43*(1), 95–103.

Shafi, S., & Gentilello, L. (2005). Hypotension does not increase mortality in brain-injured patients more than it does in non-brain-injured Patients. *Journal of Trauma, 59*(4), 830–834; discussion 834–835.

Shephard, B. (2001). *A war of nerves: Soldiers and psychiatrists in the twentieth century.* Cambridge, MA: Harvard University Press.

Shukitt-Hale, B., Banderet, L. E., & Lieberman, H. R. (1991). Relationships between symptoms, moods, performance, and acute mountain sickness at 4,700 meters. *Aviation, Space, and Environmental Medicine, 62*(9, Pt. 1), 865–869.

Shurtleff, D., Thomas, J. R., Schrot, J., Kowalski, K., & Harford, R. (1994). Tyrosine reverses a cold-induced working memory deficit in humans. *Pharmacology, Biochemistry, and Behavior, 47*(4), 935–941.

Stansbury, L. G., Lalliss, S. J., Branstetter, J. G., Bagg, M. R., & Holcomb, J. B. (2008). Amputations in U.S. military personnel in the current conflicts in Afghanistan and Iraq. *Journal of Orthopaedic Trauma, 22*(1), 43–46.

Stein, M. B., Hanna, C., Vaerum, V., & Koverola, C. (1999). Memory functioning in adult women traumatized by childhood sexual abuse. *Journal of Traumatic Stress, 12*(3), 527–534.

Stulemeijer, M., van der Werf, S. P., Jacobs, B., Biert, J., van Vugt, A. B., Brauer, J. M., et al. (2006). Impact of additional extracranial injuries on outcome after mild traumatic brain injury. *Journal of Neurotrauma, 23*(10), 1561–1569.

Sutker, P. B., Allain, A. N., Jr., Johnson, J. L., & Butters, N. M. (1992). Memory and learning performances in POW survivors with history of malnutrition and combat veteran controls. *Archives of Clinical Neuropsychology, 7*(5), 431–444.

Tan, G., Fink, B., Dao, T. K., Hebert, R., Farmer, L. S., Sanders, A., et al. (2009). Associations among pain, PTSD, mTBI, and heart rate variability in veterans of Operation Enduring and Iraqi Freedom: A pilot study. *Pain Medicine, 10*(7), 1237–1245.

Tanielian, T., & Jaycox, L. H. (Eds.). (2008). *Invisible wounds of war: Psychological and cognitive injuries, their consequences, and services to assist recovery.* Santa Monica, CA: Rand Corporation.

TBI Task Force Report. (2008). Retrieved May 17, 2010, from *www.armymedicine. army.mil/reports/tbi/TBITaskForceReportJanuary2008.pdf.*

Terrio, H., Brenner, L. A., Ivins, B., Cho, J. M., Helmick, K., Schwab, K., et al. (2009). Traumatic brain injury screening: Preliminary findings in a U.S. Army brigade combat team. *Journal of Head Trauma Rehabilitation, 24*(1), 14–23.

Toomey, R., Kang, H. K., Karlinsky, J., Baker, D. G., Vasterling, J. J., Alpern, R., et al. (2007). Mental health of U.S. Gulf War veterans 10 years after the war. *British Journal of Psychiatry, 190,* 385–393.

Twamley, E. W., Hami, S., & Stein, M. B. (2004). Neuropsychological function in college students with and without posttraumatic stress disorder. *Psychiatry Research, 126*(3), 265–274.

Varney, N. R., Roberts, R. J., Springer, J. A., Connell, S. K., & Wood, P. S. (1997). Neuropsychiatric sequelae of cerebral malaria in Vietnam veterans. *Journal of Nervous and Mental Disease, 185*(11), 695–703.

Vasterling, J. J., Brailey, K., Constans, J. I., & Sutker, P. B. (1998). Attention and memory dysfunction in posttraumatic stress disorder. *Neuropsychology, 12*(1), 125–133.

Vasterling, J. J., Duke, L. M., Brailey, K., Constans, J. I., Allain, A. N., Jr., & Sutker, P. B. (2002). Attention, learning, and memory performances and intellectual resources in Vietnam veterans: PTSD and no disorder comparisons. *Neuropsychology, 16*(1), 5–14.

Vasterling, J. J., Proctor, S. P., Amoroso, P., Kane, R., Heeren, T., & White, R. F. (2006). Neuropsychological outcomes of army personnel following deployment to the Iraq War. *Journal of the American Medical Association, 296*(5), 519–529.

Virues-Ortega, J., Buela-Casal, G., Garrido, E., & Alcazar, B. (2004). Neuropsychological functioning associated with high-altitude exposure. *Neuropsychology Reviews, 14*(4), 197–224.

Wain, H., Bradley, J., Nam, T., Waldrep, D., & Cozza, S. (2005). Psychiatric interventions with returning soldiers at Walter Reed. *Psychiatric Quarterly, 76*(4), 351–360.

Warden, D. L., & Labbate, L. A. (2005). Posttraumatic stress disorder and other anxiety disorders. In J. M. Silver, T. W. McAllister, & S. C. Yudofsky (Eds.), *Textbook of traumatic brain injury* (pp. 231–243). Arlington, VA: American Psychiatric Publishing.

Weichel, E. D., Colyer, M. H., Bautista, C., Bower, K. S., & French, L. M. (2009). Traumatic brain injury associated with combat ocular trauma. *Journal of Head Trauma Rehabilitation, 24*(1), 41–50.

Weina, P. J., Neafie, R. C., Wortmann, G., Polhemus, M., & Aronson, N. E. (2004). Old world leishmaniasis: An emerging infection among deployed U.S. military and civilian workers. *Clinical Infectious Diseases, 39*(11), 1674–1680.

Wilk, J. E., Thomas, J. L., McGurk, D. M., Riviere, L. A., Castro, C. A., & Hoge, C. W. (2010). Mild traumatic brain injury (concussion) during combat: Lack of association of blast mechanism with persistent postconcussive symptoms. *Journal of Head Trauma Rehabilitation, 25*(1), 9–14.

Yehuda, R., Keefe, R. S., Harvey, P. D., Levengood, R. A., Gerber, D. K., Geni, J., et al. (1995). Learning and memory in combat veterans with posttraumatic stress disorder. *American Journal of Psychiatry, 152*(1), 137–139.

Zapor, M. J., & Moran, K. A. (2005). Infectious diseases during wartime. *Current Opinion in Infectious Disease, 18*(5), 395–399.

Zatzick, D. F., Rivara, F. P., Nathens, A. B., Jurkovich, G. J., Wang, J., Fan, M. Y., et al. (2007). A nationwide U.S. study of post-traumatic stress after hospitalization for physical injury. *Psychological Medicine, 37*(10), 1469–1480.

PART II

Mental Health and Chronic Pain

CHAPTER 6

Posttraumatic Stress Disorder in the Workplace

Gerald M. Rosen
Brad K. Grunert

In 1980, with publication of the third edition of the *Diagnostic and Statistical Manual of Mental Disorders* (DSM-III; American Psychiatric Association, 1980), the diagnosis of posttraumatic stress disorder (PTSD) was introduced. PTSD was essentially carved out of general stress studies by defining a particular subset of stressors that was presumed to create risk for a distinctive clinical syndrome. Thus, unlike most diagnoses in the DSM, PTSD was not agnostic to etiology. The subset of stressors (Criterion A) was defined to include life-threatening events and events that threatened physical integrity. The syndrome itself was defined by various symptom criteria clustered into three groups: reexperiencing symptoms such as intrusive thoughts, nightmares, and flashbacks (Criterion B); avoidance and emotional numbing symptoms (Criterion C); and hyperarousal symptoms such as irritability and poor concentration (Criterion D).

In this chapter, we review several core issues and controversies that have surrounded the PTSD diagnosis since its inception. We consider how these issues can be of particular importance when trauma occurs in the workplace and issues of compensation apply. We then consider the implications of these concerns for assessing and treating psychiatric morbidity in the aftermath of workplace injury and stress. Our discussion of treatment pays particular attention to interventions that have as their goal an employee's return to work.

POSTTRAUMATIC PSYCHIATRIC MORBIDITY

The notion that a particular class of events can be associated with a specific clinical syndrome has been advanced on many occasions. For example, terms such as "war neurosis," "soldier's heart," "combat fatigue," and "shell shock" were used in earlier times to characterize psychiatric casualties associated with combat. These terms tended to fade from usage with the passage of whatever particular war had created the original interest. In the case of PTSD, it was the Vietnam War that galvanized attention on returning veterans (Grob & Horwitz, 2010; Scott, 1990). Unlike earlier terms, interest in PTSD has not receded over time. To the contrary, PTSD has increasingly become the focus of professional attention over the last three decades; so much so that Grob and Horwitz observed: "From its delineated origin in the conditions of Vietnam veterans, PTSD was to become one of the most influential psychiatric diagnoses in history" (p. 178).

An Internet search demonstrated that the PTSD research base contains over 13,000 articles (PsychInfo: December 17, 2009). As a consequence of this large body of research, much has been learned about how people react in the aftermath of trauma. We know that while it is normal to react to adverse events, the majority of individuals are resilient and do not develop a psychiatric disorder. Among individuals whose reactions are of such severity and breadth as to constitute the symptoms of disorder, PTSD is not the most frequent diagnosis. Instead, a variety of outcomes are to be found among that substantial minority of individuals who warrant a psychiatric diagnosis after trauma. Foremost among these disorders is depression. Other diagnoses that present with some frequency are specific phobia, panic disorder, and generalized anxiety disorder (Bryant, 2010). Epidemiologic studies illustrate that only a minority of individuals who experience a single-incident civilian accident meet the criteria for PTSD (e.g., Breslau, Davis, Andreski, & Peterson, 1991; Norris, 1992), with the normal course of posttraumatic reactions characterized by rapid onset (North, 2001) and recovery over time. The finding that natural recovery occurs in the first few months postincident is specifically referenced in the DSM: "Duration of the symptoms varies, with complete recovery occurring within 3 months in approximately half of cases" (p. 466; American Psychiatric Association, 2000). Thus, chronic PTSD is more unusual than acute presentations.

CHALLENGES TO THE PTSD DIAGNOSIS

The diagnosis of PTSD has been a useful heuristic (Coyne & Thompson, 2007), insofar as it has promoted research and furthered our understanding of posttraumatic psychiatric disorders. But does the diagnosis represent a distinct disorder in nature? This essential issue continues to raise heated debates. Rosen (2004b) observed, "It is the rare moment when most every assumption and theoretical underpinning of a psychiatric disorder comes under attack, or is found to lack empirical support. Yet, this is the situation faced by PTSD" (p. xi). Spitzer, First, and Wakefield (2007) similarly noted: "Since its introduction into DSM-III in 1980, no other DSM diagnosis, with the exception of Dissociative Identity Disorder (a related disorder), has generated so much controversy in the field as to the boundaries of the disorder, diagnostic criteria, central assumptions, clinical utility, and prevalence in various populations" (p. 233).

Although a comprehensive review of various attempts to validate the PTSD diagnosis is beyond the scope of this chapter, several core issues deserve mention. Readers interested in pursuing these topics, as well as failed efforts to identify a distinctive pathogenesis for the PTSD clinical syndrome, are referred to a recent empirical evaluation of the literature (Rosen & Lilienfeld, 2008).

Criterion A and the Assumption of a Specific Etiology

The assumption of a specific etiology, as provided by Criterion A, is so fraught with difficulties that it has come to be called the Criterion A problem (Weathers & Keane, 2007). This "problem" began shortly after PTSD was introduced into the DSM-III (American Psychiatric Association, 1980), when Breslau and Davis (1987) questioned whether a distinct subset of stressors really existed. Publications then documented the occurrence of the PTSD clinical syndrome (i.e., individuals meeting requisite symptom criteria) after numerous non-Criterion A events such as failed adoption arrangements, financial stressors, and marital disruptions and divorce. The literature almost seemed to parody Criterion A, with one article entitled "Post-traumatic stress disorder without the trauma" (Scott & Stradling, 1994) and other publications discussing the occurrence of PTSD after viewing frightening Halloween television programs (Simons & Silveira, 1994), or breaking up with a best friend (Solomon & Canino, 1990).

In addition to numerous case reports, controlled studies challenged Criterion A. Surveys taken among nonclinical psychiatric populations (e.g., college students; patients seeing family physicians) found that the endorsement of PTSD symptoms was at least as high, and sometimes higher, when referencing nontraumatic, as compared to traumatic, events (Gold, Marx, Soler-Baillo, & Sloan, 2005; Mol et al., 2005). Even more convincing, studies demonstrated that depressed patients (Bodkin, Pope, Detke, & Hudson, 2007) and people with social phobia (Erwin, Heimberg, Marx, & Franklin, 2006) often met PTSD symptom criteria in the absence of any Criterion A event. Further problems arose for Criterion A when a large literature indicated that factors extraneous to trauma contributed more variance to clinical outcome than the event itself (e.g., Bowman & Yehuda, 2004). After three decades of research, it is now clear that Criterion A events are neither necessary nor sufficient to produce PTSD's defined clinical syndrome.

Uncertainty over Criterion A challenges the very logic for having "invented" PTSD (Summerfield, 2001), unless of course the diagnosis successfully carves nature at its joints and defines a distinct stress-related clinical syndrome. This situation turns our attention to PTSD's symptom criteria.

The Symptom Criteria

Most clinicians are familiar with the 17 symptom criteria that define PTSD in the DSM-IV. There are five "re-experiencing symptoms" (Criterion B) that include intrusive thoughts, dreams of the traumatic event, flashbacks, and psychological and/or physiological reactivity to cues that serve as reminders. An individual must report only one of the B symptoms to meet the criterion. Then there are seven "avoidance" and "emotional numbing" symptoms (Criterion C) that include efforts to not think or talk about the traumatic event, and to avoid people or situations that serve as reminders; failure to recall some important part of what happened; loss of interest in usual activities; feelings of disconnectedness from others; inability to have strong or loving feelings; and a sense of a foreshortened future. An individual must endorse three or more of these symptoms to meet Criterion C. Lastly, there are five "hyperarousal" symptoms (Criterion D) that include sleep problems, irritability, concentration difficulties, hypervigilance, and exaggerated startle responses. An individual must have two or more of the hyperarousal symptoms to meet Criterion D. Thus, there are multiple ways for an individual to achieve the diagnosis of PTSD, and groups of diagnosed patients can actually be quite heterogeneous in their presentations.

Rosen and Lilienfeld (2008) noted that marked variability in symptom presentation does not by itself undermine the validity of a PTSD diagnosis, because variable presentations can be alternative manifestations of a shared etiology. As an example from medicine, one gastrointestinal problem, celiac disease, has so many symptom profiles it has been called the "great imposter" (Lee & Green, 2006). However, in the case of celiac disease, a specific etiology has been identified (intolerance to a grain protein) and linked to a distinct pathophysiology change (damage to small intestine). This clear causal link is in sharp contrast to the "Criterion A problem" faced by PTSD.

Without a specific etiology, variable symptom presentations among PTSD patients pose a challenge to the diagnostic construct. This situation is particularly concerning because PTSD's symptom criteria overlap with other disorders with which PTSD is highly comorbid (Spitzer et al., 2007). In fact, the overlap of symptoms for the combination of major depression and specific phobia is absolutely complete with PTSD. Consider, for example, two of PTSD's reexperiencing symptoms—B4 and B5. Criterion B4 reads "intense psychological distress at exposure to internal or external cues that symbolize or resemble an aspect of the traumatic event." Criterion B5 reads "physiological reactivity on exposure to internal or external cues that symbolize or resemble an aspect of the traumatic event." Compare these definitions with Criteria A and B for specific phobia. Criterion A for specific phobia states, "marked and persistent fear that is excessive or unreasonable, cued by the presence or anticipation of a specific object or situation." Criterion B for specific phobia states, "exposure to the phobic stimulus almost invariably provokes an immediate anxiety response."

Criterion Creep and Extensions of the "PTSD Model"

One might think that in the face of challenges to the PTSD diagnosis (e.g., failure to support a specific etiology; questions regarding a distinct syndrome), clinicians would be cautious in applying the construct. To the contrary, the diagnosis has been enthusiastically embraced and extended worldwide to an ever expanding array of events and reactions. Characterized as "criterion creep" (Rosen, 2004c) or "conceptual bracket creep" (McNally, 2003), this expansion of the "PTSD model" has resulted, in part, from official changes in the DSM's listed criteria. For example, in the DSM-III, traumatic events (Criterion A) had to be directly experienced or witnessed. For DSM-IV (American Psychiatric Association, 1994), simply hearing about a life-threatening event befalling a loved one could be considered traumatic. Breslau and Kessler (2001) demonstrated that expanded definitions of Criterion A increased by 59% the total number of events considered traumatic. With the expanded definition, individuals who viewed horrific events on the news were possibly at risk for developing PTSD (e.g., Ahern, Galea, Resnick, & Vlahov, 2004) as a consequence of "vicarious traumatization" (Sabin-Farrell & Turpin, 2003).

Criterion creep has also resulted from "unofficial" expansions of Criterion A, such as Avina and O'Donohue's (2002) suggestion that crude jokes in the workplace might be traumatic because victims could worry, "since he is doing this to me, what else is he capable of?" (p. 72). By extending the range of events subsumed under Criterion A to the realm of expectations, these authors effectively created the equivalent of "pretraumatic" stress disorder (Rosen, 2004c). Grob and Horwitz (2010) observed, "The expansion of the criteria defining what situations counted as 'traumatic' meant that virtually the entire population could be viewed as vulnerable to developing PTSD" (p. 186).

Expansion of the PTSD model has also occurred with the disorder's symptom criteria. Publications on "subsyndromal," "subthreshold," and "partial-PTSD," serve the notable purpose of identifying individuals who suffer posttraumatic reactions that fall short of PTSD's criteria (Grubaugh et al., 2005). At the same time, these terms blur the lines between normal reactions to adversity and symptoms of disorder (Wakefield & Horwitz, 2010). In this way, individuals who were understandably anxious or angry after the terrorist attacks of 9/11 were said to have developed symptoms (Schuster et al., 2001). Such reasoning provides a logical leap akin to labeling normal reflexive coughing in a smoky tavern as a symptom of respiratory disease (Rosen, Spitzer, & McHugh, 2008).

There also have been multiple extensions of the PTSD "model" to other areas of emotion and functioning. Linden (2003) introduced (in all seriousness) the diagnosis of posttraumatic embitterment disorder (PTED) to further the identification and treatment of individuals who suffer insulting or humiliating events. Other extensions of the model include posttraumatic relationship syndrome (Vandervoort & Rokach, 2004), posttraumatic grief disorder (Prigerson & Jacobs, 2001), posttraumatic dental care anxiety (Bracha, Vega, & Vega, 2006), and posttraumatic abortion syndrome (Gomez & Zapata, 2005). These "disorders" rest on the linkage of a particular class of events with a presumably distinct syndrome. As such, they extend, rather than address, all the underlying problems that have befallen the original construct of PTSD.

Important issues accompany criterion creep and further extensions of the PTSD diagnosis. In addition to unwarranted medicalization of normal reactions to circumstance, there is the risk of diminishing the significance of true psychiatric morbidity. Shepard (2004) observed, "Any unit of classification that simultaneously encompasses the experience of surviving Auschwitz and that of being told rude jokes at work must, by any reasonable lay standard, be a nonsense, a patent absurdity" (p. 57). In a similar vein, Sparr (1990) cautioned, "PTSD should be diagnosed if the facts fit, but only if they fit. To do otherwise dilutes and trivializes the diagnosis" (p. 259).

PTSD, Litigation, and Workers' Compensation Claims

Several considerations likely have contributed to the popularity of the PTSD diagnosis, criterion creep, and extensions of the model. From a clinical perspective, the diagnosis is a highly useful one that has helped therapists conceptualize their patients' problems. With the use of this single diagnosis, patients' problems are accounted for by a parsimonious etiological model, and treatment goals are defined. The PTSD diagnosis also is attractive to patients because they do not have to feel stigmatized for having a psychiatric disorder. By putting the responsibility for problems on an external event, PTSD confers "victim status" and relieves the individual of any inherent weakness for failing to cope. Nancy Andreasen (1995), one of the framers of PTSD in the DSM-III, observed, "It is rare to find a psychiatric diagnosis that anyone likes to have, but PTSD seems to be one of them" (p. 964).

Because a diagnosis of PTSD determines the issue of causality and conveys victim status to its recipient, the diagnosis has become particularly desirable in matters involving compensation and claims of personal injury. Slovenko (1994) observed:

> In tort litigation, PTSD is a favored diagnosis in cases of emotional distress because it is incident specific. It tends to rule out other factors important to the determination of causation. Thus plaintiffs can argue that all of their psychological problems issue from the alleged traumatic event and not from myriad other sources encountered in life. A diagnosis of depression, in contrast, opens the issue of causation to many factors other than the stated cause of action. (p. 441)

Lees-Haley (1986) considered PTSD's attractiveness when issues of compensation apply and observed with a wry sense of wit, "If mental illnesses were rated on the New York Stock Exchange, Post-traumatic Stress Disorder would be a growth stock to watch" (p. 17).

It is useful to maintain a historical perspective when discussing posttraumatic psychiatric morbidity, issues of compensation, and concerns over malingering. These topics have a long history in the courtroom (Grob & Horwitz, 2010; Rosen, 2004a). In the late 1800s, claims of "railway spine" were made against insurance companies, and the nature of posttraumatic disorders was hotly contested between plaintiff and defense experts (Erichsen, 1882; Page, 1891). Within this historical context, it is noteworthy that the DSM-IV introduced a specific and cautionary guideline that clinicians were to rule out malingering in situations in which "financial remuneration, benefit eligibility, and forensic determinations play a role" (p. 467; American Psychiatric Association, 1994). Those familiar with the DSM will appreciate that similar instructions are not provided for depression, panic disorder, or a host of other diagnostic categories. Related to DSM's concern is a large literature that addresses general issues (e.g., Simon, 2003; Young, Kane, & Nicholson, 2007), documents the occurrence of feigned events and/or symptoms (e.g., Frueh et al., 2005; Rosen, 1995; Sparr & Pankratz, 1983), and considers the impact of falsified reporting on the PTSD database (e.g., Frueh et al., 2005; Rosen, 2006).

ASSESSING PSYCHIATRIC MORBIDITY
AFTER WORKPLACE INJURY AND STRESS

Several areas of concern apply to the assessment of posttraumatic psychiatric morbidity. First is the matter of whether an assessment is being conducted for clinical or forensic purposes. Next is a consideration of assessment modalities and instruments. Then, there are general issues concerning how clinicians and experts apply their findings and arrive at case formulations. Lastly, there is the matter of how findings should be presented to a trier of fact (e.g., jury, judge, arbitrator) when patients or plaintiffs seek compensation.

Clinical versus Forensic Contexts

The role of a treating mental health professional differs from, and is incompatible with, the role of a forensic expert. Treating professionals strive to establish rapport with a patient, develop a therapeutic alliance, and work with the patient's reported belief model. Forensic experts, on the other hand, recognize that plaintiffs may misreport information in the context of litigation. Forensic experts do not develop a therapeutic alliance, but instead question a person's self-report, consider all relevant hypotheses, review other sources of data, and conduct psychological testing when appropriate. In light of these differences, it has been recommended that mental health professionals should not perform both treating and forensic roles on the same case, unless special circumstances apply (Greenberg & Shuman, 1997; Specialty Guidelines for Forensic Psychologists Committee on Ethical Guidelines for Forensic Psychologists, 1991; Strasburger, Gutheil, & Brodsky, 1997).

Despite differences, the assessment goals of a clinician (who provides therapy to a patient) and those of a forensic expert (who provides analysis to a court) are essentially the same: to provide an accurate diagnosis and case formulation for an individual's presenting complaints. Accordingly, the DSM's dictum to rule out malingering applies to all. The real difference, then, is in a professional's approach to the use of available methods and instruments. Although the full range of assessment options is immediately available to the forensic expert, clinicians tread more lightly and rely, at least initially, on a patient's self-report and perhaps selected testing. However, when patients fail to respond to treatment within the range of reasonable expectations, clinicians should consider additional assessment efforts or referral to a colleague for consultation and a second opinion. This can be necessary for patients with Munchausen's or other factitious disorders (Pankratz, 1998), patients with contributing personality disorders, and patients who for reasons of secondary gain are not properly motivated to benefit from treatment (Lacoursiere, 1993).

Interviews and Instruments

Clinicians and forensic experts can assess traumatic events and posttraumatic symptoms during a general interview, with the aid of structured interviews, and with a variety of symptom checklists and general psychometrics. For a comprehensive review of available instruments, the reader is referred to Elhai, Ford, and Naifeh (2010). Our discussion will be limited to highlighting a few basic considerations.

Both clinicians and forensic experts are encouraged to conduct a structured interview (e.g., CAPS, SCID) to ensure that the full range of PTSD symptom is assessed (Keane, Buckley, & Miller, 2003). At the same time, clinicians and forensic experts are advised to first inquire about symptoms in the context of a general and open-ended interview, before proceeding to specific probes. If a client fails to report PTSD symptoms in response to general questions, but proceeds to endorse these problems during a structured interview, then the clinician has reason to question whether this later symptom reporting is valid (Pitman, Sparr, Saunders, & McFarlane, 1996). This concern relates back to the DSM's dictum concerning feigned PTSD.

With regard to the need to rule out malingering, it can be observed that the DSM does not clarify just how that task should be accomplished. As it turns out, there is no preferred method to detect malingering among PTSD claimants (Frueh, Elhai, & Kaloupek, 2004; Guriel & Fremouw, 2003; Taylor, Frueh, & Asmundson, 2007). The MMPI-2 contains validity scales to identify individuals motivated to malinger, but coaching on these scales reduces their effectiveness (Bury & Bagby, 2002; Storm & Graham, 2000). Coaching is a serious concern because it has been shown that attorneys consider it their ethical responsibility to instruct clients on what is known about psychological tests (Wetter & Corrigan, 1995). Therefore, clinicians and experts are advised to not disclose in advance the tests they plan to administer.

Simple symptom checklists are problematic because individuals can easily feign a disorder by simply endorsing the face-obvious items (e.g., Lees-Haley, 1990). In recognition of this limitation and the need to assess response sets, some psychological tests contain validity scales. Unfortunately, the development and validation of these scales can be inadequate, with poorly established levels of specificity and sensitivity (e.g., Trauma Symptom Inventory; Rosen et al., 2006). Therefore, clinicians and forensic experts should be cautious about overinterpreting "valid" test results— particularly on tests for which the validity scales have item content that is so extreme or bizarre as to be obvious to most every respondent that is motivated to exaggerate.

Other assessment strategies are available to clinicians and forensic experts who want to consider a multimodal approach to assessment. Neuropsychologists will be familiar with symptom validity tests (SVTs), and these can be employed with PTSD claims that involve presenting problems with concentration and/or memory (Merten, Thies, Schneider, & Stevens, 2010; Rosen & Powel, 2003). Physiological assessment of reactions to trauma-relevant stimuli is another approach that has been recommended (Orr, Metzger, Miller, & Kaloupek, 2004) and is even noted in the DSM-IV (American Psychiatric Association, 2000, p. 465). However, there are no current decision rules for physiological data to allow a determination of PTSD-caseness with established levels of specificity and sensitivity (Rosen, Lilienfeld, & Orr, 2010).

It should be clear from this brief review that multiple sources of data can be considered when planning a thorough assessment of posttraumatic psychiatric morbidity. Clinicians and forensic experts will be well served if they are familiar with the benefits and limitations of each of these methods and instruments.

Case Formulations

McHugh and Treisman (2007) pointed out that the PTSD diagnosis encourages a "top-down" assessment model that lumps most posttraumatic reactions under the rubric of a single term. In this approach to assessment, patients are diagnosed in checklist fashion following decision trees provided by the DSM. One problem with this "top-down" method is that it can miss the full context of situational circumstances and other considerations that impact a patient's presenting symptoms. McHugh and others have encouraged clinicians to take a broad view, or "bottom-up" approach to assessment—one that takes into account an individual's full biography and the full range of disorders that follow traumatic events.

Rosen, Spitzer, and McHugh (2008) discussed the hypothetical case of a boat captain whose fishing vessel sank with resulting loss of life. Upon returning home, the captain experienced grief over friends who died, fears of returning to work, and situational depression. Clinicians can consider whether joining these varied concerns into a single diagnosis (PTSD) actually improves our understanding of the captain's clinical and adjustment issues. In at least some portion of cases, a patient's presentation may be better explained by providing a broad case formulation that takes into account multiple contributing factors and processes. As observed by Bryant in relation to posttraumatic phobias (2010), "It is important to consider the full range of symptom criteria that constitutes a PTSD diagnosis, and not reflexively apply the diagnosis whenever posttraumatic anxiety presents" (pp. 212–213).

Testifying to the Trier of Fact

Forensic experts have their own specialty guidelines and ethical standards that should guide their performance when conducting assessments and offering testimony (American Academy of Psychiatry and the Law, 2005; American Psychology Law Society, 1991). Clinicians, on the other hand, may have little experience with matters of the court. Therefore, clinicians who treat patients involved in litigation will want to acquaint themselves with a large literature on malingering, the proper conduct of forensic assessments, and the limitations of relying on a patient's self-reports (e.g., Simon, 2003; Williams, Lees-Haley, & Djanogly, 1999). If called upon to testify, clinicians can nondefensively explain that they have objectively determined neither the existence of subjectively reported complaints nor the truthfulness of their patient's reporting. In other words, a clinician should not go beyond the actual foundation of their knowledge. Thus, a clinician might testify in court that a patient has reported severe nightmares, and this reporting contributed to the diagnosis of PTSD. At the same time, the clinician should *not* tell the trier of fact (e.g., jury, judge, arbitrator) that there has been an independent determination that the patient "has" nightmares. To do otherwise would mislead the court and create an "echo attribution" (Rosen & Davison, 2001), whereby the professional prestige of a clinician's "finding" is confused with the patient's reporting and the true source of the message.

Many clinicians believe that clinical assessment interviews and additional treatment contacts provide a sufficient basis to detect malingering, despite evidence to the contrary. In one study (Hickling, Blanchard, Mundy, & Galovski, 2002), six actors presented to a clinic that specialized in the assessment and treatment of motor vehicle accident victims. All six individuals were diagnosed with PTSD, thereby demonstrating the successful feigning of both the nonoccurring accident and the disorder's symptoms. It sometimes is argued that therapists can detect malingering because of their extended contact with a patient over multiple therapy sessions. This position is without empirical support (Wetter & Deitsch, 1996) and appears difficult to defend. After all, an individual who falsely reports the occurrence of nightmares at the time of an intake session can just as easily misreport the same phenomenon weeks later. Other studies fail to support the popular notion that "clinical experience" adds to a clinician's ability to detect who is falsely reporting (e.g., Ekman & O'Sullivan, 1991). Truth be told, clinicians may have many areas of expertise, but they are not lie detectors (Slovenko, 2002). Consequently, clinicians are encouraged to be less than certain when testifying to a trier of fact on the actual occurrence of subjective symptoms, or on the truthfulness of a patient's reporting.

TREATING WORKPLACE PTSD

Treatment of individuals who experience life-threatening or other horrific events can be provided both for acute reactions in the immediate aftermath of trauma and for longer term psychiatric concerns. A brief overview of interventions for each of these time frames is provided, followed by more detailed consideration of specific interventions that have had as their goal the return to employment of individuals who suffer workplace injuries.

Interventions in the Immediate Aftermath of Trauma

As previously reviewed, most individuals who experience life-threatening trauma do not develop reactions of such severity and breadth as to meet criteria for diagnosing PTSD. Among survivors who meet these criteria, about two-thirds recover within 3 months. Unfortunately, this leaves a substantial minority of individuals at risk for chronic psychiatric morbidity (Kessler, Sonnega, Bromet, Hughes, & Nelson, 1995), suggesting the need for effective and early interventions in the aftermath of trauma.

Beginning in the 1980s, the most widely adopted model for early intervention employed critical incident stress debriefings (CISD) as described by Mitchell (1983). Mitchell's model called for a semistructured group intervention to be provided shortly after a traumatic event, with the goal of reducing initial distress and preventing later psychological problems. Over time, Mitchell expanded his model to include a number of techniques under the rubric of critical incident stress management (CISM; Everly & Mitchell, 1999). As a result of the model's intuitive appeal, and/or aggressive marketing (Dineen, 1998), Mitchell's model was widely accepted. An example of the widespread enthusiasm held for CISD/M could be found just a few years ago on a website (*www.magellanhealth.com/mbh/products/employee_assistance.html*) maintained by Magellan Behavioral Health Services (January 2003). At that time, this employee assistance program made the claim that its CISM practices could "improve employee productivity, decrease work-related accidents, lessen absenteeism and turnover, lessen health insurance and Worker's Comp claims and promote workplace cooperation and morale." Accompanying the widespread acceptance of Mitchell's CISD/M model was the belief that companies could risk liability if they did not provide appropriate support and interventions to alleviate psychiatric distress after work-related trauma. The executive director of the International Critical Incident Stress Foundation was asked in an e-mail, "Is it ever suggested to a company that they might be liable if appropriate debriefings are NOT provided subsequent to a critical incident?" The answer was "Yes" (Howell, personal communication with Rosen, October 24, 2001).

As it turns out, enthusiasm for, and widespread acceptance of, Mitchell's CISD/M model was premature. By the turn of the millennium, multiple studies, reviews of the literature, and organizational recommendations cautioned against the use of debriefings (e.g., McNally, Bryant, & Ehlers, 2003; Rose, Bisson, & Wessley, 2001). With the changing tides, the issue of liability also shifted (Devilly & Cotton, 2003; Devilly, Gist, & Cotton, 2006). As observed by Devilly and Cotton (2004), "While the buyer should beware (*caveat emptor*) when buying debriefing services, the evidence of a defective product is mounting to the point where it may be

time for the seller to beware (*caveat venditor*)" (p. 40). With professionals turning away from the CISD/M model, a search began for alternative
frameworks that might guide professionals in the immediate aftermath of
trauma. For example, "Psychological First Aid" (PFA) emphasizes support
and resource identification without requiring discussion of the traumatic
event, as occurs with CISD/M. Approaches such as PFA have been referred
to as "evidenced-informed" because they rely on current knowledge to generate what is hoped to constitute best available practices. Unfortunately,
good intentions have already been demonstrated to be insufficient when it
comes to early interventions in the aftermath of trauma (Bryant, 2010; Gist
& Devilly, 2010). Until further research is conducted, it remains unclear if
PFA provides an effective response. Amidst this uncertainty, one finding
does stand out: individuals with high levels of symptomatic distress, who
are identified shortly after trauma, can receive considerable benefit from
cognitive-behavioral therapies (Bryant, 2007; Foa, Hearst-Ikeda, & Perry,
1995).

Exposure-Based Treatments and Return to Work

Cognitive-behavioral therapies have been shown to be effective in the treatment of PTSD over a wide range of randomized controlled studies (Cahill,
Rothbaum, Resick, & Follette, 2009; Foa, Keane, Friedman, & Cohen,
2009). Hembree and Foa (2010) recently reviewed several treatments that
fall under the rubric of "cognitive-behavioral": exposure-based methods
including prolonged exposure, cognitive-oriented techniques, and combinations of exposure with anxiety management and/or cognitive restructuring. Variants of exposure-based treatments also exist, such as eye movement desensitization and reprocessing (EMDR). In EMDR it appears that
novel but unnecessary ingredients (e.g., bilateral stimulation) have been
added that do not alter the effectiveness of previously accepted principles of
behavior change (Davidson & Parker, 2001; Devilly, 2002; Rosen & Davison, 2003). Thus, the essential elements of cognitive-behavioral techniques
provide strongly supported and evidenced-based approaches for the treatment of posttraumatic psychiatric morbidity.

　　Treatment outcome studies typically provide pre- and postassessments
with regard to the presence or absence of symptoms, and the number of
participants who meet PTSD-caseness. Although these measures are essential, it is important to consider that when injury occurs in the workplace,
one of the key goals of rehabilitation is an individual's successful return
to work. On this issue, most treatment outcome studies are mute. For this
reason, we next focus on the development of a cognitive-behavioral-based
program that has been proven successful in returning the majority of workers to their original employers.

DESCRIPTION OF A SPECIFIC TREATMENT PROGRAM FOR WORK-RELATED PTSD

The description of intervention techniques and return-to-work rates in this section are based on the outcomes of 1,056 patients treated for work-related PTSD by the second author over a nearly 30-year period. This patient group consists primarily of individuals experiencing mutilating hand/upper extremity injuries (813 individuals), lower extremity mutilating injuries (102 individuals), truck drivers involved in accidents with severe injuries or deaths occurring to the participants (46 individuals), robbery victims working as store employees (67 individuals), and assaults occurring in the workplace (28 individuals). All of these individuals were referred for treatment by either treating physicians or workers' compensation insurance adjusters. Most individuals were covered by the workers' compensation (WC) laws of Wisconsin, Illinois, and Michigan. There were a few referrals covered by the WC laws of Texas, Oklahoma, Florida, Colorado, Iowa, and Minnesota. It is important to note that compensation laws vary between states; whether this impacts treatment remains unassessed.

Patients who met the criteria for PTSD, on the basis of a structured interview, were initially provided with psychoeducation that explained the maladaptive nature of symptoms and an understanding of exposure-based treatments. In this phase, we often discussed with patients how, at the time of their injury, things occurred very rapidly and they experienced a myriad of emotions. Although they may have made intellectual sense of what had happened, their emotional processing had lagged behind. In the model we discussed the goals of exposure therapy and the process of desensitizing anxiety reactions. In addition, we discussed how WC laws promote a return to work with the same employer as the most desirable outcome following work injury. We then laid out a plan for eventual return to work if this was at all feasible. In some cases, physical injuries were such that they precluded a return with the same employer (e.g., a worker who suffered loss of both arms). In these cases we focused on other resources, including retraining through the Division of Vocational Rehabilitation or volunteer work for individuals totally disabled under the WC laws. Regardless of the approach, the goal was to return each injured worker to as normal a lifestyle as could be accomplished.

Imaginal Exposure

After the initial education and goal-setting phase, we began exposure-based treatment. Typically, we initiated treatment with imaginal exposure in the office setting following a framework provided by Foa and her colleagues (1998, 2007). The goal of imaginal exposure was to reduce the fear and anxiety surrounding the trauma while facilitating a change in cognitive schemas and correcting misattributions (Foa, Steketee, & Rothbaum, 1989). Workers were typically asked to imagine and describe what they experienced the day of their traumatic injury. We obtained subjective units of distress (SUDS) ratings during the exposure to determine the most traumatic portions of the event. When patients came to the most emotionally charged part of the trauma, they were asked to describe in as much detail as possible their thoughts, images, and emotions. We stressed the fact that they were only experiencing a memory and they had already survived the event itself. In this regard we attempted to help patients discriminate between the trauma and memories in a manner consistent with Foa's emotional processing theory (Foa & Cahill, 2001; Foa, Huppert, Cahill, & Riggs, 2006; Foa & Kozak, 1986; Foa et al., 1989). We also incorporated questions that helped workers reprocess the event, in order to reinforce whatever sense of control they could have.

Our program's use of imaginal exposure has provided a powerful intervention for injured workers, particularly in terms of bringing intrusive thoughts under control. At the same time, many of our patients failed to benefit from this treatment component. This failure appeared particularly true when workers experienced anger or guilt as a primary emotional reaction to thought intrusions (Grunert, Smucker, Weis, & Rusch, 2003; Grunert, Weis, Smucker, & Christianson, 2007; Smucker, Grunert, & Weis, 2003). In such cases, we have found it useful to utilize cognitive reprocessing interventions embedded within imaginal exposure. These interventions included imagery rescripting and reprocessing therapy (IRRT). The goal of IRRT was to alter maladaptive trauma-related schemas such as vulnerability or victimization while replacing them with mastery images (Smucker, Grunert, & Weis, 2001; Smucker & Neideree, 1995). With IRRT, workers could "tell themselves" what they knew in the present. This method promoted the development of "mastery" imagery and led to more realistic appraisals of current circumstances, as opposed to past events. IRRT has proven to be a potent intervention for those workers who have failed to benefit from traditional imaginal exposure. It has been particularly effective when injured workers have been the victim of someone else's actions (e.g., a coworker negligently started machinery that the injured worker was using).

The above interventions appear less effective when workers do not have a complete narrative as to how they were injured (Grunert, Devine, Matloub, Sanger, & Yousif, 1988; Grunert & Dzwierzynski, 1997). For example, in "appraisal" flashbacks the worker may reexperience only a photographic image of the mutilated body part as it was initially seen. In such cases, it was often necessary to re-construct the injury process so that effective appraisal of risk factors that contributed to the injury, and rescue procedures that followed, could be appreciated (Grunert, 2005). In this way, workers could "make sense" out of what happened, emotional processing was facilitated, and realistic appraisals of "future threat" could be formed.

In Vivo *Exposure*

Once workers had gained more control over thought intrusions and had reduced their emotional impact, our program addressed avoidant behaviors by implementing graded *in vivo* exposure (Grunert et al., 1992). For highly avoidant workers we started with having them drive to the street on which their employer was located. We then had them park and spend 20–30 minutes in that surrounding. After doing this for several days, they could drive into the company's parking lot, again spending 20–30 minutes. This was followed by having them walk up to the building entrance and remain in that area for 20–30 minutes. Later, they entered the building, first going into the human resources area. At this point we began having them enter the production area. For their first actual workweek we simply had them observe for an hour other employees in the area in which they would be working. This step was followed by an hour per day of actual work and then by regular increases in daily work time over the next several weeks until full-time work hours had been achieved. Many of our workers initially returned to light-duty or office work. Some workers needed to have the schedule repeated with a blend of duties, not completing final job responsibilities until they had healed physically. Employer cooperation was paramount to the effectiveness of these efforts.

Despite the above treatments, some individuals were too distraught to accomplish a graded work return. In these cases we found it useful to actually accompany them when they reentered the workplace for the first time (Grunert et al., 1989). The worker and therapist typically entered the factory (or truck, etc.) together, with the therapist coaching on various coping techniques and encouraging cognitive reappraisals to counter avoidance. As the worker gained confidence, the area of proposed work was approached, again with ongoing coaching by the therapist. During this procedure more than 90% of our workers have actually gone to the machine at which their injury occurred and discussed what happened to them. As with imaginal exposure, many workers recalled details of the events that had previously gone unreported. Actively processing the trauma within the work setting has allowed us to facilitate the work return of over 80% of our most avoidant workers.

Treatment Program Outcome Data

Because of the nature of the WC system, we have been able to obtain follow-up data on our workers for at least 1 year postinjury. This was the typical time at which permanent disability ratings were reported. This follow-up data showed that we have been able to return 84% of our workers to their previous employers (887/1,056). Further breakdown of this finding illustrates the challenges faced in treating severely injured and psychologically traumatized individuals. Among the 887 workers who returned to their previous employers, only 38 (4.3%) returned to their same machine or job. With decreasing levels of exposure to the stimuli associated with the injuries, the numbers increase: 267 (30.1%) workers returned to the same department on a similar job; and 507 (57.2%) returned to the same building with at least some exposure to the cause of their injury. The remainder (75; 8.4%) worked in a different building or in a setting in which they had minimal to no exposure to the cause of injury. It also should be noted that 144 of the 887 workers were unable to return to their previous job due to physical factors (e.g., cold intolerance, loss of strength and or/sensation) that interfered with the worker's ability to tolerate task conditions.

Of the 169 workers who failed to return to their original employers, 94 (55.6%) were able to be retrained to obtain alternate positions. Thus, a total of 981/1,056 (92.9%) of our sample of injured workers were able to achieve some level of gainful employment. Among the 75 workers who did not return to any type of work, 56 were considered disabled due to the severity of their physical injuries, rather than as a consequence of psychological barriers. A small group of 19 were considered totally disabled due to both physical and psychological factors.

Current outcome findings indicate the need for individually tailored exposure-based methods and ongoing cooperation with an employer's human service department. With appropriate efforts, substantial gains can be achieved, with return to work occurring in the majority of cases.

CONCLUDING COMMENTS

PTSD is an important diagnosis to consider when individuals present with psychiatric dysfunction in the aftermath of trauma. At the same time, clinicians should not reflexively provide this diagnosis whenever anxiety or depression presents after an adverse event. This cautionary point may be particularly important when injuries occur in the workplace, where a host of situational factors may impact symptom presentation and motivation to recover. By approaching assessment with a broad view toward case formulation, clinicians and forensic experts can provide a sound basis for the diagnosis and treatment of posttraumatic psychiatric conditions. In those cases that meet the criteria for a PTSD diagnosis, effective treatments can be provided in the form of cognitive-behavioral therapies, primarily based on imaginal and real-life exposure to anxiety-evoking stimuli. Researchers who evaluate treatment efficacy are encouraged to routinely employ return-to-work measures so that more may be learned about this important outcome variable.

REFERENCES

Ahern, J., Galea, S., Resnick, H., & Vlahov, D. (2004). Television images and probable posttraumatic stress disorder after September 11: The role of background characteristics, event exposures, and perievent panic. *Journal of Nervous and Mental Disease, 192*(3), 217–226.

American Academy of Psychiatry and the L-aw. (2005). *Ethics guidelines for the practice of forensic psychiatry.* Retrieved from *www.aapl.org/ethics.htm.*

American Psychiatric Association. (1980). *Diagnostic and statistical manual of mental disorders* (3rd ed.). Washington, DC: Author.

American Psychiatric Association. (1994). *Diagnostic and statistical manual of mental disorders* (4th ed.). Washington, DC: Author.

American Psychiatric Association. (2000). *Diagnostic and statistical manual of mental disorders* (4th ed., text rev.). Washington, DC: Author.

American Psychology Law Society. (1991). Specialty guidelines for forensic psychologists. *Law and Human Behavior, 15,* 655–665.

Andreasen, N. C. (1995). Posttraumatic stress disorder: Psychology, biology, and the manichaean warfare between false dichotomies. *American Journal of Psychiatry, 152*(7), 963–965.

Avina, C., & O'Donohue, W. (2002). Sexual harassment and PTSD: Is sexual harassment diagnosable trauma? *Journal of Traumatic Stress, 15*(1), 69–75.

Bodkin, J. A., Pope, H. G., Detke, M. J., & Hudson, J. I. (2007). Is PTSD caused by traumatic stress? *Journal of Anxiety Disorders, 21*(2), 176–182.

Bowman, M. L., & Yehuda, R. (2004). Risk factors and the adversity-stress model. In G. M. Rosen (Ed.), *Posttraumatic stress disorder: Issues and controversies* (pp. 39–61). Chichester, UK: Wiley.

Bracha, H. S., Vega, E. M., & Vega, C. B. (2006). Posttraumatic dental-care anxiety (PTDA): Is "dental phobia" a misnomer? *Hawaii Dental Journal, 37*(5), 17–19.

Breslau, N., & Davis, G. C. (1987). Posttraumatic stress disorder: The stressor criterion. *Journal of Nervous and Mental Disease, 175*(5), 255–264.

Breslau, N., Davis, G. C., Andreski, P., & Peterson, E. (1991). Traumatic events and posttraumatic stress disorder in an urban population of young adults. *Archives of General Psychiatry, 48*(3), 216–222.

Breslau, N., & Kessler, R. C. (2001). The stressor criterion in DSM-IV posttraumatic stress disorder: An empirical investigation. *Biological Psychiatry, 50*(9), 699–704.

Bryant, R. A. (2007). Early intervention in posttraumatic stress disorder. *Early Intervention in Psychiatry, 1,* 19–26.

Bryant, R. A. (2010). Treating the full range of posttraumatic reactions. In G. M. Rosen & B. C. Frueh (Eds.), *Clinician's guide to posttraumatic stress disorder* (pp. 205–234). Hoboken, NJ: Wiley.

Bury, A. S., & Bagby, R. M. (2002). The detection of feigned uncoached and coached posttraumatic stress disorder with the MMPI-2 in a sample of workplace accident victims. *Psychological Assessment, 14*(4), 472–484.

Cahill, S. P., Rothbaum, B. O., Resick, P. A., & Follette, V. M. (2009). Cognitive-behavioral therapy for adults. In E. B. Foa, T. M. Keane, M. J. Friedman, & J. A. Cohen (Eds.), *Effective treatments for PTSD: Practice guidelines from the International Society of Traumatic Stress studies* (2nd ed., pp. 139–122). New York: Guilford Press.

Coyne, J. C., & Thompson, R. (2007). Posttraumatic stress syndromes: Useful or negative heuristics? *Journal of Anxiety Disorders, 21*(2), 223–229.

Davidson, P. R., & Parker, K. C. H. (2001). Eye-movement desensitization and repro-cessing (EMDR): A meta analysis. *Journal of Consulting and Clinical Psychology, 191*, 48–51.

Devilly, G. J. (2002). Eye movement desensitization and reprocessing: A chronology of its development and scientific standing. *Scientific Review of Mental Health Practices, 1*, 113–138.

Devilly, G. J., & Cotton, P. (2003). Psychological debriefing and the workplace: Defin-ing a concept, controversies and guidelines for intervention. *Australian Psycholo-gist, 38*, 144–150.

Devilly, G. J., & Cotton, P. (2004). Caveat emptor, caveat venditor, and critical incident stress debriefing/management (CISD/M). *Australian Psychologist, 39*, 35–40.

Devilly, G. J., Gist, R., & Cotton, P. (2006). Ready! Aim! Fire! Psychological debriefing services and intervention in the workplace. *Review of General Psychology, 10*, 318–345.

Dineen, T. (1998). *Manufacturing victims: What the psychology industry is doing to people.* Montreal: Davies.

Ekman, P., & O'Sullivan, M. (1991). Who can catch a liar? *American Psychologist, 46*, 913–920.

Elhai, J. D., Ford, J. D., & Naifeh, J. A. (2010). Assessing trauma exposure and post-traumatic morbidity. In G. M. Rosen & B. C. Frueh (Eds.), *Clinician's guide to posttraumatic stress disorder* (pp. 119–151). Hoboken, NJ: Wiley.

Erichsen, J. E. (1882). *On concussion of the spine, nervous shock, and other obscure injuries of the nervous system, in their clinical and medico-legal aspects.* New York: Birmingham.

Erwin, B. A., Heimberg, R. G., Marx, B. P., & Franklin, M. E. (2006). Traumatic and socially stressful life events among persons with social anxiety disorder. *Journal of Anxiety Disorders, 20*(7), 896–914.

Everly, G. S., & Mitchell, J. T. (1999). *Critical incident stress management.* Ellicott City, MD: Chevron.

Foa, E. B., & Cahill, S. P. (2001). Psychological therapies: Emotional processing. In N. J. Smelser & P. B. Bates (Eds.), *International encyclopedia of the social and behavioral sciences* (pp. 12363–12369). Oxford, UK: Elsevier.

Foa, E. B., Hearst-Ikeda, D., & Perry, K. J. (1995). Evaluation of a brief cognitive-behavioral program for the prevention of chronic PTSD in recent assault victims. *Journal of Consulting and Clinical Psychology, 63*(6), 948–955.

Foa, E. B., Hembree, E. A., & Rothbaum, B. O. (2007). *Prolonged exposure therapy for PTSD: Emotional processing of traumatic experiences.* New York: Oxford University Press.

Foa, E. B., Huppert, J. D., Cahill, S. P., & Riggs, D. S. (2006). Emotional processing theory: An update. In B. O. Rothbaum (Ed.), *The nature and treatment of patho-logical anxiety* (pp. 3–24). New York: Guilford Press.

Foa, E. B., Keane, T. M., Friedman, M. J., & Cohen, J. A. (Eds.). (2009). *Effective treatments for PTSD: Practice guidelines from the International Society for Trau-matic Stress studies* (2nd ed.). New York: Guilford Press.

Foa, E. B., & Kozak, M. J. (1986). Emotional processing of fear: Exposure to corrective information. *Psychological Bulletin, 99*(1), 20–35.

Foa, E. B., & Rothbaum, B. O. (1998). *Treating the trauma of rape.* New York: Guil-ford Press.

Foa, E. B., Steketee, G., & Rothbaum, B. O. (1989). Behavioral/cognitive conceptual-izations of post-traumatic stress disorder. *Behavior Therapy, 20*, 155–176.

Frueh, B. C., Elhai, J. D., Grubaugh, A. L., Monnier, J., Kashdan, T. B., Sauvageot, J. A., et al. (2005). Documented combat exposure of US veterans seeking treatment for combat-related post-traumatic stress disorder. *British Journal of Psychiatry, 186*, 467–472; discussion 473–465.

Frueh, B. C., Elhai, J. D., & Kaloupek, D. G. (2004). Unresolved issues in the assessment of trauma exposure and posttraumatic reactions. In G. M. Rosen (Ed.), *Posttraumatic stress disorder: Issues and controversies* (pp. 63–84). Chichester, UK: Wiley.

Gist, R., & Devilly, G. J. (2010). Early intervention in the aftermath of trauma. In G. M. Rosen & B. C. Frueh (Eds.), *Clinician's guide to posttraumatic stress disorder* (pp. 153–175). Hoboken, NJ: Wiley.

Gold, S. D., Marx, B. P., Soler-Baillo, J. M., & Sloan, D. M. (2005). Is life stress more traumatic than traumatic stress? *Journal of Anxiety Disorders, 19*(6), 687–698.

Gomez, L. C., & Zapata, G. R. (2005). Diagnostic categorization of post-abortion syndrome [Spanish]. *Actas Españolas de Psiquiatria, 33*, 267–272.

Greenberg, S. A., & Shuman, D. W. (1997). Irreconcilable conflict between therapeutic and forensic roles. *Professional Psychology: Research and Practice, 28*, 50–57.

Grob, G. N., & Horwitz, A. V. (2010). *Diagnosis, therapy, and evidence: Conundrums in modern American medicine.* New Brunswick, NJ: Rutgers University Press.

Grubaugh, A. L., Magruder, K. M., Waldrop, A. E., Elhai, J. D., Knapp, R. G., & Frueh, B. C. (2005). Subthreshold PTSD in primary care: Prevalence, psychiatric disorders, healthcare use, and functional status. *Journal of Nervous and Mental Disease, 193*(10), 658–664.

Grunert, B. K. (2005). Hand trauma. In D. B. Sarwer, T. Pruzinsky, T. F. Cash, R. M. Goldwyn, J. A. Persing, & L. A. Whitaker (Eds.), *Psychological aspects of reconstructive and cosmetic plastic surgery* (pp. 145–159). New York: Lippincott Williams & Wilkins.

Grunert, B. K., Devine, C. A., Matloub, H. S., Sanger, J. R., & Yousif, N. J. (1988). Flashbacks after traumatic hand injuries: Prognostic indicators. *Journal of Hand Surgery, 13*(1), 125–127.

Grunert, B. K., Devine, C. A., McCallum-Burke, S., Matloub, H. S., Sanger, J. R., & Yousif, N. J. (1989). On-site work evaluations: Desensitisation for avoidance reactions following severe hand injuries. *Journal of Hand Surgery, 14*(2), 239–241.

Grunert, B. K., Devine, C. A., Smith, C. J., Matloub, H. S., Sanger, J. R., & Yousif, N. J. (1992). Graded work exposure to promote work return after severe hand trauma: A replicated study. *Annals of Plastic Surgery, 29*(6), 532–536.

Grunert, B. K., & Dzwierzynski, W. W. (1997). Prognostic factors for return to work following severe hand injuries. *Techniques in Hand and Upper Extremity Surgery, 1*(3), 213–218.

Grunert, B. K., Smucker, M. R., Weis, J. M., & Rusch, M. D. (2003). When prolonged imaginal exposure fails: Adding an imagery-based cognitive restructuring component in the treatment of industrial accident victims suffering from PTSD. *Cognitive and Behavioral Practice, 10*(4), 333–346.

Grunert, B. K., Weis, J. M., Smucker, M. R., & Christianson, H. F. (2007). Imagery rescripting and reprocessing therapy after failed prolonged exposure for posttraumatic stress disorder following industrial injury. *Journal of Behavior Therapy and Experimental Psychiatry, 38*(4), 317–328.

Guriel, J., & Fremouw, W. (2003). Assessing malingered posttraumatic stress disorder: A critical review. *Clinical Psychology Review, 23*(7), 881–904.

Hembree, E. A., & Foa, E. B. (2010). Cognitive behavioral treatments for PTSD. In G.

M. Rosen & B. C. Frueh (Eds.), *Clinician's guide to posttraumatic stress disorder.* Hoboken, NJ: Wiley.

Hickling, E. J., Blanchard, E. B., Mundy, E., & Galovski, T. E. (2002). Detection of malingered MVA related posttraumatic stress disorder: An investigation of the ability to detect professional actors by experienced clinicians, psychological tests, and psychophysiological assessment. *Journal of Forensic Psychology Practice, 2,* 33–54.

Keane, T. M., Buckley, T. C., & Miller, M. W. (2003). Forensic psychological assessment in PTSD. In R. I. Simon (Ed.), *Posttraumatic stress disorder in litigation* (2nd ed.). Washington, DC: American Psychiatric Press.

Kessler, R. C., Sonnega, A., Bromet, E., Hughes, M., & Nelson, C. B. (1995). Posttraumatic stress disorder in the National Comorbidity Survey. *Archives of General Psychiatry, 52*(12), 1048–1060.

Lacoursiere, R. B. (1993). Diverse motives for fictitious post-traumatic stress disorder. *Journal of Traumatic Stress, 6,* 141–149.

Lee, S. K., & Green, P. H. (2006). Celiac sprue (the great modern-day imposter). *Current Opinion in Rheumatology, 18*(1), 101–107.

Lees-Haley, P. R. (1986, Winter). Pseudo post-traumatic stress disorder. *Trial Diplomacy Journal,* 17–20.

Lees-Haley, P. R. (1990). Malingering mental disorder on the Impact of Events Scale (IES): Toxic exposure and cancer phobia. *Journal of Traumatic Stress, 3,* 315–321.

Linden, M. (2003). Posttraumatic embitterment disorder. *Psychotherapy and Psychosomatics, 72*(4), 195–202.

McHugh, P. R., & Treisman, G. (2007). PTSD: A problematic diagnostic category. *Journal of Anxiety Disorders, 21*(2), 211–222.

McNally, R. J. (2003). Progress and controversy in the study of posttraumatic stress disorder. *Annual Review of Psychology, 54,* 229–252.

McNally, R. J., Bryant, R. A., & Ehlers, A. (2003). Does early psychological intervention promote recovery from posttraumatic stress? *Psychological Science in the Public Interest, 4,* 45–79.

Merten, T., Thies, E., Schneider, K., & Stevens, A. (2009). Symptom validity testing in claimants with alleged posttraumatic stress disorder: Comparing the Morel Emotional Numbing Test, the Structured Inventory of Malingered Symptomatology, and the Word Memory Test. *Psychological Injury and Law, 2,* 284–293.

Mitchell, J. T. (1983). When disaster strikes . . . the critical incident stress debriefing process. *Journal of Emergency Medical Services, 8*(1), 36–39.

Mol, S. S., Arntz, A., Metsemakers, J. F., Dinant, G. J., Vilters-van Montfort, P. A., & Knottnerus, J. A. (2005). Symptoms of post-traumatic stress disorder after non-traumatic events: Evidence from an open population study. *British Journal of Psychiatry, 186,* 494–499.

Norris, F. H. (1992). Epidemiology of trauma: Frequency and impact of different potentially traumatic events on different demographic groups. *Journal of Consulting and Clinical Psychology, 60*(3), 409–418.

North, C. S. (2001). The course of post-traumatic stress disorder after the Oklahoma City bombing. *Military Medicine, 166*(12, Suppl.), 51–52.

Orr, S. P., Metzger, L. J., Miller, M. W., & Kaloupek, D. G. (2004). Psychophysiological assessment of PTSD. In J. P. Wilson & T. M. Keane (Eds.), *Assessing psychological trauma and PTSD* (2nd ed., pp. 69–97). New York: Guilford Press.

Page, H. W. (1891). *Railway injuries: With special reference to those of the back and nervous system, in their medico-legal and clinical aspects.* London: Charles Griffin & Co.

Pankratz, L. (1998). *Patients who deceive: Assessment and management of risk in providing health care and financial benefits.* Springfield, MA: Charles C. Thomas.

Pitman, R. K., Sparr, L. F., Saunders, L. S., & McFarlane, A. C. (1996). Legal issues in posttraumatic stress disorder. In B. A. van der Kolk, A. C. McFarlane, & L. Weisaeth (Eds.), *Traumatic stress: The effects of overwhelming experience on mind, body, and society.* New York: Guilford Press.

Prigerson, H. G., & Jacobs, S. C. (2001). Traumatic grief as a distinct disorder: A rationale, consensus criteria, and a preliminary empirical test. In M. S. Stroebe, R. O. Hansson, W. Stroebe, & H. Schut (Eds.), *Handbook of bereavement research: Consequences, coping, and care* (pp. 613–645). Washington, DC: American Psychological Association.

Rose, S., Bisson, J., & Wessley, S. (2001). Psychological debriefing for preventing posttraumatic stress disorder (PTSD), Cochrane Review. In *The Cochrane Library, 3.* Oxford, UK: Update Software.

Rosen, G. M. (1995). The Aleutian Enterprise sinking and posttraumatic stress disorder: Misdiagnosis in clinical and forensic settings. *Professional Psychology: Research and Practice, 26,* 82–87.

Rosen, G. M. (2004a). Malingering and the PTSD database. In G. M. Rosen (Ed.), *Posttraumatic stress disorder: Issues and controversies.* Chichester, UK: Wiley.

Rosen, G. M. (2004b). Preface. In G. M. Rosen (Ed.), *Posttraumatic stress disorder: Issues and controversies.* Chichester, UK: Wiley.

Rosen, G. M. (2004c). Traumatic events, criterion creep, and the creation of pretraumatic stress disorder. *The Scientific Review of Mental Health Practice, 3,* 39–42.

Rosen, G. M. (2006). DSM's cautionary guideline to rule out malingering can protect the PTSD data base. *Journal of Anxiety Disorders, 20*(4), 530–535.

Rosen, G. M., & Davison, G. C. (2001). "Echo attributions" and other risks when publishing on novel therapies without peer review. *Journal of Clinical Psychology, 57*(10), 1245–1250; discussion 1251–1260.

Rosen, G. M., & Davison, G. C. (2003). Psychology should list empirically supported principles of change (ESPs) and not credential trademarked therapies or other treatment packages. *Behavior Modification, 27*(3), 300–312.

Rosen, G. M., & Lilienfeld, S. O. (2008). Posttraumatic stress disorder: An empirical evaluation of core assumptions. *Clinical Psychology Review, 28*(5), 837–868.

Rosen, G. M., Lilienfeld, S. O., & Orr, S. P. (2010). Searching for PTSD's biological signature. In G. M. Rosen & B. C. Frueh (Eds.), *Clinician's guide to posttraumatic stress disorder* (pp. 97–116). Hoboken, NJ: Wiley.

Rosen, G. M., & Powel, J. E. (2003). Use of a symptom validity test in the forensic assessment of posttraumatic stress disorder. *Journal of Anxiety Disorders, 17*(3), 361–367.

Rosen, G. M., Sawchuk, C. N., Atkins, D. C., Brown, M., Price, J. R., & Lees-Haley, P. R. (2006). Risk of false positives when identifying malingered profiles using the trauma symptom inventory. *Journal of Personality Assessment, 86*(3), 329–333.

Rosen, G. M., Spitzer, R. L., & McHugh, P. R. (2008). Problems with the post-traumatic stress disorder diagnosis and its future in DSM V. *British Journal of Psychiatry, 192*(1), 3–4.

Sabin-Farrell, R., & Turpin, G. (2003). Vicarious traumatization: Implications for the mental health of health workers? *Clinical Psychology Review, 23*(3), 449–480.

Schuster, M. A., Stein, B. D., Jaycox, L., Collins, R. L., Marshall, G. N., Elliott, M. N., et al. (2001). A national survey of stress reactions after the September 11, 2001, terrorist attacks. *New England Journal of Medicine, 345*(20), 1507–1512.

Scott, M. J., & Stradling, S. G. (1994). Post-traumatic stress disorder without the trauma. *British Journal of Clinical Psychology, 33*, 71–74.

Scott, W. (1990). PTSD in DSM-III: A case in the politics of diagnosis and disease. *Social Problems, 37*, 294–310.

Shepard, B. (2004). Risk factors and PTSD—A historian's perspective. In G. M. Rosen (Ed.), *Posttraumatic stress disorder: Issues and controversies* (pp. 39–61). Chichester, UK: Wiley.

Simon, R. I. (2003). *Posttraumatic stress disorder in litigation: Guidelines for forensic assessment* (2nd ed.). Washington, DC: American Psychiatric Publishing.

Simons, D., & Silveira, W. R. (1994). Post-traumatic stress disorder in children after television programmes. *British Medical Journal, 308*(6925), 389–390.

Slovenko, R. (1994). Legal aspects of post-traumatic stress disorder. *Psychiatric Clinics of North America, 17*(2), 439–446.

Slovenko, R. (2002). *Psychiatry in Law/Law in Psychiatry*. New York: Brunner-Routledge.

Smucker, M. R., Grunert, B. K., & Weis, J. M. (2001). Imagery rescripting for the treatment of posttraumatic stress disorder. In A. Sheik (Ed.), *Handbook of therapeutic imagery techniques* (pp. 85–97). Amityville, NY: Baywood.

Smucker, M. R., Grunert, B. K., & Weis, J. M. (2003). Overcoming roadblocks in cognitive-behavioral therapy with PTSD: A new algorithm treatment model. In R. L. Leahy (Ed.), *Overcoming roadblocks in cognitive therapy practice: Transforming challenges into opportunities for change* (pp. 175–194). New York: Guilford Press.

Smucker, M. R., & Neideree, J. L. (1995). Treating incest-related PTSD and pathognomic schema through imaginal exposure and rescripting. *Cognitive and Behavioral Practice, 2*, 63–93.

Solomon, S. D., & Canino, G. J. (1990). Appropriateness of DSM-III-R criteria for posttraumatic stress disorder. *Comprehensive Psychiatry, 31*(3), 227–237.

Sparr, L., & Pankratz, L. D. (1983). Factitious posttraumatic stress disorder. *American Journal of Psychiatry, 140*(8), 1016–1019.

Sparr, L. F. (1990). Legal aspects of posttraumatic stress disorder: Uses and abuses. In M. E. Wolf & A. D. Mosnain (Eds.), *Posttraumatic stress disorder: Etiology, phenomenology, and treatment*. Washington, DC: American Psychiatric Press.

Specialty Guidelines for Forensic Psychologists Committee on Ethical Guidelines for Forensic Psychologists. (1991). Specialty guidelines for forensic psychologists. *Law and Human Behavior, 15*, 655–665.

Spitzer, R. L., First, M. B., & Wakefield, J. C. (2007). Saving PTSD from itself in DSM-V. *Journal of Anxiety Disorders, 21*(2), 233–241.

Storm, J., & Graham, J. R. (2000). Detection of coached general malingering on the MMPI-2. *Psychological Assessment, 12*(2), 158–165.

Strasburger, L. H., Gutheil, T. G., & Brodsky, A. (1997). On wearing two hats: Role conflict in serving as both psychotherapist and expert witness. *American Journal of Psychiatry, 154*(4), 448–456.

Summerfield, D. (2001). The invention of post-traumatic stress disorder and the social usefulness of a psychiatric category. *British Medical Journal, 322*(7278), 95–98.

Taylor, S., Frueh, B. C., & Asmundson, G. J. (2007). Detection and management of malingering in people presenting for treatment of posttraumatic stress disorder: Methods, obstacles, and recommendations. *Journal of Anxiety Disorders, 21*(1), 22–41.

Vandervoort, D., & Rokach, A. (2004). Abusive relationships: Is a new category for traumatization needed? *Current Psychology: Developmental, Learning, Personality, Social, 23,* 68–76.

Wakefield, J. D., & Horwitz, A. V. (2010). Normal reactions to adversity or symptoms of disorder? In G. M. Rosen & B. C. Frueh (Eds.), *Clinician's guide to posttraumatic stress disorder.* Hoboken, NJ: Wiley.

Weathers, F. W., & Keane, T. M. (2007). The Criterion A problem revisited: Controversies and challenges in defining and measuring psychological trauma. *Journal of Traumatic Stress, 20*(2), 107–121.

Wetter, M. W., & Corrigan, S. K. (1995). Providing information to clients about psychological tests: A survey of attorneys' and law students' attitudes. *Professional Psychology: Research and Practice, 26,* 474–477.

Wetter, M. W., & Deitsch, S. E. (1996). Faking specific disorders and temporal response consistency on the MMPI-2. *Psychological Assessment, 8*(1), 39–47.

Williams, C. W., Lees-Haley, P. R., & Djanogly, S. E. (1999). Clinical scrutiny of litigants' self-reports. *Professional Psychology: Research and Practice, 30,* 361–367.

Young, G., Kane, A. W., & Nicholson, K. (Eds.). (2007). *Causality of psychological injury: Presenting evidence in court.* New York: Springer.

CHAPTER 7

Depression in the Context of Workplace Injury

Kyle E. Ferguson
Grant L. Iverson
Scott A. Langenecker
Allan H. Young

Major depressive disorder is a common psychiatric disorder and a leading cause of disability for young adults. Depression in the workforce has enormous implications, not only in human suffering, but for society as well (i.e., in absenteeism and lost productivity). Depression has a high degree of comorbidity with other psychiatric (e.g., posttraumatic stress disorder [PTSD] and other anxiety disorders) and medical disorders (e.g., diabetes, rheumatoid arthritis, chronic pain, and traumatic brain injury). Comorbid depression often complicates diagnosis, treatment planning, and prognosis in numerous health conditions (Prince et al., 2007). Moreover, as a comorbid condition, depression is also associated with delays in injured employees returning to work, even in seemingly uncomplicated cases of musculoskeletal injuries (Sullivan, Adams, Thibault, Corbiere, & Stanish, 2006).

There is a body of evidence that depression can be triggered by stressful life events (Farmer & McGuffin, 2003; Friis, Wittchen, Pfister, & Lieb, 2002; Kendler, Hettema, Butera, Gardner, & Prescott, 2003; Kendler, Karkowski, & Prescott, 1999), especially in vulnerable individuals. Moreover, there might be a genetic–environment interaction that partially mediates this relation. Researchers have reported that adults with a history of childhood trauma, coupled with predisposing genetic influences (e.g., polymorphisms in the *FKBP5* gene[1]), are more likely to develop major depression and anxiety-related disorders (e.g., PTSD) in response to significant stressful life events (Binder et al., 2008; Bradley et al., 2008; Heim et al., 2009). In other words, given gene × environment interactions of child abuse during development, the stress-response pathways of certain individuals might have been more sensitized (vulnerable) to the adverse effects of stress.

Work-related accidents, which result in significant physical or psychological injuries, can be very stressful for some individuals. Of course, other stressful life events can also occur in the interim, which may not be injury-related, and these stressful events can accumulate to become a primary etiologic factor in the person's depression. Depression, therefore—whether wholly related, partially related, or unrelated to the injury—can be an underlying cause of subjective and/or objective impairment in social and occupational functioning. If adequately treated, the majority of people with depression can experience a substantial improvement in their day-to-day functioning.

Clearly, depression is prevalent and important in the context of workplace injuries. Depression can be a preexisting condition, occurring singly, episodically, or chronically. Depression can arise de novo, or it can be partially or mostly related to physical injuries sustained in the workplace. As a primary or comorbid condition, depression can have an adverse effect on social, cognitive, and occupational functioning.

This chapter provides an overview of depression in the context of workplace injuries. We define depression broadly to include major depressive disorder, depression secondary to a medical condition, and to include mood disorder, not otherwise specified where a subsyndromal, yet problematic, level of depressive symptoms can be present. We acknowledge that the heterogeneous nature of depression as a construct may make this broad definition too generic. Nonetheless, the present state of research does not allow for a more specific subclassification strategy, based on symptoms and causes, to be explicitly delineated. The chapter is organized into the following seven sections: (1) epidemiology and risk factors, (2) healthcare costs and presenteeism, (3) neurobiology of depression, (4) effects of depression on cognition, (5) depression associated with other workplace injuries, (6) treatment, and (7) new screening battery for cognitive impairment in depression.

EPIDEMIOLOGY AND RISK FACTORS

Major depressive disorder is one of the most common psychiatric disorders and is the leading cause of disability in the United States for individuals between 15 and 44 years of age (World Health Organization, 2004). The average age of onset is in the mid-20s, with an estimated lifetime risk in community samples ranging from 10 to 25% for women and 5 to 12% for men (Alonso et al., 2004; American Psychiatric Association, 2000; Kruijshaar et al., 2005; Patten et al., 2006; Waraich, Goldner, Somers, & Hsu, 2004). The lifetime prevalence in African Americans is generally lower than other racial and ethnic groups (e.g., Caucasians, Hispanics, or others); and individuals between 35 and 44 years of age are more likely to develop comorbid depression than other age cohorts (i.e., Odds Ratio: 3.57, $p < 0.05$; Blazer, Kessler, McGonagle, & Swartz, 1994).

It has been estimated that a 2-week prevalence of major depression, major depression in partial remission, or dysthymia in the United States workforce is 9.4% (Stewart, Ricci, Chee, Hahn, & Morganstein, 2003). High prevalence rates of depression in the workforce have huge implications, not only in human suffering for individuals and their families, but for society as well. It has been estimated that depression costs the United States over $80 billion annually, mostly in absenteeism and lost productivity (Greenberg et al., 2003).

According to the biopsychosocial model, certain individuals are more likely to develop depression due to one or more risk factors, including biogenetic, psychological, somatic, and sociocultural risk factors (Schotte, Van Den Bossche, De Doncker, Claes, & Cosyns, 2006). Biogenetic risk factors are inherited vulnerabilities to environmental stress. For example, compared to the general population, individuals with a first-degree biological relative with major depressive disorder (MDD) are 1.5 to 3 times more likely to develop MDD, have an increased risk of Alcohol Dependence, and/or develop an anxiety disorder (American Psychiatric Association, 2000). In some families, this increased risk might be maternally inherited[2] (Bergemann & Boles, 2010). Psychological risk factors involve cognitive appraisals and evaluation (Segal & Dobson, 1992). For example, depressed individuals tend to make stable, internal, global attributions for negative life events (e.g., failing a test or getting a poor performance appraisal; Abramson, Seligman, & Teasdale, 1978). Somatic risk factors concern elevated vulnerability in persons who are medically ill. For example, depression is commonly comorbid with general medical conditions. Individuals with chronic medical conditions are two to three times more likely to develop depression when compared to healthy people (Egede, 2007). Sociocultural risk factors include such things as the importance of family values, local crime, social networks, and access to treatment (Schotte et al., 2006). For example, some ethnic minority groups (e.g., African Americans and Hispanics) might suffer from greater mental health problems, more generally, in part because they are not receiving sufficient care or are receiving a poorer quality of care (U.S. Department of Health and Human Services, 2001).

HEALTHCARE COSTS AND PRESENTEEISM

As noted earlier, the total annual societal cost of depression in the United States has been estimated at $83 billion (Greenberg et al., 2003). The direct costs of inpatient, outpatient, and other forms of treatment only account for approximately 25% of this estimate. Interestingly, it has been shown that lower direct costs are generally not attributable to a lack of treatment availability. That is to say, despite the availability of effective treatments, only a minority of depressed individuals are being adequately treated (e.g., taking antidepressants at therapeutic levels; Wang, Simon, & Kessler, 2008). In contrast, 62% of this figure was due to indirect costs, including absenteeism and presenteeism. Absenteeism refers to missed workdays on account of health-related problems. Depressed individuals, for example, have been found to have between 1.5 and 3.2 more short-term disability days over a 30-day period (Kessler et al., 1999), or a mean of 9.86 sick days annually, when compared to nondepressed coworkers (Druss, Rosenheck, & Sledge, 2000).

Presenteeism relates to diminished productivity at work, which is usually estimated in terms of lost productive time (Johnston, Westerfield, Momin, Phillippi, & Naidoo, 2009). Depression is a strong predictor of diminished work performance (Kessler et al., 2008). For example, depressed individuals reported significantly more total health-related lost productive time than individuals who were not depressed (i.e., an average of 5.6 hours per week versus 1.5 hours per week; Stewart et al., 2003). Of course, given that this was self-reported lost productive time, and depressed individuals had to recall a period of 2 weeks, these estimates might not have been accurate. Among other things, depressed individuals are more inclined to evaluate past performance negatively, even in situations where they performed adequately or well.

Examining the actual labor products of depressed individuals is a more accurate measure of presenteeism than estimated time working. One study of a large U.S. insurance claims processing company, for example, utilized the agency's computer tracking of the number of claims processed each day at work per each employee[3] (Berndt, Bailit, Keller, Verner, & Finkelstein, 2000). After factoring out absentee days, they found no differential effect of one or more mental disorders on average at-work productivity. In contrast, although there was no statistically significant difference between one mental disorder and healthy normal controls, comorbid depression with another mental disorder resulted in 37% more absentee days, annually, when compared to the no-mental-disorder group. In other words, while missing more workdays due to illness, persons with certain types of mental disorders may not be less productive when present at work. Accordingly, this lends some support to the claim that presenteeism in the previous studies might have been overestimated due to reporting biases in depressed employees. It is common for people with depression to show negative biases when evaluating their performance.

NEUROBIOLOGY OF DEPRESSION

Depression is a complex disorder of multiple, interactive biological systems comprising molecular, cellular, neuroanatomical, neurochemical, neuroendocrinological, and neuropsychological factors, which, in concert, are influenced by an individual's genetic makeup, prenatal development, and exposure to environmental stressors (Mossner et al., 2007; Ramasubbu & MacQueen, 2008). Moreover, depressive illness is more common in women, which suggests, to some extent, different or additional gender-related processes (Hastings, Parsey, Oquendo, Arango, & Mann, 2004). For example, it has been reported that the protective effects of the A allele of the rs 110402 SNP is associated with reduced symptoms of depression in males exposed to significant childhood abuse, but not in females exposed to similar childhood trauma (Heim et al., 2009). The sources of sex differences in the etiology of depression, however, are not fully explained, despite considerable ongoing research in this area (Desai & Jann, 2000; Hammen, 2003; Noble, 2005).

Because depression is often a recurrent and progressive illness, whereby depressive episodes are triggered more readily over an individual's lifespan—so-called stress-sensitization—the evidence tends to support a "kindling hypothesis" (Maletic et al., 2007; Ramasubbu & MacQueen, 2008). That is to say, individuals with certain biological susceptibilities appear to be more adversely affected by stressful life events than the general population, and hence more likely to develop such affective disturbances as depression (Monroe & Harkness, 2005). For example, people who suffer a single episode of major depression are at high risk for a future episode, with estimates of recurrence ranging from 50 to 80% (Bockting et al., 2005; Frank et al., 1990; Keller et al., 1992; Mulder, Joyce, Frampton, Luty, & Sullivan, 2006; Pettit, Lewinsohn, & Joiner, 2006). People who have had two or more episodes of depression are at extremely high risk for a future episode (American Psychiatric Association, 2000, p. 372; Bockting et al., 2005; Kessing, Hansen, Andersen, & Angst, 2004; Solomon et al., 2000; Williams, Crane, Barnhofer, Van der Does, & Segal, 2006). In addition, with recurrences of depression, the relative strength of a stressful situation, life event, or injury, necessary as a trigger for a new episode, appears to diminish over time[4] (Kendler, Thornton, & Gardner, 2001). In other words, the threshold for triggering a subsequent depressive episode is lowered.

Possible biological mechanisms of depression have been discussed in the literature for decades. However, these mechanisms have been poorly understood until recent times. Technological advances in neuroimaging have bolstered our understanding to some extent of the physiological and functional mechanisms of depression. Using structural and functional brain mapping techniques, researchers have identified prefrontal and limbic areas as structures putatively involved in affective regulation (Maletic et al., 2007). This richly interconnected neuroanatomic circuit involved in memory, and affect processing and regulation, is part of the limbic–cortical–striatal–pallidal–thalamic circuit (LCSPT), involving cellular signaling pathways, which interact at multiple levels forming complex signaling networks (Manji, Drevets, & Charney, 2001; Swerdlow & Koob, 1987). In addition, a dorsolateral prefrontal–inferior parietal–striatal–

thalamic–cerebellar circuit associated with executive functioning has been implicated in depression (Cummings, 1993; Henriques & Davidson, 1991; Langenecker et al., 2007b; Wagner et al., 2006). Specific neuroanatomical areas implicated in depressive illness include: ventromedial prefrontal cortex (VMPFC), lateral orbital prefrontal cortex (LOPFC), dorsolateral prefrontal cortex (DLPFC), anterior and posterior insula, dorsal, rostral, and subgenual anterior cingulate cortex (ACC), ventral striatum, thalamus, amygdala, and the hippocampus (Drevets & Raichle, 1992; Maletic et al., 2007; Phillips, Drevets, Rauch, & Lane, 2003; Pizzagalli et al., 2001). Measurable atrophy and reduced activation in one or more of these structures has been shown to correlate with poor treatment response and reduced interval time between depressive episodes (Langenecker et al., 2007b; Sheline, Sanghavi, Mintun, & Gado, 1999; Videbech & Ravnkilde, 2004).

There is considerable methodological heterogeneity in the literature on the neurobiology of depression, making this literature difficult to summarize. First, adult research participants can range considerably in age, from very young adults to elderly individuals; the ratios of females to males can vary widely; studies can examine first-episode depression versus recurrent episodes[5]; age-at-illness onset often varies; it is difficult (if not impossible) to control for acute depressed or euthymic states in study participants[6]; some studies only examine treatment-resistant individuals (which appear to differ fundamentally from treatment-responders); participants are either medicated, unmedicated, or medicated only some of the time; and depression is often a comorbid condition—not a "pure" clinical illness—which is highly correlated with other psychiatric, medical, neurological, and substance-related disorders (e.g., some studies suggest that depression occurs in most individuals (> 50%) with chronic pain; Arnow et al., 2006). Second, regarding methodology, studies can vary considerably in how and what structures and functional processes are measured,[7] which, obviously, can affect a study's outcome(s). Employing different neuroimaging techniques and analysis strategies also introduces measurement error and effect size variance to differing degrees, which is too often ignored in the discussion of results.

Given the rapid proliferation of research over the last decade, reviewing all or even most of these biological influences on depression is beyond the scope of the present chapter. Rather, we will briefly summarize several key molecular, structural, and functional correlates that are most germane to understanding depression from a neurobiological perspective.

Neurotransmitters and Depression

One of the earliest theories of depression is the monoamine deficiency hypothesis. According to this theory, because patients with depression appear to have depleted serotonin, norepinephrine, and/or dopamine levels in the central nervous system (CNS), targeting faulty monoaminergic neurotransmission with an antidepressant should restore normal function (Ordway, Klimek, & Mann, 2002). The support for this theory comes from drug treatment development, which began in the late 1950s, when the effects of tricyclic antidepressants (TCAs) and monoamine oxidase inhibitors (MAIOs) were discovered accidentally. However, this theory has undergone modifications, as it was inadequate in its original form. In particular, it is now recognized that a significant discrepancy exists between when antidepressants may change the monoamine level at the synapse, which can occur in a matter of days, and when there is a gradual modification in the number of postsynaptic receptors, thought to occur over the course of weeks. The change in number and location of postsynaptic receptors with treatment is thought to better match the typical timeline of treatment response in depression, but evidence to this effect is still quite weak. As Hindmarch (2001) noted, among other things, the original theory did not provide an adequate explanation for therapeutic action,[8] nor could it explain why antidepressants are effective in other seemingly unrelated disorders as well (e.g., social phobia).

Many drugs may affect the brain by either increasing or decreasing neurotransmitter activity (Goldberg, 2006). For example, most antidepressant medications affect norepinephrine and serotonin in the brain, which, functionally, appear to correct for abnormal signaling implicated in mood regulation and cognition (Ordway et al., 2002). Tricyclic antidepressants block reuptake of serotonin and norepinephrine; selective serotonin reuptake inhibitors (SSRIs) block reuptake of serotonin; and monoamine oxidase inhibitors (MAOIs), another class of antidepressants, block the breakdown of serotonin, norepinephrine, and sometimes dopamine, enabling these agents to remain active in the brain (Lieberman & Tasman, 2006). Antipsychotic medication appears to be effective in psychotic depression (possibly due to dopamine involvement; Schatzberg, Garlow, & Nemeroff, 2002).

More recently, research shows that the signaling pathways, which are involved in cell survival (i.e., cellular resilience in neuroplasticity) and cell death, may be affected by long-term treatment with antidepressants (Manji et al., 2003). As a corollary, it has been suggested that the longer an individual with major depression goes untreated, the more likely there will be significant cellular loss in specific regions of the brain (e.g., hippocampus; Sheline, Gado, & Kraemer, 2003). Stress and threat paradigms have been associated with decreased hippocampal and increased amygdala dendritic arborization in animal models (Magarinos, McEwen, Flugge, & Fuchs, 1996; Mitra & Sapolsky, 2008). Animals exposed to these paradigms have shown increased expression of depressive- and anxiety-like behaviors (Magarinos et al., 1996; Manolides & Baloyannis, 1984; Mitra & Sapolsky, 2008; Sapolsky, Uno, Rebert, & Finch, 1990; Vyas, Bernal,

& Chattarji, 2003). Emerging literature in humans suggests that there is decreased hippocampal volume with extensive illness burden (van Eijndhoven et al., 2009). Furthermore, it has been reported that decreased hippocampal volume appears to be more pronounced in persons experiencing multiple depressive episodes relative to individuals experiencing their first episode of depression (MacQueen et al., 2003).

Structural and Functional Changes in Depression

These neurochemical processes, affecting cellular resilience and cell death, are implicated in structural changes in the brain that appear to occur in chronically depressed individuals. Among the structures of the two circuits most affected by these neurochemicals (described above), reduced amygdala, hippocampal, and prefrontal volume have been shown in a number of neuroimaging studies. The amygdala, which is richly interconnected with the hypothalamus, is involved in vegetative and protective drives, emotional learning, patterned movements, emotional responses, and memory processes (Kolb & Whishaw, 2008; LeDoux, 1993; Murray, 2007). Regarding sex differences, the hippocampal volume of healthy males appears to be larger than females and is more likely to show volumetric reductions over the lifespan (Lupien et al., 2007; Pruessner, Collins, Pruessner, & Evans, 2001). The hippocampus is intimately involved in the consolidation of new memories and spatial organization, among other functions (Mesulam, 2000). The prefrontal cortex, the most rostral area of the frontal lobe, plays a critical role in attention, planning, decision making, emotion, and personality (Morecraft & Yeterian, 2002). Campbell and colleagues conducted a meta-analysis of studies using magnetic resonance imaging to measure volumetric differences in hippocampal and related structures (amygdala) in persons with major depressive disorders and healthy control subjects (Campbell et al., 2004). Overall, their study revealed significantly lower volume in depressed individuals relative to healthy controls in the bilateral hippocampus plus combined hippocampus and amygdala. There is an additional meta-analysis to suggest that amygdala volume was increased in medicated, but decreased in nonmedicated, participants with depression (Hamilton & Gotlib, 2008). A more recent study reported increased amygdala volume in the early, but not late stages of depression (van Eijndhoven et al., 2009).

Videbech and Ravnkilde (2004) examined 12 studies of unipolar depression, comprising 351 patients and 279 healthy controls. The average volume reduction was 8% in the left hippocampus and 10% in the right. Of course, as the study authors maintain, reduced hippocampal volume is not specific to depression, but is also seen in progressive dementias like Alzheimer's disease, which might have been a potential confound (i.e., maturation) in those studies involving much older research participants.

In a review of the literature, Drevets, Price, and Furey (2008) concluded that volumetric abnormalities, resulting in measurable reductions in gray matter in individuals with major depressive illness, have also been shown in the left anterior cingulate cortex, and orbital/ventrolateral and polar/dorsal anterolateral prefrontal lobes. They also noted reductions in white matter in the genu of the corpus callosum. In contrast, some subgroups have shown enlarged pituitary and adrenal glands.

Abnormalities of cerebral blood flow and glucose metabolism as measured by functional magnetic resonance imaging (fMRI) and positron emission tomography (PET) have been observed in persons with mood disorders (see Drevets et al., 2008; Ressler & Mayberg, 2007). Although many brain areas are associated with depressive symptoms, a number of findings seem to show increased metabolism in the prefrontal cortex, subgenual cingulate cortex, subcortical hippocampus, and amygdala (Drevets, 2000; Mayberg, 2003; Mayberg et al., 1999; Milad et al., 2007; Ressler & Nemeroff, 2000). Moreover, a reduction in gray matter volume in certain structures has been found to contribute to inconsistencies in activation/metabolism across studies (for examples see Drevets & Price, 2005; Drevets & Raichle, 1992; Ketter et al., 2001).

Some functional imaging studies show that depressed individuals engaging in cognitive tasks requiring working memory and executive functioning demonstrate increased cortical activity (see Thomas & Elliott, 2009 for a review). Harvey and colleagues proposed a cortical inefficiency model, such that additional neuronal resources are required to achieve accurate performance in depressed individuals (Harvey et al., 2005). In particular, a number of recent studies have shown increased frontal and temporal activation in depressed subjects compared to healthy control subjects, using fMRI paradigms, in the context of preserved or nonsignificantly enhanced performance, consistent with this theory (Holmes et al., 2005; Langenecker et al., 2007b; Wagner et al., 2006).

Depressed patients also demonstrate a bias toward negative emotional information. For example, compared to normal controls, studies have shown that depressed patients exhibit amygdala hyperactivity with exposure to negative words (Siegle, Carter, & Thase, 2006; Siegle, Steinhauer, Thase, Stenger, & Carter, 2002; Siegle, Thompson, Carter, Steinhauer, & Thase, 2007), negative facial expressions (Dannlowski et al., 2007), and pictures of negative valence (Hamilton & Gotlib, 2008). Emotional biases can contribute to cognitive dysfunction in depression through such processes as abnormal responses to negative performance feedback (Elliott, 1998; Murphy, Michael, Robbins, & Sahakian, 2003) and negative memory biases (Direnfeld & Roberts, 2006). Such biases are thought to be produced by a hyperactive amygdala (Abercrombie et al., 1998; Taylor Tavares et al., 2008) coupled with an attenuation of the anterior cingulate cortex (Steele, Kumar, & Ebmeier, 2007). It is also possible that increased occurrence of negative life events sensitizes individuals to negative information, whereby there is increased orbital frontal activation for negative words in those depressed individuals with increased negative life events (Hsu, Langenecker, Kennedy, Zubieta, & Heitzeg, 2010).

Given that there is double the incidence of depression in women relative to men, it is notable that gender-by-diagnosis imaging studies have not been conducted. There is some evidence to support subtle activation differences between the sexes in healthy control studies of emotion processing and verbal fluency (Mak, Hu, Zhang, Xiao, & Lee, 2009). For example, Koch and colleagues examined potential sex-related neural correlates of cognition and emotion using fMRI methods, they found that during a processing task of negative emotions, there was greater involvement of the amygdala and the orbitofrontal cortex (OFC) in female participants than in males, who showed greater involvement of the prefrontal and superior parietal regions (Koch et al., 2007). They concluded that this finding provided some evidence for increased emotional reactivity in women. Regarding individuals with a remitted episode of MDD, although men did not differ from controls, women in one recent study had smaller paracingulate volumes than sex-matched controls (Yucel et al., 2009). Goswami, May, Stockmeier, and Austin (2009) also found sex-specific changes in gene expression of the presynaptic 5-HT1D autoreceptors and 5-HT-related transcription factors, NUDR[9] and REST,[10] in dorsal raphe nucleus neurons of women with MDD, which was not found in their male counterparts. Another study showed an interaction between 5HT1A receptor binding potential and polymorphic variation in the X-linked MAO-A gene influences (Mickey et al., 2008), whereby females with the putative higher expressing genotype showed higher levels of 5HT1a binding potential, while men with this genotype did not, regardless of depressive status.

Inflammation and Depression

Chronic inflammation has been linked to cancer (Wu & Zhou, 2009), cardiovascular risk (Bray, Clearfield, Fintel, & Nelinson, 2009), and the pathogenesis and complications in diabetes mellitus (Cao, Wan, Chen, & Wu, 2009), to name only a few. Immune irregularities in stress-response pathways (e.g., hypothalamic-pituitary-adrenal axis), involving the neuroendocrine and autonomic nervous systems, have also been linked to depression (De Kloet, 2004; Miller & Raison, 2008). There is evidence to suggest that some individuals with major depression, particularly when comorbid with anxiety disorders, show high levels of the stress hormone cortisol with flattened diurnal rhythm (Manji et al., 2003; Young, Abelson, & Cameron, 2004; Young, Lopez, Murphy-Weinberg, Watson, & Akil, 2000). For example, there is evidence that medically healthy depressed individuals, across the adult lifespan, show activated inflammatory pathways, as evidenced by increased proinflammatory cytokines, increased acute-phase proteins, and elevated plasma concentrations of chemokines and adhesion molecules during both depressive episodes and euthymic states (Raison, Capuron, & Miller, 2006).

Among other effects, proinflammatory cytokines may reduce neurotropic support and monoamine neurotransmission, which is believed to cause neuronal apoptosis and glial damage (Maletic et al., 2007). Moreover, some studies suggest that depressive symptom severity is associated with increasing concentrations of these inflammatory mediators (Alesci et al., 2005; Miller, Stetler, Carney, Freedland, & Banks, 2002) and that patients who are generally unresponsive to antidepressants show elevated plasma concentrations of interleukin (IL)-6 and acute-phase proteins relative to treatment responders (Maes et al., 1997; Sluzewska, Sobieska, & Rybakowski, 1997). Understanding the reasons for these differential effects, of course, has significant clinical implications for improving prognostic accuracy and, more importantly, improving treatment efficacy.

Neuroanatomic Anomalies May Precede the Onset of Depression

The hippocampus has been shown to be vulnerable to the adverse effects of stress (Thomas, Hotsenpiller, & Peterson, 2007). In particular, elevated levels of stress hormones (i.e., corticosteroids) are associated with atrophy and/or cell death of hippocampal neurons (Gilbertson et al., 2002). Moreover, such vulnerability might be greatest in early life, at a time of high neuronal plasticity (Rao et al., 2010).

Although smaller hippocampal volume has been reported in both adult and pediatric clinical populations, it is unknown whether these changes precede illness onset or are a consequence of major depressive disorder (Rao et al., 2010). Some studies suggest, for example, that appreciable differences in hippocampal volume are usually only found in those individuals who have had major depressive disorder for over 2 years, or otherwise have had more than one depressive episode (see McKinnon et al., 2009 recent meta-analysis).

In contrast, some studies suggest that neuroanatomic anomalies may precede the onset of depressive illness, in a subset of young people who are at high-familial risk of developing the illness (MacMaster et al., 2008). Chen and colleagues, for example, examined the brain structure volume of girls (between the ages of 9 and 15 years) at high- and low-familial risk of developing depression (Chen, Hamilton, & Gotlib, 2010). It is important to note that the girls did not have a history of psychopathology prior to or at the time of the study. Girls considered at high lifetime risk of developing depression were daughters of mothers with recurrent episodes of depression (N = 23). Girls considered at low risk of developing depression were daughters of mothers with no history of psychopathology (Axis I). According to voxel-based morphometry analyses, girls at high risk of depression showed significantly less gray matter density, bilaterally, compared to the girls in the low-risk group. Moreover, manual tracing revealed significant volumetric reductions in the left hippocampus in the high-risk group. In a related study, Rao and colleagues examined hippocampal volume in 29 adolescents with unipolar major depressive disorder (10 males and 19 females), 22 adolescent with no history of psychopathology but were at high familial risk (i.e., with at least one biological parent with a history of unipolar major depressive disorder; 13 males and 9 females), and 32 healthy adolescent controls (19 males and 13 females; Rao et al., 2010). Depressed adolescents and those individuals in the high-risk group had significantly smaller hippocampal volumes, bilaterally, when compared to controls. Higher levels of early-life adversity, as indicated on a semistructured interview, were associated with smaller hippocampal volumes.

Minor Physical Anomalies

Researchers have reported that some people with unipolar depression may manifest subtle, minor physical anomalies (MPA), which may have resulted from abnormal fetal development (Lohr, Alder, Flynn, Harris, & McAdams, 1997). Culav-Sumic and Jukic (2010), for example, examined 50 female subjects with recurrent unipolar depression with psychotic symptoms, 50 female subjects with recurrent unipolar depression without psychotic symptoms, and 50 healthy female controls for the presence of 51 MPAs (on various regions of the head, eyes, ears, mouth, hands, and elsewhere on the body). Both groups had significantly greater mean total MPA scores compared to control subjects (e.g., abnormal philtrum, furrowed tongue, thin upper lip, blepharophimosis, and large pigment nevi and café-au-lait spots). Of course, as Culav-Sumic and Junkic maintain, further research is necessary to determine the extent to which these changes might have resulted from genetic factors or from environmental influences (in utero). Moreover, there are very few studies of MPAs in persons with depression, one of which reported no increase in MPA prevalence in unipolar depression (see Tenyi, Trixler, Csabi, & Jeges, 2004). Accordingly, though intriguing, caution is in order when speculating about aberrant neurodevelopment in some people with recurrent depression.

EFFECTS OF DEPRESSION ON COGNITION

Subjectively experienced problems with concentration, memory, problem solving, and thinking skills are cardinal diagnostic features of major depressive disorder (American Psychiatric Association, 1994, 2000). Patients with depression are expected to have cognitive complaints. However, the relation between depression and cognitive difficulty goes much further. The co-occurrence of subjectively experienced cognitive problems and symptoms of depression (not necessarily a clinical diagnosis of depression) has been reported repeatedly in the literature in community-dwelling adults (Bassett & Folstein, 1993; Cutler & Grams, 1988; Ponds, Commissaris, & Jolles, 1997) and specific clinical groups, such as patients with cancer (Cull et al., 1996), chronic fatigue syndrome (Wearden & Appleby, 1997), HIV (Rourke, Halman, & Bassel, 1999; van Gorp et al., 1991), major noncardiac surgery (Dijkstra, Houx, & Jolles, 1999), epilepsy (Sawrie et al., 1999; Thompson & Corcoran, 1992), chronic pain (McCracken & Iverson, 2001; Schnurr & MacDonald, 1995), and sleep apnea (Jennum & Sjol, 1994). This is a consistent finding across different cultural and ethnic groups, including Chinese (Wang et al., 2000), French (Derouesne, Lacomblez, Thibault, & LePoncin, 1999), Dutch (Comijs, Deeg, Dik, Twisk, & Jonker, 2002), and African Americans (Bazargan & Barbre, 1994). Therefore, broad and diverse research converges to illustrate clearly that the diagnosis of depression, or a depressive experience that does not meet criteria for a diagnosis, is likely to be accompanied by perceived cognitive problems in otherwise healthy adults or in adults with a variety of medical conditions.

The effects of depression on formal neuropsychological testing can range from striking and extreme to virtually nonexistent (Newman & Sweet, 1992). Some researchers have reported clear evidence of reduced neurocognitive test scores associated with more severe forms of depression (e.g., Austin et al., 1999; Channon & Green, 1999; Degl'Innocenti, Agren, & Backman, 1998; Merriam, Thase, Haas, Keshavan, & Sweeney, 1999; Politis, Lykouras, Mourtzouchou, & Christodoulou, 2004). However, the effects of mild depression on cognition appear to be small (Grant, Thase, & Sweeney, 2001; Langenecker et al., 2005; Rohling, Green, Allen, & Iverson, 2002).

Regarding specific cognitive domains, deficits have been found in (1) information processing (e.g., Tsourtos, Thompson, & Stough, 2002); (2) sustained and selective attention (e.g., Landro, Stiles, & Sletvold, 2001; Porter, Gallagher, Thompson, & Young, 2003); (3) episodic memory (e.g., Porter et al., 2003), semantic memory (e.g., Preiss et al., 2009), and spatial memory (e.g., Elliott et al., 1996); and (4) executive functions (e.g., cognitive inhibition, Gohier et al., 2009; e.g., verbal fluency, Henry & Crawford, 2005; Langenecker et al., 2005, 2007a). However, as McDermott and Ebmeier (2009) point out, there have been inconsistent findings in these domains, including though not limited to, information processing (e.g., Boone et al., 1995), memory (e.g., Baune, Suslow, Engelien, Arolt, & Berger, 2006), and executive functions (e.g., Elderkin-Thompson, Mintz, Haroon, Lavretsky, & Kumar, 2006). Accordingly, the scientific community has yet to find agreement as to what specific deficits are associated with depressive illness. Moreover, in light of considerable heterogeneity of this disorder, individuals vary widely in the degree of impairment within domains (Hammar & Ardal, 2009). Impairment, if present on any given domain, can range from very mild deficits to frank impairment.

There is substantial evidence that cognitive function is compromised in the acute phase of the illness (Elliott, 1998). The long-term effects of depression on cognition, however, are poorly understood, largely because of the methodological diversity in longitudinal research (Hammar & Ardal, 2009). For example, investigators often employ different sampling procedures and utilize different instruments, among others differences—all of which can affect the outcomes of studies to varying degrees. Regarding inclusion criteria, participants vary widely in terms of symptom severity, age, comorbidity, medication use, and so forth. Accordingly, the literature on the enduring effects of depression on cognition is mixed. Some studies show residual effects, even during remission (e.g., Majer et al., 2004; Nakano et al., 2008; Neu et al., 2005), particularly in attention and working memory (e.g., Paelecke-Habermann, Pohl, & Leplow, 2005; Weiland-Fiedler et al., 2004), whereas other studies show no such effect (e.g., Biringer et al., 2005; Lahr, Beblo, & Hartje, 2007).

There is also no consensus on a standard neuropsychological profile of depression. Rather, several hypotheses have been proffered in the literature in an effort at explaining, more broadly, cognitive deficits in depression (Hammar & Ardal, 2009). These include (1) the global-diffuse hypothesis (e.g., Veiel, 1997), (2) the deficit-specific hypothesis (e.g., Elliott, 1998), and (3) the cognitive-effort hypothesis (e.g., Hammar, Lund, & Hugdahl, 2003; Hasher & Zacks, 1979).

The global-diffuse hypothesis postulates that deficits found in major depression are similar to those deficits one finds in diffuse neurological injuries, as in the case of moderate traumatic brain injury. In particular, consistent with this view, persons with major depression generally have a lowered neurocognitive profile, overall, deficient reaction time, problems with cognitive flexibility, and subjectively experienced cognitive deficits—all of which are akin to global-diffuse impairment of brain function (Veiel, 1997). Moreover, given that in some studies 50% of individuals with major depression score two or more standard deviations below the mean on certain executive tasks (e.g., Trail Making Test Part B), proponents of this view also argue that, in addition to diffuse impairment, there is particular involvement of the frontal lobes (see Austin et al., 1999; Veiel, 1997, p. 599 ff.).

The deficit-specific hypothesis also emphasizes the role of executive functioning in major depression, though to a much larger extent. In contrast with the global-diffuse hypothesis, however, proponents of this view maintain that poor performance on certain tasks across a battery of tests is mostly due to deficient executive functioning. Elliott and colleagues, for example, posit that the "general processes influencing cognitive perfor-mance in depressed patients is a *highly specific form of deficit involving an abnormal response to negative feedback*" (Elliott, Sahakian, Herrod, Robbins, & Paykel, 1997, p. 79, emphasis ours). In other words, depressed individuals have a tendency to overreact to their mistakes, thus affecting overall performance (Gualtieri, Johnson, & Benedict, 2006).

The cognitive-effort hypothesis is premised on the notion that infor-mation processing falls along a continuum between automatic and effort-ful processing (Hasher & Zacks, 1979). On one end of the continuum, automatic processing does not require many cognitive resources. Naming a relatively simple stimulus is one such example. On the other end, effortful processing is self-directed and thus requires greater attention and energy (Hammar et al., 2003). Accordingly, more demanding tasks, regardless of what they purportedly measure, are "differentially sensitive" to depres-sion (Elliott, 1998, p. 449). For example, on a visual search task, although depressed individuals performed similar to healthy controls when there was only one type of distractor present, they required significantly longer visual search time when the target search required a more complex atten-tive search strategy (Hammar et al., 2003).

At present, the theories of MDD are attempting to integrate cognitive, emotional and activation findings into a coherent model (e.g., Phillips et al., 2003). Unfortunately, the cognitive findings have yet to be well integrated with emotion reactivity results, and activation/metabolism reports are too often limited by small sample sizes and methodologies that do not integrate well with classic neuropsychological models of depression. Nonetheless, there is a strong theme of disrupted cognitive/emotional integration (Fales et al., 2008; Hare et al., 2008). Some theories posit a disruption of emo-tion processing, overactive threat and aversion systems such that there is constant disruption of cognitive processes (Davidson, Pizzagalli, Nitschke, & Putnam, 2002; Northoff et al., 2000; Siegle et al., 2002). Attention to internal and external distractors, emotional, interpersonal, or other, takes the focus away from sustained cognitive activities (Langenecker, Lee, & Bieliauskas, 2009). This is a reconstruction of the classic bottom-up theory of disruption in depression. An alternative theory relates the relative mis-match between regulatory needs, emotional or cognitive, and the demands placed on the individual by the environment (Harvey et al., 2005; Lange-necker et al., 2007b). In support for a temporary "bottom-up" theory of depression, studies to date suggest that this hyperreactivity to emotional or salient information might be reversible with treatment (Brody et al., 2001; Davidson, Abercrombie, Nitschke, & Putnam, 1999; Davidson, Irwin, Anderle, & Kalin, 2003; Fu et al., 2004; Kalin et al., 1997; Sheline et al., 2001).

This is a top-down theory of disruption, which in its strictest form would suggest that regulatory resources are weak or insufficient to meet current demands, with weaker attention and executive functioning performance as well as diminished ability to regulate and reappraise emotions and emotional responses to potentially threatening information and situations. As noted earlier, the bulk of imaging research has been devoted to the bottom-up theory of depression with mixed support. More limited, yet promising, results support the top-down theory, a theory that is more easily integrated with neuropsychological findings of attention, processing speed, and executive functioning decrements in depression (Langenecker et al., 2007b; Paelecke-Habermann, Pohl, & Leplow, 2005; Pizzagalli et al., 2001; Weiland-Fiedler et al., 2004).

DEPRESSION CO-OCCURRING WITH OTHER WORKPLACE INJURIES

Traumatic Brain Injury

Most traumatic brain injuries occur from closed-head injuries. Less frequently, brain injuries also arise from open-head injuries due to objects penetrating the skull. The term *brain injury* refers to a significant disruption in brain function due to acceleration–deceleration forces, blunt trauma, or both; the results can include both primary and secondary damage (Silver, McAllister, & Arciniegas, 2009). Primary damage involves immediate axonal injury, vascular injury, and hemorrhage. Secondary damage arises from the endogenous evolution of cellular damage or from nonbrain-related injuries or processes, such as hypotension or hypoxia. The endogenous secondary pathophysiologies include: (1) ischemia, excitotoxicity, energy failure, and cell death cascades (e.g., necrosis and apoptosis), (2) edema, (3) gradually evolving axonal damage with possible secondary axotomy, and (4) inflammation (Kochanek, Clark, & Jenkins, 2007).

Depression is the most common psychiatric disorder following TBI of all severities and exceeds rates of depression in the population at large (Bay, 2009; Kreutzer, Seel, & Gourley, 2001; Seel et al., 2003). For example, in one retrospective study tracing persons with TBI ($N = 100$, with 87 informants) for 5 years, although MDD occurred in 17% of the sample before injury, the frequency of MDD rose to 45% postinjury (Whelan-Goodinson, Ponsford, Johnston, & Grant, 2009). Moreover, over two-thirds of those individuals with postinjury depression and anxiety were new cases.

Although depression occurs most often during the first year postinjury, the risk of developing depression might remain elevated for even decades following the injury (Silver et al., 2009). Furthermore, depression is important to identify and treat following TBI because those individuals with comorbid depression evidence greater functional impairment, are more likely to manifest postconcussive symptoms, and perceive greater disability relative to individuals with TBI who are not depressed (Fann,

Katon, Uomoto, & Esselman, 1995). Moreover, depression can mimic a postconcussion syndrome (Iverson, 2006). Clinicians should therefore be very cautious to not misdiagnose a person with depression as someone who is suffering the long-term effects of a mild TBI. Finally, it is important to consider that depression in the context of workplace injuries may be expressed differently. First, it could be an expression of illness related to a stress–diathesis model and thus meet criteria for major depressive disorder. Second, depression may arise gradually over time with the loss of status and income associated with workplace injury. Third, depression could be mimicked by a "sustained misery" or anger, yet not meet the full criteria for major depressive disorder. Finally, as postinjury insurance and legal claims can drag on for years, this may insidiously promote physical or psychological decompensation.

Chronic Pain

Back pain affects as many as 85% of individuals at some point during their lifetime (Walker, Shores, Trollor, Lee, & Sachdev, 2000). In the United States, it is the most common reason for reduced activity levels in persons under 45 years of age and the second leading cause of primary care visits (Andersson, 1999). In one national telephone survey of the U.S. workforce, it was shown that a 2-week prevalence of back pain in employees between 40 and 65 years of age ($N = 320$) was 15.1% (Ricci et al., 2006). Moreover, 42% of employees who endorsed having significant back pain also indicated that it had exacerbated during that time. Workers who reported exacerbations[11] were significantly more likely than those individuals with back pain not reporting such exacerbations to report activity limitation (88.4% vs. 60.7%; $p < .0001$) and pain-related lost productive time (22.1% vs. 13.0%; $p = .0259$). Although most individuals recover from back injuries, a sizable minority does not. Hestbaek and colleagues, for example, reported that, after a 6-month follow-up, between 3 and 40% of injured employees who had been off work were still off work, and more than 40% of employees endorsed having recurrent pain at 1 year postinjury (Hestbaek, Leboeuf-Yde, & Manniche, 2003).

It is widely held that fear and avoidance are the central psychological mechanisms underlying chronic pain (Lethem, Slade, Troup, & Bentley, 1983; Vlaeyen & Linton, 2000). In fact, avoidance has been shown to predict depression and disability in patients with chronic pain (McCracken, 1998). For example, while the prevalence of major depression in the general population is estimated at 5–17%, 30–54% of patients with chronic pain are estimated to suffer from major depression (Banks & Kerns, 1996), and a substantial number have significant distress and associated symptoms not meeting the full criteria for MDD. Moreover, pain-related avoidance behavior is also associated with poor prognosis—individuals simply do not respond as well to treatment as those individuals who evidence less avoidance behavior (Asmundson, Norton, & Norton, 1999).

Subjectively experienced cognitive problems are common following soft tissue injuries, such as whiplash (Kischka, Ettlin, Heim, & Schmid, 1991), and a substantial minority of patients remain symptomatic at 1-year postinjury (Ettlin et al., 1992; Radanov, Sturzenegger, De Stefano, & Schnidrig, 1994). Perceived cognitive problems frequently are reported by patients with other forms of chronic pain. McCracken and Iverson (2001) reported that 54% of chronic pain patients from a university pain management center endorsed at least one subjective cognitive complaint (e.g., forgetfulness, difficulty finishing tasks, or difficulty with attention). Roth and colleagues found that 62% of chronic pain patients from a university hospital pain management program reported experiencing at least one subjective cognitive complaint as being a moderate to severe problem, and 28% of the patients endorsed 5 out of 5 cognitive complaints as being a moderate to severe problem (i.e., trouble remembering, need to recheck things, difficulty making decisions, mind going blank, and trouble concentrating; Roth, Geisser, Theisen-Goodvich, & Dixon, 2005). Jamison, Sbrocco, and Parris (1988) found that 54.5% of chronic pain patients reported having moderate to extreme problems with both memory and concentration. Some researchers have suggested that the subjectively experienced cognitive problems in chronic pain patients may be associated with depression, anxiety, and fatigue (e.g., McCracken & Iverson, 2001; Muñoz & Esteve, 2005; Roth et al., 2005). Similarly, these complaints may be influenced by factors including the pain experience itself, comorbid psychiatric disorders, medication side effects, iatrogenic factors, and possible malingering.

In a meta-analytic review of the literature, Kessels, Aleman, Verhagen, and van Luijtelaar (2000) concluded that cognitive functioning, as measured by neuropsychological tests, can be adversely affected following whiplash—a relatively common injury resulting from work-related accidents. Not all studies, of course, report neuropsychological changes associated with whiplash injury (e.g., Guez, Brannstrom, Nyberg, Toolanen, & Hildingsson, 2005). The cause of cognitive complaints or measured cognitive decrements in a subset of patients with whiplash is unknown; researchers suggest these problems might be related to damage to the brain (Kischka et al., 1991), somatisation (Guez et al., 2005), distraction due to pain (Antepohl, Kiviloog, Andersson, & Gerdle, 2003), or a combination of factors.

Cognitive decrements identified on neuropsychological tests, albeit often subtle in nature, have also been noted as a result of other causes of pain, such as nonmigraineous headaches (O'Bryant, Marcus, Rains, & Penzien, 2006), chronic lower back pain (Apkarian et al., 2004; Weiner, Rudy, Morrow, Slaboda, & Lieber, 2006), multiple-site pain (Hart, Martelli, & Zasler, 2000; Iezzi, Archibald, Barnett, Klinck, & Duckworth, 1999; Iezzi, Duckworth, Vuong, Archibald, & Klinck, 2004), and laboratory-induced pain (Etherton, Bianchini, Ciota, Heinly, & Greve, 2006). However, similar to the whiplash injury literature, the results are highly variable or inconclusive in many studies (Lake, Branca, Lutz, & Saper, 1999; O'Bryant et al., 2006; Tsushima & Tsushima, 1993). Moreover, poor effort or exaggeration can confound test performance in those with chronic pain (e.g., Green, 2001; Meyers & Diep, 2000; Schmand et al., 1998).

It is important to appreciate that chronic pain can mimic a postconcussion syndrome (Gasquoine, 2000; Guez et al., 2005; Haldorsen et al., 2003; Iverson, King, Scott, & Adams, 2001; Iverson & McCracken, 1997; Jamison et al., 1988; Smith-Seemiller, Fow, Kant, & Franzen, 2003). Moreover, depression is also common in patients with chronic pain (Atkinson, Slater, Patterson, Grant, & Garfin, 1991; Campbell, Clauw, & Keefe, 2003), and it is associated with increased disability in these patients (Ericsson et al., 2002; Wilson, Eriksson, D'Eon, Mikail, & Emery, 2002). Thus, it is not surprising that patients with chronic pain often complain of diverse physical, cognitive, and psychological symptoms and problems (e.g., Guez et al., 2005; Haldorsen et al., 2003; Iverson et al., 2001; Iverson & McCracken, 1997; Jamison et al., 1988; Muñoz & Esteve, 2005; Parmelee, Smith, & Katz, 1993; Roth et al., 2005; Smith-Seemiller et al., 2003).

Posttraumatic Stress Disorder

PTSD can arise from workplace injuries in civilians and in military personnel. Depression is very common in patients who suffer from PTSD (Foa, Cashman, Jaycox, & Perry, 1997; Franklin & Zimmerman, 2001; Kessler, Sonnega, Bromet, Hughes, & Nelson, 1995; Shalev et al., 1998). For example, Blanchard and colleagues reported that 53% of their patients with PTSD at 1-year post-motor vehicle collision also had major depression (Blanchard et al., 2004). However, for those patients who never met the criteria for PTSD, only 3.7% had major depression at 1-year postcollision (Blanchard et al., 2004).

PTSD includes subjectively experienced cognitive difficulty (i.e., difficulty concentrating) as a core diagnostic criterion (American Psychiatric Association, 1994). In a sample of 128 patients with PTSD, 56% reported memory problems and 92% reported concentration problems (Foa et al., 1997). Depression, substance abuse, or both, frequently co-occur with PTSD, and these co-occurring conditions also are associated with cognitive problems. If the PTSD arose within the context of a life-threatening accident, and the individual sustained orthopedic and soft tissue injuries, he or she is a heightened risk of developing comorbid chronic pain as well (Jenewein et al., 2009). Therefore, it is very likely that a person with PTSD following a serious work-related injury will have subjectively experienced cognitive problems, and perceived cognitive difficulty is virtually guaranteed if the person has co-occurring depression, chronic pain, or substance abuse.

Researchers have reported that patients with PTSD perform more poorly on neuropsychological tests than healthy adults (Buckley, Blanchard, & Neill, 2000; Jelinek et al., 2006; Jenkins, Langlais, Delis, & Cohen, 2000). The most consistent finding has been worse performance on some tests of verbal learning and memory (Bremner et al., 1993, 1995; Sutker, Allain, Johnson, & Butters, 1992; Vasterling, Brailey, Constans, & Sutker, 1998; Yehuda et al., 1995). Some, however, have not found neurocognitive decrements associated with PTSD (Crowell, Kieffer, Siders, & Vanderploeg, 2002; Stein, Hanna, Vaerum, & Koverola, 1999; Twamley, Hami, & Stein, 2004).

Previous studies have reported differences in intelligence (IQ) in people who develop PTSD versus those who do not (Macklin et al., 1998; Vasterling et al., 2002). That is, those with PTSD are more likely to have average or below-average IQs, whereas those people exposed to traumatic events who do not develop PTSD are more likely to have high-average or superior IQs. It has been speculated that having a higher IQ might be "protective" against developing PTSD (Vasterling et al., 2002).

Increasingly, researchers are noting that people with PTSD might have lower neuropsychological test scores as a preexisting characteristic (Gilbertson et al., 2006; Parslow & Jorm, 2007). Thus, the clinician might mistakenly assume that low cognitive test scores are the result of PTSD, when in fact they preceded the onset of PTSD.

Without question, assessing cognition in people with PTSD is extraordinarily complex in regards to (1) subjective symptoms, (2) objective test results, and (3) determining the cause of any particular findings. People with PTSD can have preexisting or co-occurring depression, substance abuse, chronic pain, early trauma history, and Axis II comorbidities. Moreover, they can have preexisting lower scores on intellectual and neuropsychological tests. It is unlikely that PTSD itself would lower general intelligence scores. Therefore, it is essential to interpret neuropsychological test scores in people with PTSD carefully, not by simply comparing them to normative data corrected for age, but by considering their educational attainment and level of intelligence. These factors can have a substantial impact on the interpretation of cognitive test results.

Anoxic Injury Due to Cardiac Arrest

Cardiac arrest occasionally happens in the workplace. Cardiac arrest is caused by acute myocardial infarction (AMI); certain types of arrhythmias; severe blood loss (hypoperfusion); electric shock; lack of oxygen due to choking, drowning, or a severe asthma attack (hypoxia and anoxia); cardiogenic shock; stroke; heart valve or heart muscle disease and genetic disorders that affect the heart (Torpy, Lynm, & Glass, 2006).

Cognitive impairment following complete cardiac arrest is common. For example, only 5% of resuscitated patients achieve full remission of cognitive impairment within the first month, and as many as 50% suffer from significant long-term (> 1 year) cognitive deficits and functional impairment (Prohl, Bodenburg, & Rustenbach, 2009). Cognitive impairment following cardiac arrest is generally consistent with the well-known neuropsychological effects of cerebral anoxia, which includes impaired attention and concentration, memory, and executive functioning (Lim, Alexander, LaFleche, Schnyer, & Verfaellie, 2004; Roine, Kajaste, & Kaste, 1993).

Depression and cardiovascular disease appear to share a bidirectional relation (Carney, Freedland, Rich, & Jaffe, 1995). That is to say, depression increases the likelihood of experiencing a cardiovascular event, and, likewise, individuals who have suffered a cardiovascular event are three times more likely to develop a comorbid depressive illness when compared to the general population (Lippi, Montagnana, Favaloro, & Franchini, 2009). The prevalence of depressive symptoms among patients after AMI, for example, generally ranges from 15 to 32% (Carney et al., 1987; Fielding, 1991; Frasure-Smith et al., 2000; Schleifer et al., 1989). This bidirectional relationship results in higher morbidity at one year in those with a comorbid presentation, suggesting the critical importance of monitoring and treating both conditions when workplace injuries occur (Carney et al., 1995). In sum, in the context of a workplace injury involving cardiac arrest, depression can contribute to cognitive deficits and to overall functional impairment.

Electrical Injuries

The psychiatric effects of electrical injury are well documented in the literature. In a recent study, for example, 52% of individuals with electrical injuries met diagnostic criteria for a single psychiatric diagnosis, 26% of whom had two psychiatric diagnoses (Ramati et al., 2009). The two most prominent single diagnoses were depression (13%) and PTSD (13%). Moreover, 34% of the sample presented with comorbid depression and PTSD. Although not exclusive to comorbid depression, participants who meet diagnostic criteria for two psychiatric diagnoses performed significantly worse on objective cognitive testing (e.g., on measures of attention, verbal memory, and executive functioning) relative to those individuals with a single diagnosis. Ramati and colleagues' overall findings were generally consistent with those described elsewhere in the literature (Duff & McCaffrey, 2001; Pliskin et al., 1998; Primeau, Engelstatter, & Bares, 1995).

Neurotoxicology

Many occupations involve exposure to toxic chemicals. The neurotoxicants lead and mercury, certain pesticides, and industrial solvents have been shown to impact neuroendocrine functioning, which result in significant depressive symptoms, sleep disturbance, and cognitive difficulties (Genuis, 2008). In a study examining the effects of organic solvent exposure, for example, Morrow and colleagues found that a significantly higher number of solvent-exposed participants in their sample met the criteria for a current DSM-IV Axis-I diagnosis (71%; $N = 38$) compared to control subjects (10%; $N = 39$; Morrow et al., 2000). In particular, among the 71% of solvent-exposed participants who met diagnostic criteria, 58% were diagnosed with an anxiety disorder, 50% were diagnosed with a mood disorder (depression), and 36% met the criteria for both disorders.

Chronic exposure can result in what is commonly referred to in the literature as solvent-induced encephalopathy, occupational solvent encephalopathy, or chronic toxic encephalopathy (van Valen, Wekking, van der Laan, Sprangers, & van Dijk, 2009). Regarding cognitive effects of solvent exposure, in a recent meta-analysis, significant negative effect sizes were found on 12 test variables measuring attention, memory, visual-constructional abilities, and motor functioning (Meyer-Baron et al., 2008). The largest proportion of lower scores was found on tests of attention [with significant effect sizes ranging from very small to medium ($d = -0.16$ to $d = -0.46$)].

NEW SCREENING BATTERY FOR COGNITIVE IMPAIRMENT IN DEPRESSION

There is no standard battery of neuropsychological tests that is recommended for use to assess cognition in people who suffer from depression. Some neuropsychological domains that should be assessed include attention and concentration, speed of processing, learning and memory, and executive functioning. Iverson, Brooks, Ferguson, and Young (2009) developed a new time- and cost-effective neuropsychological screening battery for use in clinical practice and research with patients suffering from depression. Participants were 1,263 healthy adults between 18 and 79 years of age (mean age = 55.1, $SD = 17.8$) selected from the Neuropsychological Assessment Battery (NAB; Stern & White, 2003a) normative sample. The full NAB requires 3–3.5 hours of testing. The new screening battery requires approximately 1 hour of testing. Including an intellectual screening test and an effort test in this battery adds approximately 30 minutes. The new screening battery includes co-normed measures of attention, speed of processing, expressive language, learning, memory, and executive functioning that were selected based on a review of the depression literature (see Table 7.1). Sixteen individual test scores are derived from this battery.

Base-rate analyses allow us to determine the prevalence of low scores across the entire battery of tests. This helps us (1) guard against overinterpreting isolated low test scores, and (2) determine if a person has widespread

■ TABLE 7.1. Tests Included in the New Depression Screening Battery

Test	Description	Possible interpretation of impairment[a]
Attention, speed of processing, and executive functioning		
Numbers and Letters	Four timed tasks (Parts A, B, C, and D) involving letter cancellation, letter counting, serial addition, and letter cancellation plus serial addition, respectively	Difficulties in psychomotor speed, concentration, sustained attention, focused or selective attention, divided attention, and information processing speed
Mazes	Seven timed paper-and-pencil mazes of increasing difficulty	Difficulties with planning and foresight, but may also be associated with reduced impulse control and decreased psychomotor speed
Categories	Classification and categorization task in which the examinee generates different two-group categories based on photographs and verbal information (e.g., name, occupation, place of birth, date of birth, marital status) about six people	Poor concept formation, cognitive response set, mental flexibility, and generativity
Word Generation	Timed task in which the examinee creates three-letter words from a group of eight letters (two vowels, six consonants) that are presented visually	Reduced generativity or verbal fluency, poor self-monitoring, and perseverative tendencies
Expressive language		
Oral Production	Speech output task in which the examinee orally describes a picture of a family scene	Diminished speech output or fluency
Learning and memory		
List Learning	Verbal list learning task involving three learning trials of a 12-word list, followed by an interference list, and then short delay free recall, long delay free recall, and long delay forced-choice recognition tasks; the word list includes three embedded semantic categories with 4 words in each category	Difficulties with the learning, storage, and 10- to 15-minute delayed free recall and recognition of discrete pieces of verbal information
Story Learning	Verbal learning task involving immediate and delayed free recall of a five-sentence story; two learning trials are provided, and recall is scored for both verbatim and gist elements	Compromised initial learning and 10- to 15-minute delayed free recall of logically organized, orally presented verbal information
Daily Living Memory	Verbal learning task involving three-trial learning with immediate recall, delayed recall, and delayed multiple-choice recognition of information encountered in daily living, including medication instructions, and a name, address, and phone number	Difficulties with the learning, storage, and 5- to 10-minute delayed free recall and recognition of information frequently encountered in daily living

Note. Adapted from Stern and White (2003b). Copyright 2003 by PAR, Inc. Reprinted by permission. Further reproduction is prohibited without permission from PAR, Inc.
[a]There are several possible explanations for poor performance on a measure, which must be carefully considered when interpreting any neuropsychological test.

cognitive difficulties. The prevalence of low scores across the new screening battery, for adults in the NAB standardization sample, is provided in Table 7.2.

The most sophisticated interpretation of this battery of tests is stratified by intelligence. Most people seen in our outpatient laboratory for a neuro-psychological evaluation are likely to have *premorbid* intellectual abilities in the average or high-average classification range. We use the Reynolds Intellectual Screening Test (RIST) to estimate *current* intellectual abilities. After determining their current RIST score, we combine this information with clinical judgment to estimate their premorbid RIST *classification category* (e.g., low average, average, high average, or superior). We usually use

▦ **TABLE 7.2. Number of Low Scores in the Total Standardization Sample (*N* = 1,263; Cumulative Percentages)**

No. of low scores	Cutoff scores		
	<25th percentile	<1 *SD*	<10th percentile
15	0.3	—	—
14	1.0	0.2	—
13	2.0	0.5	0.2
12	3.1	1.0	0.2
11	5.1	1.6	0.4
10	7.4	1.9	0.6
9	11.2	3.5	1.3
8	14.9	4.9	2.0
7	21.1	7.8	2.9
6	27.1	11.0	4.9
5	36.7	15.8	7.5
4	49.0	23.8	12.9
3	61.5	34.9	20.8
2	74.0	51.3	32.3
1	88.6	72.4	56.8
0	100.0	100.0	100.0

Note. This represents the prevalence of low scores (cumulative percentages) across the entire battery of tests using different cutoffs (i.e., <25th percentile, <1 *SD*, and <10th percentile). *Test scores relating to attention, speed of processing, and executive functioning*: Numbers & Letters A (Speed and Errors T Scores); Numbers & Letters B (Efficiency T Score); Numbers & Letters C (Efficiency T Score); Numbers & Letters D (Efficiency and Disruption T Score); Mazes (T Score); Categories (T Score); Word Generation (T Score). Note: The following score is not included in the Profile Analyses: Numbers & Letters A Efficiency. *Test scores relating to expressive language*: Oral Production. *Test scores relating to learning and memory*: List Learning (Immediate Recall and Long Delayed Recall T Scores); Story Learning (Immediate and Delayed Recall T Scores); Daily Living Memory (Immediate and Delayed Recall T Scores). Note: The following scores are not included in the base rates: List Learning Short Delayed and List B. This research program was supported by Lundbeck Canada.

the obtained RIST as the best estimate of premorbid RIST classification. However, when we believe that the obtained RIST underestimates premorbid ability, we might choose one classification higher. An example would be if a person with obvious brain damage or cognitive impairment obtained a RIST of 109. We might assume that his or her premorbid RIST was more likely to fall in the high-average than in the average classification range. The prevalence rates of low scores across the screening battery, stratified by intelligence (RIST scores), are presented in Tables 7.3 and 7.4.

This new screening battery allows the clinician to use psychometrically derived and testable guidelines for identifying cognitive impairment in depression using (1) a clearly specified neuropsychological battery with a fixed number of tests, (2) a single set of demographically adjusted normative data, and (3) stratification by level of intelligence. This is a psychometrically sophisticated approach to identifying cognitive impairment in patients with depression. The base-rate information presented in Tables 7.2–7.4 are ready for clinical use. A clinician could give this battery and use the information in the tables to assist with interpretation. Some case studies involving this battery are summarized below.

▨ **TABLE 7.3. Prevalence of Low Scores for Adults with Below-Average or Average Intelligence**

No. of low scores	Low-average intelligence (N = 134; RIST = 80–89)			Average intelligence (N = 673; RIST = 90–109)			No. of low scores
	<25th percentile	<1 SD	<10th percentile	<25th percentile	<1 SD	<10th percentile	
15	1.5	—	—	0.3	—	—	15
14	4.5	0.7	—	0.4	0.1	—	14
13	11.2	1.5	—	0.7	0.3	0.1	13
12	12.7	4.5	0.7	1.6	0.4	—	12
11	22.4	6.7	—	2.5	0.6	0.3	11
10	29.9	7.5	2.2	4.5	0.7	—	10
9	38.1	14.2	5.2	9.1	1.6	0.7	9
8	48.5	17.2	9.0	12.3	3.0	—	8
7	58.2	30.6	12.7	19.6	5.3	1.0	7
6	64.9	40.3	18.7	26.0	8.3	3.4	6
5	72.4	46.3	26.9	36.8	14.6	5.8	5
4	82.1	60.4	39.6	50.5	22.7	11.0	4
3	91.8	70.1	52.2	64.9	35.2	19.6	3
2	96.3	84.3	66.4	77.9	54.2	33.3	2
1	97.8	94.8	85.1	91.1	76.4	60.0	1
0	100.0	100.0	100.0	100.0	100.0	100.0	0

▪ **TABLE 7.4. Prevalence of Low Scores for Adults with Above-Average Intelligence**

No. of low scores	High-average intelligence (N = 289; RIST = 110–119)			Superior intelligence (N = 138; RIST = 120+)			No. of low scores
	<25th percentile	<1 SD	<10th percentile	<25th percentile	<1 SD	<10th percentile	
12	0.3	—	—	—	—	—	12
11	0.7	—	—	0.7	—	—	11
10	1.4	—	—	1.4	—	—	10
9	2.4	0.3	—	2.2	—	—	9
8	4.5	1.0	—	4.3	—	—	8
7	8.0	2.1	—	7.2	—	—	7
6	13.1	2.4	—	11.6	1.4	—	6
5	23.2	3.8	1.0	18.8	5.1	—	5
4	34.6	10.7	3.1	29.7	8.7	3.6	4
3	47.4	21.8	10.0	37.7	15.2	6.5	3
2	60.6	33.6	18.3	57.2	32.6	11.6	2
1	83.0	60.2	42.2	77.5	52.2	37.0	1
0	100.0	100.0	100.0	100.0	100.0	100.0	0

Case Studies: Depression Screening Battery

We present four case examples of patients with perceived cognitive impairment following workplace injuries who had complicated recoveries due to problems with depression. These case examples illustrate the use of the new psychometric criteria for determining the presence of cognitive impairment. The RIST and NAB test data and profile analyses for these case examples are presented in Table 7.5.

Case 1

Mr. Smith is a 52-year-old office manager who sustained a back injury at work. He developed a chronic pain condition. Over the course of several months, he evolved a depressive episode. He denied a history of depression prior to his back injury. He was taking Sertraline for depression and Gabapentin for pain at the time he was tested. He was referred into one of our studies due to his perception that he was cognitively impaired. On the Ruff Neurobehavioral Inventory (RNBI), Mr. Smith perceived himself as having severe difficulties with learning and memory, moderate difficulties with executive functioning, and mild difficulties with attention and concentration.

On the screening battery, Mr. Smith evidenced broadly normal (or better) functioning on all measures. There was a mismatch between his

▨ TABLE 7.5. RIST and NAB Test Data for Four Subjects with Depression

	Subject			
	1	2	3	4
Demographics and test scores				
Age	52	43	27	36
Education (years)	17	9	12	12
Gender	M	M	F	M
RNBI—Cognitive Composite (T)	75	65	79	87
RNBI—Attention and Concentration (T)	66	59	78	90
RNBI—Speech and Language (T)	52	58	66	66
RNBI—Learning and Memory (T)	92	66	81	89
RNBI—Executive Functioning (T)	79	69	75	83
Intelligence				
RIST Index	117	114	105	98
Guess What	59	50	51	47
Odd Item Out	59	65	54	50
Attention, speed of processing, and executive functioning				
Numbers and Letters A Speed	54	58	63	56
Numbers and Letters A Errors	44	46	36	32
Numbers and Letters B Efficiency	44	47	56	46
Numbers and Letters C Efficiency	48	44	53	64
Numbers and Letters D Efficiency	67	41	58	60
Numbers and Letters D Disruption	65	34	43	54
Mazes	62	55	57	57
Categories	58	57	62	47
Word Generation	68	60	50	47
Expressive language				
Oral Production	56	61	41	34
Learning and memory				
List Learning A Total Immediate	56	73	26	44
List Learning A Long Delay Recall	61	74	31	38
Story Learning Immediate Recall	49	66	36	42
Story Learning Delayed Recall	55	70	44	43
Daily Living Memory Immediate	65	63	34	29
Daily Living Memory Delayed	60	62	55	19
Base rates				
No. below 25th percentile	0	1	7	7
No. below 1 *SD*	0	1	5	5
No. below 10th percentile	0	1	5	4

Note. RNBI, Ruff Neurobehavioral Inventory. Higher T scores indicate more problems with perceived cognitive abilities.

subjective experience of cognitive impairment and his objective test results. Of course, we have no way of knowing how, precisely, he would have performed on these tests prior to developing depression—and it is possible that some of his scores are mildly diminished. It is also possible, if less likely, that the controlled testing environment is free of the social, occupational, and interpersonal challenges and stressors that may serve to interfere with or distract from optimal performance in a noncontrolled environment. We encouraged his psychiatrist to reassure him that he performed well on testing.

Case 2

Mr. Anderson is a 43-year-old bank teller who sustained a knee injury at work. He was on a waiting list for surgery at the time of testing. His injury seemed to have worsened his preexisting depressive illness. Moreover, he had been very concerned about his cognition and his ability to return to work. He was taking Cipralex for depression and Imovane for sleep problems. On the RNBI, Mr. Anderson perceived himself as having mild difficulties with memory and executive functioning. He perceived himself as having broadly normal attention, concentration, speech, and language. On the screening battery, Mr. Anderson performed very well. Moreover, his learning and memory abilities were clearly superior to that of healthy men his age. He performed poorly on a single test of processing speed and divided attention. Overall, he did not show evidence of cognitive impairment.

Case 3

Ms. Jones was working as a parking lot attendant. She got into an altercation while approaching someone trying to break into a parked car. She was punched multiple times on the left side of her head, was shaken, and thrown to the ground. She did not lose consciousness but she felt dazed for a few days postinjury. Her recall of events seemed continuous, suggesting that she did not likely experience frank retrograde or posttraumatic amnesia. She appeared to have sustained a mild concussion in this fight. At the time of her evaluation (12 weeks postassault), her perceived cognitive problems included slow processing speed, reduced vocabulary skills, mild word-finding difficulties, and reduced concentration. She met the diagnostic criteria for major depressive disorder, recurrent (mild-to-moderate); and anxiety disorder not otherwise specified (NOS; she had features of PTSD and GAD).

Ms. Jones has a complicated medical and psychiatric history. She was in a motor vehicle accident when she was 6 years old. She suffered a skull fracture, moderate-severe TBI, internal organ injuries (e.g., fractured spleen), and medical complications (e.g., septic shock). She required speech therapy and physiotherapy for almost a year postinjury. She thought it took her nearly 2 years to recover from her injuries. She had to repeat the first grade because she missed so much school. However, she described herself as an average student in elementary school and high school. She recalled first experiencing symptoms of "anxiety" at 12 years of age. Childhood symptoms included restlessness and fidgety behavior. She added that these symptoms had been recurring—on and off—since then. Ms. Jones stated that she had been depressed since age 14, at which time she was "feeling detached from other kids."

Ms. Jones's intellectual abilities were average (RIST Index = 105). On the screening battery, she had 7 scores that were below average, 6 of which were below 1 *SD* and 4 of which were below the 10th percentile. Her overall performance on the test battery is considered unusually low, based on having 6 scores below 1 *SD* or 4 scores below the 10th percentile (when compared to people with average intelligence). Given her complicated neuropsychiatric history, we did not assume that her poor performance on the screening battery was caused by her workplace injury. In general, this case was very difficult in regards to estimating the recovery from her concussion, but we assumed that recovery had likely occurred and that mental health problems were her primary problem. A few weeks after our evaluation, she gradually returned to work. Although she had not returned to working full time, her psychological problems, in particular, had improved considerably, enabling her to work part time. She had been seeing a counselor, weekly, for her mental health issues, and it was anticipated that she would increase her hours to full time in the near future.

This case illustrates the specific challenge in ascertaining the true effects of workplace injury when there is preexisting psychiatric and neurological illness. A woman with this history may have diminished cognitive and coping skills and social resources for coping with stress. When a stressor and injury of this type occurs, it can result in secondary effects because of the exacerbation of the underlying condition. When the likelihood of an actual current brain injury is low, as in the present instance, it is easier to attribute these evaluation findings to preexisting weaknesses. Or it is also possible that the situation proves to worsen depression, which may then result in objective and/or subjective cognitive difficulties. There are instances, however, when a neuropsychologist will evaluate an individual with a preexisting depression, questionable CNS injury with limited details to support or disconfirm this injury, and clear worsening of the depressive condition. At present, it is not possible to accurately differentiate the validity of any subjective or objective cognitive difficulties in such circumstances, as illustrated in Case 4.

Case 4

Mr. Hughes was working as an electrician's helper. A large beam fell and struck him on the top of his head. He was not wearing a hard hat at the time of injury. He believed he lost consciousness for several seconds. He denied any frank posttraumatic amnesia but reported some initial confusion about what struck him on the head. He reported having clear memory of being transported via ambulance and being in the hospital. According to the crew report, his Glasgow Coma Scale score was 15, and he was described as alert and oriented. It appears that he sustained a mild traumatic brain injury (concussion) in this workplace accident.

At the time of his evaluation (8 weeks postinjury), Mr. Hughes reported having substantial physical (e.g., headaches, dizziness, ringing in his ears), psychological (e.g., anger and irritability), and cognitive problems (e.g., trouble following thoughts, easily distracted, forgetfulness, and feeling slow). He presented with restricted affect, and his mood appeared depressed. He was diagnosed with a major depressive episode, and it was very difficult to disentangle symptoms of depression from residual symptoms associated with his concussion. His situation was very complicated because he had a history of (1) attention and learning problems in school, (2) anxiety problems in childhood, and (3) three prior concussions and one moderate-severe traumatic brain injury (involving a 1-week hospitalization and self-reported personality change thereafter). He had a strong family history of psychiatric illness (depression and schizophrenia in several family members).

His intellectual abilities were average (RIST Index = 98). On the screening battery, he had 7 scores that were below average, 5 of which were below 1 SD, and 4 were below the 10th percentile. His overall performance on the test battery is considered unusually low, based on having 4 scores below the 10th percentile (when compared to people with average intelligence). He perceived himself as having extreme difficulty with attention and concentration, learning and memory, and executive functioning. He endorsed having mild difficulty with speech and language. Given his complicated history of learning problems and multiple brain injuries, we did not assume that his poor performance on the screening battery was caused by his workplace injury.

Mr. Hughes received intensive multidisciplinary rehabilitation services, on an outpatient basis, for 3 weeks. He also received six individual counseling and psychoeducation sessions regarding recovery from MTBI (over a 4-week period). He also saw a therapist for his depression and anger (10 sessions). It took about 6 months before he began a gradual return-to-work program, and after 3 weeks he returned to full-time work. His outcome highlights an important goal in workplace injury where depression is also present. A return to premorbid functional capacity with effective treatment, support, and workplace rehabilitation/reintegration can be the most effective way to ameliorate depression secondary to, or exacerbated by workplace injury.

TREATMENT

Evidence-based treatment of depression should involve pharmacotherapy, psychotherapy, and/or allied therapies (Sonawalla & Fava, 2001). Because as many as two-thirds of individuals with major depression do not respond to the first medication prescribed (Little, 2009), and between 60 and 70% of all individuals do not respond to adequate courses of at least two antidepressant medications (Trivedi & Daly, 2008), treatment is usually provided in a series of stages (Adli, Rush, Moller, & Bauer, 2003). Remission rates generally decline over successive treatments (Biggs et al., 2000; Crismon et al., 1999; Ereshefsky, 2001).

When an individual presents with depression for the first time, it is recommended that the first stage involve some form of monotherapy, employing either pharmacotherapy or psychotherapy (Trivedi & Kleiber, 2001). Later options include combination therapy, electroconvulsive therapy, atypical antipsychotics, and allied treatments. However, regarding more complicated or severe depression, which is more difficult to treat, there are no specific treatment algorithms, and, as Sonawalla and Fava (2001) note, "there does not seem to be a 'best' approach to its management" (p. 773).

Pharmacotherapy, Psychotherapy, or Both

Antidepressants are the most popular mode of therapy for unipolar depression in the United States (Antonuccio, Danton, DeNelsky, & Garland, 1995). If the first stage of the intervention involves pharmacotherapy, newer selective serotonin reuptake inhibitor (SSRI) antidepressants are usually indicated. These have been shown to be as effective as tricyclic agents, with fewer side effects, and are thus associated with slightly lower dropout rates (i.e., 8% vs. 13%; Mulrow et al., 2000). In a recent meta-analysis, Cipriani and colleagues examined 12 new-generation antidepressants in 117 randomized controlled trials from 1991 to 2007, comprising 25,928 participants (Cipriani et al., 2009). They found that, at therapeutic doses, mirtazapine, escitalopram, venlafaxine, and sertraline were significantly more efficacious than duloxetine, fluoxetine, fluvoxamine, paroxetine, and reboxetine.

Dosage often varies with symptom severity. For example, higher doses of SSRIs are often required in treating persons with severe or treatment-resistant depression (Sonawalla & Fava, 2001). Individuals are said to have recovered if remission lasts for 6 months or more. Accordingly, it is recommended that individuals who have been treated to the point of remission should continue treatment for at least 6 months (DeRubeis, Siegle, & Hollon, 2008). Regarding treatment-resistant depression, a number of factors affect treatment response including substance use disorders, Axis II comorbidity, duration of illness before treatment, pretreatment severity, treatment modality employed, and treatment adherence (Sonawalla & Fava, 2001).

If adequately treated, some people with depression can experience a substantial improvement in their cognitive functioning. For example, escitalopram or duloxetine administered for 24 weeks in a sample of antidepressant-drug naïve participants, between 20 and 50 years of age, resulted in improvements in episodic memory and, to a lesser degree, working memory, information-processing speed, and motor performance (Herrera-Guzman et al., 2009); Levkovitz and colleagues have demonstrated that the SSRI fluoxetine improves memory performance in persons with major depression (but not tricyclic antidepressant desipramine; Levkovitz, Caftori, Avital, & Richter-Levin, 2002); Ferguson and colleagues have shown that reboxetine (but not paroxetine) improves processing speed (Ferguson, Wesnes, & Schwartz, 2003); and quetiapine-augmented pharmacotherapy was associated with improved performance on verbal learning and executive functioning tasks (verbal fluency) in a small sample of adults (N = 18) 40 years of age (+/– 6 years) who, initially, showed a partial response to SSRI antidepressants (Olver, Ignatiadis, Maruff, Burrows, & Norman, 2008).

Although antidepressants are the most popular mode of therapy for unipolar depression in the United States and may be slightly more effective in treating dysthymia, the evidence suggests that psychological interventions are generally as effective, even in the most severe cases (Antonuccio et al., 1995; Bortolotti, Menchetti, Bellini, Montaguti, & Berardi, 2008; Cuijpers, van Straten, van Oppen, & Andersson, 2008; Imel, Malterer, McKay, & Wampold, 2008; Robinson, Berman, & Neimeyer, 1990; Wolf & Hopko, 2008). Ideally, therefore, it is best to provide individuals with the option of either a psychological or medical intervention. Moreover, such patient-centered approaches have been associated with better treatment adherence (Dwight-Johnson, Sherbourne, Liao, & Wells, 2000). In addition, existing research suggests that medication may have a more rapid treatment effect, but be more prone to relapse[12] if treatment is discontinued (Hollon et al., 2005; Hollon, Thase, & Markowitz, 2002).

Given newer available technologies, more individuals will have access to psychological interventions. Kessler and colleagues, for example, developed an online CBT program, delivered by therapists in real time (Kessler et al., 2009). Similarly, Simon and colleagues developed a telephone care management intervention, allowing individuals less familiar with computers access to outpatient care (Simon, Ludman, & Rutter, 2009).

Neuromodulation Therapies

There is a rapidly increasing repertoire of neuromodulation therapies being piloted for depression, including deep brain stimulation, vagal nerve stimulation, and repetitive transcranial magnetic stimulation, although approval for reimbursement through insurance has been limited. Validation studies are still underway, and a limited number of trials have thus far been conducted. A longstanding, highly effective, neuromodulation therapy is electroconvulsive therapy (ECT). ECT may be indicated in cases of severe psychotic depression, severe depression with melancholic features, and in individuals who cannot tolerate antidepressant medications due to a medical illness such as renal, cardiac, or hepatic disease (Sonawalla & Fava, 2001). ECT is contraindicated in persons with pacemakers, with certain types of neurological conditions (e.g., brain tumors), and other medical illnesses, which may be exacerbated by this treatment procedure. A meta-analysis suggests that ECT is effective as a short-term treatment for depression, and bilateral ECT is moderately more effective than unilateral ECT (The UK ECT Review Group, 2003). The typical side effects of ECT include, though are not limited to, headache, temporary confusion, delirium, and transitory memory impairment (Sonawalla & Fava, 2001). The transient memory impairment can include time-limited retro- and anterograde amnesia.

Alternative Therapies

Physical inactivity has been linked to depressed mood, lower self-esteem, and poor quality of life in healthy nondepressed individuals and in persons with depression (Camacho, Roberts, Lazarus, Kaplan, & Cohen, 1991; Farmer et al., 1988; Lampinen, Heikkinen, & Ruoppila, 2000; Mobily, Rubenstein, Lemke, O'Hara, & Wallace, 1996; Paffenbarger, Lee, & Leung, 1994). Although the relation between depressed mood and physical activity levels has been investigated for decades, only recently has exercise been explored as a viable option in the treatment of depression (Brosse, Sheets, Lett, & Blumenthal, 2002). In addition, light therapy and behavioral sleep interventions have been piloted successfully in the treatment of depression. In clinical populations, exercise has been shown to be a good adjunctive treatment in the long-term management of mild-to-moderate unipolar depression (Dunn, Trivedi, Kampert, Clark, & Chambliss, 2005; Martinsen, Hoffart, & Solberg, 1989; Mead et al., 2008; Nabkasorn et al., 2006; Penninx et al., 2002; Smith et al., 2007).

CONCLUSIONS

Depression is the most costly health-related condition that affects our workforce (Stewart et al., 2003). It is estimated that it costs American society over $80 billion annually (Greenberg et al., 2003). Most of these expenses are due to indirect costs, including absenteeism and presenteeism.

With the average age of onset in the mid-20s, major depressive disorder is one of the most common psychiatric disorders and is the leading cause of disability in the United States for most individuals between 15 and 44 years of age (World Health Organization, 2004). According to the biopsychosocial model, certain individuals are more likely to develop depression due to one or more risk factors, which include biogenetic risk factors, psychological risk factors, somatic risk factors, and sociocultural risk factors (Schotte et al., 2006). Accordingly, depression can be a preexisting condition, singly, episodically, or chronically.

Depression can arise de novo, or it can be partially or mostly related to injuries sustained in the workplace. As a primary or comorbid condition (e.g., with TBI, chronic pain, or PTSD), depression can have an adverse effect on social, cognitive, and occupational functioning. Depression can also interfere with treatment-relevant behaviors such as help-seeking and treatment adherence. Depression can mimic the postconcussion syndrome, so it is easy to misdiagnose chronic problems relating to a remote mild traumatic brain injury in adults who suffer primarily from depression.

Depression is a complex disorder of multiple, interactive biological systems including molecular, cellular, neuroanatomical, neurochemical, neuroendocrinological, and neuropsychological factors. In concert, these systems are influenced by an individual's genetic makeup, prenatal development, and exposure to environmental stressors (Mossner et al., 2007; Ramasubbu & MacQueen, 2008). Furthermore, although mood and affective disturbance are the cardinal features of depression (American Psychiatric Association, 2000), there has been considerable evidence that cognitive functioning is also affected (Elliott, 1998). For example, deficits in processing speed, episodic memory, and executive functioning, as measured on objective testing, have been shown to correlate with depression severity (McDermott & Ebmeier, 2009).

Regarding cognitive deficits, there is often considerable variability among persons with depression. The effects of depression on formal neuropsychological testing can range from frank impairment to broadly normal functioning (Newman & Sweet, 1992). Some researchers have reported clear evidence of reduced neurocognitive test scores associated with more severe forms of depression (e.g., Austin et al., 1999; Channon & Green, 1999; Degl'Innocenti et al., 1998; Merriam et al., 1999; Politis et al., 2004). However, the effects of mild depression on neurocognition appear to be small (Grant et al., 2001; Rohling et al., 2002).

Persons with depression are also expected to present with subjective cognitive complaints. For example, individuals with depression usually complain about problems with concentration, memory, problem solving, and thinking skills which, often, are incongruent with their performance on objective measures (American Psychiatric Association, 1994, 2000).

Evidence-based treatment of depression should involve pharmacotherapy, psychotherapy, and/or allied therapies (Sonawalla & Fava, 2001). Because as many as two-thirds of individuals with major depression do not respond to the first medication prescribed (Little, 2009), and between 60 and 70% of all individuals do not respond to adequate courses of least two antidepressant medications (Trivedi & Daly, 2008), treatment is usually provided in a series of stages. Remission rates generally decline over successive treatments (Biggs et al., 2000; Crismon et al., 1999; Ereshefsky, 2001).

Neuropsychological evaluation services are essential for measuring objective and subjective cognitive functioning. Neuropsychological evaluations are especially helpful for determining whether there has been cognitive decline following a workplace injury and for evaluating the extent to which various treatments improve functioning. Without question, assessing cognition in persons with depression, following a work-related injury, is extraordinarily complex in regards to (1) subjective symptoms, (2) objective test results, and (3) determining the cause of any particular findings. People with depression can have preexisting or co-occurring medical problems, psychiatric conditions, and/or substance abuse. Moreover, they can have preexisting lower scores on intellectual and neuropsychological tests. In some cases, individuals might exaggerate symptoms and/or underperform on neuropsychological tests. Therefore, it is essential to interpret neuropsychological test scores in people with depression carefully, not by simply comparing them to normative data corrected for age, but by considering their educational attainment and level of intelligence and by carefully assessing effort, potential exaggeration, and self-fulfilling prophecy. These factors can have a substantial impact on the interpretation of cognitive test results.

NOTES

1. The *FKBP5* gene appears to be involved in glucocorticoid signal transduction, which may alter the stress-response pathways during neurodevelopment (Binder et al., 2008).
2. This genetic risk might be maternally inherited on the mitochondrial DNA (mtDNA). Inherited only from the mother, the child thus carries the identical mtDNA sequence in the absence of a new mutation.
3. Out of the 2,222 employees, they examined the work output of 1,712 full-time employees.

4. In other words, new episodes can arise independently of external stressors.
5. One study suggests that structural changes only occur with depressed individuals who have had the illness for longer than 2 years or have had more than one depressive episode (McKinnon, Yucel, Nazarov, & MacQueen, 2009).
6. Some neurophysiological abnormalities have been shown to be mood-dependent (see Drevets, 2000).
7. For example, studies often combine the amygdala and hippocampus because white matter delineation between these two structures is often difficult to detect (Campbell, Marriott, Nahmias, & MacQueen, 2004).
8. Why, for example, does it usually take 2 to 3 weeks for antidepressants to take effect?
9. NUDR is the human homologue of Drosophila DEAF-1.
10. Repressor element-1 silencing transcription factor.
11. Exacerbations were defined as at least a 2-point increase over usual pain severity on a 0 to 10 scale, where 0 indicated "no pain" and 10 depicted "pain as bad as it could be" (Ricci et al., 2006).
12. Relapse is not to be confused with the discontinuation syndrome. The discontinuation syndrome is time-limited, with acute symptoms disappearing within about 2 weeks (see Shelton, 2006).

REFERENCES

Abercrombie, H. C., Schaefer, S. M., Larson, C. L., Oakes, T. R., Lindgren, K. A., Holden, J. E., et al. (1998). Metabolic rate in the right amygdala predicts negative affect in depressed patients. *NeuroReport, 9*(14), 3301–3307.

Abramson, L. Y., Seligman, M. E., & Teasdale, J. D. (1978). Learned helplessness in humans: Critique and reformulation. *Journal of Abnormal Psychology, 87*(1), 49–74.

Adli, M., Rush, A. J., Moller, H. J., & Bauer, M. (2003). Algorithms for optimizing the treatment of depression: Making the right decision at the right time. *Pharmacopsychiatry, 36*(Suppl. 3), S222–S229.

Alesci, S., Martinez, P. E., Kelkar, S., Ilias, I., Ronsaville, D. S., Listwak, S. J., et al. (2005). Major depression is associated with significant diurnal elevations in plasma interleukin-6 levels, a shift of its circadian rhythm, and loss of physiological complexity in its secretion: Clinical implications. *Journal of Clinical Endocrinology and Metabolism, 90*(5), 2522–2530.

Alonso, J., Angermeyer, M. C., Bernert, S., Bruffaerts, R., Brugha, T. S., Bryson, H., et al. (2004). Prevalence of mental disorders in Europe: Results from the European Study of the Epidemiology of Mental Disorders (ESEMeD) project. *Acta Psychiatrica Scandinavica. Supplementum* (420), 21–27.

American Psychiatric Association. (1994). *Diagnostic and statistical manual of mental disorders* (4th ed.). Washington, DC: Author.

American Psychiatric Association. (2000). *Diagnostic and statistical manual of mental disorders* (4th ed., text rev.). Washington, DC: Author.

Andersson, G. B. (1999). Epidemiological features of chronic low-back pain. *Lancet, 354*(9178), 581–585.

Antepohl, W., Kiviloog, L., Andersson, J., & Gerdle, B. (2003). Cognitive impairment in patients with chronic whiplash-associated disorder: A matched control study. *NeuroRehabilitation, 18*(4), 307–315.

Antonuccio, D., Danton, W. G., DeNelsky, G. Y., & Garland, Y. (1995). Psychotherapy versus medication for depression: Challenging the conventional wisdom with data. *Professional Psychology: Research and Practice, 26*(6), 574–585.

Apkarian, A. V., Sosa, Y., Krauss, B. R., Thomas, P. S., Fredrickson, B. E., Levy, R. E., et al. (2004). Chronic pain patients are impaired on an emotional decision-making task. *Pain, 108*(1–2), 129–136.

Arnow, B. A., Hunkeler, E. M., Blasey, C. M., Lee, J., Constantino, M. J., Fireman, B., et al. (2006). Comorbid depression, chronic pain, and disability in primary care. *Psychosomatic Medicine, 68*(2), 262–268.

Asmundson, G. J., Norton, P. J., & Norton, G. R. (1999). Beyond pain: The role of fear and avoidance in chronicity. *Clinical Psychology Review, 19*(1), 97–119.

Atkinson, J. H., Slater, M. A., Patterson, T. L., Grant, I., & Garfin, S. R. (1991). Prevalence, onset, and risk of psychiatric disorders in men with chronic low back pain: A controlled study. *Pain, 45*(2), 111–121.

Austin, M. P., Mitchell, P., Wilhelm, K., Parker, G., Hickie, I., Brodaty, H., et al. (1999). Cognitive function in depression: A distinct pattern of frontal impairment in melancholia? *Psychological Medicine, 29*(1), 73–85.

Banks, S. M., & Kerns, R. D. (1996). Explaining high rates of depression in chronic pain: A diathesis-stress framework. *Psychological Bulletin, 119*, 95–110.

Bassett, S. S., & Folstein, M. F. (1993). Memory complaint, memory performance, and psychiatric diagnosis: A community study. *Journal of Geriatric Psychiatry and Neurology, 6*(2), 105–111.

Baune, B. T., Suslow, T., Engelien, A., Arolt, V., & Berger, K. (2006). The association between depressive mood and cognitive performance in an elderly general population—the MEMO Study. *Dementia and Geriatric Cognitive Disorders, 22*(2), 142–149.

Bay, E. (2009). Current treatment options for depression after mild traumatic brain injury. *Current Treatment Options in Neurology, 11*(5), 377–382.

Bazargan, M., & Barbre, A. R. (1994). The effects of depression, health status, and stressful life-events on self-reported memory problems among aged blacks. *International Journal of Aging and Human Development, 38*(4), 351–362.

Bergemann, E. R., & Boles, R. G. (2010). Maternal inheritance in recurrent early-onset depression. *Psychiatric Genetics, 20*(1), 31–34.

Berndt, E. R., Bailit, H. L., Keller, M. B., Verner, J. C., & Finkelstein, S. N. (2000). Health care use and at-work productivity among employees with mental disorders. *Health Affairs (Project Hope), 19*(4), 244–256.

Biggs, M. M., Shores-Wilson, K., Rush, A. J., Carmody, T. J., Trivedi, M. H., Crismon, M. L., et al. (2000). A comparison of alternative assessments of depressive symptom severity: A pilot study. *Psychiatry Research, 95*(1), 55–65.

Binder, E. B., Bradley, R. G., Liu, W., Epstein, M. P., Deveau, T. C., Mercer, K. B., et al. (2008). Association of FKBP5 polymorphisms and childhood abuse with risk of posttraumatic stress disorder symptoms in adults. *Journal of the American Medical Association, 299*(11), 1291–1305.

Biringer, E., Lundervold, A., Stordal, K., Mykletun, A., Egeland, J., Bottlender, R., et al. (2005). Executive function improvement upon remission of recurrent unipolar depression. *European Archives of Psychiatry and Clinical Neuroscience, 255*(6), 373–380.

Blanchard, E. B., Hickling, E. J., Freidenberg, B. M., Malta, L. S., Kuhn, E., & Sykes, M. A. (2004). Two studies of psychiatric morbidity among motor vehicle accident survivors 1 year after the crash. *Behavior Research and Therapy, 42*(5), 569–583.

Blazer, D. G., Kessler, R. C., McGonagle, K. A., & Swartz, M. S. (1994). The prevalence and distribution of major depression in a national community sample: The National Comorbidity Survey. *American Journal of Psychiatry, 151*(7), 979–986.

Bockting, C. L., Schene, A. H., Spinhoven, P., Koeter, M. W., Wouters, L. F., Huyser, J., et al. (2005). Preventing relapse/recurrence in recurrent depression with cognitive therapy: A randomized controlled trial. *Journal of Consulting and Clinical Psychology, 73*(4), 647–657.

Boone, K. B., Lesser, I. M., Miller, B. L., Wohl, M., Berman, N., Lee, A., et al. (1995). Cognitive functioning in older depressed outpatients: Relationship of presence and severity of depression to neuropsychological test scores. *Neuropsychology, 9*, 390–398.

Bortolotti, B., Menchetti, M., Bellini, F., Montaguti, M. B., & Berardi, D. (2008). Psychological interventions for major depression in primary care: A meta-analytic review of randomized controlled trials. *General Hospital Psychiatry, 30*(4), 293–302.

Bradley, R. G., Binder, E. B., Epstein, M. P., Tang, Y., Nair, H. P., Liu, W., et al. (2008). Influence of child abuse on adult depression: Moderation by the corticotropin-releasing hormone receptor gene. *Archives of General Psychiatry, 65*(2), 190–200.

Bray, G. A., Clearfield, M. B., Fintel, D. J., & Nelinson, D. S. (2009). Overweight and obesity: The pathogenesis of cardiometabolic risk. *Clinical Cornerstone, 9*(4), 30–40; discussion 41–32.

Bremner, J. D., Randall, P., Scott, T. M., Capelli, S., Delaney, R., McCarthy, G., et al. (1995). Deficits in short-term memory in adult survivors of childhood abuse. *Psychiatry Research, 59*(1–2), 97–107.

Bremner, J. D., Scott, T. M., Delaney, R. C., Southwick, S. M., Mason, J. W., Johnson, D. R., et al. (1993). Deficits in short-term memory in posttraumatic stress disorder. *American Journal of Psychiatry, 150*(7), 1015–1019.

Brody, A. L., Saxena, S., Stoessel, P., Gillies, L. A., Fairbanks, L. A., Alborzian, S., et al. (2001). Regional brain metabolic changes in patients with major depression treated with either paroxetine or interpersonal therapy: Preliminary findings. *Archives of General Psychiatry, 58*(7), 631–640.

Brosse, A. L., Sheets, E. S., Lett, H. S., & Blumenthal, J. A. (2002). Exercise and the treatment of clinical depression in adults: Recent findings and future directions. *Sports Medicine, 32*(12), 741–760.

Buckley, T. C., Blanchard, E. B., & Neill, W. T. (2000). Information processing and PTSD: A review of the empirical literature. *Clinical Psychology Review, 20*(8), 1041–1065.

Camacho, T. C., Roberts, R. E., Lazarus, N. B., Kaplan, G. A., & Cohen, R. D. (1991). Physical activity and depression: Evidence from the Alameda County Study. *American Journal of Epidemiology, 134*(2), 220–231.

Campbell, L. C., Clauw, D. J., & Keefe, F. J. (2003). Persistent pain and depression: A biopsychosocial perspective. *Biological Psychiatry, 54*(3), 399–409.

Campbell, S., Marriott, M., Nahmias, C., & MacQueen, G. M. (2004). Lower hippocampal volume in patients suffering from depression: A meta-analysis. *American Journal of Psychiatry, 161*(4), 598–607.

Cao, C., Wan, X., Chen, Y., & Wu, W. (2009). Metabolic factors and microinflammatory state promote kidney injury in type 2 diabetes mellitus patients. *Renal Failure, 31*(6), 470–474.

Carney, R. M., Freedland, K. E., Rich, M. W., & Jaffe, A. S. (1995). Depression as a risk factor for cardiac events in established coronary heart disease: A review of possible mechanisms. *Annals of Behavioral Medicine, 17*(2), 142–149.

Carney, R. M., Rich, M. W., Tevelde, A., Saini, J., Clark, K., & Jaffe, A. S. (1987). Major depressive disorder in coronary artery disease. *American Journal of Cardiology, 60*(16), 1273–1275.

Channon, S., & Green, P. S. (1999). Executive function in depression: The role of performance strategies in aiding depressed and non-depressed participants. *Journal of Neurology, Neurosurgery and Psychiatry, 66*(2), 162–171.

Chen, M. C., Hamilton, J. P., & Gotlib, I. H. (2010). Decreased hippocampal volume in healthy girls at risk of depression. *Archives of General Psychiatry, 67*(3), 270–276.

Cipriani, A., Furukawa, T. A., Salanti, G., Geddes, J. R., Higgins, J. P., Churchill, R., et al. (2009). Comparative efficacy and acceptability of 12 new-generation antidepressants: A multiple-treatments meta-analysis. *Lancet, 373*(9665), 746–758.

Comijs, H. C., Deeg, D. J., Dik, M. G., Twisk, J. W., & Jonker, C. (2002). Memory complaints; the association with psycho-affective and health problems and the role of personality characteristics: A 6-year follow-up study. *Journal of Affective Disorders, 72*(2), 157–165.

Crismon, M. L., Trivedi, M., Pigott, T. A., Rush, A. J., Hirschfeld, R. M., Kahn, D. A., et al. (1999). The Texas Medication Algorithm Project: Report of the Texas Consensus Conference Panel on medication treatment of major depressive disorder. *Journal of Clinical Psychiatry, 60*(3), 142–156.

Crowell, T. A., Kieffer, K. M., Siders, C. A., & Vanderploeg, R. D. (2002). Neuropsychological findings in combat-related posttraumatic stress disorder. *The Clinical Neuropsychologist, 16*(3), 310–321.

Cuijpers, P., van Straten, A., van Oppen, P., & Andersson, G. (2008). Are psychological and pharmacologic interventions equally effective in the treatment of adult depressive disorders? A meta-analysis of comparative studies. *Journal of Clinical Psychiatry, 69*(11), 1675–1685; quiz 1839–1641.

Culav-Sumic, J., & Jukic, V. (2010). Minor physical anomalies in women with recurrent unipolar depression. *Psychiatry Research, 176*(1), 22–25.

Cull, A., Hay, C., Love, S. B., Mackie, M., Smets, E., & Stewart, M. (1996). What do cancer patients mean when they complain of concentration and memory problems? *British Journal of Cancer, 74*(10), 1674–1679.

Cummings, J. L. (1993). Frontal–subcortical circuits and human behavior. *Archives of Neurology, 50*(8), 873–880.

Cutler, S. J., & Grams, A. E. (1988). Correlates of self-reported everyday memory problems. *Journal of Gerontology, 43*(3), S82–S90.

Dannlowski, U., Ohrmann, P., Bauer, J., Kugel, H., Arolt, V., Heindel, W., et al. (2007). Amygdala reactivity to masked negative faces is associated with automatic judgmental bias in major depression: A 3 T fMRI study. *Journal of Psychiatry and Neurosciences, 32*(6), 423–429.

Davidson, R. J., Abercrombie, H., Nitschke, J. B., & Putnam, K. (1999). Regional brain function, emotion and disorders of emotion. *Current Opinion in Neurobiology,* *9*(2), 228–234.

Davidson, R. J., Irwin, W., Anderle, M. J., & Kalin, N. H. (2003). The neural substrates of affective processing in depressed patients treated with venlafaxine. *American Journal of Psychiatry, 160*(1), 64–75.

Davidson, R. J., Pizzagalli, D., Nitschke, J. B., & Putnam, K. (2002). Depression: Perspectives from affective neuroscience. *Annual Review of Psychology, 53,* 545–574.

De Kloet, E. R. (2004). Hormones and the stressed brain. *Annals of the New York Academy of Sciences, 1018,* 1–15.

Degl'Innocenti, A., Agren, H., & Backman, L. (1998). Executive deficits in major depression. *Acta Psychiatrica Scandinavica, 97*(3), 182–188.

Derouesne, C., Lacomblez, L., Thibault, S., & LePoncin, M. (1999). Memory complaints in young and elderly subjects. *International Journal of Geriatric Psychiatry, 14*(4), 291–301.

DeRubeis, R. J., Siegle, G. J., & Hollon, S. D. (2008). Cognitive therapy versus medication for depression: Treatment outcomes and neural mechanisms. *Nature Reviews. Neuroscience, 9*(10), 788–796.

Desai, H. D., & Jann, M. W. (2000). Major depression in women: A review of the literature. *Journal of the American Pharmaceutical Association, 40*(4), 525–537.

Dijkstra, J. B., Houx, P. J., & Jolles, J. (1999). Cognition after major surgery in the elderly: Test performance and complaints. *British Journal of Anaesthesiology, 82*(6), 867–874.

Direnfeld, D. M., & Roberts, J. E. (2006). Mood congruent memory in dysphoria: The roles of state affect and cognitive style. *Behavior Research and Therapy, 44*(9), 1275–1285.

Drevets, W. C. (2000). Functional anatomical abnormalities in limbic and prefrontal cortical structures in major depression. *Progress in Brain Research, 126,* 413–431.

Drevets, W. C., & Price, J. L. (2005). Neuroimaging and neuropathological studies of mood disorders. In J. Lincinio & M.-L. Wong (Eds.), *Biology of depression: From novel insights to therapeutic strategies* (pp. 427–466). Weinheim, Germany: Wiley-VCH Verlag GmbH & Co.

Drevets, W. C., Price, J. L., & Furey, M. L. (2008). Brain structural and functional abnormalities in mood disorders: Implications for neurocircuitry models of depression. *Brain Structure and Function, 213*(1–2), 93–118.

Drevets, W. C., & Raichle, M. E. (1992). Neuroanatomical circuits in depression: Implications for treatment mechanisms. *Psychopharmacological Bulletin, 28*(3), 261–274.

Drevets, W. C., Videen, T. O., Price, J. L., Preskorn, S. H., Carmichael, S. T., & Raichle, M. E. (1992). A functional anatomical study of unipolar depression. *Journal of Neuroscience, 12*(9), 3628–3641.

Druss, B. G., Rosenheck, R. A., & Sledge, W. H. (2000). Health and disability costs of depressive illness in a major U.S. corporation. *American Journal of Psychiatry, 157*(8), 1274–1278.

Duff, K., & McCaffrey, R. J. (2001). Electrical injury and lightning injury: A review of their mechanisms and neuropsychological, psychiatric, and neurological sequelae. *Neuropsychology Reviews, 11*(2), 101–116.

Dunn, A. L., Trivedi, M. H., Kampert, J. B., Clark, C. G., & Chambliss, H. O. (2005). Exercise treatment for depression: Efficacy and dose response. *American Journal of Preventative Medicine, 28*(1), 1–8.

Dwight-Johnson, M., Sherbourne, C. D., Liao, D., & Wells, K. B. (2000). Treatment preferences among depressed primary care patients. *Journal of General Internal Medicine, 15*(8), 527–534.

Egede, L. E. (2007). Major depression in individuals with chronic medical disorders: Prevalence, correlates and association with health resource utilization, lost productivity and functional disability. *General Hospital Psychiatry, 29*(5), 409–416.

Elderkin-Thompson, V., Mintz, J., Haroon, E., Lavretsky, H., & Kumar, A. (2006). Executive dysfunction and memory in older patients with major and minor depression. *Archives of Clinical Neuropsychology, 21*(7), 669–676.

Elliott, R. (1998). The neuropsychological profile in unipolar depression. *Trends in Cognitive Sciences, 2*, 447–454.

Elliott, R., Sahakian, B. J., Herrod, J. J., Robbins, T. W., & Paykel, E. S. (1997). Abnormal response to negative feedback in unipolar depression: Evidence for a diagnosis specific impairment. *Journal of Neurology, Neurosurgery and Psychiatry, 63*(1), 74–82.

Elliott, R., Sahakian, B. J., McKay, A. P., Herrod, J. J., Robbins, T. W., & Paykel, E. S. (1996). Neuropsychological impairments in unipolar depression: The influence of perceived failure on subsequent performance. *Psychological Medicine, 26*(5), 975–989.

Ereshefsky, L. (2001). The Texas Medication Algorithm Project for major depression. *Managed Care, 10*(8, Suppl.), 16–17; discussion 18–22.

Ericsson, M., Poston, W. S., Linder, J., Taylor, J. E., Haddock, C. K., & Foreyt, J. P. (2002). Depression predicts disability in long-term chronic pain patients. *Disability and Rehabilitation, 24*(6), 334–340.

Etherton, J. L., Bianchini, K. J., Ciota, M. A., Heinly, M. T., & Greve, K. W. (2006). Pain, malingering and the WAIS-III Working Memory Index. *Spine Journal, 6*(1), 61–71.

Ettlin, T. M., Kischka, U., Reichmann, S., Radii, E. W., Heim, S., Wengen, D., et al. (1992). Cerebral symptoms after whiplash injury of the neck: A prospective clinical and neuropsychological study of whiplash injury. *Journal of Neurology, Neurosurgery and Psychiatry, 55*(10), 943–948.

Fales, C. L., Barch, D. M., Rundle, M. M., Mintun, M. A., Snyder, A. Z., Cohen, J. D., et al. (2008). Altered emotional interference processing in affective and cognitive-control brain circuitry in major depression. *Biological Psychiatry, 63*(4), 377–384.

Fann, J. R., Katon, W. J., Uomoto, J. M., & Esselman, P. C. (1995). Psychiatric disorders and functional disability in outpatients with traumatic brain injuries. *American Journal of Psychiatry, 152*(10), 1493–1499.

Farmer, A. E., & McGuffin, P. (2003). Humiliation, loss and other types of life events and difficulties: A comparison of depressed subjects, healthy controls and their siblings. *Psychological Medicine, 33*(7), 1169–1175.

Farmer, M. E., Locke, B. Z., Moscicki, E. K., Dannenberg, A. L., Larson, D. B., & Radloff, L. S. (1988). Physical activity and depressive symptoms: The NHANES I Epidemiologic Follow-up Study. *American Journal of Epidemiology, 128*(6), 1340–1351.

Ferguson, J. M., Wesnes, K. A., & Schwartz, G. E. (2003). Reboxetine versus paroxetine versus placebo: Effects on cognitive functioning in depressed patients. *International Clinical Psychopharmacology, 18*(1), 9–14.

Fielding, R. (1991). Depression and acute myocardial infarction: A review and reinterpretation. *Social Science and Medicine, 32*(9), 1017–1028.

Foa, E. B., Cashman, L., Jaycox, L., & Perry, K. (1997). The validation of a self-report measure of posttraumatic stress disorder: The Posttraumatic Diagnostic Scale. *Psychological Assessment, 9*(4), 445–451.

Frank, E., Kupfer, D. J., Perel, J. M., Cornes, C., Jarrett, D. B., Mallinger, A. G., et al. (1990). Three-year outcomes for maintenance therapies in recurrent depression. *Archives of General Psychiatry, 47*(12), 1093–1099.

Franklin, C. L., & Zimmerman, M. (2001). Posttraumatic stress disorder and major depressive disorder: Investigating the role of overlapping symptoms in diagnostic comorbidity. *Journal of Nervous and Mental Disease, 189*(8), 548–551.

Frasure-Smith, N., Lesperance, F., Gravel, G., Masson, A., Juneau, M., Talajic, M., et al. (2000). Social support, depression, and mortality during the first year after myocardial infarction. *Circulation, 101*(16), 1919–1924.

Friis, R. H., Wittchen, H. U., Pfister, H., & Lieb, R. (2002). Life events and changes in the course of depression in young adults. *European Psychiatry, 17*(5), 241–253.

Fu, C. H., Williams, S. C., Cleare, A. J., Brammer, M. J., Walsh, N. D., Kim, J., et al. (2004). Attenuation of the neural response to sad faces in major depression by antidepressant treatment: A prospective, event-related functional magnetic resonance imaging study. *Archives of General Psychiatry, 61*(9), 877–889.

Gasquoine, P. G. (2000). Postconcussional symptoms in chronic back pain. *Applied Neuropsychology, 7*(2), 83–89.

Genuis, S. J. (2008). Toxic causes of mental illness are overlooked. *Neurotoxicology, 29*(6), 1147–1149.

Gilbertson, M. W., Paulus, L. A., Williston, S. K., Gurvits, T. V., Lasko, N. B., Pitman, R. K., et al. (2006). Neurocognitive function in monozygotic twins discordant for combat exposure: Relationship to posttraumatic stress disorder. *Journal of Abnormal Psychology, 115*(3), 484–495.

Gilbertson, M. W., Shenton, M. E., Ciszewski, A., Kasai, K., Lasko, N. B., Orr, S. P., et al. (2002). Smaller hippocampal volume predicts pathologic vulnerability to psychological trauma. *Nature Neuroscience, 5*(11), 1242–1247.

Gohier, B., Ferracci, L., Surguladze, S. A., Lawrence, E., El Hage, W., Kefi, M. Z., et al. (2009). Cognitive inhibition and working memory in unipolar depression. *Journal of Affective Disorders, 116*(1–2), 100–105.

Goldberg, R. (2006). *Drugs across the spectrum* (5th ed.). Belmont, CA: Thomson Wadsworth.

Goswami, D. B., May, W. L., Stockmeier, C. A., & Austin, M. C. (2009). Transcriptional expression of serotonergic regulators in laser-captured microdissected dorsal raphe neurons of subjects with major depressive disorder: Sex-specific differences. *Journal of Neurochemistry, 112*(2), 397–409.

Grant, M. M., Thase, M. E., & Sweeney, J. A. (2001). Cognitive disturbance in outpatient depressed younger adults: Evidence of modest impairment. *Biological Psychiatry, 50*(1), 35–43.

Green, P. (2001). Comment on article "Does pain confound interpretation of neuropsychological test results?" *NeuroRehabilitation, 16*(4), 305–306; discussion 307–308.

Greenberg, P. E., Kessler, R. C., Birnbaum, H. G., Leong, S. A., Lowe, S. W., Berglund, P. A., et al. (2003). The economic burden of depression in the United States: How did it change between 1990 and 2000? *Journal of Clinical Psychiatry, 64*(12), 1465–1475.

Gualtieri, C. T., Johnson, L. G., & Benedict, K. B. (2006). Neurocognition in depression:

Patients on and off medication versus healthy comparison subjects. *Journal of Neuropsychiatry and Clinical Neurosciences, 18*(2), 217–225.

Guez, M., Brannstrom, R., Nyberg, L., Toolanen, G., & Hildingsson, C. (2005). Neuropsychological functioning and MMPI-2 profiles in chronic neck pain: A comparison of whiplash and non-traumatic groups. *Journal of Clinical and Experimental Neuropsychology, 27*(2), 151–163.

Haldorsen, T., Waterloo, K., Dahl, A., Mellgren, S. I., Davidsen, P. E., & Molin, P. K. (2003). Symptoms and cognitive dysfunction in patients with the late whiplash syndrome. *Applied Neuropsychology, 10*(3), 170–175.

Hamilton, J. P., & Gotlib, I. H. (2008). Neural substrates of increased memory sensitivity for negative stimuli in major depression. *Biological Psychiatry, 63*(12), 1155–1162.

Hammar, A., & Ardal, G. (2009). Cognitive functioning in major depression—a summary. *Frontiers in Human Neuroscience, 3,* 26.

Hammar, A., Lund, A., & Hugdahl, K. (2003). Long-lasting cognitive impairment in unipolar major depression: A 6-month follow-up study. *Psychiatry Research, 118*(2), 189–196.

Hammen, C. (2003). Social stress and women's risk for recurrent depression. *Archives of Women's Mental Health, 6*(1), 9–13.

Hare, T. A., Tottenham, N., Galvan, A., Voss, H. U., Glover, G. H., & Casey, B. J. (2008). Biological substrates of emotional reactivity and regulation in adolescence during an emotional go-no-go task. *Biological Psychiatry, 63*(10), 927–934.

Hart, R. P., Martelli, M. F., & Zasler, N. D. (2000). Chronic pain and neuropsychological functioning. *Neuropsychology Reviews, 10*(3), 131–149.

Harvey, P. O., Fossati, P., Pochon, J. B., Levy, R., Lebastard, G., Lehericy, S., et al. (2005). Cognitive control and brain resources in major depression: An fMRI study using the n-back task. *Neuroimage, 26*(3), 860–869.

Hasher, L., & Zacks, R. T. (1979). Automatic and effortful processes in memory. *Journal of Experimental Psychology: General, 108,* 356–388.

Hastings, R. S., Parsey, R. V., Oquendo, M. A., Arango, V., & Mann, J. J. (2004). Volumetric analysis of the prefrontal cortex, amygdala, and hippocampus in major depression. *Neuropsychopharmacology, 29*(5), 952–959.

Heim, C., Bradley, B., Mletzko, T. C., Deveau, T. C., Musselman, D. L., Nemeroff, C. B., et al. (2009). Effect of childhood trauma on adult depression and neuroendocrine function: Sex-specific moderation by CRH Receptor 1 gene. *Frontiers in Behavioral Neuroscience, 3,* 41.

Henriques, J. B., & Davidson, R. J. (1991). Left frontal hypoactivation in depression. *Journal of Abnormal Psychology, 100*(4), 535–545.

Henry, J., & Crawford, J. R. (2005). A meta-analytic review of verbal fluency deficits in depression. *Journal of Clinical and Experimental Neuropsychology, 27*(1), 78–101.

Herrera-Guzman, I., Gudayol-Ferre, E., Herrera-Guzman, D., Guardia-Olmos, J., Hinojosa-Calvo, E., & Herrera-Abarca, J. E. (2009). Effects of selective serotonin reuptake and dual serotonergic-noradrenergic reuptake treatments on memory and mental processing speed in patients with major depressive disorder. *Journal of Psychiatric Research, 43*(9), 855–863.

Hestbaek, L., Leboeuf-Yde, C., & Manniche, C. (2003). Low back pain: What is the long-term course? A review of studies of general patient populations. *European Spine Journal, 12*(2), 149–165.

Hindmarch, I. (2001). Expanding the horizons of depression: Beyond the monoamine hypothesis. *Human Psychopharmacology, 16*(3), 203–218.

Hollon, S. D., DeRubeis, R. J., Shelton, R. C., Amsterdam, J. D., Salomon, R. M., O'Reardon, J. P., et al. (2005). Prevention of relapse following cognitive therapy vs. medications in moderate to severe depression. *Archives of General Psychiatry, 62*(4), 417–422.

Hollon, S. D., Thase, M. E., & Markowitz, J. C. (2002). Treatment and prevention of depression. *Psychological Science in the Public Interest, 3*, 39–77.

Holmes, A. J., MacDonald, A., III, Carter, C. S., Barch, D. M., Andrew Stenger, V., & Cohen, J. D. (2005). Prefrontal functioning during context processing in schizophrenia and major depression: An event-related fMRI study. *Schizophrenia Research, 76*(2–3), 199–206.

Hsu, D. T., Langenecker, S. A., Kennedy, S. E., Zubieta, J. K., & Heitzeg, M. M. (2010). FMRI BOLD responses to negative stimuli in the prefrontal cortex are dependent on levels of recent negative life stress in major depressive disorder. *Psychiatry Research: Neuroimaging, 183*(3), 202–208.

Iezzi, T., Archibald, Y., Barnett, P., Klinck, A., & Duckworth, M. (1999). Neurocognitive performance and emotional status in chronic pain patients. *Journal of Behavioral Medicine, 22*(3), 205–216.

Iezzi, T., Duckworth, M. P., Vuong, L. N., Archibald, Y. M., & Klinck, A. (2004). Predictors of neurocognitive performance in chronic pain patients. *International Journal of Behavioral Medicine, 11*(1), 56–61.

Imel, Z. E., Malterer, M. B., McKay, K. M., & Wampold, B. E. (2008). A meta-analysis of psychotherapy and medication in unipolar depression and dysthymia. *Journal of Affective Disorders, 110*(3), 197–206.

Iverson, G. L. (2006). Misdiagnosis of persistent postconcussion syndrome in patients with depression. *Archives of Clinical Neuropsychology, 21*(4), 303–310.

Iverson, G. L., Brooks, B. L., Ferguson, K. E., & Young, A. H. (2009). Development of a new neurocognitive screening battery for depression. *Journal of the International Neuropsychological Society, 15*(S2), 79.

Iverson, G. L., King, R. J., Scott, J. G., & Adams, R. L. (2001). Cognitive complaints in litigating patients with head injuries or chronic pain. *Journal of Forensic Neuropsychology, 2*, 19–30.

Iverson, G. L., & McCracken, L. M. (1997). "Postconcussive" symptoms in persons with chronic pain. *Brain Injury, 11*(11), 783–790.

Jamison, R. N., Sbrocco, T., & Parris, W. C. (1988). The influence of problems with concentration and memory on emotional distress and daily activities in chronic pain patients. *International Journal of Psychiatry in Medicine, 18*(2), 183–191.

Jelinek, L., Jacobsen, D., Kellner, M., Larbig, F., Biesold, K. H., Barre, K., et al. (2006). Verbal and nonverbal memory functioning in posttraumatic stress disorder (PTSD). *Journal of Clinical and Experimental Neuropsychology, 28*(6), 940–948.

Jenewein, J., Moergeli, H., Wittmann, L., Buchi, S., Kraemer, B., & Schnyder, U. (2009). Development of chronic pain following severe accidental injury: Results of a 3-year follow-up study. *Journal of Psychosomatic Research, 66*(2), 119–126.

Jenkins, M. A., Langlais, P. J., Delis, D. A., & Cohen, R. A. (2000). Attentional dysfunction associated with posttraumatic stress disorder among rape survivors. *The Clinical Neuropsychologist, 14*(1), 7–12.

Jennum, P., & Sjol, A. (1994). Self-assessed cognitive function in snorers and sleep apneics: An epidemiological study of 1,504 females and males aged 30–60 years—the Dan-MONICA II Study. *European Neurology, 34*(4), 204–208.

Johnston, K., Westerfield, W., Momin, S., Phillippi, R., & Naidoo, A. (2009). The direct and indirect costs of employee depression, anxiety, and emotional disorders—an employer case study. *Journal of Occupational and Environmental Medicine, 51*(5), 564–577.

Kalin, N. H., Davidson, R. J., Irwin, W., Warner, G., Orendi, J. L., Sutton, S. K., et al. (1997). Functional magnetic resonance imaging studies of emotional processing in normal and depressed patients: Effects of venlafaxine. *Journal of Clinical Psychiatry, 58*(Suppl. 16), 32–39.

Keller, M. B., Lavori, P. W., Mueller, T. I., Endicott, J., Coryell, W., Hirschfeld, R. M., et al. (1992). Time to recovery, chronicity, and levels of psychopathology in major depression. A 5-year prospective follow-up of 431 subjects. *Archives of General Psychiatry, 49*(10), 809–816.

Kendler, K. S., Hettema, J. M., Butera, F., Gardner, C. O., & Prescott, C. A. (2003). Life event dimensions of loss, humiliation, entrapment, and danger in the prediction of onsets of major depression and generalized anxiety. *Archives of General Psychiatry, 60*(8), 789–796.

Kendler, K. S., Karkowski, L. M., & Prescott, C. A. (1999). Causal relationship between stressful life events and the onset of major depression. *American Journal of Psychiatry, 156*(6), 837–841.

Kendler, K. S., Thornton, L. M., & Gardner, C. O. (2001). Genetic risk, number of previous depressive episodes, and stressful life events in predicting onset of major depression. *American Journal of Psychiatry, 158*(4), 582–586.

Kessels, R. P., Aleman, A., Verhagen, W. I., & van Luijtelaar, E. L. (2000). Cognitive functioning after whiplash injury: A meta-analysis. *Journal of the International Neuropsychological Society, 6*(3), 271–278.

Kessing, L. V., Hansen, M. G., Andersen, P. K., & Angst, J. (2004). The predictive effect of episodes on the risk of recurrence in depressive and bipolar disorders—a life-long perspective. *Acta Psychiatrica Scandinavica, 109*(5), 339–344.

Kessler, D., Lewis, G., Kaur, S., Wiles, N., King, M., Weich, S., et al. (2009). Therapist-delivered Internet psychotherapy for depression in primary care: A randomised controlled trial. *Lancet, 374*(9690), 628–634.

Kessler, R., White, L. A., Birnbaum, H., Qiu, Y., Kidolezi, Y., Mallett, D., et al. (2008). Comparative and interactive effects of depression relative to other health problems on work performance in the workforce of a large employer. *Journal of Occupational and Environmental Medicine, 50*(7), 809–816.

Kessler, R. C., Barber, C., Birnbaum, H. G., Frank, R. G., Greenberg, P. E., Rose, R. M., et al. (1999). Depression in the workplace: Effects on short-term disability. *Health Affairs (Project Hope), 18*(5), 163–171.

Kessler, R. C., Sonnega, A., Bromet, E., Hughes, M., & Nelson, C. B. (1995). Posttraumatic stress disorder in the National Comorbidity Survey. *Archives of General Psychiatry, 52*(12), 1048–1060.

Ketter, T. A., Kimbrell, T. A., George, M. S., Dunn, R. T., Speer, A. M., Benson, B. E., et al. (2001). Effects of mood and subtype on cerebral glucose metabolism in treatment-resistant bipolar disorder. *Biological Psychiatry, 49*(2), 97–109.

Kischka, U., Ettlin, T., Heim, S., & Schmid, G. (1991). Cerebral symptoms following whiplash injury. *European Neurology, 31*(3), 136–140.

Koch, K., Pauly, K., Kellermann, T., Seiferth, N. Y., Reske, M., Backes, V., et al. (2007). Gender differences in the cognitive control of emotion: An fMRI study. *Neuropsychologia, 45*(12), 2744–2754.

Kochanek, P. M., Clark, R. S. B., & Jenkins, L. W. (2007). TBI: Pathobiology. In N. D.

Zasler, D. I. Katz, & R. D. Zafonte (Eds.), *Brain injury medicine: Principles and practice* (pp. 81–96). New York: Demos.

Kolb, B., & Whishaw, I. Q. (2008). *Fundamentals of human neuropsychology* (6th ed.). New York: Worth.

Kreutzer, J. S., Seel, R. T., & Gourley, E. (2001). The prevalence and symptom rates of depression after traumatic brain injury: A comprehensive examination. *Brain Injury, 15*(7), 563–576.

Kruijshaar, M. E., Barendregt, J., Vos, T., de Graaf, R., Spijker, J., & Andrews, G. (2005). Lifetime prevalence estimates of major depression: An indirect estimation method and a quantification of recall bias. *European Journal of Epidemiology, 20*(1), 103–111.

Lahr, D., Beblo, T., & Hartje, W. (2007). Cognitive performance and subjective complaints before and after remission of major depression. *Cognitive Neuropsychiatry, 12*(1), 25–45.

Lake, A. E., III, Branca, B., Lutz, T. E., & Saper, J. R. (1999). Headache level during neuropsychological testing and test performance in patients with chronic posttraumatic headache. *Journal of Head Trauma Rehabilitation, 14*(1), 70–80.

Lampinen, P., Heikkinen, R. L., & Ruoppila, I. (2000). Changes in intensity of physical exercise as predictors of depressive symptoms among older adults: An eight-year follow-up. *Preventive Medicine, 30*(5), 371–380.

Landro, N. I., Stiles, T. C., & Sletvold, H. (2001). Neuropsychological function in nonpsychotic unipolar major depression. *Neuropsychiatry, Neuropsychology, and Behavioral Neurology, 14*(4), 233–240.

Langenecker, S. A., Bieliauskas, L. A., Rapport, L. J., Zubieta, J. K., Wilde, E. A., & Berent, S. (2005). Face emotion perception and executive functioning deficits in depression. *Journal of Clinical and Experimental Neuropsychology, 27*(3), 320–333.

Langenecker, S. A., Caveney, A. F., Giordani, B., Young, E. A., Nielson, K. A., Rapport, L. J., et al. (2007a). The sensitivity and psychometric properties of a brief computer-based cognitive screening battery in a depression clinic. *Psychiatry Research, 152*(2–3), 143–154.

Langenecker, S. A., Kennedy, S. E., Guidotti, L. M., Briceno, E. M., Own, L. S., Hooven, T., et al. (2007b). Frontal and limbic activation during inhibitory control predicts treatment response in major depressive disorder. *Biological Psychiatry, 62*(11), 1272–1280.

Langenecker, S. A., Lee, H. J., & Bieliauskas, L. A. (2009). Neuropsychology of depression and related mood disorders. In I. Grant & K. M. Adams (Eds.), *Neuropsychological assessment of neuropsychiatric disorders* (3rd ed., pp. 523–559). New York: Oxford University Press.

LeDoux, J. E. (1993). Emotional memory systems in the brain. *Behavioral Brain Research, 58*(1–2), 69–79.

Lethem, J., Slade, P. D., Troup, J. D., & Bentley, G. (1983). Outline of a fear-avoidance model of exaggerated pain perception—I. *Behavior Research and Therapy, 21*(4), 401–408.

Levkovitz, Y., Caftori, R., Avital, A., & Richter-Levin, G. (2002). The SSRIs drug fluoxetine, but not the noradrenergic tricyclic drug desipramine, improves memory performance during acute major depression. *Brain Research Bulletin, 58*(4), 345–350.

Lieberman, J. A., & Tasman, A. (2006). *Handbook of psychiatric drugs.* Hoboken, NJ: Wiley.

Lim, C., Alexander, M. P., LaFleche, G., Schnyer, D. M., & Verfaellie, M. (2004). The neurological and cognitive sequelae of cardiac arrest. *Neurology, 63*(10), 1774–1778.

Lippi, G., Montagnana, M., Favaloro, E. J., & Franchini, M. (2009). Mental depression and cardiovascular disease: A multifaceted, bidirectional association. *Seminars in Thrombosis and Hemostasis, 35*(3), 325–336.

Little, A. (2009). Treatment-resistant depression. *American Family Physician, 80*(2), 167–172.

Lohr, J. B., Alder, M., Flynn, K., Harris, M. J., & McAdams, L. A. (1997). Minor physical anomalies in older patients with late-onset schizophrenia, early-onset schizophrenia, depression, and Alzheimer's disease. *American Journal of Geriatric Psychiatry, 5*(4), 318–323.

Lupien, S. J., Evans, A., Lord, C., Miles, J., Pruessner, M., Pike, B., et al. (2007). Hippocampal volume is as variable in young as in older adults: Implications for the notion of hippocampal atrophy in humans. *Neuroimage, 34*(2), 479–485.

Macklin, M. L., Metzger, L. J., Litz, B. T., McNally, R. J., Lasko, N. B., Orr, S. P., et al. (1998). Lower precombat intelligence is a risk factor for posttraumatic stress disorder. *Journal of Consulting and Clinical Psychology, 66*(2), 323–326.

MacMaster, F. P., Mirza, Y., Szeszko, P. R., Kmiecik, L. E., Easter, P. C., Taormina, S. P., et al. (2008). Amygdala and hippocampal volumes in familial early onset major depressive disorder. *Biological Psychiatry, 63*(4), 385–390.

MacQueen, G. M., Campbell, S., McEwen, B. S., Macdonald, K., Amano, S., Joffe, R. T., et al. (2003). Course of illness, hippocampal function, and hippocampal volume in major depression. *Proceedings of the National Academy of Sciences of the United States of America, 100*(3), 1387–1392.

Maes, M., Bosmans, E., De Jongh, R., Kenis, G., Vandoolaeghe, E., & Neels, H. (1997). Increased serum IL-6 and IL-1 receptor antagonist concentrations in major depression and treatment resistant depression. *Cytokine, 9*(11), 853–858.

Magarinos, A. M., McEwen, B. S., Flugge, G., & Fuchs, E. (1996). Chronic psychosocial stress causes apical dendritic atrophy of hippocampal CA3 pyramidal neurons in subordinate tree shrews. *Journal of Neuroscience, 16*(10), 3534–3540.

Majer, M., Ising, M., Kunzel, H., Binder, E. B., Holsboer, F., Modell, S., et al. (2004). Impaired divided attention predicts delayed response and risk to relapse in subjects with depressive disorders. *Psychological Medicine, 34*(8), 1453–1463.

Mak, A. K., Hu, Z. G., Zhang, J. X., Xiao, Z., & Lee, T. M. (2009). Sex-related differences in neural activity during emotion regulation. *Neuropsychologia, 47*(13), 2900–2908.

Maletic, V., Robinson, M., Oakes, T., Iyengar, S., Ball, S. G., & Russell, J. (2007). Neurobiology of depression: An integrated view of key findings. *International Journal of Clinical Practice, 61*(12), 2030–2040.

Manji, H. K., Drevets, W. C., & Charney, D. S. (2001). The cellular neurobiology of depression. *Nature Medicine, 7*(5), 541–547.

Manji, H. K., Quiroz, J. A., Sporn, J., Payne, J. L., Denicoff, K., N, A. G., et al. (2003). Enhancing neuronal plasticity and cellular resilience to develop novel, improved therapeutics for difficult-to-treat depression. *Biological Psychiatry, 53*(8), 707–742.

Manolides, L. S., & Baloyannis, S. J. (1984). Influence of hydrocortisone, progesterone and testosterone on dendritic growth in vitro. *Acta Oto-laryngologica, 97*(5–6), 509–522.

Martinsen, E. W., Hoffart, A., & Solberg, O. (1989). Comparing aerobic with nonaerobic forms of exercise in the treatment of clinical depression: A randomized trial. *Comprehensive Psychiatry, 30*(4), 324–331.

Mayberg, H. S. (2003). Modulating dysfunctional limbic-cortical circuits in depression: Towards development of brain-based algorithms for diagnosis and optimised treatment. *British Medical Bulletin, 65,* 193–207.

Mayberg, H. S., Liotti, M., Brannan, S. K., McGinnis, S., Mahurin, R. K., Jerabek, P. A., et al. (1999). Reciprocal limbic-cortical function and negative mood: Converging PET findings in depression and normal sadness. *American Journal of Psychiatry, 156*(5), 675–682.

McCracken, L. M. (1998). Learning to live with the pain: Acceptance of pain predicts adjustment in persons with chronic pain. *Pain, 74*(1), 21–27.

McCracken, L. M., & Iverson, G. L. (2001). Predicting complaints of impaired cognitive functioning in patients with chronic pain. *Journal of Pain and Symptom Management, 21*(5), 392–396.

McDermott, L. M., & Ebmeier, K. P. (2009). A meta-analysis of depression severity and cognitive function. *Journal of Affective Disorders, 119*(1–3), 1–8.

McKinnon, M. C., Yucel, K., Nazarov, A., & MacQueen, G. M. (2009). A meta-analysis examining clinical predictors of hippocampal volume in patients with major depressive disorder. *Journal of Psychiatry and Neurosciences, 34*(1), 41–54.

Mead, G. E., Morley, W., Campbell, P., Greig, C. A., McMurdo, M., & Lawlor, D. A. (2008). Exercise for depression. *Cochrane Database of Systematic Reviews* (4), CD004366.

Merriam, E. P., Thase, M. E., Haas, G. L., Keshavan, M. S., & Sweeney, J. A. (1999). Prefrontal cortical dysfunction in depression determined by Wisconsin Card Sorting Test performance. *American Journal of Psychiatry, 156*(5), 780–782.

Mesulam, M. M. (2000). *Principles of behavioral and cognitive neurology* (2nd ed.). Oxford, UK: Oxford University Press.

Meyer-Baron, M., Blaszkewicz, M., Henke, H., Knapp, G., Muttray, A., Schaper, M., et al. (2008). The impact of solvent mixtures on neurobehavioral performance: Conclusions from epidemiological data. *Neurotoxicology, 29*(3), 349–360.

Meyers, J. E., & Diep, A. (2000). Assessment of malingering in chronic pain patients using neuropsychological tests. *Applied Neuropsychology, 7*(3), 133–139.

Mickey, B. J., Ducci, F., Hodgkinson, C. A., Langenecker, S. A., Goldman, D., & Zubieta, J. K. (2008). Monoamine oxidase A genotype predicts human serotonin 1A receptor availability in vivo. *Journal of Neuroscience, 28*(44), 11354–11359.

Milad, M. R., Wright, C. I., Orr, S. P., Pitman, R. K., Quirk, G. J., & Rauch, S. L. (2007). Recall of fear extinction in humans activates the ventromedial prefrontal cortex and hippocampus in concert. *Biological Psychiatry, 62*(5), 446–454.

Miller, A. H., & Raison, C. L. (2008). Immune system contributions to the pathophysiology of depression. *Focus, 6,* 36–45.

Miller, G. E., Stetler, C. A., Carney, R. M., Freedland, K. E., & Banks, W. A. (2002). Clinical depression and inflammatory risk markers for coronary heart disease. *American Journal of Cardiology, 90*(12), 1279–1283.

Mitra, R., & Sapolsky, R. M. (2008). Acute corticosterone treatment is sufficient to induce anxiety and amygdaloid dendritic hypertrophy. *Proceedings of the National Academy of Sciences of the United States of America, 105*(14), 5573–5578.

Mobily, K. E., Rubenstein, L. M., Lemke, J. H., O'Hara, M. W., & Wallace, R. B. (1996). Walking and depression in a cohort of older adults: The Iowa 65+ Rural Health Study. *Journal of Aging and Physical Activity, 4,* 119–135.

Monroe, S. M., & Harkness, K. L. (2005). Life stress, the "kindling" hypothesis, and the recurrence of depression: Considerations from a life stress perspective. *Psychological Review, 112*(2), 417–445.

Morecraft, R. J., & Yeterian, E. H. (2002). Prefrontal cortex. In V. S. Ramachandran (Ed.), *Encyclopedia of the human brain* (pp. 11–26). New York: Academic Press.

Morrow, L. A., Gibson, C., Bagovich, G. R., Stein, L., Condray, R., & Scott, A. (2000). Increased incidence of anxiety and depressive disorders in persons with organic solvent exposure. *Psychosomatic Medicine, 62*(6), 746–750.

Mossner, R., Mikova, O., Koutsilieri, E., Saoud, M., Ehlis, A. C., Muller, N., et al. (2007). Consensus paper of the WFSBP Task Force on Biological Markers: Biological markers in depression. *World Journal of Biological Psychiatry, 8*(3), 141–174.

Mulder, R. T., Joyce, P. R., Frampton, C. M., Luty, S. E., & Sullivan, P. F. (2006). Six months of treatment for depression: Outcome and predictors of the course of illness. *American Journal of Psychiatry, 163*(1), 95–100.

Mulrow, C. D., Williams, J. W., Jr., Chiquette, E., Aguilar, C., Hitchcock-Noel, P., Lee, S., et al. (2000). Efficacy of newer medications for treating depression in primary care patients. *American Journal of Medicine, 108*(1), 54–64.

Muñoz, M., & Esteve, R. (2005). Reports of memory functioning by patients with chronic pain. *Clinical Journal of Pain, 21*(4), 287–291.

Murphy, F. C., Michael, A., Robbins, T. W., & Sahakian, B. J. (2003). Neuropsychological impairment in patients with major depressive disorder: The effects of feedback on task performance. *Psychological Medicine, 33*(3), 455–467.

Murray, E. A. (2007). The amygdala, reward and emotion. *Trends in Cognitive Sciences, 11*(11), 489–497.

Nabkasorn, C., Miyai, N., Sootmongkol, A., Junprasert, S., Yamamoto, H., Arita, M., et al. (2006). Effects of physical exercise on depression, neuroendocrine stress hormones and physiological fitness in adolescent females with depressive symptoms. *European Journal of Public Health, 16*(2), 179–184.

Nakano, Y., Baba, H., Maeshima, H., Kitajima, A., Sakai, Y., Baba, K., et al. (2008). Executive dysfunction in medicated, remitted state of major depression. *Journal of Affective Disorders, 111*(1), 46–51.

Neu, P., Bajbouj, M., Schilling, A., Godemann, F., Berman, R. M., & Schlattmann, P. (2005). Cognitive function over the treatment course of depression in middle-aged patients: Correlation with brain MRI signal hyperintensities. *Journal of Psychiatric Research, 39*(2), 129–135.

Newman, P. J., & Sweet, J. J. (1992). Depressive disorders. In A. E. Puente & R. J. McCaffrey (Eds.), *Handbook of neuropsychological assessment: A biopsychosocial perspective* (pp. 263–307). New York: Plenum Press.

Noble, R. E. (2005). Depression in women. *Metabolism: Clinical and Experimental, 54*(5, Suppl. 1), 49–52.

Northoff, G., Richter, A., Gessner, M., Schlagenhauf, F., Fell, J., Baumgart, F., et al. (2000). Functional dissociation between medial and lateral prefrontal cortical spatiotemporal activation in negative and positive emotions: A combined fMRI/MEG study. *Cerebral Cortex, 10*(1), 93–107.

O'Bryant, S. E., Marcus, D. A., Rains, J. C., & Penzien, D. B. (2006). The neuropsychology of recurrent headache. *Headache, 46*(9), 1364–1376.

Olver, J. S., Ignatiadis, S., Maruff, P., Burrows, G. D., & Norman, T. R. (2008). Quetiapine augmentation in depressed patients with partial response to antidepressants. *Human Psychopharmacology, 23*(8), 653–660.

Ordway, G. A., Klimek, V., & Mann, J. J. (2002). Neurocircuitry of mood disorders. In

K. L. Davis, D. Charney, J. T. Coyle, & C. Nemeroff (Eds.), *Neuropsychopharmacology: The fifth generation of progress* (pp. 1051–1064). Philadelphia: American College of Neuropsychopharmacology.

Paelecke-Habermann, Y., Pohl, J., & Leplow, B. (2005). Attention and executive functions in remitted major depression patients. *Journal of Affective Disorders, 89*(1–3), 125–135.

Paffenbarger, R. S., Jr., Lee, I. M., & Leung, R. (1994). Physical activity and personal characteristics associated with depression and suicide in American college men. *Acta Psychiatrica Scandinavica. Supplementum, 377*, 16–22.

Parmelee, P. A., Smith, B., & Katz, I. R. (1993). Pain complaints and cognitive status among elderly institution residents. *Journal of the American Geriatrics Society, 41*(5), 517–522.

Parslow, R. A., & Jorm, A. F. (2007). Pretrauma and posttrauma neurocognitive functioning and PTSD symptoms in a community sample of young adults. *American Journal of Psychiatry, 164*(3), 509–515.

Patten, S. B., Wang, J. L., Williams, J. V., Currie, S., Beck, C. A., Maxwell, C. J., et al. (2006). Descriptive epidemiology of major depression in Canada. *Canadian Journal of Psychiatry, 51*(2), 84–90.

Penninx, B. W., Rejeski, W. J., Pandya, J., Miller, M. E., Di Bari, M., Applegate, W. B., et al. (2002). Exercise and depressive symptoms: A comparison of aerobic and resistance exercise effects on emotional and physical function in older persons with high and low depressive symptomatology. *Journals of Gerontology. Series B, Psychological Sciences and Social Sciences, 57*(2), P124–P132.

Pettit, J. W., Lewinsohn, P. M., & Joiner, T. E., Jr. (2006). Propagation of major depressive disorder: Relationship between first episode symptoms and recurrence. *Psychiatry Research, 141*(3), 271–278.

Phillips, M. L., Drevets, W. C., Rauch, S. L., & Lane, R. (2003). Neurobiology of emotion perception II: Implications for major psychiatric disorders. *Biological Psychiatry, 54*(5), 515–528.

Pizzagalli, D., Pascual-Marqui, R. D., Nitschke, J. B., Oakes, T. R., Larson, C. L., Abercrombie, H. C., et al. (2001). Anterior cingulate activity as a predictor of degree of treatment response in major depression: Evidence from brain electrical tomography analysis. *American Journal of Psychiatry, 158*(3), 405–415.

Pliskin, N. H., Capelli-Schellpfeffer, M., Law, R. T., Malina, A. C., Kelley, K. M., & Lee, R. C. (1998). Neuropsychological symptom presentation after electrical injury. *Journal of Trauma, 44*(4), 709–715.

Politis, A., Lykouras, L., Mourtzouchou, P., & Christodoulou, G. N. (2004). Attentional disturbances in patients with unipolar psychotic depression: A selective and sustained attention study. *Comprehensive Psychiatry, 45*(6), 452–459.

Ponds, R. W., Commissaris, K. J., & Jolles, J. (1997). Prevalence and covariates of subjective forgetfulness in a normal population in The Netherlands. *International Journal of Aging and Human Development, 45*(3), 207–221.

Porter, R. J., Gallagher, P., Thompson, J. M., & Young, A. H. (2003). Neurocognitive impairment in drug-free patients with major depressive disorder. *British Journal of Psychiatry, 182*, 214–220.

Preiss, M., Kucerova, H., Lukavsky, J., Stepankova, H., Sos, P., & Kawaciukova, R. (2009). Cognitive deficits in the euthymic phase of unipolar depression. *Psychiatry Research, 169*(3), 235–239.

Primeau, M., Engelstatter, G. H., & Bares, K. K. (1995). Behavioral consequences of lightning and electrical injury. *Seminars in Neurology, 15*(3), 279–285.

Prince, M., Patel, V., Saxena, S., Maj, M., Maselko, J., Phillips, M. R., et al. (2007). No health without mental health. *Lancet, 370,* 859–877.

Prohl, J., Bodenburg, S., & Rustenbach, S. J. (2009). Early prediction of long-term cognitive impairment after cardiac arrest. *Journal of the International Neuropsychological Society, 15*(3), 344–353.

Pruessner, J. C., Collins, D. L., Pruessner, M., & Evans, A. C. (2001). Age and gender predict volume decline in the anterior and posterior hippocampus in early adulthood. *Journal of Neuroscience, 21*(1), 194–200.

Radanov, B. P., Sturzenegger, M., De Stefano, G., & Schnidrig, A. (1994). Relationship between early somatic, radiological, cognitive and psychosocial findings and outcome during a one-year follow-up in 117 patients suffering from common whiplash. *British Journal of Rheumatology, 33*(5), 442–448.

Raison, C. L., Capuron, L., & Miller, A. H. (2006). Cytokines sing the blues: Inflammation and the pathogenesis of depression. *Trends in Immunology, 27*(1), 24–31.

Ramasubbu, R., & MacQueen, G. (2008). Alterations in neural structures as risk factors for depression. In K. S. Dobson & D. J. A. Dozois (Eds.), *Risk factors in depression* (pp. 37–61). New York: Elsevier.

Ramati, A., Rubin, L. H., Wicklund, A., Pliskin, N. H., Ammar, A. N., Fink, J. W., et al. (2009). Psychiatric morbidity following electrical injury and its effects on cognitive functioning. *General Hospital Psychiatry, 31*(4), 360–366.

Rao, U., Chen, L. A., Bidesi, A. S., Shad, M. U., Thomas, M. A., & Hammen, C. L. (2010). Hippocampal changes associated with early-life adversity and vulnerability to depression. *Biological Psychiatry, 67*(4), 357–364.

Ressler, K. J., & Mayberg, H. S. (2007). Targeting abnormal neural circuits in mood and anxiety disorders: From the laboratory to the clinic. *Nature Neuroscience, 10*(9), 1116–1124.

Ressler, K. J., & Nemeroff, C. B. (2000). Role of serotonergic and noradrenergic systems in the pathophysiology of depression and anxiety disorders. *Depression and Anxiety, 12*(Suppl. 1), 2–19.

Ricci, J. A., Stewart, W. F., Chee, E., Leotta, C., Foley, K., & Hochberg, M. C. (2006). Back pain exacerbations and lost productive time costs in United States workers. *Spine, 31*(26), 3052–3060.

Robinson, L. A., Berman, J. S., & Neimeyer, R. A. (1990). Psychotherapy for the treatment of depression: A comprehensive review of controlled outcome research. *Psychological Bulletin, 108*(1), 30–49.

Rohling, M. L., Green, P., Allen, L. M., & Iverson, G. L. (2002). Depressive symptoms and neurocognitive test scores in patients passing symptom validity tests. *Archives of Clinical Neuropsychology, 17*(3), 205–222.

Roine, R. O., Kajaste, S., & Kaste, M. (1993). Neuropsychological sequelae of cardiac arrest. *Journal of the American Medical Association, 269*(2), 237–242.

Roth, R. S., Geisser, M. E., Theisen-Goodvich, M., & Dixon, P. J. (2005). Cognitive complaints are associated with depression, fatigue, female sex, and pain catastrophizing in patients with chronic pain. *Archives of Physical Medicine and Rehabilitation, 86*(6), 1147–1154.

Rourke, S. B., Halman, M. H., & Bassel, C. (1999). Neurocognitive complaints in HIV-infection and their relationship to depressive symptoms and neuropsychological functioning. *Journal of Clinical and Experimental Neuropsychology, 21*(6), 737–756.

Sapolsky, R. M., Uno, H., Rebert, C. S., & Finch, C. E. (1990). Hippocampal damage associated with prolonged glucocorticoid exposure in primates. *Journal of Neuroscience, 10*(9), 2897–2902.

Sawrie, S. M., Martin, R. C., Kuzniecky, R., Faught, E., Morawetz, R., Jamil, F., et al. (1999). Subjective versus objective memory change after temporal lobe epilepsy surgery. *Neurology, 53*(7), 1511–1517.

Schatzberg, A. F., Garlow, S. J., & Nemeroff, C. B. (2002). Molecular and cellular mechanisms in depression. In K. L. Davis, D. Charney, J. T. Coyle, & C. Nemeroff (Eds.), *Neuropsychopharmacology: The fifth generation of progress* (pp. 1039–1050). Philadelphia: American College of Neuropsychopharmacology.

Schleifer, S. J., Macari-Hinson, M. M., Coyle, D. A., Slater, W. R., Kahn, M., Gorlin, R., et al. (1989). The nature and course of depression following myocardial infarction. *Archives of Internal Medicine, 149*(8), 1785–1789.

Schmand, B., Lindeboom, J., Schagen, S., Heijt, R., Koene, T., & Hamburger, H. L. (1998). Cognitive complaints in patients after whiplash injury: the impact of malingering. *Journal of Neurology, Neurosurgery and Psychiatry, 64*(3), 339–343.

Schnurr, R. F., & MacDonald, M. R. (1995). Memory complaints in chronic pain. *Clinical Journal of Pain, 11*(2), 103–111.

Schotte, C. K., Van Den Bossche, B., De Doncker, D., Claes, S., & Cosyns, P. (2006). A biopsychosocial model as a guide for psychoeducation and treatment of depression. *Depression and Anxiety, 23*(5), 312–324.

Seel, R. T., Kreutzer, J. S., Rosenthal, M., Hammond, F. M., Corrigan, J. D., & Black, K. (2003). Depression after traumatic brain injury: A National Institute on Disability and Rehabilitation Research Model Systems multicenter investigation. *Archives of Physical Medicine and Rehabilitation, 84*(2), 177–184.

Segal, Z. V., & Dobson, K. S. (1992). Cognitive models of depression: Report from a consensus development conference. *Psychological Inquiry, 3*, 219–224.

Shalev, A. Y., Freedman, S., Peri, T., Brandes, D., Sahar, T., Orr, S. P., et al. (1998). Prospective study of posttraumatic stress disorder and depression following trauma. *American Journal of Psychiatry, 155*(5), 630–637.

Sheline, Y. I., Barch, D. M., Donnelly, J. M., Ollinger, J. M., Snyder, A. Z., & Mintun, M. A. (2001). Increased amygdala response to masked emotional faces in depressed subjects resolves with antidepressant treatment: An fMRI study. *Biological Psychiatry, 50*(9), 651–658.

Sheline, Y. I., Gado, M. H., & Kraemer, H. C. (2003). Untreated depression and hippocampal volume loss. *American Journal of Psychiatry, 160*(8), 1516–1518.

Sheline, Y. I., Sanghavi, M., Mintun, M. A., & Gado, M. H. (1999). Depression duration but not age predicts hippocampal volume loss in medically healthy women with recurrent major depression. *Journal of Neuroscience, 19*(12), 5034–5043.

Shelton, R. C. (2006). The nature of the discontinuation syndrome associated with antidepressant drugs. *Journal of Clinical Psychiatry, 67*(Suppl. 4), 3–7.

Siegle, G. J., Carter, C. S., & Thase, M. E. (2006). Use of FMRI to predict recovery from unipolar depression with cognitive behavior therapy. *American Journal of Psychiatry, 163*(4), 735–738.

Siegle, G. J., Steinhauer, S. R., Thase, M. E., Stenger, V. A., & Carter, C. S. (2002). Can't shake that feeling: Event-related fMRI assessment of sustained amygdala activity in response to emotional information in depressed individuals. *Biological Psychiatry, 51*(9), 693–707.

Siegle, G. J., Thompson, W., Carter, C. S., Steinhauer, S. R., & Thase, M. E. (2007). Increased amygdala and decreased dorsolateral prefrontal BOLD responses in unipolar depression: Related and independent features. *Biological Psychiatry, 61*(2), 198–209.

Silver, J. M., McAllister, T. W., & Arciniegas, D. B. (2009). Depression and cognitive complaints following mild traumatic brain injury. *American Journal of Psychiatry, 166*(6), 653–661.

Simon, G. E., Ludman, E. J., & Rutter, C. M. (2009). Incremental benefit and cost of telephone care management and telephone psychotherapy for depression in primary care. *Archives of General Psychiatry, 66*(10), 1081–1089.

Sluzewska, A., Sobieska, M., & Rybakowski, J. K. (1997). Changes in acute-phase proteins during lithium potentiation of antidepressants in refractory depression. *Neuropsychobiology, 35*(3), 123–127.

Smith, P. J., Blumenthal, J. A., Babyak, M. A., Georgiades, A., Hinderliter, A., & Sherwood, A. (2007). Effects of exercise and weight loss on depressive symptoms among men and women with hypertension. *Journal of Psychosomatic Research, 63*(5), 463–469.

Smith-Seemiller, L., Fow, N. R., Kant, R., & Franzen, M. D. (2003). Presence of postconcussion syndrome symptoms in patients with chronic pain vs. mild traumatic brain injury. *Brain Injury, 17*(3), 199–206.

Solomon, D. A., Keller, M. B., Leon, A. C., Mueller, T. I., Lavori, P. W., Shea, M. T., et al. (2000). Multiple recurrences of major depressive disorder. *American Journal of Psychiatry, 157*(2), 229–233.

Sonawalla, S. B., & Fava, M. (2001). Severe depression: Is there a best approach? *CNS Drugs, 15*(10), 765–776.

Steele, J. D., Kumar, P., & Ebmeier, K. P. (2007). Blunted response to feedback information in depressive illness. *Brain, 130*(Pt. 9), 2367–2374.

Stein, M. B., Hanna, C., Vaerum, V., & Koverola, C. (1999). Memory functioning in adult women traumatized by childhood sexual abuse. *Journal of Traumatic Stress, 12*(3), 527–534.

Stern, R. A., & White, T. (2003a). *Neuropsychological Assessment Battery.* Lutz, FL: Psychological Assessment Resources.

Stern, R. A., & White, T. (2003b). *Neuropsychological Assessment Battery: Administration, scoring, and interpretation manual.* Lutz, FL: Psychological Assessment Resources.

Stewart, W. F., Ricci, J. A., Chee, E., Hahn, S. R., & Morganstein, D. (2003). Cost of lost productive work time among U.S. workers with depression. *Journal of the American Medical Association, 289*(23), 3135–3144.

Sullivan, M. J., Adams, H., Thibault, P., Corbiere, M., & Stanish, W. D. (2006). Initial depression severity and the trajectory of recovery following cognitive-behavioral intervention for work disability. *Journal of Occupational Rehabilitation, 16*(1), 63–74.

Sutker, P. B., Allain, A. N., Jr., Johnson, J. L., & Butters, N. M. (1992). Memory and learning performances in POW survivors with history of malnutrition and combat veteran controls. *Archives of Clinical Neuropsychology, 7*(5), 431–444.

Swerdlow, N. R., & Koob, G. F. (1987). Dopamine, schizophrenia, mania and depression: Toward a unified hypothesis of cortico-striato-pallido-thalamic function. *Behavioral and Brain Sciences, 10*, 197–245.

Taylor Tavares, J. V., Clark, L., Furey, M. L., Williams, G. B., Sahakian, B. J., & Drevets, W. C. (2008). Neural basis of abnormal response to negative feedback in unmedicated mood disorders. *Neuroimage, 42*(3), 1118–1126.

Tenyi, T., Trixler, M., Csabi, G., & Jeges, S. (2004). Minor physical anomalies in nonfamilial unipolar recurrent major depression. *Journal of Affective Disorders,* 79(1–3), 259–262.

The UK ECT Review Group. (2003). Efficacy and safety of electroconvulsive therapy in depressive disorders: A systematic review and meta-analysis. *Lancet, 361*(9360), 799–808.

Thomas, E. J., & Elliott, R. (2009). Brain imaging correlates of cognitive impairment in depression. *Frontiers in Human Neuroscience, 3,* 30.

Thomas, R. M., Hotsenpiller, G., & Peterson, D. A. (2007). Acute psychosocial stress reduces cell survival in adult hippocampal neurogenesis without altering proliferation. *Journal of Neuroscience, 27*(11), 2734–2743.

Thompson, P. J., & Corcoran, R. (1992). Everyday memory failures in people with epilepsy. *Epilepsia, 33*(Suppl. 6), S18–S20.

Torpy, J. M., Lynm, C., & Glass, R. M. (2006). JAMA patient page. Cardiac arrest. *Journal of the American Medical Association, 295*(1), 124.

Trivedi, M. H., & Daly, E. J. (2008). Treatment strategies to improve and sustain remission in major depressive disorder. *Dialogues in Clinical Neuroscience, 10*(4), 377–384.

Trivedi, M. H., & Kleiber, B. A. (2001). Algorithm for the treatment of chronic depression. *Journal of Clinical Psychiatry, 62*(Suppl. 6), 22–29.

Tsourtos, G., Thompson, J. C., & Stough, C. (2002). Evidence of an early information processing speed deficit in unipolar major depression. *Psychological Medicine, 32*(2), 259–265.

Tsushima, W. T., & Tsushima, V. G. (1993). Relation between headaches and neuropsychological functioning among head injury patients. *Headache, 33*(3), 139–142.

Twamley, E. W., Hami, S., & Stein, M. B. (2004). Neuropsychological function in college students with and without posttraumatic stress disorder. *Psychiatry Research, 126*(3), 265–274.

U.S. Department of Health and Human Services. (2001). *Mental health: Culture, race, and ethnicity: A supplement to mental health: A report of the Surgeon General.* Rockville, MD: U.S. Department of Health and Human Services, Substance Abuse and Mental Health Services Administration, Center for Mental Health Services.

van Eijndhoven, P., van Wingen, G., van Oijen, K., Rijpkema, M., Goraj, B., Jan Verkes, R., et al. (2009). Amygdala volume marks the acute state in the early course of depression. *Biological Psychiatry, 65*(9), 812–818.

van Gorp, W. G., Satz, P., Hinkin, C., Selnes, O., Miller, E. N., McArthur, J., et al. (1991). Metacognition in HIV-1 seropositive asymptomatic individuals: Self-ratings versus objective neuropsychological performance. Multicenter AIDS Cohort Study (MACS). *Journal of Clinical and Experimental Neuropsychology, 13*(5), 812–819.

van Valen, E., Wekking, E., van der Laan, G., Sprangers, M., & van Dijk, F. (2009). The course of chronic solvent induced encephalopathy: A systematic review. *Neurotoxicology.*

Vasterling, J. J., Brailey, K., Constans, J. I., & Sutker, P. B. (1998). Attention and memory dysfunction in posttraumatic stress disorder. *Neuropsychology, 12*(1), 125–133.

Vasterling, J. J., Duke, L. M., Brailey, K., Constans, J. I., Allain, A. N., Jr., & Sutker, P. B. (2002). Attention, learning, and memory performances and intellectual resources in Vietnam veterans: PTSD and no disorder comparisons. *Neuropsychology, 16*(1), 5–14.

Veiel, H. O. (1997). A preliminary profile of neuropsychological deficits associated with major depression. *Journal of Clinical and Experimental Neuropsychology, 19*(4), 587–603.

Videbech, P., & Ravnkilde, B. (2004). Hippocampal volume and depression: A meta-analysis of MRI studies. *American Journal of Psychiatry, 161*(11), 1957–1966.

Vlaeyen, J. W., & Linton, S. J. (2000). Fear-avoidance and its consequences in chronic musculoskeletal pain: A state of the art. *Pain, 85*(3), 317–332.

Vyas, A., Bernal, S., & Chattarji, S. (2003). Effects of chronic stress on dendritic arborization in the central and extended amygdala. *Brain Research, 965*(1–2), 290–294.

Wagner, G., Sinsel, E., Sobanski, T., Kohler, S., Marinou, V., Mentzel, H. J., et al. (2006). Cortical inefficiency in patients with unipolar depression: An event-related FMRI study with the Stroop task. *Biological Psychiatry, 59*(10), 958–965.

Walker, A. J., Shores, E. A., Trollor, J. N., Lee, T., & Sachdev, P. S. (2000). Neuropsychological functioning of adults with attention deficit hyperactivity disorder. *Journal of Clinical and Experimental Neuropsychology, 22*(1), 115–124.

Wang, P. N., Wang, S. J., Fuh, J. L., Teng, E. L., Liu, C. Y., Lin, C. H., et al. (2000). Subjective memory complaint in relation to cognitive performance and depression: A longitudinal study of a rural Chinese population. *Journal of the American Geriatrics Society, 48*(3), 295–299.

Wang, P. S., Simon, G. E., & Kessler, R. C. (2008). Making the business case for enhanced depression care: The National Institute of Mental Health-harvard Work Outcomes Research and Cost-effectiveness Study. *Journal of Occupational and Environmental Medicine, 50*(4), 468–475.

Waraich, P., Goldner, E. M., Somers, J. M., & Hsu, L. (2004). Prevalence and incidence studies of mood disorders: A systematic review of the literature. *Canadian Journal of Psychiatry, 49*(2), 124–138.

Wearden, A., & Appleby, L. (1997). Cognitive performance and complaints of cognitive impairment in chronic fatigue syndrome (CFS). *Psychological Medicine, 27*(1), 81–90.

Weiland-Fiedler, P., Erickson, K., Waldeck, T., Luckenbaugh, D. A., Pike, D., Bonne, O., et al. (2004). Evidence for continuing neuropsychological impairments in depression. *Journal of Affective Disorders, 82*(2), 253–258.

Weiner, D. K., Rudy, T. E., Morrow, L., Slaboda, J., & Lieber, S. (2006). The relationship between pain, neuropsychological performance, and physical function in community-dwelling older adults with chronic low back pain. *Pain Medicine, 7*(1), 60–70.

Whelan-Goodinson, R., Ponsford, J., Johnston, L., & Grant, F. (2009). Psychiatric disorders following traumatic brain injury: Their nature and frequency. *Journal of Head Trauma Rehabilitation, 24*(5), 324–332.

Williams, J. M., Crane, C., Barnhofer, T., Van der Does, A. J., & Segal, Z. V. (2006). Recurrence of suicidal ideation across depressive episodes. *Journal of Affective Disorders, 91*(2–3), 189–194.

Wilson, K. G., Eriksson, M. Y., D'Eon, J. L., Mikail, S. F., & Emery, P. C. (2002). Major depression and insomnia in chronic pain. *Clinical Journal of Pain, 18*(2), 77–83.

Wolf, N. J., & Hopko, D. R. (2008). Psychosocial and pharmacological interventions for depressed adults in primary care: A critical review. *Clinical Psychology Review, 28*(1), 131–161.

World Health Organization. (2004). *The World Health report 2004: Changing history, annex Table 3: Burden of disease in DALYs by cause, sex, and mortality stratum in WHO regions, estimates for 2002.* Geneva: WHO.

Wu, Y., & Zhou, B. P. (2009). Inflammation: A driving force speeds cancer metastasis. *Cell Cycle, 8*(20), 3267–3273.

Yehuda, R., Keefe, R. S., Harvey, P. D., Levengood, R. A., Gerber, D. K., Geni, J., et al. (1995). Learning and memory in combat veterans with posttraumatic stress disorder. *American Journal of Psychiatry, 152*(1), 137–139.

Young, E. A., Abelson, J. L., & Cameron, O. G. (2004). Effect of comorbid anxiety disorders on the hypothalamic-pituitary-adrenal axis response to a social stressor in major depression. *Biological Psychiatry, 56*(2), 113–120.

Young, E. A., Lopez, J. F., Murphy-Weinberg, V., Watson, S. J., & Akil, H. (2000). Hormonal evidence for altered responsiveness to social stress in major depression. *Neuropsychopharmacology, 23*(4), 411–418.

Yucel, K., M, M. C. K., Chahal, R., Taylor, V., Macdonald, K., Joffe, R., et al. (2009). Increased subgenual prefrontal cortex size in remitted patients with major depressive disorder. *Psychiatry Research, 173*(1), 71–76.

CHAPTER 8

Neuropsychological Aspects of Chronic Pain

Lance M. McCracken
Miles Thompson

Many patients undergoing neuropsychological assessments have chronic pain, particularly those with work-related injuries. Many chronic pain sufferers report and demonstrate the types of problems with cognitive and behavioral performance that are of primary interest to clinical neuropsychologists. And yet the topic of this interface between pain and neuropsychology has received relatively little systematic attention. Rather, the clinical management of chronic pain and neuropsychological problems seems fraught with assumptions and a distinct nonuniformity in theory and method. This situation is not ideal for the best quality service for patients.

This chapter briefly presents a review of psychological and neuropsychological aspects of chronic pain. It begins by presenting research into the prevalence of chronic pain and its impacts on both emotional and general daily functioning. It next reviews the literature on complaints of impaired cognitive functioning in chronic pain, followed by a review of the literature on directly assessed neuropsychological performance. It briefly touches on an area of current controversy, effects of opioid analgesics. A review of current treatment approaches is then provided. A concluding section attempts, once again briefly, to organize these various streams around the model of behavior underlying acceptance and commitment therapy (ACT).

THE PREVALENCE OF CHRONIC PAIN

Chronic pain is pain of at least 3 months duration that has persisted beyond expected healing time. It is traditionally regarded as having both unpleasant sensory and emotional qualities, as being legitimately present whether or not there is identifiable organic pathology (International Association for the Study of Pain Subcommittee on Classification, 1986), and as being remarkably impervious to medical therapies. Over the years, many epidemiological studies have investigated the prevalence rates of both chronic and acute pain. Different researchers have assessed pain prevalence using different criteria, different methods, and in different populations. Understandably, differing research methods produce varied results. Results from this work suggest that at any one time between 25 and 49% of the population are suffering from pain (Gerdle, Bjork, Henriksson, & Bengtsson, 2004; Portenoy, Ugarte, Fuller, & Haas, 2004; Schmidt et al., 2007; Walker, Muller, & Grant, 2004; Watkins, Wollan, Melton, & Yawn, 2008) and between 19 and 22% of people are suffering from persistent or chronic pain (Breivik, Collett, Ventafridda, Cohen, & Gallacher, 2006; Eriksen, Jensen, Sjogren, Ekholm, & Rasmussen, 2003; Gureje, Von Korff, Simon, & Gater, 1998).

Persistent pain is prevalent worldwide. In 1998 the World Health Organization (WHO) assessed pain prevalence, within primary care populations, in Asia, Africa, Europe, and the Americas in 15 centers and across 14 countries (Gureje et al., 1998). This study initially screened nearly 26,000 individuals of working age and later interviewed over 5,000 adults. Investigating whether pain had been present for most of the time for at least 6 months, they found an average pain prevalence of 22% with a range from 5.5 to 33% across the different centers.

Further detail about the experience of pain is provided from a large-scale computer-assisted telephone survey conducted in 2003 (Breivik et al., 2006). The research sought to investigate pain prevalence in 15 European countries and Israel. This research initially screened 46,394 adults aged 18 or over and later carried out at least 300 in-depth interviews in each country. It found that 19% of those initially screened had "long-lasting pain," which meant that pain had been present for at least 6 months, had also been present in the last month, and was present on more than one occasion during the last week. Pain also had to be rated as a five or more on a numerical rating scale from 1 (no pain) to 10 (worst pain imaginable). Of those who rated their pain as 5 and above, 66% were described as having "moderate pain" (between 5 and 7 on the numerical rating scale) and 34% rated their pain between 8 and 10. With regard to pain history, the median period was 7.0 years, but 21% who met the study criteria had experienced their pain for 20 years or more. As with the research described earlier, regional variations in prevalence were found from 12% (Spain, $N = 3,801$) to 30% (Norway, $N = 2,018$).

IMPACTS OF CHRONIC PAIN ON MOOD AND DAILY FUNCTIONING

The impact of long-term pain can alter many varied aspects of individuals' lives aside from the body sensations they experience. This impact can include changes to what they think and feel, and importantly what they do or do not do, with regard to both pain and other important aspects of their life such as family, social and recreational activities, and work.

Impact on Mood

Research consistently shows that both emotional distress and diagnosable mood disturbance occur at high rates in conjunction with chronic pain. Of course, as with pain prevalence, the results of research into the impact on mood will be influenced by methodological factors, including the population surveyed, the methods used, and the criteria applied.

Banks and Kerns (1996) found that patients with chronic pain are much more likely to suffer from depression than those who have other chronic medical conditions. Their review of research in this area revealed that between 30 and 54% of those seeking treatment for chronic pain would also meet diagnostic criteria for a depressive disorder. Their work considered the causality of these two problems and suggested that depression is most likely to be a result of chronic pain, not the other way around. In other research, a sample of nearly 6,000 representative individuals with chronic pain from the United States determined that 20.2% of those surveyed had had an episode of depression in the last year (McWilliams, Cox, & Enns, 2003). The incidence of depression in those with "chronic back or neck problems" is estimated at 17.5% in the last 12 months (Von Korff et al., 2005). These data derive from the general population contacted through the National Comorbidity Study (Kessler et al., 1994) rather than treatment-seeking samples reported by Banks and Kerns (1996). It is informative to compare these depression rates to that in the population generally. In this regard, a large household survey conducted in Canada found that individuals with chronic pain were three times more likely to be depressed than individuals without chronic pain (Currie & Wang, 2004).

As for diagnoses of anxiety disorders, Dersh, Polatin, and Gatchel (2002) reported prevalence rates of between 16.5 and 28.8% for comorbid anxiety disorders (e.g., panic disorder and generalized anxiety disorder) in patients with chronic pain. McWilliams et al. (2003) found that 35.1% of people suffering from chronic pain also suffered from anxiety disorders. In research that has surveyed anxiety in clinical samples, the prevalence of anxiety disorders has ranged from 7.0 to 62.5% (Dersh et al., 2002; Fishbain, Cutler, Rosomoff, & Rosomoff, 1998). Data from a more specific group of people with "chronic back or neck problems" revealed a comorbidity rate with anxiety disorders of 26.5% (Kessler et al., 1994). More recent research from Kessler allows us to compare this figure to the general population without pain. Data from a U.S. household survey known as the national comorbidity survey (N = 9,282) estimated that the prevalence rate for anxiety disorders within a 12-month period was 18.1%, regardless of pain presentation (Kessler, Chiu, Demler, Merikangas, & Walters, 2005).

In other international work, a survey of over 85,000 individuals across 17 geographically diverse countries found that a number of mental health problems were more likely to be present in individuals with chronic back or neck pain than in those without (Demyttenaere et al., 2007). The odds ratios for people with chronic pain also suffering from specific disorders were for dysthymia 2.8 (CI = 2.5–3.2), for generalized anxiety disorder 2.7 (CI = 2.4–3.1), for posttraumatic stress disorder 2.6 (CI = 2.3–3.0), for major depression 2.3 (CI = 2.1–2.5), for agoraphobia or panic 2.1 (CI = 1.9–2.4), and for social phobia 1.9 (CI = 1.7–2.2).

Impact on Daily Functioning

In broad terms, the intuitive conclusion that people with chronic pain might function at a lower level than those without is supported by research. In April of 2004, the American Chronic Pain Association surveyed 800 adults with chronic pain and found impacts in the following areas: sleep (78.0%), household chores (67.0%), interference with daily routines (61.0%), decreased productivity at work (51.0%), and adverse effects on relationship with partner (28%; Roper Public Affairs and Media, 2004).

As part of a wider interview in the European survey by Breivik et al. (2006), participants were also asked to rate their ability to participate in various activities (driving, exercising, household chores, maintaining an independent lifestyle, lifting, sleeping, social activities, social relationships, sexual relationships, walking, working outside of the home). Responses were given on a 3-point scale of ability (able, less able, no longer able). Many respondents reported being "less able" to perform the above activities (percentages ranged from 22 to 56% for each activity), and many also reported being "no longer able" to do activities (range 5%–32%). The activities that pain sufferers were most likely to be "less able" to do were sleeping (56%), exercising (50%), and lifting (49%). The activities that pain sufferers were most likely to be "no longer able" to do included working outside of the home (32%), driving (23%), lifting (23%), and exercising (23%). In this study it was found that just 31% of respondents were in full-time work, with 13% employed part time, 34% retired, and 22% unemployed. A quarter (26%) of the sample said that pain had influenced their employment (32% of those who classified themselves as now being retired).

Results from Breivik et al. (2006) echo earlier work by other research groups. Gureje et al. (1998) used the Groningen Social Disability Schedule (SDS) to assess daily work activities, activities directed toward finding work, and activities of those retired. Interviewers rated disability on a scale from 0 to 3 (0 = no disability, 3 = severe disability). Their results revealed that 31% of the sample with pain were rated as having either a moderate or severe disability (compared to 13% of those without pain; odds ratio 2.12). Eriksen and colleagues (2003) reported results from national health surveys in Denmark and found that activity was reported to be restricted by an average of 21% for those with pain compared with only 2% of those from a control group (odds ratio, 9.9). Similarly, quitting work for health reasons occurred in 28% of the pain group and only 5% of the control group (odds ratio, 7.3). Results from large-scale research suggest that, on average, people free from chronic spinal pain are able to function at an average of 93.5% of their full role performance; this figure drops to 76.5% for those with chronic spinal pain (Von Korff et al., 2005). Further examination of the contributing factors suggests that a third of the difference between the groups can be explained by comorbid conditions including other chronic pain conditions, chronic physical conditions, and mental health problems (such as anxiety and depression).

Potential negative impacts of chronic pain on functioning appear to be multiplied if significant psychological difficulties are also present. A large-scale European study ($N = 21,425$) suggested that if an individual has both pain and depression they have more than double the number of days off work per month than individuals who suffer from just pain or depression in isolation. Persons with pain and depression reported taking more than five times as many days off work than individuals with neither pain nor depression (Demyttenaere et al., 2006).

IMPACT OF CHRONIC PAIN ON COGNITIVE FUNCTIONING

As previously described, the direct impacts of chronic pain on a sufferer's daily functioning can be substantial and by themselves present significant treatment challenges. Chronic pain is a great burden and significantly taxes a patient's skills and capacity. If cognitive functioning is impaired by pain, an individual's skills and capacities may be further reduced. As a result, suffering and disability could be expected to become greater still. Therefore, any additional indirect impacts on functioning exerted through changes in cognitive functioning are important to understand. In this section we explore three aspects of cognitive functioning in relation to chronic pain: the context of cognitive complaints, aspects of cognitive performance, and effects of opioids on cognitive functioning.

There are considerable difficulties inherent in attempting to investigate the effects of chronic pain on cognitive functioning. Primarily, chronic pain status is a highly confounded variable. As the literature reviewed here demonstrates, those with chronic pain do not only suffer pain in isolation. They also simultaneously experience symptoms such as depression, anxiety, fatigue, sleeping problems, varied histories of head trauma, comorbid medical conditions, and the effects of medications. Any of these variables may underlie complaints of cognitive impairment or measured cognitive impairment when it is identified. As these factors are nonmanipulated, preexisting at the time of assessment, and challenging to statistically isolate, it becomes difficult to unambiguously attribute cognitive impairment directly to the experience of chronic pain itself.

Other situations present complications too. Studies of chronic pain that eliminate cases of traumatic brain injury or central nervous system disease from the data are unable to appreciate how these conditions may interact with pain—that essentially an individual can have both chronic pain and a brain injury. In fact, the prevalence rate of chronic pain after traumatic brain injury (TBI) is estimated at 57.8% based on a systematic review (Nampiaparampil, 2008). In some settings the confounding factors may be even more complex. For example, a study of the medical records of 340 U.S. military veterans seen in recently designed "polytrauma" services showed that chronic pain, posttraumatic stress disorder, and persistent postconcussive symptoms were present in 81.5%, 68.2%, and 66.8% of veterans, respectively, with 42.1% being diagnosed with all three (Lew et al., 2009). Obviously, this combination of factors can considerably complicate both diagnosis (Halbauer et al., 2009) and treatment (Gironda et al., 2009).

Cognitive Complaints

Difficulties with concentration, memory, and other aspects of cognitive functioning appear inordinately common in persons seeking treatment for chronic pain. In one early study based on a sample of 170 adults seeking treatment for chronic pain at a university medical center (age $M = 43.8$ years, $SD = 14.6$), 42.0% of patients reported at least one problem with attention, concentration, or memory (Iverson & McCracken, 1997). In these same data, 28.8% reported frequent forgetfulness, 18.2% difficulty with attention, 16.5% difficulty with concentration, 14.7% difficulty with problem solving and decision making, and 10.6% difficulty with confusion. It should be noted that these patients had no reported history of head trauma. The primary purpose of this study was to examine the presence of "postconcussive" symptoms, and it was found that 80.6% of the sample endorsed three or more symptoms from Category C of the DSM-IV research criteria for postconcussional disorder (Iverson & McCracken, 1997). When those

Category C symptoms were combined with a complaint of impaired cognition, 39% met self-report criteria for DSM-IV postconcussional disorder.

In a larger sample from the same center, a slightly larger percentage (54%) reported at least one problem with cognitive functioning (McCracken & Iverson, 2001). Another study of 222 adult patients (age M = 39.8, SD = 9.6) also seen at a university pain center showed that 62.0% reported a moderate to severe problem in at least one of five areas of cognitive functioning (Roth, Geisser, Theisen-Goodvich, & Dixon, 2005). In that sample, 47.8% reported trouble with concentration, 41.1% trouble with remembering, and 29.3% difficulty making decisions, each at a level from moderate to extreme. The differences in percentages between these studies may derive from the way complaints were measured, as dichotomous present-absent variables in the first studies and as a 5-point rating from "not at all" to "extremely" in the latter one.

In a large population-based study of community-dwelling adults aged 50 years and older in the United Kingdom (N = 7,356), 46.5% reported at least one of ten cognitive complaints (Westoby, Mallen, & Thomas, 2009). The research noted that reports of cognitive complaints increased with age, with 41.6% of those between 50 and 59, and 63.4% of those aged 80 or over, reporting at least one complaint. The prevalence of cognitive complaints was also higher in those reporting pain in the last 4 weeks compared to those who did not (52.5% versus 30.8%).

Fibromyalgia is a syndrome diagnosed by the presence of widespread pain and reported pain upon palpation in 11 of 18 designated tender points (Wolfe et al., 1990). Fatigue, sleep disturbance, and memory and concentration difficulties are also defined symptoms of fibromyalgia. In a study of beliefs about memory, or "metamemory," 23 patients with fibromyalgia were compared with age and education-matched controls and older controls (Glass, Park, Minear, & Crofford, 2005). Those with fibromyalgia reported lower memory capacity and more memory deterioration than both control groups. They also reported more use of strategies to support memory than the age-matched controls and more anxiety about memory ability than both the age-matched controls and the older controls.

Finally, a number of studies have attempted to identify predictors of cognitive complaints as a way to understand the factors that influence them. A range of factors achieve significant correlations with summary scores for cognitive complaints, including pain severity, anxiety, and depression (McCracken & Iverson, 2001; Muñoz & Esteve, 2005; Roth et al., 2005). In multivariate analyses, depression was the strongest unique predictor of cognitive complaints in the three studies reviewed here. In these analyses, combinations of variables including depression and either pain-related anxiety or "catastrophizing" accounted for 36.0% (McCracken & Iverson, 2001), 43.0% (Muñoz & Esteve, 2005), and 52.5% (Roth et al., 2005) of the variance in cognitive complaints. In the three studies selected here, pain intensity itself was only weakly associated with cognitive complaints and was not a significant predictor when other predictors were taken into account.

Cognitive Test Performance

In a recent comprehensive review of cognitive performance and chronic pain (Hart, Martelli, & Zasler, 2000), the authors located 23 studies of patients with chronic pain, mostly without a history of a traumatic brain injury or neurological disease. These studies were conducted between 1987 and 1999, and the groups studied included people with nonspecific chronic pain, fibromyalgia, post-whiplash injury, and mixed samples. It was a narrative and not a quantitative review, and the authors' conclusion is summarized here.

> Numerous studies reviewed here have demonstrated neuropsychological impairment in patients with chronic pain, particularly on measures assessing attentional capacity, processing speed, and psychomotor speed. In some studies, impairment has been related to greater pain intensity and to the involvement of head and neck areas . . . and other symptoms often associated with pain such as mood change, increased somatic awareness, sleep disturbance, and fatigue. (Hart et al., 2000, p. 147)

A more updated survey of the literature was published in 2007 by the International Association for the Study of Pain (IASP; Kreitler & Niv, 2007). The authors divided domains of functioning into seven categories and used a simple tally system for the number of studies they identified in the published literature showing evidence for deficits in patients with chronic pain based on neuropsychological test results. A summary of the main five performance domains based on this work is presented in Table 8.1. Of the other two categories, one was called "other" and included research that demonstrated deficits in reasoning (three of four studies), construction (two of two studies), and block design and similarities (no deficits were found in two studies). Another "overall" category included results from the research using the Wechsler Adult Intelligence Scale (chronic pain patients scored lower than controls in one of two studies), the Mini-Mental State Exam (MMSE) (no significant difference in one study), and the Neurobehavioral Cognitive Status Examination (32% of patients with chronic pain scored in the range of impaired performance in one study). One limitation of this brief publication is that not all of the studies reviewed are included in the reference list, and only the presence, and not the magnitude, of the results is discussed. The overwhelming suggestion from Table 8.1 is that those with chronic pain have wide-ranging impacts on neuropsychological performance.

▦ **TABLE 8.1. Summary of Study Results in Relation to Cognitive Test Performance in Patients with Chronic Pain, based on the Study by Kreitler and Viv (2007)**

Performance domain	Studies testing this domain	Studies showing deficits in chronic pain	Percent positive results	Comments
Memory	34	30	88.2	Authors concluded that most affected aspects include delayed memory, verbal tasks, and new learning
Attention	13	9	69.2	Notable in failing to show deficits were the stroop interference task and attention task from the WMS
Verbal	9	8	88.9	Tests here included vocabulary and word or category fluency
Speed	17	14	82.3	Tests here included verbal, processing, and psychomotor speed
Mental flexibility	11	8	72.7	Included mostly task or instruction switching challenges

In a study set within a Danish pain center, both the influences of pain and pain medications on cognitive functioning were investigated (Sjogren, Christrup, Petersen, & Hojsted, 2005). The study included 91 patients with chronic pain and 64 age- and sex-matched healthy controls. The patient groups were divided into those using no pain medication (n = 21), those on long-term opioid treatment (n = 19), those on antidepressant or anticonvulsant medications (n = 18), and those on a combination of opioid and at least one of the other medications (n = 33). Sustained attention (continuous reaction time) and psychomotor speed (finger tapping) were impaired across the patient groups. However, information processing (paced auditory serial addition) was impaired in just the opioid group. Patient ratings of pain and sedation were significantly correlated with poor performance in sustained attention and information processing. The MMSE was also given, and the authors remarked that it appeared insensitive for detecting effects on cognitive performance in their sample.

Effects of Analgesic Medications on Cognitive Functioning

Primary among the analgesic medications that raise concerns for cognitive functioning are the opioids analgesics. Current clinical guidelines from the

American Pain Society and American Academy of Pain Medicine state that "chronic opioids therapy can be an effective therapy for carefully selected and monitored patients with non-cancer pain" (pp. 113–114) (Chou et al., 2009). However, the authors also noted that use of opioids can be associated with significant harms. For example, they later recommend that "clinicians should counsel patients on COT [chronic opioid therapy] about transient or lasting cognitive impairment that may affect driving and work safety" (p. 122).

A recent review concluded that both acute and chronic opioid use appear to have effects on cognitive performance that appear to be "relatively broad spectrum," including impairment in attention, concentration, visual and verbal recall, visual-spatial skills, psychomotor speed, and hand–eye coordination (Gruber, Silveri, & Yurgelun-Todd, 2007). Long-term opioid use appears to affect executive functions (e.g., the ability to shift mental set and inhibit inappropriate responses). The data reviewed in this paper included normal subjects, heroin users, and patients in methadone maintenance, as well as some samples of pain sufferers; hence, generalizability to patients with chronic pain is unclear.

In another review that excluded current or recovering substance abusers, the conclusions were far more positive: "research reflects minimal to no significant impairments in cognitive functioning . . . if impairment does occur, it is most often associated with perenteral opioids administered to opioids-naïve individuals" (p. 75) (Ersek, Cherrier, Overman, & Irving, 2004). The authors emphasized that this finding particularly holds for stable chronic opioid therapy, and they even suggested that successful opioid therapy can enhance cognitive functioning, presumably as a result of reduction of pain. The authors stated that the literature is incomplete and leaves many questions about the effects of opioids largely unanswered. Certainly in research where cognitive performances are directly tested there are data to suggest that long-term opioids are associated with decreased attention, psychomotor speed, and working memory compared with healthy volunteers (e.g., Sjogren, Thomsen, & Olsen, 2000). However other results suggest that some cognitive abilities may improve with opioids (e.g., Rowbotham et al., 2003) or that cognitive functioning can remain unaffected (e.g., Raja et al., 2002).

PSYCHOLOGICAL TREATMENT FOR CHRONIC PAIN

During the last 40 years, the dominant psychological framework that has informed chronic pain treatment has shifted. The changes in psychological treatment have been described as forming a series of waves (Hayes, 2004). Within pain, the first wave was known as the operant approach (Fordyce, 1976), and within psychology more generally it is known as behavior therapy. With this approach, principles derived from laboratory-based experiments were applied to human behavior problems including chronic pain. The second wave built on the first and included the influence of cognitive therapy methods creating what is known as cognitive behavioral therapy (CBT; e.g., Turk, Meichenbaum, & Genest, 1983). Today there is a third wave of behavioral and cognitive therapy that includes elements of the first two waves. However, it also expands on the prior approaches within a conceptual framework that is less mechanistic and more contextual. This third wave utilizes clinical technologies and a research base that advocates processes such as acceptance, mindfulness, and values. Examples of these third-wave approaches include mindfulness-based stress reduction (Kabat-Zinn, 1990), dialectical behavior therapy (Linehan, 1993), mindfulness-based cognitive therapy (Segal, Williams, & Teasdale, 2002), acceptance and commitment therapy (ACT; Hayes, Luoma, Bond, Masuda, & Lillis, 2006), and an approach to chronic pain based on ACT called contextual cognitive-behavioral therapy (CCBT; McCracken, 2005).

Psychologists from different orientations may assess the merits and drawbacks of these three waves differently. An examination of the recent pain literature reveals diverse areas of competing interests including the following: catastrophizing (e.g., Sullivan, Lynch, & Clark, 2005; Sullivan et al., 2001), coping (e.g., Romano, Jensen, & Turner, 2003), self-efficacy (e.g., Asghari & Nicholas, 2001; Nicholas & Asghari, 2006), and stages of change (e.g., Kerns, Wagner, Rosenberg, Haythornthwaite, & Caudill-Slosberg, 2005), among others (Keefe, Rumble, Scipio, Giordano, & Perri, 2004). Along with current contextual approaches, each of these particular variables of interest carries its own assumptions of ontology, causality, and epistemology. The remainder of this chapter highlights some current treatment approaches that appear to have particular promise.

Exposure

Integral to the first wave of psychological treatment for chronic pain was the inclusion of what are essentially exposure-based methods to reduce avoidance (Fordyce, 1976). The term *exposure-based* implies having the patient move toward and make contact with situations that are likely to induce both fear and avoidance. This exposure could include situations involving contact with movement and pain, or contacting situations that are assumed to involve the experience of pain. The key to the success of these methods is to assure that the exposure takes place without subtle forms of avoidance blocking that contact, such as bracing, distracting, or other covert means of attempting to suppress experiences. Typically, treatments of this nature proceed through a series of "exposure trials." Here patients begin in situations that elicit low levels of threat or fear and proceed through repeated exposure trials to situations that are associated with higher levels of challenging private experiences. The progression of treatment in this way is often known as a "graded hierarchy."

An aspect of the second wave of psychological treatment that is sometimes added to this methodological foundation is known as the "behavioral experiment." This approach involves teaching patients methods to identify and challenge irrational expectations concerning particular exposure situations (e.g., Vlaeyen, de Jong, Geilen, Heuts, & van Breukelen, 2001). In this case, repeated trials are thought to reduce the feelings of fear and correct mistaken or irrational thoughts or expectations.

In an early demonstration of these methods, Vlaeyen et al. (2001) conducted a replicated, single-case, crossover experimental design study comparing exposure (repeated explicit contact with feared experiences) with techniques designed to gradually increase activity regardless of fear. The research included four participants from the Netherlands who were selected because of their high levels of fear of movement. Procedures utilizing graphical and time series analyses recorded patient ratings of pain-related thoughts and feelings on a daily basis. This study demonstrated that improvements only took place during the exposure condition and not the activity condition. Similar research was conducted in Sweden (Boersma et al., 2004) and replicated the results above. Later research in this area suggested that it was the exposure component itself, not associated educational sessions, that appeared to be responsible for increases in participant daily activity. This research also demonstrated that treatment gains were maintained at follow-up 6 months later (de Jong et al., 2005b). Similar treatments have also been carried out for patients with complex regional pain syndrome (CRPS; de Jong et al., 2005a).

Acceptance and Commitment Therapy

Over the past 15 years or so there has been a series of studies into applications of ACT to chronic pain (McCracken, 2005). ACT includes exposure-based methods but greatly expands on these. ACT is based on the notion that a significant proportion of human suffering emerges from "psychological inflexibility," a process based in interactions between verbally based learning and direct experience that reduces the capacity for behavior to persist or change as required in the pursuit of values and the achievement of goals. Psychological inflexibility lends behavior an unworkable quality resulting from avoidance, a loss of contact with direct environmental contingencies, a behavior dominating quality of verbal/cognitive-based experiences, and failure of committed and values-based action (Hayes et al., 2006). According to the therapeutic model underlying ACT, "psychological flexibility" is the contrasting process that stems from acceptance, mindfulness, contact with present experiences outside of processes of language and thinking, and behavior change based in goals and values.

ACT points to problems that can arise when people verbally analyze, apply problem solving strategies, and seek to control relatively uncontrollable events, such as thoughts, memories, physical sensations, and emotional experiences that are based in one's own history (Hayes, Strosahl, & Wilson, 1999). Because of its application to unwanted psychological experiences, this process is referred to as experiential avoidance and is assumed to be at the root of many forms of behavior problems (Hayes, Wilson, Gifford, Follette, & Strosahl, 1996). ACT also points to what is called the "illusion of language"—the sense that we are dealing with the actual world with our thoughts when in actuality we are constructing the world within our thoughts. From these processes behavior is coordinated by experiences that we attempt to control without success and by verbally constructed versions of reality that may be misleading and can block contact with other sources of healthy and flexible behavior influence.

In practice ACT includes carefully examining, with patients, their behavior patterns and the influences being exerted on them. It includes looking for clinically relevant behavior patterns in treatment sessions, patterns of avoidance or behaviors that show other qualities of psychological inflexibility. When encountered, these patterns are managed with methods to enhance psychological flexibility, such as acceptance, mindfulness, and values.

Numerous studies support the model underlying ACT particularly for chronic pain. These include studies that illustrate the potentially adverse impacts of avoidance (Fordyce, Shelton, & Dundore, 1982; McCracken & Samuel, 2007; Vlaeyen & Linton, 2000) and the potential benefits of acceptance (McCracken, 1998; McCracken & Eccleston, 2005; McCracken, Spertus, Janeck, Sinclair, & Wetzel, 1999) and mindfulness (Kabat-Zinn, 1990; Kabat-Zinn, Lipworth, & Burney, 1985; McCracken, 2007; McCracken, Gauntlett-Gilbert, & Vowles, 2007) for patients' emotional, physical, social, and work-related functioning.

Treatment Outcome

In recent years, at least seven treatment outcome studies have been published in the field of chronic pain that have focused on processes involved in psychological flexibility and inflexibility. In these studies both mindfulness-based methods alone (Morone, Greco, & Weiner, 2008; Pradhan et al., 2007; Sephton et al., 2007) and broader packages of treatment (McCracken, MacKichan, & Eccleston, 2007; McCracken, Vowles, & Eccleston, 2005) have yielded significant results across a range of domains. These findings include average effect sizes in the area of pain-related anxiety and depression of 1.2 immediately posttreatment ($N = 171$) and above 0.90 at a 3-month follow-up ($N = 114$) (Vowles & McCracken, 2008). Research in this area still awaits a large-scale, high-quality, fully randomized, controlled trial—but promising results have come from a small randomized trial of participants "at risk" for work loss due to pain or stress (Dahl, Wilson, & Nilsson, 2004), a nonrandomized trial with a waiting phase comparison (McCracken & Eccleston, 2005), and a small-scale randomized trial in patients with whiplash-associated disorders (Wicksell, Ahlqvist, Bring, Melin, & Olsson, 2008).

Relevance of ACT and Related Processes to Neuropsychology

Many patients involved in work-related accidents are referred for neuropsychological services. They may have musculoskeletal as well as neurological problems. As reviewed in this chapter, they may suffer from pain, anger, fear, depression, poor sleep, fatigue, and other postconcussive-like symptoms, and they may demonstrate difficulties in cognitive performance. They may be in a process of resolving blame, wage replacement, or damage awards. As humans will do, they are likely to have many thoughts, beliefs, and judgments about the nature of their injuries and what they mean. And their behavior is likely to fall prey to these many experiences and their thoughts about them. The influences of potential financial settlements sometimes complicate the process of treatment, even in the most honest patients.

The methods and processes of ACT appear particularly well suited to this patient group. Although complete analysis within this area is beyond the scope of this chapter, a few particular aspects of fit are easily identified. First, many of the experiences encountered during the aftermath of work-related injuries are ultimately uncontrollable or at least uncontrollable on a timeline dictated by the patient—some may subside over a longer term. Traumatic accidents along with the confusion, ambiguity, and adversarial situations they engender can create a context of needing to analyze, understand, know, or prove what is wrong. ACT includes specific therapeutic techniques for promoting acceptance and "letting go" of the struggles with these experiences, when doing so serves the purpose of functional improvement. It is assumed that once efforts are freed from analyzing and struggling with experiences, the person is more likely to be effective and engaged in assessment and treatment services. Second, patients' injuries and the experiences engendered are likely to distract, disrupt, or disintegrate behavior patterns that require sustained attention (e.g., Eccleston & Crombez, 1999). Again, acceptance-based and mindfulness-based methods for promoting more skillful attention and awareness are likely to provide benefits. Third, patients' thoughts and beliefs postinjury may have a worried, ruminative, or catastrophizing quality (e.g., Sullivan et al., 2001). ACT has specific methods for what is called cognitive defusion for reducing the impact of overwhelming emotionally laden thoughts. Finally, as acceptance, mindfulness, and defusion methods loosen the influences on endless analysis, struggling, rumination, and distress, work on values-based methods can help patients to connect or reconnect with directions in their lives even if these directions include barriers or challenges that they did not encounter before.

SUMMARY AND CONCLUSIONS

This chapter presents many findings that can be expressed with certainty and others that cannot. Certainly, chronic pain is a very prevalent problem and a source of a great deal of suffering and disability. About 20% of the general population suffers from persistent pain. Those with persistent pain are two to three times more likely than those without pain to suffer from depression or an anxiety disorder. Rates of both depression and anxiety disorders are significantly higher in those who seek treatment for chronic pain, roughly twice as likely as in those who do not seek treatment. Approximately 30% of chronic pain sufferers report that they are no longer working or consider themselves retired as a result of their pain.

Certainly, whether it is in a chronic pain service, a neuropsychology service, or in the general community, chronic pain and neuropsychological problems frequently co-occur. For example, somewhere between 40 and just over 60% of patients seeking treatment for chronic pain also complain of some kind of difficulty with cognitive functioning; similarly, about 60% of those with traumatic brain injuries also present with chronic pain. Studies of cognitive complaints in persons with chronic pain find that they are particularly correlated with measures of emotional distress, especially depression. A number of neuropsychological impairments have been documented in the literature on those with chronic pain. There is, however, some lack of uniformity in the literature, and it is far less certain what processes are involved in impairments observed, whether these impairments arise directly from collateral problems such as low mood, sleep disturbance, or other influences, from the pain experience itself, or some combination. The role of analgesic medications provides another area of relative uncertainty. For instance, opioids are increasingly prescribed for chronic pain and even encouraged in current practice guidelines. Although opioid use certainly carries some risk of cognitive and behavioral disturbance, it is by no means clear from the literature for whom, to what extent, in what areas of functioning, and under what circumstances these problems will occur. There is some degree of acrimony in the debate surrounding opioid use for chronic nonmalignant pain, and there is a great deal of emotion behind both the push for free access to reduce suffering and the push to block access to prevent harm. This emotion can cloud the evidence.

This chapter summarized recent developments in treatment for chronic pain. These developments seem particularly effective and may be an improvement in some ways over previous treatments, although definitive trials are still needed. It is suggested that the methods and processes within these treatments may be particularly well suited to the problems experienced by persons with traumatic work-related accidents, including those with verified or suspected brain injury. It is easy to conceive a treatment service based on ACT particularly designed for the most complex of the patients within this area of clinical work, for these so-called polytrauma cases with chronic pain and brain injury.

REFERENCES

Asghari, A., & Nicholas, M. K. (2001). Pain self-efficacy beliefs and pain behaviour: A prospective study. *Pain, 94*(1), 85–100.

Banks, S. M., & Kerns, R. D. (1996). Explaining high rates of depression in chronic pain: A diathesis-stress framework. *Psychological Bulletin, 119*, 95–110.

Boersma, K., Linton, S., Overmeer, T., Jansson, M., Vlaeyen, J., & de Jong, J. (2004). Lowering fear-avoidance and enhancing function through exposure in vivo: A multiple baseline study across six patients with back pain. *Pain, 108*(1–2), 8–16.

Breivik, H., Collett, B., Ventafridda, V., Cohen, R., & Gallacher, D. (2006). Survey of chronic pain in Europe: Prevalence, impact on daily life, and treatment. *European Journal of Pain, 10*(4), 287–333.

Chou, R., Fanciullo, G. J., Fine, P. G., Adler, J. A., Ballantyne, J. C., Davies, P., et al. (2009). Opioid treatment guidelines: Clinical guidelines for the use of opioids therapy in chronic noncancer pain. *The Journal of Pain, 10*(2), 113–130.

Currie, S. R., & Wang, J. (2004). Chronic back pain and major depression in the general Canadian population. *Pain, 107*(1–2), 54–60.

Dahl, J., Wilson, K. G., & Nilsson, A. (2004). Acceptance and commitment therapy and the treatment of persons at risk for long-term disability resulting from stress and pain symptoms: A preliminary randomized trial. *Behavior Therapy, 35*, 785–802.

de Jong, J. R., Vlaeyen, J. W., Onghena, P., Cuypers, C., den Hollander, M., & Ruijgrok, J. (2005a). Reduction of pain-related fear in complex regional pain syndrome type I: The application of graded exposure in vivo. *Pain, 116*(3), 264–275.

de Jong, J. R., Vlaeyen, J. W., Onghena, P., Goossens, M. E., Geilen, M., & Mulder, H. (2005b). Fear of movement/(re)injury in chronic low back pain: Education or exposure in vivo as mediator to fear reduction? *Clinical Journal of Pain, 21*(1), 9–17; discussion 69–72.

Demyttenaere, K., Bonnewyn, A., Bruffaerts, R., Brugha, T., De Graaf, R., & Alonso, J. (2006). Comorbid painful physical symptoms and depression: Prevalence, work loss, and help seeking. *Journal of Affective Disorders, 92*(2–3), 185–193.

Demyttenaere, K., Bruffaerts, R., Lee, S., Posada-Villa, J., Kovess, V., Angermeyer, M. C., et al. (2007). Mental disorders among persons with chronic back or neck pain: Results from the World Mental Health Surveys. *Pain, 129*(3), 332–342.

Dersh, J., Polatin, P. B., & Gatchel, R. J. (2002). Chronic pain and psychopathology: Research findings and theoretical considerations. *Psychosomatic Medicine, 64*(5), 773–786.

Eccleston, C., & Crombez, G. (1999). Pain demands attention: A cognitive-affective model of the interruptive function of pain. *Psychological Bulletin, 125*(3), 356–366.

Eriksen, J., Jensen, M. K., Sjogren, P., Ekholm, O., & Rasmussen, N. K. (2003). Epidemiology of chronic non-malignant pain in Denmark. *Pain, 106*(3), 221–228.

Ersek, M., Cherrier, M. M., Overman, S. S., & Irving, G. A. (2004). The cognitive effects of opioids. *Pain Management Nursing, 5*(2), 75–93.

Fishbain, D. A., Cutler, B. R., Rosomoff, H. L., & Rosomoff, R. S. (1998). Comorbidity between psychiatric disorders and chronic pain. *Current Review of Pain, 2,* 1–10.

Fordyce, W. E. (1976). *Behavioral methods for chronic pain and illness.* Saint Louis: Mosby.

Fordyce, W. E., Shelton, J. L., & Dundore, D. E. (1982). The modification of avoidance learning pain behaviors. *Journal of Behavioral Medicine, 5*(4), 405–414.

Gerdle, B., Bjork, J., Henriksson, C., & Bengtsson, A. (2004). Prevalence of current and chronic pain and their influences upon work and healthcare-seeking: A population study. *Journal of Rheumatology, 31*(7), 1399–1406.

Gironda, R. J., Clark, M. E., Ruff, R. L., Chait, S., Craine, M., Walker, R., et al. (2009). Traumatic brain injury, polytrauma, and pain: Challenges and treatment strategies for the polytrauma rehabilitation. *Rehabilitation Psychology, 54*(3), 247–258.

Glass, J. M., Park, D. C., Minear, M., & Crofford, L. J. (2005). Memory beliefs and function in fibromyalgia patients. *Journal of Psychosomatic Research, 58*(3), 263–269.

Gruber, S. A., Silveri, M. M., & Yurgelun-Todd, D. A. (2007). Neuropsychological consequences of opiate use. *Neuropsychology Reviews, 17*(3), 299–315.

Gureje, O., Von Korff, M., Simon, G. E., & Gater, R. (1998). Persistent pain and well-being: A World Health Organization Study in Primary Care. *Journal of the American Medical Association, 280*(2), 147–151.

Halbauer, J. D., Ashford, J. W., Zeitzer, J. M., Adamson, M. M., Lew, H. L., & Yesavage, J. A. (2009). Neuropsychiatric diagnosis and management of chronic sequelae of war-related mild to moderate traumatic brain injury. *Journal of Rehabilitation Research and Development, 46*(6), 757–796.

Hart, R. P., Martelli, M. F., & Zasler, N. D. (2000). Chronic pain and neuropsychological functioning. *Neuropsychology Reviews, 10*(3), 131–149.

Hayes, S. C. (2004). Acceptance and commitment therapy, relational frame theory, and the third wave of behavior therapy. *Behavior Therapy, 35,* 639–665.

Hayes, S. C., Luoma, J. B., Bond, F. W., Masuda, A., & Lillis, J. (2006). Acceptance and commitment therapy: Model, processes and outcomes. *Behavior Research and Therapy, 44*(1), 1–25.

Hayes, S. C., Strosahl, K., & Wilson, K. G. (1999). *Acceptance and commitment therapy: An experiential approach to behavior change.* New York: Guilford Press.

Hayes, S. C., Wilson, K. G., Gifford, E. V., Follette, V. M., & Strosahl, K. (1996). Experimental avoidance and behavioral disorders: A functional dimensional approach to diagnosis and treatment. *Journal of Consulting and Clinical Psychology, 64*(6), 1152–1168.

International Association for the Study of Pain Subcommittee on Classification. (1986). Pain terms: A current list with definitions and notes on usage. *Pain, 3*(Suppl.), S215–S221.

Iverson, G. L., & McCracken, L. M. (1997). "Postconcussive" symptoms in persons with chronic pain. *Brain Injury, 11*(11), 783–790.

Kabat-Zinn, J. (1990). *Full catastrophe living: Using the wisdom of your body and mind to face stress, pain, and illness.* New York: Dell Publishing.

Kabat-Zinn, J., Lipworth, L., & Burney, R. (1985). The clinical use of mindfulness meditation for the self-regulation of chronic pain. *Journal of Behavioral Medicine, 8*(2), 163–190.

Keefe, F. J., Rumble, M. E., Scipio, C. D., Giordano, L. A., & Perri, L. M. (2004). Psychological aspects of persistent pain: Current state of the science. *Journal of Pain, 5*(4), 195–211.

Kerns, R. D., Wagner, J., Rosenberg, R., Haythornthwaite, J., & Caudill-Slosberg, M. (2005). Identification of subgroups of persons with chronic pain based on profiles on the pain stages of change questionnaire. *Pain, 116*(3), 302–310.

Kessler, R. C., Chiu, W. T., Demler, O., Merikangas, K. R., & Walters, E. E. (2005). Prevalence, severity, and comorbidity of 12-month DSM-IV disorders in the National Comorbidity Survey Replication. *Archives of General Psychiatry, 62*(6), 617–627.

Kessler, R. C., McGonagle, K. A., Zhao, S., Nelson, C. B., Hughes, M., Eshleman, S., et al. (1994). Lifetime and 12-month prevalence of DSM-III-R psychiatric disorders in the United States. Results from the National Comorbidity Survey. *Archives of General Psychiatry, 51*(1), 8–19.

Kreitler, S., & Niv, D. (2007, July). *Cognitive impairment in chronic pain—Pain: Clinical Updates 15 1–4.* Retrieved February 3, 2010, from *www.mae.umontreal.ca/acces_reserve/documents/Kreitler-Niv_ClinUpdates_IASP2007.pdf.*

Lew, H. L., Otis, J. D., Tun, C., Kerns, R. D., Clark, M. E., & Cifu, D. X. (2009). Prevalence of chronic pain, posttraumatic stress disorder, and persistent post-concussive symptoms in OIF/OEF veterans: Polytrauma clinical triad. *Journal of Rehabilitation Research and Development, 46*(6), 697–702.

Linehan, M. M. (1993). *Cognitive-behavioral treatment of borderline personality disorder.* New York: Guilford Press.

McCracken, L. M. (1998). Learning to live with the pain: Acceptance of pain predicts adjustment in persons with chronic pain. *Pain, 74*(1), 21–27.

McCracken, L. M. (2005). *Contextual cognitive-behavioral therapy for chronic pain: Progress in pain research and management, Volume 33.* Seattle, WA: IASP Press.

McCracken, L. M. (2007). A contextual analysis of attention to chronic pain: What the patient does with their pain might be more important than their awareness or vigilance alone. *Journal of Pain, 8*(3), 230–236.

McCracken, L. M., & Eccleston, C. (2005). A prospective study of acceptance of pain and patient functioning with chronic pain. *Pain, 118*(1–2), 164–169.

McCracken, L. M., Gauntlett-Gilbert, J., & Vowles, K. E. (2007). The role of mindfulness in a contextual cognitive-behavioral analysis of chronic pain-related suffering and disability. *Pain, 131*(1–2), 63–69.

McCracken, L. M., & Iverson, G. L. (2001). Predicting complaints of impaired cognitive functioning in patients with chronic pain. *Journal of Pain and Symptom Management, 21*(5), 392–396.

McCracken, L. M., MacKichan, F., & Eccleston, C. (2007). Contextual cognitive-behavioral therapy for severely disabled chronic pain sufferers: Effectiveness and clinically significant change. *European Journal of Pain, 11*(3), 314–322.

McCracken, L. M., & Samuel, V. M. (2007). The role of avoidance, pacing, and other activity patterns in chronic pain. *Pain, 130*(1–2), 119–125.

McCracken, L. M., Spertus, I. L., Janeck, A. S., Sinclair, D., & Wetzel, F. T. (1999).

Behavioral dimensions of adjustment in persons with chronic pain: Pain-related anxiety and acceptance. *Pain, 80*(1–2), 283–289.

McCracken, L. M., Vowles, K. E., & Eccleston, C. (2005). Acceptance-based treatment for persons with complex, long standing chronic pain: A preliminary analysis of treatment outcome in comparison to a waiting phase. *Behavior Research and Therapy, 43*(10), 1335–1346.

McWilliams, L. A., Cox, B. J., & Enns, M. W. (2003). Mood and anxiety disorders associated with chronic pain: An examination in a nationally representative sample. *Pain, 106*(1–2), 127–133.

Morone, N. E., Greco, C. M., & Weiner, D. K. (2008). Mindfulness meditation for the treatment of chronic low back pain in older adults: A randomized controlled pilot study. *Pain, 134*(3), 310–319.

Muñoz, M., & Esteve, R. (2005). Reports of memory functioning by patients with chronic pain. *Clinical Journal of Pain, 21*(4), 287–291.

Nampiaparampil, D. E. (2008). Prevalence of chronic pain after traumatic brain injury: A systematic review. *Journal of the American Medical Association, 300*(6), 711–719.

Nicholas, M. K., & Asghari, A. (2006). Investigating acceptance in adjustment to chronic pain: Is acceptance broader than we thought? *Pain, 124*(3), 269–279.

Portenoy, R. K., Ugarte, C., Fuller, I., & Haas, G. (2004). Population-based survey of pain in the United States: Differences among white, African American, and Hispanic subjects. *Journal of Pain, 5*(6), 317–328.

Pradhan, E. K., Baumgarten, M., Langenberg, P., Handwerger, B., Gilpin, A. K., Magyari, T., et al. (2007). Effect of Mindfulness-Based Stress Reduction in rheumatoid arthritis patients. *Arthritis and Rheumatism, 57*(7), 1134–1142.

Raja, S. N., Haythornthwaite, J. A., Pappagallo, M., Clark, M. R., Travison, T. G., Sabeen, S., et al. (2002). Opioids versus antidepressants in postherpetic neuralgia: A randomized, placebo-controlled trial. *Neurology, 59*(7), 1015–1021.

Romano, J. M., Jensen, M. P., & Turner, J. A. (2003). The Chronic Pain Coping Inventory-42: Reliability and validity. *Pain, 104*(1–2), 65–73.

Roper Public Affairs and Media. (2004). *Americans living with pain survey: Executive summary and results. Survey conducted on behalf of the American Chronic Pain Association, April 2004.* Retrieved February 11, 2010, from *theacpa.org/documents/FINAL%20PAIN%20SURVEY%20RESULTS%20REPORT.pdf*

Roth, R. S., Geisser, M. E., Theisen-Goodvich, M., & Dixon, P. J. (2005). Cognitive complaints are associated with depression, fatigue, female sex, and pain catastrophizing in patients with chronic pain. *Archives of Physical Medicine and Rehabilitation, 86*(6), 1147–1154.

Rowbotham, M. C., Twilling, L., Davies, P. S., Reisner, L., Taylor, K., & Mohr, D. (2003). Oral opioid therapy for chronic peripheral and central neuropathic pain. *New England Journal of Medicine, 348*(13), 1223–1232.

Schmidt, C. O., Raspe, H., Pfingsten, M., Hasenbring, M., Basler, H. D., Eich, W., et al. (2007). Back pain in the German adult population: Prevalence, severity, and sociodemographic correlates in a multiregional survey. *Spine (Phila Pa 1976), 32*(18), 2005–2011.

Segal, Z. V., Williams, J. M. G., & Teasdale, J. D. (2002). *Mindfulness-based cognitive therapy for depression.* New York: Guilford Press.

Sephton, S. E., Salmon, P., Weissbecker, I., Ulmer, C., Floyd, A., Hoover, K., et al. (2007). Mindfulness meditation alleviates depressive symptoms in women with fibromyalgia: Results of a randomized clinical trial. *Arthritis and Rheumatism, 57*(1), 77–85.

Sjogren, P., Christrup, L. L., Petersen, M. A., & Hojsted, J. (2005). Neuropsychological assessment of chronic non-malignant pain patients treated in a multidisciplinary pain centre. *European Journal of Pain, 9*(4), 453–462.

Sjogren, P., Thomsen, A. B., & Olsen, A. K. (2000). Impaired neuropsychological performance in chronic nonmalignant pain patients receiving long-term oral opioid therapy. *Journal of Pain and Symptom Management, 19*(2), 100–108.

Sullivan, M. J., Lynch, M. E., & Clark, A. J. (2005). Dimensions of catastrophic thinking associated with pain experience and disability in patients with neuropathic pain conditions. *Pain, 113*(3), 310–315.

Sullivan, M. J., Thorn, B., Haythornthwaite, J. A., Keefe, F., Martin, M., Bradley, L. A., et al. (2001). Theoretical perspectives on the relation between catastrophizing and pain. *Clinical Journal of Pain, 17*(1), 52–64.

Turk, D. C., Meichenbaum, D., & Genest, M. (1983). *Pain and behavioral medicine: A cognitive-behavioral perspective*. New York: Guilford Press.

Vlaeyen, J. W., de Jong, J., Geilen, M., Heuts, P. H., & van Breukelen, G. (2001). Graded exposure in vivo in the treatment of pain-related fear: A replicated single-case experimental design in four patients with chronic low back pain. *Behavior Research and Therapy, 39*(2), 151–166.

Vlaeyen, J. W., & Linton, S. J. (2000). Fear-avoidance and its consequences in chronic musculoskeletal pain: A state of the art. *Pain, 85*(3), 317–332.

Von Korff, M., Crane, P., Lane, M., Miglioretti, D. L., Simon, G., Saunders, K., et al. (2005). Chronic spinal pain and physical-mental comorbidity in the United States: Results from the national comorbidity survey replication. *Pain, 113*(3), 331–339.

Vowles, K. E., & McCracken, L. M. (2008). Acceptance and values-based action in chronic pain: A study of treatment effectiveness and process. *Journal of Consulting and Clinical Psychology, 76*(3), 397–407.

Walker, B. F., Muller, R., & Grant, W. D. (2004). Low back pain in Australian adults: Prevalence and associated disability. *Journal of Manipulative and Physiological Therapeutics, 27*(4), 238–244.

Watkins, E. A., Wollan, P. C., Melton, L. J., III, & Yawn, B. P. (2008). A population in pain: Report from the Olmsted County health study. *Pain Medicine, 9*(2), 166–174.

Westoby, C. J., Mallen, C. D., & Thomas, E. (2009). Cognitive complaints in a general population of older adults: Prevalence, association with pain and the influence of concurrent affective disorders. *European Journal of Pain, 13*(9), 970–976.

Wicksell, R. K., Ahlqvist, J., Bring, A., Melin, L., & Olsson, G. L. (2008). Can exposure and acceptance strategies improve functioning and life satisfaction in people with chronic pain and whiplash-associated disorders (WAD)? A randomized controlled trial. *Cognitive Behavioral Therapy, 37*(3), 169–182.

Wolfe, F., Smythe, H. A., Yunus, M. B., Bennett, R. M., Bombardier, C., Goldenberg, D. L., et al. (1990). The American College of Rheumatology 1990 criteria for the classification of fibromyalgia. Report of the Multicenter Criteria Committee. *Arthritis and Rheumatism, 33*(2), 160–172.

PART III

Professional Practice Issues

CHAPTER 9

Neuropsychological Evaluation and Treatment
The Clinician's Perspective

Greg J. Lamberty

Individuals injured in the workplace can present for neuropsychological evaluations in a variety of different ways. Many neuropsychologists conduct evaluations in both clinical and forensic contexts, and this is true across different areas of clinical focus (i.e., pediatric, adult, mixed adult/pediatric). According to the American Academy of Clinical Neuropsychology (AACN) practice survey (Sweet, Giuffre Meyer, Nelson, & Moberg, 2011), most neuropsychologists devote an average of 20% or less of their practice to forensic evaluations. Nonetheless, it is important to consider that many cases involving workplace injuries are not necessarily or primarily referred as forensic cases, and it is not unusual for a clinically referred evaluation report to be used in medicolegal proceedings. The motivation behind a referral is not always clear, though "stealth" referrals seem to be increasingly common.[1]

In addition to differences in referral sources, the nature of clinical and forensic assessments can vary dramatically. For instance, Sweet, Giuffre Meyer, Nelson, and Moberg (2011) reported that a forensic evaluation typically took more than 4 hours longer than a clinical evaluation to conduct. These data suggest some interesting contrasts in the way that clinical and forensic evaluations/practices are conducted. Few neuropsychologists would say that clinical evaluations are somehow less important than forensic evaluations. However, the amount of time and effort spent on a forensic case is usually far greater than that spent on a clinical case. This difference

266 PROFESSIONAL PRACTICE ISSUES

often has to do with greater preparation time, more extensive testing, lengthier reports, and the possibility of additional time spent in depositions or the courtroom (Larrabee, 2005b). In addition, forensic assessments are often paid at the neuropsychologist's full fee, often in advance of the actual assessment. As a result of many of these factors, neuropsychologists conduct clinical and forensic evaluations in a significantly different manner.

The range of roles taken by neuropsychologists with clinically referred patients is broad (Lamberty, Courtney, & Heilbronner, 2003), though there is a common goal of thoroughly assessing neuropsychological functioning. In clinical cases, neuropsychologists might act as individual practitioners, members of an interdisciplinary team, hospital staff members, or consultants with a medical or rehabilitation service. The permutations and nuances of such roles are potentially numerous, but the patient and the referral sources are considered the primary "customers." In forensically referred assessments there is a clear distinction in roles (American Academy of Clinical Neuropsychology, 2007; Bush et al., 2005a; Malina, Nelson, & Sweet, 2005) wherein parties are aware of the neuropsychologist's charge to be an unbiased independent expert.

The terms *clinician* or *treating doctor* are often used to describe the neuropsychologist's role in a typical assessment, but this can be misleading. Because a minority of neuropsychologists actually provide direct care or treatment for the clients they assess (Sweet et al., 2011), there is some question about whether the neuropsychologist can or should serve as an *advocate* for the patients they see. If, on the other hand, the neuropsychologist sees a patient for psychotherapy or rehabilitation services subsequent to an assessment, he or is more clearly identifiable as a treating clinician. In such instances it is presumed that the neuropsychologist would be more suited to take a position of advocacy for the patient being seen (Fisher, Johnson-Greene, & Barth, 2002; Johnson-Greene, 2005). Yet again, some argue that advocating objectivity and truth is ultimately in the patient's best interests and that this does not always mean that there is a specific effort to sway the court's opinion in favor of a specific outcome (Bush, 2005; Malina et al., 2005). To be sure, this is a complex question and one that a treating neuropsychologist often encounters when their clinical work is referenced in a medicolegal matter.

In this chapter I focus on the practice of clinical neuropsychology in the modal clinical (i.e., nonforensic) setting and circumstance. The intent is not to provide a comprehensive reference regarding the ethical and legal aspects of the various portions of the assessment process. There are many chapters and casebooks on these topics (e.g., Bush, 2007; Grote, 2005). Rather, the focus is on the "usual and customary" practice of neuropsychology in the clinical context. In the end, the overarching goal of neuropsychological assessment should be to provide an objective data-oriented evaluation (American Academy of Clinical Neuropsychology, 2007).

INFORMED CONSENT

Most clinical neuropsychologists adhere to the American Psychological Association's (2002) Ethical Principles and Code and Conduct, either as members of that organization or as a function of their state's licensing standards. Specific sections of the Code cover the issue of informed consent (3.10 Informed Consent), and other professional organizations provide guidance specific to a particular practice area (Johnson-Greene, 2005). In routine clinical practice, neuropsychologists often provide both written and oral explanations of the nature of the neuropsychological evaluation. The fundamental issue with informed consent is that competent patients, or proxies for patients lacking competence, need to be aware of the nature of the exam they are submitting to and that their participation is voluntary. A patient's acknowledgment of this basic understanding is often made in writing, via a signed release/form, or by providing their verbal consent or, for patients who are unable to give consent, their assent. This process is typically noted in the narrative report. Even in instances where consent is initially granted, patients can withdraw for any reason. Such withdrawals are seen in cases where a patient might not have anticipated the difficulty or stressful nature of an evaluation.

Informed consent in forensic evaluations is often regarded in a different manner because the patient is not technically the consumer (American Psychological Association, 2002). Malina, Nelson, and Sweet (2005) noted that it is often not practical or reasonable to have a patient sign a consent form because many evaluations are not technically voluntary, such as those that are court-ordered or part of a broader medicolegal proceeding. In these instances it is helpful to have a standard procedure or checklist (Malina et al., 2005) that provides information about informed consent for both the patient and the provider. Most professional liability insurers also make such forms available (e.g., Youngren, Harris, & Bennett, 2001), and these can be altered to suit the neuropsychologist's needs or specific procedures. The provision of such information is referred to as notification of purpose (Bush, Connell, & Denney, 2006).

METHODS/PROCEDURES

Practically speaking, the greatest difference between a routine clinical evaluation and a forensic evaluation is in test selection. The ends of this spectrum are anchored by those who administer a brief screening measure or two on one end and those who administer multiple and overlapping measures of different realms of cognitive and psychological functioning on the other. Most neuropsychologists would not deem the use of screening measures alone as an adequate assessment in outpatient contexts. Screening measures and abbreviated forms are usually employed in circumstances when it is not clear whether a full assessment is warranted, or when time constraints or patients' financial resources do not allow the administration of lengthier measures, such as intelligence tests or full memory batteries (Axelrod, Ryan, & Ward, 2001; Lezak, Howieson, & Loring, 2004; Mitrushina, 2009). In contrast, forensic evaluations often seem to take a "more is better" approach with regard to test selection.

The AACN practice guidelines (2007) suggest that "a comprehensive neuropsychological evaluation should be thorough but also efficient and respectful of a patient's time and resources" (p. 221). Therefore, the neuropsychologist must exercise discretion in the selection of test measures in the service of thoroughness and the needs of the patient/client. This reliance on clinician discretion appears to leave the door open for markedly different assortments of tests. Some authors have suggested that the composition of the neuropsychological evaluation should be determined by known scientific standards (Larrabee, 2005a; Rohling, Meyers, & Millis, 2003; Wedding & Faust, 1989), though there is, of course, debate regarding what "scientific standards" means. In practical terms, there is no such thing as a clearly agreed upon set of test measures that constitute an "ideal" assessment. Rather, the realms of cognitive functioning assessed, the characteristics of the tests employed, and the normative databases used in interpretation are the important parameters (American Academy of Clinical Neuropsychology, 2007). Table 9.1 provides examples of measures used in typical clinical and forensic evaluations in the author's practice. For most practitioners, the measures that are ultimately used are determined by some combination of training/experience, knowledge of the literature, time constraints, availability of appropriate normative data, and practice resources. As such, the lists of tests offered in Table 9.1 will likely vary between neuropsychologists, though considerable overlap is expected.

One area in which substantial differences between clinical and forensic evaluations might exist is with regard to assessment of effort or "symptom validity" (American Academy of Clinical Neuropsychology, 2007; Bush et al., 2005b; Heilbronner, Sweet, Morgan, Larrabee, & Millis, 2009). The recent AACN Consensus Conference statement (Heilbronner et al., 2009) acknowledges that the context of an evaluation will likely have an impact on the nature of how effort or response bias is assessed. The number of measures employed and how they are presented throughout the course of an evaluation (Boone, 2009) is likely to vary, with a tendency for more measures to be used in the forensic context. Statements from various neuropsychological professional organizations have increasingly encouraged the use of symptom validity measures, and it appears to be the case that clinicians are increasingly using such measures in routine clinical practice. For instance, Sharland and Gfeller (2007) indicated that 57% of respondents use symptom validity measures, though this did not distinguish between forensic and clinical cases.

■ **TABLE 9.1. Neuropsychological Test Measures as a Function of the Nature of Referral Source**

Clinical neuropsychological evaluation	Forensic neuropsychological evaluation
WAIS-III/IV (7 subtests)	WAIS-III/IV (11 subtests for factor scores)
WRAT-4 (Reading subtest)	WRAT-4 (all subtests)
Word Memory Test	Word Memory Test
	Test of Memory Malingering
Controlled Oral Word Association	Rey Fifteen Item Test
Animal Naming	
Wisconsin Card Sorting Test	Finger Tapping
Trail Making Test	Grip Strength
Stroop Color and Word Test	
	Conners' Continuous Performance Test–II
Rey Auditory Verbal Learning Test	Trail Making Test
WMS-III/IV Logical Memory I & II	Stroop Color and Word Test
Rey Complex Figure Test	Controlled Oral Word Association Test
	Animal Naming
MMPI-2	Wisconsin Card Sorting Test
	California Auditory Verbal Learning Test–II
	WMS-III/IV Logical Memory I and II
	WMS-III/IV Visual Reproduction I and II
	Rey Complex Figure Test
	MMPI-2
	Selected symptom-oriented measures

Limitations in time and resources are largely responsible for neuropsychologists' decisions about how to shorten their clinical evaluations. To an increasingly greater extent, third-party payers and consultants are making decisions about the amount of time and sometimes even the specific measures, that can be used for a given referral question (e.g., *www.aetna.com/cpb/medical/data/100_199/0158.html*). Despite such limitations posed by third-party payers, if additional testing appears to be necessary, clinicians have an obligation to discuss service and payment options (e.g., out-of-pocket payment) with patients and/or their proxies.

In contrast, forensic evaluations are not typically constrained in this manner, so neuropsychologists are able to use whatever measures they deem appropriate. As a result, forensic evaluations typically include more comprehensive batteries and more symptom validity tests. This disparity almost guarantees that there will be substantial differences in the measures administered in clinical and forensic assessments. The extent to which batteries of markedly different lengths affect diagnostic accuracy and the quality of recommendations made is not clear, though at some point this question will need to be answered as part of the field's efforts to assess the value of neuropsychological services. These pressures are not necessarily negative because they will compel neuropsychology to make a study of the value of their services, with the goal being improved efficiency and continued access to services. Such pressures might also bring reason to forensic evaluations that can spin out of control given the often "blank check" nature of that enterprise.

Finally, as mentioned in the introduction, reports from clinically referred cases are sometimes used in medicolegal proceedings. It is not unusual for patients to get advice suggesting that a neuropsychological evaluation should be requested by their primary care physician or a medical specialist so that the expense of the evaluation can be covered by their insurance. This situation is a win–win for attorneys because they do not have to pay for the expense of an evaluation and they can assess the strength of a case based on the evaluation findings. Such an approach might be reasonable from a legal advocacy standpoint, but it borders on fraud in instances when the rationale for a neuropsychological evaluation is not fully clear or supportable by the clinical history in a case.

RECORD REVIEW

Reviewing records associated with cases referred for neuropsychological evaluation is a common task for neuropsychologists, regardless of the nature of the case. Given the differences between clinical settings, it is conceivable that the neuropsychologist might have as little as a single-sentence referral question to nearly to a lifetime's worth of clinical records available for their review. In clinically referred cases, records usually provide a history and the context of the assessment request. The records may guide the interview process and make it more efficient because the difficulties in question are usually described in some detail. When there is an issue of a work-related injury, this information might also be described in varying degrees of detail.

A clinical report does not usually involve an exhaustive review of records beyond what is typically included in a referral or history section. Discrepancies between the record and the patient interview presentation can be illuminating and are usually noteworthy. In forensically referred cases, there is typically a request to review copious records from medical providers, therapists, previous assessments, schools attended, and accident reports. In addition to the time taken to review the records, some neuropsychologists include an exhaustive written description of the records. Most often the review will focus on history and findings relevant to a patient's reported cognitive difficulty, but this is a matter of personal preference. Because of the demands of an exacting record review, some neuropsychologists charge a different (i.e., higher) rate for record review in forensically referred cases. In clinically referred cases this is more often included within the customary charges for the neuropsychological assessment code (CPT

96118). Record review alone could add anywhere from 1 or 2 to more than 10 hours of charges in a forensically referred case. Such charges are not always feasible in clinical cases, and payment for chart review billing codes (e.g., 90885, 99358) is frequently denied or reimbursed at a much lower rate than what is considered a usual and customary neuropsychological fee

CONSULTATION WITH COLLATERAL SOURCES

In clinically referred cases, patients are often accompanied by a spouse or family member who can be a valuable source of information regarding clinical history and relevant behaviors. These collateral sources of information can be very helpful in bringing together different elements of complex clinical cases. Family members are often aware of details in a patient's history and behavior that are simply not known to referral sources, not reflected in available records, and perhaps not even known to the patient. The subjectivity of interview information can be mitigated to some extent by scales and inventories that rely on family members' ratings of important behaviors. These scales tend to be more routinely employed in assessments of older (e.g., Johnson, Barion, Rademaker, Rehkemper, & Weintraub, 2004) and younger (e.g., Conners, Sitarenios, Parker, & Epstein, 1998) patients, particularly when it is difficult to rely on patients' self-report because of their cognitive limitations. Although some scales have been researched extensively, few have validity scales, and they are subject to the motivation of the person completing the measure. As such, data from these measures is used clinically to augment, rather than replace, personality or other self-report measures. They are often used in a descriptive manner that helps to support diagnoses with strong behavioral components, such as ADHD and different dementia syndromes.

In forensically referred cases, reports from collaterals are also regarded as important, but there is a general sense of skepticism regarding whether such data can be reasonably used in arriving at a diagnosis (Heilbrun, Warren, & Picarello, 2003). Involved collateral sources, such as close family members, may have their own agendas or may share an agenda that emphasizes litigation outcome. This broad general issue is one with which forensic psychology has struggled for many years (Rogers, 2008). Advances in symptom validity assessment have facilitated clinicians' ability to make determinations about the validity of data collected from patients, but the symptom validity research for measures used with collateral sources has lagged behind. Thus, as valuable as interview and history data can be in case formulation, such information can obfuscate appropriate diagnosis if it is relied upon in an uncritical manner. When information derived from collateral interviews is included in reports, it is often in a history or an interview section, suggesting to the reader that the information is susceptible to personal biases. When data from test measures given to collaterals is presented, it should be qualified by acknowledging that the data is self-reported. Most neuropsychologists understand that such data can be biased by a number of personal and relationship factors that are nearly impossible to account for.

RESULTS AND INTERPRETATION

Reporting the results of neuropsychological evaluations is a major part of the clinical enterprise. The crafting of a report and subsequent feedback session with the patient and family members or collaterals is often the last stage of the neuropsychological evaluation process. Regardless of whether in-person feedback is given, the APA Ethics Code (9.10, Explaining Assessment Results) states the following:

> Psychologists take reasonable steps to ensure that explanations of results are given to the individual or designated representative unless the nature of the relationship precludes provision of an explanation of results (such as in some organizational consulting, preemployment or security screenings, and forensic evaluations), and this fact has been clearly explained to the person being assessed in advance.

In routine clinical practice, neuropsychologists typically offer to meet with patients and family members to review assessment results. In-person meetings allow the neuropsychologist to explain results in detail and gauge the patient's or collateral source's understanding of the findings. In feedback sessions, patients are often provided a copy of the consultation report. There are instances when returning to the office for a feedback session is not feasible or practical for a patient. In such instances the narrative report can be sent with an offer to provide a telephone consultation for questions that might arise. Another option is for neuropsychologists to provide an "executive summary" of the evaluation in layperson's terms. Ultimately, the findings of the evaluation are very important to the patient, their family members, and the referral source. Neuropsychologists should strive to assure that the findings are conveyed in an understandable manner and that any recommendations made are facilitated to the extent possible (American Academy of Clinical Neuropsychology, 2007). Gorske and Smith (2009) presented a specific model for neuropsychological feedback that emphasizes practical and relevant information. They emphasize the importance of respectful collaboration with patients in service of enhancing cognitive and emotional well-being.

In forensic evaluation contexts, as stated by Ethical Standard 9.10 (Explaining Assessment Results), feedback is often precluded, making this general issue moot. Typically, referring parties do not want neuro-psychological evaluations to be anything beyond an assessment in search of diagnostically relevant facts. This situation is sometimes difficult for neuropsychologists who are oriented toward giving routine feedback and recommendations in their usual clinical practice. Furthermore, it can also be quite difficult for forensic examinees who might be hopeful that some recommendations will be forthcoming. In reality, patients are often able to access the results of an evaluation to the extent that they are used in the medicolegal proceeding. The inability to provide what is regarded as adequate traditional clinical service in these cases is one reason that some neuropsychologists prefer not to do medicolegal work. In the end, this aspect of the neuropsychological assessment process provides a stark contrast between clinical and forensic cases. Namely, clinical cases often involve the sharing of feedback and recommendations, whereas forensic cases typically do not.

HANDLING INVALID RESULTS

The emergence and use of symptom validity tests (SVTs) in routine clinical practice has dramatically changed some aspects of the neuropsychological assessment process (Larrabee, 2005a; Sweet, 1999). An increasing reliance on SVTs has facilitated more definitive statements about the validity of assessment results, even if the clinician does not necessarily regard failed SVTs as indicators of malingering. The majority of psychometric symptom validity measures have been developed in forensic or quasi-forensic con-texts, and there is still a good deal to be learned about the performance of clinically referred patients who do not have substantial secondary gain issues (Lamberty et al., 2008).

When patients "fail" SVTs or underperform on other indexes of effort, the neuropsychologist is left with the dilemma of how to describe the results. The interpretively simple route is to follow the test results and say that the evaluation is invalid because of questionable or poor effort. Going a step beyond that, the neuropsychologist might determine that the patient is malingering—that is, performing poorly on purpose in order to achieve a specific (and known) goal. Recent recommendations are clearly appre-ciative of the complexity of the phenomenon and do not recommend that a label of malingering be applied without clear and converging evidence (Heilbronner et al., 2009). Determining that a patient is a malingerer is appealing to some, though others are clearly appreciative of the difficulties with such a "diagnosis" (Boone, 2007).

In the clinical setting, patients are referred for many reasons, though presumably there is an interest in obtaining information about the nature of a person's reported symptoms and difficulties. The prudent neuropsychologist is wise to spend time trying to understand the nature of a patient's presentation beyond simply stating that an evaluation was invalidated by test results (Lamberty, 2007). Although equivocal or clearly invalid results cannot be ignored, neither can the clinician's responsibility to provide a service of worth. This service may involve a frank discussion about the invalidity of test results, a discussion about what might be behind those results, and recommendations for steps to take to move the patient to a more productive place. Carone, Iverson, and Bush (2010) offered recommendations for providing feedback to clinical patients who provide invalid symptom presentations during neuropsychological evaluations. In forensic contexts, such an analysis typically has little use because there is often a primary question regarding the validity of a patient's complaints. Invalid test results are often regarded as synonymous with a specious personal injury claim, in which case the primary purpose of the (defense oriented) referral has been met.

To the extent that forensic referral sources are seeking recommendations, the recommendations usually involve issues such as return-to-work and treatment modalities that might facilitate that goal. However, the neuropsychologist rarely conveys such information to a patient directly, given the nature of the relationship between the neuropsychologist and the referral source (Malina et al., 2005). Whether there is any possibility for a constructive discussion about invalid test results in forensically referred cases is debatable. Such findings are likely to be viewed as damaging to one's legal case, resulting in the findings being minimized (in plaintiff referrals) or treated as evidence of a baseless claim (in defense referrals).

TREATMENT RECOMMENDATIONS

For most clinically referred cases there is an assumption that treatment recommendations will be offered based on assessment findings (American Academy of Clinical Neuropsychology, 2007; Lezak et al., 2004; Vanderploeg et al., 2000). Whether this occurs in the form of a written report or face-to-face feedback is a matter of clinical expediency and patient preference. The extent to which specific treatment recommendations are made will also differ based on the clinical setting in which the assessment occurs. For example, evaluations prepared in an acute hospital or rehabilitation setting might contain recommendations for follow-up with occupational and physical therapy, individual psychotherapy, and psychiatric care for neuropsychiatric symptoms. Evaluations done in a more typical outpatient setting often focus on referrals for specialty medical care (e.g., neurology or psychiatry) and psychotherapy for a range of clinical concerns. Some neuropsychologists also provide treatment for their patients' cognitive and emotional issues.

Neuropsychologists sometimes refer patients for services that go beyond cognitive and neuropsychiatric difficulties. Services such as case management through the county, financial counseling, and respite care are often needed, and neuropsychologists who are aware of these resources can provide a valuable service to their patients. There is no clear-cut set of expectations for the kinds of treatment recommendations neuropsychologists should provide. The quality and extent of treatment recommendations made is usually more a function of the individual clinician's skill, experience, and knowledge of local resources. In recent times, the importance of functional characterization of clinical problems has become clearer, and the *psychological* part of neuropsychological is reemerging as an important focus in the field.

It is relatively uncommon for neuropsychologists to make a *specific* referral for treatment in an attorney-referred case. However, in some cases involving work-related injuries, referral sources (e.g., workers' compensation board or disability insurance carriers) ask for *generic* recommendations regarding treatment to help return a patient to work. The recommendations in such cases are usually general and involve services similar to those mentioned previously (e.g., psychotherapy, referral to psychiatry or neurology). It is not typical for the neuropsychologist to take responsibility for making such referrals; rather, such recommendations serve as basic suggestions based on the findings of the case.

SUMMARY

Neuropsychological evaluations vary considerably depending on the initiating referral source. Basic elements of the evaluation process are similar in both clinically and forensically referred cases. However, differences emerge as a function of the purpose and goals, resources available, and identified client. In clinically referred cases, insurers and other payers often limit the amount of testing that will be approved, which narrows the test selection and other elements of the evaluation process. In forensically referred cases, reimbursement is typically not a limiting factor for the extensiveness of evaluations. The other major contributor to differences between clinical and forensic cases is the nature of the relationship between the neuropsychologist and the primary "customer." In clinical cases the neuropsychologist's responsibility to the patient entails more ongoing interaction with collaterals, more regular follow-up, and provision of treatment recommendations. In forensic cases, there is usually more extensive review of records, lengthier assessments, increased focus on symptom validity, and more detailed reports. Table 9.2 contrasts some of the principal differences between neuropsychological services provided in clinical and forensic contexts.

■ TABLE 9.2. Differences in Common Practices as a Function of Referral Source

Clinically referred cases	Forensically referred cases
Informed consent	
Patients provided written and verbal descriptions of procedures and the nature of the evaluation process.	Patients provided written and verbal descriptions of procedures and the nature of the evaluation process.
Patient or proxy signs a consent form acknowledging their understanding of the evaluation process and their various rights.	Form may or may not be signed by patient.
	Checklist of informed consent procedures kept in patient file.
Methods/procedures (see Table 8.1)	
Tests are chosen to provide a thorough assessment of a range of cognitive and psychological functioning areas, mindful of time and resource limitations.	Tests are chosen to provide a thorough assessment, with multiple and overlapping measures. Time constraints are generally less emphasized.
One or two psychometric SVTs are employed along with "embedded" measures.	Several psychometric SVTs are administered along with "embedded" measures.
Record review	
Very few to a large number of records are reviewed to provide background information for the clinical interview and appropriate sections of the clinical report.	A large number of records are commonly forwarded by the referral source for review, with an expectation that the history will be reviewed and included in the narrative report.
Records are read, but not necessarily in exacting detail or with copious note-taking.	Records are read thoroughly with abstracting for the purpose of including in the narrative report.
Absent or less specific and detailed record review section in reports; rather, information from records is integrated into the narrative.	A record review section is commonly included in forensic reports, with a complete summary of relevant records and findings.
Consultation with collaterals	
Family members or relevant collaterals are interviewed to the extent they are available, and the information is considered beneficial to understanding the patient. This might include verbal reports, checklists, or history forms.	Collaterals are interviewed depending on their availability, but also as a function of the referral source's preference. Checklists and history forms may be used in addition to verbal reports.
Phone or other contact may be initiated in cases where such information is deemed essential for an understanding of the case.	Phone contact may be initiated and statements from depositions may be included as part of a more general record review.
Collateral reports are often regarded as important clinical data that inform the assessment process.	Collateral reports are regarded as important data, though the context of the evaluation is important, and these data are not considered in the same manner as test data.

(cont.)

▨ **TABLE 9.2.** *(cont.)*

Clinically referred cases	Forensically referred cases
Findings/interpretation	
Findings are provided to patients and/or their families in an accessible manner, including face-to-face feedback and/or a narrative report.	Findings are generally not shared with the patient via the neuropsychologist, but may be available through counsel.
Ideally, patients have an opportunity to ask questions directly of the neuropsychologist.	No communication with the neuropsychologist beyond the interview and evaluation.
Invalid results	
Patients are informed that the assessment results are not valid via review of report or meeting with neuropsychologist.	Patients are informed of the nature of assessment results via their attorney or other representative.
Neuropsychologist provides information about the invalid results and makes recommendations regarding appropriate courses of treatment.	Results regarding invalid effort or symptom exaggeration are often minimized, challenged, or emphasized depending upon the referral source.
Treatment recommendations	
Recommendations regarding treatment options are made in the clinical report and in person, when possible.	Recommendations are not commonly solicited, though if they are they are not shared directly with the patient.

Note. Differences may vary somewhat according to jurisdiction.

In the final analysis, differences between clinical and forensic contexts appear likely to grow as reimbursement for clinical services faces greater downward pressure. What this portends for the general practice of clinical neuropsychology is not clear, though one would hope that challenges will facilitate and not impede efficient and accurate practices.

NOTE

1. A "stealth" referral is one that comes through a clinical referral source, even though it is fairly clear that an attorney prompted the referral and will attempt to use the assessment report in a legal proceeding or hearing.

REFERENCES

American Academy of Clinical Neuropsychology. (2007). American Academy of Clinical Neuropsychology (AACN) practice guidelines for neuropsychological assessment and consultation. *The Clinical Neuropsychologist, 21*(2), 209–231.
American Psychological Association. (2002). *Ethical principles of psychologists and code of conduct.* Washington, DC: Author.

Axelrod, B. N., Ryan, J. J., & Ward, L. C. (2001). Evaluation of seven-subtest short forms of the Wechsler Adult Intelligence Scale-III in a referred sample. *Archives of Clinical Neuropsychology, 16*(1), 1–8.

Boone, K. B. (2007). A reconsideration of the Slick et al. (1999) criteria for malingered neurocognitive dysfunction. In K. B. Boone (Ed.), *Assessment of feigned cognitive impairment: A neuropsychological perspective* (pp. 29–49). New York: Guilford Press.

Boone, K. B. (2009). The need for continuous and comprehensive sampling of effort/response bias during neuropsychological examinations. *The Clinical Neuropsychologist, 23*(4), 729–741.

Bush, S. S. (2005). Ethical challenges in forensic neuropsychology: Introduction. In S. S. Bush (Ed.), *A casebook of ethical challenges in neuropsychology* (pp. 10–14). New York: Psychology Press.

Bush, S. S. (2007). *Ethical decision making in clinical neuropsychology.* New York: Oxford University Press.

Bush, S. S., Barth, J. T., Pliskin, N. H., Arffa, S., Axelrod, B. N., Blackburn, L. B., et al. (2005a). Independent and court-ordered forensic neuropsychological examinations: Official statement of the National Academy of Neuropsychology. *Archives of Clinical Neuropsychology, 20*, 997–1007.

Bush, S. S., Connell, M. A., & Denney, R. L. (2006). *Ethical issues in forensic psychology: A systematic model for decision making.* Washington, DC: American Psychological Association.

Bush, S. S., Ruff, R. M., Troster, A. I., Barth, J. T., Koffler, S. P., Pliskin, N. H., et al. (2005b). Symptom validity assessment: Practice issues and medical necessity NAN Policy and Planning Committee. *Archives of Clinical Neuropsychology, 20*(4), 419–426.

Carone, D. A., Iverson, G. L., & Bush, S. S. (2010). A model to approaching and providing feedback to patients regarding invalid test performance in clinical neuropsychological evaluations. *The Clinical Neuropsychologist, 24*(5), 759–778.

Conners, C. K., Sitarenios, G., Parker, J. D., & Epstein, J. N. (1998). The revised Conners' Parent Rating Scale (CPRS-R): Factor structure, reliability, and criterion validity. *Journal of Abnormal Child Psychology, 26*(4), 257–268.

Fisher, J. M., Johnson-Greene, D., & Barth, J. T. (2002). Evaluation, diagnosis, and interventions in clinical neuropsychology in general and with specific populations: An overview. In S. S. Bush & M. L. Drexler (Eds.), *Ethical issues in clinical neuropsychology* (pp. 3–22). Lisse, Netherlands: Swets & Zeitlinger.

Gorske, T. T., & Smith, S. R. (2009). *Collaborative Therapeutic Neuropsychological Assessment.* New York: Springer Science.

Grote, C. (2005). Ethical practice of forensic neuropsychology. In G. Larrabee (Ed.), *Forensic neuropsychology* (pp. 92–114). New York: Oxford University Press.

Heilbronner, R. L., Sweet, J. J., Morgan, J. E., Larrabee, G. J., & Millis, S. R. (2009). American Academy of Clinical Neuropsychology Consensus Conference Statement on the neuropsychological assessment of effort, response bias, and malingering. *The Clinical Neuropsychologist, 23*(7), 1093–1129.

Heilbrun, K., Warren, J., & Picarello, K. (2003). Third party information in forensic assessment. In A. M. Goldstein (Ed.), *Handbook of psychology: Forensic psychology* (Vol. 11, pp. 69–86). Hoboken, NJ: Wiley.

Johnson, N., Barion, A., Rademaker, A., Rehkemper, G., & Weintraub, S. (2004). The Activities of Daily Living Questionnaire: A validation study in patients with dementia. *Alzheimer's Disease and Associated Disorders, 18*(4), 223–230.

Johnson-Greene, D. (2005). Informed consent in clinical neuropsychology practice: Official statement of the National Academy of Neuropsychology. *Archives of Clinical Neuropsychology, 20*(3), 335–340.

Lamberty, G. J. (2007). *Understanding somatization in the practice of clinical neuropsychology.* New York: Oxford University Press.

Lamberty, G. J., Courtney, J., & Heilbronner, R. L. (Eds.). (2003). *The practice of clinical neuropsychology.* Lisse, Netherlands: Swets & Zeitlinger.

Lamberty, G. J., Nelson, N. W., Brogger, M. L., Henriksen, C. A., Condit, D., & Sweet, J. J. (2008). Further examination of FBS in secondary and non-secondary gain samples. *The Clinical Neuropsychologist, 22,* 413–414.

Larrabee, G. J. (2005a). Assessment of malingering. In G. J. Larrabee (Ed.), *Forensic neuropsychology: A scientific approach* (pp. 115–158). New York: Oxford University Press.

Larrabee, G. J. (2005b). A scientific approach to forensic neuropsychology. In G. J. Larrabee (Ed.), *Forensic neuropsychology: A scientific approach* (pp. 3–28). New York: Oxford University Press.

Lezak, M. D., Howieson, D. B., & Loring, D. W. (2004). *Neuropsychological Assessment* (4th ed.). New York: Oxford University Press.

Malina, A. C., Nelson, N. W., & Sweet, J. J. (2005). Framing the relationships in forensic neuropsychology: Ethical issues. *Journal of Forensic Neuropsychology, 4,* 21–44.

Mitrushina, M. (2009). Cognitive screening methods. In I. Grant & K. M. Adams (Eds.), *Neuropsychological evaluation of neuropsychiatric and neuromedical disorders* (pp. 103–126). New York: Oxford University Press.

Rogers, R. (2008). *Clinical assessment of malingering and deception* (3rd ed.). New York: Guilford Press.

Rohling, M. L., Meyers, J. E., & Millis, S. R. (2003). Neuropsychological impairment following traumatic brain injury: A dose-response analysis. *The Clinical Neuropsychologist, 17*(3), 289–302.

Sharland, M. J., & Gfeller, J. D. (2007). A survey of neuropsychologists' beliefs and practices with respect to the assessment of effort. *Archives of Clinical Neuropsychology, 22*(2), 213–223.

Sweet, J., Giuffre Meyer, D., Nelson, N., & Moberg, P. (2011). The TCN/AACN "Salary Survey": Professional practices, beliefs, and incomes of U.S. neuropsychologists. *The Clinical Neuropsychologist, 25,* 12–61.

Sweet, J. J. (1999). Malingering: Differential diagnosis. In J. J. Sweet (Ed.), *Forensic neuropsychology: Fundamentals and practice.* Lisse, Netherlands: Swets & Zeitlinger.

Vanderploeg, R. D., Schinka, J. A., Jones, T., Small, B. J., Graves, A. B., & Mortimer, J. A. (2000). Elderly norms for the Hopkins Verbal Learning Test—Revised. *The Clinical Neuropsychologist, 14*(3), 318–324.

Wedding, D., & Faust, D. (1989). Clinical judgment and decision making in neuropsychology. *Archives of Clinical Neuropsychology, 4*(3), 233–265.

Youngren, J. N., Harris, E. H., & Bennett, B. E. (2001). *Forensic informed consent contract*, from *www.apait.org/resources/riskmanagement/finf.htm.*

CHAPTER 10

The Neuropsychological IME

Shane S. Bush
Robert L. Heilbronner

Neuropsychologists have traditionally been called upon to evaluate patients in clinical settings. In such settings, neuropsychologists work for, or on behalf of, their patients. In the past decade, however, the value of neuropsychological consultation and assessment in forensic contexts has become increasingly evident (Heilbronner, 2008; Larrabee, 2005a; Sweet, 1999). Common types of litigation include criminal proceedings, civil cases (e.g., personal injury, medical malpractice), and administrative law, such as those involving disability insurance carriers, workers' compensation, Social Security Disability determinations, and other contexts in which neuropsychological findings assist in the administrative decision-making process about the allocation of benefits. Work-related accidents and injuries commonly lead to involvement in one or more of those forensic contexts, particularly the pursuit of workers' compensation benefits.

In forensic contexts, neuropsychologists, like doctors from other medical specialties, are sometimes retained by, and on behalf of, a party other than the person being evaluated. Because they do not have clinical, emotional, or financial obligations to the person being examined, the evaluations performed by neuropsychologists in such forensic contexts are often referred to as *independent*; this term is often applied to the examiner as well as the examination. The term *independent* is sometimes not applied to examinations performed by experts who are retained by a third party that represents or is otherwise working on behalf of the examinee, such as a plaintiff attorney in a personal injury case or a defense attorney in a criminal matter. However, neuropsychologists who have been retained by plaintiff attorneys, like those retained by defense attorneys or disability insurance companies, should have the same commitment to objectivity as do neuropsychologists retained by other parties.

The medical examination of a person involved in forensic matters by an independent doctor is commonly referred to as an *independent medical examination*, or *IME*. These terms are used even for evaluations performed by professionals who do not hold medical degrees. The specialty of the professional who performs an IME is typically used to describe the nature of the same, such as orthopedic IME, psychiatric IME, or, in this case, neuropsychological IME. Sometimes the terms *independent neuropsychological examination* or *independent neuropsychological evaluation* are used to further differentiate the neuropsychological evaluation from other types of medical examinations. However, *neuropsychological IME* is the term most commonly used by attorneys, disability insurance carriers, and others involved with this type of evaluation in the United States. Therefore, we use the term *neuropsychological IME* throughout this chapter.

As with the terminology used to describe the evaluation, the language used to refer to the persons being evaluated differs in IME contexts. Whereas in clinical contexts, the person who undergoes a neuropsychological evaluation is referred to as the *patient* or *client*, in IME contexts the person is referred to as the *examinee, claimant, or plaintiff*. Using different terms to describe persons who undergo neuropsychological evaluations in these different contexts helps all parties to remain clear about the nature of the roles and relationships of those involved. More specifically, describing someone as an examinee promotes an understanding that the usual doctor–patient relationship does not exist in forensic contexts (Bush et al., 2005a).

DIFFERENCES BETWEEN CLINICAL EVALUATIONS AND IMEs

When workers are injured on the job, they typically are taken to a local hospital or they go to their own doctors for evaluation and treatment. In such clinical contexts, there is usually some urgency for neuropsychologists and other clinicians to complete evaluations quickly so that treatment decisions can be made or modified as soon as possible. Treating doctors are invested in providing, or helping their patients get, appropriate care. Because of the need to respond relatively quickly, evaluation procedures may necessarily be truncated. It is the rare clinical evaluation that equals in breadth and depth the typical forensic neuropsychological evaluation. In addition, in clinical contexts, neuropsychologists often accept patient self-report as accurate.

In contrast, neuropsychologists performing IMEs tend to view patient self-report more skeptically because of the higher prevalence of dissimulation in forensic contexts. Questions and procedures (explained in more detail later in this chapter) are selected and applied in ways that avoid placing sole emphasis on patient self-report in IME contexts and that help examiners to identify their own potential biases (cf. Sweet & Moulthrop,

1999). These differences between clinical and independent evaluations are also reflected in the neuropsychological report (described in more detail later in the chapter).

DIFFERENCES BETWEEN DIFFERENT NEUROPSYCHOLOGICAL IMEs

Not all neuropsychological IMEs are the same. The nature of the IME can vary according to the referral question(s) and limitations (such as funding) from the referral source. For example, some disability insurance carriers may want a very thorough neuropsychological evaluation to address a wide range of complex questions regarding diagnosis, neurocognitive and functional capacities, emotional states and personality traits, and symptom validity. In contrast, some governmental agencies (e.g., Social Security) may be content with a more circumscribed evaluation and may pay relatively little for the neuropsychological service. In all instances, neuropsychologists are responsible for utilizing the methods and procedures that are deemed necessary to address a given referral question in a particular evaluation context, mindful that adversarial contexts provide opportunities for inadequate evaluations to be exposed.

INCREASED FREQUENCY OF NEUROPSYCHOLOGICAL IMEs

The application of neuropsychological knowledge and procedures to forensic questions has experienced considerable growth over the past couple of decades, and continued growth is expected (Heilbronner, 2004; Kaufmann, 2009; Sweet, King, Malina, Bergman, & Simmons, 2002). Attorneys, the courts, disability insurance carriers, the Social Security Administration, workers' compensation, and other administrative bodies are increasingly seeking the services of neuropsychologists to determine the presence, nature, and extent of brain-related problems that have been attributed to work-related injuries. Because neuropsychology has "the essentially unique role of providing quantitative measurements of behavioral consequences of various underlying neuropathological, pathophysiological and pathochemical processes that may arise across the broad spectrum of neurological and neuropsychiatric diseases" (Meier, 1999, p. xi), neuropsychologists are well positioned to answer questions about cognitive, sensory–motor, linguistic, psychiatric, and behavioral problems that may have emerged or worsened as a result of injuries sustained at work. In addition, with the proliferation of psychological and neuropsychological research addressing issues of effort, response bias, and malingering (Heilbronner, Sweet, Morgan, Larrabee, Millis, & Conference participants, 2009) in recent years, neuropsychologists are well prepared to address questions of symptom exaggeration and fabrication with multiple methods, including empirically based tests and questionnaires. Given the current litigation and economic climates, the need for neuropsychological services in the context of work-related accidents and injuries has never been greater, and it will likely continue to increase for the foreseeable future.

PREPARATION FOR PERFORMING NEUROPSYCHOLOGICAL IMEs

Professional competence as a clinical neuropsychologist is required, but not sufficient, for competent performance of IMEs. Performing neuropsychological IMEs requires a unique skill set, and clinicians who intend to perform IMEs have an ethical obligation to develop that skill set (American Psychological Association, 2002; Ethical Standard 2.01, Boundaries of Competence). Except for the rare neuropsychologist who completes a forensic postdoctoral residency, clinicians interested in performing IMEs must obtain their forensic knowledge and skills through self-study, continuing education courses, formal supervision, consultation, and/or working with a mentor (an online APA-approved IME course is available at *www.PsyBar.com*). Because different neuropsychological IMEs vary in their nature, scope, and populations encountered, competent neuropsychologists prepare for the specific types of IMEs that they are likely to perform.

INTERACTIONS WITH THE RETAINING PARTY

Referrals for neuropsychological IMEs come from a variety of sources, including attorneys, government agencies, disability insurance carriers, automobile insurance carriers, workers' compensation carriers, and IME companies or vendors. Such parties often differ in their familiarity with neuropsychology, and contact persons representing such referral sources often vary widely in their understanding of the nature and role of neuropsychology. For these reasons, neuropsychologists commonly need to educate the retaining party about the nature of the neuropsychological IME in the context in which a given IME is requested. Some retaining parties employ experienced in-house neuropsychologist consultants to facilitate the retention of other neuropsychologists who perform IMEs and/or review neuropsychological IME reports and provide feedback to the examiner. Such peer-to-peer interaction often makes the IME process smoother and more rewarding for all parties. However, when third parties employ inexperienced or unqualified psychologist consultants to help with the retention of independent examiners or to review the work product of independent neuropsychologists, the process can be frustrating and less productive.

ESTABLISHING THE PARAMETERS OF THE IME

It is important for neuropsychologists who perform IMEs to establish procedures for performing such examinations. These parameters are conveyed to the retaining party and agreed upon *at the outset* of the neuropsychologist's involvement in a given case. Similarly, retaining parties often have requirements to which neuropsychologists are asked to adhere (see Table 10.1). In some instances, negotiations between the neuropsychologist and retaining party can help address misunderstandings or conflicting practices. Typically, the agreed upon parameters are clarified in writing and signed by the neuropsychologist and the retaining party. When the established parameters of an IME are challenged by an examinee or his or her representative, the neuropsychologist needs to resolve the problem, often by contacting the retaining party, prior to performing the examination.

Billing

The amount and nature of payment vary among practitioners and among retaining parties. Preferences vary regarding hourly or flat fees, and regarding whether fees are paid in advance or following the examination. Neuropsychologists who perform IMEs typically have a fee schedule that lists basic examination fees, no show or late cancellation fees, testimony fees, and interest to be accrued if payment is not made in a timely manner. Additional fees for record review and report writing may also be listed if they are not encompassed by the basic fees. Because fees change over time, it can be helpful to date the fee schedule so that there is no confusion about which fees are in effect for a given IME. Fee schedules are commonly provided to referral sources, and some practitioners require the retaining party, or are required by the retaining party, to sign a statement of agreement regarding the fees. The American Psychological Association (American Psychological Association, 2002) Ethics Code (Standard 6.04, Fees and Financial

▪ **TABLE 10.1. Parameters of Neuropsychological IMEs**

Established by the neuropsychologist	Established by the retaining party
• Fees	• Fees
• Anticipated time requirements	• Time frame for report
• Informed consent/notification of purpose	• Informed consent/notification of purpose
• Methods/tests used	• Specific tests or types of tests
• Third-party observers	• Questions to be answered
• Recording	
• Avoiding conflicts of interest	
• Record retention	

Relationships) requires that compensation and billing arrangements are agreed upon as early as possible in the professional relationship. See Appendix 10.1 for a sample fee schedule.

THE EVALUATION

The methods and procedures used in neuropsychological IMEs and the focus of reports vary depending on the goals and nature of the IME and on the training and background of the neuropsychologist. IMEs in the context of litigation typically focus on diagnosis, causality, presence or degree of neuropsychological impairment and disability, prognosis, and the need for future neuropsychological services. In contrast, in the context of disability insurance claims, neuropsychologists emphasize examinees' functional activities and abilities and typically do not address disability status. Disability status is instead determined by the insurance carrier based on the insurance policy and consideration of multiple sources of information, of which the neuropsychological IME results are only one.

Jurisdictional laws limit the extent to which neuropsychologists can address causality of brain injury (e.g., Florida; see *Tomlian v. Grenitz*, 2001). Criteria for establishing causation have been proposed and may assist neuropsychologists in jurisdictions in which causality determinations are allowed (van Reekum, Streiner, & Conn, 2001). Regarding causation, these authors stated, "Demonstration of an association between the causative agent and the outcome, consistency of the findings, a biologic rationale, and the appropriate temporal sequence are all necessary criteria that are feasible to achieve (although not without potential difficulties)" (p. 324). A multisource, multimethod approach to neuropsychological IMEs increases the likelihood of making accurate diagnostic and causality determinations. Cross-checking various sources of information helps to determine the degree of confidence that can be placed in the information.

Describing the Parameters of the IME

At the beginning of the evaluation, neuropsychologists typically confirm the identity of the examinee via a driver's license or other photo identification. The neuropsychologist also informs the examinee that the usual doctor–patient relationship will not be established, and details the limitations of confidentiality, who the report is to be directed to, and the importance of best effort and honesty. Neuropsychologists often ask examinees whether they have been coached about how to respond or perform during the neuropsychological IME, and they often inform examinees that specific measures of effort and honesty will be used. Neuropsychologists often (but are not required to) ask examinees to sign a written consent form or other documentation detailing the nature and parameters of the IME (see Bush et al., 2005a for a sample consent form).

Review of Records

The record review is an extremely important part of the neuropsychological IME because examinee self-report is, intentionally or unintentionally, often unreliable for both biographical and injury-related information (Greiffenstein, Baker, & Johnson-Greene, 2002; Gunstad & Suhr, 2001; Mittenberg, DiGiulio, Perrin, & Bass, 1992). The occurrence and severity of a brain injury is typically established based on the characteristics of the injury (Ruff, Iverson, Barth, Bush, & Broshek, 2009). Patients who experience posttraumatic amnesia (PTA) cannot report whether they experienced a loss of consciousness, unless they were informed by others. Moreover, those who were emotionally traumatized, experienced significant physical pain, or were treated with sedation or strong pain medications often do not know why they have trouble remembering details of the accident or surrounding events and may attribute such gaps in memory to a loss of consciousness from a brain injury. Thus, police accident reports, emergency medical personnel records, and emergency department records are particularly informative for verifying and providing the context for examinees' self-reported experiences. With very mild brain injuries, neurological signs or symptoms may initially go undetected because of the focus on physical injuries and/or emotional reactions. Such mild brain injuries tend to resolve quickly and completely unless "complicated by preexisting psychiatric or substance abuse problems, poor general health, concurrent orthopedic injuries, or comorbid problems (e.g., chronic pain, depression, substance abuse, life stress, unemployment, and protracted litigation)" (Iverson, 2005, p. 301).

The reports of prior neuropsychological evaluations provide important information that can be particularly valuable when making diagnostic determinations and judgments regarding causality. Given recovery or deterioration trajectories for many disorders, comparing current results to previous test results can help confirm or rule out working hypotheses. Reviewing prior neuropsychological test data for scoring accuracy can be beneficial, particularly when the results do not seem to make "neuropsychological sense." Medical and mental health records can also reveal a history of significant injuries, illnesses, and problems that predate the current work-related injury.

Educational, vocational, military, and other biographical records can also be of considerable value for understanding and verifying background information, particularly given the tendency of examinees as a group to misrepresent their background (Gunstad & Suhr, 2001; Mittenberg, Di Giulio, Perrin, & Bass, 1992). For example, education level is often used in

selecting normative data, and examinees commonly overreport their education level (Greiffenstein et al., 2002), which can lead neuropsychologists to
overpathologize normal results (e.g., misattribute deficits to brain damage).
"No examiner in any discipline is required to simply accept self-reported
facts and history of examinees. The validity of *self-reported* disability and
symptoms needs to be evaluated, especially when such complaints occur in
a forensic context" (Heilbronner et al., 2009, p. 1102). It is often helpful
to review records prior to seeing the examinee because the information
contained in the records can help guide the clinical interview. In situations
in which the retaining party does not initially provide records, neuropsychologists request that the retaining party does provide relevant records
before the report is completed.

Interviews

Interviews provide an opportunity to gather and clarify background information, details about the injury and the examinee's experience of the injury,
subsequent symptoms and changes in functioning, treatments, and, for
those who are not working, plans regarding return to work (see Table 10.2).
Neuropsychologists interview the examinee and may interview significant
others, employers, healthcare providers, and others who have information
about the examinee's history and neuropsychological and functional status
before and following the work-related injury. For example, one examinee
reported having significant global cognitive deficits, including an inability
to identify letters or read, after a work-related mild traumatic brain injury
(TBI). When his wife was interviewed about his daily routine, she reported
that the first thing he did each morning was to have a cup of coffee and read
the newspaper, which they then discussed. The discrepancy between the
examinee's reported functional limitations and his wife's description of his
daily activities helped inform the diagnostic decision-making process.

　　Neuropsychologists are aware that collateral sources of information
who have a personal or financial stake in the outcome of the case may
provide biased information. Neuropsychologists must advise spouses,

▨ **TABLE 10.2. General Topics Covered during Neuropsychological IME
Clinical Interviews**

• Demographic variables and handedness	• Use of assistive devices
• Description of the accident and injuries	• Family medical/psychiatry history
• Current symptoms	• Education
• Functional limitations	• Work history and status
• Injury-related problems and treatments	• Work-related stressors
• Medical/psychiatric history	• Plans to return to work
• Substance abuse history	• Family background and social activities
• Medications	• Past and current daily activities

employers, treating doctors, and other collateral sources that the information they convey will not be held in confidence but will likely be included in the neuropsychological report. Collateral sources must also understand that the conversation does not imply the establishment of a treating doctor relationship. The clinical interview of the examinee precedes test administration because information gained from the interview helps determine whether testing is needed and, if so, informs the test selection process. In some contexts, the clinical interview may be sufficient for answering the referral questions. But, most often, testing is a necessary component of the neuropsychological IME.

Observations

The presentations of examinees during IMEs can provide valuable information regarding diagnosis and functional status. The observations made during IMEs typically include the usual observations made in clinical contexts, such as appearance, sensory and motor functions, language, cognition, affect, behavior, and effort. In addition, in the course of IMEs, neuropsychologists are more likely to observe behaviors outside of the office setting, such as observing interactions between examinees and others in a waiting area or observing examinees leaving the office and going to their cars. IME referral sources may also provide neuropsychologists with surveillance recordings of examinees outside of their homes or in the community. Observations outside of the office setting, and surveillance recordings, provide information about examinees engaged in daily activities when they are not aware that they are being observed, which may be the same as, or different from, the activities reported by examinees or observed in office settings. Neuropsychologists determine whether to use and rely on such materials as part of their examination process.

Observations combined with history and test results can provide converging information that helps clarify the diagnostic picture. Similarly, discrepancies between observations and history or test results raise questions about symptom validity that may warrant further exploration or confirm working hypotheses. For example, an examinee who reports having severe memory problems and performs very poorly on memory tests but who leaves the office during a lunch break, follows verbally presented directions to a local restaurant, and returns on time (without using a global positioning system) presents the neuropsychologist with a discrepancy that must be considered. Observations that occur across settings on multiple occasions can help maximize the reliability of the information obtained from the behaviors being observed. Establishing patterns of consistency adds confidence to diagnostic decisions and helps reveal disingenuous claims. However, obtaining observations across multiple settings and occasions is usually not practical during the independent evaluation process.

Neuropsychologists may be asked to allow a third party, usually an attorney, to observe or record an IME. The motivations underlying such requests vary, from wanting to ensure that an appropriate evaluation is performed to attempts to intimidate examiners. In some jurisdictions, examinees have a legal right to have a third party present during IMEs. When such requests are received, a distinction needs to be made between the clinical interview and test administration aspects of the IME. Allowing a third party to be quietly and unobtrusively present during the clinical interview does not affect test security or neurocognitive performance, which are concerns during testing. However, the presence of that third party can affect the rapport, flow, and dynamics of the interview process, especially if the third party is the plaintiff's lawyer. Some examiners allow third parties to be present during clinical interviews, whereas others do not; this decision is entirely up to the examining neuropsychologist. If examinees have, and exercise, the right to record clinical interviews, neuropsychologists are well served by also recording the interaction so that any edited or altered examinee recordings can be challenged.

Neuropsychology as a profession has taken the position that, with few exceptions, allowing third parties to observe neuropsychological testing is inappropriate (American Academy of Clinical Neuropsychology, 2001; National Academy of Neuropsychology, 2000). The presence of someone other than the examiner and the examinee during neuropsychological evaluation can affect the results, often in unknown ways; the effects also extend to audio and video recording devices (see McCaffrey, 2005, for a review). Although some jurisdictions grant examinees the right to have another person present during IMEs or to record IMEs, neuropsychologists do not have to work under conditions that knowingly compromise the validity of the results. When requests for observation of the neuropsychological IME are made, neuropsychologists are well served by educating all involved parties. However, if the requesting party does not acquiesce, or if a judge orders the evaluation to proceed with the third party present, it is entirely appropriate for the neuropsychologist to decline the referral.

Selecting Measures

The 2002 APA Ethics Code states, "Psychologists base the opinions contained in their recommendations, reports, and diagnostic or evaluative statements, including forensic testimony, on information and techniques sufficient to substantiate their findings" (Ethical Standard, 9.01a). The assumptions, roles, and goals inherent in neuropsychological IMEs necessitate use of a comprehensive evaluation methodology, consisting of systematic utilization of multiple data sources (Bush, Connell, & Denney, 2006). For admissibility in court proceedings, tests need to have an established scientific foundation or at least be generally accepted within the profession (see, e.g., *Daubert v. Merrell Dow Pharmaceuticals, Inc.*, 1993; *Frye v. United States*, 1923). Commercially available psychological and neuropsychological tests typically meet those criteria.

Most neuropsychologists use a flexible battery approach (Rabin, Barr, & Burton, 2005; Sweet, Moberg, & Suchy, 2000). That is, a variety of measures are combined into a core battery that is used relatively consistently by the neuropsychologist, with tests added or removed as needed for a given examinee. Tables 10.3 and 10.4 provide sample neuropsychological IME test batteries. The batteries are based on the flexible (vs. fixed) battery model, with tests removed, substituted, or added as needed to comprehensively assess the neuropsychological status of a given examinee. Table 10.3 lists a sample of tests for use with a fairly comprehensive battery, whereas Table 10.4 lists a sample of tests for use in IME contexts in which the parameters are limited in time and funding (e.g., some Medicare disability determination contexts).

Interpretation, Diagnosis, and Determinations

The interpretation of test data begins with decisions about the validity of the examinee's presentation, including effort on tests and honesty in responding to questions. Larrabee (2005a, p. 9) proposed a four-component consistency analysis for neuropsychological decision making. The four components, centering around consistency, are as follows:

1. Consistency within and between neuropsychological domains.
2. Consistency between the neuropsychological profile and the suspected etiological condition.
3. Consistency between the neuropsychological data and the documented severity of the injury.
4. Consistency between the neuropsychological data and the examinee's behavioral presentation.

Inconsistencies raise questions about symptom validity, with more, or more significant, inconsistencies providing stronger evidence of an invalid presentation. When the examinee's approach to the IME, including the cognitive test results, is determined to be invalid, it is common practice to describe the findings as not reliable or valid, or at most representing the examinee's minimum ability level. In such cases, the differential diagnosis typically involves a somatoform disorder (unintentional) versus malingering (intentional) using probabilistic language (e.g., Slick, Sherman, & Iverson, 1999). Of course, examinees with well-documented neurological injuries and valid deficits can still exaggerate their problems, thereby invalidating the test results. In clinical contexts, some neuropsychologists

▪ TABLE 10.3. Sample Comprehensive Neuropsychological IME Test Battery

Estimate premorbid intelligence

1. North American Adult Reading Test (NAART), Wechsler Test of Adult Reading (WTAR), Test of Irregular Word Reading Efficiency (TIWRE), or Test of Premorbid Functioning (ToPF): Reading of irregularly spelled words; estimate of premorbid intellectual ability.

Symptom validity

2. Test of Memory Malingering
3. Word Memory Test
4. Embedded indicators
5. Minnesota Multiphasic Personality Inventory—2nd edition

Intellectual functioning

6. Wechsler Adult Intelligence Scale—3rd edition or 4th edition

Language

7. Boston Naming Test
8. Complex Ideational Material
9. Token Test

Attention/Working memory

10. Wechsler Adult Intelligence Scale—3rd edition/4th edition, Working Memory Index
11. Seashore Rhythm Test

Processing speed

12. Wechsler Adult Intelligence Scale—3rd edition/4th edition, Processing Speed Index
13. Trail Making Test, Part A
14. Stroop Color and Word Test, Word Reading and Color Naming

Visuospatial skills

15. Wechsler Adult Intelligence Scale—3rd edition/4th edition, Perceptual Organization Index
16. Rey Complex Figure Test

Memory

17. California Verbal Learning Test—2nd edition
18. Wechsler Memory Scale—3rd edition or 4th edition

Executive functions

19. Controlled Oral Word Association Test/FAS
20. Trail Making Test, Part B
21. Stroop Color and Word Test, Interference
22. Wisconsin Card Sorting Test

(cont.)

■ **TABLE 10.3.** *(cont.)*

Sensory–motor functions

23. Double Simultaneous Stimulation: Sensory extinction
24. Finger Tapping Test
25. Hand Dynamometer
26. Lafayette Grooved Pegboard Test

Academic achievement

27. Wide Range Achievement Test—4th edition

Mood/personality

28. Minnesota Multiphasic Personality Inventory—2nd edition

Note. This test list is not intended to represent all of the measures or necessarily the optimal measures for assessing each domain across examinees. Each clinician is responsible for selecting the tests or test battery most appropriate for assessing a given examinee based on the available research and clinical judgment.

discontinue test administration when there is strong evidence of insufficient effort; however, with IMEs, the customary practice is to complete most or all of the test administration.

When test data are determined to be valid, neuropsychologists pursue an interpretive process that is similar to that used in clinical evaluations. The level of impairment (e.g., 1.5 or 2 standard deviations below the mean) to be used is selected *a priori*, the examinee's level of performance is compared to estimated preinjury levels and appropriate normative data, base rates of impaired scores are considered, patterns of strengths and weaknesses are compared to established patterns for various neurological disorders, and determinations about underlying brain functioning are made. Diagnosis, causality, prognosis, and, if requested, recommendations are addressed.

Hill (1965) proposed nine factors to consider when inferring causation (see Table 10.5). In the interpretive process, neuropsychologists consider the difference between test results, diagnosis, and functioning, and as Larrabee (2005b) so concisely stated, "everything must make 'neuropsychological sense' " (p. 13).

THE REPORT

Forensic neuropsychological reports, including IME reports, differ in important ways from reports generated in clinical contexts (Greiffenstein & Cohen, 2005, p. 59). Neuropsychological IME reports describe all of the prior steps in the evaluation process, as outlined in Table 10.2. The writing needs to be clear and concise, avoiding or operationally defining

■ TABLE 10.4. Sample Brief Neuropsychological IME Test Battery

Estimate premorbid intelligence

1. North American Adult Reading Test (NAART), Wechsler Test of Adult Reading (WTAR), Test of Irregular Word Reading Efficiency (TIWRE), or Test of Premorbid Functioning (ToPF): Reading of irregularly spelled words; estimate of premorbid intellectual ability; or
2. Wide Range Achievement Test—4th edition, Word Reading

Symptom validity

3. Embedded Indicators

Intellectual functioning

4. Reynolds Intellectual Assessment Scales

Language

5. Boston Naming Test
6. Complex Ideational Material

Attention/working memory

7. Wechsler Adult Intelligence Scale—3rd edition/4th edition, Digit Span subtest
8. Seashore Rhythm Test (SRT): Auditory discrimination and sustained attention

Processing speed

9. Trail Making Test, Part A
10. Stroop Color and Word Test, Word Reading and Color Naming

Visuospatial skills

11. Rey Complex Figure Test
12. Reynolds Intellectual Assessment Scales, Nonverbal subtests

Memory

13. California Verbal Learning Test—2nd edition
14. Reynolds Intellectual Assessment Scales, Memory subtests

Executive functions

15. Controlled Oral Word Association Test/FAS
16. Stroop Color and Word Test, Interference
17. Trail Making Test, Part B

Sensory–motor functions

18. Double Simultaneous Stimulation: Sensory extinction
19. Lafayette Grooved Pegboard Test (GP): Speeded fine motor coordination

Academic achievement

20. Wide Range Achievement Test—4th edition

Mood

21. Beck Anxiety Inventory
22. Beck Depression Inventory—Second Edition or Mood Assessment Scale

Note. This test list is not intended to represent all of the measures or necessarily the optimal measures for assessing each domain across examinees. Each clinician is responsible for selecting the tests or test battery most appropriate for assessing a given examinee based on the available research and clinical judgment.

■ **TABLE 10.5. Factors for Inferring Causation from Association**

• Strength of the association	• Biological gradient or dose–response
• Consistency of the observed association	curve
• Specificity of the association	• Biological plausibility
• Temporal relationship of the association	• Coherence
• Analogy	• Experiment

Note. Based on information presented by Hill (1965).

professional jargon. The primary focus of a given report depends on the purpose of the IME and the specific questions being asked. For example, neuropsychological IME reports in the context of disability determinations have strong emphasis on functional daily activities (capacity to manage hygiene, finances, etc.). Commonly, IME referral sources provide a list of specific questions to be answered (see Table 10.6); answers to the questions are often provided in place of a summary/conclusions section, although some examiners prefer to include both.

Sources of information are clearly labeled in neuropsychological IME reports. For example, in the absence of records to corroborate the examinee's report of loss of consciousness, the report should state, "The examinee reported that he was unconscious for 15 minutes" rather than "The examinee was unconscious for 15 minutes." It is also helpful for readers when neuropsychologists describe their method for determining "impaired" test scores (e.g., 1.5 or 2 standard deviations below the mean). A DSM or ICD diagnosis may be requested; care must be taken to base DSM Axis V (GAF: Global Assessment of Functioning) determinations only on psychological problems, not physical problems or environmental limitations.

Psychological and neuropsychological treatment recommendations are often not included unless specifically requested, and medical treatment recommendations are almost never provided as these are the domains of physicians. Limitations of the data or significant reservations about the findings (e.g., based on poor examinee effort) are described. Speculative statements regarding functional capabilities tend to weaken neuropsychological IME reports; statements should be based on objective evidence and data to the extent possible. Citations from the scientific literature often help substantiate conclusions but are not mandatory. Standardized scores for all tests administered may be appended to the report, although some practitioners also include some or all of the scores in the body of the report.

Some IME referral sources, such as disability insurance carriers and IME vendors, employ or retain neuropsychologists to review, edit, and comment on the reports of the independent neuropsychologist. The value of such peer review varies considerably based on the qualifications and experience of the reviewing colleague. With some referrals sources, the feedback provided by the reviewing neuropsychologist helps to clarify the

■ TABLE 10.6. Sample Neuropsychological IME Referral Questions

1. What is the claimant's current medical/neuropsychological status?

2. What are the claimant's current areas of neuropsychological and psychological strength and weakness? Please clearly state to what extent the pattern of current test scores is likely due to normal variation, impairment, or other factors.

3. Is there evidence to suggest that symptom exaggeration or feigning was present during the evaluation? Is there evidence to suggest that the insured was malingering? Is so, please integrate this information throughout your responses to these questions.

4. Provide current DSM-IV diagnoses.

5. Please comment regarding whether the etiology of any validated impairments found appears to be solely organically based in nature, solely affective (psychiatric) in nature, or combined organic and affective. If there is a combined organic and affective basis for existing deficits, please comment on which one makes overall impairment levels greater and which is the greater overall factor.

6. Please address causal relationship.

7. If impairments are found, what is your opinion regarding their underlying cause? For example, are the impairments consistent with emotional factors, motivational factors, neurological disease, medication effects, or distraction due to pain, fatigue, or substance use?

8. If cognitive or psychological impairments are present, do they reach a level that would limit the claimant's functioning? How would they limit functioning and to what degree? Would modifications or adaptations ameliorate these limitations? (*Note*: Limitation refers to an activity that cannot be performed as usual due to impairment). Please do not comment upon whether the claimant is disabled from her occupation. Determination of disability status is a process that requires the application of contractual language to the medical data.

9. Is the claimant's reported cognitive capacity consistent with your observation and test findings? Please provide a detailed explanation of your opinion.

10. Please explain how your sources of evidence above are consistent or inconsistent with each other. For example, is the examinee self-report consistent with your observations and with test data?

11. Is the claimant experiencing valid psychological or cognitive symptomatology that results in occupational impairment? In addition, is there evidence to suggest that the claimant is experiencing valid sequelae of pain and/or fatigue? Please explain.

12. If the claimant is experiencing occupational impairment, is there evidence to suggest the claimant could perform some occupational duties with appropriate accommodations?

13. Is the claimant motivated to attempt a return to gainful employment?

14. Is there a further need for neuropsychological treatment? If so, please state length and frequency.

15. What is your opinion regarding the accuracy of the claimant's current psychological/psychiatric diagnosis or diagnoses? Is the current treatment appropriate and adequate for the condition being claimed? What are your recommendations for additional or future treatment?

16. What is your opinion as to whether any of the following factors might be influencing the claimant's continuing claim for disability: (a) choice, (b) career dissatisfaction, (c) attitude of entitlement, (d) adoption of the sick role, (e) secondary gain (monetary and/or emotional), or (f) lack of motivation to return to work?

writing and strengthen the report, whereas the feedback from, and interaction with, other reviewers can be cumbersome and unproductive. In all cases, the conclusions of the independent neuropsychologist remain his or her own.

REQUESTS FOR FEEDBACK

Neuropsychological IMEs do not include feedback sessions. Examinees are advised at the outset of the evaluation that the neuropsychologist will not provide them with the results directly. They are informed that copies of the report are typically available from the referring party.

MAINTAINING AND RELEASING RECORDS

The retention and release of records is governed by jurisdictional law and professional ethics and guidelines. The APA (2007) *Record Keeping Guidelines* state the following:

> In the absence of a superseding requirement, psychologists may consider retaining full records until 7 years after the last date of service delivery for adults or until 3 years after a minor reaches the age of majority, whichever is later. In some circumstances, the psychologist may wish to keep records for a longer period, weighing the risks associated with obsolete or outdated information, or privacy loss, versus the potential benefits associated with preserving the records (See Guideline 8). (p. 999)

However, not all authoritative sources differentiate between records generated and obtained in clinical and forensic contexts; this lack of differentiation limits the IME practitioner's certainty about which records to keep and how long to keep them. In the course of performing IMEs, neuropsychologists commonly receive extensive records to review, and significant records may be generated in the course of a comprehensive neuropsychological evaluation. Some practitioners consider it an unrealistic burden to retain multiple boxes of historical information. Some third-party referral sources request practitioners to retain records for a specified period of time, usually a certain number of months, which is less than the requirements posed by state law or professional organizations. The APA recognizes the "inherent tensions" that arise in determining when to dispose of records and encourages practitioners to carefully weigh the advantages and disadvantages of retention and disposal when making such decisions. Some practitioners have found that maintaining records in an electronic format helps manage some of the logistical problems with storage. However, considerable care must be taken to ensure the security of electronic records and the confidentiality of examinee information (American Psychological Association, 2002, Ethical Standard 6.02, Maintenance, Dissemination, and Disposal of Confidential Records of Professional and Scientific Work; Bush, Naugle, & Johnson-Greene, 2002).

Neuropsychologists who perform IMEs understand that they will release copies of reports to retaining parties, and such information is conveyed to examinees at the outset, during the informed consent process (Bush & Martin, 2009; Committee on the Revision of the Specialty Guidelines for Forensic Psychology, 2008). IME companies, disability insurance carriers, and other retaining parties may request that independent examiners provide copies of raw test data to neuropsychologist consultants employed by such companies or to others. Neuropsychologists release raw test data to colleagues upon request and to others in a manner consistent with ethical and professional guidelines (see Bush, Rapp, & Ferber, 2009 for a review).

When practitioners are requested to re-release records that were obtained from other healthcare professionals, they must consider the nature of the request and the information contained in the records. When a subpoena for "any and all records" is received, "it is generally necessary to re-release any third-party information included in the record" (American Psychological Association, 2007, p. 998). However, the neuropsychologist may notify the client (i.e., retaining party) so that an objection can be raised, if desired, before the records are released.

PITFALLS

Awareness of common pitfalls (see, e.g., Fisher & Beckman, 2003) encountered in IME contexts allows neuropsychologists who perform, or who are considering performing, IMEs to provide competent services and minimize the likelihood of professional misconduct.

Not Staying Current with Trends in the Field

The practice of neuropsychology, like all healthcare professions, has evolved over time. Failure to remain abreast of evidence-based changes in the field limits the accuracy of conclusions and the value of the service for the decision maker. For example, empirically based symptom validity assessment is now a standard of practice in neuropsychology (Bush et al., 2005b; Heilbronner et al., 2009). Failure to include multiple empirically based symptom validity tests and/or indicators in a neuropsychological IME is a serious omission that can severely lessen the confidence that can be placed in the neurocognitive test data; such evaluation results would be essentially meaningless.

Clinical Judgment versus Objective Data

A primary advantage of neuropsychological IMEs compared to evaluations performed by other healthcare disciplines is the inclusion of multiple objective measures of the constructs of interest, which provide data that can be compared to appropriate normative groups. Neuropsychology's unique emphasis on empirically based measures of cognition and psychological status limits reliance on more subjective and potentially biased clinical judgments or limited cognitive screening measures (e.g., Mini-Mental State Exam). Independent examiners who place greater emphasis on their subjective clinical judgment compared to the objective evidence risk being unable to defend challenges to the scientific bases of their conclusions.

Confusing Symptoms and Function

Symptoms such as forgetfulness, distractibility, or crying episodes do not mean that someone cannot perform daily activities in the home or work setting. Many individuals can work through or compensate for such symptoms, allowing them to perform productive or social activities. In contrast, some people with mild symptoms are not able to perform tasks that require high levels of proficiency, such as a surgeon with a mild hand tremor (Fisher & Beckman, 2003). It is important in neuropsychological IME reports to distinguish between symptoms and function. In fact, disability carriers make it a point to emphasize that the examiner make efforts to link symptoms and objective evidence of impairment to limitations in functioning whenever possible.

Equating Diagnosis with Disability

Having a psychological or cognitive problem does not automatically mean that personal, social, or productive activities cannot be performed. The specific requirements of the tasks to be performed, rather than the diagnosis, determine whether the examinee's psychological problems or cognitive deficits will pose functional limitations and lead to a determination that the examinee is or is not able to perform daily activities.

Slipping into the Treating Doctor Role

Statements of advocacy on behalf of the examinee cross the line into the treating doctor role. Efforts to avoid biased statements, such as advocating for or against the allotment of benefits to the examinee, help preserve the independent examiner role.

Straying Outside One's Areas of Expertise

Inexperienced independent neuropsychological examiners may be tempted to draw conclusions about the impact of orthopedic injuries or other medical problems on the examinee's functioning. However, such determinations are best left to other healthcare specialists. For example, neuropsychologists are within the boundaries of their expertise by stating that an examinee cannot perform certain work-related tasks because his grief over the traumatic amputation of a leg results in depressed mood and crying episodes throughout much of the day. In contrast, neuropsychologists stray beyond the typical bounds of expertise by making determinations such as an examinee cannot work because of the physical limitations posed by the traumatic amputation of a leg. Such determinations are best left to the appropriate healthcare specialists.

CONCLUSIONS

Neuropsychologists are increasingly being called upon to provide independent evaluations of persons who have sustained work-related injuries. The goals, methods, and reports of neuropsychological IMEs differ in important ways from neuropsychological evaluations of individuals with alleged work-related injuries that are performed in clinical contexts. The results of neuropsychological IMEs help administrative decision makers and triers of fact make determinations about disability status, benefits, and monetary awards. By understanding the differences between clinical neuropsychological evaluations (see Lamberty, Chapter 9, this volume) and neuropsychological IMEs, and by preparing in advance to perform IMEs, neuropsychologists can provide competent, ethical services in an expanding and interesting area of practice.

REFERENCES

American Academy of Clinical Neuropsychology. (2001). Policy statement on the presence of third party observers in neuropsychological assessments. *The Clinical Neuropsychologist, 15*(4), 433–439.

American Psychological Association. (2002). Ethical principles of psychologists and code of conduct. *American Psychologist, 57*(12), 1060–1073.

American Psychological Association. (2007). Record keeping guidelines. *American Psychologist, G2*, 993–1004.

Bush, S., Naugle, R., & Johnson-Greene, D. (2002). Interface of information technology and neuropsychology: Ethical issues and recommendations. *The Clinical Neuropsychologist, 16*(4), 536–547.

Bush, S. S., Barth, J. T., Pliskin, N. H., Arffa, S., Axelrod, B. N., Blackburn, L. B., et al. (2005a). Independent and court-ordered forensic neuropsychological examinations: Official statement of the National Academy of Neuropsychology. *Archives of Clinical Neuropsychology, 20*, 997–1007.

Bush, S. S., Connell, M. A., & Denney, R. L. (2006). *Ethical practice in forensic psychology: A systematic model for decision making.* Washington, DC: American Psychological Association.

Bush, S. S., & Martin, T. A. (2009). Privacy, confidentiality, and privilege in forensic neuropsychology. In A. M. Horton Jr. & L. C. Hartlage (Eds.), *Handbook of forensic neuropsychology* (2nd ed., pp. 235–244). New York: Springer.

Bush, S. S., Rapp, D. L., & Ferber, P. S. (2009). Maximizing test security in forensic neuropsychology. In A. M. Horton, Jr. & L. C. Hartlage (Eds.), *Handbook of forensic neuropsychology* (2nd ed., pp. 177–195). New York: Springer.

Bush, S. S., Ruff, R. M., Troster, A. I., Barth, J. T., Koffler, S. P., Pliskin, N. H., et al. (2005b). Symptom validity assessment: Practice issues and medical necessity NAN Policy and Planning Committee. *Archives of Clinical Neuropsychology, 20*(4), 419–426.

Committee on the Revision of the Specialty Guidelines for Forensic Psychology. (2008). Specialty Guidelines for Forensic Psychology. Third Official Draft, released on 2.27.08, at *www.ap-ls.org/links/22808sgfp.pdf.*

Daubert v. Merrell Dow Pharmaceuticals, Inc. (509 U.S. 579 1993).

Fisher, D., & Beckman, L. (2003). Psychological and psychiatric assessment of individual for disability insurers. Retrieved from *www.psybar.com/training_material.*

Frye v. United States, 293 F. 1013 (D.C. Cir 1923).

Greiffenstein, M. F., Baker, W. J., & Johnson-Greene, D. (2002). Actual versus self-reported scholastic achievement of litigating postconcussion and severe closed head injury claimants. *Psychological Assessment, 14*(2), 202–208.

Greiffenstein, M. F., & Cohen, L. (2005). Neuropsychology and the law: Principles of productive attorney–neuropsychologist relations. In G. J. Larrabee (Ed.), *Forensic neuropsychology: A scientific approach* (pp. 29–91). New York: Oxford University Press.

Gunstad, J., & Suhr, J. A. (2001). "Expectation as etiology" versus "the good old days": Postconcussion syndrome symptom reporting in athletes, headache sufferers, and depressed individuals. *Journal of the International Neuropsychological Society, 7*(3), 323–333.

Heilbronner, R. L. (2004). A status report on the practice of forensic neuropsychology. *The Clinical Neuropsychologist, 18*(2), 312–326.

Heilbronner, R. L. (2008). *Neuropsychology in the courtroom: Expert analysis of reports and testimony.* New York: Guilford Press.

Heilbronner, R. L., Sweet, J. J., Morgan, J. E., Larrabee, G. J., Millis, S. R., & Conference participants (2009). American Academy of Clinical Neuropsychology Consensus Conference Statement on the neuropsychological assessment of effort, response bias, and malingering. *The Clinical Neuropsychologist, 23*(7), 1093–1129.

Hill, A. B. (1965). The environment and disease: Association or causation? *Proceedings of the Royal Society of Medicine, 58*, 295–300.

Iverson, G. L. (2005). Outcome from mild traumatic brain injury. *Current Opinion in Psychiatry, 18*, 301–317.

Kaufmann, P. M. (2009). Protecting raw data and psychological tests from wrongful disclosure: A primer on the law and other persuasive strategies. *The Clinical Neuropsychologist, 23*(7), 1130–1159.

Larrabee, G. J. (2005a). A scientific approach to forensic neuropsychology. In G. J. Larrabee (Ed.), *Forensic neuropsychology: A scientific approach* (pp. 3–28). New York: Oxford University Press.

Larrabee, G. J. (Ed.). (2005b). *Forensic neuropsychology: A scientific approach.* New York: Oxford University Press.

McCaffrey, R. J. (2005). Third party observers. *Journal of Forensic Neuropsychology, 4*(2).

Meier, M. J. (1999). Foreword. In J. J. Sweet (Ed.), *Forensic neuropsychology: Fundamentals and practice* (p. xi). Lisse, Netherlands: Swets & Zeitlinger.

Mittenberg, W., DiGiulio, D. V., Perrin, S., & Bass, A. E. (1992). Symptoms following mild head injury: Expectation as aetiology. *Journal of Neurology, Neurosurgery and Psychiatry, 55,* 200–204.

National Academy of Neuropsychology. (2000). Presence of third party observers during neuropsychological testing: Official statement of the National Academy of Neuropsychology. *Archives of Clinical Neuropsychology, 15,* 379–380.

Rabin, L. A., Barr, W. B., & Burton, L. A. (2005). Assessment practices of clinical neuropsychologists in the United States and Canada: A survey of INS, NAN, and APA Division 40 members. *Archives of Clinical Neuropsychology, 20*(1), 33–65.

Ruff, R. M., Iverson, G. L., Barth, J. T., Bush, S. S., & Broshek, D. K. (2009). Recommendations for diagnosing a mild traumatic brain injury: A National Academy of Neuropsychology education paper. *Archives of Clinical Neuropsychology, 24*(1), 3–10.

Slick, D., Sherman, E. M., & Iverson, G. L. (1999). Diagnostic criteria for malingered neurocognitive dysfunction: Proposed standards for clinical practice and research. *The Clinical Neuropsychologist, 13*(4), 545–561.

Sweet, J. J. (Ed.). (1999). *Forensic neuropsychology: Fundamentals and practice.* Lisse, Netherlands: Swets & Zeitlinger.

Sweet, J. J., King, J. H., Malina, A. C., Bergman, M. A., & Simmons, A. (2002). Documenting the prominence of forensic neuropsychology at national meetings and in relevant professional journals from 1990 to 2000. *The Clinical Neuropsychologist, 16*(4), 481–494.

Sweet, J. J., Moberg, P. J., & Suchy, Y. (2000). Ten-year follow-up survey of clinical neuropsychologists: Part I. Practices and beliefs. *The Clinical Neuropsychologist, 14*(1), 18–37.

Sweet, J. J., & Moulthrop, M. A. (1999). Self-examination questions as a means of identifying bias in adversarial assessments. *Journal of Forensic Neuropsychology, 1*(1), 73–88.

Tomlian v. Grenitz, 782 So. 2d 905 (Fla. 4th DCS 2001).

van Reekum, R., Streiner, D. L., & Conn, D. K. (2001). Applying Bradford Hill's criteria for causation to neuropsychiatry: Challenges and opportunities. *Journal of Neuropsychiatry and Clinical Neurosciences, 13*(3), 318–325.

APPENDIX 10.1. INDEPENDENT NEUROPSYCHOLOGICAL EVALUATION SAMPLE FEE SCHEDULE

1. Neuropsychological examination (full day) $ _____
   - Includes clinical interview; behavioral observations; test administration, scoring, interpretation, and report; and record review (up to 1 hour)
   - Additional record review (per hour) $ _____
   - Consultation/discussion with attorney (per hour) $ _____
   - No show/cancellation less than 5 business days $ _____
2. Case review or peer review, with report (per hour) $ _____
   - Retainer amount established based on amount of records and estimated time involvement
3. Depositions or court appearance $ _____
   - Preparation for legal proceeding (per hour) $ _____
   - Travel (per hour) $ _____

   Depositions: A retainer of $

   Court appearances: A retainer of $ _____ is required seven (7) days prior to the date of deposition. The time will not be reserved if a retainer is not received. The party that has retained the services of the doctor must pay any outstanding balance. This fee does not include time spent preparing for testimony. ***Retainers are not refundable***.
4. Prompt payment is always appreciated. Billing occurs on a monthly basis and payment is required in full within 30 days of the billing date. All past due invoices are subject to a finance charge of 1.5 percent per month.

I, _____, on behalf of _____, certify that the above fees are acceptable.

_____   _____
Signature   date

CHAPTER 11

Neuropsychological Assessment and Consultation in Forensic Practice

A Practical Approach to Work-Related Injuries

Robert L. Heilbronner
George K. Henry

The purpose of this chapter is to provide readers insight into many of the salient issues and points that emerge in the practice of forensic neuropsychology, particularly in the context of work-related injuries. Although the relevance of many of these issues will vary according to one's professional experiences, in our 20+ years of experience working as consultants to the legal system we have found that these issues invariably emerge at one time or another. Thus, we regard these issues as important for neuropsychologists who evaluate persons who have sustained injuries at work and particularly important for clinicians who are new to this specialty practice.

This chapter is not intended to serve as a review of the relevant literature devoted to the practice of forensic neuropsychology, as this has already been done (Greiffenstein, 2008; Greiffenstein & Cohen, 2005; Larrabee, 2000, 2005; Sweet, 1999). Nor is the chapter intended to demonstrate the value and worth of what we do; this too, has already been adequately documented (Heilbronner & Pliskin, 2003). It is also not written as a "how-to" guide to the practice of forensic neuropsychology. Indeed, all clinicians and experts must decide for themselves how they want to practice and manage the tasks that are the mandate of forensic neuropsychology.

As scientist-practitioners, clinical neuropsychologists are familiar with disciplined scrutiny (i.e., peer review), clinical procedures emphasizing data-based decision making (i.e., accountability), and a hypothesis-testing approach (i.e., objective differential diagnosis) to answer questions (Sweet,

1999). The perceived strengths of clinical neuropsychologists include multifaceted analytic abilities (nomothetic, quantitative, idiographic), a non-
adversarial and objective ethos, and a multidisciplinary knowledge base
(e.g., neuroanatomy, clinical neurology, medical terminology, psychometric
methods). The case analysis of neuropsychologists may even be a micro-
cosm of the jury process, namely, reasoning directed toward a conclusion
based on conflicting data, that is, differential diagnosis (Bush, 2003).

Forensic neuropsychology involves the "application of neuropsychology to civil and criminal legal proceedings" (Larrabee, 2000). It includes
those "activities of neuropsychologists that involve rendering an opinion
that will be 'argued' or, in some manner, adjudicated by others" (Sweet,
Grote, & van Gorp, 2002). From a practical standpoint, the following may
help to define the topic even more clearly: clinical neuropsychology can be
described as an integration of psychology and neurology. Similarly, forensic neuropsychology can be regarded as a hybrid, combining neuropsychological science and practice with forensic science and practice (Heilbronner,
2004). Because of the frequency of litigation following work-related injuries, neuropsychological evaluations of individuals who have been injured
at work are commonly forensic in nature. Neuropsychologists who evaluate such individuals or otherwise consult on such cases are well served by
being prepared for forensic involvement. Readers will also find the chapter
on neuropsychological independent medical examinations (IMEs) (Bush &
Heilbronner, Chapter 10, this volume) relevant to the present topic.

EDUCATION AND TRAINING

At present, there are no formal doctoral or postdoctoral training programs
in forensic neuropsychology. Furthermore, there is no board certification in
forensic neuropsychology requiring a competency evaluation by one's peers.
Those who currently engage in the practice of forensic neuropsychology
typically begin their careers as clinical psychologists or neuropsychologists,
evaluating and treating patients with various central nervous system (CNS)
disorders. Their first involvement in a legal case often arises as treaters—that
is, after having evaluated or treated patients and serving as their advocate or
as fact witnesses. Over time, they may be retained as consultants or experts
in legal cases where brain injury is at issue. When neuropsychologists serve
as experts, they are an advocate of the facts of the case. There are significant differences in the roles of treating clinicians versus forensic experts
(Greenberg & Shuman, 1997) which will not be the focus of this chapter.
Yet, it is important for clinicians who engage in forensic neuropsychological practice to recognize that there are important role differences between
being a treater and an expert and between clinical and forensic assessments
(Greiffenstein, 2008; Melton, Petrila, Poythress, & Slobogin, 2007).

Neuropsychologists operating in the forensic arena need to be familiar with various psycholegal issues and terms. As an example, it is advisable that forensic practitioners know and understand terms such as the Frye Rule (*Frye v. United States*, 1923) and Daubert proceedings (*Daubert v. Merrell Dow Pharmaceuticals, Inc.*, 1993). Of course, this does not mean that neuropsychologists act as attorneys. They should remain uninvolved in the outcome of the case and should not be caught up in advocating for one side or another. The goal is to advocate and represent oneself and one's opinion in the most objective and scientifically valid manner possible. Toward this end, it is important to be familiar with the literature on the subject in question, whether it is a traumatic brain injury (TBI) case, electrical injury (EI), cerebral anoxia, or some other condition or topic. It is also critical to be up to date with the most psychometrically sound versions of tests, norms, and other tools of the trade—and to be able to explain to the triers of fact in a way that they can understand—the meaning of the neuropsychological assessment results.

REFERRAL PROCESS

Forensic referrals typically start with a phone call from a party (e.g., attorney, case manager, paralegal) interested in retaining the services of a neuropsychologist. The interested party often begins by asking about availability and fees, and requesting a current copy of your curriculum vitae. In this initial contact, attorneys often make an effort to impress on neuropsychologists the case from their point of view; some call this process advocacy and others, impression management. When accepting a forensic referral, it is important that you feel confident that you can serve as a consultant and potential expert witness because you possess the requisite credentials and experience to assist the trier of fact. You should also be mindful that you are not an advocate for the side (plaintiff or defense) that has retained you. Attorneys are advocates for their client. You are not. You are an advocate of the facts and for the science of neuropsychology.

During the initial contact, it is often helpful to clarify the nature of the referral question to determine whether this is the type of case you are qualified to accept. Examinees who speak English as a second language may present with some challenging assessment decisions that may better be addressed by a neuropsychologist proficient in both languages (Judd et al., 2009). For example, if the potential examinee is bilingual (i.e., speaks both Spanish and English), it may be helpful to gather additional information, such as country of origin, degree of acculturation, and level of education, that may help with determinations about your competence to perform the evaluation.

Refusal of a referral may result in foregoing some practice revenues in the future, but selective acceptance of forensic referrals should be a guiding principle. Adhering to this guideline will not only assist the trier of fact but also reduce the potential fallout to one's credibility later at the time of deposition or appearance at trial. It is easier to deal with the loss of a referral than a loss of one's credibility.

Once the referral has been accepted, a discussion with the referral source will take place. During this discussion, it is important to address the following: payment of fees, availability for the examination and duration of the evaluation, any associated travel costs if the exam is to be conducted away from the office, no show or late cancel fees, receipt of records, whether the examinee has undergone a similar exam, and if so, tests administered, and, if possible, test results. In situations where the neuropsychologist has been retained by the defense, the examiner will sometimes be informed that the plaintiff's attorney has set forth conditions for the independent neuropsychological examination, such as providing in advance a complete list of all tests to be administered, or the right to be present and/or record the exam. These provisions can sometimes be "deal breakers," but they do not necessarily have to be. When encountering these demands, it is always prudent to be respectful but informative and firm.

Any form of recording of the evaluation should be discouraged. Nonetheless, sometimes after careful discussion, the attorneys for both sides will "stipulate" or agree that the interview may be recorded, but not the test procedures because of security concerns. Also, the demand for a list of tests often falls by the wayside after it is explained that it is not possible to say with any degree of confidence which tests will be administered, as it depends on the examinee's complaints during the interview or at the time of the exam. If the attorneys fail to reach an agreement on this point, then the neuropsychologist may consider presenting a "test battery" representing a universe of tests from which some or none of the tests may be selected. Remember, you are the expert retained to offer opinions, and in order to do so, and to have confidence in your opinions, you need reliable and valid data. Threats to test reliability and validity compromise your opinions.

In pediatric referrals, it is important to request that a parent or an adult who is familiar with the child attend the exam to provide important historical information as well as express any current psychosocial concerns. In adult referrals, it is often important to identify collateral sources (e.g., spouse, siblings, relatives, friends) who may provide additional behavioral data concerning the examinee. Collateral sources of information are often readily available when consulting on plaintiff cases, but are often not permitted when examining a plaintiff at the request of the defense. In fact, some plaintiff lawyers will attempt to limit the scope of your interview or examination procedures by refusing to allow their client to answer questions pertaining to the incident before the court or not allowing them to fill out test forms.

INTERVIEW AND REVIEW OF RECORDS

The foundation of the forensic neuropsychological evaluation rests on a comprehensive and thorough interview and review of records. The information pursued should address not only premorbid factors, such as medical, psychosocial, educational, and work histories, but also the objective evidence and examinee's recall of events surrounding an alleged incident, interim life events, and level of current functioning. According to the American Academy of Clinical Neuropsychology (AACN) Practice Guidelines for Neuropsychological Assessment and Consultation (2007; hereafter referred to as the AACN Guidelines), "A clinical interview and gathering background information, often including neuroimaging or other medical findings, is critical" (p. 219). In pediatric cases, interviewing a parent is essential; in adult examinations, collateral interviews with other family members, relatives, and/or friends may yield useful information not otherwise available from a single interview with the examinee.

MEDICAL/PSYCHIATRIC HISTORY

Medical history should include questions relative to any prenatal or perinatal complications, prematurity, Apgar scores, postnatal complications, and hospitalization. Developmental milestones may suggest delays in development as well as early childhood illnesses (e.g., frequent ear infections with tube placement), which could disrupt maturation and skill acquisition. The medical history should also explore for evidence of prior medical conditions or experiences (e.g., head injury, substance abuse, toxic exposure, hypertension, diabetes, seizures, or psychiatric disorder) that could serve as moderating variables to influence current test performance. The examiner should also obtain information on the medical history of first-degree relatives (i.e., parents, grandparents, siblings). A history of physical and/or sexual abuse and neglect should be explored. Handedness, especially left-handedness, may be important, especially if there is no family history of left-handedness; in this case it may suggest a condition of "pathological left-handedness," a phenotype for possible cerebral reorganization.

EDUCATIONAL AND VOCATIONAL HISTORY

It is important to review academic records, with special attention to standardized scores from annual state testing, teacher comments, and presence or absence of learning difficulties including learning disability (LD) or attention-deficit/hyperactivity disorder (ADHD). The examiner should inquire if the examinee has ever repeated a grade, received special education services, had tutoring, or dropped out of school. Asking about favorite and least favorite subjects can often provide useful insight into potential areas of academic strengths and weaknesses, which may be reflected in current test scores. Also important is inquiry about the individual's grade point average (GPA) and how it compares to current scores on measures of intellectual and academic functioning. A reported GPA < 3.00 in the context of above-average scores may indicate a person who underachieved in school. The results of college or graduate school entrance exams (e.g., SAT, GRE) may also offer valuable information about premorbid or optimal cognitive abilities. Family education in first-degree relatives may also be informative and may shed light on learning difficulties or ADHD.

TESTING

Test Selection

Test selection tends to be dictated by the nature of the referral question but generally includes tests of various cognitive and behavioral domains including attention, learning and memory, intelligence, academic skills, visuospatial abilities, language, sensory-motor skills, executive functions, behavior, personality, and effort. Testing should typically include at least two measures of each domain for purposes of convergent validity (AACN Guidelines, 2007). Short forms of certain tests (i.e., Wechsler Abbreviated Scale of Intelligence, Wisconsin Card Sorting Test, 64 card version, Wechsler Memory Scale, Third Edition, Abbreviated) may be appropriate when time or presenting condition precludes a more extensive sampling of behavior. Test selection should also be guided by reliability and validity considerations, as well as normative standards relative to an examinee's personal characteristics (i.e., age, gender, and sociocultural background). Selection of co-normed tests allows for comparison of performance differences between two or more cognitive domains (e.g., attention vs. memory, intellectual functions vs. memory). Determining whether to continue to use a current version of a test once a revision of the test has been published should be based on consideration of multiple factors, including the psychometric properties of both versions for the purposes of the present evaluation (Bush, 2010). Additional guidelines for test selection are articulated in the *Standards for Educational and Psychological Testing* (American Educational Research Association, American Psychological Association, and National Council on Measurement in Education, 1999).

Because the assessment of effort is a critical component for determining credibility of test performance, and because effort often fluctuates over the course of the examination process, it is important that this aspect of performance be sampled throughout the assessment. According to the AACN Guidelines (2007), "Approaches for assessing motivation and effort include: behavioral observations from interviews or testing of behaviors

such as avoidance, resistance, hostility, and lack of cooperation; examination of the pattern of performance using traditional neuropsychological
measures; identification of unexpected or unusually slow and/or impaired
levels of performance; identification of cognitive profiles that do not fit with
known patterns typical of brain disorders; and consideration of suspect
performance on objective measures of effort" (p. 201). The AACN Consensus Conference Statement on the Neuropsychological Assessment of Effort,
Response Bias, and Malingering (Heilbronner, Sweet, Morgan, Larrabee,
& Millis, 2009) further describes the parameters associated with this particular component of the neuropsychological assessment process.

Technicians

Some examiners utilize technicians to administer and score psychometric
tests. This is an acceptable practice supported by both the AACN (1999) and
the National Academy of Neuropsychology (Axelrod et al., 2000b; Puente
et al., 2006). Some professionals have argued that a potential drawback to
this approach is that the neuropsychologist loses out on an opportunity to
directly observe the examinee's approach to tasks, responses to failure, and
various other qualitative aspects of test behavior that complement the assessment process. Observing how a subject achieves a certain score or attains a
solution can often add rich information above and beyond the quantitative
features of the exam. However, qualified technicians are typically able to
assess qualitative aspects of performance. Using a technician may also help
reduce possible bias associated with the party (e.g., plaintiff vs. defense)
who has retained the services of the neuropsychologist because the technician has not reviewed records in advance, may not know the particulars of
the case, and usually has little interest in the outcome of the case.

Interpreters

Whenever possible, the use of interpreters should be avoided because they
introduce an added element of variability into the examination process and
represent a deviation from standardized test administration procedures.
However, there may be occasions when the only viable option is to proceed with an interpreter. Under this scenario, examiners should attempt to
secure the services of an independent certified interpreter and meet with
the interpreter prior to the exam to explain procedural issues (e.g., that the
instructions should be read verbatim and the examinee's responses repeated
literally) and clarify roles. Utilizing family members as interpreters is not
recommended but may be unavoidable in some situations. Reports of neuropsychological evaluations conducted via an interpreter should describe
both the deviations from standardized test administration and the usual
threats to validity (i.e., appropriateness, or lack thereof, of the tests administered and normative database).

Scoring and Interpretation

After all tests have been administered, neuropsychologists (or their technicians) usually require several hours to score the tests, and then it takes neuropsychologists additional time to interpret the results. This component of the evaluation forms part of the objective database on which experts form their opinions. With few exceptions (e.g., accommodations for persons with significant disabilities), scoring and interpretation should adhere to the guidelines provided in published test manuals, where such materials exist, and may involve automated scoring and interpretive services, with careful attention to data entry. If an initial review of the data reveals scores that are inconsistent with most of the other test results, then the examiner should rescore and recheck score transformations to confirm or disconfirm the accuracy of the test data.

It is typically prudent to utilize normative data that most closely match the examinee's characteristics (i.e., culture, race, gender, age, and educational level), when such data exist. However, in some instances comparisons to a general adult population or other group may be more appropriate than comparison to the examinee's demographic peers. According to the AACN Guidelines (2007), "In general, tests published with large stratified normative samples—"Heaton norms" (Heaton, Avitable, Grant, & Matthews, 1999) . . . provide a sound foundation for accurate interpretation" (p. 220). There may be times when previous tests that are the same or similar have been administered. Comparing current scores to previous ones can provide some useful information in tracking the effects or recovery trajectory of the presenting condition (i.e., whether it be recovery from an acute neurologic event such as a cerebrovascular accident or a TBI or to evaluate treatment efficacy), or lack thereof. Assessment of ethnic minority populations requires special consideration. For example, it is prudent not to assume that so-called nonverbal tests are more culture-fair or culturally unbiased (Rosselli & Ardila, 2003). According to the AACN Guidelines (2007), "The inferences made by neuropsychologists in interpreting the evaluation findings include judgments regarding: (1) the nature of the cognitive deficits or patterns of strengths and weaknesses, (2) the likely sources of, or contributors to, these deficits or patterns, and (3) their relation to the examinee's presenting problems and implications for treatment and prognosis" (p. 223).

FEEDBACK TO ATTORNEY

Once the available records, including deposition transcripts, have been reviewed, the examinee interviewed, and tests administered, scored, and interpreted, the examiner is typically asked to provide some preliminary opinions. This is a critical moment in the attorney–consultant relationship.

At such times, it is incumbent upon neuropsychologists to provide not only their opinions but also the basis for the opinions, their reasoning, and the limits, if any, of their opinions. Probably one of the biggest mistakes neophyte forensic neuropsychologists make at such moments is not knowing when or how to limit their opinions. For example, if one is going to provide an opinion on toxic encephalopathy, then one should be prepared to discuss mechanisms of pathophysiology in both animal and human models, the dose required for lethality, half-life, and other matters. It is not unusual at this point for retaining attorneys to probe the nexus of the opinions in order to determine if any opinions can be broadened, modified, or excluded. These attorney probes are frequently cloaked in hypothetical statements, "Doctor, would you agree with Mr. Jones' employer who believes he can continue to work?" or "Would you agree with the life care planner that Ms. Smith will need 24-hour attendant care for the rest of her life?" Neuropsychologists should be careful to not allow the attorney to influence their opinions. Opinions relating to vocational functioning and care needs should be considered thoughtfully, and the foundations for opinions on these matters should be clearly stated.

When giving feedback to retaining attorneys, neuropsychologists are an advocate of the science (e.g., the facts of the case) and not for the retaining party or examinee. Neuropsychologists performing forensic evaluations in the context of work-related injuries base opinions on sound empirical evidence and make a point to be aware of potential biases. It takes years to build credibility but seconds to destroy it by adopting anything other than an unbiased and comprehensive approach to the question at hand. It is also perfectly reasonable, and frequently warranted, to recognize the limits of one's opinions and knowledge base and to inform the retaining attorney, "I don't know the answer to that question." At some point, feedback to the attorney commonly includes an analysis and critique of the opposing expert's methodology, test data, and/or report, conclusions, and recommendations.

WRITTEN REPORT

In our experience, written reports in forensic neuropsychology are quite varied, but they are often longer and more detailed than reports from clinical practice. This difference is because of the higher demands placed on the expert in terms of thoroughness, consideration of alternative hypotheses and theories, as well as the amount of time spent in review and consultation. According to Greiffenstein and Cohen (2005), the amount of detail should "include enough to establish important facts or track essential inferences; it should not include all of the neurocognitive or psychological observations that could be made" (p. 61). Forensic reports differ from clinical reports in terms of content as well as length (Greiffenstein & Cohen, 2005). For example, forensic reports are written for individuals with administrative and legal backgrounds (e.g.., judges and lawyers) and address legal issues such as causation, damages, and competency. Clinical reports are typically less focused on such issues. Language in forensic reports, like clinical reports, should limit the use of technical terms. Invoking a specific DSM-IV multiaxial diagnosis may be less helpful than summarizing examinee behavior and test results in descriptive, probabilistic statements. When providing expert opinions in civil litigation, neuropsychological opinions must be "more likely than not" or "within a reasonable degree of neuropsychological certainty," both of which assume a ≥51% level of confidence.

DEPOSITIONS

Neuropsychologists who provide forensic consultation and expert services are eventually deposed. Prior to deposition, it is common to receive a deposition subpoena identifying all of the documents that are to be brought to the deposition. However, there is no need to be intimidated by such subpoenas because deposition subpoenas, at times, represent a shotgun approach to document production. That is, "ask for everything and get something." If no written request is provided (i.e., list of all depositions and trials in which you have testified as an expert in the last five years), then there is no need to create and bring such a document. (Of note, experts are required to keep a list of previous testimony for federal cases.)

Depositions are recorded by a court reporter and may be videotaped. Depositions are taken by the opposing party's attorney to determine all of the opinions that the expert intends to give at the time of trial and the bases for those opinions. According to Federal Rules of Evidence (FRE) #702, experts are qualified based on their education, training, or experience (Federal Rules of Evidence for the United States Courts and Magistrates, 1987). Experts are typically asked how much of their practice is devoted to medical–legal matters, ratio of plaintiff versus defense retention, and occasionally what percentage of their income is derived from forensic practice. These types of questions are foundational to infer or suggest potential bias. It is important to be honest when responding, consistent with the oath "to tell the truth, the whole truth, and nothing but the truth." It is also common to be asked to bring the entire examinee file, including records and depositions reviewed, raw test data and test protocols, handwritten notes, billing statements, and attorney correspondence, including e-mails.

Experts may be asked to attach their entire file (including raw data) as an exhibit to the deposition. This practice should be avoided whenever possible due to potential threats to test security. Rather, it is often possible to reach an agreement whereby the neuropsychologist copies and mails the raw test data directly to the identified opposing neuropsychologist, and to have them do likewise. If an agreement cannot be worked out, then the attorneys may have to go to court for a motion to compel. If this happens, the expert can provide the retaining attorney with a Declaration citing the basis for invoking the privilege, and, where applicable, citing relevant jurisdictional law, and providing copies of position papers as exhibits to the Declaration in support of keeping the raw test data out of the public domain. If the court orders release of the raw test data to the opposing attorney, then the expert must follow the court order but can request that distribution of the materials be limited and the records sealed and/or returned to the expert following conclusion of the case.

Toward the end of depositions, it is common for experts to be asked whether they have given all of the opinions that are intended to be rendered at the time of trial. An appropriate answer is to state that while all of the main opinions that have been considered to that point have been provided, there may be other opinions that have not yet been considered but that may come up at the time of trial based on the nature of the questions asked. It is also important for experts to add that they will continue to be available to review any additional records, including deposition transcripts, which may be sent, and should any opinions change, then availability would be made for another deposition.

Questioning during depositions is typically conducted to elicit Yes/No responses. However, sometimes a question will not permit a simple Yes/No response, and it is entirely acceptable to state that you cannot answer the question as phrased, which will usually lead the attorney to rephrase the question. If an attorney persists with efforts to elicit a Yes/No response, it may be helpful to state, for the benefit of all parties present, that "it would be misleading to simply state 'yes' or 'no' in response to the question." Experts have a duty to explain their opinions clearly and to not let their opinions be distorted.

The deposition transcript does not reveal if an expert paused and reflected prior to answering or responded immediately, so it is appropriate and often advisable to take all the time needed to answer questions. Neuropsychologists benefit from listening to the questions and formulating a concise answer. It is generally advisable to not volunteer information. When questions are not understood, it is appropriate to ask the attorney to rephrase it. There may be times when an expert provides an answer to a question that is slightly different from an answer provided to a similar question earlier in the deposition. Under these circumstances, the opposing attorney may attempt to discredit the expert by saying, "Well, doctor, you now testified you 'studied X.' But earlier when I asked you if you had 'studied X' you said no. So that wasn't true, was it, doctor?" These alleged discrepancies are often a product of semantics. Thus, rather than arguing with the attorney, the word meanings (e.g., "studied") should be clarified.

If it appears there was a misunderstanding due to semantics, then admit the discrepancy with a comment like, "Well, earlier when you asked me if I had 'studied *X*' I interpreted that to mean if I had ever published any studies of *X*, which I have not. But if by 'studied' you mean read published articles on *X*, then that is true."

Neuropsychologists often benefit from taking breaks throughout the deposition. This practice is especially relevant for depositions that last many hours or an entire day. The opposing attorney will not typically offer to provide a break, so the expert must periodically request breaks.

TRIAL TESTIMONY

Providing testimony at trial can be anxiety provoking, especially the cross-examination component. However, adequate preparation can help reduce any pretrial anxiety, though probably not eliminate it entirely. The deposition serves as the template for the cross examination by the opposing attorney, so reviewing the deposition transcript can be a valuable part of trial preparation. It is important to establish procedural guidelines with the retaining attorney pertaining to preparation, payment, and appearance. For example, try to establish the date for testimony well in advance (i.e., 7 days) of the appearance. Request payment in full on the account for the time spent on the case to date, estimated hours for trial preparation, and trial appearance prior to (e.g., at least 72 hours) the scheduled appearance. This way, after leaving the courtroom, there is no outstanding balance due on the account. Failure to demand payment in full prior to providing testimony, with attempts to bill after the trial appearance, often results in payment being delayed, reduced, or withheld.

Forensic neuropsychologists do not accept a work-related injury case on a lien. Rather, neuropsychologists with forensic experience create Professional Service Agreements that outline fees, services, and conditions of payment. In the case of a dispute where the retaining attorney either refuses to pay, or denies ever retaining the neuropsychologist, then the co-signed Professional Service Agreement will go a long way in rendering a court judgment in the neuropsychologist's favor.

RELEVANT FORENSIC ISSUES

A number of issues customarily arise in forensic cases, and it is important to shed light on a few of them: (1) the effects of third-party observers; (2) release of raw test data; and (3) the assessment of effort. Each of these issues has been discussed extensively elsewhere. What follows is a very brief explanation of the critical issues and recommended methods for management.

The Effects of Third-Party Observers

The presence of third-party observers during the administration of formal test procedures is inconsistent with recommendations put forth in the *Standards for Educational and Psychological Testing* (American Educational Research Association et al., 1999; American Psychological Association, 1992) that the psychological testing environment be distraction free. Standardized test manuals, statements from the developers of psychological tests, and several neuropsychological organizations (American Academy of Clinical Neuropsychology, 2001; Axelrod et al., 2000a) have specifically stated that, with few exceptions, third-party observers should be excluded from the examination room. The Canadian Psychological Association has adopted a strong position on this matter and posted the following Policy Statement on their website in 2009: "It is not permissible for involved third parties to be physically or electronically present during the course of neuropsychological or similar psychological evaluations of a patient or plaintiff. Exceptions to this policy are only permissible when in the sole professional opinion of the assessing psychologist, based on their clinical judgment and expertise, that a third party would allow more useful assessment data to be obtained. Typical examples may include the inclusion of a parent or caregiver until a full rapport is gained. The presence of these observers should be cited as a limitation to the validity of the assessment."

One of the most important reasons that third-party observation is discouraged is because of the reliance on normative data. Neuropsychological test measures have not been standardized in the presence of an observer; therefore, the presence of an observer introduces an unknown variable into the testing environment. Third-party presence can prevent the examinee's performance from being compared to established norms, thereby potentially precluding valid interpretation of the test results (McCaffrey, 2005; McCaffrey, Fisher, Gold, & Lynch, 1996). Furthermore, if an observer is present for a forensic evaluation or for purposes of a second opinion and was not present during a previous clinical evaluation, the situations would be different. This could create an adversarial atmosphere, thereby increasing the motivational effects related to secondary gain. This possibility is particularly relevant when the observer is an "interested party" (e.g., attorney) in the outcome of a lawsuit. The presence of a third party, including electronic recording devices (e.g., audio or videotape), also raises test security problems, which further supports the avoidance of such practices (McCaffrey, 2005).

Release of Raw Test Data

In the course of neuropsychological practice, particularly in forensic cases, neuropsychologists may receive requests from attorneys for copies of test protocols (e.g., raw test data). The American Psychological Association's

Ethical Principles of Psychologists and Code of Conduct (2002) makes it very clear that release of test materials to a nonpsychologist is a violation because it may place confidential test procedures in the public domain and raise a risk of making the tests available to persons unqualified to interpret them. As stated in an official position statement of the National Academy of Neuropsychology (Axelrod et al., 2000c), "the potential disclosure of test instructions, questions, and items . . . can enable individuals to determine or alter their responses in advance of actual examination. Thus, a likely and foreseeable consequence of uncontrolled test release is widespread circulation, leading to the opportunity to determine answers in advance, and to manipulation of test performance."

One example is the airline pilot who has a stroke with significant cognitive compromise and who is making an effort to return to work (e.g., flying commercial flights). With advanced knowledge of the correct responses, the results may suggest that he has recovered or at least does not have significant impairments that would preclude him from returning to work. Yet, prominent deficits (e.g., visual neglect, slow reaction time, problems processing information rapidly), may remain, thereby placing the life of himself, his crew, and passengers at risk. Another scenario, which occurs more commonly in the forensic cases, is the examinee who gains access to symptom validity measures (including the theoretical underpinnings of forced choice tests) and who can then be more likely to circumvent methods for detecting test manipulation. They may perform well on measures of effort (to show adequate response validity), but then purposefully do poorly on other measures as a means by which to demonstrate cognitive impairment.

When requests to release test data or recorded examinations place neuropsychologists in possible conflict with ethical principles, it is incumbent upon them to take reasonable steps to maintain test security and thereby fulfill professional obligations. Solutions for problematic requests for the release of test material are possible (e.g., see NAN position statements, Axelrod et al., 2000c).

The Assessment of Effort

Effort exerts significant influence on test performance. In fact, the impact of effort on test performance is probably the most intensely investigated area of research in forensic neuropsychology; it is also one of the most hotly contested issues that arises in litigation. Quite simply, the evaluation of effort is critical in forensic cases (Bush et al., 2005). In the absence of effort testing, the validity of the test results must rest on clinical judgment that has been shown to be not much better than chance (Faust, 1995; Faust, Hart, Guilmette, & Arkes, 1988; Heaton, Chelune, & Lehman, 1978). In 2009, a consensus panel of neuropsychologists created a consensus statement summarizing the importance of evaluating effort throughout the examination process (Heilbronner et al., 2009).

Symptom validity testing may incorporate both free-standing and embedded effort measures to evaluate examinee effort. Within cognitive domains, forced-choice testing has been the predominant method, incorporating tests such as the Word Memory Test, Test of Memory Malingering, and the Victoria Symptom Validity Test. Embedded measures, such as the Reliable Digit Span and the Finger Tapping Test, have also added incremental validity. The MMPI-2 has been the primary instrument utilized to investigate the validity of somatic and psychological symptom reporting. Although the traditional MMPI-2 validity scales have shown sensitivity to overreporting of psychiatric disturbance (e.g., F scale), underreporting of normal human frailties (e.g., L and K scales), and variable or systematic response biases (e.g., VRIN and TRIN), the Fake Bad Scale (FBS; Lees-Haley, English, & Glenn, 1991), which was renamed the Symptom Validity Scale (SVS) in the MMPI-2 RF, has shown superiority in identifying symptom overreporting along a physical dimension. Over the past few years, several additional MMPI-2 specialty scales for investigating effort and symptom reporting have been empirically derived. These scales include the Response Bias Scale (RBS; Gervais, Ben-Porath, Wygant, & Green, 2007), Henry–Heilbronner Index (HHI; Henry, Heilbronner, Mittenberg, & Enders, 2006), and Malingered Mood Disorder Scale (MMDS; Henry, Heilbronner, Mittenberg, Enders, & Stanczak, 2008).

The motivation to exhibit suboptimal effort may be observed under conditions of external incentives (i.e., personal injury litigation or disability claims) or under conditions with no known external incentives, as in factitious disorder. Research has also shown evidence of insufficient effort in clinical patients with no known external incentive to perform poorly (i.e., nonepileptic seizures; Williamson, Drane, & Stroup, 2007).

There has been considerable debate within the neuropsychological community as to the meaning of poor effort. Discussions have typically invoked conscious and/or unconscious determinants to explain the reasons underlying poor effort. Because further clarification may prove to be quite difficult, if not impossible, to achieve, there is general agreement in the neuropsychological community that when effort indicators are positive (indicating insufficient effort), the examinee's performance is judged to be noncredible and therefore any opinions derived from the data would be limited in reliability and validity. In the absence of external incentives, performance on tests of effort does not appear to be unduly influenced by psychological factors such as depression (Rohling, Green, Allen, & Iverson, 2002) or physical factors such as chronic pain (Meyers & Diep, 2000). Effort tests also tend to be fairly insensitive to a variety of neurologic conditions, including TBI (Green, Rohling, Lees-Haley, & Allen, 2001) and stroke (Green & Allen, 1999). Neuropsychologists engaged in forensic practice and professional organizations (e.g., American Academy of Clinical Neuropsychology, 2007; Bush et al., 2005) generally agree that the assessment of effort is a critical component of the neuropsychological assessment process, and failure to include measures to assess effort represents a serious omission that should be avoided.

SUMMARY

This chapter provides the reader with useful information that will assist with preparation in becoming a neuropsychological expert in cases involving work-related injury. Good clinical practice provides a solid foundation for good forensic practice. Thus, it is critical that forensic experts be familiar with the best methods of practice in clinical neuropsychology in general and remain objective in their approach to assessment and interpretation of the data. Education, consultation, and experience in forensic activities further solidify the foundation for achieving competent forensic practice. Representing oneself and one's opinions in an honest and unimpassioned manner and not getting caught up in the outcome of the case is the best way to ensure a long career as a forensic expert.

REFERENCES

American Academy of Clinical Neuropsychology. (1999). Policy on the use of non-doctoral-level personnel in conducting clinical neuropsychological evaluations. *The Clinical Neuropsychologist, 13,* 385.

American Academy of Clinical Neuropsychology. (2001). Policy statement on the presence of third party observers in neuropsychological assessments. *The Clinical Neuropsychologist, 15*(4), 433–439.

American Academy of Clinical Neuropsychology. (2007). American Academy of Clinical Neuropsychology (AACN) practice guidelines for neuropsychological assessment and consultation. *The Clinical Neuropsychologist, 21*(2), 209–231.

American Educational Research Association, American Psychological Association, and National Council on Measurement in Education. (1999). *Standards for educational and psychological testing.* Washington, DC: Author.

American Psychological Association. (1992). Ethical principles of psychologists and code of conduct. *American Psychologist, 47,* 1597–1611.

American Psychological Association. (2002). Ethical principles of psychologists and code of conduct. *American Psychologist, 57*(12), 1060–1073.

Axelrod, B., Barth, J., Faust, D., Fisher, J., Heilbronner, R., Larrabee, G., et al. (2000a). Presence of third party observers during neuropsychological testing: Official statement of the National Academy of Neuropsychology. Approved May 15, 1999. *Archives of Clinical Neuropsychology, 15*(5), 379–380.

Axelrod, B., Heilbronner, R., Barth, J., Larrabee, G., Faust, D., Pliskin, N., et al. (2000b). The use of neuropsychology test technicians in clinical practice: Official statement of the National Academy of Neuropsychology. *Archives of Clinical Neuropsychology, 15,* 381–382.

Axelrod, B., Heilbronner, R., Barth, J., Larrabee, G., Faust, D., Pliskin, N., et al. (2000c). Test security: Official position statement of the National Academy of Neuropsychology. Approved October 5, 1999. *Archives of Clinical Neuropsychology, 15*(5), 383–386.

Bush, D. (2003). On the practice of forensic neuropsychology. In G. L. Lamberty, J. C. Courtney, & R. L. Heilbronner (Eds.), *The practice of clinical neuropsychology.* Lisse, Netherlands: Swets & Zeitlinger.

Bush, S. S. (2010). Determining whether or when to adopt new versions of psychological and neuropsychological tests: Ethical and professional considerations. *The Clinical Neuropsychologist, 24*(1), 7–16.

Bush, S. S., Ruff, R. M., Troster, A. I., Barth, J. T., Koffler, S. P., Pliskin, N. H., et al. (2005). Symptom validity assessment: Practice issues and medical necessity NAN Policy and Planning Committee. *Archives of Clinical Neuropsychology, 20*(4), 419–426.

Daubert v. Merrell Dow Pharmaceuticals, Inc. (509 U.S. 579 1993).

Faust, D. (1995). The detection of deception. *Neurology Clinics, 13*(2), 255–265.

Faust, D., Hart, K., Guilmette, T. J., & Arkes, H. R. (1988). Neuropsychologists' capacity to detect adolescent malingerers. *Professional Psychology: Research and Practice, 19*, 508–515.

Federal Rules of Evidence for the United States Courts and Magistrates. (1987). *Section 702.* St. Paul, MN: West Publishing Company.

Frye v. United States, 293 F. 1013 (D.C. Cir 1923).

Gervais, R. O., Ben-Porath, Y. S., Wygant, D. B., & Green, P. (2007). Development and validation of a Response Bias Scale (RBS) for the MMPI-2. *Assessment, 14*(2), 196–208.

Green, P., & Allen, L. M. (1999). *Performance of neurologic patients on the Word Memory Test and Computerized Assessment of Response Bias (CARB): Supplement to the WMT and CARB '97 Manuals.* Durnham, NC: Cognistat.

Green, P., Rohling, M. L., Lees-Haley, P. R., & Allen, L. M., III. (2001). Effort has a greater effect on test scores than severe brain injury in compensation claimants. *Brain Injury, 15*(12), 1045–1060.

Greenberg, S. A., & Shuman, D. W. (1997). Irreconcilable conflict between therapeutic and forensic roles. *Professional Psychology: Research and Practice, 28*, 50–57.

Greiffenstein, M. F. (2008). Basics of forensic neuropsychology. In J. E. Morgan & J. H. Ricker (Eds.), *Textbook of clinical neuropsychology* (pp. 905–941). New York: Taylor & Francis.

Greiffenstein, M. F., & Cohen, L. (2005). Neuropsychology and the law: Principles of productive attorney-neuropsychologist relations. In G. J. Larrabee (Ed.), *Forensic neuropsychology: A scientific approach* (pp. 29–91). New York: Oxford University Press.

Heaton, R. K., Avitable, N., Grant, I., & Matthews, C. G. (1999). Further crossvalidation of regression-based neuropsychological norms with an update for the Boston Naming Test. *Journal of Clinical and Experimental Neuropsychology, 21*(4), 572–582.

Heaton, R. K., Chelune, G. J., & Lehman, R. A. (1978). Using neuropsychological and personality tests to assess the likelihood of patient employment. *Journal of Nervous and Mental Disease, 166*(6), 408–416.

Heilbronner, R. L. (2004). A status report on the practice of forensic neuropsychology. *The Clinical Neuropsychologist, 18*(2), 312–326.

Heilbronner, R. L., & Pliskin, N. H. (2003). The value of neuropsychological services in the forensic area. In G. Prigatano & N. Pliskin (Eds.), *Clinical neuropsychology and cost outcome research: A beginning.* Brighton, UK: Psychology Press.

Heilbronner, R. L., Sweet, J. J., Morgan, J. E., Larrabee, G. J., & Millis, S. R. (2009). American Academy of Clinical Neuropsychology Consensus Conference Statement on the neuropsychological assessment of effort, response bias, and malingering. *The Clinical Neuropsychologist, 23*(7), 1093–1129.

Henry, G. K., Heilbronner, R. L., Mittenberg, W., & Enders, C. (2006). The Henry-Heilbronner Index: A 15-item empirically derived MMPI-2 subscale for identifying probable malingering in personal injury litigants and disability claimants. *The Clinical Neuropsychologist, 20*(4), 786–797.

Henry, G. K., Heilbronner, R. L., Mittenberg, W., Enders, C., & Stanczak, S. R. (2008). Comparison of the Lees-Haley Fake Bad Scale, Henry-Heilbronner Index, and restructured clinical scale 1 in identifying noncredible symptom reporting. *The Clinical Neuropsychologist, 22*(5), 919–929.

Judd, T., Capetillo, D., Carrion-Baralt, J., Marmol, L. M., Miguel-Montes, L. S., Navarrete, M. G., et al. (2009). Professional considerations for improving the neuropsychological evaluation of Hispanics: A National Academy of Neuropsychology education paper. *Archives of Clinical Neuropsychology, 24*(2), 127–135.

Larrabee, G. J. (2000). Forensic neuropsychological assessment. In R. D. Vanderploeg (Ed.), *Clinician's guide to neuropsychological assessment* (2nd ed., pp. 301–336). Mahwah, NJ: Erlbaum.

Larrabee, G. J. (Ed.). (2005). *Forensic neuropsychology: A scientific approach.* New York: Oxford University Press.

Lees-Haley, P. R., English, L. T., & Glenn, W. J. (1991). A Fake Bad Scale on the MMPI-2 for personal injury claimants. *Psychological Reports, 68*(1), 203–210.

McCaffrey, R. J. (2005). Some final thoughts and comments regarding the issue of third party observers. *Journal of Forensic Neuropsychology, 4*, 83–91.

McCaffrey, R. J., Fisher, J. M., Gold, B. A., & Lynch, J. K. (1996). Presence of third parties during neuropsychological evaluation. Who is evaluating whom? *Clinical Neuropsychologist, 10*, 435–449.

Melton, G. B., Petrila, J., Poythress, N. G., & Slobogin, C. (2007). *Psychological evaluations for the courts, Third Edition.* New York: Guilford Press.

Meyers, J. E., & Diep, A. (2000). Assessment of malingering in chronic pain patients using neuropsychological tests. *Applied Neuropsychology, 7*(3), 133–139.

Puente, A. E., Adams, R., Barr, W. B., Bush, S. S., Ruff, R. M., Barth, J. T., et al. (2006). The use, education, training and supervision of neuropsychological test technicians (psychometrists) in clinical practice. Official statement of the National Academy of Neuropsychology. *Archives of Clinical Neuropsychology, 21*(8), 837–839.

Rohling, M. L., Green, P., Allen, L. M., & Iverson, G. L. (2002). Depressive symptoms and neurocognitive test scores in patients passing symptom validity tests. *Archives of Clinical Neuropsychology, 17*(3), 205–222.

Rosselli, M., & Ardila, A. (2003). The impact of culture and education on non-verbal neuropsychological measurements: A critical review. *Brain and Cognition, 52*(3), 326–333.

Sweet, J. J. (Ed.). (1999). *Forensic neuropsychology: Fundamentals and practice.* Lisse, Netherlands: Swets & Zeitlinger.

Sweet, J. J., Grote, C., & van Gorp, W. G. (2002). Ethical issues in forensic neuropsychology. In S. S. Bush & M. L. Drexler (Eds.), *Ethical issues in clinical neuropsychology* (pp. 103–133). Lisse, Netherlands: Swets & Zeitlinger.

Williamson, D. J., Drane, D. L., & Stroup, E. S. (2007). Symptom validity tests in the epilepsy clinic. In K. Boone (Ed.), *Detection on noncredible cognitive performance* (pp. 346–365). New York: Guilford Press.

CHAPTER 12

The Behavioral Health Provider as a Participant in the Disability Determination Process
Evaluations, Terminology, and Systems

David W. Lovejoy
Howard J. Oakes

There are clear indications that rates of disability have been increasing. Statistics have indicated that a 20-year-old person is estimated to have a 30% chance of becoming disabled (Social Security Administration, 2003). Estimates have also indicated that between 35 and 46 million Americans could be considered "disabled" at any time (Demeter, Andersson, & Smith, 2001). This increase has become so apparent that authors (Melhorn, Lazarovic, & Roehl, 2005) have analyzed this trend in relation to formal criteria for a health epidemic, emphasizing epidemiologic terms such as outbreak, transmission, causation, links, and diagnosis. The etiologic underpinnings of this phenomenon are thought to be multifactorial and include socioeconomic variables such as aging, national employment rates, family support, and changing legislative and definitional criteria. The latest economic crisis has added another facet to this already complicated picture.

The definitional concept of "disability" differs across settings. For instance, the definition used to determine disability may differ across private and public entities. Moreover, it is possible for a private entity to offer multiple contracts, each with a different definition of "disability." Because disability typically represents a contractual or legal concept, it is rarely established by the behavioral health specialist. Instead, the behavioral health specialist serves as a source of information for those seeking to determine "disability."

Behavioral health specialists, including neuropsychologists, are increasingly recognized as essential for making determinations of impairments, limitations, and restrictions as they apply to behavioral health disability. Private and public entities frequently call on such professionals to provide evaluations and opinions to help understand some of the complex intraindividual and contextual issues involved with respect to the presence of potential work-related impairments.

This chapter describes the roles of behavioral health specialists in helping private and public entities with the process of disability determination, and provides a review of some of the more salient issues that behavioral health specialists may struggle with during this process. The independent psychological/psychiatric/neuropsychological examination is one of the most important methods employed in determining impairments, limitations, and restrictions as they apply to the behavioral health disability setting and is used in this chapter as an avenue through which to understand some of the concepts and processes associated with determination of "disability." Because this chapter focuses on general concepts, the clinician may need to gain a more individualized understanding of the issues surrounding "disability," on a case-by-case basis. The authors of this chapter have experience consulting to private entities about behavioral health issues and their impact on work-related functionality. However, we wish to assert that the opinions offered in this chapter do not necessarily reflect the opinions or procedures of the companies or institutions with which they are or have been associated.

STRUGGLING TO UNDERSTAND "DISABILITY"

From a behavioral health perspective, recent concerns about increasing rates of disability have been particularly salient. A study conducted by the World Health Organization, World Bank, and Harvard University reported that there has been a longstanding tendency to underestimate the burden caused by mental illness in relation to both health and productivity (Murray & Lopez, 1996). The study found that mental illness accounts for over 15% of the burden of disease (both direct and indirect costs) in established market communities such as the United States. When this statistic is seen in perspective, it represents a greater disease burden than if the disease burden were estimated by combining all forms of cancer. Moreover, the study reported that depression is expected to become the leading cause of global disability by the year 2020. Insurance industry statistics related to behavioral health disability claims within the United States have also indicated that there has been a significant increase in such claims. Hurrell and Murphy (1996) observed that claims associated with mental stress composed the fastest growing segment of work-related illness. Statistics from California further revealed that claims related to work stress increased 700% from 1979 to 1988 (California Workers' Compensation Institute, 1990). Finally, Warren (2005) reported a greater than 300% increase in overall behavioral health claims over the past decade.

Over the past decade, the medical and scientific communities have experienced significant expansion related to research and clinical understanding associated with behavioral health conditions. This proliferation has been broadly evident through emphases on the "decade of the brain" followed by the more recent "decade of behavior," the human genome project, and the proliferation of functional neuroimaging techniques (e.g., single photon emission computer tomography, position emission tomography, and functional magnetic resonance imaging) in understanding how behavioral health conditions are manifested and most optimally treated. However, despite growing insights in relation to the identification, diagnosis, and treatment of these conditions, the current corpus of research lacks appropriate depth to help in further elucidating direct relationships between clinical impairment and occupational disability for any particular behavioral health or physical condition. For instance, research has found that, at any particular time, roughly 45% of actively employed individuals suffer from conditions potentially severe enough to warrant the filing of a work-related disability claim (Biddle, Roberts, Rosenman, & Welch, 1998). However, disability statistics indicate that the majority of the individuals who are actively suffering from physical or emotional discomfort adapt and persevere within their jobs and lives, without making a claim of disability (Biddle et al., 1998).

Findings such as these underscore an important multifactorial question within the field of disability that empirical research has not yet been able to clarify. That is, how do *clinical, personality, social, financial, legal, and political variables combine* in a comprehensive fashion for any one person to create a disability? At a basic level, statistics such as these also emphasize the inappropriateness of conceptual models that assume a direct or linear relationship between the simple presence of a symptom or disorder and the downstream experience of work-related impairment and/or disability.

Within the most recent version of the *Diagnostic and Statistical Manual of Mental Disorders* (DSM-IV-TR), the American Psychiatric Association (2000) acknowledged the complex relationship between disorder and disability, stating: " In determining whether an individual meets a specified legal standard (e.g., for competence, criminal responsibility or disability), additional information is usually required beyond that contained in the DSM-IV diagnosis" (p. xxxiii). Empirical studies have supported this contention, finding that neither diagnosis nor specific symptoms effectively predicts work performance/ability (Anthony & Jansen, 1984; Yelin & Cisternas, 1997).

The sociological, psychological, and medical literatures are replete with studies that identify a myriad of predictor variables associated with the risk and potential maintenance of work-related impairment and/or disability. Demographic factors, psychosocial factors, economic factors, contractual and/or entitlement definitions, personality factors, job satisfaction, and symptom presentation have all been identified as possible contributors to complaints of persistent impairment and/or disability (Franche, Frank, & Krause, 2005). Unfortunately, the specific roles, relative contributions, and interactions among these variables, in the development and long-term maintenance of work-related impairments and/or disability, remains poorly understood. Emerging from this body of literature, however, is a clear understanding that a focus on both external and intraindividual variables will likely offer the most complete picture of who may be most vulnerable to developing a disability.

In addition, available explanatory models have not yet proved efficacious in the development and initiation of protocols and methods for early identification, intervention, and treatment for those at risk for persistent disability-related difficulties. As a result, the growing costs to compensation systems (public and private), legal systems, healthcare, work sites (especially in relation to lost productivity), and society as a whole continue to increase.

Claims for disability benefits related to behavioral health conditions may be viewed as particularly challenging for those attempting to adjudicate such claims (Waldron, 2003). In addition to the difficulties associated with understanding how multiple factors interact to predict a general picture of disability, some authors (Hadjistavropoulos & Bieling, 2001; Piechowski, 2006) have noted that the subjective nature of behavioral health complaints also contributes to the overall challenge in evaluating such claims. Indeed, there remains no litmus test or lab assay to determine the existence or nonexistence of a behavioral health condition. There are also no clear empirically based guidelines or models for reliably establishing degree of occupational impairment associated with behavioral health conditions.

At present, a thorough individual evaluation by a behavioral health specialist is considered to be the most comprehensive method for clarifying the often complex and multifactorial presentations of individuals reporting work-related impairments and/or disability secondary to behavioral health conditions. Private and public entities are growing in their understanding that the complexities discussed in this section related to understanding behavioral health impairments and/or disability underscore the need for an individualized assessment approach. The broad goal of such assessments is to examine, at an individual level, variables identified as being important clinical and contextual contributors to the experience of work-related impairment and/or disability (e.g., variables related to symptom constellations, symptom severity, motivation, work setting, economic circumstances, and job satisfaction).

THE INDEPENDENT MEDICAL EXAMINATION
IN BEHAVIORAL HEALTH: FOUNDATIONAL CONCEPTS

In its most basic form, a behavioral health independent medical examination (IME) could be defined as follows: A behavioral health assessment conducted by a behavioral health specialist, not otherwise involved in the care or treatment of the individual, at the request of a third party that is not the behavioral health specialist's general employer (Baum, 2005). In this chapter we employ the conventional uses of the term *IME* as it is employed in a variety of settings. Others might argue that an "independent medical evaluation" by its very terminology is limited to evaluations completed by physicians. Individuals deemed qualified to comment on work-related impairments may be defined by contractual language and/or statute or by the utility of the unique information that they offer; the behavioral health specialist is encouraged to be aware of these issues in any particular case. Although at first blush this definition appears fairly straightforward, within the broad nature of this definition emerge multiple foundational areas worthy of further discussion. These areas, presented in question form, are discussed next.

In what context is the behavioral health IME conducted?

Guidotti (2003) indicated that IMEs are gaining in importance as referral sources increasingly appreciate the advantages of opinions offered by professionals who are not involved in a patient's or claimant's care and that this process can improve adjudication of claims. IMEs are often performed within the context of an adjudication process and/or dispute resolution typically associated with some aspect of employment or work-related functionality. These processes are typically viewed by both the retaining party and the party undergoing a behavioral health IME as having very real financial (e.g., issues related to earning capacity, benefit amount, and/or settlement amount) and personal (e.g., questions of honesty, integrity, and accuracy) consequences. Moreover, an IME may be requested within the ongoing context of a formal legal dispute. As such, the conceptual issues and practical application of services associated with a behavioral health IME are best viewed within the context of a forensic evaluation (Anfang & Wall, 2006; Bush, 2005; Committee on Ethical Guidelines for Forensic Psychologists, 1991). Vore (2007) observed that the critical reasoning associated with a behavioral health IME is most similar to that of forensic personal injury evaluations that involve highly specialized behavioral health knowledge, skills, and techniques.

Within a forensic context, there are multiple issues that the behavioral health specialist should consider prior to entering into an agreement to perform an IME. These evaluations require specialized knowledge as well as specialized procedures that make them distinctly different from clinical evaluations. Guidotti (2003) offered a broad-based description of the basic

326 PROFESSIONAL PRACTICE ISSUES

differences between clinical and forensic behavioral health evaluations. These differences are characterized in relation to nine primary areas: (1) the professional role of the examiner as it differs from that of clinician and/ or patient advocate, (2) a decreased emphasis on diagnosis, (3) the manner in which human behavior is conceptualized within the evaluation, (4) the nature of the work product that follows from the professional relationship, (5) the perceived level of trust/credibility in relation to the individual's responses, (6) the level of proof needed in support of the opinions that arise from the evaluation, (7) the temporal focus of the evaluation, (8) the level of professional and/or ethical accountability, and (9) accurate determination of which party is the client.

It is important that the behavioral health specialist providing an IME maintain familiarity with these issues, as they apply to the IME process. Familiarity with these issues gives rise to more thorough preparation and a form of critical thinking that serves to protect the objectivity of the evaluation and the reliability of resulting conclusions and opinions. Ignoring such issues places the IME process at risk.

Who are potential third parties that may request a behavioral health IME?

The referral source requesting a behavioral health IME often defines the type of IME to be performed. Evaluations that address the topic of disability or employment/work functionality have been described as falling within two broad categories: evaluations related to an individual's inability to work and evaluations related to an individual's capacity to resume or to continue to working (Anfang & Wall, 2006).

The first of these categories encompasses what many practitioners have come to know as the classic disability evaluation. This referral is typically initiated by a government entity such as Social Security or the Veterans Administration, a private insurance company administering disability or workers' compensation insurance, or, more infrequently, an attorney representing a claimant. Referral questions associated with this category typically revolve around the degree of work/employment-related impairment associated with a potential behavioral health condition.

The second category of IME-related evaluations is more typically associated with an individual's desire to maintain employment. For instance, an individual may seek work-related accommodations under the Americans with Disabilities Act (ADA) or may be contesting a work-related dismissal associated with a perceived behavioral health condition. Referral questions in this category may also relate to safety concerns in the workplace. Referrals in this category are typically initiated by an employer, a licensing board, or an attorney representing an individual's interests in association with these matters. These types of evaluations have also been referred to as fitness-for-duty evaluations and return-to-work evaluations.

Issues from both IME categories may comingle. Such an example might include finding, within the context of conducting a disability-related behavioral health IME on behalf of a private insurance company, that an insured is also involved in an administrative action with the employer, in association with perceived threatening behaviors in the workplace. In such situations, examiner role confusion becomes a distinct possibility, with overlapping employment issues and multiple definitions of disability involved. It is essential that evaluators faced with such situations try to maintain clear conceptual boundaries.

How are the concepts of mental health and/or disability typically framed within a definitional and/or legal context?

Considerable areas of ambiguity and complexity exist in relation to definitions of disability and how such definitions address behavioral health conditions. For instance, there are broad contextual differences in how basic concepts such as disability, impairment, and mental health conditions are operationalized from definition to definition. Such differences often stem from whether impairment and/or disability are being viewed from a clinical, administrative, contractual and/or legal, or research-related perspective. Differences also exist depending on whether definitions were drafted from a public policy perspective (e.g., Social Security Disability Insurance, American with Disabilities Act) or from the perspective of a private entity (e.g., long-term disability, short-term disability, individual disability), with public policy definitions typically employing language that is more inclusive. Unfortunately, the majority of disability-related definitions offer little specific guidance for conceptualization and assessment of behavioral health issues. In addition, legal and/or contractual definitions of disability may vary radically depending on the context in which a behavioral health IME is performed.

The typical behavioral health IME includes a thorough evaluation of clinical, motivational, and contextual (e.g., job setting) factors that contribute to an overall understanding of potential functional impairments. From a definitional standpoint, *impairments* are broadly viewed as functional difficulties caused by sickness or injury. Impairments essentially reduce functional capacity by two mechanisms: *limitations* (what a person cannot do) and *restrictions* (what a person should not do). LoCascio (2005) asserted, "A disability decision is a supply and demand decision, where supply is functional capacity as modified by a medical condition; demand is the sum of the required tasks of the occupation; and the balancing procedure is defined in the contract" (p. 115).

In an attempt to operationalize a behavioral health definition of impairment, Anfang and Wall (2006) noted that, in relation to particular referrals, an impairment might be viewed as the inability to perform required occupational duties, secondary to behavioral health symptomatology, with reasonable skill and safety. The behavioral health IME then can be viewed as a forensic functional capacity evaluation with a focus on emotional and/or cognitive functioning.

These definitions are fairly broad and offer little insight in relation to some of the more specific aspects of work or employment-related functionality that an evaluator may be asked to address within the course of an IME. For instance, the behavioral health specialist may be asked to address a variety of questions pertaining to behavioral health impairments (see Table 12.1).

As the concept of "disability" or the state of being "disabled" is viewed by referring sources as a legal and/or contractual concept, it is exceedingly rare for a referral source to ask an evaluator to comment directly on disability. Instead, such determinations are ultimately decided by an adjudicator or the trier of fact. The final opinions and the information gathered during the course of a behavioral health IME are typically considered, sometimes in association with other information, by the adjudicator or trier of fact in relation to the definition of disability in question.

As behavioral health specialists struggle with the boundaries and definitions surrounding the concepts of impairment and disability, it is not uncommon for practitioners to turn to familiar clinical sources for guidance. These sources might include the DSM-IV-TR (American Psychiatric Association, 2000) as well as the multiple adjunctive texts associated with the current version. In addition, the American Medical Association's *Guides for the Evaluation of Permanent Impairment* (American Medical Association, 2008) can be a valuable source of information, particularly in light of the evolving schema regarding the assessment of impairment in behavioral health conditions and pain-related symptomatology. Schultz (2005) observed that, within the clinical realm, definitions of disability typically focus on the identification and quantification of pathology. As the AMA noted, the precise measurability of functional impairments within the realm of behavioral health is often a difficult proposition. Although in its sixth edition (American Medical Association, 2008), the prior edition of the *Guides for the Evaluation of Permanent Impairment* continues to be the guide of choice in many settings.

The DSM-IV-TR actually begins with a questionably appropriate blending of the terms *mental disorder, impairment*, and *disability*. The

■ **TABLE 12.1. Referral Questions Related to Behavioral Health Impairments**

- Is the individual able to work at all?
- Is the individual able to work within his or her current occupation?
- Is there a decrease in work-related efficiency?
- Is there decreased earning capacity?
- Does the individual have the ability to maintain work-essential relationships?
- Is the individual able to function in the workplace safely, without being a danger to others or to self?

American Psychiatric Association (2000) conceptualized a mental disorder as "a clinically significant behavioral or psychological syndrome or pattern that occurs in an individual and that is associated with present distress (e.g., a painful symptom) or disability (i.e., impairment in one or more important areas of functioning) or with a significantly increased risk of suffering death, pain, disability, or an important loss of freedom" (p. xxxi).

Indeed, it is not uncommon in clinical practice to observe a merging of the separate concepts of diagnosis, impairment, and disability. This merging may arise, in part, from the DSM-IV-TR's evolving emphasis on the need for "clinically significant distress or impairment in social, occupational, or other areas of functioning" as a criterion associated with certain diagnoses. An experience of clinically significant distress without evident work-related impairment would fulfill such criteria.

Some clarification is offered later in the DSM-IV-TR that helps to separate clinical thinking as it relates to disability from forensic conceptualizations of disability. Using the DSM-IV-TR categories, criteria, and textual descriptions for forensic purposes poses significant risks that diagnostic information will be misused or misunderstood. Such dangers arise because of the "imperfect fit between the questions of ultimate concern to the law and the information contained in a clinical diagnosis. In determining whether an individual meets a specified legal standard (e.g., for competence, criminal responsibility, or disability), additional information is usually required beyond that contained in the DSM-IV diagnosis. This might include information about the individual's functional impairments and how these impairments affect the particular abilities in question" (p. xxxiii).

The AMA (2001) defined disability as an "alteration of an individual's capacity to meet personal, social or occupational demands or statutory or regulatory requirements because of an impairment" (p. 8). *Impairment*, in turn, was defined as "a loss, loss of use or derangement of any body part, organ system, or organ function" (p. 2). The AMA directly acknowledged some of the difficulties associated with these definitions as they relate to the accurate determination of impairment, secondary to behavioral health conditions. For instance, it was noted that the translation of specific impairments directly and precisely into functional limitations remains a complex and poorly understood process and that there is no available evidence to support any method for assigning a percentage of impairment related to a behavioral health condition. As a result, a broader five-category system was offered to help behavioral health specialists grossly conceptualize behavioral health impairment and associated functional limitations.

What are some common definitions of impairment and disability?

Commonly encountered legal and/or contractual definitions of disability and impairment are provided below. The definitions vary greatly in how disability is defined, with the legal definitions stemming from public policy being noticeably broad. For instance, work-related impairment is not necessarily required to establish a disability under the Americans with Disabilities Act (Americans with Disabilities Act of 1990). Foote (2003) pointed out that an impairment constitutes a disability under the ADA when it adversely affects one or more major life activities and that an ADA evaluation may appropriately begin with an evaluation of nonwork-related activities. At the other end of the spectrum are examples of contractual definitions typically seen within the private disability industry. Such definitions are often quite specific about work-related impairments as a necessary factor in determining disability status.

Satisfying the legal definition for disability in association with one entity may not satisfy the definitional criteria for disability for another entity. Moreover, the thresholds for proof of disability also differ significantly among referral sources. For instance, the threshold of proof of impairment for Social Security Disability claims can be fairly low, with the simple submission of medical records often sufficing (Anfang & Wall, 2006). In contrast, behavioral health IME referrals from the private insurance industry or from employers concerned about workplace safety often require a far more comprehensive evaluation (Anfang & Wall, 2006; Vore, 2007).

• *The Americans with Disabilities Act* The ADA (Americans with Disabilities Act of 1990) includes a three-prong definition of disability: "(1) A physical or mental impairment that substantially limits one or more of the major life activities of such individuals; (2) a record of such an impairment; (3) being regarded as having such an impairment" (29 C.F.R. Chapter XIV, Part 1630.2 (g(1)–(3)). The language associated with the ADA identifies a *qualified individual with a disability* as a person with a disability who has the proper skills, experience, education, and other job-related abilities required by the job that the person either currently holds or wishes to obtain. The ADA directly identifies a range of mental conditions that qualify as a mental impairment. Within the ADA, an *impairment* constitutes disability when it adversely impacts one or more major life activities.

Equal Employment Opportunity Commission (EEOC) regulations make direct reference to the DSM-IV as an appropriate nosology for identification and categorization of mental disorders. The EEOC regulations offer further clarification in relation to mental disorders that may qualify in relation to a mental impairment. For instance, the EEOC language is inclusive of personality disorders, but excludes conditions such as sexual behavior disorders, compulsive gambling, kleptomania, pyromania, and substance abuse disorders resulting from current illegal use of drugs (United States Equal Employment Opportunity Commission, 1997).

• *The Rehabilitation Act of 1973* The Rehabilitation Act prohibits discrimination on the basis of disability in programs conducted by federal agencies, in programs receiving federal financial assistance, in federal employment, and in the employment practices of federal contractors. The standards for determining employment discrimination under the Rehabilitation Act are the same as those used in Title I of the ADA.

• *Social Security Administration* The Social Security Administration defines disability as "the inability to engage in any substantial gainful activity (SGA) by reason of any medically determinable physical or mental impairment(s) which can be expected to result in death or which has lasted or can last for a continuous period of not less than 12 months."

• *Private Disability Insurance: Own Occupation (Hypothetical Definition)* Total Disability is an inability to perform the primary duties of one's occupation because of an injury or sickness.

• *Private Disability Insurance: Any Occupation (Hypothetical Definition)* Total Disability is the inability to perform the primary duties associated with any occupation for which the individual is qualified by education, training, and/or experience.

• *Private Disability Insurance: Catastrophic Disability (Hypothetical Definition)* The individual is unable to perform at least two activities of daily living (ADLs) without assistance.

• *Private Disability Insurance: Residual Disability (Hypothetical Definition)* The individual is unable to perform some work functions and suffers an income loss as a result. Benefits are payable when the individual returns to work after a covered disability and suffers a loss of earnings due to the sickness or injury.

The definitions associated with private disability insurance policies such as those found within group short-term disability (STD), long-term disability (LTD), and individual disability (IDI) may also have a number of provisions associated with them that may be meaningful to the behavioral health specialist during an IME. Different private disability policies may require any combination of the disability criteria (see Table 12.2). Behavioral health conditions may be excluded completely as a basis for disability or limited (typically 24 months) in relation to the amount of time benefits can be collected. Certain policies may also restrict benefits for physical

▪ **TABLE 12.2. Examples of Disability Criteria for Private Disability Policies**

• There is a demonstrated relationship between the work-related impairments and a behavioral health condition.

• An impairing condition has existed for a particular time frame prior to payment of benefits (usually for periods of 30, 60, 90, or 180 days).

• The individual making a claim is under the care of a doctor.

• The treatment is appropriate.

• The condition is not preexisting.

• The individual is not currently working in another occupation.

conditions that have associated impairments that are caused or contributed to by a behavioral health condition.

Who typically conducts a Behavioral Health IME?

Behavioral health IMEs are typically conducted by professionals with doctoral-level training in the field. These professionals fall within two groups: Those who have undergone formal medical training and hold an MD (i.e., psychiatrists) or those who have undergone formal training in clinical psychology and hold PhDs, PsyDs, or EdDs (i.e., clinical psychologists and neuropsychologists).

Both psychologists and psychiatrists are able, through licensure parameters, to practice independently in relation to the diagnosis and treatment of behavioral health conditions. Moreover, the training and credentials of both psychologists and psychiatrists allow for their testimony as experts in court, consistent with Federal Rule of Evidence 702. This rule provides that an expert may give opinion testimony if (1) the testimony will assist the trier of fact to understand evidence or to determine a fact in issue; (2) the specialist has scientific, technical, or other specialized knowledge; and (3) the specialist is qualified based on knowledge, skill experience, training, or education (*United States v. Allen*, 2001). However, issues related to the selection of the type of IME provider may be contractually constrained.

For those parties seeking to obtain or provide IME-related services, it is important to have an *a priori* understanding of the forensic ramifications associated with *Daubert* and the *Daubert* "progeny" as they apply to the structure of IMEs and the potential defense of IME findings and opinions (*Daubert v. Merrell Dow Pharmaceuticals, Inc.*, 1993; *General Electric Company v. Joiner*, 1997; *Kumho Tire Co. Ltd. v. Carmichael*, 1999). In many states these landmark cases form the foundation for the regulation and admissibility of expert testimony by requiring opinions to extend beyond *ipse dixit* ("he himself said it"; based on more than the fact that the expert said it). Post-*Daubert* standards currently require behavioral health specialists to address the scientific validity that forms the bases of their evaluations and opinions. The admissibility of testimony/evidence is particularly salient in disability evaluations because IMEs are often conducted within the context of adversarial relationships (e.g., a claimant suing a disability insurance company or an employee suing an employer) or an ongoing legal dispute.

Although there is a great deal of overlap with regard to areas of expertise with psychologists and psychiatrists (such as the ability to provide diagnostic conceptualizations and develop behavioral health treatment plans), there are also areas of expertise that are both unique and distinct to each of these professions. Such areas of expertise should be considered carefully by retaining parties when selecting an IME provider and by clinicians when considering whether to participate as an independent examiner in a given case.

Careful consideration of disability-related issues and the examinee's clinical presentation are essential prior to selecting a behavioral health specialist as an IME provider for a particular case. The overall goal should to be to obtain a specialist who has the appropriate background and expertise to provide a competent assessment of disability-related issues. Conversely, these are also issues that should be considered carefully by the behavioral health specialist, prior to agreeing to perform an IME to ensure that an IME is of optimal quality (see Table 12.3).

By virtue of their medical training and licensure, psychiatrists are uniquely able to prescribe medications as part of treatment paradigms and to understand appropriate treatment protocols. This area of expertise may be important if there are salient questions related to medication management. By virtue of training in clinical psychology and/or neuropsychology, psychologists are uniquely qualified to administer and interpret tests that offer objective, empirically based measurements of psychological/psychiatric symptomatology, cognitive functioning, and symptom validity.

There are competent IMEs performed individually by psychologists and psychiatrists. However, it is often worth considering utilizing both a psychiatrist and a psychologist to perform a joint IME. Psychologists and psychiatrists often work together in this fashion with complementary approaches and evaluation results that, when combined, may represent a more comprehensive picture of an individual's functioning (American Academy of Neurology, 1996; American Medical Association, 2001; Meyer & Price, 2006; Torrem, 2003).

APPROACHING THE BEHAVIORAL HEALTH IME

Whether a behavioral health IME is conducted by a psychiatrist, a psychologist, or a combination of the two, the basic approach to an evaluation often hinges on the types of referral questions that are posed to an

---

▥ TABLE 12.3. Disability-Related Considerations for Examiner–Examinee Matching

- The nature of the examinee's diagnosis or condition associated with the reported disability-related complaints.
- The nature of the examinee's reported functional difficulties (emotional or cognitive).
- The nature of any ongoing psychiatric or psychological treatment that the examinee receives and the potential need for comment in this area.
- The forensic skill level and past experience of the examiner with regard to performing IMEs.
- The perceived need for psychological testing or neuropsychological testing for objective documentation of behavioral health symptom patterns, symptom severity, and potential exaggeration of symptom presentation.

evaluator. The types of questions tend to differ somewhat depending on the context in which behavioral health concerns arise and the administrative, contractual, and/or the legal definition of disability being addressed. For instance, the questions posed during a Social Security Disability evaluation typically differ from those associated with an evaluation focusing on long-term disability. However, there may also be overlap among referral questions, as primary concerns for all of the previously mentioned referral sources relate to how behavioral health conditions impact work-related abilities or the setting in which work takes place.

There is a core group of questions that, if addressed thoroughly, create a strong platform for most behavioral health IMEs. These questions can be ordered hierarchically and can serve as organizational guideposts when structuring an evaluation and discussing IME-related results and opinions. Behavioral health IMEs that have not adequately addressed these topics may be open to criticism and fatal flaw arguments. These hierarchically organized questions are listed in the following sections.

Are the data being relied upon for an accurate picture of a behavioral health condition and possible associated impairments credible?

The answer to this question must be established before all others. Without an understanding of the validity of the information and data collected during an evaluation, the behavioral health specialist is essentially unable to given an opinion with any degree of confidence on the nature of the behavioral health condition at hand and any associated impairments.

In a review of the psychological literature associated with the evaluation of compensation-seeking populations, Larrabee (2005) reported that the base rates associated with motivated performance deficits that were suggestive of symptom exaggeration ranged from 33.51 to 40% for conditions such as mild traumatic brain injury, fibromyalgia, chronic fatigue, and pain or somatoform disorders. These base rates were essentially replicated in a study that focused on the prevalence of cognitive symptom exaggeration (42%) in an IME sample primarily characterized by soft tissue injuries, fibromyalgia, and orthopedic injuries (Richman et al., 2006). Sumanti, Boone, Savodnik, and Gorsuch (2006) observed similar base rates (approximately 30%) for noncredible behavioral health symptom presentations in workers' compensation claims for emotional stress. There are also growing concerns that individuals who attempt to malinger during behavioral health IMEs are developing more sophisticated strategies to evade current detection methods (Bauer & McCaffrey, 2005). Compounding this concern is the finding that half the attorneys and law students surveyed feel that it is appropriate to coach their clients in this regard (Wetter & Corrigan, 1995; Youngjohn, 1995).

This body of research indicates that behavioral health specialists need to be highly attuned to the possibility of symptom exaggeration, impression management, and the active promotion of suffering during the behavioral health IME. The findings also emphasize that clinical judgment alone is insufficient to accurately identify such behaviors.

Is there objective evidence of an identifiable behavioral health condition? If so, does the behavioral health condition cause or contribute to identifiable objective impairments in employment/ work-related functioning?

Together, these questions constitute the core of most behavioral health IMEs. We have intentionally used the term *behavioral health condition* in association with these questions to move the reader away from the notion that the establishment of a formal *behavioral health diagnosis* is a necessary criterion for an opinion as to whether impairment exists. Indeed, a valid and reliably established behavioral health diagnosis is often useful in guiding expectations related to symptom presentation, treatment, and overall prognosis. However, as noted earlier in this chapter, a diagnosis alone does not necessarily inform the behavioral health specialist as to the existence of employment/work-related impairments, or to the ability to provide accommodations for such impairments. Conversely, it is possible for individuals to experience work-related impairments secondary to behavioral health symptoms that do not rise to the level of syndromal or diagnostic significance, such as isolated complaints of work-related stress, pain, or cognitive difficulties (e.g., problems with attention, memory, information-processing speed). Nevertheless, because diagnostic formulations in the field of behavioral health are a prominent feature in the clinical realm and are often a point of significant consideration during the IME process, they clearly warrant attention.

There are strengths and weaknesses of behavioral health diagnostic decision making within a forensic context. Behavioral health diagnoses and/or disorders are established by symptom report or symptom identification. Groups of meaningful and related symptoms are known as symptom constellations. Within the DSM-IV nomenclature, when a symptom constellation is thought to have a high degree of clinical significance, it is referred to as a disorder. In clinical practice, if the volume of behavioral symptoms identified within a diagnostic category meets or exceeds syndromal threshold criteria, a diagnosis is thought to be established.

The diagnostic methodology used to identify behavioral health conditions differs significantly from methodologies typically employed to diagnose or identify certain other medical conditions or disease states. For instance, the diagnosis of conditions such as tumors, cerebrovascular accidents, cancers, or a broken bone are made with the aid of diagnostic techniques (e.g., neuroimaging, lab assays, and X-ray) that allow for the positive (and often visual) identification of underlying pathology.

Studies that have employed diagnostic techniques such as magnetic resonance imaging (MRI), SPECT, PET, and fMRI often show group differences in cerebral structure and functioning when individuals suffering from behavioral heath conditions are compared with subjects who lack the condition. Such studies have certainly broadened our understanding of behavioral health conditions. The results of such neuroimaging techniques are also sometimes proffered as diagnostic evidence for a behavioral health condition. However, the diagnostic classification rates (sensitivity, specificity, positive predictive power, and negative predictive power) for these techniques, in association with specific behavioral health conditions, have been poor, with unacceptably high false positive and false negative rates. Unfortunately, such difficulties have prevented the use of these techniques as widely accepted diagnostic tools for behavioral health conditions such as depression.

The reliance on subjective symptom reports, without clear evidence of underlying pathology in individual cases, does not, in and of itself, prevent one from rendering a behavioral health diagnosis that is both valid and reliable. Such procedures are regularly employed in nonforensic settings that lack the clear potential for secondary gain (American Psychiatric Association, 2006). However, within the forensic context of a behavioral health IME, sole reliance on this form of information can certainly make matters far more difficult, especially given the high base rates reported earlier for symptom exaggeration/distortion within this population.

Compounding difficulties associated with symptom distortion are reports that for some DSM-IV diagnostic categories, standardized syndromal thresholds may not adequately discriminate between groups believed to suffer from a particular behavioral health condition and those that are believed to be free of the condition. For instance, Murphy, Gordon, and Barkley (2002) surveyed 719 people applying for driver's license renewal at a Department of Motor Vehicles in accordance with DSM-IV criteria for attention-deficit/hyperactivity disorder (ADHD). Of this nonclinical sample, 80% endorsed six or more symptoms as occurring "at least sometimes" during their childhood, and 75% indicated that they currently experienced six or more symptoms.

Research has also found that the difficulties associated with reliance on self-report extend well beyond the accuracy of symptom reporting and the ability to establish a meaningful diagnosis. A body of research exists that demonstrates people's tendency to inaccurately report a number of pertinent historical factors. For instance, studies have found that people generally have difficulty with the accurate recall of past medical events/history and associated sick leave (Rogler, Malgady, & Tryon, 1992). Studies have also found difficulties with the accurate recollection/reporting of psychological and neuropsychological histories (Henry, Moffit, Caspi, Langly,

& Silva, 1994; Hilsabeck, Gouvier, & Bolter, 1998; Simon & VonKorff, 1995; Widom & Morris, 1997), as well as past academic performance (Greiffenstein, Baker, & Johnson-Greene, 2002). In most cases, the mentioned recall biases reflect an underestimation of past problems or difficulties in these domains. However, symptom distortion in the opposite direction is also frequently a prominent feature of psychopathology. For example, social psychology studies have revealed that current mood state can contribute to a recall bias (i.e., Direnfeld & Roberts, 2006).

These difficulties reflect some of the inherent drawbacks, within a forensic context, associated with sole reliance on the categorical approach to diagnosis espoused by the DSM-IV and with reliance on subjective self-reporting in general. The difficulties require that the behavioral health specialist retained to perform an IME strive to obtain the most objective data possible to help with the elimination of biases associated with self-report and with the formulation of the most accurate final opinions.

It is no accident that the term *objective* was used in both of the overarching IME questions associated with this section. Vore (2007) noted that the behavioral health specialist retained to perform an IME can expect to be questioned about the data used to formulate diagnostic and impairment-related opinions, as it falls along a continuum extending from subjective to objective. For the purposes of this chapter, these anchors are defined below, with different forms of data grouped along such a conceptual continuum. Separate or subcontinua could also be constructed in relation to certain forms of data listed below. For instance, one could rate different psychological measures in relation to adequacy of psychometric properties. The data elements could also be rated in relation to the degree of utility in establishing a relationship between a behavioral health condition and employment/work related impairments.

Subjective–Objective Data Continuum

Subjective refers to data that can be modified or affected by personal views, arising out of or identified by means of one's perception of one's own states. *Objective* refers to expressing or dealing with facts or conditions as perceived without distortion by personal feelings, prejudices, or interpretations.

Most Subjective

The information in this category reflects the point at which most claims or complaints begin. The information gathered typically reflects an individual's self-statements related to a perceived behavioral health difficulty. The information is based on the claimant's, insured's, or patient's simple self-report of complaints/symptoms, without any attempt to formally assess the complaints/symptoms. Examples include statements related to states that are difficult to observe (e.g., "I feel hopeless;" "I have trouble concentrating") or difficult to validate in the context of an office visit (e.g., agoraphobia, trouble focusing at work). The information also consists of medical records submitted by treaters that offer a recapitulation of self-report, without any formulations related to diagnosis, impairment, or documentation of observed behaviors.

Subjective/Objective

These procedures serve to quantify and organize subjective symptom reports and typically offer a cross-sectional view of an individual's functioning from a behavioral health perspective. These procedures, compared to the most subjective procedures, offer a broader and more cohesive conceptualization of behavioral health issues. However, these procedures remain heavily dependent on an individual's self-report. Information in this group also typically lacks external corroboration or validation. The information is gained from formal/structured behavioral health interviews or measures that offer conceptualizations related to diagnosis, impairment, treatment, and prognosis (e.g., formal psychological/psychiatric interviews conducted by treaters). The information may consist of psychometric testing that has not employed controls for symptom exaggeration/distortion (i.e., Mini-Mental State Exam, various tests of neurocognitive functioning, Beck Depression Inventory).

Most Objective

The information in this section often serves as external corroboration and/or validation for an individual's self-report. The information may relate either to underlying pathology, diagnosis, functional impairment, or a combination of the foregoing. The data elements in this section all share in common a separation from self-report or formal controls for biases in self-report (see Table 12.4).

■ TABLE 12.4. Most Objective Data Sources

- Academic records.
- Formal work/performance evaluations that include references to specific workplace behaviors.
- Interviews with co-workers that have little vested interest in evaluation outcome (Some caution is required here because these reports may contain bias due to other issues, such as job competition, sexism, and racism).
- Diagnostic studies, including MRI, CT, EEG, and psychometric testing, which include known diagnostic accuracy rates, sensitivity/specificity data, relevant normative data, and controls for symptom exaggeration/distortion.
- Surveillance data that includes descriptions of behaviors without additional interpretation that inserts perceptions related to an individual's functional capacity.

▦ **TABLE 12.5. Common Referral Questions in Disability IME Contexts**

- Are the behavioral health impairments of sufficient duration or intensity to cause a partial or a complete cessation of work?
- Are there reasonable accommodations that would mitigate behavioral health impairments in the workplace?
- If this individual is unable to function within his or her previous occupation, would the impairments limit this individual from functioning within a different occupation?
- Are there nonbehavioral health conditions that also contribute to the work/employment-related limitations in question?
- If an active behavioral health condition contributes to work/employment-related impairments and limitations, is there evidence to suggest that the behavioral health condition preceded the claim of disability and/or legal or administrative action?
- Is current treatment reasonable, or would adjustments in treatment result in a change in prognosis for functional difficulties?

Once answers to these initial questions have been established, the behavioral health specialist is able to answer other more specific and pertinent questions for the referral source (see Table 12.5). Referring sources may provide a series of more general behavioral health-related questions or more targeted questions to the case at hand. In either case, the IME provider should be prepared to provide responses to these types of questions with reasonable certitude.

The categorical approach to diagnostic classification employed by the DSM-IV essentially ignores the dimensionality of human behavior and/or symptom presentation. It is within the dimensional approach to diagnosis that behavioral symptoms are viewed as falling along a continuum. With this approach, the examiner can begin to address behavioral symptom severity or diagnostic severity by determining where someone falls on a continuum in comparison to normal or clinical populations. It is here that examiners can begin to make active decisions as to whether an individual's symptom presentation is inside or outside of the realm of normal experience. These are, in essence, some of the basic theoretical and empirical tenets that underlie psychometric approaches to assessment.

THE ROLE OF THE BEHAVIORAL HEALTH TREATMENT PROVIDER

Given the sensitive nature of behavioral treatment and the strong foundation of confidentiality that underlies such treatment, the presence of discomfort, confusion, and frustration is frequently experienced once a behavioral health specialist is called upon to offer opinions, records, and/or testimony with respect to his or her patient's functional limitations and/

or work capacity. Much like an IME provider, the treating provider should be aware of the process of disability determination in the specific context of the patient and the relative value of differing pieces of information that may be offered as evidence. Many individuals in the process of making a claim for disability may in fact be asserting claims in multiple contexts (i.e., workers' compensation, Social Security, and private disability) each of which has its own definitions, terminology, and processes.

The most commonly requested information from behavioral health providers are copies of treatment records and the completion of disability-related forms. With respect to records, the Health Insurance Portability and Accountability Act (1996) is frequently and sometimes errantly cited by providers as a barrier to providing records for the purpose of disability determination. The regulations specifically note disability determination as an excepted transaction and in no way prohibit the release of such information with a signed authorization for this purpose. Given the complexity and variations in federal regulations and state laws with respect to the release of behavioral health records, we can only caution behavioral health providers to be keenly aware of these issues and to take a proactive stance with their patients regarding the potential for conflict balanced with the need to provide clinical information in relation to a potential claim.

The variations in forms soliciting certification of disability and description of functional impairment from federal, state, and private disability-related entities could easily fill this entire chapter. However, there are several consistent themes that are worthy of comment. First, for nonphysicians, the forms are often labeled as "Attending Physician Statement" or "Certification of Medical Disability." These headings generally do not preclude the behavioral health provider from offering opinions. It is quite common for such forms to be completed by nonphysicians with due notation of the actual credentials of the individual completing the form. It is generally in the interest of a claimant for the provider treating the condition that is causing impairment to respond rather than defer to a nonbehavioral health provider for such an opinion and/or description of symptoms. Opinions from multiple providers may also be helpful within the comprehensive adjudication process.

CONCLUSIONS

This chapter begins to address some of the basic premises and complexities likely to be encountered by behavioral health providers as they interact within the larger process of disability determination. Whether serving as IME providers or treating clinicians, behavioral health specialists interacting with disability claimants should be aware of their relative position and potential responsibilities within the disability determination process.

As discussed in this chapter, when behavioral health specialists become involved with the disability determination process, by choice or by request, they often find themselves at the crossroads of clinical science, clinical judgment, and the formality and legal underpinnings of the system of disability determination.

As private and public entities continue to struggle with the interaction between behavioral health conditions and work-related impairments, behavioral health specialists will likely take on an increasing role in the provision of information in the adjudication process of behavioral health claims. Familiarity with the context of these issues, the terminology used in the process, and the associated system issues can only serve to increase the value of behavioral health specialists in the process. This chapter, though in no way exhaustive, hopefully serves as an introduction and starting point for further inquiry for the interested behavioral health specialist.

REFERENCES

American Academy of Neurology. (1996). Assessment: Neuropsychological testing of adults. Considerations for neurologists. Report of the Therapeutics and Technology Assessment Subcommittee of the American Academy of Neurology. *Neurology, 47*(2), 592–599.

American Medical Association. (2001). *Guides for the evaluation of permanent impairment* (5th ed.). Chicago: Author.

American Medical Association. (2008). *Guides for the evaluation of permanent impairment* (6th ed.). Chicago: Author.

American Psychiatric Association. (2000). *Diagnostic and statistical manual of mental disorders* (4th ed., text rev.). Washington, DC: Author.

American Psychiatric Association. (2006). *Practice guidelines for the psychiatric evaluation of adults* (2nd ed.). Washington, DC: Author.

Americans with Disabilities Act of 1990 (42 U.S.C. _ _ 12101–12213 et seq. 1990).

Anfang, S. A., & Wall, B. W. (2006). Psychiatric fitness-for-duty evaluations. *Psychiatric Clinics of North America, 29*(3), 675–693.

Anthony, W. A., & Jansen, M. A. (1984). Predicting the vocational capacity of the chronically mentally ill. Research and policy implications. *The American Psychologist, 39*(5), 537–544.

Bauer, L., & McCaffrey, R. J. (2005). Coverage of the test of Memory Malingering, Victoria Symptom Validity Test, and Word Memory Test on the Internet: Is test security threatened? *Archives of Clinical Neuropsychology, 21*(1), 121–126.

Baum, K. (2005). Independent medical examinations: An expanding source of physician liability. *Annals of Internal Medicine, 142*(12, Pt. 1), 974–978.

Biddle, J., Roberts, K., Rosenman, K. D., & Welch, E. M. (1998). What percentage of workers with work-related illnesses receive workers' compensation benefits? *Journal of Occupational and Environmental Medicine, 40*(4), 325–331.

Bush, S. S. (2005). Independent and court-ordered forensic neuropsychological examinations: Official statement of the National Academy of Neuropsychology. *Archives of Clinical Neuropsychology, 20*(8), 997–1007.

California Workers' Compensation Institute. (1990). *Mental stress claims in*

California Workers' Compensation-incidence, costs, and trends. San Francisco, CA: Author.

Committee on Ethical Guidelines for Forensic Psychologists. (1991). Specialty guidelines for forensic psychologists. *Law and Human Behavior, 15*(6), 655–665.

Daubert v. Merrell Dow Pharmaceuticals, Inc. (509 U.S. 579 1993).

Demeter, S. L., Andersson, G. B. J., & Smith, G. M. (2001). *Disability evaluation.* St. Louis, MO: Mosby.

Direnfeld, D. M., & Roberts, J. E. (2006). Mood congruent memory in dysphoria: The roles of state affect and cognitive style. *Behavior Research and Therapy, 44*(9), 1275–1285.

Foote, W. E. (2003). Forensic evaluation in Americans with Disabilities Act cases. In A. M. Goldstein & I. B. Weiner (Eds.), *Handbook of psychology: Volume 11 forensic psychology* (pp. 279–300). Hoboken, NJ: Wiley.

Franche, R. L., Frank, J., & Krause, N. (2005). Prediction of occupational disability. In I. Z. Schultz & R. J. Gatchel (Eds.), *Handbook of complex occupational disability claims* (pp. 93–116). New York: Springer.

General Electric Company v. Joiner (522 U.S. 136 1997).

Greiffenstein, M. F., Baker, W. J., & Johnson-Greene, D. (2002). Actual versus self-reported scholastic achievement of litigating postconcussion and severe closed head injury claimants. *Psychological Assessment, 14*(2), 202–208.

Guidotti, T. L. (2003). Evidence-based medical dispute resolution. In S. L. Demeter & B. J. Gunnar (Eds.), *Disability evaluation* (pp. 86–94). Washington, DC: American Medical Association.

Hadjistavropoulos, T., & Bieling, P. (2001). File review consultation in the adjudication of mental health and chronic pain disability claims. *Consulting Psychology: Practice and Research, 53*, 52–63.

Henry, B., Moffit, T. E., Caspi, A., Langly, J., & Silva, P. A. (1994). On the remembrance of things past: A longitudinal evaluation of the retrospective method. *Psychological Assessment, 6*, 92–101.

Hilsabeck, R. C., Gouvier, W. D., & Bolter, J. F. (1998). Reconstructive memory bias in recall of neuropsychological symptomatology. *Journal of Clinical and Experimental Neuropsychology, 20*(3), 328–338.

Hurrell, J. J., Jr., & Murphy, L. R. (1996). Occupational stress intervention. *American Journal of Industrial Medicine, 29*(4), 338–341.

Kumho Tire Co. Ltd. v. Carmichael (526 U.S. 137 1999).

Larrabee, G. J. (2005). Assessment of malingering. In G. J. Larrabee (Ed.), *Forensic neuropsychology: A scientific approach* (pp. 115–158). New York: Oxford University Press.

LoCascio, J. (2005). Can this patient work? A disability perspective. In J. B. Talmage & M. J. Melhorn (Eds.), *A physician's guide to return to work* (pp. 113–132). Washington, DC: American Medical Association.

Melhorn, J. M., Lazarovic, J., & Roehl, W. K. (2005). Do we have a disability epidemic? In I. Z. Schultz & R. J. Gatchel (Eds.), *Handbook of complex occupational disability claims* (pp. 7–24). New York: Springer.

Meyer, D. J., & Price, M. (2006). Forensic psychiatric assessments of behaviorally disruptive physicians. *Journal of the American Academy of Psychiatry and the Law, 34*(1), 72–81.

Murphy, K. R., Gordon, M., & Barkley, R. A. (2002). To what extent are ADHD symptoms common? A reanalysis of standardization data from a DSM-IV checklist. *ADHD Report, 8*, 1–5.

Murray, C. J., & Lopez, A. D. (Eds.). (1996). *The global burden of disease and injury series, volume 1: A comprehensive assessment of mortality and disability from diseases, injuries and risk factors in 1990 and projected to 2020.* Cambridge, MA: Harvard University Press.

Piechowski, L. D. (2006). Forensic consultation in disability insurance matters. *Journal of Psychiatry and Law, 34,* 151–167.

Richman, J., Green, P., Gervais, R., Flaro, L., Merten, T., Brockhaus, R., et al. (2006). Objective tests of symptom exaggeration in independent medical examinations. *Journal of Occupational and Environmental Medicine, 48*(3), 303–311.

Rogler, L. H., Malgady, R. G., & Tryon, W. W. (1992). Evaluation of mental health: Issues of memory in the Diagnostic Interview Schedule. *Journal of Nervous and Mental Disease, 180*(4), 215–222; discussion 223–216.

Schultz, I. Z. (2005). Impairment and occupational disability in research and practice. In I. Z. Schultz & R. J. Gatchel (Eds.), *Handbook of complex occupational disability claims* (pp. 25–42). New York: Springer.

Simon, G. E., & VonKorff, M. (1995). Recall of psychiatric history in cross-sectional surveys: Implications for epidemiologic research. *Epidemiologic Reviews, 17*(1), 221–227.

Social Security Administration. (2003). *Social Security Administration online.* Washington, DC: Author.

Sumanti, M., Boone, K. B., Savodnik, I., & Gorsuch, R. (2006). Noncredible psychiatric and cognitive symptoms in a workers' compensation "stress" claim sample. *The Clinical Neuropsychologist, 20*(4), 754–765.

Torrem, M. S. (2003). Psychiatric diagnostic techniques. In S. L. Demeter & B. J. Gunnar (Eds.), *Disability evaluation* (pp. 86–94). Washington, DC: American Medical Association.

United States Equal Employment Opportunity Commission. (1997). *EEOC enforcement guidance on the Americans with Disability Act and psychiatric disabilities. (EEOC Notice Number 915.002 ed.).* Washington, DC: U.S. Government Printing Office.

United States v. Allen (269 F.3d 842 845-846 7th Cir. 2001).

Vore, D. A. (2007). The disability psychological independent medical evaluation: Case law, ethical issues and procedures. In A. Goldstein (Ed.), *Forensic psychology: Emerging topics and expanding roles* (pp. 489–510). Hoboken, NJ: Wiley.

Waldron, C. (2003). Trends in morbidity: Pricing and reserving individual disability insurance is no walk in the park. *The Actuary, 37*(6), 7–8, 15.

Warren, P. A. (2005). *The management of workplace mental health issues and appropriate disability prevention strategies.* San Diego, CA: Work Loss Data Institute.

Wetter, M. W., & Corrigan, S. K. (1995). Providing information to clients about psychological tests: A survey of attorneys' and law students' attitudes. *Professional Psychology: Research and Practice, 26,* 474–477.

Widom, C. S., & Morris, S. (1997). Accuracy of adult recollections of childhood victimization, Part 2: Childhood sexual abuse. *Psychological Assessment, 9*(1), 34–46.

Yelin, E. H., & Cisternas, M. G. (1997). Employment patterns among persons with and without mental conditions. In R. J. Bonnie & J. E. Monahan (Eds.), *Mental disorder, work disability, and the law* (pp. 25–54). Chicago: University of Chicago Press.

Youngjohn, J. R. (1995). Confirmed attorney coaching prior to a neuropsychology evaluation. *Assessment, 2,* 279–283.

CHAPTER 13

Applying Neuropsychology in Vocational Rehabilitation Intervention

Issues in Work Access and Work Return

Robert Fraser
David Strand
Erica Johnson
Curt Johnson

A vocational assessment that carefully integrates neuropsychological information is critical to the occupational success of individuals with brain impairment. However, both vocational and neuropsychological academic programs commonly neglect the integration of vocational and neuropsychological evaluations. This chapter seeks to inform neuropsychologists, rehabilitation psychologists, vocational rehabilitation counselors, and other rehabilitation personnel about the contributions that each type of evaluation offers and the elements of the neuropsychological evaluation process that are critical to client success in work entry or reentry. This chapter contributes to previous scholarly contributions on the integration of vocational and neuropsychological services (e.g., Uomoto, 2000).

VOCATIONAL REHABILITATION COUNSELING

Vocational rehabilitation in the United States involves a spectrum of professional activities. Access to the field for the professional generally involves the achievement of a master's degree in rehabilitation counseling or vocational evaluation and subsequent attainment of the certified rehabilitation counselor (CRC) or certified vocational evaluator (CVE) credentials. Credentials are awarded based on master's degree completion and score on the designated national certification exam. Practice settings for CRCs and CVEs include the state–federal vocational rehabilitation system, private for-profit system (e.g., workers' compensation or forensic consultation), Veterans Administration, or community and hospital-based rehabilitation centers. The requisite qualifications for employment in the state–federal vocational rehabilitation system vary by state. In this system, primarily in urban areas, counselors are engaged primarily in case management and transferable skills analysis for identification of job goals in establishing the individualized rehabilitation plan. They are usually involved in the purchase of vocational evaluation, neuropsychological assessment, and other evaluation services through community providers.

There is a significant private practice sector in vocational rehabilitation. In this setting, counselors will in some cases provide psychometrically based vocational evaluations, as well as review an individual's education and work background in order to make recommendations for training and placement, to provide forensic employability testimony, and to serve as vocational rehabilitation experts in Social Security Administration hearings. A major private sector activity is job analysis relative to the essential functions of a job, in terms of both cognitive and physical demands. These individuals will frequently request a neuropsychological consultation to assist in determining an individual's capacity to meet essential job functions and establish a vocational plan and goals.

On a less frequent basis, some vocational rehabilitation counselors (VRCs) specialize in an area such as life-care planning following catastrophic injury or as assistive technology practitioners (ATPs)—both of which require additional national credentialing. VECs with ATP certification not only focus on the technology available for job modifications, but also may make recommendations regarding purchasing, training, and support of adaptive devices used for work activity. Local credentialed VRCs or ATPs can be identified, respectively, through the following professional organization websites: *www.crccertification.com* and *www.resna.org.*

Although not widely available, there are inpatient, residential, and outpatient rehabilitation programs in which staff vocational rehabilitation counselors are part of the multidisciplinary rehabilitation team, along with the physician, neuropsychologist, and other allied health providers (physical therapists, occupational therapists, speech–language pathologists). The VRC functions to establish, implement, and monitor the vocational plan. This area of practice is becoming less common with the advent of truncated insurance funding for postacute rehabilitation. A review of the Traumatic Brain Injury Model Systems, as partially funded by the National Institute on Disability and Rehabilitation Research, at universities and rehabilitation centers around the country indicates that most vocational programs do not provide full vocational rehabilitation intervention services and tend to provide more vocational consultation for those returning to a prior position. In sum, the quality of the partnership between vocational rehabilitation and neuropsychology is often influenced by the existing funding available and the infrastructure for rehabilitation services. For seasoned rehabilitation professionals, the nature of the partnership is "old news." For some new professionals to the field of rehabilitation, however, it can come as a surprise that they may have to expend considerable effort in securing the combined efforts of a quality vocational rehabilitation counselor and neuropsychologist in vocational planning efforts.

NEUROPSYCHOLOGICAL ASSESSMENT AND PROGNOSIS FOR WORKPLACE FUNCTIONING

There have been a number of reviews of neuropsychological assessment variables as related to employment outcome, most commonly in traumatic brain injury (TBI). A review by Nightingale, Soo, and Tate (2007) suggested that the domains in neuropsychological functioning, including executive functioning, perceptual ability, and global cognitive functioning, had moderate associations with employment status—but the evidence was too limited to support conclusive association. As noted by Fraser, Johnson, and Uomoto (2010), there are a number of challenges to assessing the impact of diverse psychosocial variables, including neuropsychological characteristics, on work access and work return. Some of these challenges are as follows.

1. With the exception of longitudinal studies, most employment outcome measures across studies involve prediction of employment status at a single point in time.

2. Machamer, Temkin, Fraser, Doctor, and Dikmen (2005) examined the association between employment stability and cognitive functioning at 3 to 5 years postinjury and found that a number of neuropsychological measures or variables were strong predictors of stability (e.g., Performance IQ, Digit Symbol Subtest, Selective Reminding Test, Trail Making Test Part B, and Finger Tapping Test with the Dominant hand; $p < .0001$). This study involved a much more stable outcome measure than a single point in time of contact in relation to employment.

3. Neuropsychological scores may show a stronger or more consistent relationship to employment outcome if assessed in relation to specific sectors of work that have some commonality relative to cognitive demands (e.g., skilled business professionals in administrative or managerial jobs, unskilled laborers, semiskilled customer service representatives).

4. Attempting to establish the empirical benefit of neuropsychological findings relative to employment is problematic when using heterogeneous

populations of individuals with neurological disability, or including individuals with varying gradients of disability in the same study.

5. The type and intensity of vocational rehabilitation services is often not considered as a mediating variable. Johnstone, Reid-Arndt, Franklin, and Harper (2006) indicated that provision of vocational rehabilitation services alone predicted successful vocational outcome, while traditional medical and neuropsychological variables do not. In studies of this type, however, it needs to be determined whether neuropsychological assessment findings were taken into consideration and may, in fact, have guided the successful vocational goal setting and placement outcomes.

In sum, the above considerations provide a number of reasons for the variance in findings regarding the utility of neuropsychological variables in relation to predicting employment outcome and need to be fully considered in future studies.

NEUROPSYCHOLOGICAL ASSESSMENT AS A "DRIVER" IN THE VOCATIONAL PLANNING PROCESS FOR CLIENTS WITH NEUROLOGICAL DISABILITIES

Although there can be some academic debate relating to the ecological validity of neuropsychological assessment for predicting vocational outcome, neuropsychological assessment has a number of advantages from a clinical perspective. Initially, neuropsychological assessment provides a baseline profile of the individual's limitations and areas of strength or preserved ability. This profile can guide further work access and reentry considerations relative to when and what level of activity a person might attempt in the job search or return to work. In addition, the neuropsychologist can conduct brief follow-up assessments in order to determine clinically significant changes in cognitive functioning as a result of neurological insult or disease. For example, in a recent case seen at our unit, a scientist, who had experienced a mild TBI after being hit by a car while cycling, presented a number of initial concerns. These concerns chiefly related to challenges with divided attention and low-average-range auditory memory. Executive functioning appeared to be well preserved. As a consequence of the testing, the CEO of the facility was convinced that after a few weeks of rest, the scientist might return on a half-time basis and transition to full time. With client authorization, there was great benefit to discussing with her line manager the scientist's probable return-to-work trajectory because her manager had some overconcern about sequelae from the injury. There was another brief neuropsychological screening assessment just before she returned to work, and, upon return, all went smoothly.

As indicated by Barisa and Barisa (2001), in addressing vocational rehabilitation concerns during neuropsychological evaluations, emphasis is placed on the patient's premorbid history of employment and education vis-à-vis the medical background, psychosocial history, personality style, and substance abuse history. This evaluation can involve a somewhat different neuropsychological clinical interview and report compared to neuropsychological evaluations performed for other purposes, as described later in this chapter. Barisa and Barisa also noted that the neuropsychologist moves away from emphasizing brain–behavior relationships, or identifying pathognomonic signs, and focuses on the manner in which specific deficits are likely to interfere with daily functioning in relation to a client's cognitive work demands (e.g., memory concerns, the ability to multitask), activities of daily living (e.g., shopping, home maintenance), and interpersonal interactions and communications. There is a very poignant emphasis on daily functionality in all realms of activity because diverse functional capacities affect work performance.

Without neuropsychological assessment information, patients and significant others are left to find their way as to strengths, areas of deficit, and how to compensate while in the workforce. This assessment is the catalyst for considering accommodation issues in the workplace. Beginning the accommodation consideration discussion during the neuropsychological evaluation process can help pave the way for a smooth transition versus a scramble to implement accommodations after a cognitively challenged individual is placed on the job. At our unit, we have encountered a number of individuals who, after sustaining a mild-moderate TBI, had no consultation at a treating hospital and, only later following neuropsychological assessment, understood the need for appropriate services to help address their complex needs. The neuropsychologist provides identification of cognitive changes and stability of functioning over a period of rehabilitation (Fuchs, 2009) and can make appropriate referrals to other members within the allied health or rehabilitation community (e.g., occupational therapy, physical therapy, speech and language pathology, rehabilitation engineering, assistive technology). Neuropsychologists can identify not only cognitive concerns, but also emotional problems, including posttraumatic stress disorder , symptoms of depression, and certain personality traits that are interwoven with cognitive challenges.

GENERATING HYPOTHESES ABOUT THE WORK ENVIRONMENT

LeBlanc, Hayden, and Paulman (2000) indicated that one of the most valuable contributions of neuropsychological assessment is the generation of hypotheses about the manner in which strengths and deficits identified on standardized testing might relate to behavior in the natural environment. A major benefit of neuropsychological evaluations in relation to work can be the generation of these hypotheses as relating to a specific job, but such evaluations can also be valuable in conducting a community-based vocational assessment. Using the 1993 U.S. Department of Labor (DOL) waiver, a situational assessment can be developed as relating to any job in the private sector on a *nonpaid basis for up to 215 hours*. Under the DOL waiver program, the client agrees to be a volunteer for a community agency, such as Goodwill Industries or Jewish Vocational Services, and is assigned a volunteer placement in a potentially targeted job at a community company. Workers' compensation insurance is paid by the community rehabilitation vendor (e.g., Goodwill Industries) as based on the specific volunteer occupational classification. The total of 215 hours is to be used for purposes of vocational exploration, client assessment, and actual job-specific training. The time can be spread out on a half-time basis and approximately 11 weeks (often a very realistic period of time for people regaining cognitive abilities, experiencing cognitive fatigue, etc.). Part-time work is often the best way to phase someone into employment demands. Some individuals have relatively preserved physical/cognitive capacity and are better prepared to return to work after several weeks of full-time volunteering, which can also be an employer's preference. These community-based volunteer experiences are also helpful for individuals who are not quite ready to return to their actual job but can profit from activity at a volunteer site. If a client begins another volunteer position at a company site, the 215-hour nonpaid tryout option begins anew.

THE OVERESTIMATION/UNDERESTIMATION ISSUE IN NEUROPSYCHOLOGICAL ASSESSMENT

As discussed by both Barisa and Barisa (2001) and Uomoto (2000), neuropsychological evaluations can overestimate or underestimate an individual's functional capability in a work setting. Neuropsychological evaluations can overestimate real-world performance because the testing occurs in a controlled environment one-on-one with the neuropsychologist or a test administrator. In actual work settings, a job may require differing demands, including issues of distraction and divided attention, time pressures, interpersonal issues, inordinate demands for accuracy, and other challenges. Such demands are not necessarily comparably tapped as a function of the neuropsychological assessment. An individual, therefore, may perform poorly on the job despite good performance on a neuropsychological evaluation (overestimation)—hence the importance of accommodation considerations.

Underestimation of real-world potential can also be problematic. Despite a severely occurring brain injury or disease, some individuals, though impaired with new learning on neuropsychological testing, will have well-preserved overlearned behavior on the job. In these cases, the employee's actual work tasks involve overlearned behavior on which the worker is able to rely and often benefit additionally from a rote sequence to the work (e.g., gift box assembly, paper machine operator, product welding). In these instances, often a number of environmental cues further facilitate adequate functioning. Another factor in underestimation is that there is usually a singular day of test administration, and this could be on a day when an individual is experiencing particular emotional difficulties, medication side effects, compromising pain, and other issues affecting performance. In some cases, injured workers might benefit from a rote list, environmental structure, reduced time pressures, and other accommodations. The neuropsychologist might encourage these accommodations during a job tryout or work sampling.

THE NEUROPSYCHOLOGIST'S CONTRIBUTION TO THE VOCATIONAL PLAN

In most instances, the VRC bears the onus for client progress relative to work return or access to a new job. In terms of efficacious and expedient client progress, the following points are important relative to the neuropsychologist's assessment and vocational contribution. These points are very important in neurological vocational rehabilitation.

Describe Cognitive Status

The neuropsychologist needs to be able to carefully describe the client's cognitive assets and deficits. It is also important to describe cognitive deficits that are likely to change or be subject to remediation over time. In the case of the food scientist, as previously described, concerns about divided attention and low-average auditory memory were immediately problematic, but were expected to remediate in a relatively short span of time. It is important for the rehabilitation counselor to understand areas in which improvement is unlikely so that compensatory approaches can be piloted and undertaken. In these instances, the neuropsychologist can suggest interventions, such as consultation with an assistive technologist, which might be helpful in compensating for deficits in abilities such as abstraction, organization, or planning.

Present Cognitive Abilities According to Job Descriptions

It is important that cognitive strengths and deficits are presented within the context of published job descriptions, but more importantly information from the client and supervisor/coworker as necessary. In many instances where an individual was employed prior to injury, is rehabilitating from injury, and is hoping to return to work, the goals of various stakeholders will be to return the individual to his or her original job with or without accommodation. If that is not possible, new work with the same employer may be explored. The neuropsychologist's ability to speak to these priorities in the evaluation is highly valuable.

Describe Relevant Psychosocial Issues

It is very helpful for the neuropsychologist to note any psychosocial issues that may affect the client's vocational performance. These issues can involve relationships with family and significant others, litigation and liability issues, substance abuse concerns, interpersonal or behavioral problems that were preexisting and may or may not have been exacerbated by a brain insult, and other psychosocial issues. Neuropsychological testing time also provides a good opportunity for observed input as to client behavioral functioning over a day.

Note Fatigue and Endurance

It is important to note problems with fatigue that are encountered over the neuropsychological evaluation. This can obviously be cognitive fatigue, but also physical fatigue for individuals with multiple disabilities or impairments. In some cases, observed capacity can parallel what an individual would be able to do over a workday and can be important in consideration of workplace accommodation needs, particularly in relation to cognitively complex jobs. After the assessment it can be helpful to discuss the issue of fatigue with the client, by phone or in person, to determine the extent to which the demanding neuropsychological evaluation might have affected the person's energy and stamina the following day.

Describe Community Supports

It is important to identify and emphasize community supports that might assist with successful, and stable, return to work. These supports could be positive social or religious networks, hobby groups, social and recreational groups, exercise activities (ideally within groups), and groups supportive of freedom from substances (e.g., Alcoholics Anonymous or Narcotics Anonymous) because these can facilitate and reinforce a positive and stable vocational outcome.

Provide Results in a Timely Manner

It is extremely important that the rehabilitation counselor receive a report in a timely manner. This can often be a problem, particularly when the neuropsychologist is quite busy. If this cannot be done expediently, it is very helpful for the counselor to have testing results rated in a checklist format within appropriate domains of cognitive functioning (see Fraser et al., 2010). Likert scale ratings are constructed within different domains of functioning such as abstractive abilities, speed of information processing, verbal and nonverbal memory, simple and complex attention, and so on. Checklist responses with additional targeted comments can enable the VRC and client to begin work return or access planning. At a minimum, if actual work access is not yet ready to be initiated, findings can help frame the parameters for information to be sought through the previously discussed nonpaid community-based assessment.

Provide Vocationally Relevant Recommendations

Vocationally relevant recommendations are critical. The neuropsychologist, often in consultation with the rehabilitation counselor, might consider recommendations relative to the type and level of supervision needed at the job site, such as the benefit of a job coach or paid coworker as trainer or the desirability of an on-the-job training relationship in which the Division of Vocational Rehabilitation subsidizes some salary support during training. Mentorship recommendations of this type can relate both to completing essential functions and work tasks, and to the need for mentorship relative to behavioral and interpersonal functioning.

Recommend Specific Modifications

Of additional importance among neuropsychologists' recommendations is specific guidance relative to basic procedural changes as to how the job might be done, physical modifications to the workstation, or assistive equipment that might enable an individual to perform within the context of memory, organizational, and other deficits. Neuropsychologists can become more proficient in making these types of recommendations over time by working with vocational rehabilitation specialists. Accommodation examples and resources in this area are reviewed in the Perspectives on Reasonable Accommodations section of this chapter.

Consider the Return-to-Work Continuum

In some cases, the neuropsychologist will be able to make recommendations along the continuum of options relative to work return, such as the following: (1) same job and employer; (2) same job, different employer; (3) same employer, less complex job; or (4) different employer, less complex job. These needs may be difficult to predict in the early months postinjury or with limited functional capacity information.

THE NEUROPSYCHOLOGIST'S NEEDS IN DELIVERING A VOCATIONALLY RELEVANT NEUROPSYCHOLOGICAL ASSESSMENT

When a neuropsychologist's report is not helpful to a VRC, problems often stem from the fact that the necessary questions were not asked of the neuropsychologist and important employment-contextual information was not provided. Uomoto (2000) has identified a number of ways in which this problem can be avoided.

The neuropsychologist needs a clear list of the referred person's problems and concerns. Target questions need to be addressed that will assist the neuropsychologist in providing vocationally relevant information. If a targeted return-to-work option or job goal has been identified, a cognitive job analysis that outlines essential job functions in terms of cognitive domains such as attention and concentration, memory, rote counting or tracking, information processing, simple and complex decision making, and ability to follow simple and complex commands can be helpful in conveying to the neuropsychologist the work demands required of the individual.

All questions posed by the neuropsychologist need to be in functional or rehabilitation oriented terms. Through this type of vocationally relevant specificity, the neuropsychologist will be deterred from a more traditional report response that may not be as helpful in the vocational planning process.

Although neuropsychologists can vary relative to the information they desire, current medical treatment and discharge reports are very important. Because the concerns are vocational in nature, educational records (both pre- and postinjury), specific information relative to the job description, prior client job performance, concerns that the employer or manager may have, and other questions relating to congruence between cognitive proficiencies and job demands are important. Letter or direct phone communication by the VRC to the neuropsychologist can also be beneficial.

Job description information with critical tasks described and important proficiency criteria delineated is essential. In the case of an existing job, current performance evaluation data related to the client is also of benefit. In many cases, the job description is not very useful because it is neither current nor well developed. In these cases, information from a manager or coworker prior to the assessment can be much more valuable if a VRC has not performed a job (essential functions) analysis. If there is no available information, some job description may be available through the Department of Labor's O-NET website (*online.onetcenter.org*). Other descriptions may be available on the Internet or through the recently revised *Occupational Outlook Handbook, 2010–2011* (U.S. Department of Labor, 2010).

JOB-RELEVANT INFORMATION FOR THE NEUROPSYCHOLOGIST'S ASSESSMENT

In some neuropsychological evaluation contexts, the client's job background and/or educational development may be relatively unimportant. This, however, is not the case with a vocationally relevant neuropsychological evaluation. In this case, detailed information related to prior educational and vocational attainment helps the neuropsychologist to extrapolate the interplay between prior attainment and the present cognitive profile. Information can help answer questions related to potential success at a prior job or a new job as applicable.

In terms of prior education, it is important to probe for specific educational achievements and prior strengths. Questions regarding academic achievement include: prior course load structure (e.g., Was the individual fully or partially invested in coursework, and how rigorous was the material? Was a core sequence in language arts, sciences, or mathematics achieved? Did overloading occur in a specific academic area relative to classes or electives? Were advanced placement courses attempted?). When individuals have major gaps in academic training, particularly at the elementary through high school levels, they are likely to perform less proficiently on a number of cognitive and academic tests, in part because of educational deficiencies as opposed to solely the effects of the injury/disability in question.

In the same vein, specific scholastic or on-the-job training certifications are helpful to note and can provide insight into areas of well-learned behaviors and skills. Individuals with prior rigorous academic coursework or job training may perform in an average range on some tests despite significant neuropsychological impairment because of residual capacity from their prior training experiences. Conversely, some individuals with less rigorous education and training experiences may perform poorly on neuropsychological tests despite having well-preserved cognitive abilities.

Vocational competency and prior work experience can often be synthesized from job description and clients' work performance data. Needed information can at times be secured in an interview with the individual and significant other or family member, a rehabilitation counselor/case manager referral source, or previous employers or coworkers. Varney and Menefree (1993), using a case involving traumatic brain injury, underscored the use of collateral informants such as family members and coworkers in shoring up the reliability of the vocational history information obtained. Interviewing these informants also provides the added benefit of assessing potential changes in interpersonal interaction or behavioral styles postinjury (Varney & Menefee, 1993).

Speaking with coworkers and employers directly is underutilized as a tool for gathering pertinent vocational data and making vocational recommendations. Contacting employers directly, with client authorization, gives the neuropsychologist a chance to ask specific questions about job performance and job demands, including rate of production, accuracy, and coworker interaction. Such information can help optimize the work experience.

In an experience from our unit, contact with prior employers/supervisors at a research facility indicated that there was a considerable amount of misinformation with regard to an individual's current capacities for pre-work return. The client, a young female scientist (previously described in this chapter), sustained a mild TBI as a function of a cycling injury. Some people in the research facility administration assumed that she was in a reasonable range of cognitive functioning to return to work, while others somehow had heard she was functioning "at a seventh-grade level." A vocationally relevant neuropsychological report summarized her strengths and limitations in the context of specific job questions. Recommendations were also made regarding necessary accommodations to dispel undue concern on the part of the employer.

PERSPECTIVES ON REASONABLE ACCOMMODATIONS

When possible, the neuropsychologist should make recommendations for accommodation relating to work return or new work access. In discussing accommodations, it can be helpful to review in three categories: changes in procedure, physical modifications to the workstation, or some type of assistive equipment or technology, ranging from low cost to high cost. The number and type of accommodations vary among individuals.

Procedural Accommodations

For many individuals with neuropsychological impairment, deficits can best be addressed by making changes in work procedures. On the low end of accommodation concerns, there might be work scheduling issues for an individual having deficits, with basic attention/concentration or divided attention. An individual, for example, might be advised to begin work earlier than other coworkers, such as coming in at 7:00 A.M. in order to have uninterrupted work time until 9:30 when phone calls and messages will be handled. Calls might then be taken for an hour, followed by return to uninterrupted, nonphone work. Another specific time (e.g., 2:00–3:15 P.M.) might then be scheduled for afternoon telephone contact. Actually, this is a common recommendation for individuals in relatively intense, professional jobs that demand complex sustained attention.

Procedural accommodations can be helpful for individuals with cognitive difficulties. An obvious change in procedure consists of having a supported employment job coach available for an individual to help chain tasks together, provide cues and prompts, offer assistance in development of problem-solving strategies, and other similar tasks. In addition to job coaching staff, other individuals such as paid coworkers can be utilized to mentor employees with neurological disabilities (Curl, Fraser, Cook, & Clemmons, 1996). State vocational rehabilitation agencies have used on-the-job training funding for decades to defray additional costs and supervisor training time for people with neurological disabilities as they learn or relearn specific occupational tasks.

Physical Modifications

For individuals with attention and concentration deficits, memory concerns, and difficulties with abstraction and speed of information processing, basic workstation organization can be simple and invaluable in achieving productivity. In some cases, the organization can involve basic desktop organization, or it can involve having a workstation developed to parallel the work activity sequence that occurs over the day. As an example, an individual with memory and sequencing difficulties was falling behind in his work activity as a bicycle assembler (Warren, 2000). As he performed different assembly tasks on a wheel, he placed the tools in different places and then forgot their location. Consequently, he was continually falling behind a coworker in productivity. An assistive technologist visited the site and color-coded each tool with a corresponding colored carrel box for placing the tool when finished with a step. As a result, as the worker finished each task, he placed the colored tool in the corresponding carrel box and had the next colored tool ready in the box sequence for his next assembly task. The outcome of this unobtrusive "work organizer" was a quick, successful, low-cost (cost of the wood carrel and paint) solution for improving and maintaining the worker's productivity. Another common physical accommodation is placement of one's office or workstation, whenever possible, outside of a noise nexus or area of mainstream employee foot traffic.

Assistive Technology

Assistive technology can have major benefits for individuals with diverse cognitive impairments. Today many kinds of technologies are readily available, including cell phones, personal data assistants (PDAs), electronic mail (e-mail), and dictation machines and software that can be used to compensate for cognitive deficits. Using Microsoft Outlook or other available digital options can be ideal relative to calendar functions. E-mail can be color coded by inbox folders to correspond to areas of importance, such as reminders, to-do lists, correspondence, and other features. Computer software, color printers, and digital cameras provide powerful visuals as memory aids, and the latest cell phones (smart phones) provide varying options for completing the previously mentioned tasks. These handheld devices allow use of video clips for training, and they can serve as a memory aid. They can provide prompt reminders of tools and materials used, as well as the sequencing of tasks. Software is now readily available for voice-to-text word processing or text-to-speech applications to improve reading and word prediction applications for those with spelling deficits. In sum, a wide range of accommodation recommendations can be made within the assistive technology category. As a caveat, it is important to match assistive technology recommendations to the needs and capabilities of the end user. As an example, a PDA may be very useful for a person with a technology background, but may not be for an older laborer with no computer skills, for whom pencil-and-paper checklists would be the better choice. If the assistive technology and user are not a "good fit," the technology will often not be used.

ACCOMMODATION RECOMMENDATION RESOURCES FOR THE NEUROPSYCHOLOGIST

In many cases, neuropsychologists are not versed in all of the potential avenues of accommodation for individuals with neurological impairment. The most established accommodation resource center is the Job Accommodation Network (JAN), which is a service provided by the U.S. Department of Labor's Office of Disability and Employment Policy (ODEP), housed at West Virginia University. Their services are available by both telephone (toll free at 1.800.526.7234) and the Internet (*www.jan.weu.edu*). Another extremely helpful informational resource that provides objective information about rehabilitation equipment and assistive technology is ABLEDATA at *www.abledata.com*; this is a search database of 19,000 assistive technology products maintained under contract from the U.S. National Institute for Disability and Rehabilitation Research.

Although many recommendations can be simply researched online, it is helpful to talk by telephone to some of the JAN consultants who have specialized information for different categories of disability (viz. cognitive, sensory, and physical). Phone discussion can provide the neuropsychologist consultant with a richer picture of client capacities and the challenges at hand.

IMPORTANCE OF CLARITY AND RETENTION OF NEUROPSYCHOLOGICAL FINDINGS

Neuropsychologists should attempt to clearly relate their evaluation results to clients' specific assets and deficits, in a vocationally relevant manner. Some neuropsychologists omit excessive text in their reports, and use a "bullet point" synopsis under the Assets and Deficits categories. Accommodations and other recommendations can follow, often in a sequenced manner relative to the vocational activities. This summary can be particularly valuable to the VRC and the client. Some clients prefer to audiotape the interpretive session. The summary of findings and recommendations are often presented at the end of the written report, so that they are detachable from the larger report and can easily be carried by the client. Neuropsychological evaluations are maximally useful if high-quality feedback and interpretive sessions are provided to the client and rehabilitation personnel.

CONCLUSIONS

VRCs operate in a number of different settings and use case management, counseling, and assessment skills to facilitate work access for individuals with disabilities. In the instance of return to work after injury, individuals are most likely to work with a VRC in the hospital setting, the private sector (i.e., workers' compensation system provides vocational rehabilitation), or the state–federal system. In all of these settings, the mutual consultation between VRC and neuropsychologist is essential in establishing vocationally relevant assessment information that facilitates vocational plan development and goal pursuit, with detailed consideration of the manner in which reasonable accommodations can support an individual's ability to work. The effective exchange of information between the VRC and neuropsychologist involves a solid understanding of the possibilities and limitations inherent in the funding systems at play; the types of information that each team member can provide in terms of clinical interview, assessment, and labor market information; and collaboration with the individual client.

REFERENCES

Barisa, M. T., & Barisa, M. W. (2001). Neuropsychological evaluation applied to vocational rehabilitation. *NeuroRehabilitation, 16*(4), 289–293.

Curl, R., Fraser, R. T., Cook, R., & Clemmons, D. (1996). Traumatic brain injury vocational rehabilitation: Preliminary findings from the Co-Worker as Trainer Project. *Journal of Head Trauma Rehabilitation, 11*, 75–85.

Fraser, R. T., Johnson, E., & Uomoto, J. M. (2010). Using neuropsychological information in vocational rehabilitation planning: Perspectives for clinical practice. In E. Arzubi & E. Mambrino (Eds.), *A guide to neuropsychological testing for health care professionals* (pp. 395–415). New York: Springer.

Fuchs, K. L. (2009). Neuropsychologist. *International Journal of MS Care, 11*, 32–37.

Johnstone, B., Reid-Arndt, S., Franklin, K. L., & Harper, J. (2006). Vocational outcomes of state vocational rehabilitation clients with traumatic brain injury: A review of the Missouri Model Brain Injury System Studies. *NeuroRehabilitation, 21*(4), 335–347.

LeBlanc, J. M., Hayden, M. E., & Paulman, R. G. (2000). A comparison of neuropsychological and situational assessment for predicting employability after closed head injury. *Journal Head Trauma Rehabilitation, 15*(4), 1022–1040.

Machamer, J., Temkin, N., Fraser, R., Doctor, J. N., & Dikmen, S. (2005). Stability of employment after traumatic brain injury. *Journal of the International Neuropsychological Society, 11*(7), 807–816.

Nightingale, E. J., Soo, C. A., & Tate, R. L. (2007). A systematic review of early prognostic factors for return to work after traumatic brain injury. *Brain Impairment, 8*, 101–142.

U.S. Department of Labor. (2010). *Occupational outlook handbook*. Indianapolis: JIST.

Uomoto, J. M. (2000). Application of the neuropsychological evaluation in vocational planning after brain injury. In R. T. Fraser & D. C. Clemmons (Eds.), *Traumatic brain injury rehabilitation: Practical vocational, neuropsychological, and psychotherapy interventions* (pp. 1–94). Boca Raton, FL: CRC Press.

Varney, N. R., & Menefee, L. (1993). Psychosocial and executive deficits following closed head injury: Implications for orbital frontal cortex. *Journal of Head Trauma Rehabilitation, 8*, 32–44.

Warren, G. (2000). Use of assistive technology in vocational rehabilitation of persons with traumatic brain injury. In R. T. Fraser & D. C. Clemmons (Eds.), *Traumatic brain injury rehabilitation: Practical vocational, neuropsychological, and psychotherapy* (pp. 129–175). Boca Raton, FL: CRC Press.

CHAPTER 14

Evidence-Based Neuropsychological Assessment Following Work-Related Injury

Grant L. Iverson
Brian L. Brooks
James A. Holdnack

Cognitive impairment following workplace injuries can be either time-limited or permanent. Traumatic brain injuries, depression, anxiety disorders, and chronic pain can be associated with subjectively reported and/or objectively documented cognitive problems. The challenge for neuropsychologists who evaluate injured workers lies in accurately identifying problems with cognition, quantifying the deficits, estimating the impact on day-to-day functioning, and apportioning causation. The purpose of this chapter is to promote and encourage evidence-based neuropsychological assessment following work-related injuries.

CONCEPTUALIZING EVIDENCE-BASED NEUROPSYCHOLOGICAL PRACTICE

In 2005, the American Psychological Association (APA) approved a policy statement relating to evidence-based practice in psychology. Excerpts from this policy statement are reprinted as follows.

> Evidence-based practice in psychology (EBPP) is the integration of the best available research with clinical expertise in the context of patient characteristics, culture, and preferences. This definition of EBPP closely parallels the definition of evidence-based practice adopted by the Institute of Medicine (2001,

p. 147) as adapted from Sackett and colleagues (2000): "Evidence-based practice is the integration of best research evidence with clinical expertise and patient values." The purpose of EBPP is to promote effective psychological practice and enhance public health by applying empirically supported principles of psychological assessment, case formulation, therapeutic relationship, and intervention.

Best research evidence refers to scientific results related to intervention strategies, assessment, clinical problems, and patient populations in laboratory and field settings as well as to clinically relevant results of basic research in psychology and related fields. (APA, 2005, p. 1)

To advance evidence-based research and practice in neuropsychology, Chelune (2010) encouraged the field to embrace two fundamental beliefs: (1) clinical outcomes are individual events characterized by a change in status, performance, or other objectively defined endpoint; and (2) to be useful in the care of patients, results from outcomes research must be analyzed and presented in such a way that they can be directly evaluated and used by clinicians and researchers. To advance evidence-based research and practice, Chelune made three suggestions:

1. Define neuropsychological outcomes in a manner that can be applied consistently in research and in day-to-day clinical practice.
2. Report base-rate information (i.e., base rates of low scores).
3. Provide contingency table analyses, odds ratios, and Bayesian analyses (e.g., sensitivity, specificity, positive predictive value, and negative predictive value) to aid in diagnostic decision making and treatment planning.

Fortunately, in the past few years a tremendous amount of research designed to better understand the prevalence of low scores (recommendation 2 above) in healthy adults and improve diagnostic accuracy have been published (Axelrod & Wall, 2007; Binder, Iverson, & Brooks, 2009; Brooks, Iverson, Holdnack, & Feldman, 2008; Brooks, Iverson, & White, 2007; Crawford, Garthwaite, & Gault, 2007; Heaton, Grant, & Matthews, 1991; Heaton, Miller, Taylor, & Grant, 2004; Ingraham & Aiken, 1996; Iverson & Brooks, 2010; Iverson, Brooks, & Holdnack, 2008b; Iverson, Brooks, White, & Stern, 2008c; Palmer, Boone, Lesser, & Wohl, 1998; Schretlen, Testa, Winicki, Pearlson, & Gordon, 2008). Researchers have been encouraging the use of Bayesian methods for many years (e.g., Barr & McCrea, 2001; Benedict et al., 2003, 2004; Iverson, Mendrek, & Adams, 2004; Ivnik et al., 2001; Labarge, McCaffrey, & Brown, 2003; Rasquin, Lodder, Visser, Lousberg, & Verhey, 2005; Sawrie et al., 1998; Shapiro, Benedict, Schretlen, & Brandt, 1999; Tierney, Szalai, Dunn, Geslani, & McDowell, 2000; Woods, Weinborn, & Lovejoy, 2003). However, Bayesian methods, and other interesting statistical methodologies (e.g., Crawford, Garthwaite, Howell, & Venneri, 2003; Godber, Anderson, & Bell, 2000; Pearson, 2001, 2009), including odds and likelihood ratios (e.g., Bieliauskas, Fastenau, Lacy, & Roper, 1997; Dori & Chelune, 2004; Ivnik et al., 2000, 2001), are rarely used in mainstream clinical practice.

Unfortunately, as a profession we do not have evidence-based, widely accepted psychometric criteria for interpreting the severity of cognitive impairment. At present, the diagnosis of cognitive impairment, and level of cognitive impairment, is based primarily on clinical judgment. Before reviewing research designed to improve our ability to detect and quantify cognitive impairment, it is important to provide a clinical framework for conceptualizing cognitive impairment.

CONCEPTUALIZING COGNITIVE IMPAIRMENT

There is no universally agreed upon *definition* of cognitive impairment or methodology for establishing the severity of cognitive impairment. The *Diagnostic and Statistical Manual of Mental Disorders*, fourth edition (DSM-IV; American Psychiatric Association, 1994) and the *ICD-10 Classification of Mental and Behavioral Disorders* (World Health Organization, 1992) offer several categories for diagnosing cognitive problems that are due to a traumatic brain injury, neurological condition, or general medical problem, such as mild cognitive disorder (ICD-10), cognitive disorder not otherwise specified (DMS-IV), and dementia.

Iverson and colleagues provided a clinical framework for conceptualizing cognitive impairment on a continuum (Iverson & Brooks, 2010; Iverson, Brooks, & Ashton, 2008a; Iverson et al., 2008b). These categories reflect levels of cognitive impairment in a face valid manner—the specific criteria for each level have not been codified or agreed upon. These categories can be helpful for conceptualizing cognitive problems following workplace injuries.

1. *Mild cognitive diminishment.* This level of difficulty is not cognitive "impairment." Instead, it represents a mild diminishment in cognitive functioning. This cognitive diminishment may or may not be identifiable using neuropsychological tests. This diminishment can, but does not always, have a mild adverse impact on a person's social and/or occupational functioning. This diminishment may or may not be noticeable by others.

2. *Mild cognitive impairment.* This level of cognitive impairment should be identifiable using neuropsychological tests. This impairment has a mild (sometimes moderate) adverse impact on a person's social and/or occupational functioning.

3. *Moderate cognitive impairment.* This level of cognitive impairment would have a substantial impact on everyday functioning. This impairment would be noticeable to others in regards to the person's social and/or occupational functioning.

4. *Severe cognitive impairment/dementia.* This cognitive impairment would have a substantial adverse impact on everyday functioning. This level of impairment would render the individual incapable of competitive employment. The person should not be driving a motor vehicle and might have difficulty with activities of daily living.

5. *Profound cognitive impairment/severe dementia.* This cognitive impairment would render the person in need of 24-hour supervision and assistance with daily activities, which he or she may receive at home, in a nursing home, or other institution.

The relation between levels of cognitive impairment, ability to work, and ability to live independently is depicted visually in Figure 14.1. In general, greater cognitive impairment is associated with a greater adverse effect on occupational functioning. The figure, of course, oversimplifies the relations among these factors. There are tremendous individual differences— reinforcing the need for individualized assessment and vocational planning. Some individuals with quite mild cognitive impairment might have difficulty functioning in their own occupation (e.g., physicians and lawyers),

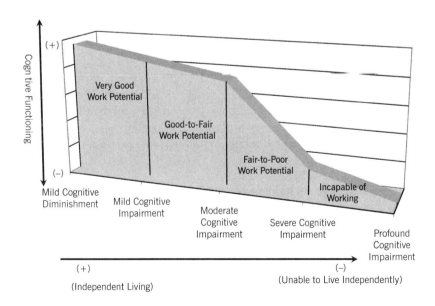

▪ **FIGURE 14.1.** Level of cognitive impairment and relative impact on daily functioning (employability and independent living).

and other people with moderate cognitive impairment might be able to work part-time in a different occupation.

Neuropsychologists are uniquely trained and qualified to identify, describe, and quantify cognitive diminishment or impairment. In fact, *deficit measurement* (Lezak, 1976, 1983) is typically one of the goals of neuropsychological assessment. The foundation of deficit measurement, psychometrically, is the normal curve, but the principles of the normal curve are frequently misunderstood in the context of a neuropsychological evaluation. Misunderstanding these principles can increase the risk for false positive diagnoses of cognitive impairment.

CAN THE BELL CURVE LEAD US ASTRAY?

In clinical practice there can be a fundamental misunderstanding, and pervasive misapplication, of the normal curve (i.e., "bell curve," Gaussian distribution). The normal curve is the foundation for interpreting intellectual and neuropsychological test scores. Many believe the curve has immutable properties and, as such, provides the clinician with confidence in test scores. Of course, clinicians appreciate that tests contain measurement error, and tests have varying degrees of reliability, so a score at the 10th percentile, for example, is only an estimate of the person's true score. That is not usually the problem that leads clinicians down the wrong path. The problem lies in applying principles of a univariate distribution (i.e., the distribution of a single score along a bell curve) to multivariate data (i.e., interpretation of numerous scores simultaneously, instead of just one).[1] By analogy, the mainstream practice of interpreting numerous test scores in clinical neuropsychology could be seen as akin to running 50- to 100 *t*-tests in an experiment. Some significant findings in the experiment might emerge by chance. This is a well-documented phenomenon in research studies, resulting in the development of procedures and adjustments (e.g., multivariate statistics, Bonferroni correction) to limit such errors from being interpreted. In the research community, such procedures have been developed and widely employed.

When a battery of cognitive tests is administered to healthy individuals, it is common to get some low scores (Axelrod & Wall, 2007; Binder et al., 2009; Brooks et al., 2007, 2008; Crawford et al., 2007; Heaton et al., 1991, 2004; Ingraham & Aiken, 1996; Iverson & Brooks, 2010; Iverson et al., 2008b, 2008c; Palmer et al., 1998; Schretlen et al., 2008). This common occurrence of obtaining some low scores exists because there is considerable intraindividual variability in the cognitive abilities of healthy people. This basic principle is illustrated using two different cutoff scores and three different test batteries in Figure 14.2. The base rate data in the figure are for healthy adults on the Neuropsychological Assessment Battery

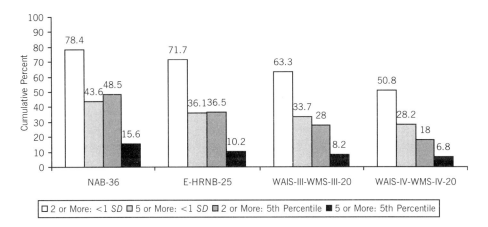

▦ **FIGURE 14.2.** Base rates of low scores across batteries with different numbers of scores being interpreted: Cutoff <1 *SD* and = ≤5th percentile. *SD*, standard deviation; NAB-36, all 36 scores from the full Neuropsychological Assessment Battery; E-HRNB-25, 25 scores from the Expanded Halstead–Reitan Neuropsychological Battery; WAIS-III-WMS-III–20, all 20 primary subtest scores from the Wechsler Adult Intelligence Scale–III and Wechsler Memory Scale–III; and WAIS-IV–WMS-IV-20, all 20 primary subtest scores from the Wechsler Adult Intelligence Scale–IV and Wechsler Memory Scale–IV. Bars represent percent of healthy adults from standardization samples who had (1) two or more or (2) five or more scores below 1 *SD* (*T* < 40; SS ≤ 7) or at or below 5th percentile (i.e., *T*-score = 34 or SS = 5).

(NAB; Stern & White, 2003a), the Expanded Halstead-Reitan Neuropsychological Battery (E-HRNB; Heaton et al., 2004), the combination of the Wechsler Adult Intelligence Scale–III (WAIS-III; Wechsler, 1997a) and Wechsler Memory Scale–III (WMS-III; Wechsler, 1997b), and the combination of the WAIS-IV (Wechsler, 2008) and WMS-IV (Wechsler, 2009). As seen in Figure 14.2, when considering a battery of tests ranging from 20 to 36 scores, the majority of healthy adults will have two or more "impaired" scores if the cutoff is set at one standard deviation (*SD*) below the mean. Across the four batteries, between 18 and 50% of healthy adults will have two or more impaired scores, with the cutoff set as ≤ 5th percentile.

What does this mean for clinical practice? The normal curve applies to normally distributed data from a single test score. However, an assumption or clinical inference relating to a single test score might be inaccurate in the context of multiple test scores. For example, if the psychometric criterion for mild cognitive impairment (MCI) is having a memory test score below 1.5 standard deviations from the mean (i.e., below the 7th percentile), then we can feel confident that if we have a memory test with excellent representative normative data (that is normally distributed), then our false positive rate for this criterion is 6%. However, neuropsychologists rarely give, and rely on, a single test. If the WMS-III, for example, is administered and the eight age-adjusted primary subtest scores are examined simultaneously, 26% of healthy older adults have one or more scores at or below the 5th percentile. If the demographically adjusted normative data are used, 39% have at least one score at or below the 5th percentile (Brooks et al., 2008). In other words, instead of a false positive rate of 5%, when interpreting eight test scores (immediate and delayed recall) derived from only four memory tests, the false positive rate for identifying memory impairment is 26–39%. In order to maintain a 5% false positive rate, the clinician needs to know that a certain number of low scores would have to be obtained—not just one (for example, see Brooks, Iverson, Feldman, & Holdnack, 2009).

DEMOGRAPHIC CHARACTERISTICS

Researchers and test publishers have illustrated repeatedly that many cognitive abilities vary in association with demographic characteristics. In some studies, women tend to perform better on tasks of verbal learning and memory, verbal fluency, and processing speed (Beatty, Mold, & Gontkovsky, 2003; Donders, Zhu, & Tulsky, 2001; Herlitz, Nilsson, & Backman, 1997; Norman, Evans, Miller, & Heaton, 2000). In contrast, men tend to perform better on motor speed (Schmidt, Oliveira, Rocha, & Abreu-Villaca, 2000), some visual-spatial and visual-constructional tasks (Beatty et al., 2003; Collaer & Nelson, 2002; Voyer, Voyer, & Bryden, 1995), and arithmetic reasoning and computations (Geary, Saults, Liu, & Hoard, 2000).

In group studies, cognitive test scores vary by level of education (Heaton et al., 2004; Heaton, Taylor, & Manly, 2003; Ivnik, Makec, Smith, Tangolos, & Peterson, 1996; Morgan et al., 2008; Rosselli & Ardila, 2003; Ryan et al., 2005). This relation, in part, is likely due to the relation between intelligence and education. In other words, intelligence, education, and neuropsychological test performance are intercorrelated. Reading ability is correlated with both education and intelligence. As such, reading ability is also correlated with other cognitive domains. Because reading is believed to be *relatively* resistant to most types of brain injury and disease (Bright, Jaldow, & Kopelman, 2002; Maddrey, Cullum, Weiner, & Filley, 1996; Strauss, Sherman, & Spreen, 2006), reading test performance has been used to estimate preinjury or predisease cognitive functioning (Bright et al., 2002; Green et al., 2008; Griffin, Mindt, Rankin, Ritchie, & Scott, 2002; Paolo, Ryan, Troster, & Hilmer, 1996).

When evaluating injured workers, it is important to consider the effects of education on the likelihood of obtaining low scores. Using demographically adjusted normative data can be helpful for estimating how a person performs relative to people with less than high school education or university degrees. This comparison is illustrated with two cases, using WMS-IV scores, in Table 14.1. Notice how the man with a university education has standard scores that are slightly lower when using demographically adjusted normative data and the man who has 10 years of education has standard scores that are somewhat higher using demographically adjusted normative data. On any given case, a clinician must decide which normative data seems most appropriate to use—given the demographic characteristics of the patient and the specific clinical questions that are being addressed in the evaluation.

It would be a mistake, however, to assume that using demographically adjusted normative data will "correct" for, or fundamentally alter, the prevalence of low scores in healthy adults. For example, the prevalence of low scores on the WMS-IV using age-adjusted versus demographically adjusted normative data is presented in Figure 14.3. Notice that having two or more scores at or below 1 *SD* occurs in 43% of healthy adults using age norms and in 37% when using demographically adjusted norms. Clinicians often assume that the demographically adjusted norms are more "refined" or "precise" and, as such, will result in fewer low scores in those with low education and greater low scores in those with university degrees. This belief, in general, is true. However, the basic principles of multivariate (i.e., multiple tests) base rates apply to age-adjusted normative data and demographically adjusted normative data.

Researchers have repeatedly demonstrated differences in cognitive test results among racial groups (Ardila, 1995; Brickman, Cabo, & Manly, 2006; Manly & Echemendia, 2007; O'Bryant, O'Jile, & McCaffrey, 2004). For example, Patton and colleagues (2003) compared 50 healthy older African-American adults to 50 Caucasians matched on age, education, and gender on the Repeatable Battery for the Assessment of Neuropsychological Status (RBANS; Randolph, 1998). The RBANS is a neuropsychological screening battery designed to measure attention/processing speed, expressive language, visual–spatial and constructional abilities, and immediate and delayed memory. The African Americans had significantly lower scores across the cognitive domains. A practical implication of this study is that if an elderly African American is being evaluated for cognitive impairment secondary to a work-related injury, the psychologist might erroneously conclude that the patient was showing frank evidence of cognitive impairment if his or her scores were compared to Caucasian normative data instead of African-American normative data.

Understanding the relation between demographic factors (e.g., sex, age, education, reading ability, and race/ethnicity) has clear implications for research and clinical practice. If the goal of testing is to identify the

■ **TABLE 14.1. Comparing Age-Adjusted and Demographically Adjusted Normative Scores on the WMS-IV**

	Age-adjusted standard scores			Demographically adjusted standard scores		
	Scaled score	Percentile rank	Classification	T score	Percentile rank	Classification
27-year-old man with 16 years education						
Logical Memory I	12	75	Average	54	66	Average
Logical Memory II	9	37	Average	44	27	Average
Verbal Paired Associates I	7	16	Low Average	37	10	Low Average
Verbal Paired Associates II	9	37	Average	44	27	Average
Designs I	12	75	Average	54	66	Average
Designs II	10	50	Average	48	42	Average
Visual Reproduction I	10	50	Average	44	27	Average
Visual Reproduction II	6	9	Unusually Low	33	4	Unusually Low
Spatial Addition	11	63	Average	47	38	Average
Symbol Span	8	25	Average	39	14	Low Average
54-year-old man with 10 years education						
Logical Memory I	5	5	Unusually Low	38	12	Low Average
Logical Memory II	4	2	Extremely Low	34	5	Unusually Low
Verbal Paired Associates I	6	9	Unusually Low	39	14	Low Average
Verbal Paired Associates II	5	5	Unusually Low	36	8	Unusually Low
Designs I	6	9	Unusually Low	42	21	Low Average
Designs II	6	9	Unusually Low	39	14	Low Average
Visual Reproduction I	6	9	Unusually Low	41	18	Low Average
Visual Reproduction II	7	16	Low Average	42	21	Low Average
Spatial Addition	5	5	Unusually Low	37	10	Low Average
Symbol Span	9	37	Average	51	54	Average

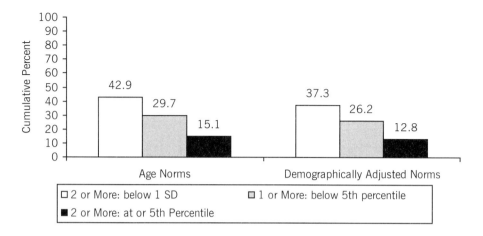

▒ **FIGURE 14.3.** Base rates of low scores on the WMS-IV using age- and demographically adjusted normative data: Cutoff <1 *SD* and = ≤5th percentile. *N* = 686. There are eight demographically adjusted memory subtest scores (Logical Memory I, Verbal Paired Associates I, Designs I, and Visual Reproduction I, Logical Memory II, Verbal Paired Associates II, Designs II, and Visual Reproduction II) that were considered for these analyses. Cutoff scores included <16th percentile (<1 *SD* or *T*-score < 40) and ≤5th percentile (*T*-score = 34). Standardization data for the WMS-IV copyright 2009 by NCS Pearson, Inc. Used with permission. All rights reserved.

presence of acquired cognitive impairment, then diagnostic accuracy will be improved if relevant demographic characteristics are considered in the interpretation of test performance.

OCCUPATIONAL GROUPS AND TEST PERFORMANCE

There is a relation between cognitive functioning and occupations, which is likely mediated to a substantial degree by education. As seen in Figure 14.4, on average general laborers perform lower on cognitive measures than managers. Similarly, as previously noted, those with university degrees tend to perform considerably better on intellectual and neuropsychological testing than those who do not graduate from high school. In general clinical practice or when evaluating injured workers, some clinicians make specific assumptions about how a person should perform on testing based on his or her occupation. For example, a clinician might say that a carpenter or skilled tradesperson should have good visual-spatial skills and a manager should have good verbal skills. Invariably, of course, those assumptions are

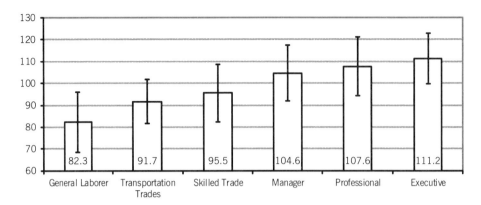

■ **FIGURE 14.4.** WAIS-IV Full Scale IQ by occupation groups. Standardization data from the WAIS-IV copyright 2008 by NCS Pearson, Inc. Used with permission. All rights reserved.

correct for some people. Finding verbal skills greater than nonverbal skills in a manager, and strengths in visual-spatial skills in a carpenter, is salient data that tends to reinforce these beliefs. The problem, of course, is that people have highly variable strengths and weaknesses that may or may not map neatly on to a clinician's assumptions about how certain occupational groups should perform. In the above examples, an injured carpenter or manager, premorbidly, might have skills that are exactly the opposite of these expectations.

Figure 14.5 illustrates the differences in cognitive abilities across various occupational groups. As can be seen, people who are in occupations that typically involve more formal education tend to have stronger cognitive abilities (i.e., verbal intelligence, nonverbal intelligence, working memory, and processing speed indexes), although it should be appreciated that there is considerable overlap between groups (the means and standard deviations are provided in Tables 14.2 and 14.3). To test the above assumption that certain occupations are associated with relative strengths or weaknesses (e.g., a tradesperson would have stronger visual than verbal skills), Figure 14.6 illustrates the verbal versus visual differences in the skilled trade/ public safety group. The differences between verbal and nonverbal skills, whether on scores of intelligence or memory, are small. Although there is a "trend" in the direction that confirms the assumption, the amount of variance in performance would be too substantial to make these differences meaningful at the group level. That being said, Tables 14.2 and 14.3 are useful to clinicians for illustrating general trends in the relation between occupational groups and cognitive test performance.

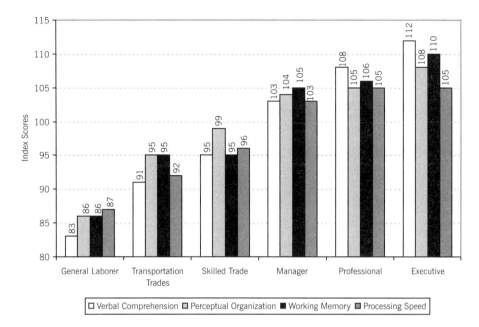

▦ **FIGURE 14.5.** WAIS-IV index scores by occupational groups. Standardization data from the WAIS-IV copyright 2008 by NCS Pearson, Inc. Used with permission. All rights reserved.

INTELLIGENCE

The number of low scores across a comprehensive battery of neuropsychological tests will vary by level of intelligence (Horton, 1999; Steinberg, Bieliauskas, Smith, & Ivnik, 2005; Steinberg, Bieliauskas, Smith, Ivnik, & Malec, 2005; Tremont, Hoffman, Scott, & Adams, 1998; Warner, Ernst, Townes, Peel, & Preston, 1987). People with below-average intellectual abilities are expected to have more low scores than people with above-average intelligence because neuropsychological test performance is correlated with intelligence. Therefore, there is a risk of misdiagnosing cognitive problems in lower-functioning persons (i.e., false positives) and a risk of missing a diagnosis of cognitive problems in persons who are higher functioning intellectually (i.e., false negatives). For example, if clinicians and researchers use a universal cutoff for memory impairment (e.g., more than 1.5 SD below the mean), then a person with superior intellectual abilities would have to experience a much greater decline to meet the criterion than a person with low-average intellectual abilities.

■ **TABLE 14.2. WAIS-IV Index Scores by Occupation Groups**

		Verbal comprehension	Perceptual reasoning	Working memory	Processing speed	General ability	Full-scale IQ
General laborer (N = 124)	Mean	82.6	86.0	86.1	87.4	82.6	82.3
	SD	13.2	13.5	15.1	15.6	13.1	13.8
Transportation trades (N = 41)	Mean	91.3	95.0	94.6	92.2	92.3	91.7
	SD	12.8	11.4	11.6	11.8	10.8	9.9
Skilled trade/ public safety (N = 192)	Mean	95.3	99.2	94.6	95.6	96.9	95.5
	SD	13.0	14.9	13.5	13.0	13.6	13.2
Manager (N = 165)	Mean	103.2	104.4	104.9	102.9	104.3	104.6
	SD	12.8	13.8	13.5	14.0	13.4	12.7
Professional/ individual contributor (N = 483)	Mean	108.4	105.1	105.5	105.4	107.6	107.6
	SD	12.9	14.3	14.1	14.0	13.5	13.5
Director; executive (N = 103)	Mean	111.8	108.4	109.8	105.1	111.5	111.2
	SD	11.6	14.2	13.0	12.5	12.2	11.6

Note. Standardization data from the WAIS-IV copyright 2008 by NCS Pearson, Inc. Used with permission. All rights reserved.

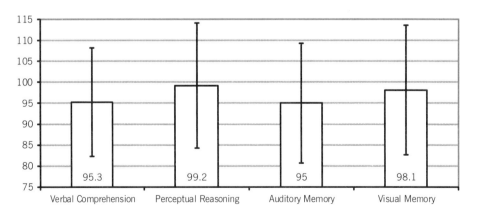

■ **FIGURE 14.6.** WAIS-IV verbal versus visual abilities within the skilled trade/ public safety group. Standardization data from the WAIS-IV copyright 2008 by NCS Pearson, Inc. Used with permission. All rights reserved.

▪ TABLE 14.3. WMS-IV Index Scores by Occupation Groups

Occupation group		Immediate memory	Delayed memory	Auditory memory	Visual memory	Visual working memory
General laborer	Mean	87.3	89.9	90.1	89.1	90.1
(N = 82)	SD	15.5	16.2	16.3	15.2	14.3
Transportation trades	Mean	95.7	97.3	96.0	98.0	95.7
(N = 27)	SD	15.0	17.8	17.1	15.3	11.9
Skilled trade/public	Mean	95.8	96.1	95.0	98.1	96.7
safety (N = 148)	SD	14.9	14.4	14.3	15.5	15.8
Manager (N = 126)	Mean	103.1	102.6	102.6	102.6	104.2
	SD	15.5	15.6	14.6	15.7	15.4
Professional/individual	Mean	105.8	104.9	105.3	104.2	106.3
contributor (N = 357)	SD	13.4	13.9	14.4	13.4	12.9
Director; executive	Mean	106.4	103.8	104.9	104.2	107.5
(N = 79)	SD	13.6	13.3	14.5	13.4	11.4

Note. A reduced number of subjects completed the Visual Working Memory Index in comparison to the other Indexes. Standardization data for the WMS-IV copyright 2009 by NCS Pearson, Inc. Used with permission. All rights reserved.

The relation between intelligence and number of low scores on the NAB is illustrated in Figure 14.7. The cumulative percentage curves illustrate the relation between level of intelligence and number of low neuropsychological test scores in healthy adults. Having five or more low scores occurs in 8.9% of healthy adults with high-average intelligence, 23% of those with average intelligence, and 61.2% of those with low-average intelligence. Approximately 30% of people with low-average intelligence will have 10 or more scores below the 10th percentile on the NAB (out of 36 scores). Stated differently, it is common for a person with low-average intelligence to have at least 1 out of every 4 of his or her neuropsychological test scores below the 10th percentile.

The prevalence of low scores on the NAB, WAIS-III/WMS-III, and WAIS-IV/WMS-IV is illustrated in Figure 14.8. Stratified by intelligence, the base rates of healthy adults who obtain two or more scores at or below the 5th percentile are presented. The base rates across levels of intelligence were higher for the NAB most likely because we analyzed 36 scores compared to 20 scores for the Wechsler scales.

Base-rate analyses across batteries of tests provide general information regarding how common it is to obtain low scores in healthy adults with different levels of intelligence. Iverson et al. (2008c) provided these base-

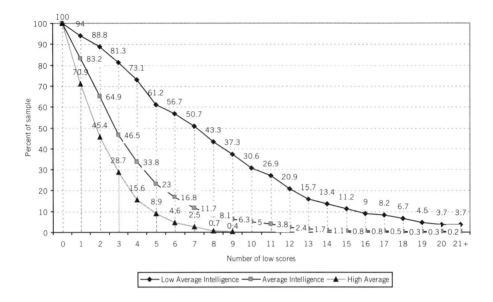

▦ **FIGURE 14.7.** Prevalence of low scores in healthy adults on the Neuropsychological Assessment Battery (NAB)—36 primary *T*-scores: low scores <10th percentile. This figure was created from data presented in: Iverson, Brooks, White, and Stern (2008c).

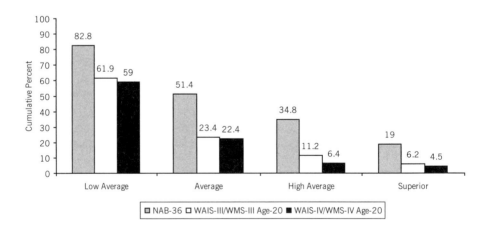

▦ **FIGURE 14.8.** Prevalence of low scores across different test batteries stratified by level of intelligence: two or more scores ≤5th percentile. NAB scores are stratified by RIST scores. WAIS/WMS scores, which are age adjusted, are stratified by either WTAR (WAIS-III/WMS-III) or ToPF (WAIS-IV/WMS-IV) scores. Numbers after the names of the tests in the legend indicate the number of subtest scores considered simultaneously.

rate tables for the NAB. In Table 14.4, we have distilled information out of those base-rate tables to illustrate a common amount of low scores in healthy adults across this battery. For example, it is common for a person of below-average intelligence to have up to 33% of his or her test scores below the 10th percentile. In contrast, it is common for a person of average intelligence to have 14% of his or her test scores in this range and a person of high-average intelligence to have 8% of his or her test scores in this range.

Similarly, Table 14.5 illustrates how common it is to obtain low scores across the entire WAIS-IV and WMS-IV, stratified by Test of Premorbid Functioning predicted intelligence (i.e., ToPF reading and demographics predicted full-scale Intelligence Quotient [FSIQ]). Defining a low score as below the 10th percentile, it is common for people with (1) unusually low predicted premorbid intelligence to have up to 65% of their scores in this range (i.e., 13/20 subtest scores), (2) low-average predicted intelligence to have up to 40% of their scores in this range, (3) average intelligence to have up to 15% of their scores in this range, and (4) high-average intelligence to have up to 10% of their scores in this range (i.e., 2/20 subtest scores).

▨ **TABLE 14.4. What Is a Normal Number of Low Scores on the Neuropsychological Assessment Battery (NAB)?**

If you have low-average intelligence:
- It is common to have up to 47% of your neuropsychological test scores below 1 *SD* from the mean.
- It is common to have up to 33% of your neuropsychological test scores below the 10th percentile.
- It is common to have up to 25% of your neuropsychological test scores at or below the 5th percentile.

If you have average intelligence:
- It is common to have up to 19% of your neuropsychological test scores below 1 *SD* from the mean.
- It is common to have up to 14% of your neuropsychological test scores below the 10th percentile.
- It is common to have up to 11% of your neuropsychological test scores at or below the 5th percentile.

If you have high-average intelligence:
- It is common to have up to 14% of your neuropsychological test scores below 1 *SD* from the mean.
- It is common to have up to 8% of your neuropsychological test scores below the 10th percentile.
- It is common to have up to 6% of your neuropsychological test scores at or below the 5th percentile.

Note. These numbers are based on the base-rate tables presented in Iverson et al. (2008c). The analyses are based on 36 primary *T*-scores. In the statements for this table, fewer than 20% of healthy adults will obtain more low scores than noted in the bulleted points. That means 80% of healthy adults will obtain that percentage of low scores or fewer.

■ TABLE 14.5. What Is a Normal Number of Low Scores on the WAIS-IV and WMS-IV?

If you have unusually low intelligence:
- It is common to have up to 85% of your test scores at or below 1 *SD* from the mean.
- It is common to have up to 65% of your test scores below the 10th percentile.
- It is common to have up to 50% of your test scores at or below the 5th percentile.

If you have low-average intelligence:
- It is common to have up to 60% of your test scores at or below 1 *SD* from the mean.
- It is common to have up to 40% of your test scores below the 10th percentile.
- It is common to have up to 25% of your test scores at or below the 5th percentile.

If you have average intelligence:
- It is common to have up to 30% of your test scores at or below 1 *SD* from the mean.
- It is common to have up to 15% of your test scores below the 10th percentile.
- It is common to have up to 10% of your test scores at or below the 5th percentile.

If you have high-average intelligence:
- It is common to have up to 15% of your test scores at or below 1 *SD* from the mean.
- It is common to have up to 10% of your test scores below the 10th percentile.
- It is common to have up to 5% of your test scores at or below the 5th percentile.

Note. These numbers are based on the base-rate tables from WAIS-IV and WMS-IV (based on ToPF stratified FSIQ) reported in Brooks, Iverson, and Holdnack (2010). There were 20 subtest scores considered in the analyses. To be considered "uncommon," fewer than 25% of healthy adults will obtain more low scores than noted in the bulleted points. For example, if it was considered "uncommon" for a person with unusually low intelligence to have 17/20 (85%) scores <1 *SD*, then it would be considered "common" to have up to 85% of the scores <1 *SD*.

DOMAIN-SPECIFIC BASE RATES OF LOW SCORES

It is helpful to know how often healthy people obtain low scores across a battery of tests, as illustrated in the previous section. Neuropsychologists are particularly interested, however, in how often healthy adults obtain low scores within specific cognitive domains such as attention, speed of processing, and memory. Domain-specific base rates can be used to determine if a certain pattern of test scores within a cognitive domain is common or uncommon in healthy adults. We illustrate this concept in this section using the normative data from the WAIS-IV and WMS-IV. The WAIS-IV contains three tests of auditory working memory (Arithmetic, Digit Span, and Letter Number Sequencing) and three tests of processing speed (Coding, Symbol Search, and Cancellation). The WMS-IV contains four tests of learning and memory (Logical Memory, Verbal Paired Associates, Designs, and Visual Reproduction) that provide four immediate and four delayed memory age-adjusted scaled scores. We conducted base-rate analyses on each domain of subtest scores, stratified by (1) ToPF-demographic predicted intelligence and (2) years of education. These base rates are presented in Tables 14.6 to 14.9.

As illustrated in these tables, it becomes readily apparent that low scores within domains are relatively common, and their prevalence varies by level of education and intelligence. For example, obtaining one or more low processing speed scores (≤5th percentile; SS ≤ 5) occurred in 25%, 8%, and 7% of adults with predicted low-average, average, and high-average intelligence, respectively (Table 14.6). Obtaining one or more low delayed memory scores (≤ 5th percentile) occurred in 34%, 22%, and 11% of adults with predicted low-average, average, and high-average intelligence, respectively (Table 14.7). The percentage obtaining one or more low working memory scores (≤ 5th percentile), stratified by years of education, was as follows: 9–11 years = 24%, 12 years = 13%, 13–15 years = 6%, and 16+ years = 1% (Table 14.8).

Of course, if a higher cutoff score is selected, the base rates increase. Obtaining one or more low-processing speed scores (< 10th percentile; SS ≤ 6) occurred in 39%, 18%, and 9% of adults with predicted low-average, average, and high-average intelligence, respectively (Table 14.6). Obtaining one or more low-delayed memory scores (< 10th percentile) occurred in 46%, 35%, and 17% of adults with predicted low-average, average, and high-average intelligence, respectively (Table 14.7). The percentage obtaining one or more low working memory scores (< 10th percentile), stratified by years of education, was as follows: 9–11 years = 42%, 12 years = 24%, 13–15 years = 14%, and 16+ years = 5% (Table 14.8).

Having comprehensive, stratified, domain-specific information can strengthen the psychometric underpinnings of clinical judgment. Two case studies illustrating the use of these domain-specific base rates are summarized in Table 14.10. The first case involves a 58-year-old man with 9 years of education who sustained a mild traumatic brain injury and a back injury in a fall at work, 2 years prior to the evaluation. He had significant problems with depression, anxiety, and insomnia. He had a long history of hypertension. An MRI of his brain revealed patchy subcortical and periventricular white matter T2 and FLAIR hyperintensities in both frontal lobes, greater on the right. The findings were considered nonspecific but compatible with small-vessel ischemic disease. The second case involved a 25-year-old woman with a university degree who was 6 months postmoderate TBI sustained in a high-speed single-vehicle car accident.

For Case 1, his WAIS-IV General Ability Index was 83, and his ToPF reading score was 82. Therefore, he might have been of low-average intelligence prior to his workplace injury and his cerebrovascular disease. However, given that his Full Scale IQ was 89 and his ToPF-Predicted FSIQ was

(text resumes on page 387)

◼ **TABLE 14.6. Base Rates of Low Auditory Working Memory and Processing Speed Subtest Scores (Age Adjusted) on the WAIS-IV and WMS-IV in Healthy Adults across Levels of Estimated Intellectual Abilities**

| No. of scores below cutoff | ToPF-demographics predicted FSIQ | | | | | | | | | | | | No. of scores below cutoff |
| | Entire adult sample | | Unusually low | | Low average | | Average | | High average | | Superior/very superior | | |
	%	C%	%	C%	%	C%	%	C%	%	C%	%	C%	
Working Memory subtests													
≤25th %ile													<25th %ile
3	13.7	13.7	77.3	77.3	36.8	36.8	9.0	9.0	0.6	0.6	—	—	3
2	13.6	27.2	18.2	95.5	25.3	62.1	13.6	22.6	1.9	2.5	—	—	2
1	20.7	47.9	4.5	100.0	20.0	82.1	25.3	47.9	10.2	12.7	4.5	4.5	1
0	52.1	100.0	—	—	17.9	100.0	52.1	100.0	87.3	100.0	95.5	100.0	0
≤16th %ile													<16th %ile
3	5.0	5.0	40.9	40.9	17.9	17.9	1.9	1.9	—	—	—	—	3
2	8.7	13.7	27.3	68.2	22.1	40.0	6.9	8.8	—	—	—	—	2
1	18.1	31.8	27.3	95.5	26.3	66.3	19.5	28.2	6.4	6.4	—	—	1
0	68.2	100.0	4.5	100.0	33.7	100.0	71.8	100.0	93.6	100.0	100.0	100.0	0
≤9th %ile													≤9th %ile
3	2.0	2.0	22.7	22.7	6.3	6.3	0.4	0.4	—	—	—	—	3
2	4.3	6.3	40.9	63.6	12.6	18.9	1.9	2.3	—	—	—	—	2
1	13.3	19.7	13.6	77.3	24.2	43.2	13.6	15.9	3.2	3.2	—	—	1
0	80.3	100.0	22.7	100.0	56.8	100.0	84.1	100.0	96.8	100.0	100.0	100.0	0
≤5th %ile													≤5th %ile
3	0.6	0.6	—	—	3.2	3.2	—	—	—	—	—	—	3
2	2.3	2.9	27.3	27.3	7.4	10.5	0.8	0.8	—	—	—	—	2
1	6.9	9.8	31.8	59.1	13.7	24.2	5.9	6.7	—	—	—	—	1
0	90.2	100.0	40.9	100.0	75.8	100.0	93.3	100.0	100.0	100.0	100.0	100.0	0
≤2nd %ile													<2nd %ile
3	—	—	—	—	—	—	—	—	—	—	—	—	3
2	0.8	0.8	13.6	13.6	3.2	3.2	—	—	—	—	—	—	2
1	2.3	3.1	13.6	27.3	5.3	8.4	1.5	1.5	—	—	—	—	1
0	96.9	100.0	72.7	100.0	91.6	100.0	98.5	100.0	100.0	100.0	100.0	100.0	0
Processing Speed subtests													
≤25th %ile													≤25th %ile
3	11.7	11.7	54.5	54.5	21.1	21.1	8.8	8.8	3.8	3.8	4.5	4.5	3
2	15.4	27.1	40.9	95.5	25.3	46.3	14.3	23.1	8.9	12.7	—	—	2
1	25.6	52.7	4.5	100.0	25.3	71.6	28.1	51.2	20.4	33.1	22.7	22.7	1
0	47.2	100.0	—	—	28.4	100.0	48.8	100.0	66.9	100.0	72.7	72.7	0

(cont.)

▨ **TABLE 14.6.** *(cont.)*

No. of scores below cutoff	Entire adult sample		Unusually low		Low average		Average		High average		Superior/ very superior		No. of scores below cutoff
	%	C%	%	C%	%	C%	%	C%	%	C%	%	C%	
					Processing Speed subtests *(cont.)*								
≤16th %ile													<16th %ile
3	5.4	5.5	27.3	27.3	13.7	13.7	3.1	3.1	—	—	4.5	4.5	3
2	11.9	17.4	31.8	59.1	23.2	36.8	9.6	12.8	7	7	—	—	2
1	18.9	36.3	31.8	90.9	18.9	55.8	19.1	31.9	14.6	21.7	9.1	13.6	1
0	63.7	100.0	9.1	100.0	44.2	100.0	68.1	100.0	78.3	100.0	86.4	100.0	0
≤9th %ile													≤9th %ile
3	2.2	2.2	9.1	9.1	6.3	6.3	1.0	1.0	—	—	—	—	3
2	6.1	8.3	22.7	31.8	10.5	16.8	4.8	5.9	2.5	2.5	4.5	4.5	2
1	13.0	21.4	36.4	68.2	22.1	38.9	12.2	18.0	6.4	8.9	4.5	9.1	1
0	78.6	100.0	31.8	100.0	61.1	100.0	82.0	100.0	91.1	100.0	90.9	100.0	0
≤5th %ile													≤5th %ile
3	0.7	0.7	4.5	4.5	2.1	2.1	0.2	0.2	—	—	—	—	3
2	3.2	3.9	13.6	18.2	11.6	13.7	1.7	1.9	0.6	0.6	—	—	2
1	8.9	12.8	31.8	50.0	11.6	25.3	6.5	8.4	6.4	7.0	4.5	4.5	1
0	87.1	100.0	50.0	100.0	74.7	100.0	91.6	100.0	93.0	100.0	95.5	100.0	0
≤2nd %ile													<2nd %ile
3	0.4	0.4	—	—	2.1	2.1	0.2	0.2	—	—	—	—	3
2	0.7	1.1	—	—	3.2	5.3	0.2	0.4	—	—	—	—	2
1	4.1	5.2	27.3	27.3	9.5	14.7	2.7	3.1	0.6	0.6	—	—	1
0	94.7	100.0	72.7	100.0	85.3	100.0	96.9	100.0	99.4	100.0	100.0	100.0	0

Note. N = 900. There are three age-adjusted working memory subtest scores (Arithmetic, Digit Span, and Letter Number Sequencing) and three age-adjusted processing speed subtest scores (Coding, Symbol Search, and Cancellation) that were considered for these analyses. C% = cumulative percentage. Cutoff scores included ≤16th percentile (≤–1 SD or SS ≤ 7); ≤9th percentile (SS ≤6); ≤5th percentile (SS ≤ 5); and below the 2nd percentile (<–2 SD or SS ≤ 4). ToPF-demographics predicted Full Scale IQ included: Unusually low (<80; *n* = 22); Low average (80–89; *n* = 95); Average (90–109; *n* = 478); High average (110–119; *n* = 157); Superior/Very superior (120+; *n* = 22). Standardization data from the WAIS-IV copyright 2008 by NCS Pearson, Inc. Used with permission. All rights reserved.

■ TABLE 14.7. Base Rates of Low Immediate and Delayed Memory Subtest Scores (Age Adjusted) on the WMS-IV in Healthy Adults across Levels of Estimated Intellectual Abilities

No. of scores below cutoff	Entire adult sample		Unusually low		Low average		Average		High average		Superior/ very superior		No. of scores below cutoff
	%	C%	%	C%	%	C%	%	C%	%	C%	%	C%	
						ToPF-demographics predicted FSIQ								
						Immediate Memory subtests								
≤25th %ile													≤25th %ile
4	5.4	5.4	36.4	36.4	9.5	9.5	3.3	3.3	0.6	0.6	—	—	4
3	11.1	16.6	31.8	68.2	20.0	29.5	10.3	13.6	3.8	4.5	—	—	3
2	19.9	36.4	18.2	86.4	25.3	54.7	22.2	35.8	12.1	16.6	—	—	2
1	26.2	62.7	13.6	100.0	28.4	83.2	28.9	64.6	24.2	40.8	27.3	27.3	1
0	37.3	100.0	—	—	16.8	100.0	35.4	100.0	59.2	100.0	72.7	100.0	0
≤16th %ile													<16th %ile
4	2.7	2.7	9.1	9.1	5.3	5.3	2.1	2.1	—	—	—	—	4
3	6.0	8.7	40.9	50.0	10.5	15.8	4.0	6.1	0.6	0.6	—	—	3
2	14.1	22.8	22.7	72.7	25.3	41.1	14.2	20.3	7.0	7.6	—	—	2
1	26.2	49.0	18.2	90.9	31.6	72.6	29.9	50.2	17.2	24.8	13.6	13.6	1
0	51.0	100.0	9.1	100.0	27.4	100.0	49.8	100.0	75.2	100.0	86.4	100.0	0
≤9th %ile													≤9th %ile
4	0.9	0.9	4.5	4.5	2.1	2.1	0.6	0.6	—	—	—	—	4
3	2.9	3.8	13.6	18.2	7.4	9.5	1.9	2.5	0.6	0.6	—	—	3
2	8.6	12.3	27.3	45.5	13.7	23.2	8.8	11.3	0.6	1.3	—	—	2
1	23.3	35.7	40.9	86.4	32.6	55.8	22.6	33.9	15.9	17.2	13.6	13.6	1
0	64.3	100.0	13.6	100.0	44.2	100.0	66.1	100.0	82.8	100.0	86.4	100.0	0
≤5th %ile													≤5th %ile
4	0.4	0.4	—	—	—	—	0.6	0.6	—	—	—	—	4
3	1.2	1.7	9.1	9.1	3.2	3.2	0.6	1.3	—	—	—	—	3
2	4.7	6.3	18.2	27.3	11.6	14.7	3.8	5.0	0.6	0.6	—	—	2
1	15.3	21.7	40.9	68.2	20.0	34.7	14.6	19.7	7.6	8.3	4.5	4.5	1
0	78.3	100.0	31.8	100.0	65.3	100.0	80.3	100.0	91.7	100.0	95.5	100.0	0
≤2nd %ile													<2nd %ile
4	0.1	0.1	—	—	—	—	0.2	0.2	—	—	—	—	4
3	0.4	0.6	4.5	4.5	1.1	1.1	0.0	2.1	—	—	—	—	3
2	2.1	2.7	18.2	22.7	3.2	4.2	1.9	2.1	0.6	0.6	—	—	2
1	10.4	13.1	40.9	63.6	16.8	21.1	9.6	11.7	2.5	3.2	4.5	4.5	1
0	86.9	100.0	36.4	100.0	78.9	100.0	88.3	100.0	96.8	100.0	95.5	100.0	0

(cont.)

■ **TABLE 14.7.** *(cont.)*

No. of scores below cutoff	Entire adult sample %	C%	Unusually low %	C%	Low average %	C%	Average %	C%	High average %	C%	Superior/ very superior %	C%	No. of scores below cutoff
					ToPF-demographics predicted FSIQ								
					Delayed Memory subtests								
≤25th %ile													≤25th %ile
4	6.4	6.4	35.3	35.3	6.8	6.8	4.6	4.6	2.7	2.7	0	0	4
3	10.6	17.0	17.6	52.9	19.3	26.1	10.9	15.4	1.4	4.1	4.8	4.8	3
2	17.1	34.1	29.4	82.4	21.6	47.7	17.5	33.0	14.3	18.4	0	4.8	2
1	25.0	59.1	5.9	88.2	31.8	79.5	28.4	61.4	19.0	37.4	19.0	23.8	1
0	40.9	100.0	11.8	100.0	20.5	100.0	38.6	100.0	62.6	100.0	76.2	100.0	0
≤16th %ile													<16th %ile
4	2.4	2.4	9.1	9.1	5.3	5.3	1.7	1.7	0.6	0.6	—	—	4
3	6.2	8.7	27.3	36.4	8.4	13.7	5.4	7.1	1.3	1.9	—	—	3
2	15.7	24.3	36.4	72.7	25.3	38.9	17.2	24.3	3.2	5.1	—	—	2
1	25.9	50.2	18.2	90.9	28.4	67.4	26.8	51.0	25.5	30.6	27.3	27.3	1
0	49.8	100.0	9.1	100.0	32.6	100.0	49.0	100.0	69.4	100.0	72.7	100.0	0
≤9th %ile													≤9th %ile
4	0.7	0.7	—	—	3.2	3.2	0.2	0.2	—	—	—	—	4
3	2.2	2.9	13.6	13.6	4.2	7.4	1.9	2.1	0.6	0.6	—	—	3
2	8.4	11.3	27.3	40.9	10.5	17.9	8.6	10.7	1.9	2.5	—	—	2
1	22.6	33.9	40.9	81.8	28.4	46.3	24.1	34.7	14.6	17.2	13.6	13.6	1
0	66.1	100.0	18.2	100.0	53.7	100.0	65.3	100.0	82.8	100.0	86.4	100.0	0
≤5th %ile													≤5th %ile
4	0.2	0.2	—	—	2.1	2.1	—	—	—	—	—	—	4
3	0.9	1.1	—	—	1.1	3.2	0.8	0.8	0.6	0.6	—	—	3
2	4.1	5.2	22.7	22.7	5.3	8.4	4.2	5.0	0.6	1.3	—	—	2
1	16.9	22.1	45.5	68.2	25.3	33.7	17.2	22.2	9.6	10.8	9.1	9.1	1
0	77.9	100.0	31.8	100.0	66.3	100.0	77.8	100.0	89.2	100.0	90.9	100.0	0
≤2nd %ile													<2nd %ile
3	0.3	0.3	—	—	1.1	1.1	0.2	0.2	—	—	—	—	3
2	1.8	2.1	9.1	9.1	4.2	5.3	1.0	1.3	0.6	0.6	—	—	2
1	11.1	13.2	31.8	40.9	11.6	16.8	11.3	12.6	6.4	7.0	9.1	9.1	1
0	86.8	100.0	59.1	100.0	83.2	100.0	87.4	100.0	93	100.0	90.9	100.0	0

Note. N = 900. There are four age-adjusted immediate memory subtest scores (Logical Memory I, Verbal Paired Associates I, Designs I, and Visual Reproduction I) and four age-adjusted delayed memory subtest scores (Logical Memory II, Verbal Paired Associates II, Designs II, and Visual Reproduction II) that were considered for these analyses. C% = cumulative percentage. Cutoff scores included ≤16th percentile (≤–1 SD or SS ≤ 7); ≤9th percentile (SS ≤ 6); ≤5th percentile (SS ≤ 5); and below the 2nd percentile (<–2 SD or SS ≤ 4). ToPF-demographics predicted Full Scale IQ included: Unusually low (<80; *n* = 22); Low average (80–89; *n* = 95); Average (90–109; *n* = 478); High average (110–119; *n* = 157); Superior/Very superior (120+; *n* = 22) Standardization data for the WMS-IV copyright 2009 by NCS Pearson, Inc. Used with permission. All rights reserved.

■ **TABLE 14.8. Base Rates of Low Auditory Working Memory and Processing Speed Subtest Scores (Age Adjusted) on the WAIS-IV and WMS-IV in Healthy Adults across Levels of Education**

No. of scores below cutoff	Levels of education										No. of scores below cutoff
	<8 years		9–11 years		12 years		13–15 years		16+ years		
	%	C%	%	C%	%	C%	%	C%	%	C%	
					Working Memory subtests						
≤25th %ile											<25th %ile
3	58.5	58.5	37.2	37.2	13.8	13.8	9.4	9.4	2.9	2.9	3
2	24.4	82.9	24.4	61.5	17.0	30.8	12.0	21.4	5.9	8.8	2
1	9.8	92.7	21.8	83.3	27.5	58.3	21.1	42.5	13.8	22.6	1
0	7.3	100.0	16.7	100.0	41.7	100.0	57.5	100.0	77.4	100.0	0
≤16th %ile											<16th %ile
3	24.4	24.4	16.7	16.7	4.0	4.0	3.8	3.8	0.4	0.4	3
2	36.6	61.0	14.1	30.8	12.3	16.3	6.4	10.2	0.4	0.8	2
1	24.4	85.4	35.9	66.7	21.7	38.0	14.3	24.4	11.3	12.1	1
0	14.6	100.0	33.3	100.0	62.0	100.0	75.6	100.0	87.9	100.0	0
≤9th %ile											≤9th %ile
3	14.6	14.6	7.7	7.7	0.7	0.7	1.1	1.1	0.4	0.4	3
2	14.6	29.3	12.8	20.5	5.8	6.5	2.6	3.8	—	—	2
1	41.5	70.7	21.8	42.3	17.4	23.9	9.8	13.5	5.0	5.4	1
0	29.3	100.0	57.7	100.0	76.1	100.0	86.5	100.0	94.6	100.0	0
≤5th %ile											≤5th %ile
3	2.4	2.4	2.6	2.6	—	—	0.4	0.4	0.4	0.4	3
2	7.3	9.8	9.0	11.5	2.9	2.9	1.1	1.5	—	—	2
1	26.8	36.6	12.8	24.4	9.8	12.7	4.9	6.4	0.4	0.8	1
0	63.4	100.0	75.6	100.0	87.3	100.0	93.6	100.0	99.2	100.0	0
≤2nd %ile											<2nd %ile
3	—	—	—	—	—	—	—	—	0.4	0.4	3
2	4.9	4.9	3.8	3.8	0.4	0.4	—	—	—	—	2
1	7.3	12.2	9.0	12.8	2.9	3.3	1.1	1.1	—	—	1
0	87.8	100.0	87.2	100.0	96.7	100.0	98.9	100.0	99.6	100.0	0
					Processing Speed subtests						
≤25th %ile											<25th %ile
3	22.0	22.0	26.9	26.9	13.5	13.5	9.4	9.4	5.4	5.4	3
2	34.1	56.1	23.1	50.0	16.0	29.5	15.4	24.8	9.2	14.6	2
1	14.6	70.7	26.9	76.9	26.5	56.0	28.6	53.4	22.6	37.2	1
0	29.3	100.0	23.1	100.0	44	100.0	46.6	100.0	62.8	100.0	0

(cont.)

▪ **TABLE 14.8.** *(cont.)*

No. of scores below cutoff	\<8 years %	\<8 years C%	9–11 years %	9–11 years C%	12 years %	12 years C%	13–15 years %	13–15 years C%	16+ years %	16+ years C%	No. of scores below cutoff
				Levels of education							
				Processing Speed subtests *(cont.)*							
≤16th %ile											\<16th %ile
3	14.6	14.6	12.8	12.8	5.8	5.8	4.5	4.5	2.1	2.1	3
2	26.8	41.5	21.8	34.6	14.5	20.4	10.9	15.4	4.2	6.3	2
1	19.5	61.0	23.1	57.7	17.8	38.2	19.2	34.6	18.4	24.7	1
0	39.0	100.0	42.3	100.0	61.8	100.0	65.4	100.0	75.3	100.0	0
≤9th %ile											≤9th %ile
3	9.8	9.8	6.4	6.4	1.5	1.5	2.3	2.3	0.4	0.4	3
2	14.6	24.4	7.7	14.1	7.6	9.1	5.6	7.9	2.9	3.3	2
1	24.4	48.8	24.4	38.5	14.5	23.6	11.7	19.5	7.1	10.5	1
0	51.2	100.0	61.5	100.0	76.4	100.0	80.5	100.0	89.5	100.0	0
≤5th %ile											≤5th %ile
3	2.4	2.4	2.6	2.6	—	—	0.8	0.8	0.4	0.4	3
2	17.1	19.5	2.6	5.1	4.0	4.0	1.9	2.6	1.7	2.1	2
1	19.5	39.0	20.5	25.6	8.4	12.4	8.6	11.3	4.2	6.3	1
0	61	100.0	74.4	100.0	87.6	100.0	88.7	100.0	93.7	100.0	0
≤2nd %ile											\<2nd %ile
3	—	—	2.6	2.6	—	—	0.4	0.4	0.4	0.4	3
2	4.9	4.9	—	—	0.7	0.7	0.8	1.1	—	—	2
1	17.1	22.0	7.7	10.3	5.1	5.8	3.0	4.1	0.8	1.3	1
0	78.0	100.0	89.7	100.0	94.2	100.0	95.9	100.0	98.7	100.0	0

Note. Sample sizes across the levels of education included: ≤8 years (*n* = 41); 9–11 years (*n* = 78); 12 years (*n* = 276); 13–15 years (*n* = 266); 16+ years (*n* = 239). There are three age-adjusted working memory subtest scores (Arithmetic, Digit Span, and Letter Number Sequencing) and three age-adjusted processing speed subtest scores (Coding, Symbol Search, and Cancellation) that were considered for these analyses. C% = cumulative percentage. Cutoff scores included ≤16th percentile (≤–1 *SD* or SS ≤ 7); ≤9th percentile (SS ≤ 6); ≤5th percentile (SS ≤ 5); and below the 2nd percentile (\<–2 *SD* or SS ≤ 4). Standardization data from the WAIS-IV copyright 2008 by NCS Pearson, Inc. Used with permission. All rights reserved.

▪ **TABLE 14.9. Base Rates of Low Immediate and Delayed Memory Subtest Scores (Age Adjusted) on the WMS-IV in Healthy Adults across Levels of Education**

No. of scores below cutoff	<8 years %	<8 years C%	9–11 years %	9–11 years C%	12 years %	12 years C%	13–15 years %	13–15 years C%	16+ years %	16+ years C%	No. of scores below cutoff
					Immediate Memory subtests						
≤25th %ile											<25th %ile
4	22.0	22.0	14.1	14.1	5.4	5.4	4.9	4.9	0.4	0.4	4
3	22.0	43.9	20.5	34.6	13.8	19.2	10.9	15.8	3.3	3.8	3
2	24.4	68.3	25.6	60.3	22.1	41.3	19.5	35.3	15.1	18.8	2
1	22.0	90.2	28.2	88.5	29.7	71.0	25.2	60.5	23.4	42.3	1
0	9.8	100.0	11.5	100.0	29.0	100.0	39.5	100.0	57.7	100.0	0
≤16th %ile											<16th %ile
4	9.8	9.8	10.3	10.3	2.5	2.5	1.5	1.5	0.4	0.4	4
3	22.0	31.7	11.5	21.8	6.5	9.1	6.0	7.5	0.8	1.3	3
2	22.0	53.7	24.4	46.2	15.6	24.6	13.5	21.1	8.4	9.6	2
1	24.4	78.0	30.8	76.9	33.7	58.3	25.6	46.6	17.2	26.8	1
0	22.0	100.0	23.1	100.0	41.7	100.0	53.4	100.0	73.2	100.0	0
≤9th %ile											≤9th %ile
4	4.9	4.9	1.3	1.3	0.7	0.7	1.1	1.1	—	—	4
3	9.8	14.6	10.3	11.5	2.5	3.3	2.3	3.4	0.4	0.4	3
2	17.1	31.7	20.5	32.1	9.8	13.0	8.3	11.7	2.1	2.5	2
1	36.6	68.3	32.1	64.1	29.0	42.0	19.2	30.8	16.3	18.8	1
0	31.7	100.0	35.9	100.0	58.0	100.0	69.2	100.0	81.2	100.0	0
≤5th %ile											≤5th %ile
4	2.4	2.4	—	—	0.4	0.4	0.8	0.8	—	—	
3	7.3	9.8	5.1	5.1	0.7	1.1	0.8	1.5	—	—	3
2	7.3	17.1	15.4	20.5	4.7	5.8	4.5	6.0	0.8	0.8	2
1	26.8	43.9	24.4	44.9	19.9	25.7	12.0	18.0	8.8	9.6	1
0	56.1	100.0	55.1	100.0	74.3	100.0	82.0	100.0	90.4	100.0	0
≤2nd %ile											<2nd %ile
4	2.4	2.4	—	—	—	—	—	—	—	—	4
3	2.4	4.9	2.6	2.6	0.4	0.4	—	—	—	—	3
2	4.9	9.8	5.1	7.7	2.5	2.9	2.3	2.3	—	—	2
1	26.8	36.6	23.1	30.8	11.6	14.5	9.4	11.7	3.3	3.3	1
0	63.4	100.0	69.2	100.0	85.5	100.0	88.3	100.0	96.7	100.0	0

(cont.)

■ **TABLE 14.9.** *(cont.)*

No. of scores below cutoff	<8 years		9–11 years		12 years		13–15 years		16+ years		No. of scores below cutoff
	%	C%	%	C%	%	C%	%	C%	%	C%	

Delayed Memory subtests

≤25th %ile											<25th %ile
4	9.1	9.1	13.9	13.9	8.0	8.0	6.4	6.4	1.7	1.7	4
3	9.1	18.2	19.0	32.9	14.5	22.5	10.9	17.4	3.0	4.6	3
2	34.1	52.3	27.8	60.8	18.5	41.1	15.8	33.2	10.1	14.8	2
1	22.7	75.0	24.1	84.8	25.8	66.9	24.5	57.7	25.3	40.1	1
0	25.0	100.0	15.2	100.0	33.1	100.0	42.3	100.0	59.9	100.0	0

≤16th %ile											<16th %ile
4	9.8	9.8	7.7	7.7	1.8	1.8	2.3	2.3	0.4	0.4	4
3	12.2	22.0	12.8	20.5	8.7	10.5	4.9	7.1	1.7	2.1	3
2	22.0	43.9	26.9	47.4	20.3	30.8	14.3	21.4	7.1	9.2	2
1	22.0	65.9	25.6	73.1	27.9	58.7	25.2	46.6	25.1	34.3	1
0	34.1	100.0	26.9	100.0	41.3	100.0	53.4	100.0	65.7	100.0	0

≤9th %ile											≤9th %ile
4	4.9	4.9	2.6	2.6	0.4	0.4	0.4	0.4	—	—	4
3	4.9	9.8	3.8	6.4	1.4	1.8	3.4	3.8	0.8	0.8	3
2	9.8	19.5	25.6	32.1	10.9	12.7	6.8	10.5	1.7	2.5	2
1	34.1	53.7	21.8	53.8	28.6	41.3	20.3	30.8	16.3	18.8	1
0	46.3	100.0	46.2	100.0	58.7	100.0	69.2	100.0	81.2	100.0	0

≤5th %ile											≤5th %ile
4	—	—	1.3	1.3	0.4	0.4	—	—	—	—	4
3	1.9	4.9	0.0	16.7	0.7	1.1	1.1	1.1	0.4	0.4	3
2	7.3	12.2	15.4	16.7	5.4	6.5	2.6	3.8	0.0	10.0	2
1	29.3	41.5	28.2	44.9	21.4	27.9	13.5	17.3	9.6	10.0	1
0	58.5	100.0	55.1	100.0	72.1	100.0	82.7	100.0	90	100.0	0

≤2nd %ile											<2nd %ile
3	4.9	4.9	1.3	1.3	—	—	—	—	—	—	3
2	2.4	7.3	5.1	6.4	2.9	2.9	0.8	0.8	0.4	0.4	2
1	14.6	22.0	19.2	25.6	13.4	16.3	10.5	11.3	5.9	6.3	1
0	78.0	100.0	74.4	100.0	83.7	100.0	88.7	100.0	93.7	100.0	0

Note. Sample sizes across the levels of education included: ≤8 years ($n = 41$); 9–11 years ($n = 78$); 12 years ($n = 276$); 13–15 years ($n = 266$); 16+ years ($n = 239$). There are four age-adjusted immediate memory subtest scores (Logical Memory I, Verbal Paired Associates I, Designs I, and Visual Reproduction I) and four age-adjusted delayed memory subtest scores (Logical Memory II, Verbal Paired Associates II, Designs II, and Visual Reproduction II) that were considered for these analyses. C% = cumulative percentage. Cutoff scores included ≤16th percentile (≤–1 *SD* or SS ≤ 7); ≤9th percentile (SS ≤ 6); ≤5th percentile (SS ≤ 5); and below the 2nd percentile (<–2 *SD* or SS ≤ 4). Standardization data for the WMS-IV copyright 2009 by NCS Pearson, Inc. Used with permission. All rights reserved.

■ **TABLE 14.10. Case Studies Illustrating the Domain-Specific Base-Rate Tables**

	Case 1: 58-year-old man; 9 years education		Case 2: 25-year-old woman; 16 years education	
	Score	Percentile rank	Score	Percentile rank
Intelligence				
WAIS-IV Verbal Comprehension Index	83	13	120	91
WAIS-IV Perceptual Reasoning Index	88	21	98	45
WAIS-IV General Ability Index	83	13	110	75
WAIS-IV Full Scale	89	23	103	58
ToPF-Demographics Predicted FSIQ-Simple	89	23	108	70
ToPF Reading Score	82	12	102	55
Verbal Working Memory Index	102	55	89	23
Attention and Working Memory (DS)*	12	75	9	37
Mental Arithmetic (AR)*	9	37	7	16
Attention and Working Memory (LNS)*	6	9	9	37
Processing Speed Index	94	34	97	42
Visual-Processing and Clerical Speed (Coding)*	9	37	7	16
Visual-Scanning and Processing Speed (Symbol Search)*	9	37	12	75
Visual-Scanning Speed (Cancellation)*	8	25	11	63
Immediate Memory Index	72	3	102	55
Immediate Memory for Stories (LM-I)*	5	5	12	75
Learning Word Pairs (VPA-I)*	6	9	7	16
Immediate Memory for Designs (Designs-I)*	6	9	12	75
Immediate Memory for Designs (VR-I)*	6	9	10	50
Delayed Memory Index	69	2	90	25
Delayed Memory for Stories (LM-II)*	4	2	9	37
Delayed Memory for Word Pairs (VPA-II)*	5	5	9	37
Delayed Memory for Designs (Designs II)*	6	9	10	50
Delayed Memory for Designs (VR-II)*	7	16	6	9

Note. ToPF, Test of Premorbid Functioning. Scores marked with an * were included in base-rate analyses. Case 1 experienced a remote mTBI, and he had small-vessel ischemic disease. Case 2 was 6 months post a moderate TBI.

89, we decided to calculate base rates in comparison to adults of *average*, not low-average, intelligence (assuming that prior to his neurological problems he would have scored at least a couple points higher on his FSIQ). The summary of this person's low scores is presented in Table 14.11, but information is derived from the base-rate tables (as indicated below). Having one or more verbal working memory scores at the 9th percentile is somewhat unusual in the general population (Table 14.6), but common for people with 9–11 years of education (Table 14.8). Having one or more processing speed scores at or below the 25th percentile is considered normal for the general population (Table 14.6), as well as those adults with similar intelligence (Table 14.6) or years of education (Table 14.8). Having four immediate memory scores at or below the 9th percentile is rare in the general population (occurring in less than 1%; Table 14.7) and among people with 9–11 years of education (i.e., occurring in 1.3%, Table 14.9). Having four delayed memory scores at or below the 16th percentile, or three or more scores at or below the 9th percentile, is rare for the general population (Table 14.7) and for people with 9–11 years of education (Table 14.9). The base-rate analyses give us more confidence in the interpretation that he has acquired memory deficits—even though he was likely of average to low-average intellect premorbidly.

For Case 2 (see Table 14.10), it is difficult to estimate her preinjury level of intelligence. Her ToPF score, ToPF-Demographics Predicted FSIQ, and WAIS-IV FSIQ scores were all average. However, her Verbal Comprehension Index was superior, and her General Ability Index was High Average. Therefore, we assumed that it is more likely that she was high average, intellectually, prior to her TBI.

The summary of base-rate analyses for this person is presented in Table 14.12. It can be challenging to confidently identify cognitive deficits in people with above-average premorbid intelligence. Notice that having one or more verbal working memory subtest at or below the 16th percentile occurs in 31.8% of the general population (Table 14.6), but only 12.1% of those with university degrees (Table 14.8) and 6.4% of those with estimated high average intelligence (Table 14.6). Interestingly, having two or more delayed memory scores less than or equal to the 25th percentile is also somewhat uncommon in those with university degrees (14.8%; Table 14.9) or above-average intelligence (18.4%; Table 14.7). The base-rate analyses provide support for the clinical inference that she has acquired cognitive difficulties in those two domains.

POOR EFFORT AND THE POTENTIAL FOR MISDIAGNOSIS

Neuropsychological test scores are significantly influenced by motivational factors. The accuracy of neuropsychological test results is largely dependent

▪ **TABLE 14.11. Case 1: Base-Rate Analyses (Age = 58, Education = 9, Predicted Premorbid Intelligence = Lower Portion of Average) (Base Rates of Low Scores Extracted from Tables 6–9)**

Domain/comparison group	≤25th percentile (Subtest ≤ 8)	≤16th percentile (Subtest ≤ 7)	≤9th percentile (Subtest ≤ 6)	≤5th percentile (Subtest ≤ 5)	≤2nd percentile (Subtest ≤ 4)
Verbal Working Memory subtests					
Number of low scores for Case 1 (3 max)	1 low score	1 low score	1 low score	None	None
Base rates of low scores from new tables:					
• Total WMS-IV Sample (Table 14.6)	47.9%	31.8%	19.7%	—	—
• Education-stratified sample (Table 14.8)	83.3%	66.7%	42.3%	—	—
• ToPF-Demo. Predicted FSIQ (Table 14.6)	47.9%	28.2%	15.9%	—	—
Processing Speed subtests					
Number of low scores for Case 1 (3 max)	1 low score	None	None	None	None
Base rates of low scores from new tables:					
• Total sample (Table 14.6)	52.7%	—	—	—	—
• Education-stratified sample (Table 14.8)	76.9%	—	—	—	—
• ToPF-demo. predicted FSIQ (Table 14.6)	51.2%	—	—	—	—
Immediate Memory subtests					
Number of low scores for Case 1 (4 max)	4 low scores	4 low scores	4 low scores	1 low score	None
Base rates of low scores derived from new tables:					
• Total sample (Table 14.7)	5.4%	2.7%	0.9%	21.7%	—
• Education-stratified sample (Table 14.9)	14.1%	10.3%	1.3%	44.9%	—
• ToPF-demo. predicted FSIQ (Table 14.7)	3.3%	2.1%	0.6%	19.7%	—
Delayed Memory subtests					
Number of low scores for Case 1 (4 max)	4 low scores	4 low scores	3 low scores	2 low scores	1 low score
Base rates of low scores derived from new tables:					
• Total sample (Table 14.7)	6.4%	2.4%	2.9%	5.2%	13.2%
• Education-stratified sample (Table 14.9)	13.9%	7.7%	6.4%	16.7%	—
• ToPF-Demo. Predicted FSIQ (Table 14.7)	4.6%	1.7%	2.1%	5.0%	12.6%

Note. There are three age-adjusted working memory subtest scores (Arithmetic, Digit Span, and Letter Number Sequencing), three age-adjusted processing speed subtest scores (Coding, Symbol Search, and Cancellation), four age-adjusted immediate memory subtest scores (Logical Memory I, Verbal Paired Associates I, Designs I, and Visual Reproduction I), and four age-adjusted delayed memory subtest scores (Logical Memory II, Verbal Paired Associates II, Designs II, and Visual Reproduction II) that were considered in this table.

▨ **TABLE 14.12. Case 2: Base-Rate Analyses (Age = 25, Education = 16, Predicted Preinjury Intelligence = High Average) (Base Rates of Low Scores Extracted from Tables 14.6–14.9)**

Domain/comparison group	≤25th percentile (Subtest ≤ 8)	≤16th percentile (Subtest ≤ 7)	≤9th percentile (Subtest ≤ 6)	≤5th percentile (Subtest ≤ 5)	≤2nd percentile (Subtest ≤ 4)
Verbal Working Memory subtests					
Number of low scores for Case 2 (3 max)	1 low score	1 low score	None	None	None
Base rates of low scores from new tables:					
• Total WMS-IV sample (Table 14.6)	47.9%	31.8%	—	—	—
• Education-stratified sample (Table 14.8)	22.6%	12.1%	—	—	—
• ToPF-Demo. Predicted FSIQ (Table 14.6)	12.7%	6.4%	—	—	—
Processing Speed subtests					
Number of low scores for Case 2 (3 max)	1 low score	1 low score	None	None	None
Base rates of low scores from new tables:					
• Total sample (Table 14.6)	52.7%	36.3%	—	—	—
• Education-stratified sample (Table 14.8)	37.2%	24.7%	—	—	—
• ToPF-demo. predicted FSIQ (Table 14.6)	33.1%	21.7%	—	—	—
Immediate Memory subtests					
Number of low scores for Case 2 (4 max)	1 low score	1 low score	None	None	None
Base rates of low scores derived from new tables:			—	—	—
• Total sample (Table 14.7)	62.7%	49.0%	—	—	—
• Education-stratified sample (Table 14.9)	42.3%	26.8%	—	—	—
• ToPF-demo. predicted FSIQ (Table 14.7)	40.8%	24.8%			
Delayed Memory subtests					
Number of low scores for Case 2 (4 max)	2 low scores	1 low score	1 low score	None	None
Base rates of low scores derived from new tables:					
• Total sample (Table 14.7)	34.1%	50.2%	33.9%	—	—
• Education-stratified sample (Table 14.9)	14.8%	34.3%	18.8%	—	—
• ToPF-demo. predicted FSIQ (Table 14.7)	18.4%	30.6%	17.2%	—	—

Note. There are three age-adjusted working memory subtest scores (Arithmetic, Digit Span, and Letter Number Sequencing), three age-adjusted processing speed subtest scores (Coding, Symbol Search, and Cancellation), four age-adjusted immediate memory subtest scores (Logical Memory I, Verbal Paired Associates I, Designs I, and Visual Reproduction I), and four age-adjusted delayed memory subtest scores (Logical Memory II, Verbal Paired Associates II, Designs II, and Visual Reproduction II) that were considered in this table.

upon effort. Effort, a state not a trait, can be variable during a neuropsychological evaluation. Most of the time, people likely provide "good" or "adequate" effort for the purposes of evaluation. Sometimes people are not motivated to perform well on testing, and the obtained results can be misinterpreted as reflecting cognitive deficits (acquired or longstanding).

Lange and colleagues studied 63 injured workers who were slow to recover from a mild traumatic brain injury. All were referred by the Workers' Compensation Board to a specialty assessment and treatment program (Lange, Iverson, Brooks, & Ashton Rennison, 2010). All were evaluated within 6 months of injury. Approximately one in four failed simple effort testing [i.e., 23.8%; Test of Memory Malingering (TOMM; Tombaugh, 1996)]. Those who failed effort testing reported more postconcussion-like symptoms, and more severe symptoms, than those who passed effort testing. A subgroup of 37 patients underwent neuropsychological screening evaluations (Stern & White, 2003b). Those who failed effort testing performed very poorly on neuropsychological screening, as illustrated in Figure 14.9.

In another study, Iverson and colleagues examined the "good old days" bias in workers who were slow to recover from a mild traumatic brain injury. The "good old days" bias refers to the tendency to view oneself as healthier in the past and to underestimate past problems. In that study, the injured workers retrospectively endorsed the presence of fewer preinjury symptoms compared to a healthy community control group. Workers

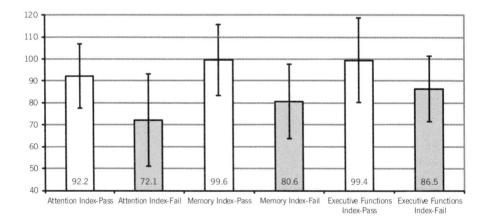

▪ **FIGURE 14.9.** Relation between poor effort and neuropsychological test performance in workers' compensation patients who are slow to recover from mild traumatic brain injury. Scores are for the Attention, Memory, and Executive Functions Indexes from the NAB Screening Module. The sample size is 37, 8 of whom failed the Test of Memory Malingering (TOMM; Tombaugh, 1996).

who failed effort testing tended to retrospectively report fewer symptoms preinjury compared to those workers who passed effort testing. Many of the workers reported their preinjury functioning as better than the average person (Iverson, Lange, Brooks, & Rennison, 2010).

Taken together, these two studies illustrate clearly that poor effort is a critical variable to consider when conducting a neuropsychological assessment of an injured worker. Poor effort is associated with (1) reporting fewer symptoms and better functioning than the average person before being injured (i.e., the "good old days" bias), (2) reporting more symptoms after being injured, (3) reporting more severe symptoms after being injured, and (4) very poor performance on cognitive testing. As such, individuals providing poor effort are much more likely to be diagnosed (i.e., arguably *misdiagnosed*) as having cognitive impairment and a postconcussion syndrome than individuals who pass effort testing.

RETURN-TO-WORK CONSIDERATIONS

A person's ability to return to work following an injury can be affected by physical, psychological, cognitive, and motivational factors. First, a person needs to be physically capable of performing the job duties, or have modifications in place to accommodate physical limitations. Examples of physical limitations include motor problems; sensory problems (e.g., vision or hearing); or significant problems with strength, stamina, or endurance. Physical problems can result in occupational limitations or restrictions.

Second, the person must have the emotional stability, adaptive personality, and resilience[2] to cope with the demands of work. From a psychological perspective, a person could have significant interpersonal problems (e.g., argumentativeness or disinhibition) or emotional problems (e.g., depression or anxiety) that might interfere with normal workplace functioning. Emotional problems can make people less enthusiastic and motivated employees. These problems can reduce their ability to tolerate stress or conflict in the workplace, and lead to increased absenteeism and "presenteeism."[3] Emotional problems can reduce effectiveness in customer service or sales occupations.

Third, if a person has cognitive deficits, he or she must be able to cope with and compensate for these deficits in a work setting. Cognitive problems can affect work requiring constant attention and concentration, such as assembly lines, heavy equipment operations, use of power tools, and working on ladders. Cognitive problems can adversely affect a person's ability to learn on the job, remember assignments for the day, or regulate his or her behavior. Finally, the person must be motivated to make the effort to be successful on the job. Some people are highly motivated, and other people are only marginally motivated to reenter the workforce.

Neuropsychological assessment following workplace injuries can be very useful for documenting the cognitive and psychological consequences of these injuries. Early assessment can help guide specific treatment and rehabilitation strategies. Moreover, these evaluations can be useful for identifying preexisting problems (e.g., ADHD, learning disability, specific cognitive strengths and weakness, substance abuse, or mental health problems) that can interact with, and complicate our understanding of, the acute consequences and recovery course from injury. Abbreviated serial assessments can be useful for tracking progress in treatment and rehabilitation. The use of neuropsychological assessment in the context of vocational rehabilitation is discussed in detail by Fraser and colleagues in this book (see Chapter 13).

Without question, neuropsychologists provide important services to individuals who suffer life-altering workplace injuries. Complex questions and decisions need to be addressed, relating to the accurate identification and quantification of deficits, the assessment of causality, and recommendations for rehabilitation and/or accommodation. As such, it is important for clinicians to have access to, and apply, scientifically grounded data to inform their conclusions. The understanding and application of multivariate base rates enables the clinician to reduce potential false positive identification of acquired cognitive impairment in some patients and yet, also increase sensitivity to cognitive impairment in others.

CAVEATS AND CONSIDERATIONS

In this chapter, we have illustrated how low scores are commonly observed in healthy adults and how the number of low scores varies by demographic characteristics and level of intellectual functioning. A number of points regarding the prevalence of low scores in the general population, and in injured workers, are important to consider.

First, variability in cognitive functioning is not meaningless. Rather, the nature and extent of variability in cognitive functions can have direct implications for an individual's educational and occupational functioning. Deficits in specific cognitive domains (e.g., verbal intellectual ability or memory) will have more or less impact on daily functioning depending on the cognitive demands of the person's work and psychosocial environment.

Second, inclusion in the "healthy" normative sample does not imply an absence of any problems in educational, occupational, or psychosocial functioning; it merely implies that any difficulties experienced by the individual have not resulted in a specific developmental, psychiatric, or neurological diagnosis. For example, young or middle-aged adults who completed 8 or fewer years of education probably experienced some academic difficulties, but they did not necessarily qualify for a specific diagnosis. Therefore, having low scores suggests possible problems or limitations with cognitive functioning in daily life regardless of whether or not the number of low scores is unusual for the person's level of education. Stated differently, a person with limited education or low intelligence might have a "normal" number of low scores when compared to people with similar education or intellectual abilities—but have quite significant cognitive limitations in daily life.

Third, it can be very difficult to interpret the neuropsychological test results of people who have developmental disorders (e.g., intellectual disability or learning disability) and then experience a workplace injury. For these individuals, it can be challenging to quantify the nature and extent of acquired cognitive deficits.

Fourth, the absence of a significant number of low scores does not necessarily indicate the absence of mild cognitive impairment. It is possible, of course, to fail to detect mild cognitive impairment when relying on base-rate analyses.

Finally, the presence of a significant number of low scores does not necessarily indicate the presence of acquired cognitive impairment following a workplace injury. The low scores could represent longstanding cognitive limitations. They could also reflect, in part, poor or variable effort.

CONCLUSIONS

Cognitive diminishment or impairment, be it temporary or permanent, is relatively common following certain types of workplace injuries. The purpose of this chapter was to provide clinicians with information to improve their accuracy for identifying and quantifying acquired cognitive problems in daily practice. This information is designed to strengthen the scientific underpinnings of clinical judgment.

The foundation of deficit measurement, psychometrically, is the normal curve. In daily practice we rely heavily on the curve. But the principles of the normal curve are frequently misunderstood in the context of a neuropsychological evaluation, increasing the risk for false positive diagnoses of cognitive impairment. The problem lies in applying principles of a univariate distribution to multivariate data. One solution, therefore, is to have the necessary base-rate information to simultaneously interpret multiple test scores.

We believe that variability in cognitive functioning is a human phenotype; it arises from the interaction of our genetics and environment. As such, test score scatter, discrepancies, strengths and weaknesses, and low scores can be developmental, acquired (e.g., due to a workplace traumatic brain injury), or both. Many clinicians underappreciate that a substantial minority of healthy adults, with no known neurological, psychiatric, or developmental problem, will have multiple low scores on testing. These low scores could be due to situational factors (e.g., test anxiety or lapses in attention), their phenotype (i.e., inherent weaknesses), or both. Therefore, it is important to consider the possibility that some low scores are situational or longstanding, and not attributable to an acquired injury.

Practitioners interpreting multiple neuropsychological scores should appreciate that: (1) test-score scatter or variability is common; (2) having some low scores occurs in a substantial minority of healthy adults; (3) the number of low scores is related to the cutoff score used for interpretation (e.g., 1 *SD* or the 5th percentile); (4) the number of low scores depends on the number of tests administered; and (5) the number of low scores varies by characteristics of the examinees (such as education, race/ethnicity, and intelligence). Therefore, an assumption or clinical inference relating to a single test score might be inaccurate in the context of multiple test scores. Failing to consider these fundamental psychometric principles when interpreting multiple test scores can result in false positive or false negative diagnoses of cognitive impairment.

In our view, we need to move toward robust decision-making algorithms to augment and improve clinical judgment and diagnostic accuracy. These algorithms need to account for differences in test results that are attributable to demographic factors and level of intelligence—and be informed by base rates of low scores. The translation of clinical research in this area to clinical practice will facilitate evidence-based neuropsychological assessment.

Neuropsychological assessment following workplace injuries can provide important information for understanding the nature and extent of cognitive difficulties associated with the injury, combined with estimating preinjury strengths and weaknesses—to maximize the rehabilitation team's understanding of the person's overall strengths and limitations. Comprehensive evaluation data can provide useful information as to whether the person might face cognitive challenges on the job. Evaluations are most helpful if they focus on the relations between specific problems and deficits, and real-world social and occupational functioning. Neuropsychological assessment can facilitate accommodations in the workplace. Moreover, brief follow-up assessments can be used to monitor treatment progress and recovery. We advocate a scientific approach to neuropsychological assessment that is akin to the rigorous research models of our field and yet simultaneously meets the specific needs of the patients who need our help.

NOTES

1. The belief that all traditional neuropsychological tests are normally distributed—when in fact some distributions are highly skewed—creates additional psychometric problems when clinicians use local or research norms (i.e., computing Z-scores from means and standard deviations, then assigning a percentile rank). On tests where the distribution is normal, the linear derivation of

Z-scores provides an accurate estimation of the individual's relative position in the normative sample (i.e., the calculated z-score and the actual Z-score yield the sample percentile rank). However, when the distribution is skewed (e.g., many neuropsychological tests are negatively skewed), the linear transformation of means and standard deviations to Z-scores results in a mismatch between the calculated percentile rank and the actual percentile rank. For example, a Z-score of (–1) in a normal sample is consistent with the 16th percentile; however, in a negatively skewed distribution the (–1) will actually have a higher percentile rank but the clinician will not know it because he is often not aware of the extent of the skewness. In a skewed distribution, the variance above and below the mean can vary considerably. Therefore, using the averaged standard deviation presented in research studies can be a misrepresentation of the actual distribution of scores above and below the mean. Therefore, using skewed normative data from the research literature could artificially inflate the number of low scores obtained by an examinee.

2. Resilience comprises a broad, diverse set of psychological, social, and biological factors that confer some degree of protection from poor outcome following workplace injuries (e.g., positive coping style, high self-efficacy, hardiness, positive emotions and optimism, humor, social and occupational support, genetics, serotonin transport and binding, norepinephrine biosynthesis and availability, dopaminergic brain reward systems, sympathetic nervous system regulation, neuropeptides, hypothalamic–pituitary–adrenal axis, cortisol, and other stress hormones) (Feder, Nestler, & Charney, 2009; Hoge, Austin, & Pollack, 2007; Southwick, Vythilingam, & Charney, 2005).

3. Presenteeism relates to diminished productivity at work, which is usually estimated in terms of lost productive time.

REFERENCES

American Psychiatric Association. (1994). *Diagnostic and statistical manual of mental disorders* (4th ed.). Washington, DC: Author.

American Psychological Association. (2005). *Policy Statement on Evidence-Based Psychological Practice*. Retrieved February 7, 2011, from *www.apa.org/practice/ resources/evidence/evidence-based-statement.pdf*.

Ardila, A. (1995). Directions of research in cross-cultural neuropsychology. *Journal of Clinical and Experimental Neuropsychology, 17*(1), 143–150.

Axelrod, B. N., & Wall, J. R. (2007). Expectancy of impaired neuropsychological test scores in a non-clinical sample. *International Journal of Neuroscience, 117*(11), 1591–1602.

Barr, W. B., & McCrea, M. (2001). Sensitivity and specificity of standardized neurocognitive testing immediately following sports concussion. *Journal of the International Neuropsychological Society, 7*(6), 693–702.

Beatty, W. W., Mold, J. W., & Gontkovsky, S. T. (2003). RBANS performance: Influences of sex and education. *Journal of Clinical and Experimental Neuropsychology, 25*(8), 1065–1069.

Benedict, R. H., Cox, D., Thompson, L. L., Foley, F., Weinstock-Guttman, B., & Munschauer, F. (2004). Reliable screening for neuropsychological impairment in multiple sclerosis. *Multiple Sclerosis, 10*(6), 675–678.

Benedict, R. H., Munschauer, F., Linn, R., Miller, C., Murphy, E., Foley, F., et al. (2003). Screening for multiple sclerosis cognitive impairment using a self-administered 15-item questionnaire. *Multiple Sclerosis, 9*(1), 95–101.

Bieliauskas, L. A., Fastenau, P. S., Lacy, M. A., & Roper, B. L. (1997). Use of the odds ratio to translate neuropsychological test scores into real-world outcomes: From statistical significance to clinical significance. *Journal of Clinical and Experimental Neuropsychology, 19*(6), 889–896.

Binder, L. M., Iverson, G. L., & Brooks, B. L. (2009). To err is human: "Abnormal" neuropsychological scores and variability are common in healthy adults. *Archives of Clinical Neuropsychology, 24*, 31–46.

Brickman, A. M., Cabo, R., & Manly, J. J. (2006). Ethical issues in cross-cultural neuropsychology. *Applied Neuropsychology, 13*(2), 91–100.

Bright, P., Jaldow, E., & Kopelman, M. D. (2002). The National Adult Reading Test as a measure of premorbid intelligence: A comparison with estimates derived from demographic variables. *Journal of the International Neuropsychological Society, 8*(6), 847–854.

Brooks, B. L., Holdnack, J. A., & Iverson, G. L. (2011). Advanced clinical interpretation of the WAIS-IV and WMS-IV: Prevalence of low scores varies by level of intelligence and years of education. *Assessment, 18*(2), 156–167.

Brooks, B. L., Iverson, G. L., Feldman, H. H., & Holdnack, J. A. (2009). Minimizing misdiagnosis: Psychometric criteria for possible or probable memory impairment. *Dementia and Geriatric Cognitive Disorders, 27*(5), 439–450.

Brooks, B. L., Iverson, G. L., Holdnack, J. A., & Feldman, H. H. (2008). The potential for misclassification of mild cognitive impairment: A study of memory scores on the Wechsler Memory Scale-III in healthy older adults. *Journal of the International Neuropsychological Society, 14*(3), 463–478.

Brooks, B. L., Iverson, G. L., & White, T. (2007). Substantial risk of "Accidental MCI" in healthy older adults: Base rates of low memory scores in neuropsychological assessment. *Journal of the International Neuropsychological Society, 13*(3), 490–500.

Chelune, G. J. (2010). Evidence-based research and practice in clinical neuropsychology. *The Clinical Neuropsychologist, 24*(3), 454–467.

Collaer, M. L., & Nelson, J. D. (2002). Large visuospatial sex difference in line judgment: Possible role of attentional factors. *Brain and Cognition, 49*(1), 1–12.

Crawford, J. R., Garthwaite, P. H., & Gault, C. B. (2007). Estimating the percentage of the population with abnormally low scores (or abnormally large score differences) on standardized neuropsychological test batteries: A generic method with applications. *Neuropsychology, 21*(4), 419–430. Test Software *www.abdn.ac.uk/~psy086/dept/PercentAbnormKtests.htm.*

Crawford, J. R., Garthwaite, P. H., Howell, D. C., & Venneri, A. (2003). Intraindividual measures of association in neuropsychology: Inferential methods for comparing a single case with a control or normative sample. *Journal of the International Neuropsychological Society, 9*(7), 989–1000.

Donders, J., Zhu, J., & Tulsky, D. (2001). Factor index score patterns in the WAIS-III standardization sample. *Assessment, 8*(2), 193–203.

Dori, G. A., & Chelune, G. J. (2004). Education-stratified base-rate information on discrepancy scores within and between the Wechsler Adult Intelligence Scale—Third Edition and the Wechsler Memory Scale—Third Edition. *Psychological Assessment, 16*(2), 146–154.

Feder, A., Nestler, E. J., & Charney, D. S. (2009). Psychobiology and molecular genetics of resilience. *Nature Reviews. Neuroscience, 10*(6), 446–457.

Geary, D. C., Saults, S. J., Liu, F., & Hoard, M. K. (2000). Sex differences in spatial cognition, computational fluency, and arithmetical reasoning. *Journal of Experimental and Child Psychology, 77*(4), 337–353.

Godber, T., Anderson, V., & Bell, R. (2000). The measurement and diagnostic utility of intrasubtest scatter in pediatric neuropsychology. *Journal of Clinical Psychology, 56*(1), 101–112.

Green, R. E., Melo, B., Christensen, B., Ngo, L. A., Monette, G., & Bradbury, C. (2008). Measuring premorbid IQ in traumatic brain injury: An examination of the validity of the Wechsler Test of Adult Reading (WTAR). *Journal of Clinical and Experimental Neuropsychology, 30*(2), 163–172.

Griffin, S. L., Mindt, M. R., Rankin, E. J., Ritchie, A. J., & Scott, J. G. (2002). Estimating premorbid intelligence: Comparison of traditional and contemporary methods across the intelligence continuum. *Archives of Clinical Neuropsychology, 17*(5), 497–507.

Heaton, R. K., Grant, I., & Matthews, C. G. (1991). *Comprehensive norms for an extended Halstead-Reitan Battery: Demographic corrections, research findings, and clinical applications.* Odessa, FL: Psychological Assessment Resources.

Heaton, R. K., Miller, S. W., Taylor, M. J., & Grant, I. (2004). *Revised comprehensive norms for an expanded Halstead-Reitan Battery: Demographically adjusted neuropsychological norms for African American and Caucasian adults professional manual.* Lutz, FL: Psychological Assessment Resources.

Heaton, R. K., Taylor, M. J., & Manly, J. (2003). Demographic effects and use of demographically corrected norms with the WAIS-III and WMS-III. In D. S. Tulsky, D. H. Saklofske, G. J. Chelune, R. K. Heaton, R. J. Ivnik, R. Bornstein, et al. (Eds.), *Clinical interpretation of the WAIS-III and WMS-III* (pp. 183–210). San Diego, CA: Academic Press.

Herlitz, A., Nilsson, L. G., & Backman, L. (1997). Gender differences in episodic memory. *Memory and Cognition, 25*(6), 801–811.

Hoge, E. A., Austin, E. D., & Pollack, M. H. (2007). Resilience: Research evidence and conceptual considerations for posttraumatic stress disorder. *Depression and Anxiety, 24*(2), 139–152.

Horton, A. M., Jr. (1999). Above-average intelligence and neuropsychological test score performance. *International Journal of Neuroscience, 99*(1–4), 221–231.

Ingraham, L. J., & Aiken, C. B. (1996). An empirical approach to determining criteria for abnormality in test batteries with multiple measures. *Neuropsychology, 10*, 120–124.

Institute of Medicine. (2001). *Crossing the quality chasm: A new heath system for the 21st century.* Washington, DC: National Academy Press.

Iverson, G. L., & Brooks, B. L. (2010). Improving accuracy for identifying cognitive impairment. In M. R. Schoenberg & J. G. Scott (Eds.), *The black book of neuropsychology: A syndrome-based approach* (pp. 923–950). New York: Springer.

Iverson, G. L., Brooks, B. L., & Ashton, V. L. (2008a). Cognitive impairment: Foundations for clinical and forensic practice. In M. P. Duckworth, T. Iezzi, & W. O'Donohue (Eds.), *Motor vehicle collisions: Medical, psychosocial, and legal consequences* (pp. 243–309). Amsterdam: Academic Press.

Iverson, G. L., Brooks, B. L., & Holdnack, J. A. (2008b). Misdiagnosis of cognitive impairment in forensic neuropsychology. In R. L. Heilbronner (Ed.), *Neuropsychology in the courtroom: Expert analysis of reports and testimony* (pp. 243–266). New York: Guilford Press.

Iverson, G. L., Brooks, B. L., White, T., & Stern, R. A. (2008c). Neuropsychological Assessment Battery (NAB): Introduction and advanced interpretation. In A.

M. Horton, Jr. & D. Wedding (Eds.), *The neuropsychology handbook* (3rd ed., pp. 279–343). New York: Springer Publishing.

Iverson, G. L., Lange, R. T., Brooks, B. L., & Rennison, V. L. (2010). "Good old days" bias following mild traumatic brain injury. *The Clinical Neuropsychologist, 24*(1), 17–37.

Iverson, G. L., Mendrek, A., & Adams, R. L. (2004). The persistent belief that VIQ-PIQ splits suggest lateralized brain damage. *Applied Neuropsychology, 11*(2), 85–90.

Ivnik, R. J., Makec, J. F., Smith, G. E., Tangolos, E. G., & Peterson, R. C. (1996). Neuropsychological tests' norms above age 55: COWAT, BNT, MAE Token, WRAT-R Reading, AMNART, STROOP, TMT, and JLO. *The Clinical Neuropsychologist, 10*, 262–278.

Ivnik, R. J., Smith, G. E., Cerhan, J. H., Boeve, B. F., Tangalos, E. G., & Petersen, R. C. (2001). Understanding the diagnostic capabilities of cognitive tests. *The Clinical Neuropsychologist, 15*(1), 114–124.

Ivnik, R. J., Smith, G. E., Petersen, R. C., Boeve, B. F., Kokmen, E., & Tangalos, E. G. (2000). Diagnostic accuracy of four approaches to interpreting neuropsychological test data. *Neuropsychology, 14*(2), 163–177.

Labarge, A. S., McCaffrey, R. J., & Brown, T. A. (2003). Neuropsychologists' abilities to determine the predictive value of diagnostic tests. *Archives of Clinical Neuropsychology, 18*(2), 165–175.

Lange, R. T., Iverson, G. L., Brooks, B. L., & Ashton Rennison, V. L. (2010). Influence of poor effort on self-reported symptoms and neurocognitive test performance following mild traumatic brain injury. *Journal of Clinical and Experimental Neuropsychology,* 1–12.

Lezak, M. D. (1976). *Neuropsychological assessment.* New York: Oxford University Press.

Lezak, M. D. (1983). *Neuropsychological assessment* (2nd ed.). New York: Oxford University Press.

Maddrey, A. M., Cullum, C. M., Weiner, M. F., & Filley, C. M. (1996). Premorbid intelligence estimation and level of dementia in Alzheimer's disease. *Journal of the International Neuropsychological Society, 2*(6), 551–555.

Manly, J. J., & Echemendia, R. J. (2007). Race-specific norms: Using the model of hypertension to understand issues of race, culture, and education in neuropsychology. *Archives of Clinical Neuropsychology, 22*(3), 319–325.

Morgan, E. E., Woods, S. P., Scott, J. C., Childers, M., Beck, J. M., Ellis, R. J., et al. (2008). Predictive validity of demographically adjusted normative standards for the HIV dementia scale. *Journal of Clinical and Experimental Neuropsychology, 30*(1), 83–90.

Norman, M. A., Evans, J. D., Miller, W. S., & Heaton, R. K. (2000). Demographically corrected norms for the California Verbal Learning Test. *Journal of Clinical and Experimental Neuropsychology, 22*(1), 80–94.

O'Bryant, S. E., O'Jile, J. R., & McCaffrey, R. J. (2004). Reporting of demographic variables in neuropsychological research: Trends in the current literature. *The Clinical Neuropsychologist, 18*(2), 229–233.

Palmer, B. W., Boone, K. B., Lesser, I. M., & Wohl, M. A. (1998). Base rates of "impaired" neuropsychological test performance among healthy older adults. *Archives of Clinical Neuropsychology, 13*(6), 503–511.

Paolo, A. M., Ryan, J. J., Troster, A. I., & Hilmer, C. D. (1996). Utility of the Barona demographic equations to estimate premorbid intelligence: Information from the WAIS-R standardization sample. *Journal of Clinical Psychology, 52*(3), 335–343.

Patton, D. E., Duff, K., Schoenberg, M. R., Mold, J., Scott, J. G., & Adams, R. L. (2003). Performance of cognitively normal African Americans on the RBANS in community dwelling older adults. *The Clinical Neuropsychologist, 17*(4), 515–530.

Pearson. (2001). *Wechsler Test of Adult Reading.* San Antonio, TX: NCS Pearson.

Pearson. (2009). *Advanced clinical solutions for the WAIS-IV/WMS-IV: ACS clinical and interpretative manual.* San Antonio, TX: NCS Pearson.

Randolph, C. (1998). *Repeatable battery for the assessment of neuropsychological status manual.* San Antonio, TX: Psychological Corporation.

Rasquin, S. M., Lodder, J., Visser, P. J., Lousberg, R., & Verhey, F. R. (2005). Predictive accuracy of MCI subtypes for Alzheimer's disease and vascular dementia in subjects with mild cognitive impairment: A 2-year follow-up study. *Dementia and Geriatric Cognitive Disorders, 19*(2–3), 113–119.

Rosselli, M., & Ardila, A. (2003). The impact of culture and education on non-verbal neuropsychological measurements: A critical review. *Brain and Cognition, 52*(3), 326–333.

Ryan, E. L., Baird, R., Mindt, M. R., Byrd, D., Monzones, J., & Bank, S. M. (2005). Neuropsychological impairment in racial/ethnic minorities with HIV infection and low literacy levels: Effects of education and reading level in participant characterization. *Journal of the International Neuropsychological Society, 11*(7), 889–898.

Sackett, D. L., Straus, S. E., Richardson, W. S., Rosenberg, W., & Haynes, R. B. (2000). *Evidence based medicine: How to practice and teach EBM* (2nd ed.). London: Churchill Livingstone.

Sawrie, S. M., Martin, R. C., Gilliam, F. G., Roth, D. L., Faught, E., & Kuzniecky, R. (1998). Contribution of neuropsychological data to the prediction of temporal lobe epilepsy surgery outcome. *Epilepsia, 39*(3), 319–325.

Schmidt, S. L., Oliveira, R. M., Rocha, F. R., & Abreu-Villaca, Y. (2000). Influences of handedness and gender on the grooved pegboard test. *Brain and Cognition, 44*(3), 445–454.

Schretlen, D. J., Testa, S. M., Winicki, J. M., Pearlson, G. D., & Gordon, B. (2008). Frequency and bases of abnormal performance by healthy adults on neuropsychological testing. *Journal of the International Neuropsychological Society, 14*(3), 436–445.

Shapiro, A. M., Benedict, R. H., Schretlen, D., & Brandt, J. (1999). Construct and concurrent validity of the Hopkins Verbal Learning Test-revised. *The Clinical Neuropsychologist, 13*(3), 348–358.

Southwick, S. M., Vythilingam, M., & Charney, D. S. (2005). The psychobiology of depression and resilience to stress: Implications for prevention and treatment. *Annual Review of Clinical Psychology, 1,* 255–291.

Steinberg, B. A., Bieliauskas, L. A., Smith, G. E., & Ivnik, R. J. (2005). Mayo's older Americans normative studies: Age- and IQ-adjusted norms for the trail-making test, the Stroop Test, and MAE Controlled Oral Word Association Test. *The Clinical Neuropsychologist, 19*(3–4), 329–377.

Steinberg, B. A., Bieliauskas, L. A., Smith, G. E., Ivnik, R. J., & Malec, J. F. (2005). Mayo's older Americans normative studies: Age- and IQ-adjusted norms for the Auditory Verbal Learning Test and the Visual Spatial Learning Test. *The Clinical Neuropsychologist, 19*(3–4), 464–523.

Stern, R. A., & White, T. (2003a). *Neuropsychological Assessment Battery.* Lutz, FL: Psychological Assessment Resources.

Stern, R. A., & White, T. (2003b). *Neuropsychological Assessment Battery:*

Administration, scoring, and interpretation manual. Lutz, FL: Psychological Assessment Resources.

Strauss, E., Sherman, E. M. S., & Spreen, O. (2006). *A compendium of neuropsychological tests: Administration, norms, and commentary* (3rd ed.). New York: Oxford University Press.

Tierney, M. C., Szalai, J. P., Dunn, E., Geslani, D., & McDowell, I. (2000). Prediction of probable Alzheimer disease in patients with symptoms suggestive of memory impairment: Value of the Mini-Mental State Examination. *Archives of Family Medicine, 9*(6), 527–532.

Tombaugh, T. N. (1996). *Test of memory malingering.* North Tonawanda, NY: Multi-Health Systems.

Tremont, G., Hoffman, R. G., Scott, J. G., & Adams, R. L. (1998). Effect of intellectual level on neuropsychological test performance: A response to Dodrill (1997). *The Clinical Neuropsychologist, 12,* 560–567.

Voyer, D., Voyer, S., & Bryden, M. P. (1995). Magnitude of sex differences in spatial abilities: A meta-analysis and consideration of critical variables. *Psychological Bulletin, 117*(2), 250–270.

Warner, M. H., Ernst, J., Townes, B. D., Peel, J., & Preston, M. (1987). Relationships between IQ and neuropsychological measures in neuropsychiatric populations: Within-laboratory and cross-cultural replications using WAIS and WAIS-R. *Journal of Clinical and Experimental Neuropsychology, 9*(5), 545–562.

Wechsler, D. (1997a). *Wechsler Adult Intelligence Scale* (3rd ed.). San Antonio, TX: Psychological Corporation.

Wechsler, D. (1997b). *Wechsler Memory Scale* (3rd ed.). San Antonio, TX: Psychological Corporation.

Wechsler, D. (2008). *WAIS-IV Wechsler Adult Intelligence Scale* (4th ed.): *Administration and scoring manual.* San Antonio: NCS Pearson.

Wechsler, D. (2009). *Wechsler Memory Scale* (4th ed.). San Antonio, TX: Psychological Corporation.

Woods, S. P., Weinborn, M., & Lovejoy, D. W. (2003). Are classification accuracy statistics underused in neuropsychological research? *Journal of Clinical and Experimental Neuropsychology, 25*(3), 431–439.

World Health Organization. (1992). *International statistical classification of diseases and related health problems* (10th ed.). Geneva, Switzerland: World Health Organization.

Index

outcome from, 134–136
wartime hazards, 127
See also Combat-related PTSD; Iraq/
Afghanistan conflict; Polytrauma
military patients
Minnesota Multiphasic Personality
Inventory–2 (MMPI-2), 317
Minnesota Multiphasic Personality
Inventory (MMPI), 92, 95
Minor physical anomalies (MPA), 198
Misdiagnosis, 387, 390–391
Mitochondrial DNA, 221*n*2
Moderate cognitive impairment, 363
Monoamine deficiency hypothesis,
192–193
Monoamine oxidase inhibitors (MAIOs),
193
Mood, impact of chronic pain on, 245–246
Motivation, changes following traumatic
brain injuries, 24–25
Motor impairments, 20

N

National Academy of Neuroscience, 316
National Football League, 69–71
National Hockey League. *See* Ice hockey
National Institute of Occupational Safety
and Health (NIOSH), 108, 109
Nervous system
effects of neurotoxic chemicals on,
115–116
See also Central nervous system
Neurodiagnostic testing, of electrical
injuries, 87–88
Neurofilaments, 16
Neuroimaging
in behavioral IMEs, 336
diffusion tensor imaging, 18–20
magnetic resonance imaging, 18
Neuromodulation therapies, 219
Neurons
diffuse axonal injury, 70
traumatic axonal injury, 15–16, 17
Neuropsychological assessment
advocacy for the patient, 266
consultation with collateral sources,
271–272
deficit measurement and, 364
in depression, 221

differences between clinical and forensic
cases, 265–266, 275–277
differences between clinical evaluations
and neuropsychological IMEs,
281–282
differences in referral sources, 265
of electrical injuries, 81, 96–98
evidence-based. *See* Evidence-based
neuropsychological assessment
handling invalid results, 273–274
informed consent, 267
methods/procedures, 267–270
misunderstanding and misapplication of
the normal curve, 364–366
of neurotoxic exposure injuries, 120–122
record review, 270–271
results and interpretation, 272–273
of sports-related concussion, 68–77
"stealth" referrals, 265, 277*n*1
treatment recommendations, 274–275
vocationally relevant. *See* Vocationally
relevant neuropsychological
assessment
of work-related traumatic brain injuries,
32–33
See also Neuropsychological IMEs
Neuropsychological Assessment Battery
(NAB), 208
base rate data, 364–365
normal number of low scores, 375
prevalence of low scores, 373, 374
Screening Module, 35, 36
Neuropsychological decision making, 290
Neuropsychological IMEs
billing, 284–285, 302
common pitfalls, 297–299
differences with clinical evaluations,
281–282
different types of, 282
establishing the parameters of, 284
evaluation methods and procedures
causality determinations, 285
describing the parameters to
examinees, 285–286
interpretation, diagnosis, and
determinations, 290, 292
observations, 288–289
review of records, 286–287
test selection, 289–290, 291–292, 293
third party presence, 289
in forensic contexts, 280–281
increased frequency of, 282–283